Lecture Notes
in Business Information Processing 235

More information about this series at http://www.springer.com/series/7911

Jolita Ralyté · Sergio España
Óscar Pastor (Eds.)

The Practice of
Enterprise Modeling

8th IFIP WG 8.1. Working Conference, PoEM 2015
Valencia, Spain, November 10–12, 2015
Proceedings

 Springer

Editors
Jolita Ralyté
CUI, Battelle - Batiment A
University of Geneva
Carouge
Switzerland

Sergio España
Utrecht University
Utrecht
The Netherlands

Óscar Pastor
Department of Information Systems
and Computation
Universitat Politècnica de València
Valencia
Spain

ISSN 1865-1348   ISSN 1865-1356 (electronic)
Lecture Notes in Business Information Processing
ISBN 978-3-319-25896-6   ISBN 978-3-319-25897-3 (eBook)
DOI 10.1007/978-3-319-25897-3

Library of Congress Control Number: 2015952066

Springer Cham Heidelberg New York Dordrecht London

Printed on acid-free paper

Springer International Publishing AG Switzerland is part of Springer Science+Business Media
(www.springer.com)

Preface

Welcome to the proceedings of the 8th Working Conference on the Practice of Enterprise Modelling (PoEM 2015) that was held during November 10–12 in the beautiful and modern city of Valencia, Spain, and hosted by the Research Center in Software Production Methods (PROS) of the Universidad Politécnica de Valencia.

Enterprise modelling (EM) encloses a set of activities by which several perspectives of an organization are elicited, documented, analyzed, and communicated, typically through a structured, iterative, stakeholder-centric, and model-based approach. This way, the knowledge of the enterprise is made explicit and further actions can be performed, such as making strategic decisions, undertaking organizational reengineering, standardizing ways of working, developing or acquiring information and communication technology, etc. As a consequence, EM has an impact on large economic markets such as consulting and information system development, making it a relevant field of research and industrial practice.

The PoEM series of conferences started in 2008 aiming at providing a forum for sharing experiences and knowledge of EM between the academic community and practitioners from industry and the public sector. PoEM is supported by the IFIP WG8.1 and is a very interesting and dynamic event where new research challenges emerge from EM practices – success and failure stories related by practitioners, and vice versa, practitioners take the opportunity to learn about new EM solutions.

This year, PoEM was very successful by receiving 72 submissions covering a large variety of EM topics. Each paper was evaluated by at least three Program Committee members and got constructive recommendations for further improvement. After examining the reviews, 23 papers were selected for presentation at the conference and are included in these proceedings. They are organized in eight sections corresponding to the conference sessions: Evolving Enterprises, Securing Enterprises, Making Empirical Studies, Investigating Enterprise Methods, Acquiring User Information, Managing Risks and Threats, Engineering Methods, and Making Decisions in Enterprises.

In addition to full research papers, we selected nine short papers presenting research works in progress and case studies. During the conference they were presented in dedicated sessions and are published in the CEUR online proceedings (CEUR-WS. org).

The conference audience also enjoyed three outstanding keynote presentations: two from academia and one from industry. Professor Pericles Loucopoulos from the Manchester Business School of the University of Manchester (UK) gave a talk on "What Could the Role of Enterprise Modelling Be During the 5th Economic Phase?" Professor Larry Constantine, a Fellow of the Association for Computing Machinery and a Life Member of the Industrial Designers Society of America, delivered a lecture on "Missing Models: Understanding Human Activity in the Enterprise." Finally, a presentation with a practitioner perspective was given by a representative from industry, Rafael Montes, from TecnoGram Procesos, on "Event Sourcing Implementation of a BPM System: A Practical Experience."

This year's PoEM introduced a few novelties – a traditionally two-day conference was extended by one day and complemented with three additional events: a workshop named AMINO (TowArds the Model drIveN Organization), a doctoral consortium, and a Young Entrepreneur Seminar (yes!PoEM 2015). We hope that all participants, both from academia and industry, enjoyed the scientific and social program of the conference and received inspiration for their research and industrial innovations.

To conclude, we would like to express our gratitude to a number of people who spent their time and energy in organizing and successfully running PoEM 2015. First of all we thank the Program Committee members and additional reviewers for their help in selecting the papers for the scientific program of the conference, the authors of the papers for their confidence in PoEM, and the presenters and session chairs for lively presentations and discussions. We are grateful to the PoEM Steering Committee chairs for their continuous assistance, and the chairs of workshops, doctoral consortium, and yes!PoEM for creating an exciting event. Finally, we extend our gratitude to the local organizing team at the Universidad Politécnica de Valencia for their hospitality and the organization of the social events of the conference.

November 2015   Jolita Ralyté
                                                          Sergio España
                                                          Óscar Pastor

Conference Organization

Steering Committee

Anne Persson   University of Skövde, Sweden
Janis Stirna   Stockholm University, Sweden
Kurt Sandkuhl   The University of Rostock, Germany

General Chair

Óscar Pastor   Universitat Politècnica de València, Spain

Program Committee Chairs

Jolita Ralyté   University of Geneva, Switzerland
Sergio España   Utrecht University, The Netherlands

Organising Chairs

Tanja Vos   Universitat Politècnica de València, Spain
Marcela Ruiz   Universitat Politècnica de València, Spain

Doctoral Consortium Chairs

Pnina Soffer   University of Haifa, Israel
Jelena Zdravkovic   Stockholm University, Sweden

Workshops Chairs

Charlotte Hug   Université Paris 1 Panthéon-Sorbonne, France
Francisco Valverde   Universitat Politècnica de València, Spain

Publicity Chair

Fáber Giraldo   University of Quindío, Colombia

Program Committee

Raian Ali   Bournemouth University, UK
Dimosthenis Anagnostopoulos   Harokopio University of Athens, Greece
Hernán Astudillo   Universidad Técnica Federico Santa María, Chile

Marko Bajec	University of Ljubljana, Slovenia
Judith Barrios Albornoz	University of Los Andes, Colombia
Giuseppe Berio	Université de Bretagne Sud, France
Robert Andrei Buchmann	University of Vienna, Austria
Rimantas Butleris	Kaunas University of Technology, Lithuania
Albertas Caplinskas	Institute of Mathematics and Informatics, Lithuania
Juan Pablo Carvallo	Universidad del Azuay, Equator
Jaelson Castro	Universidade Federal de Pernambuco, Brazil
Tony Clark	Middlesex University, UK
Jose Luis de La Vara	Carlos III University of Madrid, Spain
Wolfgang Deiters	Fraunhofer Institute for Software and Systems Engineering, Germany
Dulce Domingos	FCUL, Portugal
Sergio España	Utrecht University, The Netherlands
Xavier Franch	Universitat Politècnica de Catalunya, Spain
Ulrich Frank	Universität of Duisburg Essen, Germany
Giovanni Giachetti	Universidad Andres Bello, Facultad de Ingeniería, Chile
Jēnis Grabis	Riga Technical University, Latvia
Stijn Hoppenbrouwers	HAN University of Applied Sciences, The Netherlands
Paul Johannesson	Royal Institute of Technology, Sweden
Juergen Jung	DHL Global Mail, Germany
Håvard Jørgensen	Commitment AS, Norway
Monika Kaczmarek	University Duisburg Essen, Germany
Ron Kenett	KPA Ltd. and University of Torino, Italy
Lutz Kirchner	Scape Consulting GmbH, Germany
Marite Kirikova	Riga Technical University, Latvia
John Krogstie	IDI, NTNU, Norway
Birger Lantow	University of Rostock, Germany
Ulrike Lechner	Universität der Bundeswehr München, Germany
Pericles Loucopoulos	University of Manchester, UK
Beatriz Marín	Universidad Diego Portales, Chile
Florian Matthes	Technische Universität München, Germany
Raimundas Matulevicius	University of Tartu, Estonia
Graham Mcleod	Inspired.org, South Africa
Jan Mendling	Wirtschaftsuniversität Wien, Austria
Christer Nellborn	Nellborn Management Consulting AB, Sweden
Andreas L Opdahl	University of Bergen, Norway
Óscar Pastor	Universitat Politècnica de València, Spain
Anne Persson	University of Skövde, Sweden
Michael Petit	University of Namur, Belgium
Ilias Petrounias	University of Manchester, UK
Henderik Proper	Luxembourg Institute of Science and Technology, Luxembourg
Jolita Ralyté	University of Geneva, Switzerland
Colette Rolland	Université Paris 1 Panthéon-Sorbonne, France
Daniel Romero	Universidad Nacional de Asunción, Paraguay

Francisco Ruiz	University of Castilla la Mancha, Spain
Irina Rychkova	Université Paris 1 Panthéon-Sorbonne, France
Kurt Sandkuhl	University of Rostock, Germany
Ulf Seigerroth	Jönköping University, Sweden
Khurram Shahzad	Royal Institute of Technology, Sweden
Nikolay Shilov	SPIIRAS, Russian Federation
Pnina Soffer	University of Haifa, Israel
Janis Stirna	Stockholm University, Sweden
Darijus Strasunskas	DS Applied Science, Norway
Stefan Strecker	University of Hagen, Germany
Victoria Torres	Universitat Politècnica de València, Spain
Francisco Valverde	Universitat Politècnica de València, Spain
Olegas Vasilecas	Vilnius Gediminas Technical University, Lithuania
Pablo Villarreal	Universidad Tecnológica Nacional - Facultad Regional Santa Fe, Argentina
Frank Wolff	DHBW-Mannheim, Germany
Eric Yu	University of Toronto, Canada
Jelena Zdravkovic	Stockholm University, Sweden

Additional Reviewers

Nadia Abdu	Universität der Bundeswehr München, Germany
Nathalie Aquino	Universidad Nacional de Asunción, Paraguay
Marija Bjeković	Public Research Centre Henri Tudor, Luxembourg
Alexander Bock	Universität of Duisburg Essen, Germany
Anis Boubaker	University of Quebec at Montreal, Canada
Paulius Danenas	Kaunas University of Technology, Lithuania
Mohammad Hossein Danesh	University of Toronto, Canada
Sybren De Kinderen	Luxembourg Institute of Science and Technology, Luxembourg
Khaled Gaaloul	Luxembourg Institute of Science and Technology, Luxembourg
Fáber Giraldo	University of Quindío, Colombia
Jens Gulden	Technische Universität München, Germany
Matheus Hauder	Technische Universität München, Germany
Elena Kushnareva	Université Paris 1 Panthéon-Sorbonne, France
Alexei Lapouchnian	University of Toronto, Canada
Karolyne Oliveira	Universidade Federal de Pernambuco, Brazil
Audrius Rima	Vilnius Gediminas Technical University, Lithuania
Marcela Ruiz	Universitat Politècnica de València, Spain
Alexander W. Schneider	Technische Universität München, Germany
Tomas Skersys	Kaunas University of Technology, Lithuania
Dirk van der Linden	Luxembourg Institute of Science and Technology, Luxembourg
Jéssyka Vilela	Universidade Federal de Pernambuco, Brazil

Contents

Aquiring User Information

Investigating Enterprise Models

Managing Risks and Threats

Making Decisions in Enterprises

Engineering Methods

Keynote

What Could the Role of Enterprise Modelling be During the 5th Economic Phase?

An Extended Abstract of Keynote Talk

Pericles Loucopoulos[✉]

University of Manchester, Manchester, UK
pericles.loucopoulos@manchester.ac.uk

Enterprise Modelling (EM) has emerged as one of the key techniques in externalising and analysing the factors underpinning the intertwining of Information Technology (IT) systems to their enterprise environment. This intertwining [1] is central to achieving sustainability of IT systems [2, 3]. Sustainability has been studied in strategic management [4] and more recently in Information Systems Engineering (ISE) [5, 6].

In EM there is a large number of languages on offer to assist in capturing and conveying particular information for the understanding of the aforementioned intertwining [7], approaches such as goal modelling [8], business process modelling [9], business rules modelling [10], social modelling [11], to name but a few. In parallel with these initiatives, a number of associated tools has emerged e.g. ADONIS, Archimate, ARIS, GRADE, as well as meta-tools such as ADOxx, MetaEdit + and Metis.

Current EM approaches can deal with facets of modelling that makes requirements traceable to any aspect of the enterprise under study. There is a significant body of empirical evidence that EM approaches and tools have had a positive impact on organizational and information systems development efficiency c.f. [12–14].

Research in ISE has attempted to address changing requirements by proposing scalable service delivery platforms such as Services Oriented Architecture (SOA) and cloud computing, or using Model Driven Development (MDD), or analysing large amounts of data [15, 16]. Such engineering approaches more often than not assume a relatively stable enterprise environment, an assumptions that is increasingly being challenged by macroeconomic factors. As enterprises compete in fast-paced changing financial ecosystems they need to constantly adapt their service/product offerings to gain and sustain competitiveness.

The need for dynamically changing software systems has highlighted three challenges. First, in order to develop useful software one must deal with the complexities of the natural world in which the application resides [17–19]. Second, in order to understand the orchestration and configuration of different individual systems one must understand the requirements of different organizations that own the individual systems, the interplay between the collaborating components and the dynamics of the overall system [1, 20]. Third, in order to maintain a high level of quality and utility, software needs to evolve in tandem with the evolution of user requirements [1]. Users, designers and other stakeholders need to be assured that the system will continue to satisfy their emerging goals.

© IFIP International Federation for Information Processing 2015
J. Ralyté et al. (Eds.): PoEM 2015, LNBIP 235, pp. 3–7, 2015.
DOI: 10.1007/978-3-319-25897-3_1

Could IT be the source of sustainable advantage? There is much debate about it with the prevailing view that IT does not possess uniqueness and inimitability characteristics [21, 22]. Competitive advantage cannot be gained by considering IT as a resource based artifact, but rather by considering the way that IT capabilities are *coupled and aligned* with organizational capabilities [21–23] provides such opportunities.

The paradigm of EM is currently facing a challenge of semantic integration across multiple levels of abstraction and of detail. While traditionally EM emerged from bottom-up approaches, by applying semantic extensions to some core concern (e.g. business process models extended with information about the organizational responsibilities) we are now facing a need to represent enterprise architecture holistically, to support a decomposition of the high level business view down to requirements representation and low level system designs.

Current EM approaches have been used in practice mostly in a reactive mode in the sense that they are deployed a long time after enterprise strategies have been decided upon and adopted. As we enter a new world economic cycle – in the Kondradief sense of analysis of economic lifecycle - the question is whether EM should and could play a more significantly strategic role in this cycle. Could EM play a role over and above the support role it has assumed to date in facilitating IT solutions to solving enterprise problems? Could EM be used for shaping up enterprise strategy and if so what kinds of conceptual frameworks need to be developed so that useful techniques and tools can be of high value? Is it indeed relevant to even ask these questions that after all are driven by macroeconomic considerations when EM is confined to a specific technological paradigm?

The anticipated 5th economic cycle is likely to be dominated by technological innovation [24] and one such innovation of interest to the EM community is the use of information which, because of its increasing social value and use, has the potential of changing the way enterprises react to a new economic era, for example, the opportunities for developing non-market collaborative ventures, the non-formal sharing of information-centric "goods", etc. As Mason argues there is already profound changes in work processes (fuelled by this information-centric view) that is transforming our established notions of work, production and value [25]. This macroeconomic transformation will impact on the way that enterprises need to view a whole new set of key levers affecting their business models and in such a setting the issue is no longer the alignment between an enterprise and its IT system but rather about the opportunities that may arise in an emergent manner.

To address dynamic requirements of today's business environments, one should go beyond static design of services that are aligned to organizational objectives and business requirements. We argue in [26, 27] that we need in EM to begin thinking of conceptual frameworks that can integrate the contextual, service, operational and teleological views and relate these to the enterprise ecosystem. Such a conceptual framework will need to deal with the different but intertwined perspectives of *description, relation, and evaluation* that will empower designers – business as well as IT designers – to come up with solutions that will fit this new macroeconomic landscape.

The *design requirements* problem clearly articulated by Brooks [28] poses the challenge of "What is the emergent behaviour and dynamics of the software artifact and its environment in their evolutionary trajectory?" Users, designers and other stakeholders need to ask "will the system continue to satisfy our emergent goals, and what are these goals be expected to be during the artifact's lifetime?", in contrast to the older question of "what are the (fixed) goals of the system and what is it expected to do in relation to these goals?".

The *predictability problem* of designs raises the question of "how does the artifact and its behaviour change the environment as to make our predictions of system behaviours faithful?" In other words, now designers need to attend more closely to the continuous dynamic composition of the system and its environment, and how they together differ from the environment in separation. Designers need to predict faithfully the impact of the system on the environment, and vice versa. This is a different problem from those faced earlier where the system was assumed to not affect the environment, or the environment the system, with rare exceptions.

These research challenges can only be satisfactorily addressed through multi-disciplinary approaches that, in addition to the traditional ISE disciplines exploited in EM (conceptual modelling, development methods etc.) consider also the possibilities offered by for example, socio-economic analysis, systems thinking, architectural impact analysis, design rationale, etc.

EM should strive to offer enterprises the opportunity of developing meta-capabilities, that is routines and mechanisms that bring about changes to enterprise capabilities and depict different abstraction levels. The significance of meta-capabilities is that by modelling and analysing meta-capabilities, their needs and relations to other capabilities, processes and services, will facilitate identification of potential social and technical inflexibilities towards change and hence play a significant role in sustainability of competitive advantages. Developing these meta-capabilities will require enterprises to engage in a continuous knowledge enhancement cycle and in this the EM research and practice community could play a significant role.

Acknowledgement. The author wishes to thank Eric Yu and Mohammad Danesh of the University of Toronto for their collaboration on the work presented in [26, 27] on which some of the ideas in this extended abstract are based.

References

1. Jarke, M., Loucopoulos, P., Lyytinen, K., Mylopoulos, J., Robinson, W.: The brave new world of design requirements. Inf. Syst. **36**(7), 992–1008 (2011)
2. Bleistein, S.J., Cox, K., Verner, J., Phalp, K.T.: B-SCP: a requirements analysis framework for validating strategic alignment of organisational it based on strategy, context and process. Inf. Softw. Technol. **2006**(46), 846–868 (2006)
3. Sousa, H.P., do Prado Leite, J.C.S.: Modeling organizational alignment. In: Yu, E., Dobbie, G., Jarke, M., Purao, S. (eds.) ER 2014. LNCS, vol. 8824, pp. 407–414. Springer, Heidelberg (2014)
4. Teece, D.J., Pisano, G., Shuen, A.: Dynamic capability and strategic management. Strateg. Manag. J. **1997**(18), 509–533 (1997)
5. Ulrich, W., Rosen, M.: The business capability map: the "rosetta stone" of Business/IT alignment. Enterpr. Archit. 14(2) (2014)

6. Zdravkovic, J., Stirna, J., Henkel, M., Grabis, J.: Modeling Business Capabilities and Context Dependent Delivery by Cloud Services. In: Salinesi, C., Norrie, M.C., Pastor, Ó. (eds.) CAiSE 2013. LNCS, vol. 7908, pp. 369–383. Springer, Heidelberg (2013)

7. Sandkuhl, K., Stirna, J., Persson, A., Wißotzki, M.: In: Dietz, J.L.G., Proper, E., Tribolet, J. (eds.) Enterprise Modeling: Tackling Business Challenges with the 4EM Method. The Enterprise Engineering Series (2014)

8. Lamsweered, A.V.: Requirements Engineering: From System Goals to UML Models for Software Specifications. Wiley, New york (2009)

9. OMG (2009), Business Process Modeling Notation (BPMN) Version 2.1, Object Management Group (2009)

10. Loucopoulos, P., Wan-Kadir, W.M.N.: BROOD: business rules-driven object oriented design. J. Database Manag. **19**(1), 41–73 (2008)

11. Yu, E., Giorgini, P., Maiden, N., Mylopoulos, J., Fickas, S. (eds.): Social Modeling for Requirements Engineering. Cooperative Information Systems. MIT Press, Cambridge (2010)

12. Nilsson, A., Tolis, C., Nellborn, C.: Perspectives on Business Modelling: Understanding and Changing Organisations. Springer Verlag, Heidelberg (1999)

13. Stirna, J., Persson, A.: Purpose driven competency planning for enterprise modeling projects. In: Ralyté, J., Franch, X., Brinkkemper, S., Wrycza, S. (eds.) CAiSE 2012. LNCS, vol. 7328, pp. 662–677. Springer, Heidelberg (2012)

14. Krogstie, J.: Model-Based Development and Evolution of Information Systems: A Quality Approach. Springer, London (2012)

15. Stirna, J., Grabis, J., Henkel, M., Zdravkovic, J.: Capability driven development – an approach to support evolving organizations. In: Sandkuhl, K., Seigerroth, U., Stirna, J. (eds.) PoEM 2012. LNBIP, vol. 134, pp. 117–131. Springer, Heidelberg (2012)

16. Yu, E., Deng, S., Sasmal, D.: Enterprise architecture for the adaptive enterprise – a vision paper. In: Aier, S., Ekstedt, M., Matthes, F., Proper, E., Sanz, J.L. (eds.) PRET 2012 and TEAR 2012. LNBIP, vol. 131, pp. 146–161. Springer, Heidelberg (2012)

17. Lyytinen, K., Loucopoulos, P., Mylopoulos, J., Robinson, B. (eds.): Design Requirements Engineering. LNBIP, vol. 14. Springer, Heidelberg (2009)

18. Turski, W.M.: And no philosopher's stone either. In: IFIP 10th World Computer Congress, pp. 1077–1080. North-Holland, Dublin (1986)

19. Jackson, M.: Why software writing is difficult and will remain so. Inf. Process. Lett. **88**(1–2), 13–25 (2003)

20. Cleland-Huang, J., Jarke, M., Liu, L., Lyytinen, K.: Requirements Management – Novel Perspectives and Challenges, Dagstuhl Seminar Series (2010)

21. Bhatt, G.D., Grover, V.: Types of information technology capabilities and their role in competitive advantage: an empirical study. J. Manag. Inf. Syst. **22**, 253–277 (2005)

22. Nevo, S., Wade, M.: The formation and value of IT-Enabled resources: antecedents and consequences. Manag. Inf. Syst. Q. **2010**(34), 163–183 (2010)

23. Henderson, J.C., Venkatraman, N.: Strategic alignment: leveraging information technology for transforming organizations. IBM Syst. J. **32**(1), 4–16 (1993)

24. Perez, C.: Technological Revolutions and Financial Capital: The Dynamics of Bubbles and Golden Ages. Elgar, London (2002)

25. Mason, P.: PostCapitalism: A Guide to our Future. Allen Lane, London (2015)

26. Danesh, M.H., Loucopoulos, P., Yu, E.: Dynamic capabilities for sustainable enterprise IT – a modeling framework. In: 34th International Conference on Conceptual Modeling (ER 2015). Stockholm, Sweden (2015)

27. Loucopoulos, P., Stratigaki, C., Danesh, M.H., Bravos, G., Anagnostopoulos, D., Dimitrakopoulos, G.: Enterprise capability modeling: concepts, method and application. In: 3rd International Conference on Enterprise Systems. Basel, Switzerland (2015)
28. Brooks, F.P.: The Design of Design: Essays from a Computer Scientist. Addison-Wesley, New York (2010)

Evolving Enterprises

Towards Guiding the Use of Enterprise Modeling in the Context of Business and IT Alignment

Julia Kaidalova[1(✉)], Ulf Seigerroth[1], and Anne Persson[2]

[1] School of Engineering, Jönköping University, P.O. Box 1026, 55111 Jönköping, Sweden
{julia.kaidalova,ulf.seigerroth}@ju.se
[2] University of Skövde, School of Informatics, Högskolevägen Box 408,
541 28 Skövde, Sweden
anne.persson@his.se

Abstract. Today's dynamic business environment presents enterprises that wish to stay competitive with a great challenge. This is further complicated by rapidly advancing IT capabilities and the crucial role that IT plays in most organizations - a backbone for realizing visions and goals. The problem of eliminating the gap between business and IT within enterprises, i.e. the problem of Business and IT Alignment (BITA), has been acknowledged as a contemporary challenge and actively elaborated by academics and practitioners. One practice that is used to facilitate BITA is Enterprise Modeling (EM), which is considered as a catalyzing practice for capturing, visualizing and analyzing different aspects of enterprises. This paper presents a framework that illustrates the role of EM in the context of BITA and suggests recommendations to deal with EM challenges.

Keywords: Business and IT alignment · Enterprise modeling · Enterprise modeling challenges · Enterprise modeling recommendations

1 Introduction

IT can be used to change the way companies organize their business processes, how they communicate with their customers and the means by which they deliver their services [1]. However, while it is undeniable that suitable IT solutions are required in order to reach organizational goals, effective support of business operations with appropriate IT solutions is complicated due to the dynamic nature and intertwined relation between business operations and IT solutions [2]. In order to conceptualize this problem – how to align business and IT – practitioners and researchers have used a variety of terms such as harmony, linkage, fusion, fit, match, and integration, but in the long run the term alignment has gained widespread acceptance. In early studies, Business and IT Alignment (BITA) implied linking business strategy and IT strategy. Later, the view on BITA has expanded and current research recognizes many dimensions of alignment in BITA [3].

In the context of BITA, Enterprise Modeling (EM) can be considered as a useful practice. EM facilitates the creation of a number of integrated models which capture and represent different aspects (focal areas) of an enterprise, for example business processes,

© IFIP International Federation for Information Processing 2015
J. Ralyté et al. (Eds.): PoEM 2015, LNBIP 235, pp. 11–26, 2015.
DOI: 10.1007/978-3-319-25897-3_2

business rules, concepts, information, data, vision, goals and actors [4, 5]. The essential ability of enterprise models to represent an enterprise from different perspectives allows EM to be used for providing a multidimensional view on an enterprise and to integrate these multiple dimensions into a coherent structure [4]. These capabilities of enterprise models also provide a powerful mechanism for dealing with the strategic and structural dimensions of BITA. On the other hand, EM is also able to provide solid support when there is a need to develop a common understanding of the current multidimensional praxis and an agreement on future vision and strategies [4, 5]. These characteristics of EM make it applicable for BITA when there is a need to consider the multiple views of stakeholders and to create a shared understanding between them [6–8].

Despite the fact that the literature recognizes various benefits of using EM to achieve BITA [4, 9–13], there are no studies that in an extensive way illustrate the role of EM in improving BITA. Thus, the research question of this work is the following:

How can EM contribute to business and IT alignment?

The main objective of the paper is to present a framework that includes EM challenges and recommendations that are relevant for BITA. It describes the existing results so far of a research project aiming to generate prescriptive guidelines for practitioners dealing with EM in the BITA context.

The remainder of the paper is structured in the following way: Sect. 2 describes the research approach. In Sect. 3 the theoretical foundation that served as a basis for this research is presented. It covers the BITA and EM domains. The overview of the EM framework is introduced in Sect. 4, while Sect. 5 describes the related challenges and recommendations in more detail. Finally, Sect. 6 concludes the paper.

2   Research Approach

The research process in this study has included three iterations in order to refine the EM framework. The framework has evolved through three versions: a preliminary EM framework, an intermediate EM framework and the final EM framework. Both theoretical and empirical foundations have been used to generate and validate the results iteratively. The theoretical foundation includes relevant theories from EM, BITA and other related domains. The empirical foundation has included interview data on the practice of EM.

A stepwise representation of the research process of this study is shown in Fig. 1. The figure schematically represents three parallel tracks of the research process: theoretical work, conceptualization work, and empirical work. Elements with white filling represent steps of the research, whereas elements with grey filling represent results (knowledge contributions).

In the *theoretical work* of this paper four literature reviews have been performed (steps 1, 2a, 3a, 4 in Fig. 1). The *empirical work* involved two rounds of interviews with EM practitioners, the results of which were the basis for developing the framework (steps 2b, 3b). In total, eight semi-structured interviews have been carried out in two rounds. The main criterion when choosing respondents was that they had significant experience

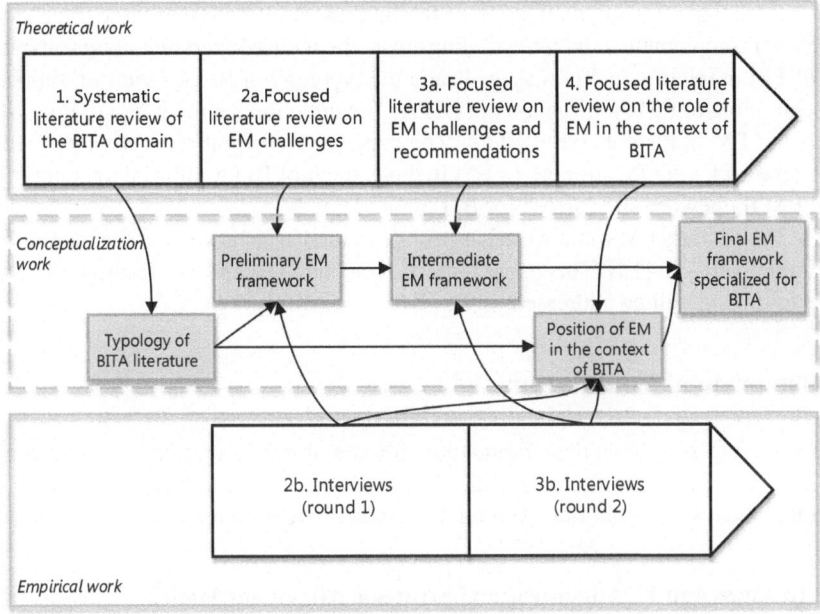

Fig. 1. Research process – theoretical, empirical and conceptualization work

in EM, including both managing modeling sessions and using created models for various purposes. All the chosen respondents had at least 5 years of experience in EM within enterprise transformation, systems development and other types of projects. The analysis of the collected data was done incrementally with analysis following each interview. The last interviews revealed to reach informational saturation. The respondents from the first and the second rounds of interviews will be addressed as *Respondent 1-x* and *Respondent 2-x* respectively in the remainder of the paper. The *conceptualization work* that resulted in the EM framework involved the continuous analysis and synthesis of various theoretical and empirical research results as well as their integration and refinement.

As Fig. 1 shows, the research started with a systematic literature review of the BITA domain (step 1), which allowed the generation of a typology of the BITA literature representing the main interest areas and identified existing knowledge gaps. The typology also provided an initial idea of the role of EM in relation to BITA, which in turn allowed the investigation of EM practice in the frame of the BITA domain. After that, on the basis of the typology of BITA literature, a Preliminary EM framework has been generated using a focused literature review on EM challenges (step 2a) in combination with the first round of interviews (step 2b). The intention behind these two steps was to investigate EM practice in terms of challenges that EM practitioners face. After that, using the Preliminary EM framework as a foundation, a focused literature review on EM challenges and recommendations (step 3a) and the second round of interviews (step 3b) enabled generation of the Intermediate EM framework. Here the intention was to investigate EM practice with particular attention to EM challenges and corresponding recommendations. Conceptualization of the findings from both interview rounds (step 2b and 3b) complemented with the findings from the focused literature review about the role of EM in relation to BITA (step 4) and the typology of BITA literature supported the positioning of EM in the context of BITA. The intention behind it was to investigate the role of EM in the context of BITA. The conceptual integration of the Intermediate EM framework with Positioning of EM in the context of BITA allowed to generate the Final EM framework specialized for BITA.

The Preliminary EM framework has been presented in [14], whereas the Intermediate EM framework – in [15]. This paper aims to focus on the Final EM framework, which in the following will be addressed as *the EM framework*.

3   Theoretical Foundation

In this section the theoretical foundation for the study is presented. First, general description and relevant theories of the BITA domain are introduced in Subsect. 3.1. After this the relevant theories from the EM domain are presented in Subsect. 3.2

3.1   Business and IT Alignment and Strategic Alignment Model

One of the key factors for the success of an enterprise is the alignment between IT support and business strategies and processes. The importance of business and IT alignment is discussed and recognized by both academics and practitioners [1]. The challenge of business and IT alignment is not new though, as it came with the use of information systems in organizations. There are two conceptual views on BITA – a process, i.e. a set of activities to reach a certain state of alignment, and a state, i.e. the amount of alignment [9]. The first view implies that BITA is an ongoing process, which requires specific IT management capabilities, includes specific actions and has distinct patterns over time [9]. The second view implies that it is a state, for which it is possible to identify antecedents, measures, and outcomes.

BITA as a state is often criticized for being a "fuzzy" target, as according to [16] practitioners are often facing an ambiguity: what exactly in the business should be aligned with IT? When focusing on the strategic alignment, the suggestion would be a business strategy. However, in practice business strategy is often an unclear target, since strategy provides a direction, not a final destination. Significant attention in the current literature is given to strategic alignment. This refers to the degree to which the business strategy and plans, and the IT strategy and plans, complement each other [9]. Henderson and Venka-traman in [17] presented one of the most cited alignment frameworks - Strategic Alignment Model (SAM). This model defines alignment as the degree of fit and integration between four elements: business strategy, IT strategy, business infrastructure, and IS infrastructure. The multivariate alignment of SAM main elements includes six alignment perspectives: (1) strategic fit on business side - the alignment of business strategy and business structure, (2) strategic fit on IT side - the alignment of IT strategy and IT struc-ture; (3) strategic integration - the alignment of business and IT strategies; (4) functional integration - the alignment of business and IT structures; (5) automation – cross-domain perspective that implies the alignment of business strategy and IT structure; (6) linkage - cross-domain perspective that implies the alignment of IT strategy and business structure [17]. The SAM framework has some limitations, however. For example, depending on how IT-intensive an enterprise or an industry is, the applicability of SAM may vary, as the underlying assumptions of the SAM model may not hold [18]. In addition, when aiming at functional integration in SAM, there is a need to understand the business processes and organization [16]. The business requirements often change and the information about them is limited. Therefore, functional integration requires dealing with a moving target. Moreover, the SAM framework considers the environment of an enterprise only partially, although there are many external factors that can influence BITA. Despite these limitations, the SAM framework represents the four essential elements of an enterprise and divides them between the strategic and operational levels, and the areas of business and IT, therefore in this study we will employ the SAM as a basis for the EM framework.

3.2 Enterprise Modeling – the Process and Intentional Perspective

There is a clear need to capture both organization (business) and technology issues during the design and implementation of IS [19]. Moreover, capturing these dimensions in a valid and comprehensive way requires the involvement of a large number of stakeholders. In this respect EM can serve as an effective practice. EM (sometimes also called business modeling, c.f. [20]) is a practice for developing, obtaining, and communicating enterprise knowledge, like strategies, goals and requirements to different stakeholders [20, 21].

EM is often used during development or refinement of enterprise IS. Researchers pay significant attention to the applicability of EM for software requirements engineering [21, 22]. According to [23], EM is an activity where integrated and commonly shared models describing different aspects of an enterprise are created. Enterprise models focus on some aspect of the problem domain, such e.g. processes, business rules, concepts/information/data, vision/goals, or actors. Therefore the core capability of enterprise models is to capture different aspects (focal areas) of the enterprise practice in terms of procedures, operations, management etc. A model plays an important role as a visual mapping of perception of the enterprise practice and thus it fosters communication. It is a compact abstraction and thus it allows coping with complexity. Models are usually based on shared concepts and thus they facilitate shared understanding [24].

According to [4, 5, 24], collaboration, participation, and interaction among a large group of stakeholders is highly beneficial in the practice of modeling, as it enables more effective and efficient model derivation and it also increases the validity of models. The participative approach also implies involvement of stakeholders in modeling for better understanding of enterprise processes [4, 25]. One problem, which might occur here, is that the resulting enterprise models are often not enough formalized, which in some cases might complicate their further application. Therefore, the role of the EM practitioner who leads this kind of EM effort becomes vital for the efficient creation and use of enterprise models [4, 26].

In terms of the modeling process itself, [15] propose a model according to which EM process includes three basic activities that are usually performed in sequential order, but in some cases can roll back (Fig. 2). After having started the EM effort the EM practitioner, often together with the domain experts, needs to analyze what information should be collected in order to reach the goal of the modeling effort. Therefore, the first activity of EM is to collect information about the enterprise at hand.

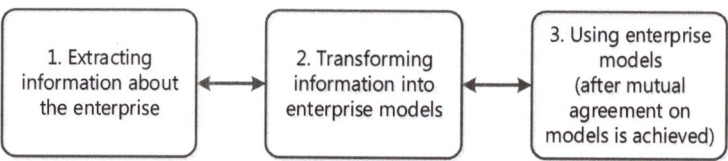

Fig. 2. EM activities [15]

During participative EM, where domain experts play an important role, the main source for getting information are modeling sessions or workshops. During such sessions the EM practitioner has a leading role in eliciting and integrating opinions about various aspects of the enterprise. The ability of the EM practitioner to facilitate this process is crucial in order to extract the necessary information and then to transform this information into enterprise models (activity 2 in Fig. 2). Models are created during modeling sessions together with domain experts to make sure that existing viewpoints are considered and consolidated. A common practice is to iterate between the first and the second activity several times when creating models to make sure that all the needed information has been captured and documented. It is important to emphasize that documentation of models is a continuous process, which will continue until a common agreement on the created models is achieved among the involved participants. There are various challenges that are specific for all three activities of EM. Common agreement among the stakeholders on creating enterprise models is crucial in order to use the created enterprise models for any purpose (activity 3 in Fig. 2).

Apart from development or refinement of an enterprise IS, EM can be used to create shared domain knowledge [8, 27, 28]. Both of these abilities play an important role in BITA, although the results of using EM depend on the purpose behind EM in a particular case. In [27] a hierarchy of EM intentions has been presented (Fig. 3), which shows possible purposes of using EM. It has been further refined in [29]. This model has been also used to generate the EM framework presented in this paper.

The hierarchy of EM intentions differentiates between three high-level intentions. The first intention deals with ensuring the quality of the business, primarily focusing on two issues: (1.1) ensuring acceptance of business decisions through committing the stakeholders to the decisions made, and (1.2) maintaining and sharing knowledge about the business, its vision, and the way it operates. With respect to knowledge sharing EM plays an important role, since it provides a multifaceted map of the business as a platform for communicating between stakeholders. The second group of EM intentions is developing the business, which can be considered as one of the most common intentions of EM. EM can be used in the early stages of IS development as an effective practice for

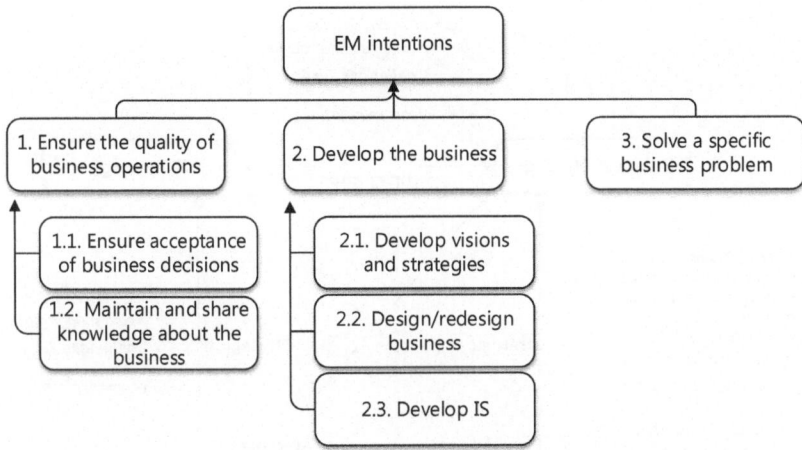

Fig. 3. The main elements of the EM intentions hierarchy, adapted from [27]

gathering business needs and high-level requirements. Developing the business might include (2.1) developing business vision and strategies, (2.2) redesigning business operations, and (2.3) developing the supporting information systems.

The third top-level intention in the hierarchy is to use EM as a problem-solving tool, where EM is only used for supporting the discussion among a group of stakeholders trying to analyze a specific problem. In such cases EM can be helpful for capturing, delimiting, and analyzing the initial problem situation and in order to decide on further actions. Various intentions behind an EM initiative can aim for different results, and subsequently can affect various perspectives of BITA [30].

4   Overview of the EM Framework

The EM framework consists of (1) positioning of EM intentions in the SAM model and (2) challenges and recommendations when using EM for BITA. The challenges (numbered 1–4) and recommendations will be introduced in detail in Sect. 5. In order to position EM in the context of BITA, the elements of hierarchy of EM intentions according to (Fig. 3) have been positioned in the SAM framework (Fig. 4).

The presented positioning of EM intentions in SAM indicates that EM can facilitate BITA in a number of ways. First, it allows the alignment of business strategy with IT strategy, i.e. *strategic integration*, when EM is applied for developing business vision and strategies. In this relation EM is used as a tool for clarification and documentation of business and IT strategies for an enterprise.

> *"It is quite time-consuming to create and communicate a vision and strategy. It is especially tricky to really make people understand and accept vision and strategies. The way we approach it is an EM workshop." (Respondent 2–1)*

Using EM for developing supporting IS allows the alignment of IT strategy with underlying IT structure, i.e. *strategic fit on the IT side*. EM provides a description of

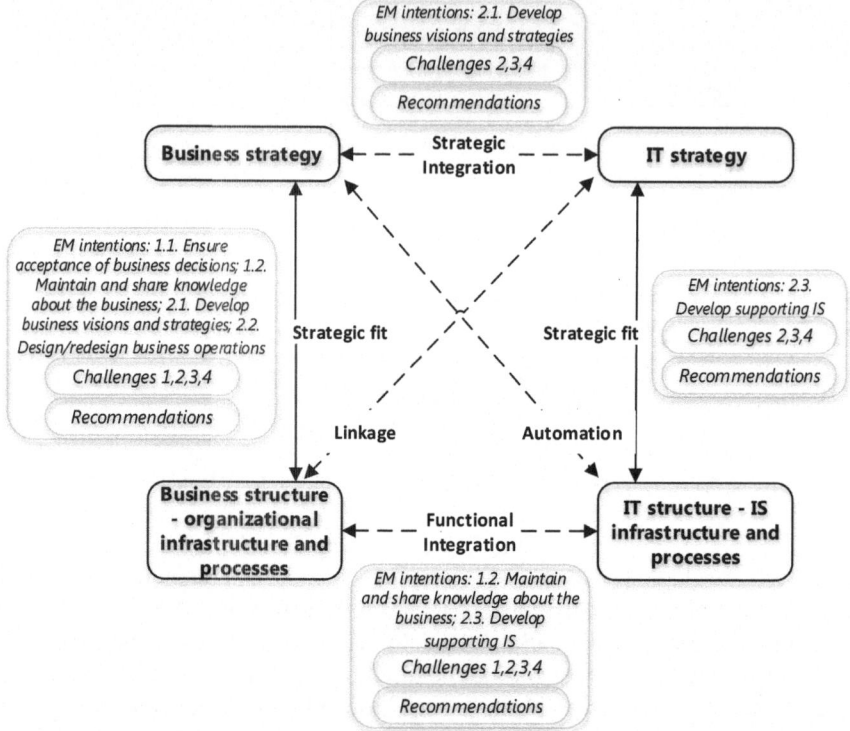

Fig. 4. Positioning of Enterprise Modeling within the Business and IT Alignment context

the AS-IS state of the business, possibly including a description of the business processes. In other words, EM provides a clear picture of how the business operates, which then serves as a basis for developing the required IS.

> *"Mostly you use enterprise models to show smarter ways of working that enterprise can realize. Often implementation of new IT system is one way of fulfilling these changes." (Respondent 2–4)*

Alignment of business and IT structures, i.e. ***functional integration***, can be facilitated by applying EM for developing IS, as it helps to develop IS according to particular requirements from the business side.

> *"I have used EM a lot to identify the need for some kind of IT solution. When such a need exists I have to create a functionality description based on business processes. Based on it I can see possible business use cases." (Respondent 2–3)*

> *"You need to visualize IS – parts of it that are useful and those parts which are not useful. Then it can be possible to take actions regarding those, which are not useful anymore." (Respondent 2–1)*

> *"We start from creating process models. After that we add a resource layer, where we can indicate the main areas for setting demands on new IS." (Respondent 2–2)*

Also, functional integration can be facilitated by using EM for maintaining or sharing knowledge about the business, as it provides a common ground for the dialogue between the business and IT sides. In this case, EM can describe the way the business works and the types of infrastructure that exists to support it.

"If you would like to share knowledge about business operations then EM, i.e. creating models together during particularly EM workshops, is an excellent way to do that!" (Respondent 2–4)

EM can facilitate the alignment of business strategy and business structure, i.e. **strategic fit on business side**, in a number of ways. In order to redesign business operations EM can be used to define the way the business should work in coherence with the existing business strategy. For this purpose a number of business process models can be created, taking into account the vision and the strategy. Additionally, a clearly modeled and documented business strategy has a better chance to be followed by enterprise employees than one that is not.

"Often company would like to pick up some opportunities on the market. In some cases the board should make a decision if the company should enter another market. In other cases – the board should decide if the company should start producing another type of products. In both cases we start EM by going through the vision and strategy. Based on that it is possible to set goals for new things." (Respondent 2–2)

Using EM to ensure acceptance of business decisions is a way to make people committed to the business decisions, which in turn helps to actually realize strategical decisions in practice. Communication between stakeholders that happens during EM sessions can play an important role in stakeholders' commitments and can help to carry out the discussed business decisions.

"The owner of created model should be committed to apply and realize it in the business." (Respondent 2–1)

Realizing business strategy can also be facilitated by using EM as a tool for creating shared knowledge and understanding, as enterprise models can serve as a compact source for articulating business strategy. An articulated and documented vision and strategy can then be discussed, refined and referred to if needed. In some cases, clearly modeled and documented visions and strategies can help people to actually follow them in their daily work.

"Good visualization (a model) of business vision and strategy might work as a self-playing piano, since there will be no need for instructions for making people follow these vision and strategy in day-to-day operations." (Respondent 2–1)

5   Guiding EM in the Context of BITA

The positioning of EM intentions in the context of BITA as presented in Fig. 4 provides a structure for discussing EM challenges and recommendations. Related EM challenges and recommendations are presented in Table 1, which is followed by their detailed description in the subsequent sections below.

Table 1. EM challenges and recommendations relevant for the context of BITA

Challenges	Recommendations
1. In time discussion of technical solutions	- Start modeling with a group of participants who have strong domain knowledge of problematic areas
	- Make sure that IT experts are involved in the process only after the key areas have been identified and a general understanding of WHAT should be changed has been created
2. Reuse of enterprise models	- Make sure the existing models are maintained in a repository and that they are kept up to date
	- The benefit of models maintenance should be clarified for enterprise management
3. Dealing with diverse backgrounds, knowledge and interpretations	- Provide the participants with a brief reminder of the purpose of the models being presented and with a summary of the notation
	- When using models as a basis for explanation and discussions, the diverse backgrounds and knowledge of the involved stakeholders should be considered and consolidated
4. Presenting relevant information in an understandable way	- Take benefit from the power of a good visualization when using models for different purposes
	- Make sure that the targeted audience can understand the models

In Time Discussion of Technical Solutions. During EM there is a tendency to involve technical people in the discussion process quite early, which can divert the discussions and create a risk of getting stuck in implementation details instead of discussing alternative solutions from the business perspective. The respondents highlight the inclination of IT specialists to take over the analysis as soon as they get involved in the modeling sessions. That is why it is important to not let technical specialists dominate the modeling sessions.

> *"In many cases IT representatives want to take over the analysis too early. First experts from operations should make models explaining how operations are running (process models, concept model, etc.). If that is ready, then we start the dialogue with IT representatives." (Respondent 2–2)*

"It is hard to get beyond discussion of particular IT solutions. People representing different part of the business end up talking about IT solutions. It is really hard to make people say what they want to achieve in the business, and only after this look at what type of IT support is needed." (Respondent 2–3)

The analysis of the interviews have shown that EM practitioners recommend to start the modeling efforts with a smaller group with strong domain knowledge that can identify key areas for continuing work. The analysis also shows that it is recommended that people with technical domain knowledge (IT experts) should not be involved until the key areas and problematic issues have been identified. Then the EM effort can move on and focus on HOW to deal with these key areas, which then could initiate the involvement of IT experts.

"It is good to have technical details, but not before enterprise models are ready and have good quality. This is the best basis that you could have in order to set demands for the IT." (Respondent 2–2)

This challenge is typical for scenarios where EM is used with the following intentions: (2.1) developing business vision and strategies, (2.2) redesigning business operations, and (2.3) developing the supporting information systems.

Recommendations:

- Start modeling with a group of participants who have strong domain knowledge of problematic areas.
- Make sure that IT experts are involved in the process only after the key areas have been identified and a general understanding of WHAT should be changed has been created.

Reuse of Enterprise Models. This challenge is related to the fact that enterprise models are mainly only used once for a specific purpose and for the project for which they were created. This is highly inefficient but unfortunately, in many cases, a common practice.

"Resulting enterprise models might be hard to reuse. They can be too specific or incomplete, since they were aimed to be used for developing one particular IT system." (Respondent 2–4)

It requires considerable effort to ensure the continuous value of enterprise models over time. One way to deal with this could be to appoint someone responsible for model maintenance and reuse through the use of model repositories. The respondents have emphasized the importance of repositories to store and maintain enterprise models. Enterprise models maintenance is an important task due to the dynamic nature of today's business environment, especially if the enterprise is captured and described in models that represent different parts and states of the enterprise. The reuse of enterprise models from previous modeling projects can be facilitated by the adoption of a restricted set of notation rules for modeling, covering methods and tools.

"Explain to people what is the value of models maintenance!" (Respondent 2–4)

"What is really needed is a repository that is used in the whole company, so that all new models can be related to old ones." (Respondent 2–4)

"For one company (sometimes for a business unit) you need to select a modeling technique, notation and tool to document and store models and put them into place. Then you can use enterprise models efficiently." (Respondent 2–4)

This challenge is relevant when using EM for: (1.1) ensuring acceptance of business decisions throughcommitting the stakeholders to the decisions made, and (1.2) maintaining and sharing knowledge about the business, its vision, and the way it operates, (2.1) developing business vision and strategies, (2.2) redesigning business operations, and (2.3) developing the supporting information systems.

Recommendations:

- Make sure the existing models are maintained in a repository and that they are kept up to date.
- The benefit of models maintenance should be clarified for enterprise management.

Dealing with Diverse Backgrounds, Knowledge and Interpretations. Stakeholders that are involved in EM projects usually have different backgrounds and knowledge. For example, the skills and abilities of people from administration differ from those of staff working in operations. This means that different groups of stakeholders may have significantly different interpretations of the situation facing the enterprise. Creating mutual agreements about different enterprise aspects is therefore crucial during any EM effort. This means that an EM practitioner has to consider the varied backgrounds of involved stakeholders and to negotiate between people in order to create mutual agreements.

"If you have a workshop with people with different backgrounds - financial persons, engineers, HR department, operations, product development - they are looking at reality differently. They often have different solutions depending on their preferences, backgrounds and knowledge." (Respondent 2–1)

Diverse backgrounds and interpretations among stakeholders might affect EM and this can be an obstacle for using models for any purpose. It is crucial to have a mutual understanding about the meaning of different models before analyzing or implementing them. To deal with this diversity it is therefore suggested to explain what the models really represent in the enterprise. It can also be useful to start with a brief explanation of the adopted modeling notation and/or method to get everyone on the same page. However, the respondents have emphasized that at this stage of using enterprise models (both for developing the business and for ensuring the quality of the business), it is reasonable to keep such introductions quite short.

"Some participants might know how to read models, others might not. If you mix them together you have to do a "warm-up" – a short method introduction, so that all know how to understand the models." (Respondent 2–2)

This challenge is relevant when using EM for: (1.1) ensuring acceptance of business decisions through committing the stakeholders to the decisions made, and (1.2) maintaining and sharing knowledge about the business, its vision, and the way it operates, (2.1) developing business vision and strategies, (2.2) redesigning business operations, and (2.3) developing the supporting information systems.

Recommendations:

- Provide the participants with a brief reminder of the purpose of the models being presented and with a summary of the notation.
- When using models as a basis for explanation and discussions, the diverse backgrounds and knowledge of the involved stakeholders should be considered and consolidated.

Presenting Relevant Information in an Understandable Way. This challenge is closely related to the previous one. It emphasizes the need for EM practitioners to represent and deliver relevant information to stakeholders and to decision makers in a clear and understandable way. This can be challenging due to the diversity of stakeholders' backgrounds and requires that EM practitioners have relevant pedagogical and communication abilities.

"It is hard to implement a model, since first people need to really understand it." (Respondent 2–1)

"We are more likely to make decisions to act if we have clear understanding about the subject matter. If we do not understand then we resist making decisions. It is important to make the situation clear for key decision makers." (Respondent 2–2)

"If you are really into the model you can fail to explain it. People are not here to learn the model, but to solve the problem." (Respondent 2–3)

The interviews have shown that enterprise models are often used for decision making. One suggestion in this context is to use illustrative models of satisfactory quality. It was also suggested by the respondents to use models as a foundation for explanation. The main reason for this is that models have greater explanatory power than ordinary textual and verbal descriptions. However, textual and verbal explanations are still important, since models themselves also need to be explained. One thing to keep in mind is to contextualize the explanations when presenting the models to the stakeholders.

"Good visualizations might work as a self-playing piano, since you will not need to give instructions – people can act by themselves if they have clear directions (regarding how to implement models)." (Respondent 2–1)

"Use their language and talk their talk! Try to see, feel and understand their perspectives of the company and environment. Then you can have a dialogue and communicate." (Respondent 2–1)

"Ask yourself: How would I communicate this to [management position X]? What is the suitable language? What is on the agenda? How do I translate things into the [management position X] situation?" (Respondent 2–1)

"You need to explain in other words!" (Respondent 2–3)

This challenge is relevant when using EM for: (1.1) ensuring acceptance of business decisions through committing the stakeholders to the decisions made, and (1.2) maintaining and sharing knowledge about the business, its vision, and the way it operates,

(2.1) developing business vision and strategies, (2.2) redesigning business operations, and (2.3) developing the supporting information systems.

Recommendations:

- Take benefit from the power of a good visualization when using models for different purposes.
- Make sure that the targeted audience can understand the models.

6   Conclusions

In the broad sense, this work investigated the role of EM in the context of BITA. To position EM in the context of BITA, the Strategic Alignment Model was used as a frame. The positioning was done considering the intentions of EM use, since the effect of EM is highly dependent on the purpose behind a particular EM effort. The resulting positioning suggests that EM can facilitate BITA in a number of ways. Particularly, it contributes to strategic alignment and functional integration, and what is more it facilitates fit between infrastructure and processes (both business and IS) and corresponding strategies. In addition to the positioning of EM in the context of BITA, this paper identifies challenges that EM practitioners face when using EM for BITA and suggested recommendations to deal with these challenges. Together these results are presented as the framework with a set of conceptually structured EM challenges and recommendations that are specific for different alignment perspectives. The framework provides a detailed view on the implication of EM in the light of various alignment perspectives, which so far has not been described in a structured manner in the literature.

An important characteristic of the study is related to the aspects of EM being considered. Most contemporary studies on EM challenges and recommendations focus on either (1) the collaborative nature of EM or (2) the required characteristics of created enterprise models, whereas only a few provide a combined view. Consideration of both of these aspects gives an opportunity to get a broader view on EM practice and to generate more comprehensive support for EM practitioners. This study considered both. Various aspects of collaboration in EM were analyzed when investigating the extraction of information about the enterprise in participative settings and the creation and the usage of enterprise models. The desired characteristics of enterprise models have been taken into account when investigating how extracted enterprise-related information is usually transformed into enterprise models and how created models can be used for various purposes. The result of this study, the EM framework, contains challenges and recommendations for using enterprise models for various intentions, which imply both of the aforementioned aspects.

References

1. Silvius, A.J.G.: Business and IT alignment: what we know and what we don't know. In: The Proceedings of International Conference on Information Management and Engineering, pp. 558–563 (2009)

2. Luftman, J.: Assessing IT-Business Alignment. Inf. Syst. Manage. **20**(4), 9–15 (2003)
3. Schlosser, F., Wagner, H.-T., Coltman, T.: Reconsidering the dimensions of business-IT alignment. In: The Proceedings of the 45th Hawaii International Conference on System Science, pp. 5053–5061 (2012)
4. Sandkuhl, K., Stirna, J., Persson, A., Wissotzki, M.: Enterprise Modeling– Tackling Business Challenges with the 4EM Method. Springer, Heidelberg (2014)
5. Stirna, J., Persson, A.: Anti-patterns as a means of focusing on critical quality aspects in enterprise modeling. In: Halpin, T., Krogstie, J., Nurcan, S., Proper, E., Schmidt, R., Soffer, P., Ukor, R. (eds.) BPMDS 2009 and EMMSAD 2009. LNBIP, vol. 29, pp. 407–418. Springer, Heidelberg (2009)
6. Jonkers, H., Lankhorst, M., van Buuren, R., Hoppenbrouwers, S., Bonsangue, M., van der Torre, L.: Concepts for modelling enterprise architectures. Int. J. Coop. Inf. Syst. **13**(3), 257–287 (2004)
7. Kearns, G.S., Lederer, A.L.: A resource-based view of strategic IT alignment: how knowledge sharing creates competitive advantage. Decis. Sci. **34**(1), 1–29 (2003)
8. Reich, B.H., Benbasat, I.: Factors that influence the social dimension of alignment between business and information technology objectives. MIS Q. **24**(1), 81–113 (2000)
9. Chan, Y.E., Reich, B.H.: IT alignment: what have we learned? J. Inf. Technol. **22**(4), 297–315 (2007)
10. Gregor, S., Hart, D., Martin, N.: Enterprise architectures: enablers of business strategy and IS/IT alignment in government. Inf. Technol. People **20**(2), 96–120 (2007)
11. Wegmann, A., Regev, G., Rychkova, I., Le, L.-S., de la Cruz, J.G., Julia, P.: Business-IT alignment with SEAM for enterprise architecture. In: Proceedings of the 11th IEEE International EDOC Conference, pp. 111–121 (2007)
12. Seigerroth, U.: Enterprise Modeling and Enterprise Architecture: the constituents of transformation and alignment of Business and IT. Int. J. IT/Business Alignment Governance (IJITBAG) **2**(1), 16–34 (2011)
13. Christiner, F., Lantow, B., Sandkuhl, K., Wissotzki, M.: Multi-dimensional visualization in enterprise modeling. In: Abramowicz, W., Domingue, J., Węcel, K. (eds.) BIS 2012 Workshops. LNBIP, vol. 127, pp. 139–152. Springer, Heidelberg (2009)
14. Kaidalova, J., Kaczmarek, T., Seigerroth, U., Shilov, N.: Practical challenges of enterprise modeling in the light of business and IT alignment. In: Sandkuhl, K., Seigerroth, U., Stirna, J. (eds.) PoEM 2012. LNBIP, pp. 31–45. Springer, Heidelberg (2012)
15. Kaidalova, J., Seigerroth, U., Bukowska, E., Shilov, N.: Enterprise modeling for business and IT alignment: challenges and recommendations. Int. J. IT/Business Alignment Governance **5**(2), 43–68 (2014)
16. Silvius, A.J.G.: Business & IT alignment in theory and practice. In: The Proceedings of the 40th Hawaii International Conference on Systems and Sciences, p. 211b (2007)
17. Henderson, J., Venkatraman, N.: Strategic Alignment: A model for organizational transformation through information technology. In: Kocham, T.A., Useem, M. (eds.) Transforming Organizations, pp. 97–117. Oxford University Press, New York (1992)
18. Chan, Y.E., Reich, B.H.: IT alignment: an annotated bibliography. J. Inf. Technol. **22**(4), 316–396 (2007)
19. Gibson, C.F.: IT-enabled business change - an approach to understanding and managing risk. MIS Q. Executive **2**(2), 104–115 (2003)
20. Kirikova, M.: Explanatory capability of enterprise models. Data Knowl. Eng. **33**(2), 119–136 (2000)
21. Persson, A.: Enterprise Modelling in Practice: Situational Factors and their Influence on Adopting a Participative Approach (Doctoral Dissertation). Department of Computer and Systems Sciences, Stockholm University (2001). ISSN 1101-8526

22. Rolland, C., Prakash, N.: From conceptual modelling to requirements engineering. Ann. Softw. Eng. **10**, 151–176 (2000)
23. Stirna, J., Persson, A., Sandkuhl, K.: Participative enterprise modeling: experiences and recommendations. In: Krogstie, J., Opdahl, A.L., Sindre, G. (eds.) CAiSE 2007 and WES 2007. LNCS, vol. 4495, pp. 546–560. Springer, Heidelberg (2007)
24. Barjis, J.: CPI modeling: collaborative, participative, interactive modeling. In: Jain, S., Creasey, R.R., Himmelspach, J., White, K.P., Fu, M. (eds.) Proceedings of the 2011 Winter Simulation Conference, pp. 3099–3108. IEEE, Piscataway (2011)
25. Front, A., Rieu, D., Santorum, M.: A participative end-user modeling approach for business process requirements. In: Bider, I., Gaaloul, K., Krogstie, J., Nurcan, S., Proper, H.A., Schmidt, R., Soffer, P. (eds.) BPMDS 2014 and EMMSAD 2014. LNBIP, vol. 175, pp. 33–47. Springer, Heidelberg (2014)
26. Rosemann, M., Lind, M., Hjalmarsson, A., Recker, J.: Four facets of a process modeling facilitator. In: The Proceedings of the 32nd International Conference on Information Systems, pp. 1–16 (2011)
27. Persson, A., Stirna, J.: Why enterprise modelling? an explorative study into current practice. In: Dittrich, K.R., Geppert, A., Norrie, M. (eds.) CAiSE 2001. LNCS, vol. 2068, pp. 465–468. Springer, Heidelberg (2001)
28. Lind, M., Seigerroth, U.: Team-based reconstruction for expanding organizational ability. J. Oper. Res. Soc. **54**(2), 119–129 (2003)
29. Bubenko Jr., J.A., Persson, A., Stirna, J.: An intentional perspective on enterprise modeling. In: Salinesi, C., Nurcan, S., Souveyet, C., Ralyté, J. (eds.) Intentional Perspectives on Information Systems Engineering, pp. 215–237. Springer, Heidelberg (2010)
30. Kaidalova, J.: Positioning Enterprise Modeling in the context of Business and IT alignment. In: Abramowicz, W., Kokkinaki, A. (eds.) BIS 2014 Workshops. LNBIP, vol. 183, pp. 202–213. Springer, Heidelberg (2014)

Towards a Generic Goal Model to Support Continuous Improvement in SME Construction Companies

Anne Persson[1(✉)], Anniken Karlsen[2], and Kristens Gudfinnsson[1]

[1] School of Informatics, University of Skövde,
P.O. Box 408, 541 28 Skövde, Sweden
{anne.persson,kristens.gudfinnsson}@his.se
[2] Aalesund University College, Postboks 1517, 6025 Aalesund, Norway
ak@hials.no

Abstract. Small and medium sized (SME) construction companies are often good at bricks, mortar and carpentry but not at management. However, it is often bad management that hinders companies to become financially sustainable over time and to grow. This paper presents a generic goal model aiming to support SME construction companies to systematically work with continuous improvement towards the overarching goal of becoming thriving businesses. The goal model has been developed based on the principles of lean, balanced scorecards and the business canvas, as well as on a management consultant's experiences from working with this kind of companies for many years.

Keywords: Goal model · Enterprise modeling · Continuous improvement · SME construction companies

1 Introduction

Small and medium sized (SME) enterprises are a key driver for economic growth in Europe [1]. In order to stay competitive and profitable, SMEs, like larger organizations, must meet the requirements and demands of a rapidly changing market. SME construction companies are no different. For many years, construction companies have had a poor reputation for coping with the adverse effects of change with many projects unable to meet deadlines, cost and quality targets [2]. Even more serious is the fact that many companies, particularly small ones, are going bankrupt in an industry that has a great influence on nations' gross domestic product [3].

Due to this, top-level concerns for both business executives and national authorities are how to turn construction companies into profitable and well-run businesses and to keep them that way over time. Particularly the SME construction companies, struggle with low profits and many are going bankrupt, adding people to the unemployment lines. In many cases this is due to lack of control systems and proper information for decision-making.

In the work leading up to this paper we have noticed that for a small construction company one or two problematic projects can actually tip the scale towards severe

© IFIP International Federation for Information Processing 2015
J. Ralyté et al. (Eds.): PoEM 2015, LNBIP 235, pp. 27–42, 2015.
DOI: 10.1007/978-3-319-25897-3_3

financial crisis. Practitioners have reported to us that many SME construction companies are good at "bricks, mortar and carpentry", but not at management. This becomes devastating in a situation where companies not only have to manage each project individually, but must also be able to handle project portfolios with complex dependencies between projects. Hence, the potential for improving the management aspect of construction companies is great. Such improvement should, however, be done orderly and with a long-term perspective, which implies setting up orderly schemes for continuous improvement.

In this paper we propose a generic goal model that is aimed to somewhat alleviate this problematic situation in SME construction companies by providing a framework for continuous improvement. The model is the backbone of a method for continuous improvement to be used in SME construction companies, the SmallBuild + method. The method has been developed within a EUREKA Eurostars project.

The remainder of the paper is organized as follows. Section 2 provides the theoretical background of the work. In Sect. 3 the approach to developing the proposed goal model is described. The generic goal model is presented in Sect. 4, together with some suggestions on how to use it, also in relation to tool support. Finally, some aspects of further evaluation and future outlook are discussed in Sect. 5.

2   Theoretical Background

In this section we describe the background to the work presented in this paper. We describe the situation of SME construction companies and some challenges they face in their continuous improvement efforts. The approach proposed in the paper is based on a generic goal model. The use of such models to support continuous improvement is also discussed.

2.1   Challenges of SME Construction Companies

The building and property industry is a large, fragmented and complex industry. It is also an important policy area affecting all sectors of the society. The wealth creation of society is among others dependent on the construction industry delivering well-functioning buildings and infrastructure to businesses, industry, public entities, private individuals and society [4]. As an example, in 2014 the construction of 25,404 homes was initiated in Norway alone.

Continuing with Norway as an example, the following list indicates some major challenges facing the industry [4]. We believe that it is fair to assume that the situation is similar in other countries.

1. Productivity growth seems to be too weak.
2. Building and construction processes are characterized by many quality deviations, errors and omissions.
3. The industry is characterized by fragmented purchasing and low procurement expertise leading to a non-holistic overall cost focus, contributing to short-term investments.

4. The industry has a too low rate of innovation. There is broad consensus in the industry that the industry must get better at taking innovations in use.
5. Parts of the industry are characterized by too many unethical practices.
6. Production processes are characterized by weak interaction. Widespread use of detailed contracts, selecting suppliers based on the lowest price, combined with split purchasing, provides many changes, additions and conflicts that generate distrust and weakened interactions.
7. The construction process is hampered by too many delayed and costly regulations and rules and different interpretations of these.

In addition to this, a sector study by e-Business W@tch [5] identified the issues of improving ICT skills, increasing the awareness of ICT benefits and potentials, and facilitating interoperability are identified as relevant construction sector policy initiatives. Although the study is 10 years old, our experience shows that this is still the case.

Olawale and Sun [6] conducted a survey of 250 construction project organizations in the UK, which was followed by face-to-face interviews with experienced practitioners from fifteen of these organizations. They found that the top five factors inhibiting effective project cost and time control, are all project internal elements and that quite often programs are drawn upon gut feeling. This is in contrast to previous studies where many external aspects are cited as the most important factors, such as inflation, material shortage, unforeseen ground conditions, inclement climate, etc. [6].

For many years construction companies have had a poor reputation for coping with the adverse effects of change with several projects unable to meet deadlines, cost and quality targets [2]. Even more serious is the matter that many are going bankrupt within an industry that possibly influences an economy's gross domestic product more than any other [3]. This is particularly the case with small and medium sized companies (SME). Due to this, top-level concerns for both business executives and others are how to turnaround the construction companies to profitable and well-run businesses and keep them that way.

Morris and Pinto [7] investigated data on project overruns from 3600 projects and concluded that project managers also need to look into the organizational business contexts within which projects are managed. This aspect is highlighted by Aarseth [8] who presents findings from interviews conducted with hundreds of project managers and project team members suggesting that the task perspective, time schedule and scope, is not sufficient when the context of the project is complex. Just as important are focus on business relationship management, cooperation between the project, the people and companies in the project and the external environment, organizations and context [8].

Obviously, construction projects seldom can be handled one by one along a timeline. Instead they are usually parts of project portfolios where a number of projects continually must be analyzed, invested in and developed in concert [9]. Within these portfolios each project are likely to be subject to uncertainty and risk as regards cost, time and quality [2]. Therefore, managers must know which projects the company is involved in, which stage each project has reached, who is involved in each project, capital-binding in each project, and how each project is related to and dependent on other project schedules. As regards the highest ranked factor inhibiting both cost and time control it is obvious that there is a need for controlling and restricting the influence of this factor.

In summary, SME construction companies face big challenges, not only in Norway, which means that the potential for improving the management aspect of construction companies is great. Such improvement should, however, be done orderly and with a long-term perspective, which implies setting up orderly schemes for continuous improvement.

2.2   Challenges to Continuous Improvement in SME Enterprises

SME enterprises are a key driver for economic growth in Europe [1]. In order to stay competitive and profitable, SMEs, like larger organizations, must meet the requirements and demands of a rapidly changing market. One strategy to achieve this is to implement different continuous improvement initiatives, such as, e.g., Lean. However, despite the well-known theories, only a few SMEs succeed in their continuous improvement initiatives [10].

Ogunbiyi, Oladapo and Goulding [11] have done an empirical study of the impact of lean construction techniques on sustainable construction in the UK. Results from their study indicate that there are many benefits associated with implementation of lean construction and sustainable construction such as improved corporate image and sustainable competitive advantage, improved productivity and process flow, improvement in environmental quality and increased compliance with customer's expectations. The study also identifies several areas of linkage between lean and sustainability such as waste reduction, value maximization, environmental management and health and safety improvement among others.

SMEs are generally defined by their number of employees, but there are other variables than size that influence leadership, strategic planning and culture in companies [12]. A majority of SMEs are privately held and family-owned. Research has shown that this affects how the company is managed and operated. Family firms are run by reasons other than financial and rational and reflect a different view of ownership, based on the owner's values and beliefs [13]. This implies that non- economic (family) goals may take precedence over economic goals in family firms [14]. These circumstances have implications both on the design of business support services and SMEs' willingness to participate in continuous improvement as well as their objectives to do so [15].

There are several factors that have shown to be critical for a successful implementation of different continuous improvement initiatives. The most common are management and leadership [16], but also performance evaluation [17] and supporting information systems have shown to play an important roll particularly now with the growing use of business intelligence [18].

Performance Measurement Systems (PMS) support performance management by communicating and transforming different performance measurements between different organizational levels and employees. Ukko et al. [19] conclude that association between goals on the strategic level and on the operational level is important in order to achieve the strategic goals, and that performance measurement should be enabled on the operational level. They also state that since many companies today apply performance measurement on the operational level, one of the major challenges for managers is to achieve understandable and accessible communication about the goal of the organization. There is also a need to better understand challenges in transforming performance measurement on the operational level to usable information on the strategic level. It is critical that managers on different levels have relevant decision support of good quality.

2.3 Using Generic Goal Models to Support Continuous Improvement

Goals have been important to businesses for a long time. In 1954 Peter Drucker published the book *The Practice of Management*, being recognized as the first book to write about *objectives*, to define *key result areas*, to outline how to set objectives, and to describe how to use them to direct and steer a business and to measure its performance while looking at management as a whole [20]. The time dimension is essential in management because management is concerned with decisions for action, and action is always aimed at results in the future [20]. This clearly points to the need to take a continuous improvement perspective when working towards goal achievements.

A goal model is a structure of interrelated goals that describe the strategic direction of an enterprise towards a desired state of the enterprise. Goals models provide an analytical instrument for a number of purposes, e.g. decision-making and planning in order to achieve consistence, coherence and increased understanding among [21].

Goal models are often considered to be a part of the enterprise modeling process, where a number of integrated models capturing and representing different aspects (focal areas) of an enterprise, for example business processes, business rules, concepts, information, data, vision, goals and actors [22]. The systematic use of process models for various purposes is a quite common practice in all types of organizations. We have observed, however, that the systematic use of goal models in practice is less common even though goals are needed as a driver in all kinds of organizational development work.

A number of goal modeling techniques are described in the literature. Some examples can be found in [22–25]. They are reported to have a number of weaknesses, e.g. being complex to understand, requiring a huge amount of time to implement and as such being unable to support business analysts in a rapidly changing business environment [26] Nevertheless, since goals are essential for business development, there is a need to find fairly simple and practical approaches that support businesses in working with goals.

One of the more critical aspects in goal modeling is the creative process of formulating the goals, negotiating them between the stakeholders involved, defining relationships between goals, and documenting the model. It takes quite a bit of competence to manage this process [27]. Using reference goal models or generic goal models can be a useful starting-point to alleviate some of the risk in such situations. The aim of reference models typically is to unify and integrate the body of knowledge or best practice in a certain area. In the work reported in this paper, this approach was considered relevant, since the level of management maturity in SME construction companies is relatively low. A reference goal model in this case then provides learning and insight into which elements make up an enterprise and which areas must be in focus to ensure long-term survival and company growth.

3   Approach to Develop the Proposed Generic Goal Model

In a pilot study carried out in a Norwegian SME construction company [28] enterprise modeling was used in a turnaround operation together with business management methods in an effort to change the way of working in the company. The company was at the time at severe risk to go bankrupt. The combination of these approaches yielded some very encouraging results (Fig. 1).

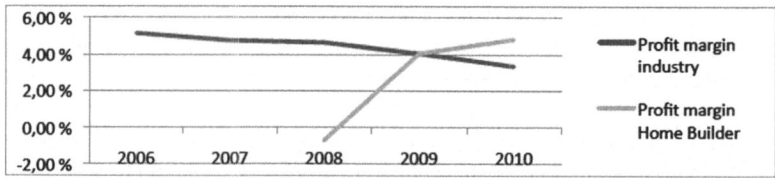

Fig. 1. Profit margin in industry in Norway compared to that in the SME construction company [28]

These results motivated an initiative to develop a process surveillance and control method that combines enterprise modeling and business management methods, the SmallBuild + method. The aim of the method is to support companies in their continuous improvement towards sustainability and economic growth. It has been developed in collaboration between practitioners and researchers in a project funded by the EUREKA Eurostars programme[1].

The Norwegian SME construction company previously mentioned has been involved as a case study setting for developing and testing the method. During the project, the company needed to carry out a second turnaround project to save the company from going bankrupt, again. This shows that awareness of the status of a company and related risks needs to be part of day-to-day business.

During that work, the need for defining relevant goals related to various business areas became a central theme to ensure survival and growth after a period where most of the energy had been put into handling urgent issues and putting out fires, due to the danger of bankruptcy. Motivated by the writings of [9] and the work by [6], relevant goals for ensuring long-term sustainability were formulated. The goals were documented in the form of a simple hierarchical goal model. The goal model was developed in close cooperation between practitioners and researchers in the SmallBuild + project. The manager of the company experienced great value in putting the goals and objectives into an orderly "system". He stated that it helped him to get an overview of the

---

[1] https://www.eurostars-eureka.eu.

situation: "When everything is burning around you, it is difficult to raise your head and look at the situation from a bird's eye perspective."

This specific goal model was generalized to be applicable to other SME construction companies and then became the backbone of the SmallBuild + method for continuous improvement (Fig. 2).

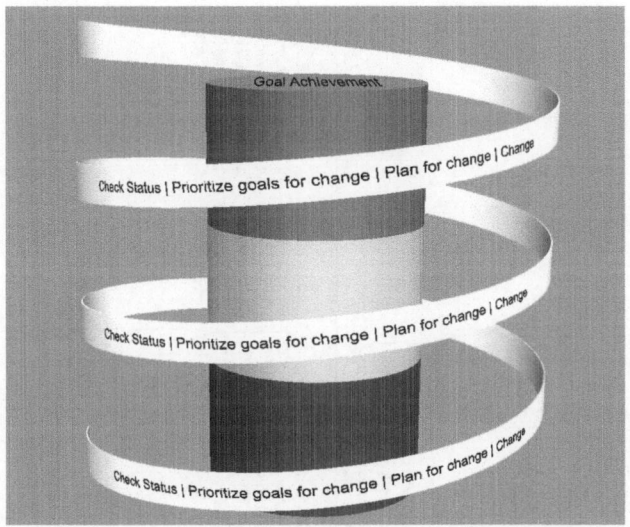

Fig. 2. Goal oriented continuous improvement in the SmallBuild + method

The development of the goal model was built on the following three approaches: (1) Lean [29], (2) Balanced Scorecard [30], and (3) the Business Model Canvas [31]. It also builds on a management consultant's experiences from working with this kind of companies for many years. The consultant participated in the project.

4   The Generic Goal Model and its Use

In this section the developed generic goal model is presented. Since the model targets improving the effectiveness of the organization as a whole, including various focus areas, its subcomponents are many and varied, corresponding to the common target components addressed in change literature [32] and targeted by consultants with years of experience as change facilitators. To address this complexity in an orderly fashion and to increase readability of the model, we chose to present each focus area in separate sub-models.

In the top-level model (Fig. 3), the main goals are presented that need to be achieved in order to ensure sustainable SME construction companies. Each of them represents an essential focus area. Each of these top goals are decomposed in a separate sub-model (Figs. 4, 5, 6, 7, 8 and 9), except for the goal focusing on health and safety, which are covered in national regulatory documents.

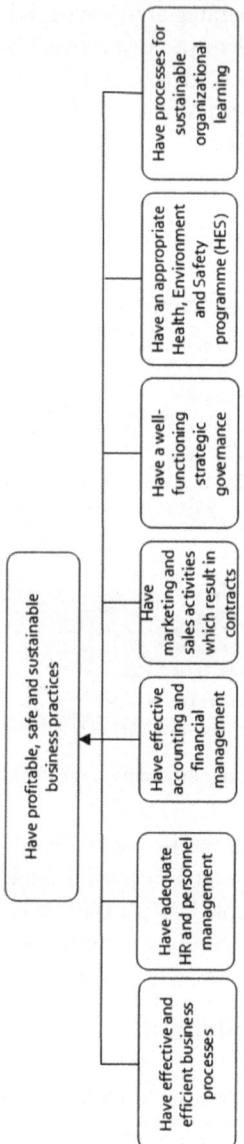

Fig. 3. Top-level goal model

When assessing the status of a specific SME construction company, the goals of each focus area assessed one by one. The status is set to red, yellow or green. Red means that the goal needs urgent attention. Yellow means that the status of the goal is partially satisfactory and needs attention but not urgently. Green means that the status of the goal is satisfactory. For each of the goals needing attention Fig. 10 provides an example of defined criteria for setting the status of a goal, in this case a goal concerning

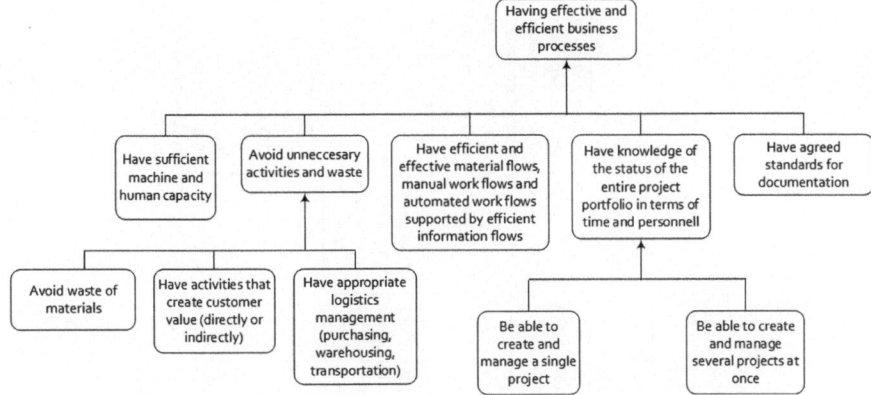

Fig. 4. Sub-model on having effective and efficient business processes

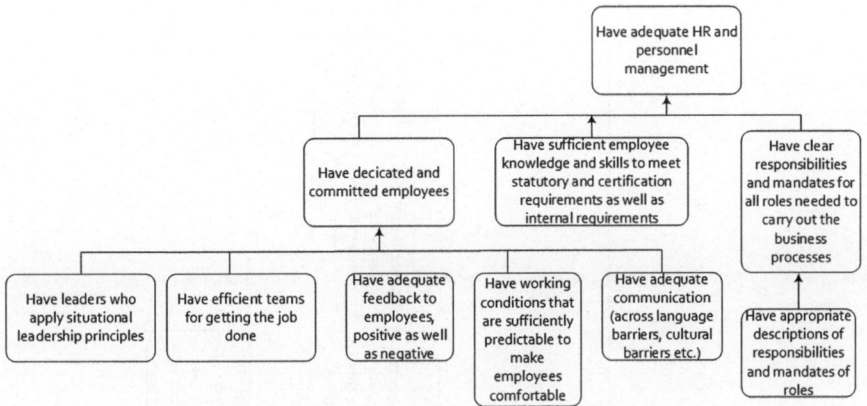

Fig. 5. Sub-model on having good HR and personnel management

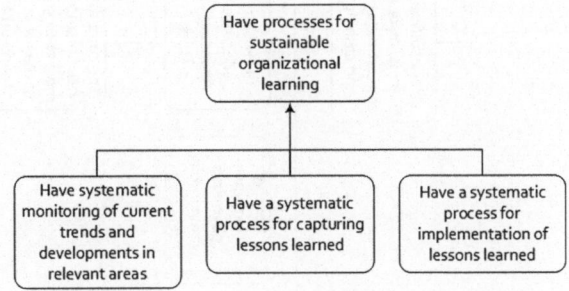

Fig. 6. Sub-model on having sustainable organizational learning

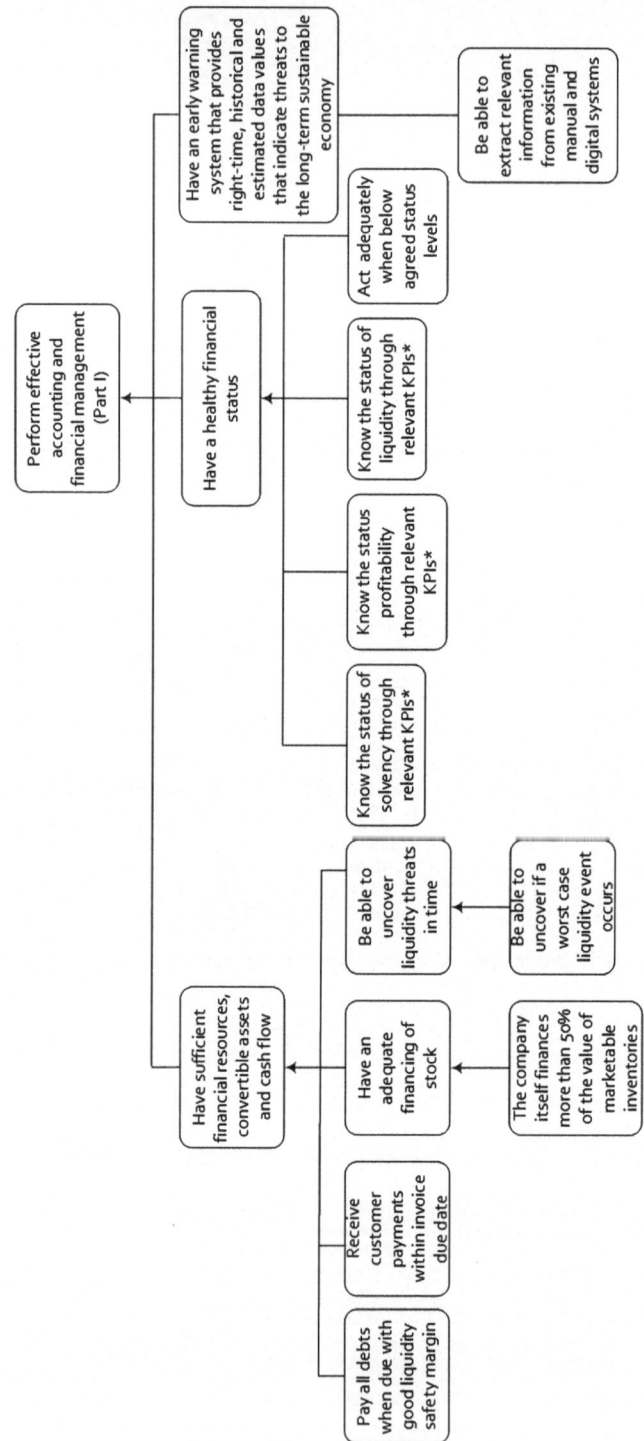

Fig. 7. Sub-model on having effective accounting and financial management

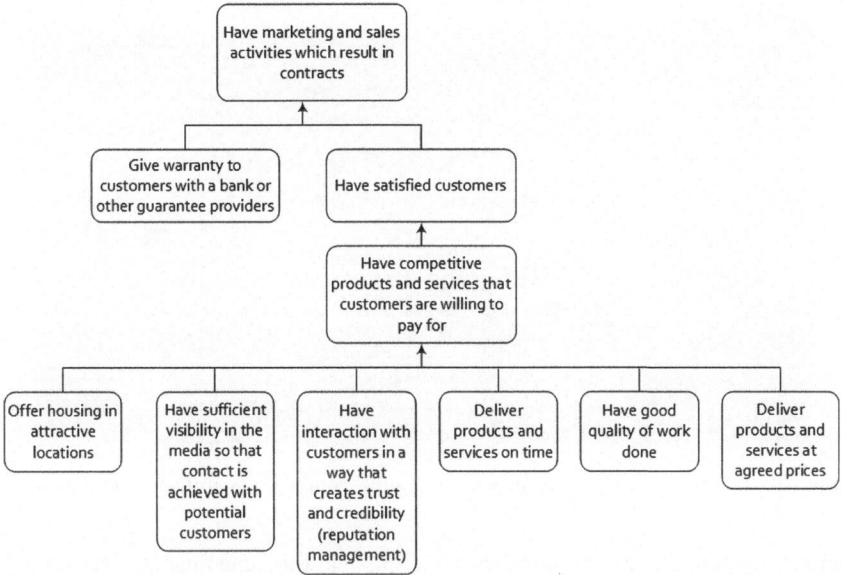

Fig. 8. Sub-model on having marketing and sales activities, which results in contracts

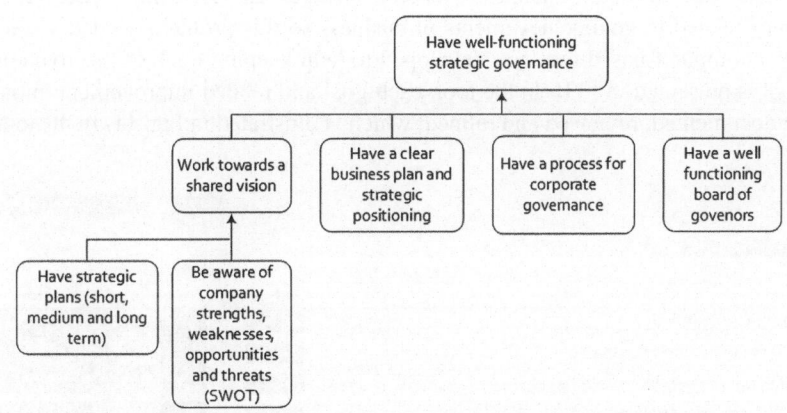

Fig. 9. Sub-model on having well-functioning strategic governance

the liquidity of the company. This supports the user of the model in estimating the status of the company in question. Similar criteria are developed for the other focus areas. Goals specific the company in question can be added to model. After the assessment of each of the goals, the model becomes a specific goal model relevant for the company in question.

In order to ensure that goals were followed by relevant improvement initiatives, a paper-based scheme was developed in the project where each goal was listed, categorized due to the status of goal achievement, linked to an improvement initiative with a start and end-date and motivated by strategy and other formal company decisions.

Liquidity			
Measurement Parameter	Indicator of satisfactory or good condition	Indicator weak condition	Indicator serious condition
Payment of debt when due	Pay all your debts when due and has a good safety margin	Paying almost all debt when due, but has almost no reserves to meet unforeseen events	Paying almost never debt when due. Often receive threats of debt collection experience last peak
Payments received from customers	The company's customers mostly pay when due, and now have few or no old Debts	The company has some claims where the customer rightfully hold back payment	The company has large amounts tied up in accounts receivable, where the customer refuses to pay before ... (Average credit more than 30-40 days)
Inventories	The company finances even more than 50% of the value of marketable inventories	The company finances itself ca. 40-50% of the value of marketable inventories.	The company has large amounts tied up in stocks without construction financing, where it may be expected to be a long time before it can be sold for cash receipts from customers
Discovering liquidity threat Describe a "worst case" liquidity event for the enterprise	If the incident occurs the company will now go into a weak liquidity condition	If the event occurs, the company will immediately go into a severe liquidity condition	If the incident occurs the company is now unable to pay its debts

Fig. 10. Example of criteria to support setting the status of a goal (Color figure online)

After having used the paper-based scheme in the field for some time, it became evident to the manager of the company that it was useful to ensure follow-ups of a variety of business areas, but it proved difficult and cumbersome to keep the paper-based scheme up to date, due to status changes, schedule changes etc. Evidently there are huge dynamics related to goal achievements in business so this problem needed a solution. Hence, a computer-based tool was developed to help keeping track of this dynamicity. The tool is presented in [33]. In the tool, each goal and related improvement initiatives can be documented, reviewed and refined, which is illustrated in Fig. 11. In the tool, the

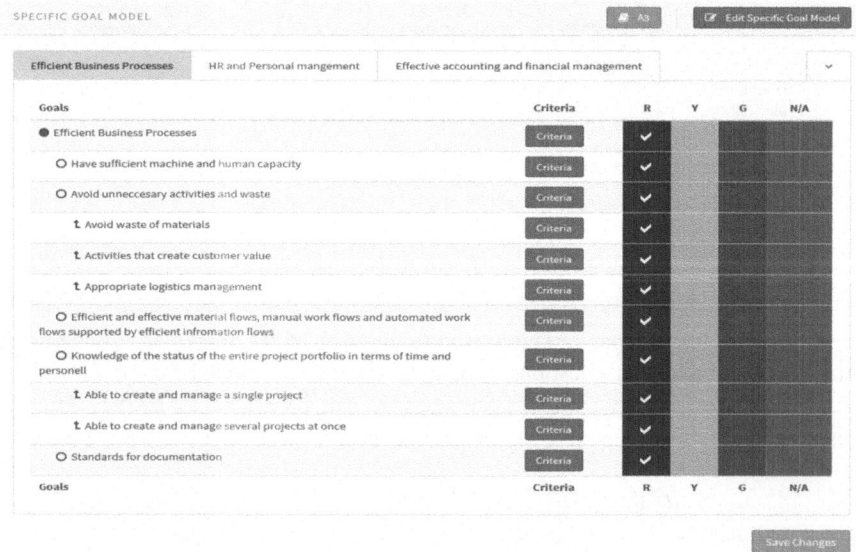

Fig. 11. Managing the goals of a specific company (Color figure online)

columns to the right are colored red (serious condition), yellow (weak condition), green (good condition) and blue (not applicable), starting from the left.

An overview of the company status can also be generated (Fig. 12), where the wheel on the right hand side illustrates the portion of red, yellow and green goals. In this case the portion of red goals is about half and the portion of red goals is the smallest.

Note that Figs. 11 and 12 are only meant to illustrate how the status of goals are presented to the user.

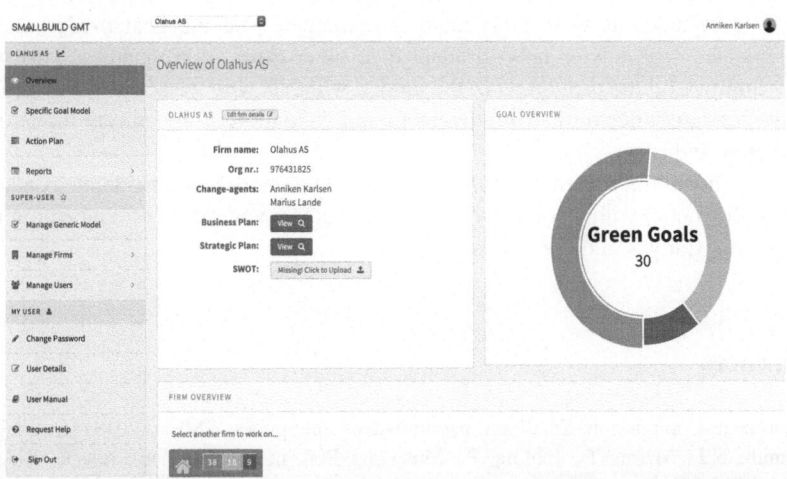

Fig. 12. Overview of goal status for a company (Color figure online)

5   Further Evaluation and Outlook

The SmallBuild + project is soon to be finished. The SmallBuild + method and tool has been tested, with positive results, in the SME construction company involved in the project. The positive results have in turn encouraged a consultancy company that is also involved in the project to start preparing for commercialization of both the method and the tool. In fact, they have founded another company aimed to support SME construction companies with capital and other support for making them sustainable over time. The SmallBuild + method and related tool will be an important part of the services offered.

The generic goal model has not only been tested in the SME construction company involved in the project. It has also been tested by the consultancy company in a turnaround operation involving another SME construction company, with positive results.

Although there are positive indications of the usefulness of the goal model and related tool, we foresee that further testing and consequent adjustments will be needed before they can be put into more widespread use.

One example of remaining work is that in the current version of the generic goal model, there is no weighting of the goals. During the use of the tool it has become evident that this needs to be done because not every goal can realistically be equally important. However, this is something that will require some research in order for such a weighting to be reliable. E.g. in initial discussions, it has turned out that the goal of having good financial management is a critical goal for SME construction companies. In any case, the complex relationships between goals in the model need to be the basis for such a weighting.

In terms of applicability of the goal model beyond the construction industry, we speculate that, since most of the goals are quite generic, it should be useful to other types of companies as well. One could also imagine that the goal model could be complemented with advice how to adapt it to other types of companies. This would hugely improve on the usefulness of the model, which is why we see it as a natural step to move forward, after further improvement and validation of the current model in the construction industry.

An additional improvement could be to extend the model with guidelines on how to integrate the model with a company's existing management practices concerning Lean, the Business Canvas and the Business Scorecard.

References

1. European Commission: Small and medium-sized enterprises (SMEs) (2013) [Online]
2. Smith, N.J., Merna, T., Jobling, P.: Managing Risk in Construction Projects. Blackwell Publishing, Oxford (2006)
3. Love, P.E.D., Irani, Z.: An exploratory study of information technology evaluation and benefits management practices of SMEs in the construction sector. Inf. Manag. **42**, 227–242 (2004). Elsevier
4. The Bygg21 strategy report (2014). http://www.dibk.no/globalassets/bygg21/bygg21 strategien/bygg21_strategirapport.pdf
5. e-Business W@tch (2006). http://ec.europa.eu/enterprise/archives/e-business-watch/studies/sectors/construction/documents/Construction_2006.pdf
6. Olawale, Y., Sun, M.: Cost and time control of construction projects: Inhibiting factors and mitigating measures in practice. Constr. Manag. Econ. **28**(5), 509–526 (2010)
7. Morris, P., Pinto, J.: The Wiley Guide to Managing Projects. John Wiley, Hoboken (2004)
8. Aarseth, W.: Project Management - A New Mindset for Success. Collaborative Business and Global Mindset. Fagbokforlaget, Trondheim (2014)
9. Hernández, C., Pajares, J., López-Paredes, A.: A portfolio inspired metric for project selection in construction management. Organ. Technol. Manag. Constr. Int. J. **3**(1), 264 (2011)
10. Bhasin, S.: An appropriate change strategy for lean success. Manag. Decis. **50**, 439–458 (2012)
11. Ogunbiyi, O., Oladapo, A., Goulding, J.: An empirical study of the impact of leanconstruction techniques on sustainable construction in the UK. Constr. Innov. **14**(1), 88–107 (2013). Permanent link to the document: http://dx.doi.org/10.1108/CI-08-2012-0045
12. Ghobadian, A., Gallear, D.N.: Total quality management in SMEs. Omega **24**, 83–106 (1996)

13. Brundin, E., Florin Samuelsson, E., Melin, L.: The Family Ownership Logic: Core Characteristics of Family-Controlled Businesses. CeFEO Working Paper 2008:1 Jönköping: Center for Family Enterprise and Ownership, Jönköping International Business School (2008)
14. Kraus, S., Harms, R., Fing, M.: Family firm research: sketching a research field. Int. J. Entrepreneurship Innov. Manag. 13(1), 32–47 (2011)
15. Bill, F., Johannisson, B., Olaison, L.: The incubus paradox: attempts at foundational rethinking of the "SME support genre". Eur. Plan. Stud. 17(8), 1135–1152 (2009). doi:10. 1080/09654310902980997
16. Achanga, P., Shehab, E., Roy, R., Nelder, G.: Critical success factors for lean implementation within SMEs. J. Manufact. Technol. Manag. 17, 460–471 (2006)
17. Alaskari, O., Ahmad, M., Dhafr, N., Pinedo-Cuenca, R.: Critical successful factors (CSFs) for Successful implementation of Lean tools and ERP systems. In: World Congress on Engineering WCE 2012. International Association of Engineers, London (2013)
18. Davenport, T., Short, J.: The new industrial engineering: Information technology and business process redesign. Sloan Manag. Rev. 31(4), 11–27 (1990)
19. Ukko, J., Karhu, J., Rantanen, H.: How to communicate target information in SMEs? In: Malmberg, P. (ed.) European Productivity Conference. Finland (2006)
20. Drucker, P.F.: The Practice of Management, Harper Business; Reissue edition 3 October 2006
21. Overbeek, S., Frank, U., Köhling, C.: A language for multi-perspective goal modeling: Challenges, requirements and solutions. Computer Standards & Interfaces 38, 1–16 (2014)
22. Sandkuhl, K., Stirna, J., Persson, A., Wißotzki, M.: Enterprise Modeling: Tackling Business Challenges with the 4EM Method. The Enterprise Engineering Series, Kindle edn. Springer, Heidelberg (2014)
23. Dardenne, A., van Lamsweerde, A., Fickas, S.: Goal-directed requirements acquisition. Sci. Comput. Program. 20(1–2), 3–50 (1993)
24. Yu, Eric S.K.: Towards modelling and reasoning support for early-phase requirement engineering. In: IEEE International Symposium Requirements Engineering, pp. 226–235 (1997)
25. Rolland, C.: Capturing system intentionality with maps. In: Krogstie, J., Opdahl, A.L., Brinkkemper, S. (eds.) Conceptual Modelling in Information Systems Engineering, pp. 141–158. Springer, Berlin Heidelberg (2007)
26. Ullah, A., Lai, R.: Modeling business goal for business/IT alignment using requirements engineering. J. Comput. Inf. Syst. 51(3), 21–28 (2011). Springer
27. Stirna, J., Persson, A.: Purpose Driven Competency Planning for Enterprise Modeling Projects. In: Ralyté, J., Franch, X., Brinkkemper, S., Wrycza, S. (eds.) CAiSE 2012. LNCS, vol. 7328, pp. 662–677. Springer, Heidelberg (2012)
28. Karlsen, A., Opdahl, A.L.: Enterprise Modeling Practice in a Turnaround Project. In: Fallmyr, T. (ed.) Norsk Konferanse for Organisasjoners Bruk Av Informasjonsteknologi, pp. 199–212. NOKOBIT-stiftelsen og Akademika forlag, Trondheim (2012)
29. Liker, J., och Morgan, J.M.: The toyota way in services: the case of lean product development. Acad. Manag. Perspect. 20, 5–20 (2006)
30. Schneiderman, Arthur M. (2006). "Analog Devices: 1986–1992, The First Balanced Scorecard". Arthur M. Schneiderman. Archived from the original on 25 December 2013. Accessed 28 May 2014
31. Osterwalder, A.: The Business Model Ontology - A Proposition in A Design Science Approach. Ph.D. thesis University of Lausanne (2004)

32. Cawsey, T.F., Deszca, G., Ingols, C.: Organizational Change – An Action-Oriented Toolkit, 2nd edn. Sage, Thousand Oaks (2012)
33. Karlsen, A., Persson, A., Gudfinnsson, K., Hauge, V., Lande, M. and Tellnes, O.: Towards a Tool to Support Goal Oriented Continuous Improvement in SME Construction Companies. In: PoEM Conference (2015, submitted)

A Risk-Based Approach Supporting Enterprise Architecture Evolution

Khaled Gaaloul[1]([✉]) and Sérgio Guerreiro[2]

[1] Luxembourg Institute of Science and Technology (LIST),
Luxembourg City, Luxembourg
khaled.gaaloul@list.lu
[2] Lusófona University, Campo Grande, Lisbon, Portugal
sergio.guerreiro@ulusofona.pt

Abstract. Enterprise architecture (EA) is a discipline driving change within organizations. The management of EA change is a challenging task for enterprise architects, due to the complex dependencies amongst EA models when evolving towards different alternatives (To-be models). In this paper, we present an approach supporting design decision during EA evolution. The idea is to reason on (To-be) models when evolving to a posterior state. To that end, we rationalize on a set of design decisions that are mapped on a non deterministic finite automaton, which is then evaluated by Markov decision processes. The idea consists of computing EA models valuations while integrating both alternatives rewards and risks metrics. In doing so, we consider risk as a correctness factor to choose the best alternative. Finally, we simulate our risk-based approach using a manufacturing scenario and discuss its usefulness and applicability.

Keywords: Enterprise architecture · Evolution · Risk · Markov theories · Simulation

1 Introduction

Enterprise architecture (EA) is a logical organization of a business and its supporting data, applications, and IT infrastructure [1]. EA clearly defines goals and objectives for the future success of the business. A typical architecture consists of models showing how aspects of your business relate. EA models have proven to be very useful for the management and governance of enterprises [2]. EA is composed of a multitude of EA models each being concurrently edited by different enterprise architects. Businesses should have an 'As-is' model that represents its current state, and planned models to show potential directions (To-be) of the business during EA evolution [3].

One of the many challenges an enterprise architect faces are risks when moving towards EA 'To-be' states. At every step in creating an enterprise design, architects need to analyze and evaluate risk. As definition, a risk is an unwanted event which can bring negative consequences to the organization. Risk management aims to identify and assess risks in order to define preventive controls to

© IFIP International Federation for Information Processing 2015
J. Ralyté et al. (Eds.): PoEM 2015, LNBIP 235, pp. 43–56, 2015.
DOI: 10.1007/978-3-319-25897-3_4

decrease the probability of occurrence of risk situations [4]. In most cases, risk assessment and treatment is done using the enterprises internal methodology or based on best practices known by the architect [5].

Current EA frameworks do not support risk appropriately due to inflexible EA models and missing guidance on risk identification and analysis [6,7]. The integration of the different risk management processes at an enterprise level is a promising and still open research topic [4]. The Open Group Architecture Framework (TOGAF) associates specific risks to each of the nine identified phases of the architecture development method, however in the absence of a formal corporate methodology, architects are only limited to best practice [1,8]. Moreover, risk management efforts operate in silos with narrowly focused, functionally driven, and disjointed activities. That fact leads to a fragmented view of risks including different models and metrics. The lack of interconnection and holistic view of risks limits an organization-wide perception of risks, where interdependent risks are not anticipated, controlled or managed [7].

In this paper, we propose a risk-based approach to support enterprise architecture evolution. The idea is to model a production/delivery process while analyzing risk factors when moving towards (To-be) models. This scenario models EA alternatives supporting outsourcing solutions. Outsourcing is an effective cost-saving solution when used properly. It can be adopted entirely or partly in the EA model. However, integrating outsourcing is not an easy task for architects. There are potential risks when dealing with outsourcing partners such as delays, privacy, and competency. In doing so, we present a reasoning method using Markov decision processes (MDP). MDP provides a mathematical framework for modeling decision making in situations where outcomes (*i.e.* risk factors) are partly random and partly under the control of a decision maker (*i.e.* enterprise architect). Our assumption consists of delivering valuations when the enterprise architect faces different EA model alternatives. These valuations are simulated using MDP and depend on both alternatives rewards and risks metrics. Based on these simulation results, enterprise architect will have the responsibility of taking a final decision whether the EA evolution should be committed to or reverted.

The remainder of this paper is structured as follows. Section 2 presents the research background. The motivating example is illustrated in Sect. 3 where we present three outsourcing options as alternatives in EA (To-be) models. Section 4 is dedicated to the approach including the reasoning method and its simulation tool. Related work are discussed in Sect. 5. Finally, Sect. 6 concludes and identifies future work to follow up this research effort.

2   Background

This section presents the background of our approach. Risk assessment is used to reason on computing best alternatives when modeling EA evolution. Further, the DEMO theory and methodology [9] are summarized, where DEMO is partially used to design risk scenarios in Sect. 3.

2.1   Risk Assessment

Today, risk management is mainly performed in a domain-specific manner. Different methods and approaches exist in the different risk-aware domains, *e.g.*, information security, environment, project management, finance. Due to the huge number of references, it is not possible to provide an exhaustive list in this paper.

The most generally agreed upon definition of risk is the one found in ISO/IEC Guide 73 [10]. The risk is defined as a combination of the probability of an event and its consequence. Following this definition, risk management is defined as coordinated activities to direct and control an organization with regard to risk [10].

The scope of this paper is limited to risk assessment which is one the process in the risk management methodology [11]. Risk assessment is executed at discrete time points (*e.g.* once a year, on demand, etc.) and until the performance of the next assessment provides a temporary view of assessed risks. Risk assessment is often conducted in more than one iteration, the first being a high-level assessment to identify high risks, while the other iterations detail the analysis of the major risks and other risks. The process can be divided in the following steps:

- Risk analysis, further divided in:
  - Risk identification: the identification of risk comprises risk scenarios and risk factors.
  - Risk estimation: it assesses the risk impacts through the valuation of business assets.
- Risk evaluation: it compares each risk level against the risk acceptance criteria and prioritize the risk list with risk treatment indications.

Our approach defines a reasoning method based on risk assessment. In doing so, we need to identify risk scenarios and factors. Scenarios are identified in Fig. 2. Risk factors define risk criteria for evaluating risk. The risk criteria should reflect the objectives and context for the risk assessment. Adequate consideration should be given to the time and resources available, stakeholder views and risk perceptions, and the applicable legal and regulatory requirements [12].

2.2   DEMO Theory and Methodology

From the business processes point of view, DEMO (Design and Engineering Methodology for Organizations) theory and methodology [9] introduce capabilities to deal rigorously with the dynamic aspects of the process-based business transactions using an essential ontology that is compatible with the communication and production, acts and facts that occur between actors in the different layers of the organization. A DEMO business transaction model [13] encompasses two distinct worlds: *(i)* the transition space and *(ii)* the state space.

On the one hand, the DEMO transition space is grounded in a theory named as Ψ-theory (PSI), where the standard pattern of a transaction includes two distinct actor roles: the Initiator and the Executor. Figure 1 depicts this basic transaction pattern. The transactional pattern is performed by a sequence of

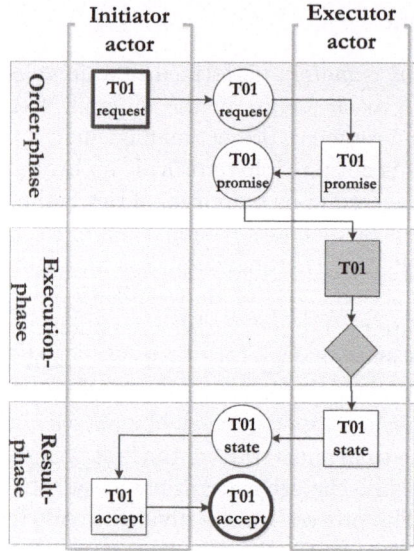

Fig. 1. The DEMO standard pattern of a transaction between two actors with separation between communication and production acts (Adapted from [9])

coordination and production acts that leads to the production of the new fact. In detail, encompasses: *(i)* order phase that involves the acts of request, promise, decline and quit, *(ii)* execution phase that includes the production act of the new fact itself and *(iii)* result phase that includes the acts of state, reject, stop and accept. DEMO basic transaction pattern aims specifying the transition space of a system that is given by the set of allowable sequences of transitions. Every state transition is exclusively dependent from the current states of all surrounding transactions. There is no memory of previous states. This memoryless property holds with Markov theories.

On the other hand, the DEMO state space delivers the model for the business transactions facts, which are products or services, and are obtained by the business transaction successful execution. Throughout the business transaction execution more intermediate facts are required.

Integrating both the DEMO transition and state spaces, we obtain the inter restrictions of systems[1], which is composed by all the information links between actors and information banks (I-banks), and the mapping of all the responsibilities between actors.

3   Motivating Example

In the manufacturing sector one of the most important factors to increase profit margins is by optimizing the production process. Moreover, there is the delivery

---

[1] Usually named as restrictions between systems.

process which is closely related to production. Without an effective production/delivery strategy, deadlines can be missed and labour costs can eat into profits. Figure 2 describes the scenario from a business perspective using a non deterministic finite automaton. Each arrow defines the set of finite possible evolutions between models. Each model is represented by DEMO. The usage of a business transaction oriented methodology, such as DEMO, has the benefit of narrowing the domain of EA models to a single and self-contained set of models. As depicted in Fig. 2, each Model has many options to evolve, showing the non deterministic nature of a decision.

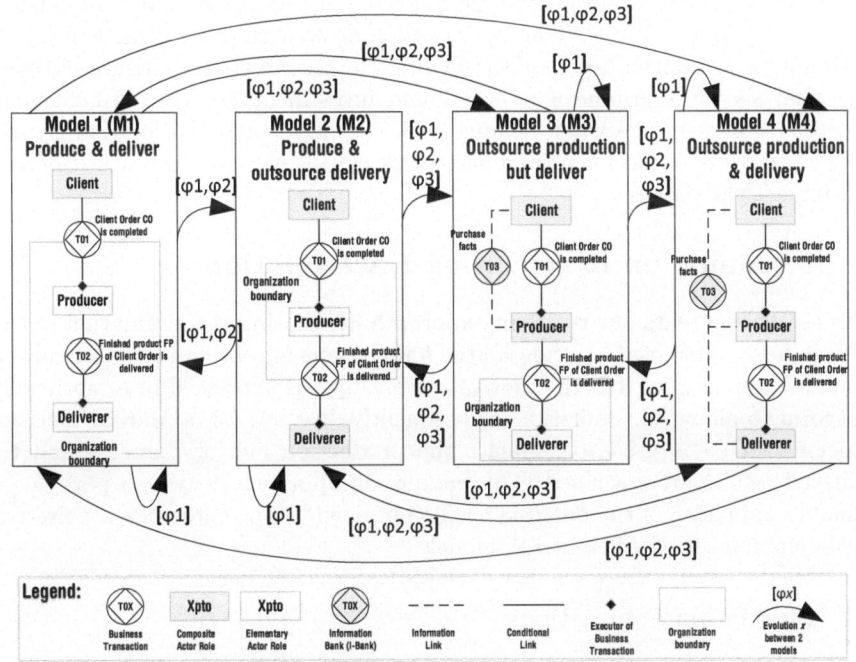

Fig. 2. Mapping the set of possible evolutions ($\varphi_{1,2,3}$) from/to Models $M_{1,2,3,4}$: a non deterministic finite automaton representation.

The production/delivery process remains generic, but focuses on different models supporting four production/delivery strategies. After identifying client's needs, we model four solutions to optimize their production scheduling and their delivery assignment. Basically, one key feature is about outsourcing both production and delivery. The main motivations which have led to outsourcing are the lack of expert-labor in some portions of the business process and the availability of cheaper labor whilst not comprising on the quality of output. Moreover, when outsourcing is introduced financial transactions become more complex and so an additional effort for information banks (I-banks) is required to synchronize financial auditing inter organizations.

Our concern in this paper is mainly about risk assessment with regards to the production/delivery strategy. It is always beneficial for an organization to consider the advantages and disadvantages before actually adopting one of these solutions (see Fig. 2). Risk can be a part of the outsourcing solution which has pros and cons to it. On the one hand, risk-sharing can be one of the advantages of outsourcing. Outsourcing certain components of your business process helps the organization to shift certain responsibilities to the outsourced distributor. Since the distributor is a specialist, they plan your risk-mitigating factors better. On the other hand, outsourcing disadvantages can be the risk of exposing confidential data or the delay in delivery time frames because of partner's deficiency.

In our approach we prioritize the following criteria: regulatory compliance, cost, and project schedule. The first criterion deals with data security/integrity to comply with information banks (I-bank). The second criterion defines benefit-cost analysis to determine if it is a sound investment/decision. Benefits may be positive or negative when dealing with partners competencies. Finally, the project schedule criteria is a time-based risk which refers to delays, if it occurs, will impact the process.

4 Reasoning on Risk During EA Evolution

This section presents our reasoning approach integrating risk evaluation during EA evolution. In Sect. 4.1, we detail the foundations for obtaining the simulation results. Next, in Sect. 4.2, the motivating example is expressed in a mathematical form to allow its simulation. Subsequently, in Sect. 4.3, a Markov Decision Process (MDP) is used to simulate the production/delivery process and the achieved results are discussed. This simulation approach delivers a partial, yet valuable, valuation of the possible results obtained by the enterprise architect to decide upon a set of different EA models.

4.1 Simulation Foundations

For simulation purposes, the reasoning approach for EA evolution is depicted in Fig. 3. Each step is enforced by the following:

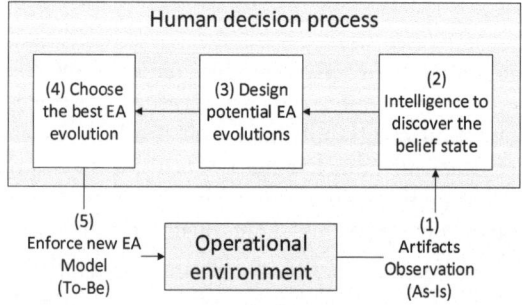

Fig. 3. EA evolution process

1. (*Figure 3(1): Observation*) the set of artifacts used at operation-time are observed and collected;
2. (*Figure 3(2): Intelligence*) this step is equal to (1) if full observation is considered. However, if *(i)* uncertainty about the artifacts exists, or if *(ii)* due to manual task-based environments is not possible to automatically collect the data about the artifacts, or if *(iii)* different perceptions coexist within the organization in regard to the artifacts; then a partial observation solution should be considered. Partial observable Markov decision processes (POMDP) [14–16] solutions have potential to estimate the belief artifacts and could be used in these situations.

   In this motivating example, we merely consider that all the artifacts are observable and then a Markov decision processes (MDP) could be used in that situation. MDP valuates a given EA transformation process maximizing the expected value (V) after discounting the decay throughout time. A MDP is usually defined by the tuple (S, A, P, R, γ) where:

   $S = \{S_1, ..., S_n\}$ is a set of states, representing all the possible underlying states the process can be in (our motivating example represents S by the models M);

   $A = \{A_1, ..., A_n\}$ is a set of actions, representing all the available control choices at each point in time (our motivating example represents A by the

   $$P_{ij}^a = \begin{array}{c} \\ i_0 \\ i_1 \\ ... \\ i_k \end{array} \begin{array}{cccc} j_0 & j_1 & \cdots & j_k \\ \begin{bmatrix} p_{00} & p_{01} & \cdots & p_{0k} \\ p_{10} & p_{11} & \cdots & p_{1k} \\ ... & ... & ... & ... \\ p_{k0} & p_{k1} & \cdots & p_{kk} \end{bmatrix} \end{array}$$

   evolutions φ); is a transition matrix that contains the probability of a state transition, whereas i is the actual state and j is the final state if a given action a that is being used;

   $R = \{R_1, ..., R_n\}$ is an immediate reward function, giving the immediate utility for performing an action that drives the system towards each state[2];

   γ is a discounted factor of future rewards, meaning the decay that a given achieved state suffers throughout time;

   $\rho = \{\rho_1, ..., \rho_n\}$ is a risk function that is taken when an action that drives the system towards a state. A risk could be considered beneficial to the organization (positive) or prejudicial (negative). In this experimental set-up, for simplification, we consider $R = R + \rho$.
3. (*Figure 3(3): EA design*) in regard to potential options, the enterprise architect need to design a new set of evolutions, *e.g.*, designing a new set of rules or adding an information bank to coordinate actors. If partial observations are occurring, then the new artifacts will depend on the belief artifacts obtained in (2);
4. (*Figure 3(4): Choose best EA evolution*) a qualitative and/or quantitative valuation of the best evolution to take. This step is the responsibility of

---

[2] The need to estimate rewards could also be found in literature, *e.g.*, [17] proposes an EA support tool where the score of a given architecture solution should be indicated by the architect.

enterprise architect. To support the architect the MDP is solved. There are many solutions available to solve a MDP. Our goal is to use MDP using a well-known solution with stable results. Therefore, to obtain the maximized V, we solve the MDP as specified by the following recursive Eq. 1:

$$V(s) := \sum_{s'} P_{\pi(s)}(s, s') \left(R_{\pi(s)}(s, s') + \gamma V(s') \right) \tag{1}$$

where: $\pi(s) := arg \; \underset{a}{max} \; \{\sum_{s'} P_a(s, s')(R_a(s, s') + \gamma V(s'))\};$

5. (*Figure 3(5): Enforce new EA model*) equal to result of (4) if full actuation considered. Whether operational environment is not completely controllable then the evolution will be only partial enforced.

4.2   Motivating Example Set-Up

The example is herein presented by the following definitions: *(i)* models (M), *(ii)* evolutions (φ), *(iii)* transition matrix (P_{ij}^a), *(iv)* rewards matrix (R) and *(v)* risks matrix.

The conceptualization of M set is explained in Sect. 3, where: M_1 - Produce & deliver, M_2 - Produce & outsource deliver, M_3 - Outsource production but deliver, and, M_4 - Outsource production & deliver.

In regard φ, an EA model transformation is triggered whenever the enterprise architect decides to evolve the organization with a known purpose. In this context, the following set of evolutions (φ) decisions are considered: φ_1 - *do not take any action*, φ_2 - *change boundary of the organization*, and, φ_3 - *change information bank (I-bank)*.

P_{ij}^a is the probabilistic estimation between the evolutions (φ) required to transit from a model M to other M is presented cf. Table 1. Let p be the probability of φ be successful. For simulation purposes, p is tested in the range $[0.1, ..., 1.0]$ with small steps of 0.1 each. This approach offers more choice possibilities to the Enterprise Architect, including the non-success φ. In the top part of Table 1 (φ_1) it is assumed that the system will stay in the same state in the majority of the situations (90 %). In the middle part of Table 1 (φ_2) it is not allowed to transit to the same state. Moreover, more probability is given to the neighbor states as depicted in Fig. 2. Finally, the bottom part of Table 1 (φ_3), follows a similar approach of (φ_2) except that transitions between M_1 and M_2 are not allowed due to nonexistent I-banks.

Moreover, the reward matrix R is presented in Table 2. The sum of rewards for φ_2 and φ_3 are the same to challenge the MDP solver in identifying which is better the value possible for p. I-banks exist only in M_3 and M_4. Therefore, an higher reward is delivered when φ_3 is considered.

Exemplifying, the probability to be in state $M3$ at time $t + 1$, being in state $M3$ and choosing $\varphi 1$ at time t, is $P(3, 3, 1) = 0.9$ and the associated reward is $R(3, 1) = 1$. Translating for the scenario language, this denotes that keeping the model of *outsourcing production but delivering in-house* after doing no action has a probability 0.9 of occurring but offers a small reward (when compared with the other reward values).

In the end, the corrected rewards matrix is presented by Table 3. Two positive ρ (risk) and two negative (ρ) are considered: ρ_1 $(-)$ data inconsistency risk, ρ_2 $(-)$ competence poor allocation, ρ_3 $(+)$ data secured in-house, and, ρ_4 $(+)$ better delivery time. Corrected rewards are presented with exaggerated values to overemphasize the impact of risk in the simulation. Again the need to risk estimation is broadly found in literature [12].

4.3   Simulation Results

The results shown below emphasize the rationale behind our approach to deliver valuation when the architect faces different EA model evolution options. This rationale is more important than the particular results obtained for the production/delivery process at hand. Moreover, this approach is used recursively: observing the reality, simulating different options, enforcing new models, and finally restarting the loop.

The MDP is computed by a $Matlab^{\copyright}$ toolbox[3] using a linear programming algorithm. Figure 4 depicts the result from the MDP simulation. The intent of this motivating example is to show the benefits of using stochastic approaches to aid the EA architect decisions. This goal can be achieved if engineers are empowered with full pertinent information to forecast the impacts of their decisions in the near future of the organization. With this proposal, the architect is able to simulate different configurations (and evaluate them) before its implementation.

In the top left corner, the value function is presented at each stage k, and each p value is separated. We observe that when $p \rightarrow 1$ then value function increases. In the top right corner, a value function is also delivered. However, the risks from Table 3 induce a correction to the Table 2. As shown, the results are the opposite from the former value function. In the bottom left corner, the elicited evolutions to fulfil the value function are depicted. For each p a different set of evolutions exist. Each set is represented by a different color. For $p \in [0.1, ..., 0.8]$ the optimal solution is given by the evolutions *Change Boundary* and then *Change I-banks*. But, for $p \in [0.8, ..., 1.0]$ the optimal solution is *Change I-banks*, then *Change Boundary* and finally back to *Change I-banks*. In the bottom right corner, for each p, we represent the percentage of time spent in each model. Here, we generally observe that changing p do not present a dramatic change in the percentage of usage of a model, except when $p \rightarrow 1$. This effect is mostly due to the balanced weights that are used in Tables 1 and 2.

Aggregating the previous results, the solution that maximizes the value function (without correction) is when $p = 1$ and leading to a major use of M_3 (*Outsource production but deliver in-house*). Therefore, in this example, the probability (p) to succeed with an evolution (φ) seems to be a relevant variable to maximize the value function. Consequently, the enterprise Architect

---

[3] Toolbox public available at http://www7.inra.fr/mia/T/MDPtoolbox.

Table 1. Transition matrix (P_{ij}^a) containing the set of possible evolutions $(\varphi_{1,2,3})$ from/to Models $M_{1,2,3,4}$

$\varphi1$ From \ To	Model 1	Model 2	Model 3	Model 4
Model 1	0.9	0.1/3	0.1/3	0.1/3
Model 2	0.1/3	0.9	0.1/3	0.1/3
Model 3	0.1/3	0.1/3	0.9	0.1/3
Model 4	0.1/3	0.1/3	0.1/3	0.9

$\varphi2$ From \ To	Model 1	Model 2	Model 3	Model 4
Model 1	0	p	$(1-p)/2$	$(1-p)/2$
Model 2	$p/2$	0	$p/2$	$1-p$
Model 3	$1-p$	$p/2$	0	$p/2$
Model 4	$(1-p)/2$	$(1-p)/2$	p	0

$\varphi3$ From \ To	Model 1	Model 2	Model 3	Model 4
Model 1	0	0	p	$1-p$
Model 2	0	0	p	$1-p$
Model 3	$1-p$	$p/2$	0	$p/2$
Model 4	$(1-p)/2$	$(1-p)/2$	p	0

Table 2. Reward matrix (R) containing the set of rewards when achieving a Model through each evolution $(\varphi_{1,2,3})$

Achieved model \ Evolution	$\varphi1$	$\varphi2$	$\varphi3$
Model 1	1	4	1
Model 2	1	4	1
Model 3	1	4	7.5
Model 4	1	4	7.5

Table 3. Corrected rewards matrix containing the set of risks $(\rho_{1,2,3,4})$ that could occur when achieving a Model through each evolution $(\varphi_{1,2,3})$

Achieved model \ Evolution	$\varphi1$	$\varphi2$	$\varphi3$
Model 1	$\rho_2 = -10$	$\rho_2 = -10$	$\rho_3 = +10$
Model 2	$\rho_2 = -10$	$\rho_4 = +10$	$\rho_3 = +10$
Model 3	$\rho_1 = -10$	$\rho_2 = -10$	$\rho_1 = -10$
Model 4	$\rho_1 = -10$	$\rho_4 = +10$	$\rho_1 = -10$

should take actions that maximize the chances of being successful. The remaining sub-optimal results are also useful, due to the occurrence of workarounds, it is not expected that any organizational operation will behave 100 % as prescribed [18,19].

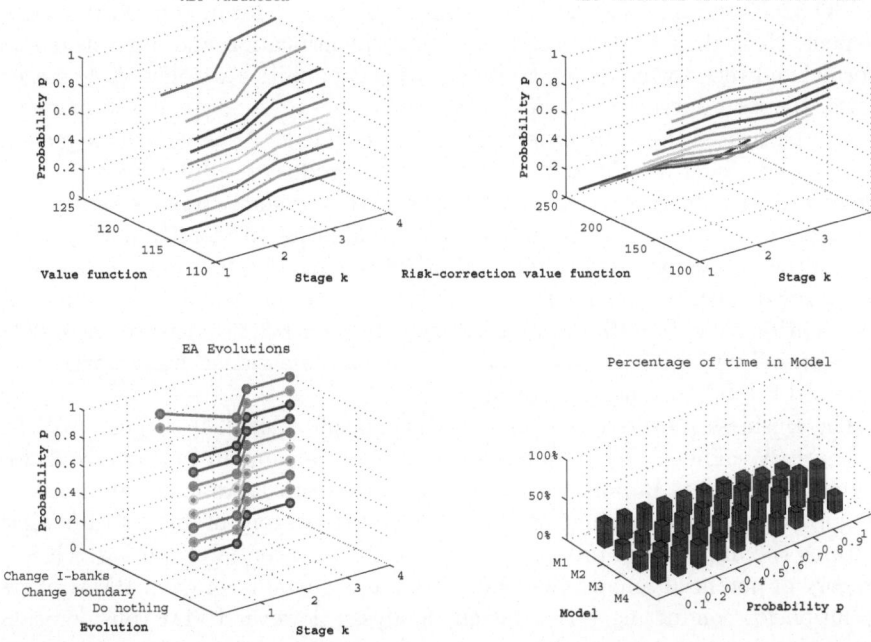

Fig. 4. MDP simulation: P_{ij}^a cf. Table 1; R cf. Table 2; ρ cf. Table 3; $\gamma = 0.95$ and $p \in [0.1, ..., 1.0 : 0.1]$

Conversely, considering that when $p \in [0.1, ..., 0.8]$ only 2 evolutions are demanded. But, for $p \in [0.8, ..., 1.0]$ there are 3 evolutions needed, then more changing costs could be incurred in this last interval of p.

Moreover, the differences between the MDP valuation graph (top left corner) and MDP valuation with risk-correction (top right corner) emphasize the great impact of risk in the EA evolution estimation process.

5   Related Work

Most of risk management methodologies are internal procedures for a company, *e.g.*, the ones found in the guidelines of the Washington State Department of Transportation [20], that "provide information on how project risk management fits into the overall project management process" and "provide guidance on how to pro-actively respond to risks". The main risk analysis is divided into a qualitative and quantitative approach: on the one hand, qualitative risk analysis assesses the impact and likelihood (high, medium, low) of the identified risks and develops prioritized lists of these risks for further analysis. On the other hand, in quantitative analysis a numerical estimation of the probability that a project will meet its cost and time objectives is made. In this paper, we integrate risks factors in the correction of design decision. Our evaluated risk values are computed with (To-be) models invariants and support different EA strategies.

ISO 31000 series of standards [4] defines the baseline for integrated risk management. Nevertheless, their guidance on risk identification and analysis is still informal and very few modeling and computing capabilities are offered. As stated in [12], the introduction of model-based approaches as support of risk management is motivated, first, by an efficiency improvement of the risk management process, and second by the enhancement of the product resulting from the performed process. Moreover, risk management methods usually provide list of common risks to consider, but do not provide capabilities to identify new risks or analyze them in depth. Regarding goal-oriented modeling frameworks, many of them provide risk management capabilities, mainly for dealing with information security risks: KAOS and its security extension [12,21], Misuse cases [22], and Secure Tropos [23]. However, none of the aforementioned frameworks have addressed the EA evolution problem.

The Business Motivation Model (BMM) specification [24] suggests SWOT (Strength, Weakness, Opportunity, Threat) as an example of an approach for making assessments. In practice, enterprises can substitute different approaches, categorizing potential impacts as a risk which is a category of impact value that indicates the impact and probability of loss, and a potential reward which is a category of potential impact that indicates the probability of gain. BMM offers a solution for conducting a risk/benefit analysis; however BMM consideration remains static when dealing with evolution factors (*i.e.* risks) within enterprises.

6   Conclusions

This paper proposes an EA-driven organizational change process. One specific transformational change in EA is that of outsourcing. In this challenging context, we consider that a fully informed decision-making approach will empower the enterprise architects with tools to forecast the impacts of their decisions when outsourcing partly or entirely their processes. Subsequently, the enterprise architects will be able to decide upon which the best (or sub-optimal), and timely, action to be enacted is.

Our proposal is demonstrated by a stochastic simulation founded in the Markov decision processes theory, using a manufacturing scenario. On the one hand, four distinct EA models to optimize their production scheduling and their delivery assignment are available. Each model has its own risks. Some risks are positive and are beneficial to the organization, whereas other risks are negative and are prejudicial. On the other hand, three distinct evolutions are also available. The challenge posed to the enterprise architect is to choose the set of evolutions that maximize the value for the organization considering the associated risks. This solution shows the valuation throughout the intermediate EA evolution stages. Therefore, the organization is able to forecast not only the final valuation to be achieved, but also the correct value that will be chosen based on risk assessment.

As future work we identify the need to explore real world scenarios to enforce an informed decision-making approach that work, side-by-side, with practitioners. Moreover, a derived research problem is also identified where most of the operational environment observations are incomplete. Therefore, the alternatives that we are pretending to research will compulsory need to address the issue of environments that are usually called partially observable.

References

1. The Open Group - TOGAF Version 9. Van Haren Publishing, Zaltbommel, The Netherlands (2009)
2. Lankhorst, M.M.: Enterprise Architecture at Work - Modelling, Communication and Analysis. The Enterprise Engineering Series, 4th edn. Springer, Heidelberg (2013)
3. Gaaloul, K., El Kharbili, M., Proper, H.A.: Secure governance in enterprise architecture - access control perspective. In: IEEE, editor, The 3rd International Symposium ISKO-Maghreb, pp. 1–6, Marrakesh, Morocco (2013)
4. ISO 31000. Risk management Principles and guidelines. International Organization for Standardization, Geneva (2009)
5. Wieringa, R., van Eck, P., Steghuis, C., Proper, H.A.: Competences of IT Architects. Academic Service - SDU, The Hague (2008)
6. Roth, S., Hauder, M., Matthes, F.: A tool for collaborative evolution of enterprise architecture models at runtime. In: 8th International Workshop on Models at Runtime, Miami, USA. IEEE Computer Society (2013)
7. Barateiro, J., Antunes, G., Borbinha, J.L.: Manage risks through the enterprise architecture. In: 45th Hawaii International Conference on System Science (HICSS), pp. 3297–3306. IEEE Computer Society (2012)
8. Gaaloul, K., Guerreiro, S.: A decision-oriented approach supporting enterprise architecture evolution. In: The 24th IEEE International Conference on Enabling Technologies: Infrastructure for Collaborative Enterprises WETICE, Larnaca, Cyprus, 15–17 June 2015. IEEE (2015)
9. Dietz, J.L.G.: Enterprise Ontology: Theory and Methodology. Springer, Heidelberg (2006)
10. ISO/IEC Guide 73. Risk management Vocabulary Guidelines for use in standards, Geneva (2002)
11. ISO/IEC 27005:2008. Information technology - Security techniques - Information security risk management (2008)
12. Mayer, N.: Model-based Management of Information System Security Risk. Ph.D. thesis, University of Namur (2009)
13. Dietz, J.L.G.: The deep structure of business processes. Commun. ACM **49**(5), 58–64 (2006)
14. Guerreiro, S.: Decision-making in partially observable environments. In: 2014 IEEE 16th Conference on Business Informatics (CBI), vol. 1, pp. 159–166, July 2014
15. Guerreiro, S.: Engineering the decision-making process using multiple markov theories and DEMO. In: Aveiro, D., Pergl, R., Valenta, M. (eds.) EEWC 2015. LNBIP, vol. 211, pp. 19–33. Springer, Heidelberg (2015)
16. Puterman, M.L.: Markov Decision Processes: Discrete Stochastic Dynamic Programming. Wiley, New York (1994)
17. Ameller, D., Franch, X.: Assisting software architects in architectural decision-making using quark. Clei Electron. J. **17**(3) (2014)
18. Guerreiro, S., Tribolet, J.: Conceptualizing enterprise dynamic systems control for run-time business transactions. In: ECIS, p. 5 (2013)

19. Alter, S.: Theory of workarounds. Commun. Assoc. Inf. Syst. **34**(55), 1041–1066 (2014)
20. Washington State Department of Transportation. Project Risk Management Guidance for WSDOT Projects. Technical report, July 2010
21. Sousa, S., Marosin, D., Gaaloul, K., Mayer, N.: Assessing risks and opportunities in enterprise architecture using an extended ADT approach. In: Gasevic, D., Hatala, M., Nezhad, H.R.M., Reichert, M. (eds.) 17th IEEE International Enterprise Distributed Object Computing Conference, EDOC 2013, Vancouver, BC, Canada, 9–13 September 2013, pp. 81–90. IEEE (2013)
22. Matulevicius, R., Mayer, N., Heymans, P.: Alignment of misuse cases with security risk management. In: Proceedings of the 4th Symposium on Requirements Engineering for Information Security (SREIS 2008), in conjunction with the 3rd International Conference of Availability, Reliability and Security (ARES 2008), pp. 1397–1404. IEEE Computer Society (2008)
23. Matulevičius, R., Mayer, N., Mouratidis, H., Martinez, F.H., Heymans, P., Genon, N.: Adapting secure tropos for security risk management in the early phases of information systems development. In: Bellahsène, Z., Léonard, M. (eds.) CAiSE 2008. LNCS, vol. 5074, pp. 541–555. Springer, Heidelberg (2008)
24. Object Management Group. Business Motivation Model (BMM) Specification. Technical report dtc/06-08-03, Needham, Massachusetts, August 2006

Securing Enterprises

Pattern-Based Security Requirements Derivation from Secure Tropos Models

Atilio Rrenja and Raimundas Matulevičius[✉]

Institute of Computer Science, University of Tartu, Tartu, Estonia
{rrenja,rma}@ut.ee

Abstract. The increasing rates of cyber-attacks have led to the subsequent need to rapidly develop secure information systems (IS). Secure Tropos is an actor and goal-oriented approach to identify security goals and to enable security requirements elicitation. This is achieved by considering system actors, their dependencies and by deriving security constraints that actors need to satisfy. Nevertheless goal-oriented modelling has proven itself to be valid it also contains few shortcomings. One of them is the high granularity of the process, which leads quickly to high complexity models. Security patterns are proven to be reusable solutions that address recurring security problems. In this paper we investigate the integration of a pattern-based security requirements derivation from the Secure Tropos models.

Keywords: Security risk management · Secure tropos · Security patterns

1 Introduction

Security concerns play an important role in nowadays enterprises. Different enterprise stakeholders have various objectives and need to collaborate to achieve them. Thus, understanding security risks and estimating their impact could envision threats, estimate their consequences, and propose countermeasures to mitigate these threats.

Secure Tropos is an agent-oriented information and enterprise system development method that helps understanding *security objectives* through *satisfying security constraints* by considering *actor dependencies* [11]. In [7, 8] Security Tropos was extended to Security Risk-aware Secure Tropos (RAST), where the original language was semantically aligned to the concepts of the domain model for information systems security risk management (ISSRM) [6, 9]. The extended language supports security requirements elicitation through understanding security risks. However, even given an IS with a rather moderate complexity, identifying and mitigating security risks could become quite a complex activity. One of the reasons is the inherited complexity of the Secure Tropos model, when the model size quickly grows with introduction of different analysis concerns.

In this paper we propose an application of security risk-oriented patterns (SRPs) [2], which could overcome the above problem by suggesting the proven security solutions for the reoccurring security problems. We analyse *how to apply SRPs and derive security*

© IFIP International Federation for Information Processing 2015
J. Ralyté et al. (Eds.): PoEM 2015, LNBIP 235, pp. 59–74, 2015.
DOI: 10.1007/978-3-319-25897-3_5

requirements from Secure Tropos models. To answer the question, firstly, we have represented SRPs using RAST. Secondly, we have proposed a process to apply SRPs to derive security requirements from the (Secure) Tropos models. Finally, we have conducted an observatory study to understand usability of the proposed method.

The rest of the paper is structured as follows: in Sect. 2 an overview of security risk management using Secure Tropos is provided. Section 3 presents security risk-oriented patterns. In Sect. 4 we consider the process for security requirements derivation from the Secure Tropos model. Section 5 outlines the observatory study conducted in order to validate the usability and understandability of the pattern application. Section 6 discusses some related work. Finally in Sect. 6 we summarise the study discussion and present some future work.

2   Security Risk Management Using Secure Tropos

In this section we, firstly, present the ISSRM domain model used to define the SRPs and to analyse the Secure Tropos models. Secondly, we overview how Secure Tropos constructs are aligned to concepts of the ISSRM domain model.

2.1   Information Systems Security Risk Management

The ISSRM domain model (see Fig. 1) defines security risk management concepts at three interrelated levels, which help developers identify specific IS security risk management constructs [6, 9].

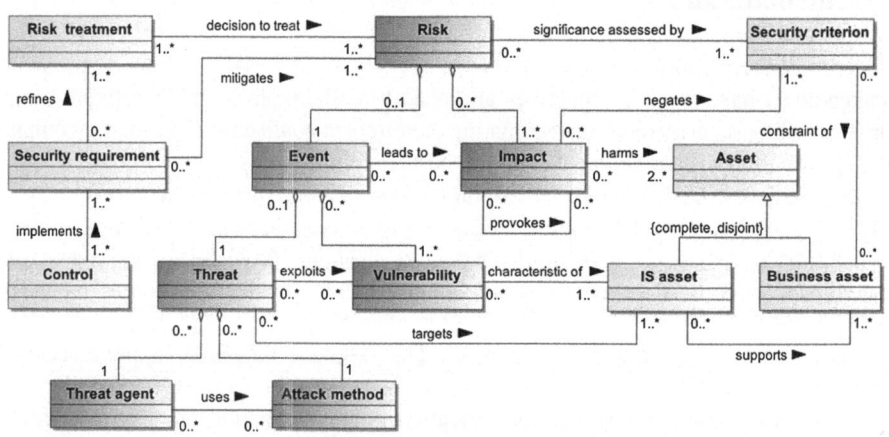

Fig. 1. The ISSRM Domain Model (adapted from [6, 9])

Asset-related concepts (i.e., *business* and *IS assets*, and *security criterion*) explain the organisation's values that need to be protected. The needed protection level is defined as the security needs, typically in terms of confidentiality, availability and integrity. *Risk-related concepts* (i.e., *risk, impact, event, vulnerability, threat, attack method*, and *threat agent*) define the risk itself and its components. Risk is a combination of threat with one or more vulnerabilities, which leads to a negative impact, harming some assets. An impact shows the negative consequence of a risk on an asset if the threat is accomplished. A vulnerability is a weakness or flaw of one or more IS assets. An attack method is a standard means by which a threat agent executes a threat. *Risk treatment-related concepts* (i.e., *risk treatment decision*, *security requirement* and *control*) describe how to treat the identified risks. A risk treatment leads to security requirements mitigating the risk, implemented as security controls.

The risk management process consists of six steps. First, it initiated by identifying analysed context and assets. The second step is security objective determination. The third step includes risk analysis. This step is followed with making a risk treatment decision. In the fifth step one suggests security requirements, which are implemented to security controls (sixth steps). The process is iterative and each previous step could be repeated if its result is not of satisfactory quality.

2.2 Security Risk-Aware Secure Tropos

Security Risk-aware Secure Tropos (RAST) is an extension of the i^* framework [13], Tropos [4] and Secure Tropos methods [11]. By aligning the modelling constructs to the concepts of the ISSRM domain model, it becomes possible to use the targeted modelling constructs to express specific concepts from the security risk management domain. This extension enables using Secure i^*/Tropos concepts wherever possible utilizing the already existing constructs, but additionally, whenever void or ambiguity exits, new constructs are introduced to address security risk management.

Asset-Related Concepts. The ISSRM *assets* are modelled using Secure Tropos constructs *Goal, Softgoal, Actor, Plan* and *Resource. Goal* is defined a desired state that an actor is determined to achieve (e.g., Data Employed in Fig. 2). *Softgoal* is a desired state that an actor is determined to achieve yet there is no clear determination of how this state is to be achieved (e.g., Confidentiality & Integrity in Fig. 2). *Actor* is an entity that is part of a system and is driven by certain goals and intentions (e.g., Server and Input Interface in Fig. 2). *Plan* is a course of action followed by an actor in order to achieve and satisfy a goal (e.g., Submit data in Fig. 2). The relationships between the assets are modelled using the constructs of *contribution, means-ends*, and *decomposition*. The ISSRM *security criterion* is represented by combining a *Softgoal* with *Security constraint(s)* (e.g., Confidentiality & Integrity and Maintain the integrity & confidentiality of the submitted data in Fig. 2). The ISSRM *constraints of* relationship can be modelled both explicitly by the *Restrict* link (see Fig. 2) and implicitly as security constraint placed on the security dependency link and restricting use of *dependum* (e.g., see connection between Server and Input Interface in Fig. 2).

Risk-Related Concepts. To distinguish risk related concepts darker colours are introduced to Secure Tropos constructs. The ISSRM *threat agent* is represented as actor (e.g., Attacker in Fig. 5). The ISSRM *attack method* – as a *plan* and the ISSRM *threat* as a combination of *goal* and *plan* (e.g., submitted data obtained and Intercept transmission in Fig. 5). The ISSRM *vulnerability* is not represented, how it is indicated through *vulnerability point* (see black circle in Fig. 5).

Risk Treatment-Related Concepts. The ISSRM *security requirements* are modelled by combining constructs of *Goal*, *Softgoal*, *Plan*, and *Security constraint* (e.g., (S) Perform Cryptographic procedures in Fig. 6). The ISSRM *mitigates* relationship is used to indicate a connection where a construct or group of constructs mitigate a certain security risk.

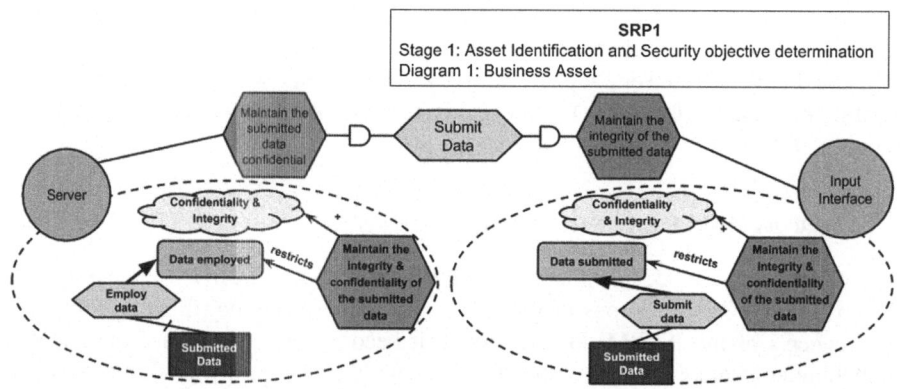

Fig. 2. SRP1: assets and security criteria

3 Security Patterns

"A security pattern describes a particular recurring security problem that arises in specific contexts, and presents a well-proven generic solution for it" [12]. Following this definition and the principles of the security risk management (see Sect. 2.1), five security risks-oriented patterns are introduced in [2]. In this section we briefly recall these patterns and illustrate how RAST could be used to represent them.

3.1 Security Risk-Oriented Patterns

SRP1 describes how to *secure the transmission of confidential data between business entities*. This pattern involves an attacker who intercepts the transmission between the input interface and the server, then obstructs and modifies the data. The attack is facilitated due to the transmission medium not being encrypted and data being stored in a plain text. The risk event leads to the loss of the confidentiality of the data and loss of the integrity of the data. The risk is mitigating by introducing cryptographic and checksum countermeasures.

SRP2 enables *validation of data submitted to a business activity, by predicting the need for a mechanism that scans and detects malicious data before the data is forwarded* *to this business activity.* This pattern counters an attacker that has information regarding the systems inner functionalities. The malicious agent attacks by submitting through the input interface a malicious script that exploits the fact that incoming data are not filtered. The attack leads at the loss of confidentiality and the integrity of the business activity that is forwarded to.

SRP3 ensures the *availability of a service in a Denial of Service* (DoS) event. The attacker sends an exponentially growing number of simultaneous requests to the system, resulting in the system crashing due to its ability to only serve a certain number of simultaneous clients. The attack leads to the loss of the service availability.

SRP4 focuses on *securing confidential information, from being accessed by unauthorised devices or people.* An attacker gains access to sensitive business data through a commonly used retrieval interface. Due to the interface not having an access control mechanism, the attacker is able to retrieve the data. The attack negates confidentiality of the business data.

SRP5 specifies how to *secure data stored into a business data store* against internal attacks. The attack occurs due to the data being stored in a plain format, and, thus, leads to the loss of the confidentiality of the stored data and the perpetual damage of the files residing in the same instance as malicious script.

3.2   Security Risk-Oriented Patterns Expressed in Secure Tropos

In this section we demonstrate how RAST could be applied to represent SRPs; more specifically we will represent SRP1. For instance, in Fig. 2 we define Submitted data as the ISSRM *business asset.* Both Server and Input Interface should collaborate in the way to achieve Confidentiality and Integrity of the submitted data. This *security criterion* is clarified by security constraint Maintain the integrity & confidentiality of the submitted data. This constraint restricts the goal of Data employed at the Server side and Data submitted at the Input interface side. Submit Data plan is the dependum between the two actors, and two constrains indicate that this double constrained dependency should be fulfilled by Server and Input Interface's activities.

Figure 3 introduces the Transmission Medium actor, which is used to transfer data from Input Interface to Server. This actor is part of the considered system (i.e., *IS asset*), thus, it is used to support the transfer of the *business asset* (i.e., Submitted data).

In Fig. 4 we identify a security *even* defined as Man in the middle attack that *impacts* the security criterion Confidentiality & integrity. In Fig. 5 this event is expanded showing how Attacker can achieve his goal Submitted data obtained by executing the *attack method* Intercept transmission.

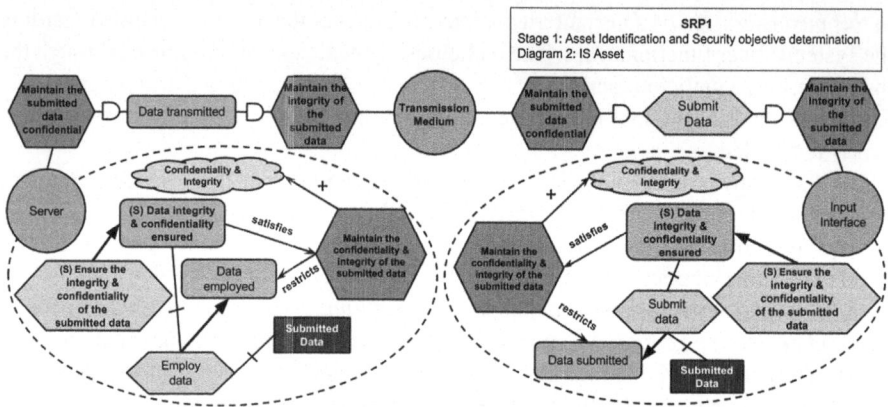

Fig. 3. SRP1: context pre-processing

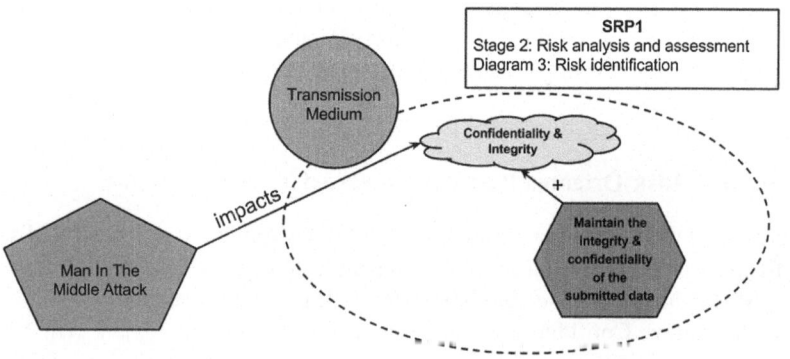

Fig. 4. SRP1: security risk identification

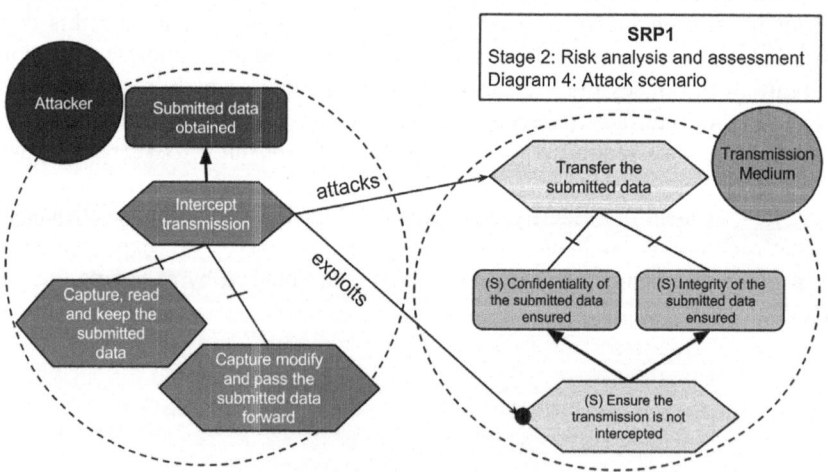

Fig. 5. SRP1: security threat

To mitigate the risk in Fig. 6 we present the implementation of *risk reduction* deci-sion. Hence there, the secure plan of the Ensure the integrity & confidentiality of the submitted data (see Fig. 3) is changed with Perform cryptographic procedures and Perform checksum procedures. The replacements are performed in the according actor of the model. Risk mitigation is indicated using the Mitigates relationships.

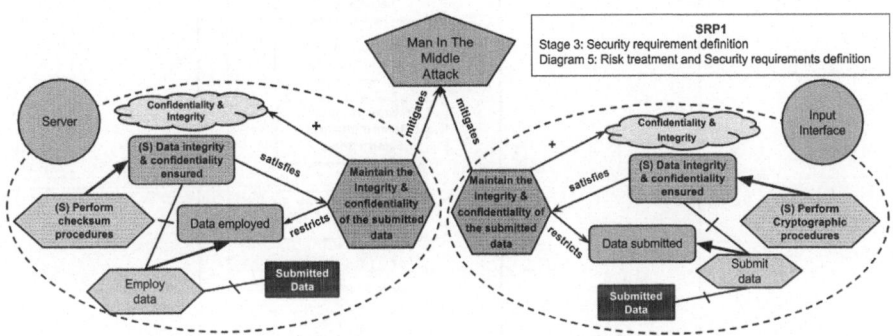

Fig. 6. SRP1: security requirements definition

Although RAST contains some limitations with respect to the ISSRM domain (as indi-cated in [7, 8]), the language allows represent the SRP description. In our example, the recurring security problem is illustrated in Figs. 4 and 5, the context in Figs. 2 and 3. Finally we present the solution in Fig. 6. We will illustrate how graphical SRP representa-tions can be used to derive security requirements from the Secure Tropos models in Sect. 4.

4   Deriving Security Requirements Using SRP's

4.1   Collaboration Between System and Security Analysts

Application of SRPs to Tropos model could stimulate collaboration between two roles (as illustrated in Fig. 7) – *system analyst*, who is responsible for system development, for example, using *i**/Tropos method, and *security analyst*, who is responsible for security solutions and could potentially apply SRPs to achieve her goals. In some cases both roles could be played by the same person. For instance, after creating system model using *i**/Tropos method, system analyst could potentially request security analyst to determine security requirements. After analysing the system model, security analyst selects and applies the relevant SRPs. The SRP application includes (1) SRP occurrence identification and asset alignment, (2) vulnerable asset identification and secure goal introduction, and (3) security requirements introduction. After this iteration, security analyst could potentially consider whether other SRPs should be applied. If not the system model with introduced security requirements is returned back to system analyst.

Next system analyst should potentially decide which security requirements could be implemented to the targeted system. In other words, system analyst needs to perform trade-off analysis to understand the cost-value benefits of the security solution. In case of necessity, system analyst could potentially request security analyst for justification

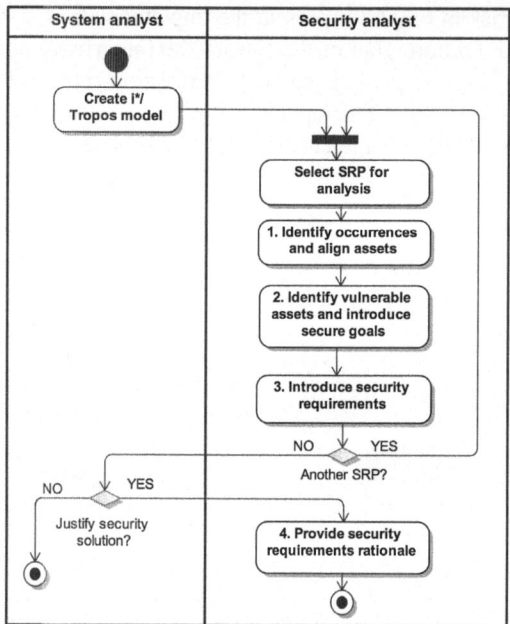

Fig. 7. SRP1: collaboration between system and security analysts

of the proposed security requirements. In the latter case, the instantiated SRP's security threat models (e.g., see Fig. 5) could be used to (4) provided security requirements rationale.

4.2 Security Requirements Derivation

Now we will illustrate how the SRPs expressed in RAST could be used to derive security requirements from the Secure Tropos models. The model [3] used to demonstrate the derivation process is presented in Fig. 8. We will use the SRP1 (illustrated in Sect. 3.2). However other SRPs can be following the same steps.

1. Occurrence identification and asset alignment. This step includes identification of the pattern occurrences in the analysed model. This is a manual activity due to the complexity of the Secure Tropos models. In Fig. 8 we aim to apply SRP1. The contextual pattern description helps to observe the following occurrences:

- The Internet Store actor aligns to the SRP1 Server actor, thus, giving the similar interactions with the other actors;
- The User (Interface) aligns to the SRP1 Input Interface due to the connection to the Internet Store/Server. Given that a 1:1 occurrence not existing between SRP1 and the scenario under investigation, we assume that the User fulfils the Send Use Info plan by using an input interface provided by the Internet Store. This is why we recall the User actor as User Interface.

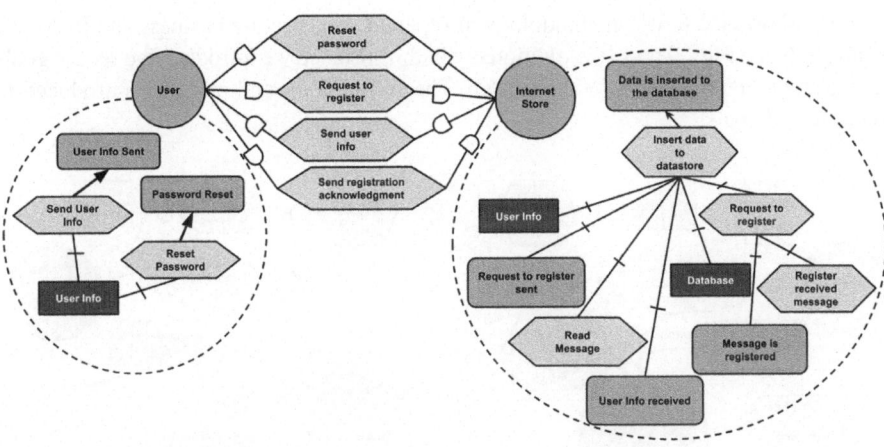

Fig. 8. Internet store registration; adapted from [3]

Following the pattern description a Transmission Medium is introduces as the intermediate actor to Send user info. This assumption is done to support the communication between the User and the Internet Store.

Next step is to consider the dependency relationship and potentially equipped it with the security constraints in order to highlight the *security objectives*. The extracted occurrence of the pattern is illustrated in Fig. 9.

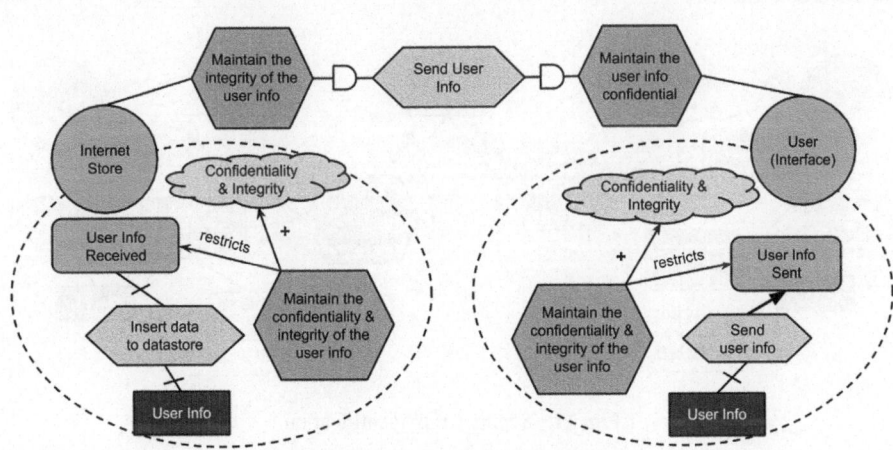

Fig. 9. Asset and security criteria analysis

2. Vulnerable asset identification and secure goal introduction. In this step vulnerable assets are identified and security criteria and constraints are explicitly introduced. The process follows the RAST methodology of separately illustrating business and IS Assets as illustrated in Figs. 9 and 10. Additionally in this instance we introduce the secure goals and secure plans suggested by the pattern. The secure goals and plans are introduced to their aligned goals.

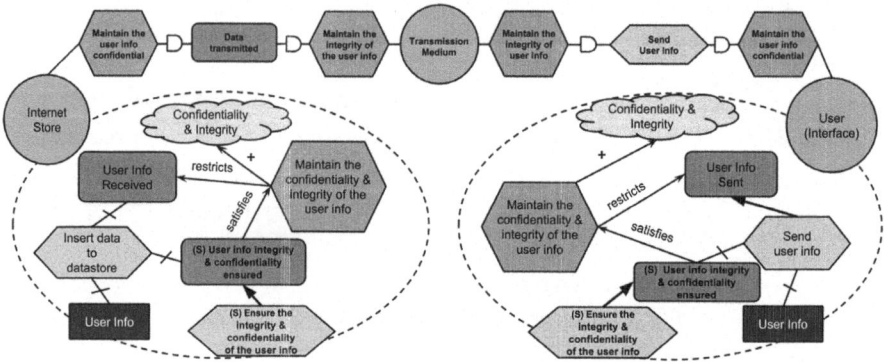

Fig. 10. Model Pre-processing

3. Security requirements introduction. Following the SRP1 risk treatment and security requirements definition, it becomes possible to introduce secure goals and plans as illustrated in Fig. 11. The previously defined model now is also equipped with *security requirements* such as Perform checksum procedures and Perform Cryptographic procedures. As illustrated in Fig. 11 both suggestions *mitigate* the security event (i.e., Man in the Middle Attack).

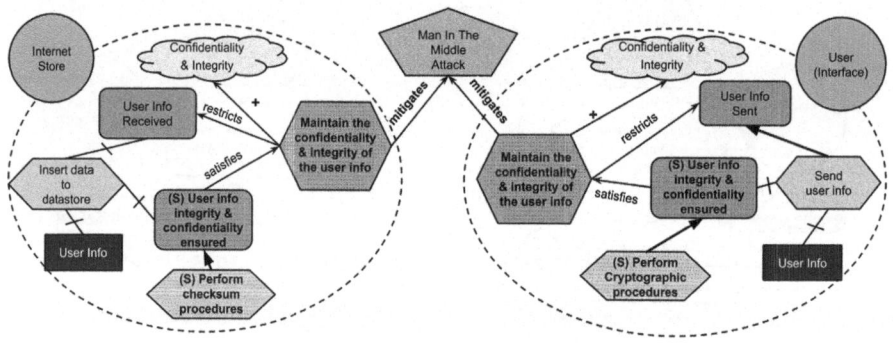

Fig. 11. Security risk identification

4. Security requirement rationale. In some cases this step could be considered as optional, but it becomes important, once one needs to understand the rationale and trade-off of the newly introduced security requirements. Following the pattern attack scenario, in this step one defines how the security threat could be carried on the targeted system. More specifically in our case, Fig. 12 illustrates how Attacker (i.e., *threat agent*) could obtain the user info by intercepting transmission.

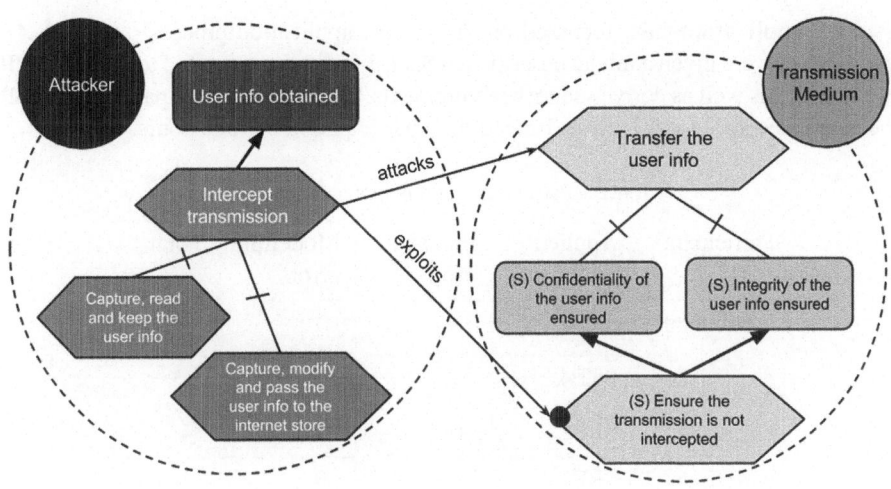

Fig. 12. Security threat

5 Validation

To validate the SRPs expressed in RAST and their application process contribution we have conducted an observatory study. Its **objectives** were (*i*) to understand *correctness* and (*ii*) *usability* the SRP application, (*ii*) to compare *understandability* of the SRP application of the participants with the ISSRM background against participants without ISSRM background.

5.1 Observatory Study Design

Participants. We have invited six individuals with the software engineering background. Three participants (i.e., *group A*) had the IS-security background as they were working in the field of enterprise security and had prior knowledge of the ISSRM concepts. Other three participants (i.e., *group B*) had no information systems security background, but nevertheless they were practitioners working in the software engineering companies.

Design. Firstly, the participants were given the introductory lecture. Secondly, they participants were given a Secure Tropos model and were asked to derive the security requirements using the SRPs. Finally, the participants filled the questionnaire on the usability of the SRPs and their application process. Each participant took approximately 3 h to complete the process.

Treatment. The lecture included an introduction of the ISSRM domain model and security risk management process (see Sect. 2.1), RAST (see Sect. 2.2), SRPs (see Sect. 3) and their application process (see Sect. 4). The lecture was concluded with an SRP application demo.

SRP application task focussed on the pattern application process (see Sect. 4). Participants were given a model described in Sect. 3 and were requested to identify SRP occurrences as well as derive security requirements. None of the participants applied all the SRPs (see Table 1), since we limited their participation to three hours.

Table 1. Participant pattern application errors

Participants	Applied SRP	Phrasing errors	Modelling errors	Total
Participant 1	SRP2	20[a]	0	20[a]
	SRP4	_[a]	_[a]	_[a]
Participant 2	SRP5	0	4	4
Participant 3	SRP1	11	0	11
	SRP3	16	0	16
Participant 4	SRP4	11	0	11
Participant 5	SRP1	26	13	39
Participant 6	SRP2	10	0	10

[a]Not eligible for error counting due to the participant not using an existing construct but assumed that the system includes the functionality.

Questionnaire. Once the SRP application was completed, participants filled the questionnaire on the usability of the RAST process, SRPs and SRP application process. Specifically in included questions on easiness, satisfaction, and understandability of used artefacts.

5.2 Threats to Validity

The following threats to validity should be taken into account:

- The number of participants is rather small (only six participants) thus the sample may not be accurate. The results might differ if we were able to attract more participants. However they all were practitioners working in the field of software security engineering.
- Given treatment could influence the received results. When applying SRPs participants had some questions, and we provided then with the answers. However otherwise they would have difficulty to complete the given task.
  Each participant conducted his task individually. If participants had opportunity to discuss and to learn from each the result potentially would be different.
- Each participant applied different SRPs. Ideally all of the participants would have to complete all SRPs for better result. However, we were limited by the time constraints (three hours per participant).
- Participants had a varying level of prior knowledge of ISSRM domain and security risk management. Having participants with the same knowledge could potentially

deliver more reliable result. We tried to mitigate this threat by provided introductory lecture.

- The majority of the participants implemented the models using an online drawing tool. Implementing the models by hand or other modelling tool method could impact the modelling outcome.
- The participants were not told that they were expected to perform in a certain way or that a specific result was expected from them. Stating expectations upfront would impact the overall performance of the participants. The performance could be enhanced in case the participant would want to perform according the expectations. Or the participant could suffer from a type of performance anxiety and his result would be negatively affected.
- Participant had prior acquaintance with the conductor of the observatory study and the first author of this paper. If no prior acquaintance would occur participants could not ask the same questions or perform in the same manner they would perform to another individual. However this acquaintance was the way to involve participants in the evaluation.
- Some SRPs were easier identified in the model comparatively to other SRPs. If all the SRPs would be identical in terms of identification ease, the result could be different. Making an SRP easier or harder to identify results in the pattern application process becoming automatically easier of harder to perform.

All the above threats had a certain effect to the overall results. We assume that in case of a more extensive study with a greater number of participants and different design, different outcomes might be received.

5.3   Observatory Study Results

Correctness of the Participant Models. Correctness of each SRP application is defined through the number of errors identified in the resulting model (i.e., the lower number indicates better model correctness). Errors are divided to two categories *phrasing* and *modelling* errors. Phrasing errors describe any error in regards to the phrasing of any of the constructs (e.g. labels of goals, plans, and etc.). Modelling errors describe errors performed in the modelling of each concept. Modelling errors include using wrong constructs when linking assets, risk components, security countermeasures and similar. Additionally, modelling mistakes also include incorrect colouring of the constructs (as the colour here brings the semantic difference between security risk concepts). Both types of errors are discovered by comparing the participants' models with the models prepared by the first author of this paper.

Table 1 presents the result of the model correctness. It was observed that *Participant 2* has made the least amount of errors compared to the other participants. It is also important is to point out that the majority of errors done by *Participant 1* were rather minor in comparison to phrasing errors of the other participants. In general the majority of the errors are phrasing errors. This could be explained by the fact that the modelling language does not provide explicit guidelines on how to name the constructs during modelling.

Understandability. As mentioned in the design description, the participants were divided to two groups – *group A* and *group B* – based on their previous experience with the security engineering. The results show that participants of *group A* were able to apply and comprehend the used patterns as well as the pattern application process. Participant of *group B* were able *moderately* to apply and to comprehend SRPs. *Group A* correctly executed all the pattern application steps. Nonetheless mistakes were made in phrasing and resource decomposition (as discussed above). But they performed all the tasks in a rather reasonable time and were confident in their results.

Group B completed the SRP application process with a *moderate* correctness. Similar to *group A*, *group B* also made mistakes in phrasing and modelling. Furthermore, noticeable difference in the results was the level of confidence in the results of the application process. Participants of *group B* were notably less confident than the participants of *group A* in their results. As conclusion we observed that the information systems security experience had some impact and helped better contributed to the understandability of the SRPs application.

Discussion and Concluding Remarks. We draw out the concluding remarks based on our observations and the participant responses marked in the questionnaire. All participants completed the application of at least one pattern. Mistakes were observed in the phrasing and modelling of various assets of the models. In comparison less mistakes were made in modelling rather than phrasing. All the participants understood the proposed SRP representations. The pattern application process was according to the majority of the participants moderately easy to be applied. RAST affects the overall process in a moderate level.

The fact that both groups were able to complete the tasks assigned, demonstrated that the process is useable as a starting point to derive security requirements in a goal-oriented environment. The easiest part in the application process according to the majority of the participants was the pattern identification and asset alignment. The hardest step to be applied by the majority of the participants was security requirement introduction and extracted model re-integration.

Having background knowledge in IS security affects the process during the first applications and speeds up moderately the security requirement derivation process. Prior knowledge of an agent-oriented language in combination ISSRM affects rather positively the outcome of modelling. Participant that had no prior knowledge were less confident about their results. The following lessons are learnt:

- Application of the SRPs helps to construct rather correct security models and derive appropriate security requirements. The major modelling mistakes are made due to the lack of guidance from the modelling language application.
- The SRP application guidelines are rather understandable and moderately usable by their users. However, a priori experience in security engineering helps to see the method purpose. Potentially some security engineering training could help to improve method application.

6   Related Work

There are few studies where the secure $i*$ framework [13] or Secure Tropos is used to capture security and privacy requirements through security patterns. Some extensions are proposed to Secure Tropos to be suited for the security pattern description language [10]. Elsewhere in [5], legal requirements are incorporated to security and privacy patterns expressed using another extension of Tropos methodology towards security. Here authors concentrate on access control, need-to-know, outsourcing, and non-repudiation patterns. In addition to these contributions, in this paper we use the Secure Tropos approach [11] to represent security risk-oriented patterns.

In [1] Ahmed has presented a method for security requirements elicitation from business processes (SREBP). This method enables security requirements derivation from BPMN models, namely value chains and business process models. The method involves collaboration between the business analyst and security analyst. In the current study we develop a method to derive security requirements from the RAST models. Hence the collaboration is defined between the security analyst and system analyst, since we consider the *late requirements* stage modelled in Secure Tropos.

7   Summary and Future Work

In this paper we analyse how to integrate security risk-oriented patterns into the goal-oriented IS development. We have developed a threefold procedure. Firstly, it is important to define and describe the SRPs in modelling language used for IS development, in our case RAST. Secondly this description is used to identify the pattern occurrences in the targeted IS model. Typically this step requires some model pre-processing. Finally, the security requirements are derived and introduced following the SRP description. To support this procedure we have presented a pattern presentation structure as well as their application process. The proposal is validated in the observatory study, which illustrates the SRP usability. Finally it was demonstrated that the proposed SRP's could potentially be the starting point for security requirements derivation and security trade-off analysis.

The future work includes expansion of the SRP list with new patterns and their representation using RAST. Also it is important to define guidelines for systematic security requirements prioritisation and their implementation to security controls. Last but not least, the software tools to support the representation of the SRPs ain RAST and their application process could potentially help to decrease the application effort.

Acknowledgement. This research is supported by the Estonian Research Council.

References

1. Ahmed N.: Deriving Security Requirements from Business Process Models, Ph.D. thesis, University of Tartu (2015)
2. Ahmed, N., Matulevičius, R.: Securing business processes using security risk-oriented patterns. Comput. Stan. Interfaces **36**(4), 723–733 (2014)

3. Altuhhova, O.: An Extension of Business Process Model and Notation for Security Risk Management, McS thesis, University of Tartu (2013)
4. Bresciani, P., Perini, A., Giorgini, P., Giunchiglia, F., Mylopoulos, J.: Tropos: an agent-oriented software development methodology. Auton. Agent. Multi-Agent Syst. **8**, 203–236 (2004)
5. Compagna, L., El Khoury, P., Krausov, A., Massacci, F., Zannone, N.: How to integrate legal requirements into a requirements engineering methodology for the development of security and privacy patterns. Artif. Intell. Law **17**(1), 1–30 (2009)
6. Dubois, E., Heymans, P., Mayer, N., Matulevičius, R.: A systematic approach to define the domain of information system security risk management. In: Nurcan, S., et al. (eds.) Intentional Perspectives on Information Systems Engineering, pp 289–306. Springer, Heidelberg (2010)
7. Matulevičius, R., Mayer, N., Mouratidis, H., Dubois, E., Heymans, P., Genon, N.: Adapting secure tropos for security risk management in the early phases of information systems development. In: Bellahsène, Z., Léonard, M. (eds.) CAiSE 2008. LNCS, vol. 5074, pp. 541–555. Springer, Heidelberg (2008)
8. Matulevičius, R., Mouratidis, H., Mayer, N., Dubois, E., Heymans, P.: Syntactic and semantic extensions to secure tropos to support security risk management. J. UCS **18**, 816–844 (2012)
9. Mayer N.: Model-Based Management of Information System Security Risk, Ph.D. thesis, University of Namur (2009)
10. Mouratidis, H., Giorgini, P., Schumacher, M., Manson, M.: Security patterns for agent systems. In: Proceedings of EuroPLop 2003 (2003)
11. Mouratidis, H., Giorgini, P.: Secure tropos: a security-oriented extension of the tropos methodology. Int. J. Softw. Eng. Knowl. Eng. (IJSEKE) **17**(2), 285–309 (2007)
12. Schumacher, M., Fernandez-Buglioni, E., Hybertson, D., Buschmann, F., Sommerlad, P.: Security Patterns: Integrating Security and Systems Engineering. Wiley, New York (2006)
13. Yu, E.: Towards modeling and reasoning support for early-phase requirements engineering. In: Proceedings of the 3rd IEEE International Symposium on Requirements Engineering, pp. 226–235. IEEE Computer Society Press (1997)

Analyzing Attack Strategies Through Anti-goal Refinement

Tong Li[1]([✉]), Jennifer Horkoff[2], Elda Paja[1], Kristian Beckers[3],
and John Mylopoulos[1]

[1] University of Trento, Trento, Italy
{tong.li,paja,jm}@unitn.it
[2] City University London, London, UK
horkoff@city.ac.uk
[3] Technische Universität München, Garching bei München, Germany
beckersk@in.tum.de

Abstract. Analyzing security from an attacker's perspective has been accepted as an effective approach for dealing with security requirements for complex systems. However, there is no systematic approach for constructing attack scenarios. As a result, the completeness of the derived attack scenarios is subject to the expertise of analysts. In this paper, we propose a systematic process for identifying attack scenarios to support security analysis, founded on anti-goal refinement. In particular, we examine three real attack scenarios in order to understand attack strategies that have been applied in reality. Based on our examination, we propose a comprehensive anti-goal refinement framework, which consists of five anti-goal refinement patterns and an analysis process for using the patterns as part of security design. Finally, we evaluate the proposed anti-goal refinement framework by applying it to a credit card theft scenario.

1 Introduction

Due to ever-increasing complexity, today's systems contain more and more security vulnerabilities, resulting in a broader range of attacks. According to data from the Common Vulnerability Enumeration (CVE)[1], 9625 vulnerabilities were added to the CVE database in 2014, a nearly 30 percent increase from 2013 (7440 vulnerabilities). Given the fast rate of emerging security vulnerabilities, it is challenging to get a comprehensive understanding of the consequences of each vulnerability, not to mention the combined consequences of multiple vulnerabilities, which may lead to multistage attacks. Taking an attacker's perspective to analyze potential security breaches has been advocated as an effective approach, as it sheds light on which vulnerabilities need to be examined, and thus avoids inspecting the full space of vulnerabilities.

Techniques, such as attack trees [1] and misuse cases [2], have been proposed to describe attack scenarios (i.e., steps that attackers use to perform their

---

[1] https://cve.mitre.org.

© IFIP International Federation for Information Processing 2015
J. Ralyté et al. (Eds.): PoEM 2015, LNBIP 235, pp. 75–90, 2015.
DOI: 10.1007/978-3-319-25897-3_6

attacks) and to guide security analysis. However, when building attack scenarios from an attacker's viewpoint, there are no specific guidelines to follow [3]. As such, different security analysts can create different, subjective attacker models, and the completeness of the derived attack scenarios is subject to the expertise of the analysts. Threat analysis approaches (e.g., STRIDE [4]) elicit and tackle threats to different parts of systems, but do not capture the attacker's intentions behind each threat and miss the connections between threats. As such these approaches are not well suited to analyze complicated multistage attacks.

Further work has explicitly captured the rationale behind attacker actions using anti-goals [5–7]. Such approaches capture not only the space of possible attacks, but an attacker's strategy, including alternative plans and combing multiple steps to achieve a malicious goal. For example, to disclose a data asset, one attack strategy can be finding out all software applications that process the data and then hacking the applications to disclose the data, or directly hacking the hardware that stores the data. By systematically developing an attack strategy against a particular scenario, analysts can effectively identify attack scenarios, and then provide corresponding countermeasures.

Our previous work captures an attacker's malicious intentions as anti-goals as part of a holistic security requirements analysis framework [6,7]. The approach takes into account security issues in various abstraction layers by using a three-layer, goal-oriented requirements model [8]. By iteratively refining root anti-goals into operationalizable anti-goals, we can create an attack strategy that implies a space of attack scenarios, from which related security controls can eventually be derived (Fig. 1). However, we have not studied in-depth how anti-goals can be refined systematically, in order to generate a comprehensive attack strategy. Thus, our primary goal is to *produce a framework, grounded in real evidence, to support systematic exploration of attack strategies, producing strategies which are more complete, leading to a more complete security analysis* (i.e., the highlighted part in Fig. 1). To achieve this goal, we perform the following steps:

1. Perform a grounded study on three real attack scenarios [9] in order to investigate how attackers elaborate their malicious intentions in reality, from which we identify five anti-goal refinement patterns.
2. Propose an anti-goal refinement framework, which systematically refines anti-goals by leveraging the identified anti-goal refinement patterns, and eventually reveals attack scenarios.
3. Evaluate the proposed refinement framework by applying it to a different credit card theft scenario [10], the result of which shows that our framework is able to generate a comprehensive attack strategy, which not only covers the reported attack scenarios, but also reveals new attack scenarios.

The remainder of this paper is structured as follows: we present the anti-goal modeling approach that we use to analyze the attacker's strategy in Sect. 2. The examination of real attack scenarios is described in Sect. 3, based on which we propose an anti-goal refinement framework in Sect. 4. We evaluate the proposed framework in Sect. 5, and discuss related issues of the framework in Sect. 6. In

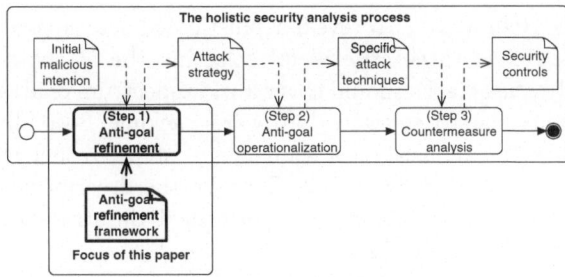

Fig. 1. Research overview

Sect. 7, we compare our proposal with related work. Finally, we conclude the paper and discuss future work in Sect. 8.

2   Anti-goal Modeling

Anti-goals were first used by van Lamsweerde to model an attacker's malicious intentions related to system assets [5]. An anti-goal model presents how the attacker's abstract anti-goals are refined to terminal anti-goals (that are realizable by attackers), which captures the attacker's strategies. By constructing anti-goal models, analysts can effectively identify system threats and use this knowledge to design secure systems.

In this paper, we leverage the anti-goal approach to analyze system threats in order to provide corresponding countermeasures. In particular, we focus on analyzing anti-goal refinements from an attacker's viewpoint by studying real attack scenarios. To this end, we adopt three concepts from a recent goal model approach, *Techne* [11], for building anti-goal models: *Goal*, *Task*, and *Domain Assumption*. A *goal* captures attacker intentions (i.e., anti-goals); a *task* presents detailed attack actions that are performed by attackers; a *domain assumption* describes an indicative property that is relevant to the system. Detailed examples of anti-goal models are presented in Fig. 2. It is worth noting that we do not introduce a new notion *anti-goal* but use the ordinary notion *goal* to model anti-goals, as anti-goals are simply goals from the attacker's viewpoint.

3   Attack Scenario Examination

We examine three real attack scenarios in order to understand attack strategies that have been applied in reality. In particular, we apply the anti-goal modeling to real attack scenarios, and then investigate the rationale behind each anti-goal refinement within the modeled scenarios, and finally extract five anti-goal refinement patterns. In the remainder of this section, we first briefly introduce the real attack scenarios that we examine, and then present our examination on these scenarios in detail.

Sample Attack Scenarios. To reveal sophisticated attack strategies from the examination, we define three criteria for selecting the attack scenarios to be examined. Firstly, the attacks should cover a wide spectrum of attack techniques, from social engineering to software/hardware hacking. Secondly, we look for multistage attacks that consist of a sequence of steps, rather than an atomic attack that is done by a single exploit. Thirdly, the description of the attacks should present not only attack actions performed by attackers, but also the intentions motivating the actions.

According to the above criteria, we select three attack scenarios that are documented in Mitnick's book [9, Chap. 11]. Each of these attack scenarios involves both social and technical issues, and consists of multiple attack steps. In this case, the author narrates the entire attack process in detail, shedding light on both the why and how for each attack step. The general problems and contexts of these attack scenarios are as follows:

- *Easy Money:* Two attackers aim to defeat a security product that is designed for access control in order to get prize money. The product applies terminal-based security technique, which identifies system users based in part on the particular computer terminal being used.
- *Dictionary as an Attack Tool:* An external attacker intends to steal the source code of a new electronic game, which is developed by a global company. The source code is stored on an unknown server of the company.
- *The Speedy Download:* An external attacker wants to obtain some confidential files of an accounting firm in order to affect the stock price of publicly traded companies. The confidential files are stored on the workstation, which can only be accessed from the company's local network.

In this paper, we illustrate the examination process using the "Easy Money" scenario. The complete set of examination results can be found online[2].

Construct Initial Anti-goal Models. We first build initial anti-goal models according to the textual description of the attack scenarios. The construction of anti-goal models is carried out by combining top-down and bottom-up analysis. The content of each node is described in natural language, using a particular part of the scenario description. Figure 2(a) presents the entire anti-goal model that is built from the "Easy Money" attack scenario. Note that we capture the attack actions as *tasks* so as to provide a full view of the scenario, but our analysis focuses on the anti-goal refinement rather than the anti-goal operationalization. To easily reference to the elements of the anti-goal model, we annotate each element with regard to the type of the element. In particular, G stands for *Goal*, T stands for *Task*, and D stands for *Domain Assumption*.

Characterize Anti-goals. It is our goal to capture anti-goals and their refinements, such as in Fig. 2(a), in a more structured and abstract way. Thus we characterize each anti-goal with a structured description language, which is specified in Table 1 by using EBNF syntax.

---

[2] http://disi.unitn.it/~li/poem15/result.pdf.

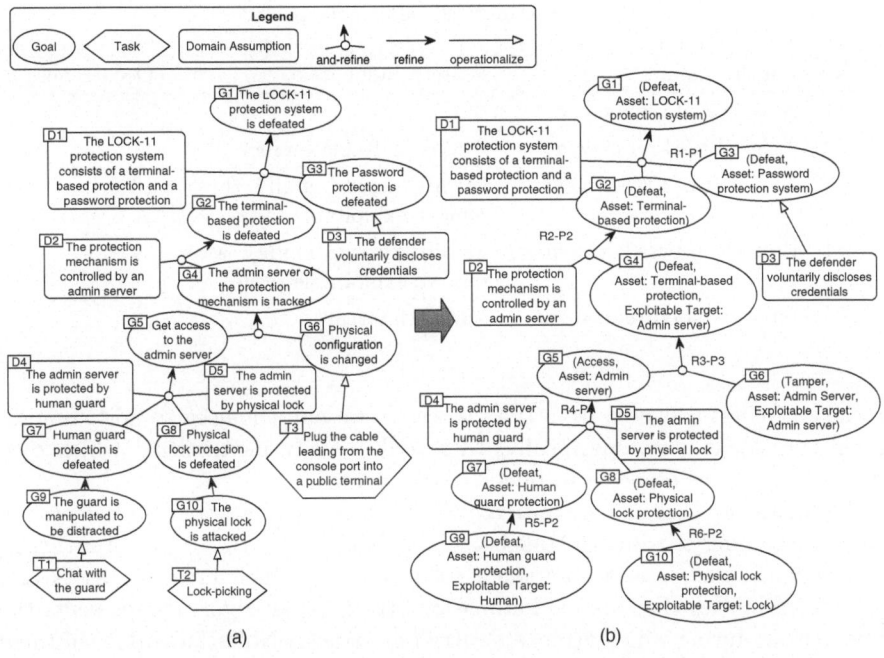

Fig. 2. Anti-goal models that are built from the "Easy Money" attack scenario

Table 1. The EBNF syntax of the structured description language

Rule_1:	\<anti−goal\> ::= \<threat\>, \<attribute−description\>+
Rule_2:	\<threat\> ::= 'tamper' | 'disclose' | 'spoof' | 'repudiate' | 'deny' | 'reach' |'access' |'control' | 'defeat'
Rule_3:	\<attribute−description\> ::= \<attribute\>, \<descriptor\>
Rule_4:	\<attribute\> ::= 'asset' | 'exploitable target' | 'interval'

Each anti-goal is characterized by one threat and one or several attributes (*Rule_1*). A *threat* presents an undesired state that an attacker wants to impose on the targeting system. We classify threats using an existing, established threat categorization, STRIDE, provided by Microsoft [4]. STRIDE is an acronym that stands for six threat categories: *Spoofing, Tampering, Repudiation, Information disclosure, Denial of service*, and *Elevation of privilege*. These threat categories provide comprehensive coverage of security threats and have been adopted and investigated in both academia and industry [4,12]. Note that we describe the threat categories in terms of their essential actions rather than the full description (*Rule_2*), as the threat actions are more succinct and intuitive when combined with other attributes. For the threat *Elevation of privilege*, we specifically consider three threat actions *reach*, *access*, and *control*, each of which implies a particular level of privilege. When comparing the available categories in STRIDE

Table 2. Summarized refinement patterns

No.	Pattern name	Pattern influences	Occurrence
P1	Asset-based refinement	Modify asset	2
P2	Target-based refinement	Add exploitable target	7
P3	Threat-based refinement	Modify asset; modify threat; remove exploitable target	10
P4	Protection-based refinement	Modify threat; modify asset; remove exploitable target	4
P5	Interval-based refinement	Modify interval	2

to the anti-goals collected from the real cases, we find the need to add an additional threat category, specifically, "defeated security mechanism" which captures the attacker intention to break system protections.

Moreover, we characterize anti-goals with three other attributes (*Rule_4*): an *asset* is anything of value to stakeholders, it is normally the object of a threat; an *exploitable target* is a component of a system, which involves assets and has vulnerabilities that are exploitable by attackers; an *interval* represents the time period, during which attackers carry out attacks. Note that values of these attributes are described in text (*Rule_3*). By using the structured description language, we characterize the anti-goals in the initial anti-goal model, resulting in a characterized model as shown in Fig. 2(b).

Identify Refinement Patterns. Once the characterized anti-goal model is obtained, we investigate each refinement relation in detail, on the basis of which we can identify refinement patterns.

We first investigate the influences of refinement relations on the refined anti-goals, i.e., what have been changed from the refined anti-goals to their sub-goals. For example, as shown in Fig. 2(b), the influence of refinement *R1* is that the asset of the anti-goals *G2* and *G3* have been modified from their parent goal *G1*. After performing such analysis on all 25 refinement relations in the three attack scenarios, we cluster refinement relations with similar influences, based on which we summarize five refinement patterns. Table 2 presents the identified refinement patterns, as well as their influences and number of occurrence in the three attack scenarios. Examples of the application of the refinement patterns can be found in Fig. 2(b), where each refinement relation is annotated with its corresponding refinement pattern.

4   An Anti-goal Refinement Framework

The extracted five anti-goal refinement patterns shed light on various ways to refine an anti-goal, based on which we propose an anti-goal refinement framework. The framework efficiently leverages the proposed refinement patterns to refine an attacker's high-level anti-goals and to generate a comprehensive attack strategy, the analysis process of which is shown in Fig. 3.

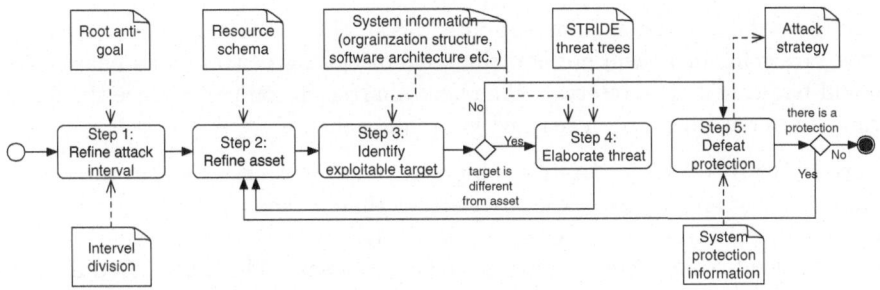

Fig. 3. An analysis process of anti-goal refinement

Each of these steps makes use of one particular refinement pattern, and the detailed guidelines for performing these steps are presented below (the steps are illustrated as part of the evaluation in Sect. 5). It is worth noting that we describe the anti-goal refinement framework from an attacker's perspective to clearly show the rationale of the strategy, but the corresponding analysis is actually performed by security analysts with a complete set of system information in order to discover all potential attack scenarios. In particular, the description of each analysis step focuses on addressing the following issues:

– *Rationale.* We first describe the rationale of each analysis step, which explains the design of the analysis process (Fig. 3). Note that the proposed anti-goal refinement framework is a specific way to analyze attack strategy, and does not exclude other possible ways (more discussions in Sect. 6).
– *Input.* We then specify the inputs that are required for performing the analysis step. It is worth noting that our proposal is a general framework, which is not associated with specific models. Thus, for inputs, we only describe the types of information that are required, and all models that capture the corresponding information can be used. In Sect. 6, we will discuss the potential of using a three-layer requirements goal model from our previous work [8] to support the analysis.
– *Sanity check.* Our framework is intended to cover various attacks and thus provides a comprehensive security analysis. As a result, a single anti-goal can lead to a very large model. To deal with this complexity, we propose to prune the model as part of its construction, i.e., performing sanity checks after each analysis step in order to reduce the refinement space.
– *Stop criteria.* Finally, we describe the stop criteria of each analysis step.

Step 1: Refine Attack Interval. The system security settings can change over time, affecting an attacker's anti-goals. As the first step, an attacker applies the interval-based refinement pattern in order to concentrate on specific time intervals. Thus, this analysis step requires specific domain knowledge regarding the division of time intervals. In particular, for each interval-based refinement, the analyst should check whether the system security settings have been changed from the original interval to its sub-intervals. If the security settings remain the same, this refinement will not contribute to disclosing new attack scenarios and should be pruned. The interval refinement analysis is completed once the finest-grained intervals have been reached via refinements.

Step 2: Refine Asset. Given a composite asset, it is easier for an attacker to attack a fine-grained part of the asset rather than attacking the composite asset as a whole. An attacker can leverage the asset-based refinement pattern to generate sub-goals that focus on more specific sub-assets. The asset-based analysis takes the system resource schema as input, which documents "part-of" relations between system resources. To identify system assets among system resources, we refer to the asset identification process that is specified in ISO27005:2011 [13, Annex B], which deals with both the primary assets and the supporting assets. In particular, the primary assets include *business processes and activities* and *information*; the supporting assets include *hardware, software, network, personnel, site,* and *organizations structure*. This analysis step is done when all identified assets in the resource schema are analyzed.

Step 3: Identify Exploitable Target. Once the an attacker has determined the assets he intends to impair, he needs to find out corresponding vulnerable system components (a.k.a. exploitable targets), by exploiting which the assets will be damaged. In particular, an asset can be involved in system components in different ways according to the type of the components, e.g., an information asset can be accessed by people, processed by software, or stored in hardware. Note that the asset and the exploitable target of an anti-goal can be the same, if the asset itself is a vulnerable system component.

We here consider the types of vulnerable system components in line with the list of supporting assets presented in ISO27005:2011 [13, Annex B.1.2]. As such, corresponding system information is required, e.g., information of system infrastructure, software architecture, and organization structures. When identifying the exploitable target, analysts should check the risk of exploiting the target, e.g., using the CORAS approach [14]. If the risk is under certain threshold, determined by the analysts, the target is assumed to be secure and is excluded from this refinement step. After using the target-based refinement pattern to identify all potential exploitable targets, this analysis step is complete.

Step 4: Elaborate Threat. If an attacker aims to impose a threat to an asset by exploiting a target, which is different from the asset, then the attacker should identify new threats that he wants to impose on the exploitable target in order to successfully impose the original threat to the asset. For example, if an anti-goal is intended to disclose (*threat*) confidential files (*asset*) that are stored in a database (*exploitable target*), then it can be refined to getting access to (*new threat*) the same database (*new asset*) by using the threat-based refinement pattern.

When applying the threat-based refinement pattern, the system information and related security knowledge are required to support the threat elaboration. Specifically, we refer to 19 STRIDE threat trees as the security knowledge sources, which describe alternative ways about how a threat category can be refined to other categories. As we specify the threats of anti-goals using the STRIDE threat categories, the application of the STRIDE threat trees can be seamlessly integrated into this analysis step. In order to discover all potential attack scenarios, once we identify the new threats to the exploitable target that can lead to the original threat to the asset, we iteratively analyze the new threats to the exploitable target through the analysis step 2 and 3, i.e., we treat the exploitable target as a new asset. Such as in the aforementioned example, the newly introduced sub-goal "getting access to (*new threat*) the database (*new asset*)" concerns the database as a new asset, which was the exploitable target in the parent anti-goal.

Step 5: Defeat Protection. From an attacker's perspective, security protections are obstacles to his attacks. If the attacker targets a system component which is protected by some security mechanisms, such as encryption and firewalls, then he needs to first defeat the mechanisms in order to achieve their anti-goals. According to the knowledge about system security design, the attacker can use the protection-based refinement pattern to generate anti-goals against related security protection mechanisms.

Each of the newly generated anti-goals concerns a specific protection mechanism as its asset and is intended to defeat it. Similar to the last analysis step, as long as new assets have been identified in the new anti-goals, subsequent analysis will iteratively refine assets and identify targets for the new anti-goals, i.e., going back to the analysis step 2. It is worth noting that during the anti-goal refinement, we focus on identifying which protection mechanisms need to be defeated by exploiting which targets, not answering which specific attack techniques to be used to defeat the mechanisms. Once there are no further security protections to be defeated, i.e., there are no new assets have been found, the analysis reaches an end as all potential attack scenarios have been obtained.

5   Evaluation

In order to evaluate the proposed anti-goal refinement framework, we apply it to a credit card theft scenario. In this section, we first introduce the evaluation scenario, and then illustrate the application of this framework to the scenario, finally, we evaluate the resulting anti-goal model. Due to space limitations, we only present part of the resulting model (Fig. 4) for illustrating the application of the framework, and the full version can be found online[3].

Credit Card Theft Scenario. This scenario presents a complicated multistage attack in reality, which is documented in Skoudis's hacking book [10, Chap. 12] and is different from the source of the previous three real attack scenarios. Specifically, in this scenario, there is a widgets corporation which operates more than 200 retail stores. Each retail store communicates with the central corporate network by using a VPN, and all credit card transactions are seamlessly moved from

---

[3] Available at http://disi.unitn.it/~li/poem15/evaluation_model.pdf.

individual stores back to the central database. Each store has several Point-of-Sale (POS) terminals, which access the local store network using wireless access points. Each store also has a store server, which processes credit card transactions and forwards the transactions back to the company server.

Fig. 4. Application of the anti-goal refinement framework to the scenario of credit card theft (excerpt)

Applying the Anti-goal Framework. As a pre-step, we first process the scenario description to extract information that is required by the analysis. Specifically, we capture the attacker's high-level malicious intention, i.e., steal customer's credit card information, and model it as his root anti-goal (*G1* in Fig. 4). In addition, we capture related domain information that is required for the analysis, such as asset relations, system infrastructure etc. Having the root anti-goal and related domain information as input, we apply the proposed framework (Fig. 3) to refine the root anti-goal into operational anti-goals and thus generate a comprehensive attack strategy. We summarize this process as follows.

1. As the scenario only deals with the credit card system in a general time span and does not describe any particular time interval, we opt not to apply the first step. In other time-sensitive cases, this step would be applied.
2. We refine the asset of the root anti-goal *G1* according to the composition relations among assets. As the entire set of credit card information is composed of information of credit cards that are processed in different retailer stores, the root-goal *G1* should be and-refined to more than 200 sub-goals, each of which is intended to disclose credit cards of one particular store. Since all the retailer stores have homogeneous design and configuration, the attack scenarios about these retailer stores are the same, i.e., the more than 200 anti-goals will be refined in the same way. Thus, as shown in Fig. 4, we only focus on the first sub-goal *G2* in later analysis.
3. We identify exploitable threats to the assets. Due to the domain knowledge that the information of credit cards that are used in store A (i.e., *CCA*) is kept in the *store server A*, *G2* is refined to *G5*, targeting the *store server A*. In addition, we refine *G1* to *G4* because the entire set of credit card information as a whole is stored in the company database. Due to space limitations, we will skip the illustration of this branch in the later analysis steps, which can be found in the online full model.
4. As the asset and the exploitable target of *G5* are not the same object, we need to elaborate *G5* to identify which threats should be imposed to the *store server A* in order to *disclose* the *CCA*. According to the threat knowledge, *G5* is and-refined to *G6* and *G7*, which are intended to reach the server and to access into the server, respectively.
5. As *G6* and *G7* introduce a new asset *store server A*, iterative analysis should be performed to these two goals from the secondly step until the analysis no longer introduces new assets. As shown in Fig. 4, the longest refinement paths {*G6, G10, G15, G17, G18, G19*} iterates three times.
6. After identifying an exploitable target, we check whether there are security mechanisms that have been applied to protect it. Take *G21* for example, it is refined to *G22* as there is an *access control mechanism* that has been applied to protect the *store server A*. Because *G22* promotes the *access control mechanism* as a new asset, another round of analysis starts from the second step.
7. Performing the iterative analysis on *G13* and *G22* results in the anti-goals *G14* and *G23*, respectively. As the iterative analysis has not introduced new assets, the anti-goal refinement reaches an end.

Results and Analysis. The evaluation finally results in an anti-goal model with 46 anti-goals and 48 refinements, which takes one author 5 h to build. By analyzing the and/or refinement operators, we identify that the final model implies a total of 11 alternative attack scenarios.

To assess the effectiveness of the proposed framework, we carry out a bottom-up analysis to check whether the documented credit card theft scenarios can be covered by the attack scenarios that are identified by our approach. Specifically, we identify all specific attack actions that have been performed by the attacker in the scenario description, including both successful and failed attack actions. Then, we check whether the intention of these actions can be linked to the leaf goals of the anti-goal model. Our examination turns out that all the attack actions documented in the scenario can be linked to the leaf goals, i.e., the identified attack scenarios completely cover the real attack scenarios. Specifically, 6 out of the 11 potential attack scenarios are reported in the scenario description (2 successful, 4 failed), while the other 5 potential attack scenarios are not mentioned in the scenario description, revealing previously unconsidered attacks.

6   Discussion

Diversity of Anti-goal Refinement. Our proposal is based on the examination of three real attack scenarios that come from the same book [9], and examining other scenarios from different sources may have different results. In addition, the examination process reflects our specific interpretation of attack strategies, and the outcome of the examination can vary from person to person. As such, the proposed anti-goal refinement framework is a particular way of refining anti-goals, which has been evaluated as effective to analyze attacker's malicious intentions in the credit card theft scenario. We believe this method can also be effective when applied to further cases, and we will continue to evaluate this method as part of our larger security analysis framework.

The Role of Anti-goal Refinement in Security Analysis. Our proposal, in this paper, serves as an important step in our holistic security analysis framework [6,7]. The resulting anti-goal model represents a comprehensive attack strategy, which discloses various potential attack scenarios. In particular, according to a comprehensive attack pattern repository (CAPEC)[4], each leaf anti-goal in the resulting model will be operationalized into concrete attack actions that use specific attack techniques and tools. Failing to operationalize a leaf anti-goal implies the corresponding attack scenario is unrealizable. Then, for each realizable attack scenario, we will assess its risk in terms of likelihood and severity (such information is available in the CAPEC attack patterns). Finally, regarding the risk of the realizable attack scenarios, we can design corresponding security controls to prevent or mitigate concrete attack actions of the attack scenarios.

In addition, to deeply integrate the anti-goal refinement framework into the holistic security requirements analysis framework, we plan to leverage the three-layer goal model [8] that is used in the holistic security framework to support the anti-goal refinement analysis. In particular, the three-layer goal model captures various system components in different abstraction layers, as well as the connections between the components. Moreover, the security protection information is also captured by the security goals and security tasks within the three-layer goal

---

[4] https://capec.mitre.org/.

model. Consequently, with only minor extensions, the three-layer goal model is able to provide the related information that is required by the anti-goal refinement framework.

Threats to Validity of the Evaluation. A major threat to the conclusion validity is that the evaluation is only performed to one single scenario. Although the scenario is relatively complicated and involves various security issues, in the future, we need to evaluate our approach with more real attack scenarios. To this end, an efficient prototype tool is required to support the analysis process. In addition, the entire evaluation is performed by only one author, imposing a threat to the external validity. Subsequent work will use multiple and varied evaluators to apply the method.

Scalability. Our framework is designed to provide a comprehensive anti-goal refinement analysis, i.e., covering all potential attack scenarios. As such, the scalability issues are raised due to the large refinement space. To deal with this problem, we have proposed sanity checks for each analysis step in Sect. 4, in order to prune the model as part of its construction.

In addition to the checks, we also observe a further phenomenon which helps to mitigate scalability. During the anti-goal refinement, it is possible to obtain repeated anti-goals, i.e., different anti-goals can be refined into the same anti-goals. This is because one anti-goal can have various influences, e.g., accessing to the server of a retailer store not only discloses credit card information stored in that server but also enables the attacker to penetrate the company internal network. As such, it is important to detect and merge the repeated anti-goals during the anti-goal analysis as new anti-goals are generated. Otherwise, the repeated anti-goals will be further refined separately and the size of the model can grow exponentially. Note that merging repeated anti-goals is performed by adding all refinement links of these anti-goals to one anti-goal and removing other anti-goals. As such, the derived model is not a tree but a directed acyclic graph (DAG).

Finally, we plan to develop a modeling and analysis tool, extending our existing tool MUSER [15] in order to (semi-)automate anti-goal refinement. In particular, we are defining formal inference rules for the five anti-goal refinement patterns that are proposed in this paper. On top of these inference rules, the tool will further implement the analysis process of anti-goal refinement (shown in Fig. 3) in order to support the automation of anti-goal refinement. To guarantee the correctness of the analysis and to reduce model complexity, the tool will interact with analysts in order to support manual revision after each analysis step, allowing the analyst to, for example, perform sanity checks (see Sect. 4) over the refinements.

7   Related Work

In this paper, we analyze attack strategies by examining three real attack scenarios that are documented in a security textbook [9]. Apart from this book, we have found other potential security knowledge sources. Attack patterns were first proposed by Moore et al. [16] to summarize reusable attack knowledge from repeated attacks in support of system security analysis. In particular, CAPEC (Common Attack Pattern Enumeration and Classification) is a comprehensive attack pattern repository, which was first released in 2008 and has accumulated 463 attack patterns [17]. However, these attack patterns indeed describe low-level attack knowledge about how to use specific attack techniques and tools to perform a particular attack, such as "exploit user-controllable input to perform a format string injection". Thus, CAPEC attack patterns do not fit our need of analyzing high-level attack strategies in this paper, but they can be used to operationalize anti-goals and support security analysis as discussed in Sect. 6. Another security threat knowledge source is the STRIDE threat trees [4], which focuses on how one threat can be refined into other threats. However, these threat trees only capture a single step of threat elaboration and cannot account for multistage attacks. As a result, we do not examine these threat trees for analyzing attack strategies, but use them as the security knowledge source to support the threat elaboration analysis in our anti-goal refinement framework.

Anti-goals were first proposed by Lamsweerde to capture attacker intentions and to construct anti models in order to provide security requirements for potential threats [5]. To refine anti-goals, apart from the ad-hoc way (asking why and how questions), the author proposed to use formal goal refinement patterns, which were designed for refining requirement goals [18]. However, the nature of attack analysis requires that the anti-goal refinement should cover all potential attack scenarios in order to provide comprehensive and reliable security design, which cannot be supported by the typical goal refinement patterns. In contrast, our anti-goal refinement framework reflects attack strategies investigated from real attacks and is designed to reveal all potential attack scenarios.

Attack trees are a typical way of representing attack scenarios. Although there is no unique way of creating attack trees, different researchers have proposed their own ways to build attack trees, which are related to our anti-goal refinement framework. Morais et al. advocate to first build the overall attack, and then identify the violated security properties and the security mechanisms to be exploited, respectively, and finally model the concrete attack actions [3]. Paul proposes a layer-per-layer approach to generate skeletons of attack trees using information comes from system architecture, risk assessment study, and related security knowledge base [19]. However, these approaches do not capture the attacker's malicious intentions and cannot analyze attack strategies as we define them.

Apart from the attack trees, attack graphs are another way of representing attack scenarios. An attack graph shows all paths through a system that end in a state where an attacker achieves his malicious intentions. Phillips and Swiler first use attack graphs to analyze network security [20]. Due to the homogeneous settings of machines in the network, the states of machines (nodes in the attack graph) and the atomic attacks to machines (transitions in the attack graph) are able to be enumerated. As such, it is possible to fully automate the generation of attack graphs using a comparatively simple attack strategy. Take the approach of Sheyener et al., for example: an attacker starts from a machine with the root permission, he then iteratively detects a new machine in the network, logs into that machine, and gets the root permission of that machine until reaching his target machine [21]. In a recent study, Beckers et al. propose to apply the attack graph approach to analyze social engineering attacks, where the states of people are modeled as nodes and social engineering attacks are captured as transitions between nodes [22]. However, the attack graph approach only applies to systems that have simple and homogeneous components, and is therefore inappropriate for security analysis of complex socio-technical systems that have heterogeneous components, such as people, software, and hardware.

8   Conclusions

In this paper, we argue that analyzing attack strategies is an efficient and systematic way of identifying all potential attack scenarios, which are essential for performing security analysis from an attacker's viewpoint. As such, we examine three real attack scenarios to understand how attackers elaborate their malicious intentions, from which we summarize five refinement patterns. Based on these refinement patterns, we further propose an anti-goal refinement framework for systematically generate attack strategies from an attacker's viewpoint. Finally, we evaluate our proposal with another scenario of credit card theft.

In the future, we plan to seamlessly integrate the anti-goal refinement framework into our holistic attack modeling and analysis framework [6,7] using the attacker's viewpoint as part of the holistic design of secure systems. Next, we aim to implement the anti-goal refinement patterns into formal logic inference rules using Datalog and extend the tool MUSER [15] to support the semi-automatic application of the framework. Finally, with the tool support, we aim to further evaluate our approach with more real attack scenarios.

Acknowledgements. Trento authors are supported by the ERC advanced grant 267856, titled "Lucretius: Foundations for Software Evolution". Jennifer Horkoff is supported by an ERC Marie Skodowska-Curie Intra European Fellowship (PIEF-GA-2013-627489), and by a Natural Sciences and Engineering Research Council of Canada Postdoctoral Fellowship (Sept. 2014 - Aug. 2016).

References

1. Schneier, B.: Attack trees. Dr. Dobb's J. **24**(12), 21–29 (1999)
2. Sindre, G., Opdahl, A.L.: Eliciting security requirements with misuse cases. Requirements Eng. **10**(1), 34–44 (2005)
3. Morais, A., Hwang, I., Cavalli, A., Martins, E.: Generating attack scenarios for the system security validation. Networking Sci. **2**(3–4), 69–80 (2013)
4. Shostack, A.: Threat Modeling: Designing for Security. Wiley, Hoboken (2014)
5. Lamsweerde, A.V.: Elaborating security requirements by construction of intentional anti-models. In: ICSE, pp. 148–157 (2004)

6. Li, T., Paja, E., Mylopoulos, J., Horkoff, J., Beckers, K.: Holistic security requirements analysis: an attacker's perspective. In: Requirements Engineering Conference (RE), 2015 IEEE 23rd International (2015, to be published)

7. Li, T., Horkoff, J., Beckers, K., Paja, E., Mylopoulos, J.: A holistic approach to security attack modeling and analysis. In: Proceedings of the Eighth International i* Workshop (2015, to be published)

8. Li, T., Horkoff, J.: Dealing with security requirements for socio-technical systems: a holistic approach. In: Jarke, M., Mylopoulos, J., Quix, C., Rolland, C., Manolopoulos, Y., Mouratidis, H., Horkoff, J. (eds.) CAiSE 2014. LNCS, vol. 8484, pp. 285–300. Springer, Heidelberg (2014)

9. Mitnick, K.D., Simon, W.L.: The Art of Deception: Controlling the Human Element of Security. Wiley, New York (2011)

10. Skoudis, E., Liston, T.: Counter Hack Reloaded: A Step-by-step Guide to Computer Attacks and Effective Defenses. Prentice Hall Press, Upper Saddle River (2005)

11. Jureta, I., Borgida, A., Ernst, N., Mylopoulos, J.: Techne: towards a new generation of requirements modeling languages with goals, preferences, and inconsistency handling. In: Proceedings of RE 2010, pp. 115–124 (2010)

12. Scandariato, R., Wuyts, K., Joosen, W.: A descriptive study of microsofts threat modeling technique. Requirements Eng. **20**(2), 163–180 (2015)

13. ISO, I., Std, I.: Iso 27005: 2011. Information technology-Security techniques-Information security risk management. ISO (2011)

14. Lund, M.S., Solhaug, B., Stølen, K.: Model-driven Risk Analysis: The CORAS Approach. Springer Science & Business Media, Heidelberg (2010)

15. Li, T., Horkoff, J., Mylopoulos, J.: A prototype tool for modeling and analyzing security requirements from a holistic viewpoint. In: The CAiSE 2014 Forum at the 26th International Conference on Advanced Information Systems Engineering (2014)

16. Moore, A.P., Ellison, R.J., Linger, R.C.: Attack modeling for information security and survivability. Technical report, CMU-SEI-2001-TN-001. CARNEGIE-MELLON UNIV PITTSBURGH PA SOFTWARE ENGINEERING INST (2001)

17. Barnum, S., Sethi, A.: Attack patterns as a knowledge resource for building secure software. In: OMG Software Assurance Workshop: Cigital (2007)

18. Letier, E., Van Lamsweerde, A.: Agent-based tactics for goal-oriented requirements elaboration. In: Proceedings of the 24th International Conference on Software Engineering, pp. 83–93. ACM (2002)

19. Paul, S.: Towards automating the construction & maintenance of attack trees: a feasibility study. arXiv preprint arXiv:1404.1986 (2014)

20. Phillips, C., Swiler, L.P.: A graph-based system for network-vulnerability analysis. In: Proceedings of the 1998 Workshop on New security paradigms, pp. 71–79. ACM (1998)

21. Sheyner, O., Haines, J., Jha, S., Lippmann, R., Wing, J.M.: Automated generation and analysis of attack graphs. In: 2002 IEEE Symposium on Security and Privacy, Proceedings, pp. 273–284. IEEE (2002)

22. Beckers, K., Krautsevich, L., Yautsiukhin, A.: Analysis of social engineering threats with attack graphs. In: Garcia-Alfaro, J., Herrera-Joancomartí, J., Lupu, E., Posegga, J., Aldini, A., Martinelli, F., Suri, N. (eds.) DPM/SETOP/QASA 2014. LNCS, vol. 8872, pp. 216–232. Springer, Heidelberg (2015)

Eliciting Security Requirements for Business Processes of Legacy Systems

Nikolaos Argyropoulos[1]([✉]), Luis Márquez Alcañiz[2], Haralambos Mouratidis[1],
Andrew Fish[1], David G. Rosado[3], Ignacio García-Rodriguez de Guzmán[3],
and Eduardo Fernández-Medina[3]

[1] University of Brighton, Watts Building, Lewes Road, Brighton BN2 4GJ, UK
{n.argyropoulos,h.mouratidis,andrew.fish}@brighton.ac.uk
[2] Spanish National Authority for Markets and Competition (CNMC), Madrid, Spain
luis.marquez@cnmc.es
[3] University of Castilla-La Mancha, Paseo de la Universidad 4,
13071 Ciudad Real, Spain
{david.grosado,ignacio.grodriguez,eduardo.fdezmedina}@uclm.es

Abstract. The modernisation of enterprise legacy systems, without compromises in their functionality, is a demanding and time consuming endeavour. To retain the underlying business behaviour during their modernisation, the MARBLE[TM] framework has been developed for the extraction of business process models from their source code. Building on top of that work, in this paper we propose an integrated approach for transforming the extracted legacy process models into Secure Tropos goal models. Such models facilitate the elicitation of security requirements in a high level of abstraction, which are then incorporated back into the process models of the modernised systems as security features. Therefore high level models can be derived from legacy source code with minimal manual intervention, where security can be elaborated by non-technical stakeholders in alignment with organisational objectives.

Keywords: Legacy systems · Business process modelling · Goal-oriented security requirements · Secure Tropos · BPMN · MARBLE

1 Introduction

The essence of legacy system migration is to move an existing, operational system to a new environment, retaining the functionality of the legacy system while causing as little disruption to the existing operational and business environment as possible [1]. Legacy system migration is a very expensive procedure which carries a definite risk of failure. Consequently before any decision to migrate is taken, an intensive study should be undertaken to quantify the risk and benefits and fully justify the redevelopment of the legacy system involved [2,3].

Reverse engineering techniques have become very important within the legacy system migration process, providing several benefits. Firstly, reverse engineering allows the retrieval of abstract representations to facilitate the comprehension

© IFIP International Federation for Information Processing 2015
J. Ralyté et al. (Eds.): PoEM 2015, LNBIP 235, pp. 91–107, 2015.
DOI: 10.1007/978-3-319-25897-3_7

of different legacy systems, such as relational databases [4] and aspect oriented systems [5]. Secondly, abstract representations obtained by reverse engineering from legacy systems can be refactored to improve their maintainability or add new functionalities to evolve legacy systems. To meet these demands, business process archaeology has emerged as a set of techniques and tools to recover business processes from source code [6]. One of the main benefits of business process archaeology is that it preserves business behaviour buried in legacy source code and it retrieves business processes, thereby providing more opportunities for refactoring due to the higher abstraction level.

During business process refactoring new security features can also be introduced to evolve the legacy business processes. Since the advantages of the early identification of security requirements are recognised by the consensus of the RE literature [7,8], it is imperative that security concerns are taken into account during the early redesign stages of such systems. An advantage of eliciting security requirements in the early (re-)development stages is the lower possibility of security issues arising when the system is already in use, which would require redesigns and significant downtimes, thus proving costly for enterprises [9].

The security objectives of an enterprise are expressed via security requirements, which are used as input during the redesign of the business processes supported by such legacy systems. The development of *"secure by design"* business processes is considered highly beneficial as information security breaches can impact enterprises both financially and in terms of reputation and trust from the customer's side. It can also be a legal obligation to regulate and ensure the security of sensitive information handled by business processes [10]. However, despite its apparent importance and the potential to greatly benefit modern business processes, security is usually considered as an afterthought during their development in practice [11] and receives little attention from business process management (BPM) approaches developed in research [12,13].

In this work we present a novel approach for the modernisation of legacy systems from an information security point of view. It facilitates the elaboration of security requirements via Secure Tropos goal models, derived from legacy business processes which are automatically extracted from their legacy source code. Therefore, by integrating existing and novel components, the proposed approach facilitates a unique transformation of the lowest abstraction level of legacy systems (i.e., source code) to highly abstract enterprise models in a largely automated manner. As a result it offers to non-technical enterprise stakeholders a platform appropriate for capturing high-level organisational security objectives in the form of security requirements, which can then be integrated back to the business processes as security features.

The rest of the paper is structured as follows; Sect. 2 presents related work in the areas of process archaeology and goal-to-process model transformations. Section 3 introduces our approach and its four building blocks: (i) the MARBLE™ framework for the derivation of a process models from legacy source code, (ii) the IBUPROFEN algorithms for the refactoring of the extracted process model, (iii) the Secure Tropos approach for security-oriented goal modelling and (iv) the transformation algorithms for the transition from process to goal models and vice versa. In Sect. 4 our approach is applied to a module extracted from a real software application, while final conclusions are provided in Sect. 5.

2   Related Work

2.1   Process Archaeology

Business process archaeology [6] studies the business processes in an organization by analysing the existing software artefacts. The objective is to discover the business forces that motivated the construction of the enterprise information systems. On the one hand, traditional archaeologists investigate several artefacts and situations, trying to understand what they are looking at, i.e., they must understand the cultural and civilizing forces that produced those artefacts. Similarly, a business process archaeologist analyses different legacy artefacts such as source code, databases and user interfaces and then tries to learn what the organization was thinking while also attempting to understand why the organization developed the information system in a particular way. The business process archaeology initiative is being progressively supported by new reverse engineering techniques and tools to retrieve and elicit the embedded business knowledge. One of these tools is MARBLE^{TM} [14,15], a business process archaeology method to rebuild business processes embedded in legacy information systems.

2.2   Aligning Business Processes with Organisational Goals

The organisational context of the enterprise enacting a business process, provides valuable input for its successful (re-)design. Since graphical process modelling standards are not fully equipped to encapsulate such context, goal-oriented modelling languages are better suited for that purpose [16] since they can capture the intentions of stakeholders as system requirements [17]. Nevertheless, while goal models can provide a high-level direction and rationale in the form of goals, they lack the ability to adequately identify the specifics of their implementation at the process level. Thus goal-oriented requirements engineering (GORE) should be used more as a starting point, rather than a complete solution for the further development of process designs [18].

To that end, a number of approaches have been developed starting from goal models and eliciting business process designs. Mappings between organisational goals and process activities are introduced by such approaches in order to facilitate the transition between goal and process models. A variety of GORE frameworks have been utilised, such as KAOS in [19,20], Tropos in [21,22] and i* in [23–25]. Such generic model transformation approaches lack a clear security orientation so they are unable to capture the essence of security requirements, which, as opposed to functional requirements, act as restrictions on the means used for the achievement of goals.

To cover that need, certain security-oriented approaches have been developed. In [26], SecureBPEL is introduced as an extension of the BPEL execution standard enriched with constructs from the Secure Tropos goal-oriented framework, to enforce delegation and trust requirements in web services used to support the designed business process. In [27] the SecCo (Security via Commitments) framework is introduced for the elicitation of security requirements that need to be fulfilled by the organisation's business processes, through the modelling and analysis of objectives, roles and social commitments between actors. Similarly in [28], transformation rules expressed in SecBPMN are used to introduce security requirements, identified using STS-ml, to existing BPMN process models.

Nevertheless, such attempts are unable to incorporate concepts and mechanisms to deal with the whole range of security requirements and also take into account elements of risk analysis (e.g., threats). As a result, in order to cover all aspects of risk and security a number of such approaches have to be used simultaneously, leading to a large overhead in time and specialised personnel and a high level of complexity. In addition, the simple annotation of existing process models with elements of security is not aligned with the notion of *"security by design"*, which requires the derivation of such process designs from high level, security- and risk-aware organisational models. Moreover such attempts cannot adequately capture and reflect the rationale behind security decisions at an appropriate level of abstraction as they usually just impose general restrictions on the interactions between participants of the process (i.e., at conversation diagram level) but not on their specific activities (i.e., workflow level).

3   Proposed Approach

3.1   MARBLE™ Framework

MARBLE™ is a technique and a tool that supports business process archaeology by retrieving business processes from legacy source code [6]. MARBLE™ utilises an extensible, ADM-based framework for recovering business processes. To achieve that: (i) the information is collected into and is used from standard KDM (Knowledge Discovery Metamodel) [29] repositories and (ii) the information of KDM repositories is used to retrieve business process models [30].

MARBLE™ focuses on the reverse engineering stage of the re-engineering process. It proposes four abstraction levels (with four different kinds of models) as well as three model transformations between them, in order to cover the whole path of the business process archaeology method between legacy information systems and business processes (see Fig. 1). The four generic abstraction levels proposed in MARBLE™ are the following:

- Level L0. As the lowest level of abstraction, L0 represents the legacy information system (LIS) in the real world as a collection of different software artefacts (e.g. source code, database, documentation).
- Level L1. This level consists of several specific models, i.e., one model for each different software artefact involved in the archaeology process (e.g., source

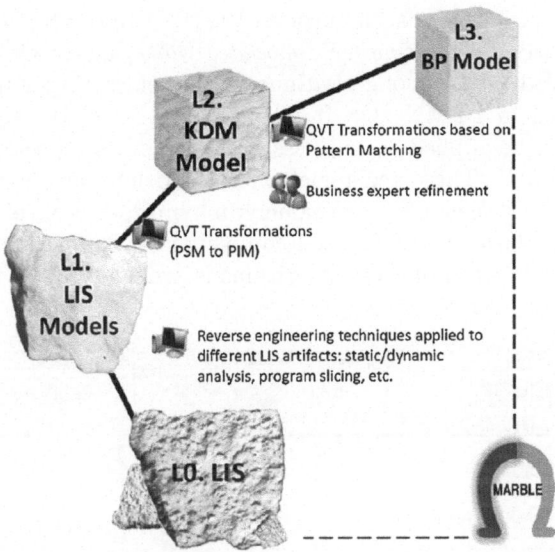

Fig. 1. MARBLE^{TM}, a framework to support business process archaeology [6]

code, database, user interfaces). These models are considered to be PSM (Platform-Specific Models) since they depict the software artefacts according to their specific technology or platforms.

- Level L2. It consists of a common PIM (Platform-Independent Model) which represents the integrated view of the set of PSM models at L1. The standard KDM metamodel is used for this purpose, since it makes it possible to model all the artefacts of the legacy system in an integrated and technological independent manner.
- Level L3. As the highest level of abstraction, L3 represents a computational independent model of the system. It depicts the business processes retrieved from the knowledge concerning legacy information systems represented in the KDM repository at L2. Business process models at L3 are represented according to the BPMN (Business Process Model and Notation) metamodel [31].

MARBLE^{TM} provides a Java parser to obtain code models, which are transformed and integrated in a model repository according to the KDM standard. After that, KDMs are transformed to business process models by applying business pattern recognition. Finally, the tool allows the discovery, visualisation and editing of business process models. An in-depth elaboration of the framework's functionality and capabilities is provided at [6,14].

3.2 IBUPROFEN

Business process models derived via the reverse engineering approach followed by MARBLE^{TM} often require some refinement before they can be utilised for further transformations. For such purposes the **IBUPROFEN** *(Improvement and BUsiness Processes Refactoring OF Embedded Noise)* approach has been developed, which introduces a set of algorithms for the refactoring of business process models expressed in BPMN [32]. It introduces a set of ten refactoring algorithms which can be applied on business process models represented by graphs, expressed in BPMN. These ten refactoring algorithms are divided into three categories regarding their purpose, namely: maximization of relevant elements, fine-grained granularity reduction and completeness. An overview of the refactoring performed by each of these algorithms is provided in Fig. 2 and in [33].

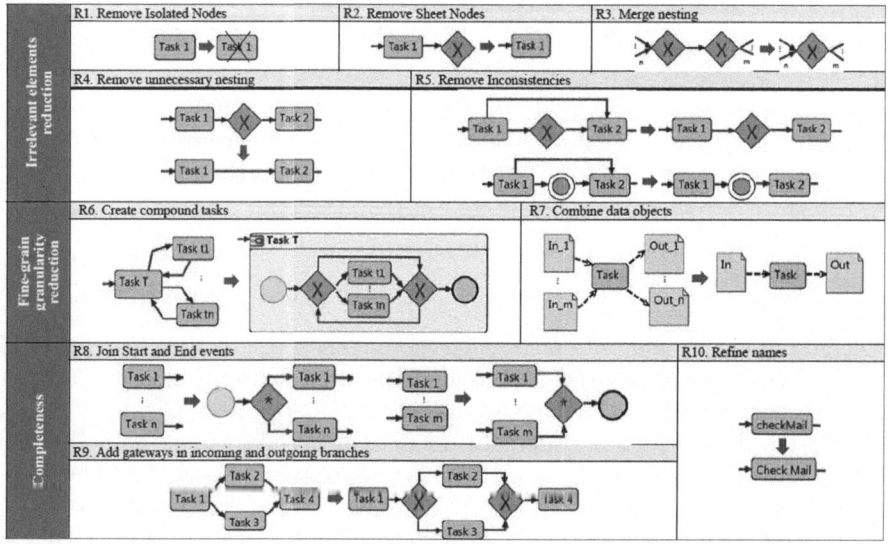

Fig. 2. Process model refactoring algorithms introduced by IBUPROFEN [33]

3.3   Secure Tropos

Secure Tropos [34] is a security-oriented extension of Tropos, a goal-oriented requirements engineering method. This extension includes the concept of security constraint which is defined as a restriction related to security issues, such as privacy, integrity, and availability [35]. Security constraints can influence the analysis and design of the information system under development by restricting some alternative design solutions, by conflicting with some of the requirements of the system, or by refining some of the system's objectives. In addition, Secure Tropos defines secure dependencies which introduces security constraints that must be fulfilled for the dependency to be satisfied. A security mechanism represents potential solutions for the implementation of the security constraints, leading to the fulfilment of security objectives. The advantages of this approach, compared to other security-oriented software engineering approaches are: (i) its ability to perform social analysis during the early requirements stage, (ii) the simultaneous consideration of security with the other requirements of the system-to-be, (iii) the support for not only requirements stages but also design stages.

3.4   Model Transformations

A series of transformation rules need to be defined in order to facilitate the transition from business process models, expressed in BPMN and derived from legacy source code using the MARBLE™ framework (Fig. 3 *Phase 1*), to Secure Tropos goal models. This process-to-goal transformation will create an additional, higher level of abstraction, represented by a goal model of the legacy system. At this level of abstraction it is easier for non-technical stakeholders to elaborate on the overall system security by defining certain easily comprehensible constraints. Such constraints can be captured by the Secure Tropos goal model and mapped back onto the process model, in order to be implemented during the redesign of the legacy systems.

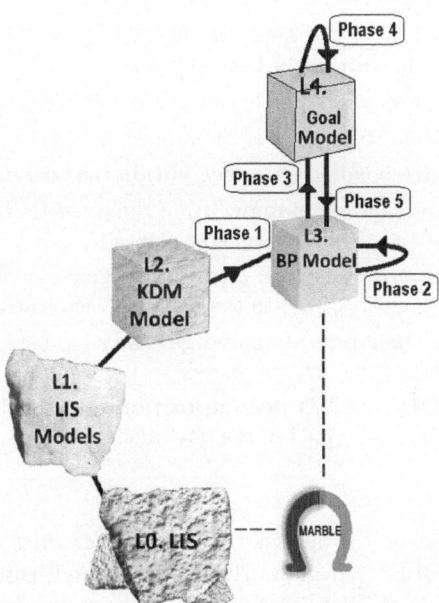

Fig. 3. Extended framework to accommodate goal model reasoning

Essentially, the proposed transformation aims to derive a goal model, on which security will be elaborated and expressed using Secure Tropos. A goal-to-process transformation can then be performed, beginning from the Secure Tropos goal model and deriving a secure business process model, used as input for the legacy system redevelopment via the MARBLE^{TM} framework. The overall process, containing an extra level of abstraction accommodating the security-oriented, goal model reasoning is illustrated in Fig. 3 and summed-up in Subsect. 3.5.

Transformation rules have been defined which map Secure Tropos and BPMN concepts to each other and provide instructions on how the transformation can take place. Such mappings are based on conceptual similarities between the paired concepts, identified after semantic analysis of the formal documentation and meta-models of the two modelling approaches [31, 34]. A process-to-goal transformation algorithm has been defined at Table 1, utilised in order to transform the refactored process model by IBUPROFEN (Fig. 3 *Phase 2*) to a Secure Tropos goal model (Fig. 3 *Phase 3*).

Table 1. Algorithm for Phase 3 of the transformation process

Step 1	*For each* **lane** (*l*) of the process model:
	Create a corresponding **actor** $a(l)$ in the goal model
Step 2	*For each* **sub-process** (*p*) of the process model:
	Create a corresponding **goal** $g(p)$ in the goal model
	For each of the **sub-activities** (p') of *p*:
	Create a corresponding **sub-goal** $g(p')$, within $g(p)$
Step 3	*For each* **data object** (*d*) of the process model:
	Create a corresponding **resource** $r(d)$ in the goal model
Step 4	*For each* **message exchange** (*m*) of the process model, between two activities (p_s, p_r) in two different lanes (l_s, l_r):
	Create a **dependency link** $dl(m)$ in the goal model, from the dependent goal $(g(p_s))$ to the dependee actor $a(l_r)$
Step 5	*For each* **exclusive** or **inclusive gateway** (*x*) between sub-activities $(p_1, ..., p_n)$ of the process model:
	Create an **OR** or **AND decomposition** $or(x)$ of the corresponding goals $(g(p_1), ..., g(p_n))$ in the goal model

By the application of the above transformation rules to a process model derived by the MARBLE^{TM} framework and refactored using the IBUPROFEN algorithms, a basic Secure Tropos goal model can be produced. This basic goal model is the main input upon which the security elaboration of the system will take place by stakeholders of the organisation. As a result of this security elaboration, security constraints, objectives and mechanisms are added to the Secure Tropos goal model to capture the security aspects that will be introduced to the legacy system during its redesign (Fig. 3 *Phase 4*).

The security-oriented concepts of Secure Tropos (i.e., security constraints, mechanisms and threats) cannot be directly mapped onto existing BPMN concepts. Therefore, some manual tasks need to be performed in order for the process

Table 2. Algorithm for Phase 5 of the transformation process

Step 1	*For each* **goal** ($g(p)$) or **resource** ($r(d)$) of the goal model, restricted by a *security constraint* (*sc*):
	Annotate the corresponding **activity** (p) or **data object** (d) of the process model
Step 2	*For each* **security mechanism** (*sm*) of the goal model:
	Create a **"secure" activity** (*sp*) in the process model, connected to the annotated activities (p) or data objects (d)
Step 3	*For each* **threat** (t) on a goal ($g(p)$) or resource ($r(d)$) of the goal model:
	Create a corresponding **error event** (e) in the process model, connected to the threatened activities (p) or data objects (d)

model to reflect the security choices captured at the goal model level (Fig. 3 *Phase 5*). Table 2 presents an algorithm providing a precise set of instructions for performing such goal-to-process refinement tasks.

3.5   Overview of Approach

As illustrated in Fig. 3, the proposed approach consists of the following phases:

1. *Extraction* of BPMN process models from the source code of the legacy system using the automated MARBLE[TM] tool [15].
2. *Refactoring* of the extracted process model using the IBUPROFEN algorithms, automated via an Eclipse plugin [32].
3. *Process-to-goal transformation* using the algorithm of Table 1 to create an initial goal model from the refactored BPMN process model.
4. *Security elaboration* for deriving security requirements, threats and security mechanisms using the Secure Tropos approach via the SecTro tool [36].
5. *Process model refinement* using the algorithm of Table 2 for the addition of the security features elaborated at the Secure Tropos goal model.

The result of the application of above approach is a secure business process model, aligned with the high-level enterprise security objectives. This process model, which operationalises the security requirements captured at the goal model level, can be then used as input for the legacy system redevelopment effort, as proposed by the MARBLE[TM] framework. Therefore the security features introduced at a high level from the organisation's stakeholders will be included at the legacy system during its modernisation.

4   Illustrative Example

4.1   System Description

JBooks[1] is a Java-based personal finance application utilising a checkbox based interface that allows users to insert and visualize transactions. It is interfaced

---
[1] Available at: http://freshmeat.net/projects/jbooks/.

with a relational database, and involves a double-entry system for all transactions (i.e., every transaction involves a transfer from one account to another). A module of the JBooks application was selected for the purposes of this example. This module receives a string as input and if it is numeric it converts it to text in order to be further utilised by other modules of the application.

4.2 Method Application

The first phase of the method application is the extraction of a process model from the source code of the JBooks application. By using the MARBLE^{TM} tool we extracted a large amount of process models for the different modules of the JBooks application. For this example we selected a relatively simple process model representing the module that converts numerical strings to text.

After the initial process model is extracted via the MARBLE^{TM} tool it is refactored by applying the algorithms of IBUPROFEN. During refactoring some elements of the process model are replaced by equivalent ones or merged to reduce the complexity of the overall model. Since the refactoring process does not fulfill the commutative property, the order of the application of the algorithms is critical as it can define the quality of the outcome model [33]. The optimal execution order that maximises the understandability and modifiability of the process model has been experimentally identified as: first applying the granularity reduction set of algorithms, then the irrelevant elements reduction set of algorithms and finally the completeness algorithms [33]. The IBUPRO-FEN algorithms are implemented as a plugin of the Eclipse^{TM} environment on the process model extracted by the MARBLE^{TM} tool. In our example, after applying the refactoring algorithms, the process model illustrated in Fig. 4 is derived.

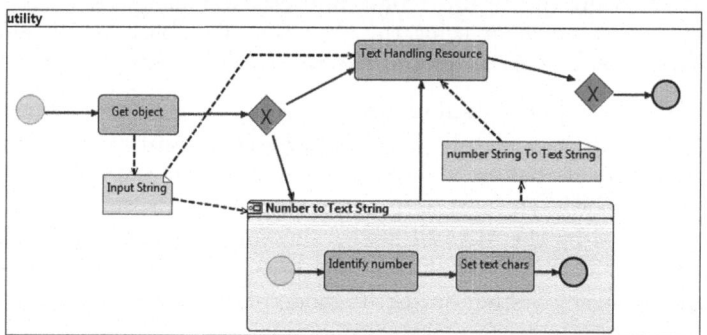

Fig. 4. Process model of JBooks module

Next, the transformation of the derived process model to a Secure Tropos goal model need to be performed. By applying the algorithm in Table 1 to our example one actor is created to correspond to the lane of the process model

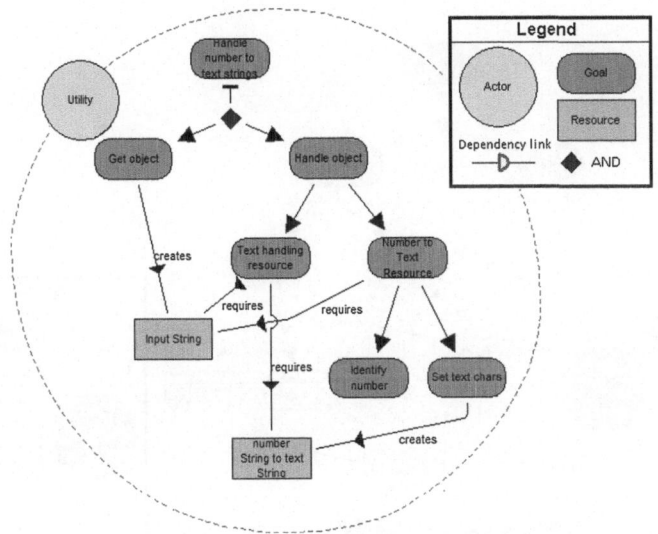

Fig. 5. Derived goal model of selected JBooks module

(Step 1), each sub-process and task is transformed to a (sub-)goal *(Step 2)* and resources are created, corresponding to the data object of the process model *(Step 3)*. In addition to the transformation steps defined by the algorithm, an extra root-level goal has been added to provide context to the derived Secure Tropos goal model, modelled using the SecTro tool [36], as illustrated in Fig. 5.

As goal models in general, and Secure Tropos in our case, do not provide the means to capture temporal dimensions (i.e., the sequence of goal achievement), the resulting models cannot always capture all the information contained in process models. In our example, the application of *Step 5* of the transformation algorithm cannot sufficiently capture in the goal model the fact that the activity "Get Object" is followed by either "Text handling resource" or "Number to Text resource". This is due to the fact that Secure Tropos does not offer special notation for illustrating OR decompositions or the specific sequence of execution of goals. In order to resolve this issue a new goal had to be manually added ("Handle object") which includes the two alternatives (i.e., "Text handling resource" or "Number to Text resource") as sub-goals and is connected with an AND relationship with the "Get Object" sub-goal.

During security elaboration process the system stakeholders can express their security requirements and define the basic mechanisms to implement them, using the goal model as a high level representation of the application. For simplicity purposes, our example includes one security constraint, concerning the validity of the input. It is related to the integrity of the input data and can be implemented by a security mechanism validating that it has not been altered before it reached the module. A threat has also been included in the goal model representing the malicious alteration of the module's input by a third party. The complete, security-annotated goal model is presented in Fig. 6.

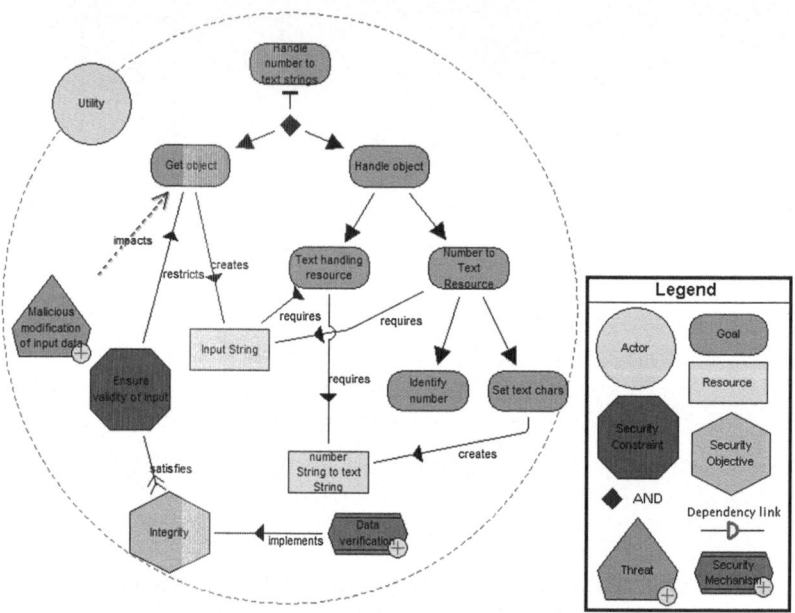

Fig. 6. Security-annotated goal model of JBooks module

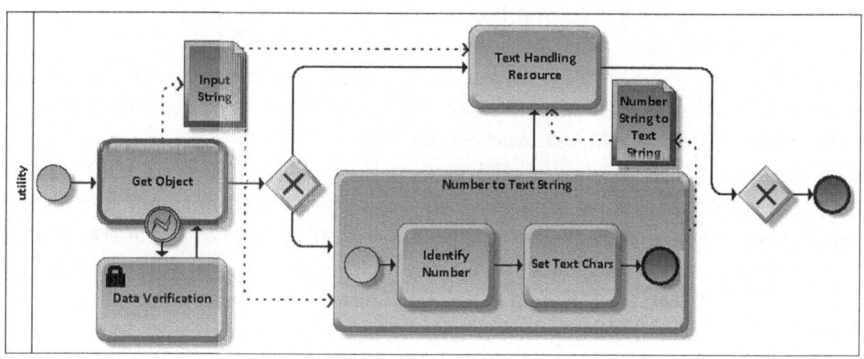

Fig. 7. Secure BPMN process model of JBooks module (Color figure online)

Finally, the security introduced at the goal model level has to be transferred back to the initial process model, by following the steps defined in Table 2. The finalised secure process model, illustrated at Fig. 7, now includes a secure task, denoted by a padlock symbol, representing the data validation security mechanism. The "Get Object" task is annotated with a red border to denote that it is security constraint while it is also an error event, annotated as an orange circle, is attached to represent the malicious data modification threat.

4.3   Lessons Learned

The addition of security in a module of the JBooks legacy system provided insights concerning the completeness and applicability of the proposed approach. Even though the example used was rather limited in size and complexity, we were able to successfully complete each step of our approach without any major complications. Some manual intervention was necessary after the refactoring of the process model in order to make the produced model more readable (e.g., reshaping and spacing elements and association links). Moreover the seamless transition between its different components added to the value of the approach, facilitated by the fact that the output for each phase can be used quite effortlessly as the input of the next. The availability of CASE tools (e.g., MARBLE^{TM} tool, IBUPROFEN plugin, SecTro tool) further contributed in the aspect of automation, as most phases, with the exception of the goal-to-process transformation, required minimal manual efforts. By expanding and interfacing the available support tools, this automation can be further strengthened in the future.

Regarding the transformation process, one addition to the proposed algorithm consisted of creating a root-level goal in the produced goal model, which was decomposed to the rest of the goals and encapsulated the overall purpose of the module. This was performed for reasons of completeness and comprehensibility of the goal model by stakeholders and had no further impact on the rest of the approach. Another point requiring further attention is the inadequacy of goal models to capture the exact sequence by which their (sub-)goals should be accomplished, especially when complex branching (e.g., inclusive, exclusive gateways) is present at the process model. This led to the need for some manual intervention during the fifth step of our transformation algorithm, as explained in the previous section. To address this issue in the future, extensions at the notation of Secure Tropos will be explored, along with the refinement of the transformation rules defined in the algorithm.

5   Conclusion

The modernisation of enterprise legacy systems can be a demanding and time consuming endeavour. In order to facilitate that process, the MARBLE^{TM} framework has been developed for the extraction of process models from legacy source code. Such process models offer a more comprehensible and flexible platform for the elaboration of potential redesigns of the legacy system in question. The IBUPROFEN framework was also developed since the extracted process models often required some refinement (e.g., removal of excess notation, completeness).

In this work we extend these frameworks by introducing an algorithmic approach for the transformation of the derived business process models to goal models. Goal models provide the means necessary for the elaboration of security for the redesigned legacy system, at a high abstraction level, comprehensible by non-technical stakeholders and aligned with organisational objectives. Using a set of transformation rules, goal models can be created based on such business process models. Secure Tropos offers the means for capturing the security related aspects of the redesigned system (e.g., security constraints, mechanisms, threats), which can then be incorporated back into the process model via a set of goal-to-process transformation rules. As a result, security choices of the system's stakeholders can be operationalised by the redesigned business processes.

An illustrative example of a legacy system module was utilised as a proof of concept for the proposed transformation approach and led us to useful conclusions about its completeness and effectiveness. Its application resulted in an accurate goal model representation of the selected legacy system's module, upon which security was successfully elaborated and then introduced back into the process model. Some complications sourced from certain elements of process models (i.e., sequence of execution, branching) which cannot always be translated to goal modelling concepts without losing certain information. Nevertheless, this example provided valuable insight on the applicability of the proposed approach while it also brought into consideration aspects which require further attention.

Overall, this novel approach could be a valuable tool for both practitioners and researchers, attempting to introduce security to existing business processes, starting from a high level of abstraction, which allows the alignment of security choices with the overall organisational strategy. Despite the emphasis in business processes extracted from legacy source code, the transformation algorithms introduced by this approach can be utilised for the introduction of security to any available process model, newly designed or already existing. This approach will also be integrated in the extraction activity of a migration process of legacy systems to the cloud (SMILE2Cloud) in which we are currently working [37,38].

Future work will look into the formalisation of the existing transformation algorithms using QVT and the potential addition of further steps or activities in order to eliminate any flaws during the transition between goal and process models and vice versa. As soon as a set of concrete transformation rules has been explicitly defined via an appropriate formal language, already existing support tools (e.g. SecTro tool, Eclipse plugins) can be further extended to automate the majority of this transformation, thus limiting the need for manual intervention. Finally, the validation of this approach via a case study would add great value, especially if it involves a large and more complex enterprise legacy system along with the participation of its stakeholders and analysts.

Acknowledgments. This research is part of the following projects: SERENIDAD (PEII11-037-7035) financed by the "Viceconsejería de Ciencia y Tecnología de la Junta de Comunidades de Castilla-La Mancha" (Spain) and FEDER, and SIGMA-CC (TIN2012-36904) financed by the "Ministerio de Economía y Competitividad" (Spain).

References

1. Wu, B., Lawless, D., Bisbal, J., Grimson, J., Wade, V., O'Sullivan, D., Richardson, R.: Legacy system migration: a legacy data migration engine. In: 17th International Database Conference, pp. 129–138 (1997)
2. Bisbal, J., Lawless, D., Wu, B., Grimson, J.: Legacy information systems: issues and directions. IEEE Softw. **16**(5), 103–111 (1999)

3. Bisbal, J., Lawless, D., Wu, B., Grimson, J., Wade, V., Richardson, R., Sullivan, D.O.: A Survey of Research into Legacy System Migration. Technical report (1997)
4. Cleve, A., Hainaut, J.L.: Dynamic analysis of SQL statements for data-intensive applications reverse engineering. In: 15th IEEE Working Conference on Reverse Engineering, pp. 192–196. IEEE Computer Society (2008)
5. Bernardi, M.: Reverse engineering of aspect oriented systems to support their comprehension, evolution, testing and assessment. In: 12th IEEE European Conference on Software Maintenance and Reengineering, pp. 290–293. IEEE Computer Society (2008)
6. Pérez-Castillo, R., De Guzmán, I.G.R., Piattini, M.: Business process archeology using MARBLE. Inf. Softw. Technol. **53**(10), 1023–1044 (2011)
7. Liu, L., Yu, E., Mylopoulos, J.: Security and privacy requirements analysis within a social setting. In: 11th IEEE International Requirements Engineering Conference, pp. 151–161. IEEE Computer Society (2003)
8. Mellado, D., Fernández-Medina, E., Piattini, M.: A common criteria based security requirements engineering process for the development of secure information systems. Comput. Stan. Interfaces **29**(2), 244–253 (2007)
9. Whitman, M.E.: Enemy at the gate: threats to information security. Commun. ACM **46**(8), 91–95 (2003)
10. Leitner, M., Rinderle-Ma, S.: A systematic review on security in process-aware information systems - constitution, challenges, and future directions. Inf. Softw. Technol. **56**(3), 273–293 (2014)
11. Neubauer, T., Klemen, M., Biffl, S.: Secure business process management: a roadmap. In: 1st IEEE International Conference on Availability, Reliability and Security, Vienna, Austria, pp. 457–464. IEEE Computer Society (2006)
12. Pavlovski, C.J., Zou, J.: Non-functional requirements in business process modeling. In: 5th Asia-Pacific Conference on Conceptual Modelling, pp. 103–112 (2008)
13. Rodríguez, A., Fernández-Medina, E., Trujillo, J., Piattini, M.: Secure business process model specification through a UML 2.0 activity diagram profile. Decis. Support Syst. **51**(3), 446–465 (2011)
14. Pérez-Castillo, R., De Guzmán, I.G.R., vila Garca, O., Piattini, M.: MARBLE: modernization approach for recovering business processes from legacy information systems. In: International Workshop on Reverse Engineering Models from Software Artifacts, pp. 17–20 (2009)
15. Pérez-Castillo, R., Fernández-Ropero, M., De Guzmán, I.G.R., Piattini, M.: MARBLE. A business process archeology tool. In: 27th IEEE International Conference on Software Maintenance, pp. 578–581. IEEE Computer Society (2011)
16. Ko, R.K., Lee, S.S., Lee, E.W.: Business process management (BPM) standards: a survey. Bus. Process Manage. **15**(5), 744–791 (2009)
17. Lapouchnian, A., Yu, Y., Mylopoulos, J.: Requirements-driven design and configuration management of business processes. In: Alonso, G., Dadam, P., Rosemann, M. (eds.) BPM 2007. LNCS, vol. 4714, pp. 246–261. Springer, Heidelberg (2007)
18. Horkoff, J., Li, T., Li, F.L., Salnitri, M., Cardoso, E., Giorgini, P., Mylopoulos, J., Pimentel, J.A.: Taking goal models downstream: a systematic roadmap. In: 8th IEEE International Conference on Research Challenges in Information Science, pp. 1–12. IEEE Computer Society (2014)
19. Koliadis, G., Ghose, A.: Relating business process models to goal-oriented requirements models in KAOS. In: Hoffmann, A., Kang, B.-H., Richards, D., Tsumoto, S. (eds.) PKAW 2006. LNCS (LNAI), vol. 4303, pp. 25–39. Springer, Heidelberg (2006)

20. Ghose, A.K., Narendra, N.C., Ponnalagu, K., Panda, A., Gohad, A.: Goal-driven business process derivation. In: Kappel, G., Maamar, Z., Motahari-Nezhad, H.R. (eds.) ICSOC 2011. LNCS, vol. 7084, pp. 467–476. Springer, Heidelberg (2011)
21. Pistore, M., Roveri, M., Busetta, P.: Requirements-driven verification of web services. Electron. Notes Theor. Comput. Sci. **105**, 95–108 (2004)
22. Guizzardi, R.S.S., Guizzardi, G., Almeida, J.P.A., Cardoso, E.: Bridging the gap between goals, agents and business processes. In: 4th International i* Workshop, pp. 46–51. CEUR (2010)
23. Lo, A., Yu, E.: From business models to service-oriented design: a reference catalog approach. In: Parent, C., Schewe, K.-D., Storey, V.C., Thalheim, B. (eds.) ER 2007. LNCS, vol. 4801, pp. 87–101. Springer, Heidelberg (2007)
24. Decreus, K., Poels, G.: A goal-oriented requirements engineering method for business processes. In: Soffer, P., Proper, E. (eds.) CAiSE Forum 2010. LNBIP, vol. 72, pp. 29–43. Springer, Heidelberg (2011)
25. Ruiz, M., Costal, D., España, S., Franch, X., Pastor, O.: GoBIS: an integrated framework to analyse the goal and business process perspectives in information systems. Inf. Syst. **53**, 330–345 (2015)
26. Séguran, M., Hébert, C., Frankova, G.: Secure workflow development from early requirements analysis. In: 6th IEEE European Conference on Web Services, pp. 125–134. IEEE Computer Society (2008)
27. Paja, E., Giorgini, P., Paul, S., Meland, P.H.: Security requirements engineering for secure business processes. In: Niedrite, L., Strazdina, R., Wangler, B. (eds.) BIR Workshops 2011. LNBIP, vol. 106, pp. 77–89. Springer, Heidelberg (2012)
28. Salnitri, M., Giorgini, P.: Transforming socio-technical security requirements in SecBPMN security policies. In: 7th International i* Workshop. CEUR (2014)
29. ISO/IEC 19506: Information technology - Object Management Group Architecture-Driven Modernization (ADM) - Knowledge Discovery Meta-Model (KDM). Technical report (2012)
30. Pérez-Castillo, R., Cruz-Lemus, J.A., De Guzmán, I.G.R., Piattini, M.: A family of case studies on business process mining using MARBLE. J. Syst. Softw. **85**(6), 1370–1385 (2012)
31. Object Management Group: Business Process Model and Notation (BPMN) Version 2.0. Technical report (2011)
32. Fernández-Ropero, M., Pérez-Castillo, R., Piattini, M.: Graph-based business process model refactoring. In: 3rd International Symposium on Data-driven Process Discovery and Analysis, pp. 16–30. CEUR (2013)
33. Fernández-Ropero, M., Pérez-Castillo, R., Cruz-Lemus, J.A., Piattini, M.: Assessing the best-order for business process model refactoring. In: 28th Annual ACM Symposium on Applied Computing, pp. 1397–1402. ACM (2013)
34. Mouratidis, H., Giorgini, P.: Secure tropos: a security-oriented extension of the tropos methodology. Int. J. Softw. Eng. Knowl. Eng. **17**(02), 285–309 (2007)
35. Mouratidis, H., Jurjens, J.: From goal-driven security requirements engineering to secure design. Int. J. Intell. Syst. **25**, 813–840 (2010)
36. Pavlidis, M., Islam, S., Mouratidis, H.: A CASE tool to support automated modelling and analysis of security requirements, based on secure tropos. In: Nurcan, S. (ed.) CAiSE Forum 2011. LNBIP, vol. 107, pp. 95–109. Springer, Heidelberg (2012)
37. Márquez, L., Rosado, D.G., Mouratidis, H., Mellado, D., Fernández-Medina, E.: A framework for secure migration processes of legacy systems to the cloud. In: Persson, A., Stirna, J. (eds.) CAiSE 2015 Workshops. LNBIP, vol. 215, pp. 507–517. Springer, Heidelberg (2015)

38. Shei, S., Márquez Alcañiz, L., Mouratidis, H., Delaney, A., Rosado, D.G., Fernández-Medina, E.: Modelling secure cloud systems based on system requirements. In: 2nd Evolving Security & Privacy Requirements Engineering Workshop: Co-located with the 23rd IEEE International Requirements Engineering Conference, pp. 19–24 (2015)

Making Empirical Studies

Testing a Selection of BPMN Tools for Their Support of Modelling Guidelines

Monique Snoeck[1(✉)], Isel Moreno-Montes de Oca[2],
Tom Haegemans[1], Bjorn Scheldeman[1], and Tom Hoste[1]

[1] Research Center for Management Informatics,
KU Leuven, Naamsestraat 69, 3000 Leuven, Belgium
{monique.snoeck,tom.haegemans}@kuleuven.be,
{bjornscheldeman,hoste.tom.92}@gmail.com
[2] Department of Computer Science, UCLV, Santa Clara, Cuba
Isel@uclv.edu.cu

Abstract. BPMN has become the de facto standard notation for process modelling. Past research has demonstrated the need for modelling guidelines to improve the quality of process models. In previous research we collected a set of practical guidelines through a systematic literature survey and classified those in different categories. In this paper we test a selection of BPMN tools for their support for these guidelines, and report on existing support per category of guideline and the kinds of support used by the tool to support the different guidelines. The results give insight into which domains of guidelines are well supported and which lack support from BPMN tools. Further, different preferences of the vendors are observed regarding the methods of support they implement in their tools.

1 Introduction

The Business Process Modelling Notation (BPMN) provides a way to conceptualize business processes into a graphical representation using constructs such as events, gateways, activities, processes, sub-processes, and control-flow dependencies [1, 2]. BPMN is a means to document, model and analyse the increasingly changing business processes in a structured, logically and systematic way [3]. The growing interest in BPMN turned it into an important standard with regards to process modelling within organizations and across organizations [4, 5].

One of the main objectives of BPMN is to provide an easily understandable notation. Because there is an increasing amount of stakeholders (e.g. business users, business analysts, technical developers) using these models, it is important that other people can easily interpret the BPMN models [6]. For people who were not involved in the modelling process, understanding complex and low quality models can be problematic. Also, misinterpretations of models can be the cause of a wrong implementation. A lot of the BPMN modelling is done as part of requirements engineering in the early phase of system development. When a model with a significant amount of errors is used as a basis for implementation, this generally means a high modification cost and a lot of effort to correct these mistakes at a later point in time [1].

© IFIP International Federation for Information Processing 2015
J. Ralyté et al. (Eds.): PoEM 2015, LNBIP 235, pp. 111–125, 2015.
DOI: 10.1007/978-3-319-25897-3_8

To avoid misinterpretations and high correction costs and get the full potential out of BPMN we have to make sure the quality of the BPMN models is high and the models do not contain purposeless complexity. The problem with providing a certain level of quality is that there are no unified standards regarding BPMN model quality. So the question that arises here is: How can we ensure the quality of BPMN models? Since relying on best practices has a positive impact on the model quality [7], following guidelines provided in literature can significantly enhance the quality of BPMN models.

However, two complications arise with regard to applying the guidelines. First, there is a vast amount of guidelines published in a variety of sources, making it difficult for a modeller to study and apply them all. This problem has been addressed in previous research by the authors. A systematic literature review (SLR) on pragmatic guidelines for business process modelling quality spanning the period of 2000–2014 [8] collected 72 papers addressing different aspects of modelling quality. All the guidelines and best practices identified in these papers were extracted, classified into different categories, and for each set of similar guidelines a unified guideline was proposed. This resulted in a set of 27 problems and unified guidelines, documented in a technical report [9]. Second, the fact that guidelines exist does not automatically mean all of these guidelines are always applied by every modeller. However, practically every user of BPMN uses the language in combination with a BPMN tool [3], and it was already proven that people using these tools and receiving support from these tools are less likely to produce low quality BPMN models [3]. This means that it is possible to provide BPMN models of decent quality, but most likely only when the modeller gets some kind of support provided by a modelling tool. This raises the following question: to what extent are the unified guidelines supported by BPMN modelling tools and how do they do this?

The remainder of this paper is structured as follows: Sect. 2 introduces the research questions; Sect. 3 presents related work; Sect. 4 introduces the approach for testing the tool support for a given collection of guidelines, while Sect. 5 reports on findings; Sect. 6 presents a discussion of the results. Finally, Sect. 7 presents conclusions and future work.

2 Research Questions

In this paper, we investigate which business process modelling guidelines are supported by current BPMN tools. In particular, we answer the following main question:

RQ: How extensive is the support for the identified set of unified guidelines in a representative set of popular BPMN tools?

The extent of the support can be assessed in two different ways: by looking at the number of guidelines that are supported, and by looking at the kind of support that is given (like e.g. supporting better layout through warnings versus automatic positioning of objects). Researching these different types of support will help answering our main research question. Hence the first sub-question is formulated as:

SRQ1: Which types of support exist for best practices in the considered set of tools?

The second way to evaluate the extent of the support is to look at which guidelines have some sort of support or not. So, the second research sub-question is formulated as follows:

SRQ2: To what extent are the guidelines supported by the considered set of tools?

The guidelines that were tested for support, have been classified into different categories [9]. By analysing the support per category, we gain useful insights regarding implementation problems or shortage of support in certain domain. Therefore, the third sub-question is:

SRQ3: To what extent is each category of best practices supported by the considered set of tools?

3 Related Research

While, to the best of our knowledge, BPMN tool support for guidelines, has not yet been researched, there are many other studies that provide a framework to evaluate a tool against certain criteria (e.g. [10–15]). The most relevant paper for our research [10] proposes an approach for the selection of a modelling tool and uses best practices as its evaluation criteria. First, the author develops a methodology to evaluate the candidate tools. The criteria for evaluation are build based on the definition of a core benchmark set defined in terms of a general benchmark goal. Moreover, the methodology requires the selection of a preferential tool, which reflects the company's perception of a "best-in-class" modelling tool [10]. Second, the researcher constructs metrics that indicate the importance that a company assigns to each criterion in the benchmark set. Third, the study provides an example by applying the framework to a set of 16 tools.

The main difference with the approaches of [10–15], is that we aim at comparing BPMN tools without adopting the perspective of a particular organisation. Consequently, we will use the framework of [10] as a starting point, but, to avoid bias, we will adhere to a more objective methodology and use context-independent measures. The guidelines identified through the SLR will serve as the core benchmark set.

4 Methodology

4.1 Selection of the Set of Guidelines

As explained above, in previous work, the authors of this paper collected the available guidelines from the scientific literature through a systematic literature review [8] and made an overview available as a technical report [9]. This technical report provides extensive information per guideline such as its sources, existing variants, metrics, examples and available scientific evidence. The technical report identifies 27 unified guidelines, classified into three large categories: guidelines that count elements, morphology guidelines and presentation guidelines, which each have a number of subcategories. For example, presentation is further subdivided in layout and label guidelines. For this paper, tool support for all guidelines was investigated, irrespective of available scientific evidence for their impact on modelling quality. This is motivated by the fact that future research may still prove certain guidelines to be useful, even though experimental evaluation of the impact on model quality may currently be lacking.

4.2   Selection of the Set of Tools

A representative set of tools was selected in 4 steps. The first step constituted of defining inclusion/exclusion criteria. Due to financial resource limitations, only free tools or tools with a free trial version were considered. To ensure a fair evaluation, only full functional tools with a recent update (2013 or later) were selected. Tools that seem to be outdated or only provide a limited functionality during the trial period should be excluded to avoid wrong conclusions or distorted results. Finally, to prevent checking non-relevant tools (e.g. purely graphical tools such as yEd or Microsoft Visio), only modelling tools, or suites with a modelling component were considered. In step 2, we tried to compose a set of available tools that is as complete as possible: we consolidated market overviews and existing lists [16, 17] into a list of 117 tools, which we reduced to a list of 20 tools by applying the exclusion and inclusion criteria (step 3). In step 4, due to time restrictions, six tools were selected while ensuring the sample to be as representative as possible. First, Signavio Process Editor was selected for being known for its support of best practices: a complete overview of the numerous guidelines that are incorporated in the tool is available on their website [18]. Next, two tools stand out because of their high degree of attention for best practices as evidenced by the avail-ability of extensive documentation about best practices on the website of the vendors: Bizagi Process Modeller and Camunda Modeller [19, 20]. The fourth included mod-elling tool is Bonita [21] because it was ranked first among several open-source applications for modelling and publishing BPMN 2.0 processes [6]. Finally, the selection was expanded with two popular tools [22]: Visual Paradigm and ARIS Express.

4.3   Research Method per Subquestion

First, to identify the types of support, we followed an explorative approach, similar to grounded theory. To start, we explored the tools to get familiar with them and to discover the functionalities they offer (e.g. automatic formatting of the layout of the model, a quality check to validate the model...). Next, BPMN test models were drawn, without observing the guidelines. During this phase we identified the different ways of how the tool tries to support the user.

Second, to examine the extent to which a guideline is supported by the selected tools and to investigate to what extent each category of best practices is supported, the guidelines were tested by drawing diagrams with the tools. While each unified guideline corresponds to one problem, some guidelines could not be matched to a single test. As an example, unified guideline 5, dealing with the problem of multiple start and/or end events, has several sub-guidelines: (1) use no more than two start/end events in the top process level; (2) use one start event in subprocesses and (3) use two end events to distinguish success and fail states in subprocesses. This guideline was therefore split into atomic guidelines such as to ensure full test coverage (see items b–e for subcategory 1.2 Number of events in Table 1). Overall this resulted in 56 atomic guidelines to test.

For each atomic guideline, we constructed a BPMN test model that mimics its corresponding problem. For example, the guideline "use no more than two start/end events in the top process level" was tested by constructing a BPMN model that has three start events (see [9 p. 10]). Thus, each atomic guideline was assessed by one test and each test corresponds to exactly one atomic guideline. To reduce the possibility of mistakes, each test was performed two times per guideline, each time by a different researcher. In addition, whenever possible, the test models were exported from one tool to another by means of XML to avoid errors caused by manually redrawing the test models.

In total 56 models that evidence the violation of the unified guidelines were tested. In addition, each guideline was tested by two researchers in each of the six tools. This means 672 test were conducted.

5 Results

5.1 Identification of Types of Support

From the exploratory study it was possible to detect a certain consistency regarding the way the different tools provide support. In general, the same five different ways of support are used across the different tools:

Forced Support. In this case, the tool forces the user to follow the corresponding guideline, resulting in the inability to avoid the guideline (e.g. explicitly labelling the model as erroneous, denying the user to drag an element to a certain place, making it unable to save an invalid model, refusing unlabelled elements…).

Warning. In case of a warning, the tool gives the user a warning message after validating the model (e.g. when a user draws a model that is too large according to the tools' guidelines, when pressing the validate or save button, a message will be shown saying that the model should be smaller). This does however not restrict the user in any way to continue working on or save the model.

Suggestive Support. A suggestion means that the tool tries to direct the user in the right way (e.g. automatically suggesting a certain size for an element, drawing guides to position the element in a symmetric way…).

Documentation. The documentation of the tools contains some best practices referring to modelling guidelines which can help to enhance the quality of the model. This type of support can be combined with another type of support (e.g. a documented guideline can also be enforced by the tool). However, most of the guidelines stated in the documentation are not supported by the tool itself, resulting in only written guidance for the modeller.

Related Support. Sometimes it happens that a tool does not directly support a particular guideline but does this indirectly by supporting a related guideline. For example, a tool may not provide direct support for the guideline "Avoid models with more than 7

Table 1. Tool support per guideline

			RESULT					
LEGEND:			SIGNAVIO	BIZAGI	VISUAL PARADIGM	BONITA	ARIS EXPRESS	CAMUNDA MODELER
f	The tool forbids the user to avoid the guideline.							
w	The tool gives the user a warning when validating the model.							
s	The tool suggests following the guideline when the user is drawing the model.							
d	The documentation of the tool supports the guideline. (can be combined with other symbol)							
n	The tool does nothing related to the guideline.							
r (n)	The tool does something related to another guideline. The number n refers to the guideline listed below.							
	GUIDELINE	**TEST: Does the tool avoid ...**						
1 Guidelines that count elements								
	1.1 Number of elements	a. A high number of elements	r(1)	n	n	n	n	n
		b. Duplicate elements	n	d	n	w	n	n
		c. Unnecessary elements	w	d	n	n	n	n
	1.2 Number of events	a. A high number of events	n	n	n	n	n	n
		b. A high number of start events	w	n	n	n	n	n
		c. A high number of end events	n	n	n	n	n	n
		d. Absence of start events	w	d	n	w	n	w
		e. Absence of end events	w	d	n	w	n	w
		f. High number of intermediate events	n	n	n	n	n	n
	1.3 Number of arcs	a. A high number of arcs	n	n	n	n	n	n
	1.4 Number of gateways	a. A high number of gateways	n	n	n	n	n	n
	1.5 Number of activities	a. A high number of activities	r(1)	n	n	n	n	n
	1.6 Element complexity	a. A high number of routing paths per gateways	n	n	n	n	n	n
		b. Multiple inputs and outputs on the same gateway	w	d	n	n	n	n
		c. A high number of outgoing sequence flows from an event	f	n	n	n	n	n
2 Morphology								
	2.1 Depth (nesting)	a. A high level of depth	n	n	r(2)	n	r(3)	n
	2.2 Cyclicity	a. Cycles in the model	n	n	n	n	n	n
		b. Badly formed cycles	w	n	n	n	n	n
		c. Multiple exit points per cycle	n	n	n	n	n	n
	2.3 Parallelism	a. A high level of parallelism	n	n	r(2)	n	r(4)	n
		b. Bad parallelism in the model	w	n	n	n	n	n
	2.4 Structuredness	a. Unstructuredness (AND-Gate/xOR-Gate mismatch)	w	d	n	n	n	n
		b. Unstructuredness (xOR-Gate/AND-Gate mismatch)	w	d	n	n	n	n
		c. Unstructuredness (AND-Gate/iOR-Gate mismatch)	n	d	n	n	n	n
		d. Unstructuredness (iOR-Gate/AND-Gate mismatch)	n	d	n	n	n	n
		e. Unstructuredness (xOR-Gate/iOR-Gate mismatch)	n	d	n	n	n	n
		f. Unstructuredness (iOR-Gate/xOR-Gate mismatch)	n	d	n	n	n	n
	2.5 Diameter (longest path)	a. A large model in terms of diameter	w	n	n	n	s	n
	2.6 iOR Gateways	a. A high level of gateway diversity	s	n	n	n	n	n
		b. The use of iOR-Gates	s	n	n	n	n	n
	2.7 General complexity	a. A high level of complexity	s	n	r(2)	n	r(3,4)	n
	2.8 Modularity	a. A too large model	r(1)	d	n	n	n	n

3 Presentation							
3.1 Layout guidelines	a. A high number of crossing lines	n	d	s	n	s	d
	b. Overlapping lines	w	s	n	n	n	d
	c. Overlapping elements	w	n	s	f	s	f
	d. A high number of bends in connecting elements.	w	f	s	n	s	n
	e. Objects not drawn orthogonally / symmetric	w	s	s	s	s	s
	f. A square model (and supports a long and thin model)	n	n	s	n	s	n
	g. Elements drawn with different sizes	n	n	n	n	n	d
	h. A large drawing area	w	n	n	n	n	n
	i. The use of color highlights (not supporting the guideline for colors)	s	s	s	f	s	f
	j. Abscence of color highlights (supporting the guideline for colors)	r(8)	r(8)	r(8)	n	r(8)	n
	k. Gateways used for both splitting and merging	w	d	n	n	n	d
	l. Elements placed too close together (not overlapping)	w	n	n	f	s	n
	m. Related elements placed too far from each other	n	n	s	n	s	n
	n. Unspecified task types	n	n	n	n	s	n
	o. Absence of pools and swimlanes	n	s	n	s	n	n
	p. A model flow not from left to right	w	d	n	n	s	n
3.2 Label style	a. Labels that do not follow verb-object style	n	d	r(5)	n	n	d r(7)
	b. Long labels	n	n	n	w	n	n
	c. Gateways without labels	w	d	s	n	n	d
	d. Events without labels	w	d r(6)	s	n	n	d
	e. Tasks without labels	w	s	s	w	s	w
	f. Unlabeled outgoing sequence flows from x-OR gateways	w	d	n	n	n	d
	g. Pools (processes) without labels	w	s	s	f	s	n
	h. Short labels or abbreviations	n	d	n	n	n	n
Related Guidelines							
Nr							
1.	SIGNAVIO gives a Layout warning: The diagram is too large in size.						
2.	When VISUAL PARADIGM automatically defines the layout, a less complex view can be achieved, but not always.						
3.	When ARIS EXPRESS automatically defines the layout, depth is displayed in a clear and organized way.						
4.	When ARIS EXPRESS automatically defines the layout, parallelism is displayed in a clear and organized way.						
5.	VISUAL PARADIGM gives a 'Fair' warning when the label does not contain glossary terms.						
6.	BIZAGI Best practices (documentation) suggest not to label start and end events; only other events.						
7.	CAMUNDA Best practices (documentation) suggest 'verb + object' for task labels, but events should be labeled 'object + past'.						
8.	The tool allows you to change the color of elements, but it is suggested to use the same color.						
9.	CAMUNDA Best practices (documentation) suggest only for xOR-Gateways to label outgoing paths with a question.						

events." but may issue a warning concerning the actual size of the model. This is obviously related to each other, and therefore classified as related support.

No Support. When a tool provides no support at all, this means there is no forced support, no warning, no suggestions and nothing within the provided documentation concerning a certain guideline.

5.2 Support for Individual Guidelines

The test results are summarized in Table 1, which gives an overview of which types of support the different tools have to offer to every tested guideline. For some tools the test resulted in more than one possible type of support. In this case the strongest support was reported as result of the test. The ordering between types of support was defined as follows: forced support is stronger than a warning; a warning is 'explicit' and therefore stronger than a suggestion; since a tool actively intervenes when suggesting something, a suggestion is stronger than documentation; and the documentation of the actual guideline is stronger than some indirect support. So, when both a warning and a suggestion support a certain guideline, only the warning is reported as result in Table 1. As an example, Signavio supports the guideline, "Place elements as symmetric as possible", in two different ways. First, the tool offers a suggestion by snapping elements automatically to a symmetric position relative to the model, which is classified as a suggestion. Second, the tool gives the user a layout warning when lines are not orthogonally drawn, which is classified as a warning. Because the warning is a stronger type of support than the suggestion, the type of support was classified as a warning in Table 1. The weaker type of support is not visible in Table 1, but is still archived in the complete overview in Appendix D of [23]. Overall, on the total of 336 combinations of atomic guideline and tool, 118 (35,1%) cases revealed some type of support. Figure 1 gives an overview of the overall degree of support for the six tools.

5.3   Support per Category

A "degree of support" was calculated for every tool per category of guidelines. This degree of support indicates what proportion of the tests resulted in a positive value. As an example, if 9 out of the 15 tests in the category of guidelines that count elements return a positive result (meaning there is some kind of support), this results in a score of 60% (= 9/15). Figure 2 gives an overview of the degree of support per category for the six tools. Similarly, Fig. 3 gives an overview of the strongest types of support per category for the 118 cases where a tool offers some sort of support for a guidelines.

6   Discussion

6.1   Support of the Guidelines

Overall, the large majority of guidelines (85,71%) seems to be known by tool builders. Nevertheless there are major differences between tools (see Fig. 1). That is, some of the selected tools offer substantially more support than the others. This was already noticed during the exploratory research phase and was later confirmed in the results. Signavio was found to be the tool with the highest degree of overall support (57,14%), followed by Bizagi (50%), ARIS Express (30,36%), Visual Paradigm (28,57%), Camunda (25%) and Bonita (19,64%).

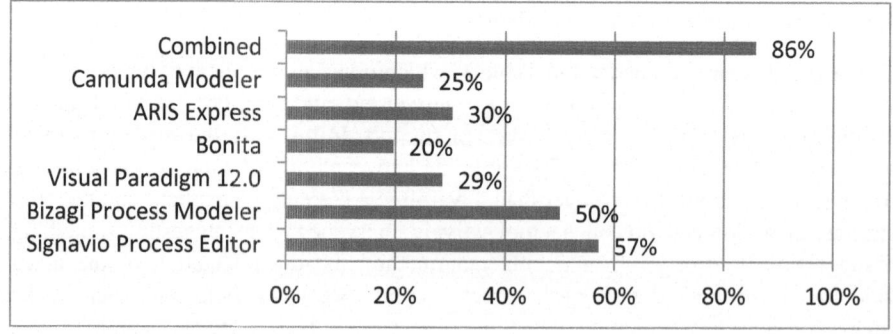

Fig. 1. Extent to which the guidelines are implemented by the set of tools

Although Signavio offers the highest level of support, it only supports 57,14% of the tested guidelines, which is relatively low. Likewise, the support that the other tools under investigation offer for the tested guidelines is less than or equal to 50%. Hence, when considering the tools separately, it can be seen that individual tools clearly lack support for a significant part of the guidelines.

6.2   Support of the Categories of Guidelines

In general, the group of presentation guidelines is the best supported category of guidelines (see Fig. 2). However, when looking at the details in Table 1, we see large differences in how this support happens concretely. Visual Paradigm and ARIS Express have the highest degree of support for the guidelines regarding the layout of the model. Furthermore, Bizagi scored best regarding label style guidelines, despite having lower degrees of support for the other domains. Also, Camunda Modeller has a strong support for the label style guidelines. Finally, Bonita seems the tool with the weakest average support although certain individual categories score fairly. The different scores per category and subcategory in Fig. 2 indicate that tools vendors each have different preferences about which categories to support.

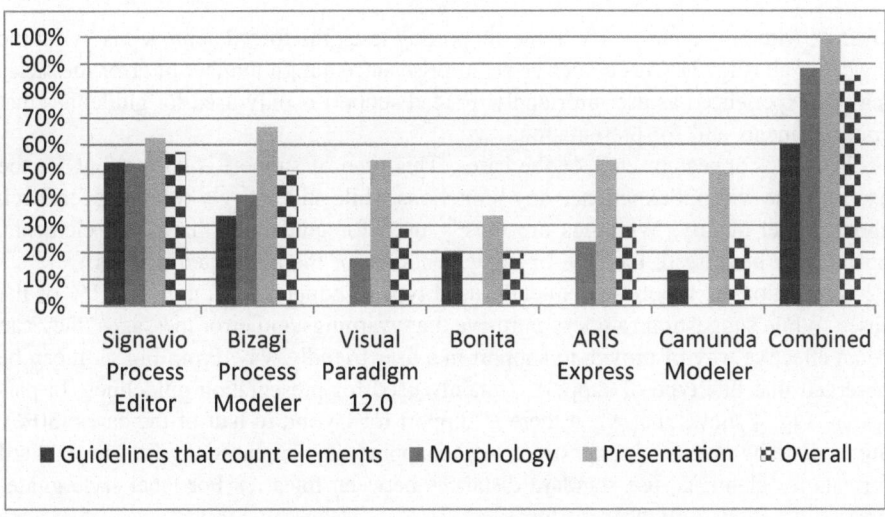

Fig. 2. Degree of support per category of guidelines

In a specific category of guidelines, the overall degree of support is always higher than the degree of support offered by the tool with the highest degree of support. For example, in Fig. 2, it can be seen that the degree of support for guidelines that count elements is 60% for the combined set of tools, while, in the same category of guide-lines, Signavio offers a degree of support of 53%, which is the highest score of a single tool within that category. This indicates that each single tool supports some guidelines that other vendors do not yet support. Thus, the different vendors of the tools can learn from each other regarding the different support offered by guidelines they have not yet implemented.

Surprisingly, the degree of support for guidelines that count elements is fairly low. Only 60% of the tested guidelines had a positive result in at least one tool (see Fig. 2) and, except for Signavio, all the tools have a degree of support lower than 35%. This low support is unexpected, because guidelines that count elements is the domain which should be the easiest to support (these guidelines have the easiest associated metrics [9]). Moreover, many of these guidelines have empirical support for their effect on model understandability [24, 25], which is a strong motive for providing tool support. A first explanation could be that tool builders fear that support in this area would restrict the user too much, e.g. when more complex models are needed, it would be irritating for the user to repeatedly receive warnings and suggestions in a situation where the high number of elements or arcs are unavoidable. A second possible explanation is that the perceived utility of automated support is perceived as low compared to e.g. the perceived utility of layout support: counting elements is fairly easy to perform manually without support, whereas the use of guides and snapping elements to a grid to optimize the layout of a diagram is considered as useful.

6.3   Types of Support

Overall, with only a use of 7% in the supporting tests, the forced approach is by far the lowest of all (Fig. 3). This comes as no surprise since a high number of error messages may be experienced as user-unfriendly. Forced support is only used for guidelines that count elements and for presentation.

Warnings appear in 26% of the cases. This type of support is convenient for the user as (s)he will not experience any limitations while still actively receiving feedback about model quality. Warnings are mostly used for guidelines that count elements, presumably because of the ease of implementation of the associated metrics.

Suggestions is the most frequently used type of support: it is used in 31% of the cases. While suggestions are less intrusive than warnings and error messages, they can be an effective way of providing support in a user friendly way. From Fig. 3, it can be observed that this type of support is mainly used for presentation guidelines. In particular, Fig. 4 shows that when there is support for layout, in half of the cases (50%), this is done by means of suggestions (e.g. snapping an element to a grid, use standard formats for elements, use standard distances between lines...). For label style guidelines, suggestions only account for 30%.

Related support is the second least used type of support: they are used in 12% of the cases. In addition, we find this type of support in 30% of the cases where there is support for morphology. A possible reason for this is that guidelines provided in this category are sometimes difficult to support in a straightforward way (e.g. "Keep the path from a start node to the end as short as possible").

Documentation appeared as a type of support in 24% of the cases. In the category of presentation guidelines, documentation accounts for 33% of the type of support for label guidelines (see Fig. 4). Furthermore, documentation is the most used type of support for morphology guidelines, next to and presumably for the same reason as for

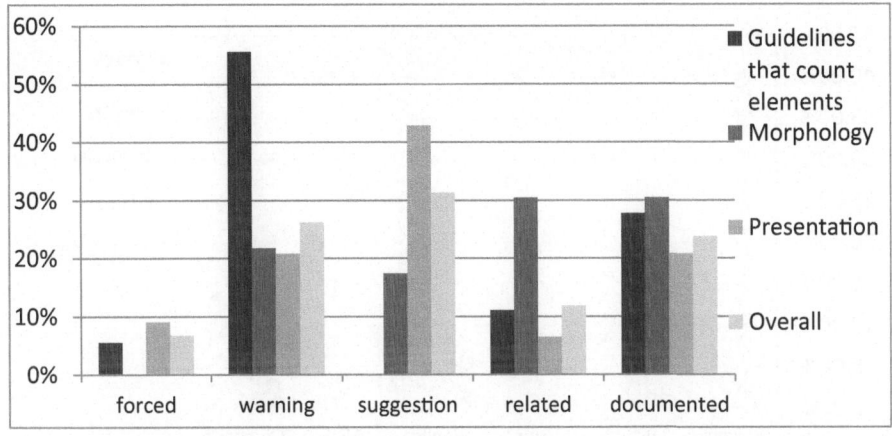

Fig. 3. Strongest types of support per category of guideline and overall

the related type of support. Nevertheless, we need to mention that in some of the cases where a stronger type of support is offered, the guideline is documented as well. As an example, some guidelines that Signavio supported were also documented on their website. As explained in Sect. 5.2, Table 1 only reports on the strongest type of support and, therefore, the additional support by means of documentation is not visible in the figures.

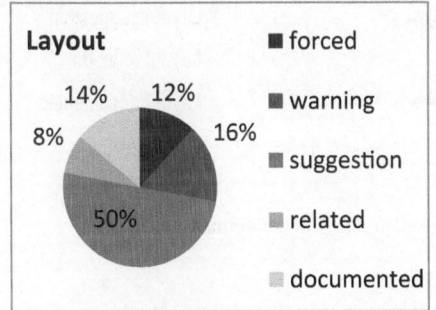 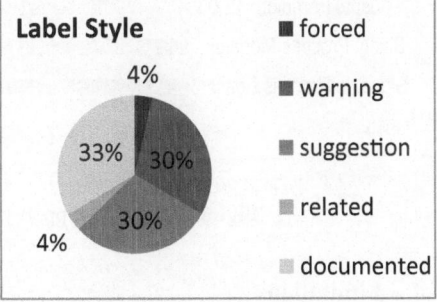

Fig. 4. Types of support per tool for layout and label style guidelines

When looking at individual tools, we can witness significant differences in types of support used by each of the tools (see Fig. 5). For presentation guidelines in particular, we can see that different tools handle support for layout and label guidelines in a very different way (see Figs. 6 and 7). While Signavio and Bizagi both have a high degree of overall support, Signavio mainly achieves this through warnings while Bizagi does this through the weaker form of support of documentation.

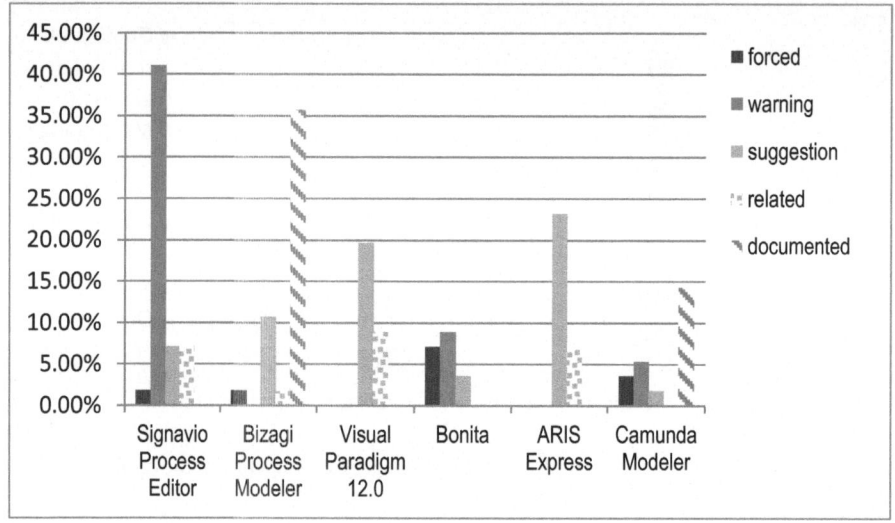

Fig. 5. Types of support per tool.

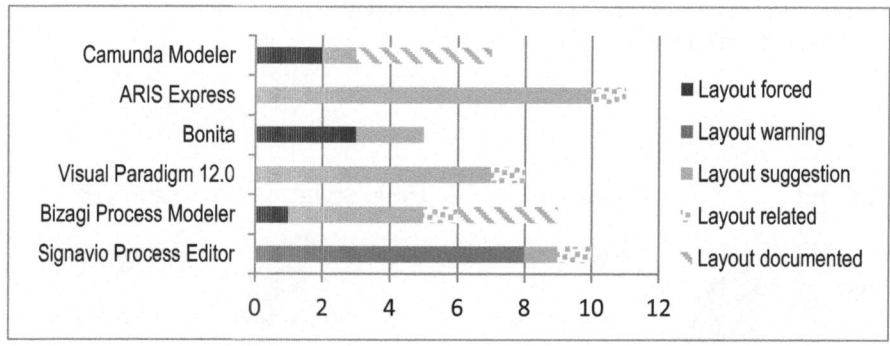

Fig. 6. Types of support per tool for layout guidelines

6.4   Limitations

The most important limitation of this research is the limited set of tools that was investigated. However, during the tool selection phase a number of other tools were briefly investigated to test the available functionality in the free version of the tool (see tool selection criteria). None of these briefly explored tools seemed to offer substantially different or more support than the tools in the sample. Based on these experiences, it seems safe to conclude that the general conclusions hold for the wider range of BPMN tools.

A second limitation relates to the performed tests. Despite researching the tool extensively during the exploratory research phase in order to get familiar with the tool and its functionalities, we might have missed some of the intended support for

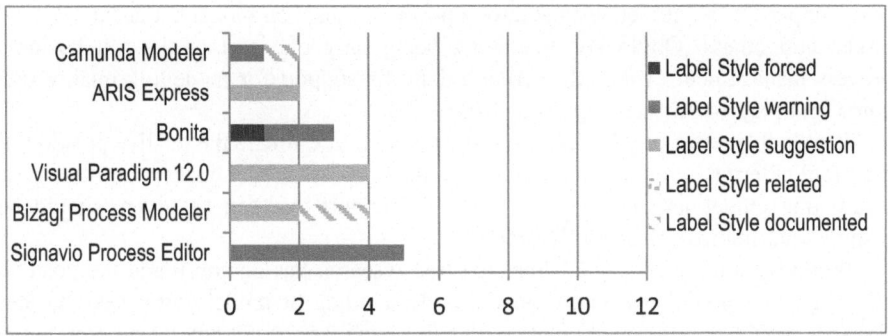

Fig. 7. Types of support per tool for label guidelines

guidelines. This was partly resolved by considering the "related guideline" as a type of support to take into account functionalities that are not a direct support for the tested guideline, but nevertheless offer relevant support related to the tested guideline.

7   Conclusion and Further Research

The goal of this research was to examine how extensive the support for the practical modelling guidelines is in a representative set of popular BPMN tools. First, we identified different types of support that indicate which level of support for a guideline is provided by a certain tool. These types of support were then used to indicate to which extent the BPMN modelling guidelines are implemented by a representative set of BPMN modelling tools. We found that almost every guideline was supported by at least one of the examined tools: only 8 out of the 56 atomic guidelines has no support at all. This leads to the conclusion that most guidelines are known by at least some of the tool builders. However, when considering the tools separately, each tool clearly lacks support for a significant part of the guidelines.

Considering the categories of guidelines, we found that the group of presentation guidelines is the best supported category. The second most supported category are the morphology guidelines, and the least supported guidelines are the guidelines that count elements. However, the extent to which a certain category is supported, is highly dependent on the tool. In terms of types of support, warning and suggestions revealed to be the favourite types of support while enforcing guidelines is the least used type of support. The proportional use of different types of support is however dependent on the investigated tool and the category of guidelines.

As existing research has already demonstrated the positive impact on model quality (e.g. on model understanding and model correctness), following guidelines provided in literature can significantly enhance the quality of BPMN models. The presented results are therefore useful in the first place for anyone who needs to select a tool for modelling purposes. For example, when teaching BPMN to students, students should benefit from tools that offer a better support for model quality to make their exercises. Also business analysts who need to communicate about business processes with end-users will benefit from support for all guidelines that have a positive impact on model understanding and model correctness. Obviously, modelling being only one part of the full business process management cycle, other criteria than the support for modelling quality will come into play when selecting a full BPM suite.

Tool builders can use the results of this research to estimate the relative position of their tool in terms of relative support for business process model quality. The overview of existing guidelines and different levels of support that can be given, should be inspirational improve their tool's support.

While for a number of guidelines existing research has demonstrated the positive effect of those guidelines on e.g. model understanding or model correctness, further research should be performed to investigate the actual effect of a type of support on the actual application of a guideline by a modeller. Also, the relation between types of support and experienced utility, user-friendliness and guidelines acceptance may be an avenue of further research.

References

1. Dijkman, R.M., Dumas, M., Ouyang, C.: Semantics and analysis of business process models in BPMN. Inf. Softw. Technol. **50**(12), 1281–1294 (2008)
2. Born, M., Kirchner, J., Müller, J.P.: Context-driven business process modeling. In: The 1st International Workshop on Managing Data with Mobile Devices (MDMD 2009), Milan, Italy (2009)
3. Recker, J., et al.: How good is BPMN really? insights from theory and practice. In: 14th European Conference on Information Systems. Association for Information Systems, Goeteborg (2006)
4. Recker, J.: BPMN modeling - who, where, how and why. BPTrends **5**, 1–8 (2008)
5. zur Muehlen, M., Recker, J.: How much language is enough? theoretical and practical use of the business process modeling notation. In: Bellahsène, Z., Léonard, M. (eds.) CAiSE 2008. LNCS, vol. 5074, pp. 465–479. Springer, Heidelberg (2008)
6. Chinosi, M., Trombetta, A.: BPMN: An introduction to the standard. Comput. Stan. Interfaces **34**(1), 124–134 (2012)
7. Lübke, D., Schneider, K., Weidlich, M.: Visualizing use case sets as BPMN processes. In: 3rd International Workshop on Requirements Engineering Visualization, REV 2008. IEEE (2008)
8. Moreno-Montes de Oca, I., et al.: A systematic literature review of studies on business process modeling quality. Inf. Softw. Technol. **58**, 187–205 (2015)
9. Moreno-Montes de Oca, I., Snoeck, M.: Pragmatic guidelines for Business Process Modeling. KU Leuven - FEB - Management Information Systems Group (2015)
10. Daneva, M.: A best practice based approach to CASE-tool selection. In: 4th IEEE International Software Engineering Standards Symposium and Forum (ISESS 1999), "Best Software Practices for the Internet Age". IEEE (1999)
11. Rivas, L., et al.: Tools selection criteria in software-developing Small and Medium Enterprises. J. Comput. Sci. Technol. **10**(1), 24–30 (2010)
12. Illes, T., et al.: Criteria for software testing tool evaluation. a task oriented view. In: Proceedings of the 3rd World Congress for Software Quality (2005)

13. IEEE, IEEE Std 1209-1992: IEEE Recommended Practice for the Evaluation and Selection of CASE Tools (1993)
14. Du Plessis, A.L.: A method for CASE tool evaluation. Inf. Manage. **25**(2), 93–102 (1993)
15. Le Blanc, L.A., Korn, W.M.: A structured approach to the evaluation and selection of CASE tools. In: Proceedings of the 1992 ACM/SIGAPP Symposium on Applied Computing: Technological Challenges of the 1990's. ACM (1992)
16. Harmon, P., Wolf, C.: Business Process Trends; Business Process Modeling Survey (2011). http://www.bptrends.com/bpt/wp-content/surveys/Process_Modeling_Survey-Dec_11_FINAL.pdf. Accessed from July 2015
17. BPMN-Forum. BPMN tool related posts and discussions (2015). http://bpmnforum.com/bpmn-tools. Accessed from July 2015
18. Signavio. Guidelines by convention: Signavio Best Practice. http://academic.signavio.com. Accessed from July 2015
19. Camunda, BPMN 2.0 Best Practices (2014)
20. Bizagi, Bizagi Process Modeler User's Guide (2015)
21. Bonita. Bonita. http://fr.bonitasoft.com. Accessed from July 2015
22. Ramakrishan, M.: Top Ten BPM tools you cannot ignore! in Wordpress (2013)
23. Scheldeman, B., Hoste, T.: The support of best practices by BPMN tools, in Faculty of Economics and Business. KU Leuven, Belgium (2015)
24. Mendling, J., Reijers, H.A., van der Aalst, W.M.P.: Seven process modeling guidelines (7PMG). Inf. Softw. Technol. **52**(2), 127–136 (2010)
25. Mendling, J., et al.: Thresholds for error probability measures of business process models. J. Syst. Softw. **85**(5), 1188–1197 (2012)

Consistently Formalizing a Business Process and its Properties for Verification: A Case Study

Michael Rathmair[✉], Ralph Hoch, Hermann Kaindl, and Roman Popp

TU Wien, Institute of Computer Technology, Vienna, Austria
{rathmair,hoch,kaindl,popp}@ict.tuwien.ac.at

Abstract. Formal verification of business process models can be done through *model checking* (also known as *property checking*), where a model checker tool may automatically find violations of properties in a process model. This approach obviously has formal representations as a prerequisite. However, a key challenge for applying this approach in practice is to consistently formalize the process and its properties, which clearly cannot be done automatically. We studied this challenge in a case study of formally verifying an informally given business process against a guideline written like a legal text. Major lessons learned from this case study are that formalizing is key to success and that in its course a semi-formal representation of properties is useful. In the course of such a step-wise and incremental formalization, problems with the given process model have been found already, apart from those found with a model checker tool that used the formal property specification. In total, our approach revealed five problems not found by the official review. In summary, this paper investigates in a case study consistently formalizing a business process and its properties for verification through model checking.

1   Introduction

Hardware and software should be free of errors, and the same applies to business processes. Usual quality assurance techniques for hardware and software in practice are reviews and tests. These have the purpose of finding errors but they can, in general, not show that there are no errors. Research both related to hardware and software investigates *model checking* for formal verification, which can, in principle, show that there are no errors with regard to certain properties. This requires both a formally specified behavioral model and formulas specifying properties to verify them against. Neither of them are usually available in practice, unfortunately.

Roughly speaking, a formal representation is one that allows (automatic) reasoning purely based on its form, which has defined semantics. In particular, illustrative diagrams or natural language are *not* formal representations. That is why formalization is necessary when something is given informally, e.g., in such diagrams or in natural language. Business process models typically are behavioral models, but usually not (really) formally defined in practice. So, their formalization is important but even more so the consistent formalization of properties

© IFIP International Federation for Information Processing 2015
J. Ralyté et al. (Eds.): PoEM 2015, LNBIP 235, pp. 126–140, 2015.
DOI: 10.1007/978-3-319-25897-3_9

to check them against. These properties are sometimes hard to get in practice and at best, informally described. The properties typically refer to the behavioral models, but this means some coupling. And if the person who formalizes properties has the behavioral model available, then there will be some influence on the properties. This is reminiscent of someone writing test cases for his own software. So, we argue for more or less independent formalization of a behavioral model and of the properties to check it against. Unfortunately, this may lead to inconsistent formalizations that do not fit together for the purpose of model checking. Therefore, consistent formalization of behavioral model and properties is a challenge, which we address in this paper.

We investigated this challenge in the context of a case study where it became apparent. The task was verifying a high-level business process of our university against a corresponding guideline, both of which were given informally. More precisely, this is a real process enacted on a regular basis (for searching and appointing a full professor). For the case study, a process diagram in informal notation was used, as given in the course of preparations for an official Quality Audit. The guideline is an official document of our university, derived from the Austrian law for universities. In particular, its writing style is like that of this legal text, i.e., a special kind of text in natural language.

So, there was informal input, but formal representations of both process and properties are needed for formal verification using model checking. Of course, there is neither an automated transformation nor a defined sequence of steps available for such a task of formalization, and we did not attempt to define something like that, either. Still, we suggest, based on the case study, to use a semi-formal representation in the course of the formalization. Its usefulness is a major lesson learned, generalized from the case at hand.

The remainder of this paper is organized in the following manner. First, we present some background material on model checking in order to make this paper self-contained. Then we discuss related work. The core part presents a case study of model checking an informally given high-level process against a guideline based on legal text, where consistent formalization was particularly studied, and concludes with lessons learned from it. After that, we discuss threats to validity. Finally, we derive general conclusions on consistently formalizing properties used for model checking business processes.

2   Background on Model Checking

Model checking (or property checking) is a formal verification technique based on models of system behavior and properties, specified unambiguously in formal languages (see, e.g., [1]). The behavioral model of the system under verification is often specified using a Finite State Machine (FSM), in our case using synchronized FSMs. Their expressiveness is sufficient for our case, but Petri nets, e.g., could be used as well, if needed (depending on the tool used). The properties to be checked on the behavioral model are formulated in a specific property specification language, usually based on a temporal language. Several tools (such as SPIN [2] or NuSMV [3]) exist for performing these checks by systematically exploring the state-space of the system. When such a tool finds a property violation, it reports it in the form of a counterexample.

In this work, we make use of *Linear Temporal Logic*, or *Linear-time Temporal Logic*, (LTL) and *Computational Tree Logic* (CTL) for property specification. More precisely, we use PLTL (LTL with past). Since a rough understanding of some of their operators is needed for understanding our formalization approach, let us briefly sketch these here. PLTL provides expressions of relations between states (path formulas) using operators referring to behavior over time. In PLTL, the set of traditional propositional logic operators is extended by time operators such as:

- G (Globally): an expression p is true at time t if p is true at all times $t' \geq t$.
- F (Future): an expression p is true at time t if p is true at some time $t' \geq t$.
- O (Once): an expression p is true at time t if p is true at some previous time $t' \leq t$.

CTL features the specification of branching time properties. While PLTL allows the specification of properties to hold for all computation paths related to a given point in time, CTL provides operators for specifying whether there exists (eventually) a computation path where a specific state property holds. In this work, we use the following CTL operators:

- EF (Eventually in the Future): an expression p is true in the initial state s_0 and there exists a state sequence $s_0 \rightarrow s_1 \rightarrow s_2 \rightarrow \cdots \rightarrow s_n$ such that p is true in s_n.
- AG (Always Globally): an expression p is true in the initial state s_0 and in each state of all transitions $s_0 \rightarrow s_1 \rightarrow s_2 \rightarrow \cdots \rightarrow s_n$.

3   Related Work

Previous related work made it absolutely clear that some representation with defined semantics is a prerequisite for formal verification, also of business processes. Given such a representation, checking correctness properties inherent in the business process itself is possible. Since we rather focus on formalizing properties given in addition to a business process, we cite only a few references here. Wynn et al. [4] verify business processes against four defined properties (soundness, weak soundness, irreducible cancellation regions and immutable OR-joins). Sbai et al. [5] show how a model checker can be used to identify problems with a specification of a business process to be automated as a workflow, and how a verification of certain correctness properties can be accomplished. Kherbouche et al. [6] propose an approach for using model checking as a mechanism to detect errors such as deadlocks or lifelocks.

Some previous work addressed the question of what to verify a business process model against, to determine possible violations of certain properties given in addition to the process model itself. Fisteus et al. [7] propose a framework for integrating BPEL4WS and the SPIN and SMV verification tools. This framework can verify a process specification against properties such as invariants and goals through model checking. Armando et al. [8] show how model checking can be used for automatic analysis of security-sensitive business processes. They propose a system that allows the separate specification of the business process workflow and of corresponding security requirements. In more recent work [9], they show how model checking can be specifically used to check authorization requirements that are implemented in parts of business processes. Barros et al. [10] propose to check business processes against execution rules incorporated in workflows with model checking techniques.

Mrasek et al. [11] point out that formalizing properties in CTL is a difficult task and strive for making it easier through so-called patterns based on textual fragments in natural language. This approach can work in a given context for entering properties, and it helped in a case study. In general, however, the interpretation of these textual patterns is subtle and error-prone. So, they have to be prepared specifically for a given problem by CTL specialists, anyway. In particular, for our case study with given legal text, such an approach would most likely require a variety of different patterns and still be hard to validate.

The focus of our work as presented in this paper is, however, consistently formalizing the business process and its properties as required for automatic verification through model checking. Still, no previous work in the context of model checking of business process models addressed it to our best knowledge, including model-based business process compliance-checking approaches [12]. Apart from [11], which addresses formalizing properties (but not formalizing the process), all the publications on model checking of business processes already assume the availability of formal representations.

4   A Case Study of Model Checking a High-Level Process Against a Guideline

We performed a case study, where we verified a high-level business process of our university against a corresponding guideline, both of which were given informally. More precisely, this is a real process enacted on a regular basis (for searching and appointing a full professor), but its 'as-is' process *diagram* has been yet under development at this time (in the course of preparations for an official Quality Audit). We used a version of this diagram that was under official review at about the same time as the case study, but in order to keep pace with the tight schedule of the overall endeavor, we only dealt with the core part of this process where the search committee is active. Figure 1 shows a selected part of this core part to be used below for illustration purposes, in the informal notation officially used. (Note, that the arrow from the task "Invite new reviewers" leads outside of this selected part.) The guideline is an official document of our university, and its text (in German) can be found at http://www.tuwien.ac.at/dle/universitaetskanzlei/satzung/berufungsverfahren/. This guideline is derived from the Austrian law for universities. In particular, its writing style is like the one of this legal text.

MAN-03-02-S Process of Appointing a Professor

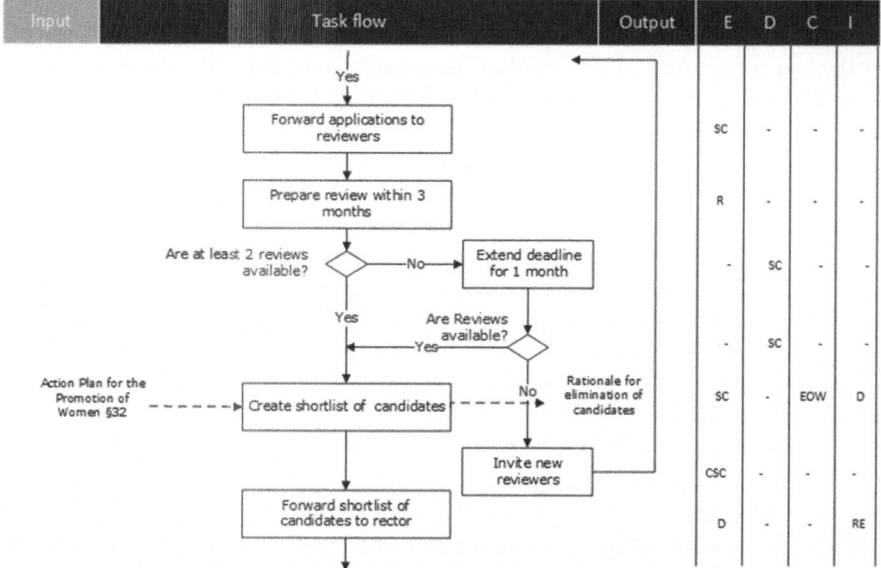

E = Executes; D = Decides; C = Contributes; I = Informed.
SC = Search Committee; R = Reviewer; EOW = Equal opportunities working party; D = Dean;
CSC = Chair Person of the Search Committee; RE = Rector.

Fig. 1. Diagram of a part of the process for appointing a professor

4.1 Stakeholders

The stakeholders involved in this case study, directly or indirectly, are the following:

- Central group responsible. A dedicated group directly assigned to the rectorate was responsible for creating business models of several high-level processes of our university, and for their review.
- Working groups. In order to acquire knowledge on these processes, several dedicated working groups were assembled, whose output was fed into the process models created by the central group responsible for that.
- Reviewers of process models. In order to get as much feedback as possible on these models, every employee of our university has been invited to participate in the review (via email).
- Case study team. The people having performed this case study are actually the same as the authors of this paper. Two of them had enacted this very process in key roles in 2013.
- Verification engineer. The first author of this paper was the verification engineer in this team and brought in know-how and experience from applying

such techniques in hardware design, more precisely circuit verification, see, e.g., [13].

4.2 Formalization of Guideline and Process Model

Initially, the verification engineer only worked on formalizing the guideline, as he did not know the process at all. Therefore, he could not formalize the process model yet, and also not completely formalize the properties to check it against, since he did not know the states of the process model. So, he created a *semi-formal* representation of properties according to the guideline first, where he used PLTL/CTL operators already, but still text fragments from the guideline to indicate, e.g., sequences of tasks. This property representation was subject to an informal manual inspection by the complete case study team. Only after that, the verification engineer was given the part of the process model, which he formalized as an FSM. Once having the FSM available, he formalized the properties based on the previously prepared *semi-formal* representations. Finally, he applied the model checking tool for checking whether the process model is inconsistent with the given guideline.

For illustrating the creation of a semi-formal representation, let us start with an example excerpt from the guideline. § 7(1) of the guideline is given in the second column of Table 1: "The chairperson of the search committee forwards ...". First, the verification engineer identified all actors and artefacts mentioned in the partial sentence and treated them as individual objects, e.g., CSC and list (of candidates). After that, he identified actions and mapped them to expressions including temporal operators, e.g., F as specifications of allowed sequences. Since this example contains two different actions with different actors, the full paragraph is actually mapped to two properties. The second of these properties in its semi-formal representation, i.e., "G (list $=$ TRUE $\rightarrow F$ Dean.state $=$ forward candidate list to rector)", expresses that globally (PLTL operator G), if the list exists, then the Dean must reach a future state (PLTL operator F), where the list of candidates is forwarded to the rector.

Especially with respect to 'time', it is interesting to give an example of what we did *not* formalize from the given guideline, even though temporal logics are employed. The guideline says, for instance, "reviews should be prepared within 3 months" (as translated from the German text). The verification engineer did not include this statement into the list of properties (not even their semi-formal representation), since he had his focus on *sequences in time*, although the so-called X operator of LTL could be used in an attempt to model this statement. In hindsight, we briefly discussed this possibility, where time units would be defined, e.g., a day. Based on that, the checker tool could simulate time slots through loops for a defined number of time units corresponding to 3 months. Obviously, there would a minor intricacy involved, since not every month has the same number of days, but this could be approximated. Another, more serious issue with this approach would be that a day would be the minimum duration of each task. All of these intricacies of this thought experiment are, however, beyond the scope of the given guideline text and the law it is based upon.

Table 1. A selection of properties as derived from the guideline, where violated properties are highlighted through various shades of gray as background

§	Guideline Text	Semi-formal Property Representation	Property Formula
§6(2)	If according to "§3 Absatz 1" of this guideline more than 2 reviews have been requested, and are 2 reviews available after 3 months, the search committee makes its decision based on these available reviews, otherwise the search committee may extend the deadline for one month ; after this deadline, the search committee makes its decision based on the available reviews	G (SC has received 2 or more reviews $\rightarrow$ F SC.state = create list with candidates) AG (SC has received less than 2 reviews $\rightarrow$ (1EF SC.state = Extend deadline for 1 month & EF SC.state = Extend deadline for 1 month) G (SC.state = Extend $\rightarrow$ F SC.state = create list with candidates)	G ((inst_process.state = Prepare & inst_review_list.i.numReviews = 2) $\rightarrow$ F inst_process.state=Create_C_L) AG (((inst_process.state = Prepare) & (inst_review_list.i.numReviews < 2)) $\rightarrow$ (1(EF inst_process.state = Extend) & (EF inst_process.state = Extend)) G (inst_process.state = Extend $\rightarrow$ F inst_process.state=Create_C_L)
§7(1)	The chairperson of the search committee forwards this list as soon as possible to the responsible dean, who forwards it to the rector.	G (list = TRUE $\rightarrow$ F CSC.state = forward candidate list to dean) G (list = TRUE $\rightarrow$ F Dean.state = forward candidate list to rector)	No refined formalization possible, since no such state exists in the FSM. G (inst_process.state = Forward_C_R $\rightarrow$ inst_process.E = Dean)

inst_process = Process of appointing a professor;
Extend = Extend deadline for 1 month;
Create_C_L = Create shortlist of candidates;
Prepare = Prepare review within 3 months;
Forward_C_R = Forward shortlist of candidates to rector.

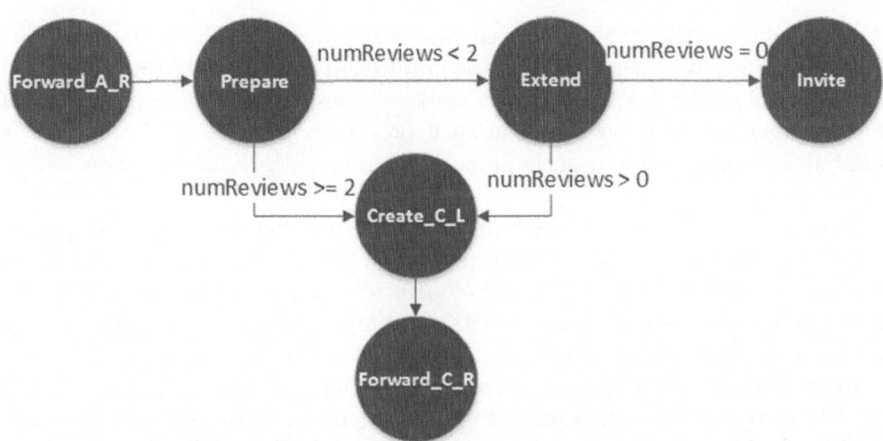

Extend = Extend deadline for 1 month; numReviews = signal number of reviews; Create_C_L =
Create shortlist of candidates; Prepare = Prepare review within 3 months; Forward_A_R =
Forward Applications to Reviewers; Forward_C_R = Forward shortlist of candidates to rector;
Invite = Invite new reviewers.

Fig. 2. FSM of the part of the process model shown in Fig. 1

A related example of what we clearly did not formalize about 'time' is the phrase "as soon as possible" (in the original German text the word "ehestmöglich") in § 7(1), see Table 1 in the last row. Without modeling time units, this cannot even be approximated.

The effort for the manual translation of the given part of the guideline to a set of semi-formally represented properties was approximately six hours. It included eleven paragraphs of the guideline, resulting in 25 semi-formally represented properties, and a meeting of the team for their informal inspection.

The informal inspection of the semi-formal property formulations was an essential part of the full verification process. The translation of a natural language text fragment as given by the guideline is an error-prone process. One or more formulated properties have to cover the textually given facts and characteristics of the described process "Appointing a Professor". At the review meeting, all 25 properties were discussed and analyzed whether they are not in conflict, covering the guideline and adequately representing it.

Based on the results of this review, the verification engineer made a few changes to the semi-formal representation of the properties. After that, he was given the process representation in the form of the excerpt shown in Fig. 1, essentially an annotated flow diagram. He constructed an FSM for the control flow, which is shown in Fig. 2 for the same excerpt. In essence, he mapped each chart element to an FSM state each. State transitions were derived from the task flow of the given process model. Since the arrow from the state "Invite new reviewers" in Fig. 1 is outside of the part selected for presentation here, it is not included in the FSM.

Constructing this FSM may even look straight-forward, especially for the excerpt used in this paper. However, the notation of diagrams like those shown in Fig. 1 is not formally specified. In fact, forks of lines can either mean procedural or concurrent flows, as we found in such process representations. So, there is essential ambiguity also in such process diagrams, which make formalization hard in general.

Data objects were extracted from the given process model and may influence control flow decisions: reviewer list, review list, application list, and list of candidates. As illustrated in Fig. 2, i_numReviews is an internal variable of the data object review list. The value of this variable (either > 0 or $= 0$) directly influences the state transition in the control flow FSM.

Roles of this process as given through the columns with the header "E / D / C / I" in the process diagram of Fig. 1 are modeled through a variable each, all of them of type enumeration, with possible values SC, CSC, etc. The values assigned depend on the given FSM state, e.g., for the state *Create_C_L* of this FSM corresponding to the task "Create shortlist of candidates", variables to be used by the model checking tool are assigned as follows: E := SC, C := EOW and I := D.

Once the FSM is defined, based on the given process diagram, it is useful to reflect again on the representation of 'time' apart from sequences. There is a task with the text "Prepare review within 3 months" in the process diagram in Fig. 1. In the FSM, it is simply a state with a corresponding identifier. So, the semantics of this text is obviously not represented. The verification engineer saw the correspondence of this text with the corresponding text of the guideline (as discussed above) in passing, but there was no formal verification based on a temporal logic.

For the creation of the FSM and the definition of related variables as derived from (the selected part of) the officially given process diagram, a time effort of approximately three hours was used.

According to the given FSM, the verification engineer manually reformulated the semi-formally represented property statements to corresponding PLTL or CTL formulas, respectively. Informal parts of the semi-formally represented property had to be replaced by expressions referencing states of the FSM and its related variables. In the example used above, the formula "G (inst_process.state = Forward_C_R $\rightarrow$ inst_process.E = Dean)" refers to the process state Forward_C_R. While the list object is not used here, the state Create_C_L before Forward_C_R (in the FSM) creates it.

If a semi-formal representation of a property could not be translated to an adapted PLTL or CTL formula, two cases were to be distinguished:

1. The granularity of the given model was partially not compatible with the level of detail specified in the guideline. Hence, if the verification engineer was unable to redefine some semi-formally represented property, this is not necessarily a violation of the given guideline.

2. An error in the model was identified. A subsequent detailed manual inspection of the model uncovered errors like missing or improper states, undefined variables, etc.

An example of a missing state is the first semi-formally represented property of § 7(1). It cannot be translated into a refined formula because there is no state in the given model denoting that "The chairperson of the search committee forwards this list as soon as possible to the responsible dean", i.e., the sentence highlighted in light-gray of the guideline in Table 1 and the corresponding semi-formal property representation. More precisely, there is also a confusion in the process model about the actors SC and CSC involved here, which means a second violation of this property. Yet another task was identified to be missing (with respect to preparing and submitting the final report, which were mixed up in the process model), similarly to the one indicated above. So, a total of three violations were found by the verification engineer already in the course of modeling.

After this final formalization effort of approximately two hours, both the model in the form of an FSM and the set of formalized properties were defined and ready for model checking with the tool.

4.3   Tool-Supported Model Checking and its Results

For the tool-supported model checking, the formalized process model (in the form of the FSM and its associated variables) and the set of refined properties from the guideline (in the form listed in the fourth column of Table 1) were input to the model checker tool NuSMV. For any property violation found by the model checker tool, it returns a *counterexample* listing. This is presented as a possible execution sequence violating a specific property formulation. These results had to be manually analyzed by the verification engineer to locate the violations in detail and, finally, to interpret them in terms of the given process model and the guideline it has been verified against.

Table 1 contains examples of such violations found by the NuSMV tool, indicated in dark-gray and mid-gray, respectively. Let us explain the violation shown in mid-gray first. Listing 1 shows a selected part of the counterexample report for this violated property formula. Such listings refer to states, but these are different from the states of the FSM. In fact, NuSMV enumerates its *execution* states, whose sequence forms a trace. In this example, State 1.1 denotes that the variable i_numReviews, which is a local variable of the data object review_list, has the value 0. The control flow FSM reaches its FSM state Prepare at (execution) State 1.13. At State 1.14, the control flow FSM reaches its state Extend because the condition "Are at least 2 reviews available" is not fulfilled. The violation of this property is indicated by the following unspecified transition from the FSM state Extend (State 1.14) to Invite (State 1.16). This FSM state sequence is in conflict with the partial sentence "after this deadline, the search committee makes its decision based on the available reviews" (textual part highlighted in mid-gray of column one). In fact, the guideline does not define what to do if i_numReviews = 0. As a consequence, the model checking tool automatically indicates that the given formal property is not satisfied on the formalized input model, and hence the guideline is not consistent with the process model.

```
-- specification  G (inst_process.state = Extend -> F
     inst_process.state = Create_C_L)   is false
-- as demonstrated by the following execution sequence Trace
     Type: Counterexample
-> State: 1.1 <-
...
inst_review_list.i_numReviews = 0
...
-> State: 1.13 <-
inst_process.state = Prepare
-> State: 1.14 <-
inst_process.state = Extend
-> State: 1.16 <-
inst_process.state = Invite
...
```

Listing 1. Counterexample Tool Output Reporting a Property Violation

For the second property violation found by the tool, highlighted in dark-gray in Table 1, the same counterexample as shown in Listing 1 is returned (possibly with different execution states, but this does not matter). In fact, the value 0 is the cause of the contradictions of both properties. In addition, the property highlighted in dark-gray is also violated if the variable i_numReviews is assigned to 1. This has actually been checked with the tool by the verification engineer by forcing it to evaluate an example with the value 1, where the tool tells that this is a counterexample as well.

This second property violation is especially interesting, since it expresses that shifting of the deadline for the submission of Reviews is optional and not mandatory if i_numReviews < 2. This is formalized as a CTL formula, which enables the combination of path and state operators. Since the property states that the task "Extend the deadline for 1 month" is optional, it has to be checked whether both paths, one including the task and one not, are reachable. In terms of formalization, simply using the EF operator in one direction is not sufficient, therefore, since it defines that a path *exists*. This would also include the case of a mandatory extension as given in the process model. So, it is necessary to have a conjunction with the same part of the formula negated, see Table 1.

For the dedicated final adaptation and debugging of the formalized model and properties, a final interpretation, and location of the two violations found by the tool, a time effort of approximately two hours was used.

4.4   Summary of Results and Lessons Learned

In total, five problems were revealed in the selected part of the process for appointing a professor. In fact, no problems at all were found in this part by the official review, for which all employees of the university had been invited.

Now let us briefly generalize from the case at hand and try to indicate lessons learned that may be useful for similar endeavors:

- *Possibly conflicting roles.* Specifying the process model and the properties to be used for verifying it, should be done by different people. The process model should also not be known in advance by the one(s) formalizing the properties. Having it available, however, imposes the risk that knowing the process already may influence the verification engineer in the semantic interpretation of properties. We think that this is reminiscent of a test-case writer who knows the internal details of the program to be tested. In our case study, this helped the verification engineer to avoid related pitfalls.
- *Usefulness of a semi-formal representation of properties.* Introducing a semi-formal representation of properties appears to be helpful, when the final formulas cannot be directly stated because the process model is not (yet) available to the verification engineer. In addition, the semi-formal representation was useful for the informal inspection, since not the whole team had to be familiar with the actual modeling language.
- *Finding violations in the course of formalization.* While usually the emphasis is on finding violations through a model checker tool, already in the course of formalizing properties, certain violations can be revealed. In our case study, even three out of five violations were found in the course of trying to translate the semi-formal representation of properties to formulas fitting the FSM of the process model.
- *Mismatch of the level of abstraction of the business process model and properties to be checked.* Especially when the model and the properties are formalized separately, a mismatch of their respective levels of abstraction may occur. In our case study, several statements in the official guideline that the given process diagram was verified against were much more detailed than this diagram with its abstractions. Analyzing such cases helped to determine missing tasks in the process model.
- *Formalizing time.* It may come as a surprise first that in spite of the use of temporal logics certain aspects of 'time' were not formally represented and, therefore, not verified by the model checker tool. One issue in this regard is, again, the level of abstraction to be used for consistent formalization of the process and its properties, another the expressiveness of the given formalisms.
- *Ambiguity of legal text.* It does not come as a surprise, however, that natural language is, in principle, ambiguous. Strictly speaking, we had to deal with a kind of legal text in our case study, which is supposed to be less ambiguous. We believe that we made a reasonable formalization of the text "the search committee may extend the deadline for one month", as given in Table 1 in dark-gray, as discussed in relation to a property violation found by the checker tool. The text is, however, "otherwise the search committee may" ("andernfalls kann die Berufungskommission" in the original German text), which could even deserve a legal interpretation by an educated expert in the given context.

While some of these lessons learned have most likely been observed before and in other areas, we think that especially finding violations already in the course of formalization, as well as mismatch of the level of abstraction of the business process model and properties to be checked are new. Some of our lessons learned may even be more generally relevant for other formalization efforts, e.g., usefulness of a semi-formal representation. In fact, it was also observed in the context of requirements engineering [14].

5   Threats to Validity

Of course, there are threats to the validity, both external and internal. Regarding threats to the external validity, having performed just a single case study yet is obviously relevant. In addition, this was a relatively small case study. However, the third author is well informed about the spectrum of business processes subject to the official Quality Audit, and we can state that the chosen one is highly representative. So, for gaining first insights into issues and benefits of applying model checking to the verification of such high-level business process, this case study seems to have been appropriate, especially with regard to the formalization challenge. Still, more cases studies along these lines will be required, also in industry, to substantiate the results.

Regarding threats to the internal validity, let us consider the fact that the verification engineer (the first author) comes from the field of hardware design and verification. The work in this case study may have been easier to tackle with more background on business processes and their modeling. However, our experience shows that especially the core task of formalization was possible to be done well even without. The most important background was the know-how for model checking and its tool support as well as the prior experience with behavioral and temporal modeling, even gained in a completely different domain. In addition, a case study with inductively generalized lessons learned is clearly a weak method for gaining trustable results. However, it is a recognized method for empirical studies and for gaining experience, and we applied it according to the usual way of doing a case study according to the current state of the art. Still, for getting more reliable results for specific hypotheses (to be formulated based on our lessons learned), reproducible experiments will be necessary.

6   Conclusion

In this paper, we investigate formalizing as required for formal model checking. We present a case study of formalizing an excerpt of a high-level business process of our university and of properties derived from a guideline derived from an Austrian law. A fundamental issue involved was formalizing properties consistently with a process model (yet) unknown to the verification engineer. This has been addressed and solved by using a semi-formal intermediary specification. In this case study, problems in the process model were found already while formalizing, and later by the model checker tool. Overall, several problems were revealed by this approach to model checking that were uncovered in the official review.

In this course, we investigated a new verification option for business process owners whose processes and associated properties are given informally. There is quite some effort involved in such a formalization task, and a case study like ours helps to get an idea of the amount. It just depends on the criticality of the business process, whether the results are worth this effort. The process of our case study is one of those most critical for a university, and none of the problems found by our formalization effort and by the model checker has been found in a review by all members of the university, in principle. So, it is up to the people responsible for a given business process to judge whether this effort may pay off. Our case study shows the feasibility of such an approach and provides data on this trade-off.

Based on all that, we conclude that consistently formalizing is key for successful formal and automated verification of business processes. This has not been addressed yet in the literature. Still, much is left for future work, such as systematically extracting data objects and their life cycles from process models and additional sources, and machine support for incremental formalization (possibly building on [15,16]).

Acknowledgment. Part of this research has been carried out in the ProREUSE project (No. 834167), funded by the Austrian FFG.

References

1. Baier, C., Katoen, J.P.: Principles of Model Checking. MIT Press, Cambridge (2008)
2. SPIN: SPIN Verifying Multi-threaded Software with Spin. http://spinroot.com/spin/whatispin.html. Accessed, 01 December 2014
3. NuSMV: NuSMV: a new symbolic model checker. http://nusmv.fbk.eu/. Accessed 01 December 2014
4. Wynn, M., Verbeek, H., van der Aalst, W., ter Hofstede, A., Edmond, D.: Business process verification - finally a reality!. Bus. Process Manage. J. **15**(1), 74–92 (2009)
5. Sbai, Z., Missaoui, A., Barkaoui, K., Ben Ayed, R.: On the verification of business processes by model checking techniques. In: 2010 2nd International Conference on Software Technology and Engineering (ICSTE), vol. 1, V1–97–V1-103, October 2010
6. Kherbouche, O., Ahmad, A., Basson, H.: Using model checking to control the structural errors in bpmn models. In: 2013 IEEE Seventh International Conference on Research Challenges in Information Science (RCIS), pp. 1–12, May 2013
7. Fisteus, J.A., Fernández, L.S., Kloos, C.D.: Applying model checking to BPEL4WS business collaborations. In: Proceedings of the 2005 ACM Symposium on Applied Computing, SAC 2005, pp. 826–830. ACM, New York (2005)
8. Armando, A., Ponta, S.E.: Model checking of security-sensitive business processes. In: Degano, P., Guttman, J.D. (eds.) FAST 2009. LNCS, vol. 5983, pp. 66–80. Springer, Heidelberg (2010)

9. Armando, A., Ponta, S.E.: Model checking authorization requirements in business processes. Comput. Secur. **40**, 1–22 (2014)
10. Barros, C., Song, M.: Automatized checking of business rules for activity execution sequence in workflows. J. Softw. **7**(2), 374–381 (2012)
11. Mrasek, R., Mülle, J., Böhm, K., Becker, M., Allmann, C.: User-friendly property specification and process verification – a case study with vehicle-commissioning processes. In: Sadiq, S., Soffer, P., Völzer, H. (eds.) BPM 2014. LNCS, vol. 8659, pp. 301–316. Springer, Heidelberg (2014)
12. Becker, J., Delfmann, P., Eggert, M., Schwittay, S.: Generalizability and applicability of model-based business process compliance-checking approaches - a state-of-the-art analysis and research roadmap. BuR - Bus. Res. **5**(2), 221–247 (2012)
13. Rathmair, M., Schupfer, F., Krieg, C.: Applied formal methods for hardware Trojan detection. In: 2014 IEEE International Symposium on Circuits and Systems (ISCAS), pp. 169–172, June 2014
14. Kaindl, H.: Using hypertext for semiformal representation in requirements engineering practice. New Rev. Hypermedia Multimedia **2**, 149–173 (1996)
15. Kaindl, H.: How to identify binary relations for domain models. In: Proceedings of the Eighteenth International Conference on Software Engineering (ICSE-18), pp. 28–36. IEEE, Berlin, March 1996
16. Kaindl, H., Kramer, S., Diallo, P.S.N.: Semiautomatic generation of glossary links: a practical solution. In: Proceedings of the Tenth ACM Conference on Hypertext and Hypermedia (Hypertext 1999), pp. 3–12. Darmstadt, Germany, February 1999

Dealing with Risks and Workarounds: A Guiding Framework

João Barata[1,2,3(✉)], Paulo Rupino da Cunha[3], and Luís Abrantes[4]

[1] CTCV, Technological Center for Ceramics and Glass,
iParque – L7, 3040-540 Antanhol, Portugal
barata@dei.uc.pt
[2] ISMT, Miguel Torga Institute,
L. Cruz de Celas 1, 3000-132 Coimbra, Portugal
[3] CISUC, Department of Informatics Engineering, University of Coimbra,
Pólo II, 3030-290 Coimbra, Portugal
rupino@dei.uc.pt
[4] MIC, Mecânica Industrial de Coimbra, R. J. Adelino da Silva 73,
3045-479 Taveiro, Portugal
qualidade@mic.com.pt

Abstract. We present rISk-arounD, an enterprise-wide framework for modeling risks and workarounds in conformity with ISO 9001. The mode of inquiry is the canonical action research (CAR), conducted in a metalworking company. Our contribution suggests that (1) risks and workarounds should be jointly considered to model uncertainty in organizations, (2) participative enterprise modeling can assist process improvement and regulatory compliance, and (3) it is also necessary to address informal "shadow" practices in enterprise models. Moreover, we discuss how to adopt CAR to promote a culture of participative enterprise modeling. This framework can help organizations in their transition to the new 2015 version of ISO 9001, which endorses process oriented approaches and risk-based thinking as top priorities.

Keywords: Information systems · Participative enterprise modeling · Risks · Workarounds · rISk-arounD · ISO 9001:2015

1 Introduction

"Only those who will risk going too far can possibly find out how far one can go" (T. S. Eliot, *Preface to Transit of Venus: Poems by Harry Crosby*, 1931). In organizational practice, people can be tempted to work around the official procedures basing their decision on a risk-benefit analysis [1, 2]. When it happens, a breach occurs between the "formal" modeled system and the reality, which may hoist other, unforeseen risks. Therefore, managing uncertainty is a major concern of organizations and we argue that it can be addressed with participative enterprise modeling [3].

© IFIP International Federation for Information Processing 2015
J. Ralyté et al. (Eds.): PoEM 2015, LNBIP 235, pp. 141–155, 2015.
DOI: 10.1007/978-3-319-25897-3_10

ISO 9001 is a worldwide standard to implement a quality management system [4]. Its revised version is expected to be published by the end of 2015 and one of its major changes is the inclusion of risk-based thinking [5]. ISO 9001 suggests a process approach and documented information to ensure process visibility, problem prevention, and system auditability [4]. The lack of adherence between the designed processes and the run-time processes is a frequent cause of nonconformity in quality audits, requiring measures to guarantee compliance by reducing process friction [6]. Risk-based thinking involves antic-ipation of undesired events that affect reality and its models of expected behavior [7], ulti-mately raising improvement opportunities [8].

The importance of risk management is growing and there are several reasons to explain the fact, for example (1) regulatory pressure; (2) customer requirements; (3) public image; and (4) management attitudes, that are becoming more profes-sional to integrate risks in their strategies and operations. Moreover, risk is a key topic in the research agenda of information systems (IS), business process manage-ment (BPM), and enterprise modeling [8–10]. Risks are entangled in BPM [9], however, *"there is still a lack of research which investigates the management of risks during process execution, the exploitation of post-execution data for the purpose of risk analysis and the enablement of an integrated formal reasoning of risks in process models"* [10].

Workarounds are alternative procedures to the official process, which can result from a mismatch between people expectations and actual practice [11], receiving increased attention in IS [1, 2, 12]. According to [2], organizational employees utilize workarounds in business processes according to a risk-benefit analysis, being perceived as process improvements if the efficiency gains outweigh the exposure resulting from process violation. A recent study presented by [12] addresses the informal, unexpected, and undesired workarounds that the users of a multinational company had put in place. The authors suggest that canonical action research (CAR) is an appropriate approach to deal with the problem [12].

The literature about risks and workarounds is vast [8] and the two concepts are interrelated [2], however, they are typically studied independently [1, 8]. There is a lack of models built specifically for small and medium enterprises (SMEs), which often adopt rudimentary risk management practices and lack a risk-aware culture [13–15]. More-over, there is a shortcoming of practical cases and insufficient research in run-time risk management [10], which can be affected by changes that process participants decide to perform to the formal process model. These open issues led us to set the goal of devel-oping a guiding framework to deal with risks and workarounds [4, 5], fostering risk-based thinking in the scope of ISO 9001.

We organized the remainder of the paper as follows. Section 2 presents the literature review. Next, we present the research approach, that is the canonical action research [16]. Section 4 details our CAR cycle in a metalworking SME. In Sect. 5, we discuss the results according to the principles suggested by [17] to ensure rigor and relevance in CAR. Finally, we present the conclusions, the study limitations, and the opportunities for future research.

2   Literature Review

2.1   Risks and Workarounds

A definition for risk includes (1) a probability that the actual outcome of an event will differ from the expected outcome and (2) the impact associated with that outcome [18]. Kaplan [19] suggests a three-level hierarchy of risks. Level 3 is the most detailed and consists of the operational and compliance risks [20] that emerge from business processes (e.g., information security and privacy, regulatory issues). According to [19], level 3 risks are more predictable and related to standard operation procedures. Level 2 includes strategy risks; for example, environmental, customer relations, human resources, and IT related risks [19]. At level 1 are the global enterprise risks that may occur due to most improbable events, usually called *"black swan"*, which reveal the most adverse consequences for the firm's survival [19]. They should also be tackled by managers, for example with scenario planning and meetings [19]. Alternatively, the risk model proposed by [21] separates the IS, recognizing (level 1) the organization; (level 2) the mission and business processes; and (level 3) the IS. Although the literature offers contributions for process oriented risk models [9, 13, 22], an enterprise-wide risk framework must consider distinct layers, for example the strategic and the cultural [19], at all levels of the organization [13]. Consideration for compliance risks and operational risks should be integrated during the design-time and at run-time of business processes [20]. Dealing with both types of risks involves the definition of objectives, business rules, and internal controls [19]. What if the process is not followed as designed?

Workarounds can be seen as a change or deviation from an existing (formal) work system to overcome the problems that are preventing the achievement of the desired goals [1]. In IS, workarounds may take place as a discrepancy between the information technologies (IT) expectations and the actual practices [11], resulting in the creation of alternative ones and *"shadow applications"* [23] by the users. On the one hand, workarounds may be used to solve misfits, deficiencies, or identifying opportunities to improve the IS [12]. On the other hand, workarounds may create difficulties for IS adoption, leading to redundancies in data and applications [23], potential nonconformity with policies, inefficiencies or hazards [1], becoming a source of emergent risks or an amplification of the initial risks. The IS may even be seen as *"'scapegoats', as managers can blame the IS for not preventing workarounds"* [24].

The studies presented by [1, 25] identify workarounds that are sporadic and disappear, while others can persist over time and become the standardized formal practice. In the latter case, people consider the alternative practice more appropriate for their needs, learn with the experience, and produce a change. The breach between formal practices supported by IT and real practices may increase, requiring a timely identification of these cases and the redesign of the IS. According to [26], workarounds should not be confused with errors and mistakes. In fact, workarounds depend on the organizational culture [27] and in the existence of open discussions that are able to exploit their potential for process improvement [26]. Although some models point to the need of identifying process configurations that minimize risks [9], they do not consider the full potential of workarounds for risk identification.

2.2   Risks and Workarounds in Enterprise Modeling

Enterprise modeling is "*an activity where an integrated and negotiated model describing different aspects of the enterprise is created*" [28], comprising sub-models that can focus on different dimensions, for example, people, processes, and IT. The objective of enterprise modeling is to develop a business or to ensure its quality [28], for example, for strategy development, business process (re-)redesign, procedure communication, and IS requirements identification, ensuring that the model fits reality [3]. Enterprise models deal with two types of uncertainty: "*One uncertainty is in the values of key parameters, which are uncertain because of a lack of knowledge and a natural variability. The second uncertainty is in the structure of the model itself. Model uncertainty relates to whether the structure of the model fundamentally represents the system or decision of interest*" [29].

Information systems include different interrelated dimensions, namely the context, people, process, IT, and information/data [30, 31]. Therefore, IS modeling is a complex endeavor that tries to simplify various aspects of reality, integrating social and technical aspects [32]. Risks and workarounds are two important parts of the organizational practice that affect the IS. As we recognize the important contributions that addressed each of these parts separately [1, 2, 8, 9, 12], we argue for the opportunity to achieve synergies in their combination.

Risk modeling has been studied in the context of SMEs, for example by [33] for ERP implementation. According to [33], risks must be modeled according to the different lifecycle phases of the project. Other authors studied risk management in the lifecycle of BPM from design to post-execution; for example [10], arguing that "*most approaches [for design-time phase] do not provide principles or guidance to support risk-informed business process models*" [10]. A model of IS risk was proposed by [8], considering the facets: (1) goals and expectations; (2) risk factors and other sources of uncertainty; (3) the operation of the work system whose risks are being managed; (4) the risk management (contingency management) effort; (5) the possible outcomes and their probabilities; (6) the impacts on other systems; and (7) the resulting financial gains or losses. In [34] a framework is presented for analyzing incident management systems, providing guidance for IS risk assessment factors in critical systems.

Workaround modeling has been addressed, for example, by [35], who compared the formal processes and the workarounds, including the dimensions of (1) motivation; (2) constraints; and (3) consequences. The Workaround Process Model and Notation (WPMN) is a solution proposed by [2] to combine workarounds in business process models. The model contains different constructs for the representation of workarounds, context analysis (risk-benefit, situational factors, business rules), and the workaround impact. WPMN has potential synergies with compliance and risk model proposals, for example [9, 22]. Nevertheless, we could not find in the literature an enterprise-wide framework with the purpose of integrating risks and workarounds, not restricted to the process level, addressing the different lifecycle phases of risk-based thinking.

Processes are only one of the dimensions of the IS and there is a need to consider a strategic dimension in risk approaches [19], as presented by [36] in the scope of IT risks. Moreover, there are problems in current business process models in what regards capturing all the information that is required to audit risks [37]. Similarly, dealing with workarounds requires understanding people motivation, risk analysis, the consequences for other process activities, and the context involved [2]. We acknowledge the integration of risks and workarounds in the work presented by [2], however, the authors do not address risks that emerge from the informal workflows. To overcome these difficulties, the study conducted by [12] selected activity theory as the focal theory for their research, characterized as a cross-disciplinary framework for analyzing forms of human practice.

3   Research Approach

We considered Action Research [16] and Design Science Research [38] as two suitable approaches, because both allow the design of a new artifact or solution and to test it in practice. Action research is an approach that simultaneously aims at improving a problematic situation in the target organization and contribute to the body of scientific knowledge [16, 17]. Since our work aimed at solving concrete organizational issues in a client setting [16], we considered that it was more aligned with the dual goal of action research.

There are multiple forms of action research [39], usually represented in a cyclic combination of phases. We followed one of the most used and well documented forms that is the canonical action research (CAR), characterized by five phases of *Diagnosing, Action planning, Action taking, Evaluating, and Specifying learning* [16].

Rigorous action research is seen as one of the solutions to improve the relevance of IS, by solving real world problems [40]. To ensure rigor and validity, there are five principles that we must consider in CAR [17]: *Principle of the Researcher–Client Agreement; Principle of the Cyclical Process Model; Principle of Theory; Principle of Change through Action*; and *Principle of Learning through Reflection*. The next section describes the findings of our CAR cycle. Afterwards, we discuss those results according to each of the five principles above, adopting the structure selected by [12] for the discussion of their CAR project.

4   Framework Development

"Thinking is easy, acting is difficult, and to put one's thoughts into action is the most difficult thing in the world" (Johann Wolfgang Von Goethe).

4.1   Client-system Infrastructure

Our client is a small metalworking company founded in 1947. Its activity is conducted in the fields of mechanical engineering and industrial maintenance. Its market is mostly local, with the majority of their customers within a 100 km range. Quality is a priority to the company. ISO 9001 [4] certification is seen as a competitive advantage that distinguishes them from low cost players in the sector. Moreover, they have demanding customers regarding compliance to environmental and safety risks. The lack of resources that characterize SMEs [15] is a reality in our setting. However, the adoption of an enterprise-wide risk modeling is not an option; it is vital for the conformity to standards [5] and for the company survival.

4.2 Diagnosing the Setting

The CAR diagnosis started with semi-structured interviews [41] involving the top manager, the chief financial officer, and the quality manager. We also used data gathering techniques of document collection and observation [41] to understand the organizational processes and the current risk management practices.

According to the quality manager "*a customized industrial IS is critical for our company's future and to comply with our audits*". The top manager considered that flexibility and informality were competitive advantages; nevertheless, they also bear a higher possibility of nonconformity with the strategy and with formal practices. There were other concerns, namely (1) the lack of human resources, requiring that any methodologies be lightweight; (2) the need to redesign business processes and the underlying IT; and (3) the barriers for change that were constantly raised by the older staff. The company managers had no experience with enterprise modeling methods and tools. Their processes were designed and described in semi-structured word processor documents, which is usual in ISO 9001 certified SMEs.

We also conducted a literature review during this Diagnosing stage. Each publication was coded using the Mendeley free reference management tool and discussed with the company managers. It was during the discussion and the comparison with practice that workarounds emerged. One of the company's problems were the misalignments between: (1) formal processes (quality procedures) and actual practice; (2) IT and process support (high volume of paper and disconnected support spreadsheets); (3) market demands and staff competences (most of them were in the company since its foundation and have low IT competences and a high resistance to change); (4) regulations and business processes; and (5) insufficient information quality for decision-making needs. According to the company managers, frequent workarounds multiplied the risks and potential nonconformity in quality audits.

Our comprehensive joint diagnosis provided the foundations to our action plan, presented in the next section.

4.3 Planning our CAR Action

We prepared an overall action plan with two main objectives. First, it was necessary to identify the main dimensions to address in risks and workarounds (agreed by their stakeholders), and provide support for communication and learning in the organization [42]. Although workarounds have been studied regarding IT and business processes [1, 12, 43], it is possible to workaround other dimensions of an IS, including organizational hierarchies (people), company policies and regulations that shape its context, or required information/data of a given system. Our model should be multidimensional. Second, we had the purpose of assisting SMEs in the ISO 9001 transition to the new 2015 version. Therefore, ISO 9001 principles and suggested approaches, for example the PDCA [4], should be a part of our proposal. It was also our intention to make the framework and related models suitable for audits, because they are frequent in ISO 9001-based quality management systems. Our solution required artifacts and routines [30, 44] to assist practitioners in its adoption. Moreover, we wanted to apply participative enterprise modeling in our action, not merely to model systems but to design the underlying framework itself.

Our overall plan for this CAR cycle is inspired in the ISO_2 [45] approach, originally proposed for the joint development of IS and ISO 9001-based quality management systems. First, we conducted a literature review to create (1) a frame of reference about the problem domain. Then, we (2) diagnosed organizational practice to identify the company policies, initial risks, and potential workarounds. Next, we (3) defined the framework vision, followed by (4) its main components and the dynamic of the model for the purpose of creating change. The sequent step involved the (5) sourcing of tools such as risk matrices, process models and related procedures, and IT adaptations. Afterwards, it was time for (6) adoption in practice to respond to risks and workarounds. Finally, we (7) studied the changes that occurred with the introduction of the new framework and opportunities for future work.

The organization did not intend to buy an IT modeling platform and the mere description of risks would be a disappointment for the managers expectation. Our plan was to foster a culture of participative enterprise modeling [3, 27] in the organization, as a basis for risk-based thinking required by ISO 9001:2015 revision.

4.4 Action Taking: Proposing and Testing the rISk-arounD Framework

Figure 1 presents the framework that we built to deal with risks and workarounds. We named it the rISk-arounD framework.

The enclosing dashed line represents the dynamic of risk-based thinking in ISO 9001. Based on the sources of uncertainty (e.g., events, variability, mishaps) and certainty (e.g., quality principles, strategy, formal process maps) that are represented on the left of the model, the organization must identify the risks at three distinct levels (on the top of the figure), evaluate their local and broader impacts, including risks and opportunities to change (on the right), and respond with the focus on improvement (on the bottom). The internal part represents the aspects that must be addressed for dealing with risks and workarounds in IS [2, 6]. A workaround can be based in a risk-benefit evaluation [2] emerging from an existing friction in the business process [6]. Modeling must address five interrelated dimensions of (1) Context, (2) People, (3) Process, (4) IT, and (5) Information/data [30]. The dark circles specify the main literature references for each component of the framework. Table 1 presents practical examples of certainty/uncertainty models that can be used for each dimension.

Table 1 presents examples of models for the "formal" organization in the second column. Conversely, the rightmost column presents models of uncertainty (by risks/workarounds) that may influence the organizational goals. The examples were created, during our CAR cycle, in different formats including matrices (for black swan and risks affecting quality principles), organizational charts (e.g., alternative circuits of the official organigram), and process maps.

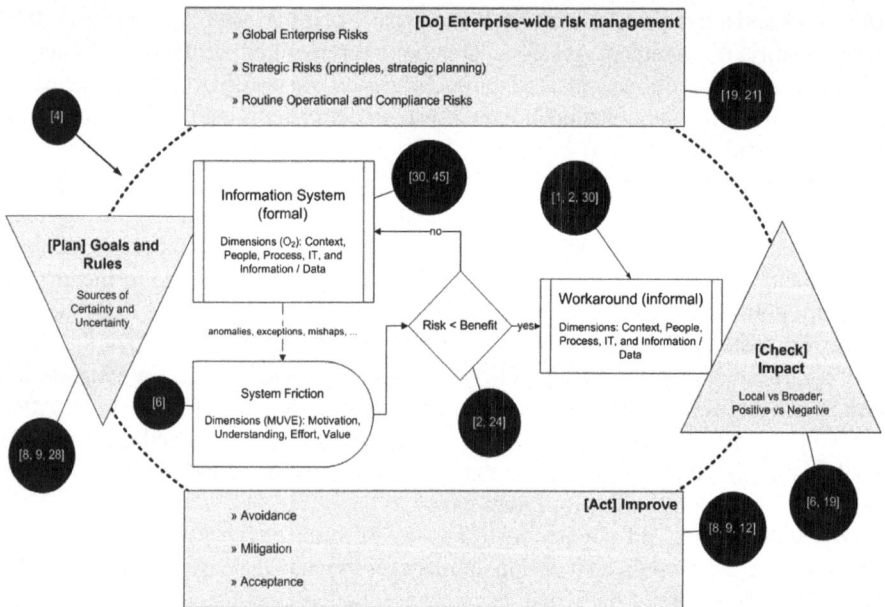

Fig. 1. The rISk-arounD Framework

Table 1. Examples of certainty/uncertainty models for each dimension.

Dimension	Models for certainty	Models for uncertainty
Context	The principles that the organization states in its quality policy;	"Black swan" list;
People	The company organigram; Functions;	Informal power structures; Informal leaders; Individual goals;
Process	Process models representing activities, roles, business rules,…;	Workarounds to improve efficiency; Misfit between "static" process maps and the dynamic of real practice;
IT	The "official" IT portfolio, for example, an ERP;	The "unofficial" applications sourced by process users (e.g., parallel spreadsheets);
Information/ Data	The organizational databases; Statutory reports.	Information/data quality issues; Omitted information/data.

Figure 2 exemplifies an operational and compliance model. It is an extract of the organizational process map for the provisioning and metal component maintenance of our organization.

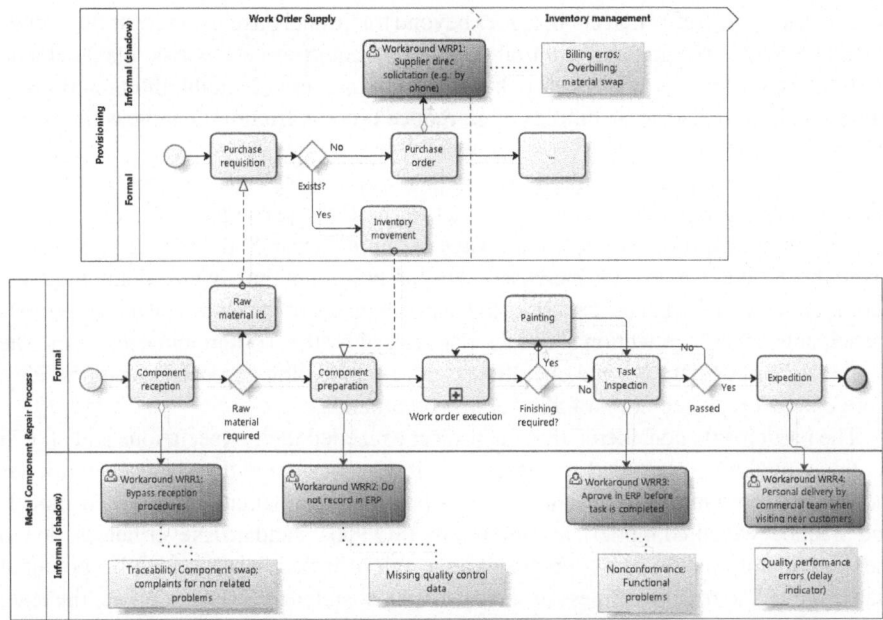

Fig. 2. Modeling workaround risks at process level

Each process in the figure has two lanes as suggested by [2], to specify the formal process according to ISO 9001 requirements and the informal aspects, which represent the potential workarounds and its associated risks.

The risks identified at process level were included in a main risk list and each one evaluated from 1 to 5 as proposed by [19]. Finally, actions were defined to accept (e.g., check insurance for "black swans"; change process to adopt the workaround), mitigate (e.g., minimize risk/workaround probability), or avoid the risk/workaround. For the example in Fig. 2, (1) the product expedition now requires a quality report that is shipped with the product, after production manager's validation and (2) the task inspection (on the right) becomes integrated in the IT platform used to record timesheets. In some cases, actions were aimed at eradicating workarounds (e.g., required fields in the IT platform), in other cases, the organization accepted them but acted to mitigate the risks (e.g., double checking quality control procedure).

4.5 Evaluating

The purpose of this CAR step is to evaluate the consequences of action taking in the organizational setting [16], and comparing them to project objectives and expectations. It was a joint evaluation conducted by researchers and practitioners.

The new models that were developed addressing distinct levels of uncertainty [19, 30] were considered by the client organization as an advance when compared to the previous practice of identifying risks based on the ISO 9001 (official) process maps. First, it was simpler to communicate risk-based thinking for the ISO 9001:2015 transition. The framework suggests that risks and workarounds are dynamic and require a continuous (cyclic) effort. Second, it goes beyond traditional business process flowcharts (1) addressing strategic and cultural aspects of enterprise-wide risk management, (2) framing informal processes in risk-based thinking, and (3) highlighting actions to address risks and also opportunities (e.g., reduce process friction to address the work-around practice).

Similarly to risks, it is required to anticipate workarounds and their possible consequences. Interestingly, it was an enjoyment to the CAR participants when they were asked to think, express, and deal with ways of "going around" the formal system. We found three main benefits: (1) increased transparency about the organizational practice; (2) anticipation of formal process risks that can trigger a workaround decision by process participants; and (3) reflection about the risks raised by the workaround execution. The combination of declarative and operational process modeling approaches can provide a more efficient representation of allowable workarounds.

The participants considered that the project exceeded their expectations and should continue involving other workers. Moreover, it was considered that the framework has the potential to contribute for adherence of process documentation (expected model) and practice (executed model), as required by ISO 9001 standard. Nevertheless, due to the participatory nature of the proposed approach, it is necessary to identify potential bias and treats to trustworthiness of the participants' statements. For example, the team structure, the sense of hierarchy, and individual goals can influence the participants' evaluation of risks and workarounds.

5   Discussion

Recalling the five principles suggested by [17] to frame our discussion:

- Principle of the Researcher–Client Agreement. The client and the researchers agreed that CAR was an appropriated approach to create a new framework and address the organizational problem of risks and workarounds. The steps of CAR were explained to the company managers, ensuring that they followed them appropriately [16, 17], independently of the physical presence of the researchers in the setting. We established weekly goals to simplify team coordination, for example: "identify how model A can be integrated with model B"; "identify potential workarounds for process C". Finally, the organization approved a scientific publication of our results.

- Principle of the Cyclical Process Model. Based on the time constraints of our project, we considered that one CAR cycle was appropriate to propose and test the enterprise-wide framework. We also agreed that it was interesting to conduct a second cycle including process participants. Although we concluded that the guiding framework would be suitable for that second cycle, new challenges emerge to: (1) promote the open debate about workarounds that occur in the organization (and managers may not be aware of); (2) train process participants about rISk-arounD; (3) make them aware of the potential risks of workarounds; (4) allow them to suggest process improvements that may avoid, mitigate, or accept risks/workarounds; and (5) foster a culture of participative enterprise modeling in the entire organization.

- Principle of Theory. Theory has an important role in CAR to guide the research and to allow discussion of the findings [46]. The creation of a theoretical frame of reference allowed us to promote a shared understanding about CAR and the recommendations for participative enterprise modeling. Moreover, it provided us the starting point to integrate and improve existing models that were independently built for risks and workarounds. It was an opportunity to compare the gaps between models and practices, according to the managers' perspective and literature guidance.

Several studies adopted action research for enterprise modeling, providing contributions to understand the modeling process and the use of specific methods, for example [47]. However, few studies addressed the role of theory in CAR for the creation of high-level frameworks with the participation of organizational users. We advocate that theory can have a central role in participative enterprise modeling for:

- *Diagnosing*. We provided a selection of articles about the problem domain to organizational managers, facilitating their active participation from early stages of the project. Interesting debates emerged when managers compared the papers' conclusions with their own experience.
- *Action planning*. The understanding of the problem from a theoretical viewpoint facilitated our plan. Practitioners understood the requirements of the approach and the need of a gradual approach to the problem. Moreover, they realized the difficulty to achieve immediate results in risk-based thinking because we could not find a framework that included all the components required for our models.
- *Action taking*. Theory guided our actions in practice. We must be aware that researchers are not always present in the research setting, therefore, it is important to empower all the practitioners with the theoretical foundations to conduct (and document) action appropriately, reflecting about the theory and daily practice.
- *Evaluating*. The outcomes of this research were constantly evaluated by researchers and practitioners according to the lens of the literature review previously conducted.
- *Specifying learning*: Sharing a guiding framework among enterprise modeling participants is an opportunity to (1) promote organizational learning (e.g., *"now I understand why model A has the component B"*; *"now I see why our risk list was scarce and ineffective for process Z: the majority of risks were hidden in multiple workarounds"*) and (2) compare the advances with current practice. The opinion that managers had about scientific projects significantly improved after CAR, according to them, due to the possibility to combine their immediate interest with scientific advances.
- Principle of Change through Action

Action taking addressed risks and workarounds in the processes of the organization. Therefore, we improved the organization readiness for ISO 9001:2015. The major changes occurred in the organizational risk plans, in process maps, and in IT improvement. The new risks that emerged from the models evaluation resulted in changes to the production and commercial modules of the company's IT systems. Additional controls were included in IT and a new mobile app was developed to assist the component repair process illustrated in Figure 2.

- Principle of Learning through Reflection. The framework is a result of joint reflection by researchers and practitioners. We learned about the benefits of participative enterprise modeling and deepened the analysis of our findings in the current discussion section.

We found advantages in a layered approach to address risks and workarounds, not strictly addressing business processes (level 3 in [19]; level 2 in [21]), usually evaluated at the operational level and according to its "formal" description of expected sequence. ISO 9001 involves cultural aspects [4, 27] aiming at a culture focused on customer satisfaction, improvement, and involvement of people in quality efforts. Enterprise-wide modeling must address informal business processes and the overall principles of the organization to capture the complexity of routines [44].

Dealing with risks and workarounds is a continuous effort, not limited to a single modeling project. Moreover, there are social aspects that advise a gradual implementation of the framework in daily practice. An open discussion about workarounds and risks is not straightforward: we are also dealing with compliance issues when we acknowledge that reality does not follow the legal or standard procedure. A possible behavior would be to deny workarounds and assume that organizations always *act* according to what they *think*, trusting that they are always capable of doing *the most difficult thing in the world*. We argue that workarounds are natural elements in the *"ways of working"* [27] of organizations and the rISk-arounD framework can contribute to finding improvement opportunities at different levels: global; organizational; operational and compliance. A culture of participative enterprise modeling can contribute to the progress of risk-based thinking.

6   Conclusions

We presented the development of an enterprise-wide framework to deal with risks and workarounds, capturing formal and (informal) "shadow" practices. The setting was an ISO 9001-certified metalworking SME that is preparing the transition for the new ISO 9001:2015 version. We discussed a scenario that aimed at (1) fostering a culture of participative enterprise modeling [3]; (2) with the creation of a guiding framework for risk-based thinking (and acting); (3) adopting it in practice with simple models. We used canonical action research that has synergies with participative enterprise modeling. It is necessary to consider five interrelated dimensions in an enterprise-wide risk framework, namely context, people, process, IT, and information/data. We confirmed the benefits of integrating workarounds in risk-based thinking to overcome the limitation of formal defined processes, which can bias the analysis of potential risks to the "visible" parts of the models.

To our knowledge, rISk-arounD is the first guiding framework in the scope of ISO 9001:2015 (planned to be released in late 2015) that integrates risks and workarounds. However, there are limitations to take into consideration. First, the framework is inspired in specific references, other models could be used. Second, we propose a high-level representation that was considered suitable for this SME, but the scenario may differ in organizations with increased modeling maturity. Nevertheless, our results can provide guidance in the initial steps of risk modeling. Third, the artifacts were built with simple tools, accessible to all the project participants, however, the representation and visualization of models that result from the framework can be improved with IT support. Forth, the project team only included managers but other process participants can participate. Fifth, the positive results in this socio-technical setting must be cautiously evaluated due to the potential risk of the Hawthorn effect, suggesting that the observed participants behavior could be *"related only to the special social situation and social treatment they received"* [48].

Future work can involve distinct sectors and more complex scenarios, for example in the highly regulated food industry, for which we already have planned interventions. It would be important to extend our study with additional standards, for example the ISO 31000. The rISk-arounD framework can be adopted to improve modeling methods and languages or to develop new models to deal with uncertainty. Although the rISk-arounD can provide methodical guidance on the steps and sources to integrated modeling of risks and workarounds, the development of new artifacts to assist organizational practice can improve the transferability of our results. A second CAR cycle will address these open issues and involve process participants in the reflection about their potential workarounds, risks, and consequences.

Acknowledgements. The authors thank the three reviewers for their comments and ideas to improve the paper. This work has been partially funded by European Regional Development Fund (ERDF), within the National Strategic Reference Framework (NSRF) – Mais Centro.

References

1. Alter, S.: Theory of workarounds. Commun. Assoc. Inf. Syst. **34**, 1041–1066 (2014)
2. Röder, N., Wiesche, M., Schermann, M., Krcmar, H.: Workaround aware business process modeling. In: Proceedings of International Conference on Wirtschaftsinformatik, pp. 482–496 (2015)
3. Stirna, J., Persson, A., Sandkuhl, K.: Participative enterprise modeling: experiences and recommendations. In: Krogstie, J., Opdahl, A.L., Sindre, G. (eds.) CAiSE 2007 and WES 2007. LNCS, vol. 4495, pp. 546–560. Springer, Heidelberg (2007)
4. ISO: ISO 9001 Quality management system – requirements. International Organization for Standardization, Geneva (2008)
5. IAF: Transition planning guidance for ISO 9001:2015. ISO/TC 176/SC2. International Accreditation Forum (2015)
6. Antunes, A., Cunha, P.R., Barata, J.: MUVE IT: Reduce the Friction in Business Processes. Bus. Process Manag. J. **20**, 571–597 (2014)
7. Sadgrove, M.K.: The Complete Guide to Business Risk Management. Ashgate (2015)
8. Alter, S., Sherer, S.A.: A general, but readily adaptable model of information system risk. Commun. Assoc. Inf. Syst. **14**, 1–28 (2004)
9. Zur Mühlen, M., Rosemann, M.: Integrating Risks in Business Process Models. In: Proceedings of ACIS, pp. 62–72 (2005)
10. Suriadi, S., Weiß, B., Winkelmann, A., ter Hofstede, A.H.M., Adams, M., Conforti, R., Fidge, C., La Rosa, M., Ouyang, C., Pika, A., Rosemann, M., Wynn, M.: Current research in risk-aware business process management - overview, comparison, and gap analysis. Commun. Assoc. Inf. Syst. **34**, 933–984 (2014)

11. Ferneley, E.H., Sobreperez, P.: Resist, comply or workaround? an examination of different facets of user engagement with information systems. Eur. J. Inf. Syst. **15**, 345–356 (2006)
12. Malaurent, J., Avison, D.: Reconciling global and local needs: a canonical action research project to deal with workarounds. Inf. Syst. J. (2015). doi:10.1111/isj.12074
13. Popescu, M., Dascalu, A.: Considerations on integrating risk and quality management. Annals of "Dunarea de Jos" University of Galati, Fascicle I, pp. 49–54 (2011)
14. Aureli, S., Salvatori, F.: The current state of risk management in italian small and medium-sized enterprises. In: Proceedings of AMIS, pp. 15–36 (2013)
15. Islam, A., Tedford, D.: Risk determinants of small and medium-sized manufacturing enterprises (SMEs) - an exploratory study in New Zealand. J. Ind. Eng. Int. **8**, 12 (2012)
16. Susman, G.I., Evered, R.D.: An assessment of the scientific merits of action research. Adm. Sci. Q. **23**, 582–603 (1978)
17. Davison, R., Martinsons, M.G., Kock, N.: Principles of canonical action research. Inf. Syst. J. **14**, 65–86 (2004)
18. Holton, G.A., Knight, F.: Defining risk. Financ. Anal. J. **60**, 19–25 (2006)
19. Kaplan, R.S.: Risk management and the strategy execution system. Balanc. Scorec. Rep. **11**, 1–6 (2009)
20. Zoet, M., Welke, R., Versendaal, J., Ravesteyn, P.: Aligning risk management and compliance considerations with business process development. In: Di Noia, T., Buccafurri, F. (eds.) EC-Web 2009. LNCS, vol. 5692, pp. 157–168. Springer, Heidelberg (2009)
21. NIST, N.I. of S. and T.: NIST SP 800-37: Guide for Applying the Risk Management Framework to Federal Information Systems: a Security Life Cycle Approach (2010)
22. Sadiq, W., Governatori, G., Namiri, K.: Modeling control objectives for business process compliance. In: Alonso, G., Dadam, P., Rosemann, M. (eds.) BPM 2007. LNCS, vol. 4714, pp. 149–164. Springer, Heidelberg (2007)
23. Handel, M.J., Poltrock, S.: Working around official applications. In: Proceedings of CSCW (2011)
24. Röder, N., Schermann, M.: Why managers tolerate workarounds - the role of information systems. In: Proceedings of AMCIS (2014)
25. Zhou, X., Ackerman, M., Zheng, K.: CPOE workarounds, boundary objects, and assemblages. In: Proceedings of CHI (2011)
26. Halbesleben, J.R.B., Wakefield, D.S., Wakefield, B.J.: Work-arounds in health care settings: Literature review and research agenda. Health Care Manage. Rev. **33**, 2–12 (2008)
27. Gallear, D., Ghobadian, A.: An empirical investigation of the channels that facilitate a total quality culture. Total Qual. Manag. Bus. Excell. **15**, 1043–1067 (2004)
28. Persson, A., Stirna, J.: An explorative study into the influence of business goals on the practical use of enterprise modelling methods and tools. In: Proceedings of ISD, pp. 275–287. Springer, New York (2001)
29. Holmes, K.J., Graham, J.A., McKone, T., Whipple, C.: Regulatory models and the environment: practice, pitfalls, and prospects. Risk Anal. **29**, 159–170 (2009)
30. Barata, J., da Cunha, P.R.: Modeling the organizational regulatory space: a joint design approach. In: Grabis, J., Kirikova, M., Zdravkovic, J., Stirna, J. (eds.) PoEM 2013. LNBIP, vol. 165, pp. 206–220. Springer, Heidelberg (2013)
31. Barata, J., Cunha, P.R.: Five dimensions of information systems: a perspective from the IS and quality managers. In: Proceedings of EMCIS, Windsor, UK (2013)
32. Baxter, G., Sommerville, I.: Socio-technical systems: from design methods to systems engineering. Interact. Comput. **23**, 4–17 (2011)

33. Ojala, M., Vilpola, I., Kouri, I.: Risks and risk management in ERP Project-cases in SME Context. In: Proceedings of 9th International Conference on Business Information Systems (BIS 2006), pp. 179–186 (2006)
34. Kim, J.K., Sharman, R., Rao, H.R., Upadhyaya, S.: Framework for analyzing critical incident management systems (CIMS). In: Proceedings of HICSS (2006)
35. Nadhrah, N., Michell, V.: A normative method to analyse workarounds in a healthcare environment: motivations, consequences, and constraints. In: Proceedings of ICISO, pp. 195–205 (2013)
36. Strecker, S., Heise, D., Frank, U.: RiskM: A multi-perspective modeling method for IT risk assessment. Inf. Syst. Front. **13**, 595–611 (2010)
37. Carnaghan, C.: Business process modeling approaches in the context of process level audit risk assessment: an analysis and comparison. Int. J. Account. Inf. Syst. **7**, 170–204 (2006)
38. Hevner, A.R., March, S.T., Park, J.: Design science in information systems research. MIS Q. **28**, 75–105 (2004)
39. Baskerville, R., Wood-Harper, A.T.: Diversity in information systems action research methods. Eur. J. Inf. Syst. **7**, 90–107 (1998)
40. Vries, E.: Rigorously relevant action research in information systems. Sprouts Work. Pap. Inf. Syst. **7**, 1–24 (2007)
41. Myers, M.D., Newman, M.: The qualitative interview in IS research: examining the craft. Inf. Organ. **17**, 2–26 (2007)
42. Bernus, P.: Enterprise models for enterprise architecture and ISO9000:2000. Annu. Rev. Control. **27**, 211–220 (2003)
43. Yang, Z., Ng, B.Y., Kankanhalli, A., Luen Yip, J.W.: Workarounds in the use of IS in healthcare: a case study of an electronic medication administration system. Int. J. Hum. Comput. Stud. **70**, 43–65 (2012)
44. Pentland, B.T., Feldman, M.S.: Designing routines: on the folly of designing artifacts, while hoping for patterns of action. Inf. Organ. **18**, 235–250 (2008)
45. Barata, J., Cunha, P.R.: ISO2: A new breath for the joint development of IS and ISO 9001 management systems. In: Escalona, M., Aragón, G., Linger, H., Lang, M., Barry, C., Schneider, C. (eds.) Information Systems Development: Improving Enterprise Communication (Proceedings of ISD), pp. 499–510. Springer, Switzerland (2014)
46. Davison, R., Martinsons, M.G., Ou, C.X.J.: The roles of theory in canonical action research. MIS Q. **36**, 763–786 (2012)
47. Luebbe, A., Weske, M.: Investigating process elicitation workshops using action research. In: Proceedings of BPM 2011 International Workshops, LNBIP 99, pp. 345–356. Springer, Heidelberg (2012)
48. French, J.R.P.: Field experiments: changing group productivity. In: Miller, J.G. (ed.) Experiments in Social Process: A Symposium on Social Psychology, pp. 81–96. McGraw-Hill, New York (1950)

Aquiring User Information

Case-Based Development of Consumer Preferences Using Brand Personality and Values Co-creation

Eric-Oluf Svee[✉] and Jelena Zdravkovic

Department of Computer and Systems Sciences, Stockholm University,
Box 7003, 16407 Kista, Sweden
{eric-sve,jelenaz}@dsv.su.se

Abstract. Consumers have preferences whose determination is outside the realm of economic rules and values. To be successful in current market conditions, product and service companies need to capture such preferences to provide best-fit support by their Information Systems (IS), sometimes by developing entirely new features. In our previous work, we have conceptualized a meta-model for incorporating consumer preferences into the development of IS —Consumer Preference Meta-Model (CPMM). This artifact was developed with the ability to be expanded with new kinds of consumer preferences, as well as their related concepts. Building upon that work, in this study we consider methodological usage of CPMM for the case of Asker's Brand Personality as the primary value framework. The framework brings both the enterprise and the consumer into dialog, with this values co-creation fostering synchronicity between the information systems that are designed as an outgrowth of this process, and the desires of both the consumers and the businesses that they will support. The case example uses the Twitter feed of a major airline, whose tweets are processed using Aaker's 5-factors and Kano's quality framework. The results complete an instantiation of CPMM that generates a feature model reflective of both brand personality and values co-creation.

Keywords: Value · Consumer value · Consumer preferences · Brand personality · Values co-creation · Requirements engineering

1 Introduction

To sustain today's highly competitive market of software applications and services, it is becoming vital for software providers to deliver the functionalities and qualities fitting and delighting their consumers. Systems analysts therefore, need the means to capture real preferences of consumers and further relate them to requirements for software customized in different ways to fit anyone. Additionally, because of immense variety of consumers' preferences and the need for efficient system development reuse, they need to be formalized and classified.

In our previous work [27], we proposed eliciting requirements for lines of IS by using a Consumer Preference Meta-Model (CPMM) as a starting point. The central aspects of CPMM concern possible segmentation of users (i.e. consumers), as well as several known user value frameworks—such as Holbrook's [4] from the marketing

© IFIP International Federation for Information Processing 2015
J. Ralyté et al. (Eds.): PoEM 2015, LNBIP 235, pp. 159–173, 2015.
DOI: 10.1007/978-3-319-25897-3_11

discipline. Because the preferences may origin even from other disciplines, be contextual, individual or characteristic of a group, and each potentially influencing the selection of system's modes of work [9], CPMM was meant to be extendable to include other user value frameworks and thus solve the problem of capturing and classification of any consumers' preferences and their related attributes.

Following our previous work, the goal of this study was to further advance in the following directions: (a) to propose a method of using CPMM as a "living" classification of consumer preferences enabling system analysts to capture the preferences on a case basis - i.e. considering different value frameworks for the preference elicitation, a business domain of interest, sources of consumers, or instruments for measuring of importance of the preferences; and (b) to test the applicability of the method on a real-world example where the Brand Personality value framework [1] is integrated into CPMM for classifying the preferences of a crowd-source and bringing the enterprise and the consumer together through value co-creation [28], and further to derive the requirements for system components using feature models [27].

The paper is structured accordingly: Sect. 2 provides a background on Values of consumers (Sect. 2.1), the Consumer Preference Meta-Model (Sect. 2.2), Brand Personality (Sect. 2.3) and Values Co-creation (Sect. 2.4). Section 3 presents a method for integrating value frameworks to CPMM for obtaining a value classification, and Sect. 4 provides an example from the airline industry that illustrates that capability of CPMM to include new value frameworks, and to relate them further to system requirements. Section 5 concludes the work with a summary of the presented research as well as a preview to future work.

2 Background

2.1 Values

At the highest level, value is viewed as the relative status of a thing, or the esteem in which it is held, according to its real or supposed worth, usefulness, or importance.

One framework is Holbrook's Typology of Consumer Value [1]. According to Holbrook, a consumer value is "an interactive, relativistic preference experience"; interactive entails an interaction between some subject and an object, relativistic refers to consumer values being comparative, preferential refers to consumer values embodying the outcome of an evaluative judgment, and experience refers to consumer values not residing in the product/service acquired but in the consumption experience. Three consumer value dimensions are the basis for his typology: *Extrinsic/Intrinsic*, *Self-oriented/Other-oriented*, and *Active/Reactive*. The Typology is used in our research within Consumer Preference Meta-Model (Sect. 2.2, class *Consumer Value*) to stream value concepts from other value frameworks towards consumer preferences, to provide them a clear consumer value focus.

2.2 Consumer Preference Meta Model (CPMM)

Our conceptualization of consumer preferences [27] included three perspectives – business modeling, addressing the core concepts related to the exchange of a value object of interest, such as a system; consumer modeling, where peoples' preferences about the product line are modeled according to existing theories; and segment modeling, which is designed to enable profiling of the consumer.

Consumer is a role representing a group of people in the consideration for the evaluation of the *System*, based on individual preferences. Any of the value frameworks can be taken into consideration, and can categorize its values as a measure (*Qualitative* or *Quantitative*) that can be quantitative and/or qualitative; these are seen as driving consumers' desires to participate in the exchange process, i.e. as *Consumer Driver*, which should be satisfied through a consumption experience of the *System*. Additionally, different value frameworks could be used integrated to combine their values or measures, and for that the *Mapping* association class is used. A *Segment* encompasses the information characterizing a subclass of consumer, further distinguishing it from demographics and context of use properties. A *Segment* is used to refine the *Measure* to elicit a variety of subclasses of consumers. *Demographics* encompass consumer characteristics, such as age, ethnicity, education, and similar. *Context of Use* reflects an individual's context, such as the location and the time of the use a system, as well as other related concepts - objects, regulations and conditions.

CPMM was developed in [26] to include the main-established value frameworks from marketing – *Consumer Value* [4] and psychology disciplines – *Basic Value* and *Human Need* [10, 19]. In this study's proposal, we elaborate CPMM's ability to process additional ranges of perceived values of consumers, by considering the value framework Brand Personality (Sect. 2.3) as a new concept for Value Co-creation (Sect. 2.4).

2.3 Brand Personality

The intensity of emotional brand connections is seen as key determinant of consumer loyalty [14]. If it is possible to align the interests of both consumers and a business through this relationship, and then continue this coordination into the development of information systems it is hypothesized that the resulting systems will better support the needs of both parties.

There are several components to consumer brand identification, or the process through which a relationship between a consumer and a business is created. Brand personality as codified by Aaker, is defined as the set of human characteristics associated with a brand, and is based on a "5-factor" personality test [2]. When the brand personality fits well with consumer's self-concept, it provides them a sense of ease and plays a considerable role in self-expression [2, 21].

Its results are culturally based, making social context an important component. The case utilized by this work is based on Aaker's original work [1] and comes from North America. Officially known as Factor Analyses or Facets, the factors are: Sincerity (down-to-earth, honest, wholesome, cheerful); Excitement (daring, spirited, imaginative, up-to-date); Competence (reliable, intelligent, successful); Sophistication (upper class, charming); and Ruggedness (tough, outdoorsy).

2.4   Values Co-creation

Co-creation was originally defined in the late 1990s by Kambil as co-creation of value by a firm's customers [6] and later extended by Prahalad in the sense of firms creating value with customers to produce a unique customer experience [15]. The operating definition adopted in this work is the creation of value by consumers [28].

Co-creation is the participation of consumers along with producers in the creation of value in the marketplace. Activities of this kind go well beyond the notion of co-creation as conceived in services that are to an extent jointly actualized by their suppliers and the receiving customers. They also go beyond the current paradigm of mass customization, as it aims to satisfy the needs and wants of a specific individual cost-effectively.

In *autonomous* co-creation considered in this study, individuals or consumer communities produce marketable value in voluntary activities conducted independently of any established organization, although they may be using platforms provided by such organizations. Thus, consumers are no longer just passive value takers, but have emerged as value makers in both individual and collective actions.

3   Method for Classifying Consumer Preferences

To construct a step-wise method for capturing of the preferences of consumers, we apply the method for taxonomy development introduced by Nickerson [11]. More concretely, we utilize Nickerson's method to guide the fulfillment of CPMM to conceptualize consumer preferences and their related properties, specific to given problem conditions – such as sources of consumers, value frameworks and measures used, etc. In this study, Nickerson's method has been used as a basis to emphasize the inherent intention of CPMM to be used itself as a taxonomy.

In the following, we describe the method in generic terms, and then apply it in Sect. 4 (Table 1).

Table 1. Development method steps

Step	Description
1. Instantiate CPMM	Use *class:Consumer Driver* for Nickerson's meta-characteristic
2. Fulfill modeling perspectives	Delineate context for CPMM by defining (Business, Segment, Consumer)
3. Refine *class:ConsumerDriver*	Review the meta-characteristic as per results of Step 2
4. Evaluate Value Framework(s) and related data set(s)	Utilize evaluation for decision between empirical or conceptual approaches
5. Map value framework(s)	Relate chosen value framework(s) to *class: ConsumerValue* to ensure consumer orientation
6. Evaluate for completeness and consistency	Check all classes derive logically from meta-characteristic *class:Consumer Driver*

3.1   Instantiate CPMM

The process begins by instantiating CPMM, in which the class *Consumer Driver* is used as the meta-characteristic in Nickerson's method [11]. The meta-characteristic is the most comprehensive characteristic of the taxonomy, and it can serve as the basis for the choice of subsequent characteristics within the taxonomy.

3.2   Fulfill Modeling Perspectives

The conceptualization of consumer preferences within CPMM includes three perspectives—business modeling, addressing the core concepts related to the value exchange surrounding a system; consumer modeling, where peoples' preferences about the system are modeled according to existing theories; and segment modeling, which is designed to enable profiling of the consumer. Fulfillment of these core concepts after the assignation of the meta-characteristic (*Consumer Driver*) populates the instance of CPMM at a basic level for later refinement, while assigning the contextual boundaries that the taxonomy will operate within upon completion. This step partly fulfills Nickerson's *Identify new subset of objects* (Empirical-to-Conceptual) and *Conceptualize characteristics and dimensions of objects* (Conceptual-to-Empirical) which is then completed in step 4.

3.3   Refine Meta-Class

The third step is to refine the meta-class (Nickerson's meta-characteristic) to a desired level of abstraction, which, as discussed previously, is based on the purpose of the taxonomy, i.e., based on the users and their expected use of the taxonomy as found via the Modeling Perspectives in the previous step.

Once populated, the instantiation of CPMM has *Consumer Driver* refined by value frameworks that might be utilized as the meta-characteristic (Consumer Value, Basic Values, Human Needs are seen in Fig. 1). Including and relating additional value frameworks to *Consumer Values* (Sect. 2.1) occurs via the *Mapping* association class.

To briefly summarize the taxonomy development method [11], the system analyst identifies characteristics of the possible objects that follow from the meta-class. These characteristics must, however, discriminate among the possible taxonomy objects; a characteristic that has the same value for all or nearly all objects is of no use in the taxonomy.

3.4   Decide on Approach

After these steps the system analyst can decide between two alternative approaches for the main development steps: Empirical-to-Conceptual or Conceptual-to-Empirical [11]. The choice approach depends on the availability of data about the possible taxonomy objects under study and the knowledge of the analyst about the domain of interest. The fulfillment of the tripartite modeling perspectives in step 2, in combination with the application of the value frameworks to refine the meta-class in step 3, drives this decision.

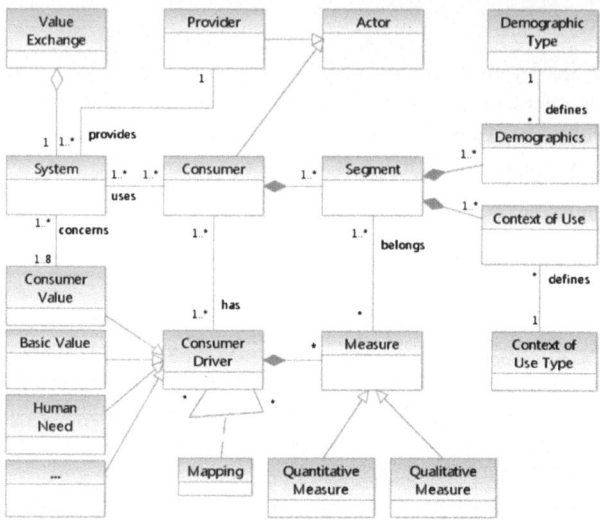

Fig. 1. Consumer preference meta-model (CPMM)

In the empirical-to-conceptual approach, the system analyst identifies a subset of objects that they wish to classify. These possible objects are likely to be the ones with which the analyst is most familiar or that are most easily accessible, possibly through a review of the literature. The subset could be a random sample, a systematic sample, a convenience sample, or some other type of sample. Next, the analyst identifies common characteristics of these objects. The characteristics must be logical consequences of the meta-characteristic.

In the conceptual-to-empirical approach, the system analyst begins by conceptualizing the dimensions of the taxonomy without examining actual objects. This process is based on the analyst's knowledge about how the possible objects are similar and how they are dissimilar. Since this is a deductive process, little guidance can be given other than to say that the analyst uses their knowledge of existing foundations, experience, and judgment to deduce what they think will be relevant dimensions.

Choosing an approach is based on the chosen value framework or the data available to the project, because every value framework produces data in a different way, and also provides different tonality to the meaning. This choice can also be driven by the real world constraints of a project, such as budget, time, and availability of data.

3.5   Map Value Frameworks

This step ensures that every value framework utilized within CPMM has a consumer orientation. This relationship is brought about because each framework must be related to the *Consumer Values* class via the *Mapping* association class. So although the choice of value framework is dependent on many factors, among them the approach decided on in the previous step, the need for an explicit consumer orientation does not drive the decision. However, an empirical-to-conceptual approach necessarily requires first choosing a value framework that produces empirical —such as Schwartz's Basic Values [20] and then mapping it accordingly, just as choosing a conceptual-to-empirical would lead to a choice of a framework such as Maslow's Hierarchy [10].

To offer an example, for Holbrook [4], the Consumer Value *Status* is sought by the consumer adjusting their consumption in a manner that affects those whom they wish to influence: by consuming products or engaging in consumption experiences so as to project a particular type of image one wishes to portray.

Each of these relate directly to the Brand Personality facet *Sophistication* described as glamorous, pretentious, charming, and romantic. A *Sophisticated* brand would attract someone seeking to fulfill the Consumer Value *Status* because they are trying to buy their way into the visibility of others to satisfy an Extrinsic (value possessed outside the value object), Active (occurring in the moment of consumption) and Other-oriented (needing an externalized locus of appreciation) value. Similarly, that same brand would appeal to a consumer seeking to fulfill Schwartz's Basic Value *Power* by displaying their ability to conspicuously consume items with little utilitarian purpose. This need-fulfillment via the approval of others is deemed *Esteem* by Maslow's Human Needs, which also has the side effect of solidifying relationships with others, providing a feeling of *Safety*.

3.6   Evaluate for Completeness and Consistency

At the end of these steps, the systems analyst asks if the ending condition(s) has/have been met with the current version of the taxonomy. Both objective and subjective conditions must be checked. If it is the first iteration, it is likely that none of the objective conditions will be met so the process will be repeated. In subsequent iterations the objective conditions must be evaluated and if not met, the process is repeated.

In repeating the method, the analyst must again decide which approach to use. Since new possible taxonomy objects—such as those identified in step 2—may have been identified or new domain knowledge may have been obtained in the previous iteration, the analyst can re-use the previous heuristics to decide which approach to apply in the next iteration. Iterations of the design process may add new dimensions and existing dimensions may be eliminated.

At this point in the process a classification in the form of an open and case-based taxonomy of consumer preferences is generated. This step will be elucidated through the case example in Sect. 4.

4   Example Case

4.1   Study Structure

Following Zwass [28], this study is classified as an exploration of the autonomous co-creation of consumer-side production through collective sentiment expression. Unpacking this, what we have is value co-creation between a business and its consumers that is emergent, and which is discovered through sentiment analysis.

For the purposes of this research, the public Twitter feed of a major airline was selected based on the availability of a nearly real-time text-based interaction between the business and the consumer. Additionally the software used by the airline often is publicly visible, although not necessarily publicly available: all passengers are impacted when an error in the route configuration system occurs, although they are not necessarily operators of the system. This ability for the consumers to comment on the efficacy of the services that the airline provides to them is intermediated through those supporting technologies and IT systems.

Technical Overview. The Twitter feed for United Airlines [25] was monitored for a period of approximately 7.5 h between 7–8 July 2015. A Twitter API [26] was created to provide security keys and access tokens for a Python [16] script that utilized modules Tweepy [24], pandas [12], re [17], and json [5]. 6873 tweets were collected: 509 between 17:23-23:22 CET on 7 July 2015 and 6364 between 14:06-17:34 CET on 8 July 2015. The discrepancy in the number of tweet collected is due to a router failure that grounded the entire United fleet for 5 h on 8 July. This technical issue led to a massive increase in the amount of user activity.

Data Analysis. A simple random sample of 250 tweets was extracted from the main data set, with these further processed to remove text that was already extant in the simple random sample (e.g., a large number of retweets were created on the day of the router failure) or that was without any substantive or actionable activity (e.g., crude comments about the airline). This left a final data set of 72 tweets.

Qualitative Data Capture. The final data set was first classified using Kano's Must-be/Expected, One-dimensional/Normal, and Attractive/Exciting attributes [8] and then further designated as a Feature, Idea, Service, or Complaint.

In Table 2 below we present few examples from the collected data set; the instantiation of CPMM based on the set is explained starting with the next sub-section and following the methodical approach presented in Sect. 3.

Table 2. Examples of tweets from data set, along with their Kano classification

Text of tweet	Kano	Code
@united is check in for tomorrow's flights still down? App is very glitchy and I can't check in.	M	S
@united UA5131 delayed for 1 h. Should I check in luggage 30 min before original time or the actual scheduled departure time?	M	S
"@united Is there a problem with online and app check-in? Either it's broken or something's wrong with my ticket. Thanks for checking."	M	S
"@united Was there any resolution to this? Why not enter our ID and 4 digit pin number instead of typing the CC# every hr?"	O	F/I
"@TheNewsHam and @united just pushed departure from #BOS to noon arrive ORD 145PM. They'd better delay #UA895 *heartracing"	O	S
Kano = Must-be/Expected (M) One-dimensional/Normal (O) Attractive/Exciting (A)		
Code = Feature (F) Idea (I) Service (S) Complaint (C)		

4.2   Instantiation of Consumer Preference Meta-Model for United Airlines

Figure 2 is an instantiation of CPMM using the case example of United Airlines. The class instances are described in further detail in the following sections.

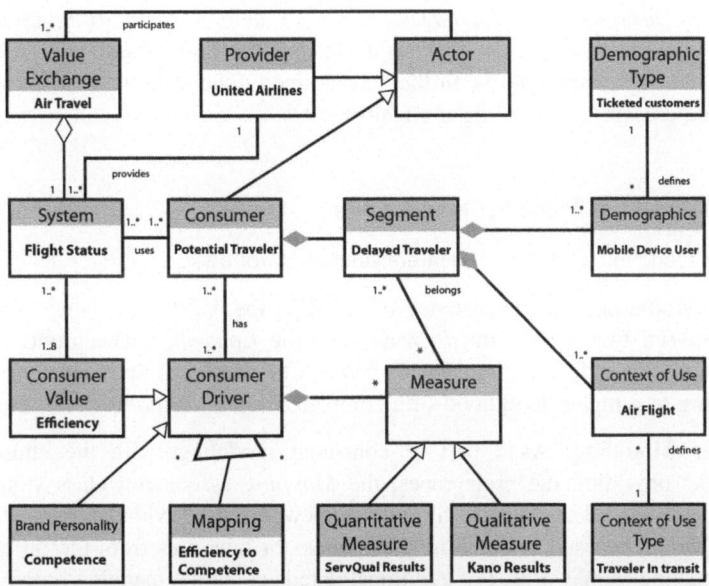

Fig. 2. Instantiation of CPMM for United Airlines case example

To offer a brief walkthrough of this instance, *Actor:Provider:UnitedAirlines* and *Actor:Consumer:PotentialTraveler* participate in *ValueExchange:AirTravel*, where the availability *System:FlightStatus* marks a decision point for the *Actor:Consumer: PotentialTraveler*. If *System:FlightStatus* fulfills the *Mapping* created between *BrandPersonality:Competence* and *ConsumerValue:Efficiency* then *ValueExchange: AirTravel* can be successfully completed: the consumer preferences of the *Consumer: PotentialTraveler* have been met by the features in the system. *Mapping* provides the *ConsumerDriver* that must be addressed by *System:FlightStatus* to successfully complete the *ValueExchange:AirTravel*.

Information to address the necessary features of *System:FlightStatus* is found in *Measure* where data about *Actor:Consumer:PotentialTraveler* has been collected through the through *QuantitativeMeasure:ServQualResults* (an implementation of a survey constructed using the ServQual methodology) and *QualitativeMeasure: KanoResults,* where the textual data was coded according to the precepts of Kano.

Measure is also important because this is where the initial stages of value co-creation occur: through their design of the survey instrument, and through the use of Kano's work as an organizing principle for the qualitative data, *Actor:Provider: UnitedAirlines* initiates and proposes the means for the co-creation to occur. Through their understanding of their own brand personality attributes, *Actor:Provider:*

UnitedAirlines necessarily decides how and where the interaction with *Actor:Consumer:PotentialTraveler* occurs.

A more precise understanding of *Actor:Consumer:PotentialTraveler* is provided in *Segment:DelayedTraveler* and that is itself further refined by: *ContentOfUse:AirFlight*, where only delays related to a ticketed air flight are managed by the system; *ContentOfUseType:TravelerInTransit* where this would be the sole use case for *Actor: Consumer; Demographics:MobileDeviceUser* to delimit *System:FlightStatus* from being designed for working on desktop devices, and *DemographicType:TicketedCustomers* where the user base is further constrained. The delimitations these classes provide are crucial for designing the feature model.

4.3   Fulfillment of Modeling Perspectives

The three modeling parts have been considered as follows:

Business Modeling: In this instance of CPMM, the *Value Exchange* (Air Travel) occurs between two *Actors*: the *Provider* and the *Consumer*. The proposed *System* (Flight Status) would be designed with features to maximize the *Consumer Drivers*, thus leading to a higher likelihood of a completed *Value Exchange*.

Consumer Modeling: As a part of consumer modeling, with the chosen value frameworks providing the preferences, the *Mapping* association class would house *Brand Personality*; designed for different frameworks used within *Consumer Driver*, *Mapping* would be used to combine their values or measures from the different consumer modeling frameworks. For additional details about the mapping process refer to Sect. 4.6. *Measure* is one of the key classes, and is used to provide the source data used in the development of the taxonomy. For this instance, it was envisioned (though not implemented) that ServQual [13] could be used to provide weightings for consumer drivers through the *Quantitative Measure* class: for instance what is the relative importance of proactive, timely notification of delay vs. reactive customer service. *Qualitative Measure* in this study was an implementation of Kano and was used to classify the source data according to these known methods of judging consumer satisfaction. It was chosen because its categories— Must-be/Expected, One-dimensional/Normal, and Attractive/Exciting—mirror those of feature models [7].

Segment Modeling: In the case example, Potential Travelers are the primary *Consumer*, but CPMM takes into account the need for specific systems to address specific consumer values. In particular providing service to a *Segment* of travelers who are delayed could rapidly increase the *Consumer Drivers* built upon *Brand Personality* Competence and the *Consumer Value* Efficiency. To further target the segment and allow for successful implementation, Demographics indicate that only *Consumers* with tickets and who have mobile phones will be the target users. There is little need for the company to provide information on flight delays except on a need-to-know basis. Being able to more closely target their messaging, rather than through widely distributed mass media such as Twitter, would allow for better management of the company's brand personality assets. *Context of Use* specifies that delayed travelers who are ticketed and have mobile phones will be able to use the system. This also provides a large design constraint, because those without smart phones will not be precluded from using the system. In essence there is no need to create a system for all travelers because ideally only a segment of the consumer base experiences delays.

4.4 Refinement of Meta-Class

The initial instantiation of CPMM provides the meta-class (Nickerson's meta-characteristic) via the class *Consumer*. *Consumer* is a role representing a group of people in the consideration for the evaluation of the *System* based on individual preferences [27].

This is further refined through *Segment* in this step. In the case example, United Airlines (*Provider*) is trying to attract Potential Travelers (*Consumer*) who are experiencing delays (*Segment*) by introducing a flight status *System* that is designed around the *Provider's* Brand Personality and that matches with the *Consumer Value* Efficiency that is held by *Consumers* of type Potential Travelers.

4.5 Decision on Approach

Nickerson's Empirical-to-Conceptual approach was selected due to the qualities of the extant data; whereas a Conceptual-to-Empirical approach could have been used as a top-down means for dimension discovery, Empirical-to-Conceptual proved to be a cleaner and more flexible approach. For example, the Brand Personality value *Competence*—a higher order concept—could have been used as a basis for coding the data for term inference and tonality, but that requires an extremely large set of training data. Given the relatively small size of corpus that was available an analysis of n-grams and usage provides a solid proof of concept. An additional benefit is that this is more likely scenario when used in situations outside of research.

4.6 Mapping Brand Personality to Consumer Drivers

In previous work [3, 22] the value frameworks from Maslow (Human Need) [10], Schwartz (Basic Value) [19, 20] and Holbrook (Consumer Value) [4] were used, and related (i.e. mapped from *any framework* to Consumer Values) through integration via CPMM. By presenting an incremental addition to the past mappings [3, 22], it is possible to see how Brand Personality could be readily used within CPMM.

This choice is also borne out by the data available for a particular instantiation: with many systems design projects being developed on an *ad hoc* basis, it is impossible to guarantee the availability of survey data from Schwartz's Portrait Values Questionnaire [27]. CPMM is designed to agnostically accept any value framework (Table 3).

In the case example, Holbrook's Consumer Value *Efficiency* and the Brand Personality *Competence* are mapped via the *Mapping* class. As a single example due to space constraints, to Holbrook, *Efficiency* results from the active use of a product or consumption experience as a means to achieve some self-oriented purpose [4]. This is a

Table 3. Mapping brand personality to Holbrook's typology of consumer values

Brand personality	Consumer value	Consumer dimensions
Competence	Efficiency	Self-oriented/Active/Extrinsic
Ruggedness competence	Excellence	Self-oriented/Reactive/Extrinsic
Sophistication	Status	Other-oriented/Active/Extrinsic
competence	Esteem	Other-oriented/Reactive/Extrinsic
Excitement	Play	Self-oriented/Active/Intrinsic
Excitement sophistication	Aesthetics	Self-oriented/Reactive/Intrinsic
Sincerity	Ethics	Other-oriented/Active/Intrinsic
Sincerity	Spirituality	Other-oriented/Reactive/Intrinsic

utilitarian value: hammers are generally prized for their usefulness and not their beauty. Aaker's *Competence* [1] encapsulates responsibility, dependability, and security. It is synonymous with reliable, responsible, dependable, and in fact, efficient.

Mapping brand personality to consumer values—two ostensibly similar frameworks—lies in the benefits derived from co-creation. Brand personality is about how a company presents itself, as well as the consumers' understanding of, and relationship to, that brand. The uniqueness of this co-creation dialog allows the two sides of the value exchange to evaluate and learn from each other.

This valuable information can be used for systems design, but only if it is refined. This refinement takes place through Holbrook's Consumer Values Typology. They are based on clear, concise logical support, and because they are less abstract than brand personality, they are better capable of supporting the development of information systems.

4.7   Evaluate for Completeness and Consistency

The subjective ending condition *Extendibility* has been used to allow for continuous refinement and development. With the source data exhausted, a natural end point was reached, while additional data could be collected using the same methods, allowing the process to resume and for the taxonomy to be extended.

4.8   Feature Model Derived from Taxonomy of Consumer Preference

Brand Personality is transformed through *Mapping* into a known consumer values framework and becomes a lens through which to review data collected through the values co-creation process. The data discussed in Sect. 4—having been transformed into a case-based taxonomy—can then be used to create a feature model.

In Fig. 3, features were derived from user tweets that had been classified according to *QualitativeMeasure:KanoResults*. The tonality of the text data produced no Attractive/Exciting features so only MustBe and One-Dimensional were utilized. Three mandatory features of *System:FlightStatus* were included, along with one optional feature.

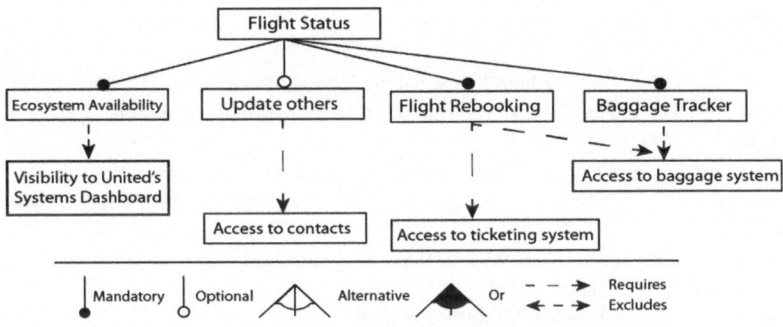

Fig. 3. Feature model for flight status system

To walk through one feature, *System:FlightStatus* must allow for flight rebooking. Because this model is written from perspective of *System:FlightStatus,* the documented features are capabilities that the system should possess. To accomplish that task, *System:FlightStatus* requires access to both the ticketing system and the baggage system. The ticketing system should be understood as not simply United's but rather one of the large computer reservation systems of SABRE/Amadeus: *Consumer: PotentialTraveler* would like the ability to find other flights to meet their needs in the event of problems with United.

5 Conclusions and Future Work

In this study, we have proposed a methodical use of the Consumer Preference Meta-Model (CPMM) for capturing and classifying any sort of consumers' preferences, which we have illustrated through the case of the Brand Personality value framework. Being recognized as a significant determinant of consumer loyalty [12] and with the ability to align the interests of both consumers and a business in terms of value co-creation, we found the framework worth analyzing for the inclusion in CPMM, along with the established ones [4, 10, 20].

The method has been based on the idea that CPMM should be able not only to capture but also to classify and relate different kinds of consumer preferences along with their related contextual and measurement properties; therefore we have aligned it with Nickerson's method for taxonomy creation within information systems [11], in Sect. 3.

The United Airlines example with the sourcing of user preferences from the Twitter social network and their classification using the Brand Personality framework demonstrated the possibility to scope preferences of company's customers and further map them, and according to relevance to integrated value facets, enable the creation of feature models for representing system requirements that support the values of the end users.

In [22, 23] we have proposed the integration of CPMM to Enterprise Architecture, and in particular TOGAF, using a linkage between stakeholder concerns and consumer preferences. Following that, one direction of future work concerns the use of CPMM in conjunction with Enterprise Modeling techniques.

References

1. Aaker, J.L.: Dimensions of brand personality. J. Mark. Res. **34**(3), 347–356 (1997)
2. Aaker, J.L.: The malleable self: The role of self-expression in persuasion. J. Mark. Res. **36** (1), 45–57 (1999)
3. Giannoulis, C., Svee, E.O., Zdravkovic, J.: Capturing consumer preference in system requirements through business strategy. Int. J. Info Syst. Model. Des. (IJISMD) **4**(4), 1–26 (2013)
4. Holbrook, M.B. (ed.): Consumer Value: A Framework for Analysis and Research. Psychology Press, London (1999)
5. Json. https://docs.python.org/2/library/json.html
6. Kambil, A., Ginsberg, A., Bloch, M: Re-inventing value propositions. Stern Working Paper IS-96–21, New York University (1996)
7. Kang, K., Cohen, S., Hess. J., Novak, W., Peterson, A.: Feature-oriented domain analysis (FODA) feasibility study. Technical report No. CMU/SEI-90-TR-21. Software Engineering Institute, Carnegie Mellon University, Pittsburgh, PA (1990)
8. Kano, N., Seraku, N., Takahashi, F., Tsuji, S.: Attractive quality and must-be quality. J. Japan. Soc. Qual. Control **14**(2), 39–48 (1984)
9. Kluckhohn, C.: Values and value-orientations in the theory of action: an exploration in definition and classification. In: Parsons, T., Shils, E. (eds.) Toward a General Theory of Action. Harvard University Press, Cambridge (1951)
10. Maslow, A.H.: A theory of human motivation. Psychol. Rev. **50**(4), 370 (1943)
11. Nickerson, R.C., Varshney, U., Muntermann, J.: A method for taxonomy development and its application in information systems. Eur. J. Inf. Syst. **22**(3), 336–359 (2013)
12. Pandas. http://pandas.pydata.org
13. Parasuraman, A., Zeithaml, V.A., Berry, L.L.: Servqual. J. Retail. **64**(1), 12–40 (1988)
14. Park, C.W., Deborah, J.M., Priester, J., Eisingerich, A.B., Lacobucci, D.: Brand attachment and brand attitude strength: conceptual and empirical differentiation of two critical brand equity drivers. J. Mark. **74**(6), 1–17 (2010)
15. Prahalad, C.K., Ramaswamy, V.: The Future of Competition: Co-Creating Unique Value with Customers. Harvard Business School Press, Boston (2004)
16. Python. https://www.python.org/
17. Re. https://docs.python.org/2/library/re.html
18. Sánchez-Fernández, R., Iniesta-Bonillo, M.Á.: The concept of perceived value: a systematic review of the research. Mark. Theor. **7**(4), 427–451 (2007)
19. Schwartz, S.H., Melech, G., Lehmann, A., Burgess, S., Harris, M., Owens, V.: Extending the cross-cultural validity of the theory of basic human values with a different method of measurement. J. Cross Cult. Psychol. **32**(5), 519–542 (2001)
20. Schwartz, S.H., Tamayo, A., Porto, J.B.: Basic human values: their content and structure across countries. Valores E Comportamento Nas organizações/Values Behav. Organ. **1**, 21–55 (2005)
21. Sirgy, M.J.: Self-concept in consumer behaviour: a critical review. J. Consum. Res. **9**(3), 287–300 (1982)
22. Svee, E.-O., Zdravkovic, J., Giannoulis, C.: Consumer value-aware enterprise architecture. In: Cusumano, M.A., Iyer, B., Venkatraman, N. (eds.) ICSOB 2012. LNBIP, vol. 114, pp. 55–69. Springer, Heidelberg (2012)
23. Svee, E.-O., Zdravkovic, J.: extending enterprise architectures to capture consumer values: the case of TOGAF. In: Persson, A., Stirna, J. (eds.) CAiSE 2015 Workshops. LNBIP, vol. 215, pp. 221–232. Springer, Heidelberg (2015)

24. Tweepy. https://github.com/tweepy/tweepy
25. Twitter. https://twitter.com/united/
26. Twitter API. https://apps.twitter.com/app/8516668/show
27. Zdravkovic, J., Svee, E.-O., Giannoulis, C.: Capturing consumer preferences as requirements for software product lines. Requir. Eng. **20**(1), 71–90 (2013)
28. Zwass, V.: Co-creation: toward a taxonomy and an integrated research perspective. Int. J. Electron. Commer. **15**(1), 11–48 (2010)

Modelling Users Feedback in Crowd-Based Requirements Engineering: An Empirical Study

Nada Sherief[1], Walid Abdelmoez[2], Keith Phalp[1], and Raian Ali[1(✉)]

[1] Faculty of Science and Technology, Bournemouth University, Poole, UK
{nsherief,kphalp,rali}@bournemouth.ac.uk
[2] The Arab Academy for Science, Technology and Maritime Transport, Alexandria, Egypt
walid.abdelmoez@aast.edu

Abstract. Most enterprises operate within a complex and ever-changing context. To ensure that requirements keep pace with changing context, users' feedback is advocated to ensure that the requirements knowledge is refreshed and reflects the degree to which the system meets its design objectives. The traditional approach to users' feedback, which is based on data mining and text analysis, is often limited, partly due to the ad-hoc nature of users' feedback and, also, the methods used to acquire it. To maximize the expressiveness of users' feedback and still be able to efficiently analyse it, we propose that feedback acquisition should be designed with that goal in mind. This paper contributes to that aim by presenting an empirical study that investigates users' perspectives on feedback constituents and how they could be structured. This will provide a baseline for modelling and customizing feedback for enterprise systems in order to maintain and evolve their requirements.

Keywords: Users' feedback · Feedback analysis · User involvement · Crowd-Based requirements engineering · Enterprise requirements evaluation

1 Introduction

Requirements management is still one of the most challenging fields in software development [1], has the most impact on project success, and is a major issue for decision makers in enterprises. Requirements are gathered from, yet must still represent, a diverse group of users; they are intrinsically volatile in nature. These issues are exacerbated by the problem that users still typically provide their feedback on the fulfilment of their requirements in a natural language and in an ad-hoc manner, which introduces a great deal of imprecision and ambiguity.

To cope with such a lack of precision, a range of semi-automated techniques have been suggested to handle such user data (this includes techniques such as text mining and/or human facilitator). These techniques may be used to gather, interpret, aggregate, and revise what users say, partly to mitigate for such issues as bias and subjectivity in their textual responses. More effective results can be reached if the feedback is written in a structured format. Structured feedback text would, arguably, allow approaches, such as text processing, to provide more accurate results within less time and with fewer

© IFIP International Federation for Information Processing 2015
J. Ralyté et al. (Eds.): PoEM 2015, LNBIP 235, pp. 174–190, 2015.
DOI: 10.1007/978-3-319-25897-3_12

human interventions. If text is structured the requirements extraction process can be more systematic, eliminating complexity and ambiguity found in natural language, and requiring less effort.

Research has identified the need to involve users in requirements engineering, but often focuses on a small number of selected users to give input and feedback in requirements related activities and afterwards in user acceptance testing [2]. Recent research has been focusing on the possibility of utilizing crowdsourcing in requirements engineering [3, 4] to cater for the dynamic contexts and the diversity of users. Moreover, in [5, 6] the collective users' feedback was also encouraged for shaping software adaptation as users are important to communicate certain information that cannot be monitored and captured by automated means and also cannot be fully specified by designers at design time, yet are necessary to plan and support adaptation. Furthermore, authors in [7] stated that the crowd can enrich and keep the precision of engineers' knowledge about software evaluation via their iterative feedback at runtime (i.e. while the software is in use). That is, users' feedback can communicate their opinion on the role of the system in meeting their requirements leading to better users' acceptance of the software. Their acceptance of the product is of a high importance for market success.

However, the literature is still limited in providing engineering approaches to developing systematic feedback acquisition [8, 9]. Our research focuses on the development of a modelling and elicitation framework of crowdsourced feedback at runtime. This includes devising mechanisms to structure such feedback in a way that makes it easy for users to express and engineers to interpret. This will allow the system to prioritize different problems reported by users. Also, it will help in evaluating the overall quality of the system and in taking evolution and maintenance decisions.

In this paper we conduct a two phase empirical study. We follow a qualitative method of two phases including two focus groups in the first phase and three forums' analysis in the second. In the first, we build on the top of our initial findings on the topic in [7] and provide more detailed results on the different aspects of the feedback design and conduct of runtime feedback acquisition. In the second phase study, we undergo a detailed analysis of users' feedback on enterprise software applications by analysing actual users' feedback through examination of their posts and responses on three online forums. We finally discuss how the results inform the process of designing feedback acquisition and increase its efficiency.

2 Research Method

We followed a qualitative approach to explore and understand how users provide feedback and their preferences on the acquisition process. The study had two phases. In the first phase study we took an empirical approach by conducting a two sessions focus group study, which is a popular technique of qualitative research in software engineering [10]. The sessions lasted 2 h and 52 min. Both sessions were audio recorded and transcribed with consent from participants. Our goal was to collect insights and experience from users who have actually given feedback before. Also, both junior and senior software engineers were invited to understand how more high-tech users give feedback and how they think a good feedback should be structured in order to be easily understandable and analysed. The main areas we wanted to explore were:

(RQ1). How users would like feedback to look like, and the criteria that judge whether the feedback is meaningful and useful?

(RQ2). How users would like to be involved in the process of providing feedback, and what encourages them to act as evaluators?

The focus groups were analysed using the thematic mapping approach [11]. The results of the focus groups analysis shown in Fig. 1 gave us a good level of understanding of users' feedback aspects. The resulted thematic areas can be viewed from two different perspectives. In the first perspective, participants gave several insights regarding the structure of the feedback and what are the characteristics they think make their feedback meaningful and useful. These ideas are covered in the environmental and structure thematic areas. In the second perspective, participants gave their perceptions regarding what they expect from a feedback acquisition method. How it can support, motivate and value their feedback. These ideas are covered in the engagement and involvement thematic areas.

Our research goal necessitates building a more concrete description for feedback structures. So in order to get the elaborated view, we conducted another study which involved the analysis of three actual online forums where people give feedback on business software. The main areas we wanted to explore in the second phase study (i.e. the three forums analysis) were:

(RQ1). What are the main concepts that constitute the feedback structure?

(RQ2). What are the designs of the identified feedback concepts?

To start with, we have taken both the environment and structure thematic areas shown in Fig. 1 of the focus groups results as our initial template. This template was edited and enhanced in the forums analysis process to come up with more details on how feedback could be structured in a meaningful and useful manner. We have analysed 200 feedback from 20 different sources found on Microsoft's TechNet, WordPress, and SAP forums. We targeted business software to avoid the noise typically found in general purpose software, as normally users tend to give a more serious and focused feedback, because of the social norms in such kind of forums. Also, business users are best fitted from the motivation perspective, because it has a direct value on their work and performance. We have chosen these three forums in order to target different types of business users with diverse technical capabilities.

We studied actual users' feedback through observation and analysis of their posts and responses on forums. The main advantage of this method is the direct examination of the experience of user's difficulties in the task of expressing their problems and opinions in using the software, the task flow and challenges. Moreover, forums provide a considerable amount of feedback that we have analysed using thematic analysis [11] with the intention to come up with the main concepts that constitute a feedback, and the outlines of the identified concepts.

Using software in the data analysis process has been believed to increase consistency and/or accuracy of qualitative research. In our research, NVivo 10 was used

Fig. 1. Focus groups final thematic map

in the data collection and analysis. Moreover, we used multi-coder arrangement [12] to reduce subjectivity and bias. Two researchers performed the coding of the same collection of sources, and analysis of forums. During the analysis new concepts and structures emerged and caused new themes, concepts, categories or codes to be added to the thematic map. After each team discussion, the members refined, merged and/ or reorganized the nodes. When a disagreement emerged a third researcher was consulted. This helps validate that a theme is not just emerging from a single coder subjective thinking.

3   Focus Groups Results

Following the recommendation of six stages of analysis [11], four thematic areas were formed, and 15 themes were identified from the analysis, which are shown in Fig. 1. The four thematic areas are: environment, structure, engagement and involvement.

Environment refers to the settings that support users so they feel confident in providing meaningful evaluation feedback. This includes Specificity, Clarity and feedback Method. In detail, participants would like to use a method they prefer to aid them in easily providing feedback. Furthermore, to improve the clarity of feedback, participants pointed out that it is preferable to add reasons and explanations in feedback to help make their viewpoints more **comprehensive**. Also, providing **structure** to the feedback will decrease misinterpretations and ease the analysis of texts afterwards. Specificity can be goal-oriented, which means by specifying the **quality attribute** in the feedback that concerns the user, such as usability, or reliability. Also, specificity can be influenced by the **feedback type** the user would like to provide, as more users tend to give feedback when they need help or when a problem occurs.

Structure refers to the attributes of a feedback which are favourable to be seen by the participants. This includes Specificity, Level of Detail, Measurement, and Timing. In detail, they thought that feedback would be more useful and accurate if it was related to a certain **feature**. It would be useful to be able to correlate feedback according to the **inter-relationships** between the features, because some features may affect the functionality of others. Moreover, it is important to provide the possibility of varying **details** in the feedback to ensure a minimum level of meaningful and useful information, and also to put into consideration other **contextual** aspects that might affect the users while giving their feedback. Furthermore, participants also suggested using simple measurements in a way to aid users in giving their feedback through and re-using the experiences of others. For example, users can **rate** how much others' feedback was meaningful or useful, and accordingly **statistics** can appear to users to show other useful feedback. Also, users can give feedback about their experience with new changes in the software to aid engineers in measuring user **satisfaction**. Finally, it is also important to consider the timing of giving the feedback. Users thought that giving a feedback **immediately** (i.e. at runtime) is important especially in reporting errors or problems, as it helps giving more accurate feedback with detailed explanations, and therefore would affect the structure of the feedback.

Engagement refers to the key merits the acquisition process provides to the involved users that encourage them to take part as evaluators. This includes some key characteristics of engaged users with the process, and also the qualities that are important to the process. This includes Recognition, Value, Channel, and Transparency. In details, participants mentioned that they would like to be recognized through their **reputation**. Reputation may be considered as a component of identity as defined by others. Reputation is a vital factor in any community where trust is important. Also, users would take recommendations, and/or solutions into consideration if they are given from **reliable** users. The reliability of users increases the weight of their feedback. Moreover, users like to be valued in a way in the participation. Participants mentioned that their feedback is valued by knowing that it taken into **consideration** for further analysis and leads to software enhancements. Also, the possibility to learn from others' experiences provides great value to users as it increases their **awareness** by knowing other possible features variations they were no aware about before. Furthermore, Channel reflects the way users want to interact through feedback. They would like the feedback acquisition process to be simple and **interactive**. Also, after giving their feedback they would appreciate if they can **chat** with the analyst to discuss their feedback. Finally, it would increase users' trust if they know the **process** in which their feedback will be handled and considered. Transparency generally implies openness, which can be achieved in different ways. The user can be **notified** through a message that the feedback will be taken into consideration. Transparency may be achieved by giving the user an **example** of other users whom their feedback was taken into consideration and their issue was resolved.

Involvement refers to a variety of aspects that motivate users to participate in the process of feedback acquisition and can directly influence the decisions and activities in using/evaluating the software. This includes Privacy, Rewards, Support, and Response. In detail, privacy issues were raised by participants. Participants differentiated between two aspects in privacy, the privacy of their **identity**, and the privacy of the **content** they provide (i.e. their feedback). Moreover, participants were particularly interested in the rewards mechanism for involvement whether through implicit or explicit incentives. **Implicit incentives** are not based on anything tangible. Social incentives are the most common form of implicit incentives. These incentives allow the user to feel good as an active member of the community for example through increasing their reputation. **Explicit incentives** refer to tangible rewards, for examples financial. Furthermore, the level of support from the feedback system was considered important. Many suggestions were raised about how a feedback acquisition tool can help them. For example, the **interaction styles** *"there can be videos to explain to the users what they can do (in order to provide feedback)"*. The ease of use of the feedback acquisition tool is important. They also suggested that the feedback tool can provide **hints** to the users about its capabilities. Moreover, if there is an **automated** detection in some steps of providing the feedback, this would further ease their job. For example if the tool can automatically detect the feature the user is having trouble with. Finally, the feedback tool response on feedback was also considered important. Two characteristics of system response were discussed, which are the **speed of response** from the system and the **language of response**.

4   Forums Analysis Results

In this section we explain the forums analysis results represented in the final thematic map shown in Fig. 2. The **first** thematic area that was founded from the analysis to the forums is our **novel classification of feedback types** that users provide. We have reached 8 distinct feedback types that users use on forums. In this section we will provide definitions for each type of feedback.

Fig. 2. Forums analysis final thematic map

Before we start defining the meaning of each feedback type, we would like to classify feedback into two types: a *simple feedback*, and a *complex feedback*. A simple feedback is a feedback that consists of a single feedback type that a user provides in his post to express a certain meaning, while the complex feedback is a structured feedback that consists of several feedback types that together form a new meaning that can be inferred from its unique structure.

Below if the list of feedback types and subtypes (i.e. cases):

1. **Confirmation or Negation** is a simple feedback type that the users use to agree or disagree on problems or opinions of other users. When these feedback types are unaccompanied with other types in a feedback, it can be inferred as voting for a problem or a given solution.

2. **Investigation** is a simple feedback type used when a user is asking a question to clarify something about another feedback posted by another user. A user may ask about some issues in a problem statement, or unclear steps in a provided solution, or clarify some contextual information that helps explain the problem more.

3. **Elaboration** is a simple feedback type where the user gives extra explanation on a feedback he already posted. There are two cases for giving extra explanations on a feedback:

   a. **Feedback Elaboration** is when a user needs to give more detailed information that he forgot to provide in his main feedback this can be added separately in the feedback where he elaborates. For Example, A user can elaborate on a problem he provided by giving explanation on some trials that he made trying to solve his problem or rephrasing the problem statement.

   b. **Investigation Elaboration** is when a user simply replies on an Investigation by giving detailed explanations to answer the posted question(s).

4. **Justification** is a simple feedback type used when users need to provide reasons to support their feedback. They may give reasons why they provided a solution/ suggestion, or it can be used with confirmations or negations to state reasons why a user agrees or disagrees on a feedback opinion of another user.

5. **Verification** is a complex feedback type where a user gives his opinion on a solution or suggestion he received on the problem that he posted. As a complex type it means that it combines several other feedback types in its structure that are mandatory in its definition. Specifically in order to verify whether a solution or a suggestion was useful or not, this feedback has to reference a certain Mitigation (i.e. Solution or Suggestion) in which the user will be giving his opinion to verify whether it solved the issue or not by using Confirmation or Negation.

6. **Problem** feedback type refers to a certain feature or group of features in the software that the user is having problem with, and a detailed explanation of the problem. Problems may use other feedback types such as Investigations to ask users some questions they need answers for. However, problems in general cannot occur in the same Feedback post with Mitigations or Verifications. In general users who post problems are not the same users who post the Mitigations, and even if this case occurred will not be contained in the same problem post.

   a. **Topic definition** is a simple feedback type that represents the first posted problem in a feedback thread where the user is seeking help. Therefore it does not reference any other feedback in the thread but can be referenced in many other posts.

   b. **Addition** is a complex feedback type where a user votes (i.e. agrees or disagrees) on any posted problem, and adds another problem in his feedback, which is not related to the main problem on which the discussion is held. This means that a feedback thread may contain multiple problems along with the replies. From the definition of this feedback type as a complex type, this implies that it must contain other feedback types in its definition, which in this case are Confirmation or Negations that must reference another problem. Therefore, it cannot reference a feedback post that contains Mitigation, because by definition we use this feedback to add a problem to a problem.

7. **Mitigation** is a complex feedback type that represents a solution or a suggestion that may help a user resolve the problem(s) he has. Since this type is intended to resolve a problem, therefore it has to reference that problem in the solution or suggestion for specificity. Also, for every Mitigation it is always expected that the user who posted the problem will Verify that Mitigation. There are two types of Mitigations:
   a. **Solution** is a well-known procedure or steps that when followed can resolve the problem or issue.
   b. **Suggestion** is a recommendation that a user provides for another user as a trial to resolve his problem. This suggestion may or may not solve the problem. This needs Verification from the problem owner (i.e. the user who posted the problem).
8. **Correction** is used when a user corrects the understanding of another user. There are two cases for this feedback type.
   a. **Problem correction** is a complex feedback type. It occurs when the user corrects the problem of another user. In a problem definition a user must refer to a feature(s) that he is having a problem with. Sometimes the user is using a feature which is not intended for the type of task he is doing, simply due to a lack of understanding of the job a feature should perform. Consequently, other users can provide corrections to this misunderstanding.
   b. **Mitigation Correction** is a *complex* feedback type. This type of feedback may occur when a user is trying to correct a Mitigation that was provided for a certain problem. Errors in Mitigations may occur due to the lack of contextual information about the tasks the user is doing or environmental information about the softwares or hardware used while applying Mitigation.

The **second** thematic area that we have reached from our forums analysis is the Level of Detail. Level of Detail represents how much information the user provides in their feedback to express their opinions or problems. The information users provide have two major categories: Detail Types and Context. A single feedback can contain a mix of contextual information and several kinds of details. By Detail Types we mean how deep and specific the user is in expressing their feedback. By Context we mean the information the user may provide about the settings of his use to the software or while providing his feedback, which may affect the problems, mitigations, other users' responses. Therefore, this thematic area is considered a complementary area to the feedback types explained in the section above, as it adds more clarity to the feedback descriptions. Below is **our novel description of the Detail Types**:

1. **Concise.** By literal meaning it is used when users provide very short feedback types with no explanations or details. From the analysis we noticed that it is used mostly, when users tend to confirm or negate by just expressing their agreement or disagreement on a feedback. Moreover, it was never used in problem statements or mitigations, since by nature these specific feedback types need explanation to be meaningful.
2. **Explanation** is the opposite of concise, as in this detail type the user is expected to provide as much details in his feedback to make it meaningful for other users. There is no restriction on the use of this detail category with any feedback type, because it is always acceptable to give more details.

3. **Exemplification** is utilized when the users need to provide examples within this text. In the forums' threads that we have analysed examples are always given within explanations especially problem explanations.

4. **Trials** is used closely with problem description where the problem owner who is explaining the problem, shows that he made many attempts to resolve the problem but have failed to reach a Solution. The user posts these trials as a kind of extra explanation of the problem and how it occurs, and also to avoid getting suggestions from other users with same trials that he already made.

5. **Scenario** is used to explain text in a list. A solution can be explained in steps. These steps if verified by the problem owner can be used as a solution scenario to solve similar problems to other users. Moreover, other users may list the problems they have in the problems statement. Other may suggest mitigation to other users in a form of a list of possible actions to try; sometimes it matters to be in a certain order.

6. **Feature Definition** is used to define a user's perception of the usage of a certain feature. This description is sometimes used in problem statements, which helps other users understand why the user is having a problem (i.e. sometimes users have wrong understanding of the usages of a feature). Moreover, users who provide Mitigation may use it a form to document how they use a feature with certain types of tasks. Finally, it is mostly used when users provide Feedback Type: Correction, specifically Problem Correction, where the user corrects the misunderstanding of another user by providing the correct feature definitions to features referenced in the problem statement.

7. **Question** is a simple detail category that is used with Investigations to indicate the question(s) posted for clarification.

Contextual information can carry valuable information that can help make the feedback more understandable or useful. There are five main categories of contextual information that were captured in the forums analysis that map to [13].

1. **Task:** It captures what the user is doing. This is specifically important when the user is describing a Problem feedback type, because it gives to the other users an idea about the context in which the problem occurred, or describing the frequent jobs that the user is involved in in his daily work which helps give an idea to other users about the importance the feature the user is having problem with.

2. **Spatio-Temporal:** In this kind of context the user specifies information related to place and time. From our forums analysis we have found an angle where such information may play useful role. Cases are when users try to explain the timing relationship between two tasks (i.e. two tasks happening together, or one feature corrupts when a user does a certain action). Another Case is when users try to specify some information about a problem in relation to where it occurs in software for example in a certain interface, or when using a certain module.

3. **Personal:** In this kind of context users express their emotional judgments, stress, or information about their expertise, which is repeated mainly with Negation feedback.

4. **Social:** we mean context information related to a user's role at work, and information about co-workers.

5. **Environmental:** is related to a software or hardware specs, versions, and architec-tures. Users can provide these kinds of information in a problem statement to specify the software version they are using which may differ in the feature with problem from older or newer ones. Therefore, this adds specificity and usefulness to add such information. Moreover, users can add also environmental context in Mitigations to specify that the suggestion or solution works on a certain version, or works well with a certain hardware configuration.

The **third** thematic area concluded from the forums analysis, it was noted that users use four different methods to provide feedback, which are: text, code snippets, snapshots and links. It was notable that some methods were associated with a certain feedback types. (a) The text method is the most commonly used method in all feedback, and even it is used with other methods such as links or snapshots. However, it is important to note that most users use text written in natural language, which leads to lots of misinterpre-tations. This motivates our goal in creating a new feedback modelling language that utilizes the same methods the users are used to provide their feedback with, but in a patterned way and with the aid of textual keywords. Therefore, this thematic area is considered a complementary area to the feedback types explained above. (b) Code snip-pets are used to show fragments of code that have problems, or fragments of code to illustrate mitigation, and same for Snapshots. (c) Finally, a further method used by users to express details in forums, is Links. Links are very useful in providing Mitigations whether solutions or suggestions. Users use them to provide all the information they need by referencing the page that contains manuals or illustration the may help the problem owner. They can also, provide extra notes or explanations in their feedback besides the Link.

Finally, we have concluded from our forums analysis this **fourth** thematic area which is measurement. By measurement we mean measuring problem occurrence frequency or voting for mitigations' usefulness. This can simply be done through confirmations and negations that reference Problems or Mitigation feedback Types. By gathering such relationships between different users' feedback, it will allow the system to (a) prioritize the problems according to its rate of occurrence; (b) Also, when the system arrives to a good Mitigation action, the feedback causing this Mitigation could be reused in similar cases.

5 Threats to Validity

Although we have carefully followed the principles in conducting mixed methods approach, our study would still have five main threats to validity: (a) In the focus groups study users were students, researchers, and engineers recruited from Egypt and UK, which might produce a population bias; (b) a common threat to validity in focus groups study is whether all the participants perceived the questions as intended. We have addressed this issue by providing scripts which went through iterative revisions and modifications by two research members and we have undergone a mock-focus group of 2 participants for questions refinements; (c) while the analysis of forums was effective in identifying and describing concepts that construct users' feedback, it is possible that it did not identify all the important aspects and factors that can affect and influence their behaviour in this regard; (d) The number of analysed feedback from the three different forums (200 feedback) could be found medium considering that numerous number of threads available online, we stopped analysis when we reached the stage of saturation; (e) We have targeted forums where business users provide feedback, future research would further investigate general purpose forums (e.g. products, social media) to discover aspects of feedback in a loosely controlled and more open feedback acquisition environments than the one we studied.

6   Architecture for Structured Feedback Acquisition

In this section we explain how we utilize our findings to propose architecture for structured feedback acquisition as presented in Fig. 3. A set of rules that define feedback elements can be derived from the observations that we have reached from the classifications defined in Sect. 4. We propose architecture for structured feedback acquisition that consists of three main components. First, to formalize the definition of rules we propose developing an ontology that constructs the building blocks of user feedback structure elements, their operation rules, and a set of reserved keywords for each concept.

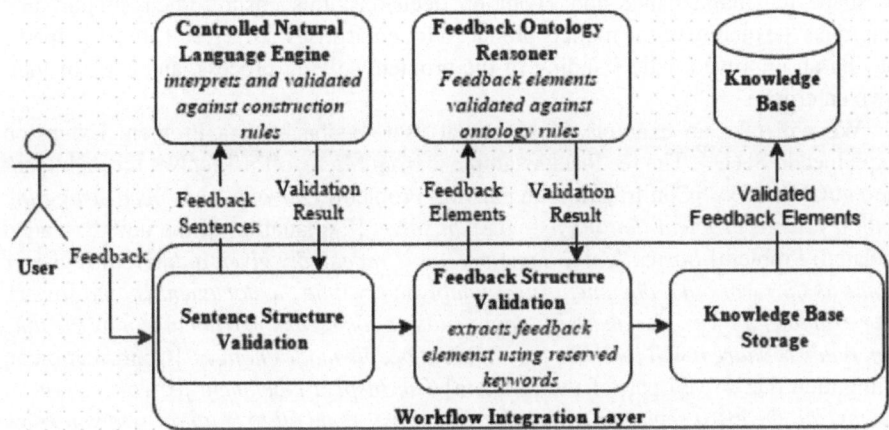

Fig. 3. An architecture for structured feedback modelling

Second, to improve clarity and enable consistent automated semantic analysis of the feedback, a feedback controlled natural language can be employed as an acquisition method for users to provide their feedback. It will restrict the user by general rules such as keeping sentences short and only use the reserved keywords to define textual blocks. This will be achieved by employing an already existing controlled natural language that will act as our text writing foundation that users will use to write their feedback more precisely.

Third, a workflow integration layer orchestrates the workflow between both controlled natural language engine and the ontology reasoner. This layer takes user feedback written in Controlled English, and sends it to the controlled natural language engine that will interpret the text and validate it against the language construction rules. Validated feedback sentences will return to this layer that will extract the feedback elements (that were presented in our findings) using the set of reserved words in the ontology. These elements will be validated against the ontology rules. Finally, this layer will be responsible for storing the validated feedback elements in a knowledge base. This knowledge base will allow engineers to have concrete and formal instances of the feedback extracted by more systematic means, which is more efficient and less error-prone. This can help in evaluating the overall quality of the system, which will help in taking evolution and maintenance decisions.

In our research we suggest employing goal models to represent the stakeholders' goals. We relate it to the feature model to represent both the functional and non-functional requirements of the system. By relating the structured feedback to the feature model, engineers can propagate through the interconnections between them to determine different levels of evaluation information. For example, by looking on the feedback and feature model they can identify most problematic features in the software according to some simple metrics like the no of negative feedback referencing that feature. Or they can look at it from a higher level to see which goals are violated keeping enterprise stakeholders unsatisfied. Stakeholders can be identified and their input can then be used to shape the maintenance and evolution decisions; this ensures their support and improves the quality of the models produced for enterprises. This results in participants having an improved understanding of the problem solving process, and even of their own enterprise.

We will take an example of an actual user feedback on a Problem Extension explained in Sect. 4. The feedback example is from Microsoft's TechNet forum https://goo.gl/CMBDJe: "[Confirmation on existing Problem] *Our office has been struggling with a related problem that maybe you can solve.* [Explanation of the new Extended (related) Problem] *Basically, the same person is repeatedly given a different reviewer name as they work in a document (presumably every time the document is auto saved). For example, if I work for an hour adding edits or comments on a document by the time I'm ready to share it will look like five different people made changes.* [Confirmation on Mitigation that solved part of the problem] *The Inspect Document fix works great to remove all the extra reviewer names, but it changes them all to 'Author'. Do you know how to then either (a) change 'Author' to the reviewer's actual name or (b) stop Office from assigning multiple names to the same reviewer? Also, we've tried checking 'Always use these values regardless of sign in' under General to no avail. Thanks - your fix is the closest we've come to a solution and it's greatly appreciated."*

In this example we show how user should write the feedback in a structured format that conforms to the feedback elements and reserved keywords defined by the ontology, the controlled natural language syntax, and the notation that we suggest that will be defined in the intermediate layer.

In this example, the feedback type is problem extension. In order to able to correctly classify this feedback as a problem extension, the user should follow some unique rules that uniquely identifies that type, such as: this feedback should confirm on a previously stated problem in the thread; it should also confirm on a previously stated mitigation in the feedback thread; but also adds a new problem in the feedback content; it should also explain trial that the user has undergone to solve the issue; and provide some environmental context which serves in favour of understanding how the mitigation was applied.

To show the benefits of using a structured format for systematically analysing feedback, we can take the first sentence in the example: "Our office has been struggling with a related problem that maybe you can solve." It can be logically inferred that the user who wrote this feedback agrees on a previously stated problem. However, to reach this conclusion it requires a human interpreter to read, understand and provide such conclusion. But when written: "*I agree* on [*@problem* refer to a previously stated problem]". First, the word "I agree" can be defined as a reserved keyword that indicates that this is a confirmation sentence. Moreover, it accurately refers to a previously stated problem in the thread, which will be validated by the workflow integration layer that handles the communication with the ontology. Therefore, writing the feedback sentence with the new notation removes redundancy, subjectivity, and also provides decisive definitions for the sentences' meanings, and thus can eliminate or remove human interventions.

The next step is the each sentence (i.e. instances content) is validated using the controlled natural language engine. The workflow layer will be responsible for retrieving the sentences that will be sent for validation, and showing the results for the user. In case that the user did not write proper controlled English, this layer will suggest how he can improve his feedback.

7   Related Work

There are several paradigms where the role of users is central such as User centred design [14], User Experience [15], Agile methodology [16], Usability Testing [17]. These techniques can aid the design of enterprise software systems, but they are expensive and time consuming when used for highly variable software designed to be used by a large number of users in contexts that are hardly predictable at design time. Furthermore, our work is similar to End-user Computing [18] in the motivation of involving users and enabling them to change in the system itself to meet their requirements and needs. However, we rely on users to provide feedback in order to decide on maintenance and evolution decisions rather than taking actions.

Recent research has been directed towards involving users in evaluating and modelling evolving requirements for large enterprise softwares. Authors in [19], main contribution is a theoretical understanding of user involvement as a key success factor in implementing and maintaining business intelligence solutions. Moreover, in [20], authors suggest users involvement in developing Business Process Management projects. Their modelling approach involves using User Requirements notation that integrates goals and usage scenarios, from which requirements can evolve. Additionally, in [21] the authors present how strategy maps can be augmented by consumer values to include goals reflecting consumer values, which can be used as requirements for new solutions. All the above work supports the importance of users in driving the enterprise business process as a lifelong activity. However, their work operates on the management of requirements at a rather strategic level to ensure goal satisfaction, and business strategy implementation. In contrast, our work aims to provide engineering approach with concrete constructs to model and acquire feedback and enable their role to take place.

Various works has been done on how to extract requirements from users' feedback. Authors in [22], extract the main topics mentioned in the feedback, along with some sentences demonstrative to those topics using sentiment analysis. Also in [23], have defined a simple domain ontology consisting of generic broad types of feedback and associations. They cluster feedback messages according to the entities they refer to, use natural language parsing and heuristic filtering that can match the detected keywords to domain ontology. Moreover, in [24], the research aims on providing an elicitation approach that can offer new opportunities for users to support them in documenting their needs using a mobile tool. In contrast, and instead of analysing given feedback, e.g. through forums and social networks, our work contributes to forward engineer the acquisition process itself making the analysis more efficient.

When engineering feedback, we need to use a language understood by users and at the same time traceable to the requirements model and knowledge. Goal Model [25], Feature Model [26] and Business Processes [27] seem to be potential models which link the space of the business to the space of users and their understanding of the system.

8   Conclusion and Future Work

This paper has presented a two phase empirical study. The first phase focus group study focused on the different aspects of the activity of interacting with users and acquiring their feedback, which gave a broad perspective for open research challenges. While the second forums analysis study examined actual users' feedback to reach a classification of feedback structures and their elements. The findings can be employed to develop a collaborative architecture that utilizes structured feedback for extracting requirements in a systemized way where the risks resulting from human interventions are minimized. Therefore, our results serve as a foundation step for a holistic approach for the structuring and use of users' feedback for crowdsourced software evaluation. Furthermore, from the feedback classification reached from the empirical study, we can derive new templates that combine multiple feedback and feedback types to form new cases that can inform the engineers by giving them a detailed view of the software's evaluation status from the users' point of view.

Acknowledgments.   The research is supported by a European FP7 Marie Curie CIG grant (the SOCIAD project) and Bournemouth University through the Graduate School PGR Development fund.

References

1. Jarke, M., Loucopoulos, P., Lyytinen, K., Mylopoulos, J., Robinson, W.: The brave new world of design requirements. Information Systems 36(7), 992–1008 (2011)
2. Cleland-Huang, J., Jarke, M., Liu, L., Lyytinen, K.: Requirements management–novel perspectives and challenges. In: Dagstuhl Reports 2, vol. 10, pp. 117–152 (2013)

3. Hosseini, M., Phalp, K., Taylor, J., Ali, R.: Towards crowdsourcing for requirements engineering. In: REFSQ 2014, Germany (2014)
4. Snijders, R., Dalpiaz, F., Hosseini, M., Shahri, A., Ali, R.: Crowd-centric requirements engineering. In: UCC 2014, pp. 614–615. IEEE, London (2014)
5. Ali, R., Solis, C., Omoronyia, I., Salehie, M., and Nuseibeh, B.: Social adaptation: when software gives users a voice. In: ENASE 2012, Poland (2012)
6. Ali, R., Solis, C., Salehie, M., Omoronyia, I., Nuseibeh, B., Maalej, W.: Social sensing: when users become monitors. In: ESEC/FSE 2011, Hungary, pp. 476–479 (2001)
7. Sherief, N., Jiang, N., Hosseini, M., Phalp, K., Ali, R.: Crowdsourcing software evaluation. In: EASE 2014, pp. 19. ACM, London (2014)
8. Almaliki, M., Ncube, C., Ali, R.: The design of adaptive acquisition of users feedback: An empirical study. In: RCIS 2014. IEEE, Morocco (2014)
9. Almaliki, M., Ncube, C. Ali, R.: Adaptive software-based Feedback acquisition: a persona-based design. In: RCIS 2015. IEEE, Greece (2015)
10. Kontio, J., Lehtola, L., Bragge, J.: Using the focus group method in software engineering: obtaining practitioner and user experiences. In: ISESE 2004. IEEE, USA (2004)
11. Braun, V., Clarke, V.: Using thematic analysis in psychology. Qual. Res. Psychol. 3(2), 77–101 (2006)
12. Crawford, H.K., Leybourne, M.L., Arnott, A.: How we ensured rigor from a multi-site, multi-discipline, multi-researcher study. In: Forum Qualitative Sozialforschung/Forum: Qualitative Social Research, vol. 1, no. 1 (2000)
13. Krogstie, J., Lyytinen, K., Opdahl, A.L., Pernici, B., Siau, K., Smolander, K.: Research areas and challenges for mobile information systems. Int. J. Mobile Commun. 2(3), 220–234 (2004)
14. Vredenburg, K., Mao, J.Y., Smith, P.W., Carey, T.: A survey of user-centered design practice. In: CHI 2002, pp. 471–478. ACM, Minneapolis, Minnesota, USA (2002)
15. Law, E.L.C., Van Schaik, P.: Modelling user experience - an agenda for research and practice. Interact. Comput. 22(5), 313–322 (2010)
16. Dybå, T., Dingsøyr, T.: Empirical studies of agile software development: a systematic review. Inf. Softw. Technol. 50(9–10), 833–859 (2008)
17. Adikari, S., McDonald, C.: User and usability modeling for HCI/HMI: a research design. In: ICIA 2006, pp. 151–154. IEEE (2006)
18. Doll, W.J., Torkzadeh, G.: The measurement of end-user computing satisfaction. MIS Q. 12, 259–274 (1988)
19. Yeoh, W., Koronios, A.: Critical success factors for business intelligence systems. J. Comput. Inf. Syst. 50(3), 23–32 (2010)
20. Pourshahid, A., Amyot, D., Peyton, L., Ghanavati, S., Chen, P., Weiss, M., Forster, A.J.: Business process management with the user requirements notation. Electron. Commer. Res. 9(4), 269–316 (2009)
21. Svee, E.-O., Giannoulis, C., Zdravkovic, J.: Modeling business strategy: a consumer value perspective. In: Johannesson, P., Krogstie, J., Opdahl, A.L. (eds.) PoEM 2011. LNBIP, vol. 92, pp. 67–81. Springer, Heidelberg (2011)
22. Galvis Carreño, L.V., Winbladh, K.: Analysis of user comments: an approach for software requirements evolution. In: ICSE 2013, pp. 582–591. IEEE Press, CA, USA (2013)
23. Schneider, K.: Focusing spontaneous feedback to support system evolution. In: RE 2011. IEEE, Italy (2011)
24. Seyff, N., Graf, F., Maiden, N.: Using mobile RE tools to give end-users their own voice. In: RE 2010, pp. 37–46. IEEE Computer Society, Sydney, Australia (2010)

25. Yu, E.S.: Social modeling and *i**. In: Borgida, A.T., Chaudhri, V.K., Giorgini, P., Yu, E.S. (eds.) Conceptual Modeling: Foundations and Applications. LNCS, vol. 5600, pp. 99–121. Springer, Heidelberg (2009)
26. Kang, K.C., Kim, S., Lee, J., Kim, K., Shin, E., Huh, M.: FORM: a feature-; oriented reuse method with domain-; specific reference architectures. Ann. Softw. Eng. **5**(1), 143–168 (1998)
27. OMG, B.P.M.N., Version 1.0. OMG Final Adopted Specification, Object Management Group (2006)

Investigating Enterprise Models

Factors Influencing Productization of Enterprise Modeling: A Qualitative Inquiry into the Scandinavian Strand of Methods and Tools

Natalie Yilmaz and Janis Stirna[✉]

Department of Computer and Systems Sciences,
Stockholm University, Postbox 7003, SE 164 07 Kista, Sweden
natalie.yilmaz@gmail.com, js@dsv.su.se

Abstract. Enterprise Modeling (EM) methods and tools have been developed and successfully used for more than two decades yet their adoption in organizations is mostly ad hoc. Only a few EM methods and tools have become successful products despite being theoretically sound and having certain success in application in practice. This grounded theory inquiry ponders on what factors influence the successful productization of EM methods and tools. Among the factors discussed are EM maturity gap, method and tool development process, application context, marketing and sales aspects, as well as product aspects.

Keywords: Enterprise modeling · EM methods · Tools · Productization

1 Introduction

Enterprise Modeling (EM) has proved to be a practicable approach that supports congruent organization and information system (IS) development by creating an integrated and commonly shared model describing different aspects of an enterprise (e.g. goals, business process, concepts, rules, etc.) More about the applicability of EM is available in [1].

In Scandinavia, Business or Enterprise Modeling were initially developed in the eighties by Plandata, Sweden [2], and later refined by the Swedish Institute for System Development (SISU). A significant innovation in this strand of EM was the notion of business goals as part of an enterprise model, enriching traditional model component types such as entities, and business processes. The SISU framework was further developed in the ESPRIT projects F3 – "From Fuzzy to Formal" and ELEKTRA – "Electrical Enterprise Knowledge for Transforming Applications" leading to an EM method called EKD – "Enterprise Knowledge Development" [3, 4]. It was used in practice for more than a decade of application in practice and continuously improved, primarily in terms of method guidance, to become the 4EM – "For Enterprise Modeling" method [5]. F3, EKD, and 4EM were mostly developed by researchers in the EU and nationally funded research projects. In parallel to these developments a number of successful consultancy businesses spun off the initial SISU EM community the experiences of which are summarized in [6]. Elsewhere in Scandinavia EM approaches have been developed in close integration with modeling tools, with Troux

© IFIP International Federation for Information Processing 2015
J. Ralyté et al. (Eds.): PoEM 2015, LNBIP 235, pp. 193–208, 2015.
DOI: 10.1007/978-3-319-25897-3_13

Architect (initially developed under the name of Metis) and Active Knowledge Modeling (AKM) being a notable example [7]. Apart from the "Scandinavian strand" of EM, a variety of other EM methods have been suggested (c.f., for instance, [8–13]).

Many EM approaches have been developed together with industry partners and successfully applied in a significant number of industrial cases. In the case of EKD and 4EM, since 2000, it has been applied to ca 40 organizations, but most of these applications have been involving the developers of the method. Similarly, i* [13] is a popular approach for goal and requirements modeling and is widely used in the scientific community, yet its industrial use beyond the research community is, to the best of our knowledge, insufficient. Some methods have been developed together with tools (e.g. AKM), for some (e.g. EKD and 4EM) several tool support solutions have been developed, and some EM approaches have adopted the strategy of using simple drawing tools (e.g. Visio) for model documentation (c.f. [6]). In summary, the current state of EM method and tool adoption is such that many potentially useful methods and tools are not used beyond the broader community (industrial and academic partners) that developed them. A possible cause could be the fact that EM methods and tools emerge from R&D projects with little or no focus on how to launch a finished product in the market. Hence, the current situation is that EM methods and tools are not generally intended and developed as commercialized products initially. i.e., they are not developed and managed as products, and we can conclude that the concept of productization within the area of EM is not addressed consciously. This may be due to the fact that the productization processes are fairly generic and do not consider the specifics of this product category. To this this end, the research question addressed in this paper is as follows: *what factors influence the successful productization of enterprise modeling methods and tools?*

This study focuses solely on success factors of EM methods and tools from a perspective of their development and management as *products*. I.e. we are not analyzing the theoretical and technological construction of EM methods and tools as design artifacts. Other methods or tools, e.g. for supporting business process management, IS analysis and design, and model-driven development are considered out of scope of this study.

The rest of the paper is organized as follows. Section 2 briefly describes the principles of EM, product development, and productization. Section 3 describes the research approach. Section 4 presents the research findings. Section 5 provides concluding remarks and issues of future work.

2   Theoretical Foundations and Related Work

This section briefly introduces the topics related to the research question, namely, EM, new product development, and productization.

2.1   Enterprise Modeling

An EM method consists of (1) a modeling language, (2) intended modeling process - including ways of working, EM project management and competency management - by which the enterprise models are produced. It also proposes (3) tools to be used during that process.

An EM language typically consists of sub-models each addressing a specific aspect of an enterprise, such as business goals, process, concepts, actors, rules, IS requirements. The components of the sub-models are related between them within a sub-model (intra-model relationships), as well as with components of other sub-models (inter-model relationships) see Fig. 1. The ability to trace decisions, components, and other aspects throughout the enterprise is dependent on the use and understanding of these relationships.

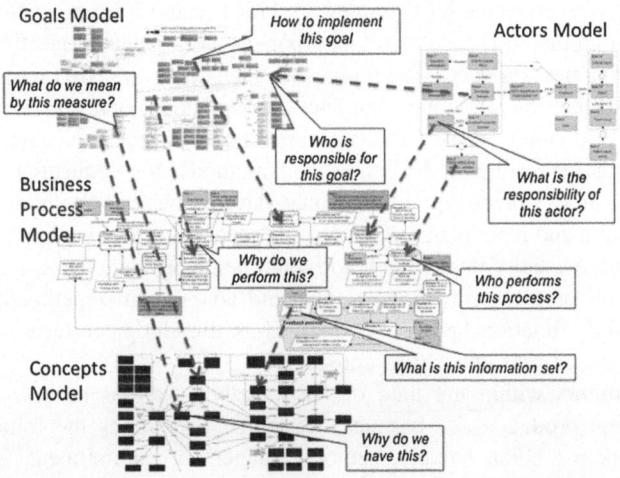

Fig. 1. Working with inter-model links (dashed arrows) through driving questions

To achieve high quality results, the EM process is as equally important as the EM language used. There are two levels of the EM process – the EM project level and the modeling level.

The EM project level, where the modeling activities, such as, defining the scope of the project, planning the modeling activities, conducting modeling seminars, are placed in a context of purpose. The modeling level is where the domain knowledge is elicited, and enterprise models created and refined. When it comes to eliciting domain knowledge to be included in enterprise models, the Scandinavian strand of EM recommends a participatory way of working – facilitated stakeholder group sessions. The modeling process is consensus-driven in the sense that stakeholders collaboratively create and "own" the models, as well as govern their contents. In contrast, consultative participation means that analysts create models and stakeholders are then consulted to validate the models; cf. [5] for more on the EM process.

The EM process needs to be supported by tools. The tool requirements depend on the organization's intentions (e.g. will the models be kept "alive") and situational factors (e.g. the presence of skillful tool operators and resources). There are several categories of tools that can be considered such as group meeting facilitation tools, model documentation tools, as well as project communication and collaboration tools. More on the kinds of tools needed as well as on how to select and introduce EM tools in organizations is available in [5, 14].

2.2 New Product Development

New Product Development (NPD) process involves a sequence of activities such as an initial idea generation, evaluation of the idea as well as subsequent development, test, and ultimately market launch [15]. This process varies in different industries, thus it must be adapted to meet the requirements of a specific industry in order to attain the best possible outcome [16]. We follow the NPD framework [15] because it is one of the most widely recognized within the NPD field and it incorporates all the main stages that are required when developing new products. The framework categorizes the NPD process into seven consecutive stages, namely, new product strategy development, idea generation, screening and evaluation, business analysis, development, testing, and commercialization.

Considering the nature of EM tools and methods, the sequential distinction of stages in [15] may not be applicable since development of methods and tools is typically iterative and incremental. This regards especially the development and testing stages as they are usually intertwined. Although being separate tasks, it is common to develop method or tool prototypes, to test and adapt them repetitively rather than developing a fully functional product at once. Thus, this study conforms to the stages in [15] as being concurrent rather than consecutive.

Several authors within the field of NPD analyze various success factors when developing new products. For instance, Lester [17] identifies the following critical success factors for NPD, namely, senior management commitment, organizational structure and processes, developing attractive new product concepts, forming a venture team, and project management. Brown and Eisenhardt [18] argue that cross-functional teams, managerial skills, and support from senior management are crucial success factors. They extend [17] by considering additional factors that are linked to the market, financial performance, and product concept effectiveness.

Bhuiyan [16] connects the critical success factors to each stage of the NPD process proposed in [15] and proposes relevant metrics to measure the achievement of those factors together with tools and techniques for applying the metrics for each stage of the NPD process (see Table 1). This is also relevant to products in the area of EM.

Good product ideas, functioning prototypes, and well-executed NPD projects are not sufficient for the success of a product. Maintenance of the new product in terms of planning, building marketing, distribution, and evolution are equally important. Hence, Software Product Management (SPM) covering both, the business and technological aspects of the product, is needed; cf., for instance [19].

2.3 Productization

Productization is a relatively novel area related to SPM and it is yet to attract a large amount of research. According to [20] *"productization means standardization of the*

Table 1. Framework for successful NPD [16].

Stage	Critical success factor	Metrics	Tools and technique
New product Strategy	Clear strategy	Return on investment	Financial analysis
	Well communicated Strategy	Degree of communication	Balanced scorecard as a communication tool
Idea generation	Customer focused idea generation	Number of customer-focused ideas generated	Lead user methodology
			Ethnographic approach
Screening and business case	Up-front homework	Expected commercial value	Financial method evaluation
		Net present value	
		Internal rate of return	
		Productivity index	
Development	Speed	Development time	Team cohesiveness
	Customer feedback	Degree of functional integration	Dynamic time to market
		Degree of team commitment	Degree of parallelism
		Concurrency of activities	
		Degree of design effort on real customer priorities	
Testing	Product functionality	Product performance	Validation testing
	Customer acceptance	Customer perceived value	User and field testing

elements in the offering." The term incorporates various technological attributes from inceptive stages of designing a product such as requirements engineering, creation of product architecture and selection of platform, to the commercial features regarding positioning, sales and distribution activities such as delivery channels, positioning and after sales activities. According to [20] the term productization is mostly used within the context of service and software industries with the aim of modifying intangible services into more defined product-like outcomes, i.e. creating defined offerings. The concept is applicable for the creation products and services in the area of EM.

Artz et al. [21] introduce a productization process for moving from developing customer specific solutions to product software. The process consists of the following six stages – (1) independent projects, (2) reuse across projects, (3) product recognition, (4) product platform, (5) standardized product platform, (6a) customizable software product, and (6b) standard product.

According to [22], the productization level increases as the maturity of an offering increases (see Fig. 2). The higher the level of maturity, the lower the abstraction level, which subsequently facilitates interaction with customers. Considering the current state of EM methods and tools, many seem to be at the lowest level, i.e. the methods and tools are developed but only used in practice by the extended group of developers and offered to a broader audience in an ad hoc manner. Several methods and tools are on the second level – the offering is well elaborated along with a clear-cut strategy of how to use it. But in most cases this is done from a technological point of view and essential business aspects for making a commercial success are missing. The latter is needed to reach the highest level of productization.

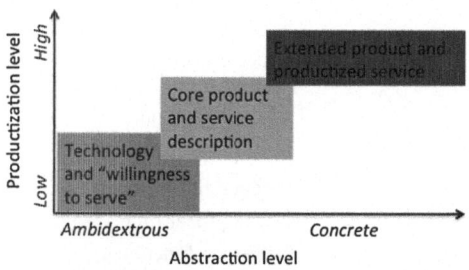

Fig. 2. Productization levels in context of service and technology (adapted from [22])

The framework of [22] stresses the importance of *inbound and outbound productization*. Inbound productization includes the tasks for harmonizing and systematizing the offering's delivery process. In the case of EM these are the processes of developing an EM method (e.g. by means of method-engineering [23]) or developing an EM tool as software. Outbound productization refers to the ability to sell, e.g. it aims at improving the visibility, compactness, and the perceived value of a product by customers. It should include brand design, licensing, training, and after-sales service. Most of the current efforts in EM are focused on inbound productization while tasks for outbound productization are considerably more neglected.

3   Research Approach

This study seeks to identify the factors that influence successful productization in the area of EM. Currently there is very little theoretical knowledge regarding this topic. Yet we have some hypothetical areas of investigation, e.g. that EM development projects are lacking inclusion of the concepts such as NPD, SPM, and productization. Furthermore, it is not always the case that methods and tools are developed as one product – an EM method can be supported by different tools and vice versa. Due to the lack of research, these assumptions are mostly based on our own experiences and observations in the field, as well as on communications with our peers. I.e. much of relevant empirical knowledge exists in "people's heads" – experts and practitioners in EM. By virtue of this, it was suitable to generate the theoretical findings by conforming to a qualitative approach. The primary reason for this was due to the exploratory characteristics of this research. It was also important that the participants shared their inner thoughts and beliefs regarding the topic and henceforth a qualitative approach was appropriate. The research strategy chosen for this study is Grounded Theory [24]. The purpose of Grounded Theory is to generate theories from data via a continual process of contrasting the ideas with existing data, and ameliorating the emerging concepts and theory by scrutinizing them against new data gathered particularly for the purpose.

The method of data collection for this approach was unstructured interviews. The following categories of EM professionals were interviewed – EM and business consultants, researchers developing EM methods, as well as a product marketing manager. Interviewees were selected based on authors' knowledge about their involvement in EM method and tool development and application in practice. Interviewee profiles are presented in Table 2. The interviews were transcribed and analyzed by the Altas.ti tool according to the principles of Grounded Theory, which included open, axial, and selective coding.

Table 2. Interview profiles

No	Interviewee profile
i1	Researcher with extensive expertise in EM. Has developed EM methods and has been involved in numerous publications and EM projects. Has worked as a modeling facilitator and a consultant.
i2	Researcher with broad skills and experience in EM, has developed EM methods and been involved in various publications and EM projects.
i3	Senior advisor at a consultancy firm. Extensive experience in various aspects of EM since several decades. Has extensive experience in R&D, consulting, and in developing EM methods and tools.
i4	Consultant in business and organizational development. Practitioner in EM with many years of experience. Has successfully developed various EM methods.
i5	Consultant in organizational development and change management. Has worked as a researcher previously, and has extensive experience of developing and applying EM methods in practice.
i6	Business and management consultant at a consultancy firm. Has been working in the area of EM for decades and has extensive knowledge of developing and applying EM methods and tools.
i7	Product marketing manager at one of the world largest IT organizations. Is responsible for numerous products within one of the organization's key areas.

Every interviewee agreed to participate freely in this study. They were fully informed of the research objective and the meaning of their involvement.

4 Factors Influencing Productization

This section presents the empirical findings in terms of factors influencing the success of productization, namely, EM maturity gap, method and tool development process, application context, marketing and sales aspects, as well as product aspects.

4.1   Reduction of EM Maturity Gap

The empirical data indicates a gap between research and practice views on EM in terms of what is important, as the following citation shows.

> *Citation 1: "I would say that we have different degrees of maturity in research and in practice. In research you get to a high level of maturity conceptual wise, you [in research] create theories and you make it very sound. It will work in a theoretical environment in an experiment environment, it will work, it is elegant. But the real world does not have those premises; you have different premises there. You have different situations where it's stickier, it's muddier, it's more convoluted, it's a different set of problems. It's those wicked problems, if you like, dirty problems, they are not clean like you can do it in research." [i4]*

What the maturity gap in this case refers to is the actual belief of what characteristics a successful EM method or tool should encompass. The empirical findings show that there are different views towards this in research and in practice. As a result, methods and tools originating from research often oversimplify problems faced in practice. Practitioners' view is that they are well designed and based on the existing research, but the fact that they are designed from a theoretical perspective leads to problems of using them in practice, as one interviewee states it below.

> *Citation 2: "The very good example for that, is the i* method...it is very difficult to get that out into practice...yeah, there are some very nice relationships, and some very nice things but very soon the models start to turn into something big, you can't really read them and there are no good tools to work with and... Not very practical...so, the practical aspect...is the method practical? Does it help me to solve my problems?" [i2]*

The different views of EM in practice and research also manifest themselves in the way people speak about EM. One of the interviewees [i5] said that in the industry people mostly talk about Enterprise Architecture, rather than EM, and that EM is merely viewed as one component of the whole enterprise architecture.

Moreover, many interviewees who were working with EM in practice claimed that using something that has not been "proven in combat" has a risk involved, since it may have a misconception of the complexity of the problems in the real world, as interviewee 4 points out.

> *Citation 3: "And the first question you will meet when you try to introduce a tool or a method to someone, let's say a practitioner, is: has this been proven? Has this been used? Do you have any reference cases? Or can you show me something that actually works? Otherwise I am taking a risk if I am going to use this thing" [i4]*

Many interviewees also pointed out that individuals from research and practice are not working together sufficiently enough to establish a shared view of EM methods and tools. Although there are various projects, usually financed as research grants that include individuals from both sides of the field, there is a lack of incentives to drive things further (in business terms) once the project is completed. From a research perspective the majority of the participants concluded that many researchers are not necessarily interested in pursuing things to the point of commercialization. Interviewees 1 and 2 point out the following:

> *Citation 4: "Very often the method developers have the interest of developing methods and not necessarily being consultants and selling...of course, we are researchers, so maybe we [personally] are not very interested in developing it into the market." [i1]*

Citation 5: "Well, because you publish a paper and then it is over. You will have another career. So, I think that the driving force behind these research - based methods is not the market, it is the research." [i2]

Another factor leading to the low adoption rate of EM is related to EM projects usually being run from an IT perspective and not from a business perspective. The projects are mostly conducted from an IT point-of-view, but IT people do not have the mandate to successfully work with the business aspects. Thus, the lacking incorporation of a business perspective, such as the inclusion people with extensive knowledge on how to manage the company, business processes, and strategic goals, negatively influences on the overall success of an EM method or tool.

Citation 7: "... the biggest problem is that it is usually run by IT departments and they focus on technology, on methods, on tools, that's not something most business are interested in. They are interested in the business. So for the few companies I know that actually manage to do this, what they all have in common is the fact that these efforts are run by business departments not the IT department. So I would say, it's sort of a managerial issue. They do not have the right teams or the right organization. They are simply not doing it right." [i5]

From a user perspective the EM method and tool maturity gap is affected by the existing competences and skills. Interviewees pointed to a high learning curve of how to apply the methodology or tools. The functionality of tools is often unexploited and they are simply used as drawing tools. Interviewees 3 and 4 described this in the following terms.

Citation 8: "We do not really have process owners that know what it means to be a process owner, so let alone, if we have this tool that we have documents and processes in, they do not know what to do with that. We have people who are skilled in using the tool itself but we're just using it as a drawing tool. We do not use the repository capabilities and all that stuff. Because we're not on that maturity level at all. And that goes for a lot of companies" [i4]

Citation 9: "One of the biggest barriers is (1) lack of education, and (2) freeing the most knowledgeable people in companies from their daily project work, working with paper flows and so on." [i3]

In summary, the EM maturity gap should be reduced by the following – (a) Individuals from research and practice working together, and (b) modeling the IT and a business perspective in congruence.

In [14] we have defined EM method and tool usage maturity as determinant of how experienced and prepared the organization is to work with EM methods and tools. A key aspect of this is competence and if the organization wants using EM without external consultants it needs a "modeling department"; for more on this c.f. [1, 5].

4.2   EM Method and Tool Development Process

There is no commonly recognized process for developing EM methods and tools. One of the potential reasons for this is the difference of views of EM in research and practice discussed previously. A common perception is that methods should evolve based on previous experiences and include well-known approaches in a manner that is easy to comprehend and grasp. I.e., method developers should extract key things from different cases, find a solution, and develop a way of structuring it to make it comprehensible and appealing. Interviewee 4 compared a possible future recognized development process for EM with the business model canvas.

Citation 10: "Now what I have seen lately, that is very interesting is that the business model canvas.... Well, that model has been very, very popular; everybody is doing canvas – "oooh canvas", like it was something new. There is nothing new in it; it is the same questions that have been asked all the time. It is just a different way of exposing it, and structuring it becomes graphical. And that is one thing that I've seen successful, a good example where ways of structuring problems becomes very popular because it does not only address the analytical part of your brain but also the structural with, for example, pictures. So, you have this business model canvas and you have those icons and pictures, and you have things like that, which makes it popular because it is just not bullet points on a PowerPoint. So it's more attractive to view, it becomes a way of structuring it. So, one way of developing that will work very well is, if you can find ways of presenting already known facts but in a way that is easier to understand and grasp; then I think you're on to something." [i4]

Moreover, interviewee 3 identified four crucial success factors that must be taken into account when developing an EM method and tool as stated in the citation below.

Citation 12: "1: which sector you're looking at, 2: the business situation, 3: the customer situation, and 4: the technological situation in the market." [i3]

Another important aspect when developing an EM method or tool is making the right decisions not only regarding the actual method or tool that is being developed but also about how the project organization is set up by ensuring that the right people with the necessary competence are involved, and that they are given defined roles. Ultimately, it is important that the development of an EM method or tool follows the same type of process as any product being developed. The primary reason for this is that EM methods and tools are used by people and hence user acceptance must be ensured. Interviewee 4 stated the following.

Citation 13: "So, if you want to produce a method, a tool or something like that for management consulting, for instance, you must follow through the same type of process as you do with any product. Here in management consulting you do not want it necessarily in a computer, the tool here has to be able to work with people. So, if people can grasp it easily, then you can run with it." [i4]

In summary, there is no commonly recognized process for the development of an EM method or tool as a product. What is commonly known and used are method engineering approaches to method development and software engineering approaches to tool development, but these merely see methods and tools as design artifacts instead of products. Hence, a successful inbound productization should have the following criteria: (a) the process of creating a core product (method/tool) must be systematic which contributes to the product being comprehensible and appealing to the users; and (b) should follow the same NPD process as any product.

4.3   Application Context of EM Methods and Tools

The success of an EM method or tool is highly influenced by the extent to which contextual factors are considered. Every interviewee stated that neglecting the application environment for an EM method or tool leads to failure. The context often contains many aspects that influence the problem that a method or a tool is designed to solve, which may only be discovered by using it in its intended setting. It is therefore crucial to understand the situation where the method or tool is to be used, which in turn requires presence in that specific context as there might be other aspects affecting the situation, as interviewee 4 exemplifies below.

> *Citation 13: "You might have to design the tool that solves the particular problem but the situation where this problem occurs contains a lot of other things that influence the problem that you haven't taken into account." [i4]*

Considering the context increases awareness of the problem that is being addressed and allows designing a method or tool that can solve that specific problem. Awareness also allows for communicating with the stakeholders in a manner that is comprehensible for them, which, in turn, enhances success of the method or tool.

The influencing aspects are not always identifiable prior to setting an EM method or tool in its context. Hence, it is vital that methods and tools are extendable. Without such an option of agile extensions the likelihood of good results is small, as interviewee 3 states it below.

> *Citation 16: "We must have capabilities to adapt and extend them. Because they change during the lifecycle. You need an agile approach, model-based, architecture driven workplaces and that the evolution of them is stored in the architecture itself. The tool I am talking about is a multidimensional platform where all dimensions are agile approaches, adaptive methods (potentially throughout the whole life-cycle), adaptive tools and holistic design. Because the way we are handling properties and parameters in ICT today is completely wrong." [i3]*

In summary, the factor influencing productization regarding the application context is the need for an EM method or tool to be extendable in an agile way.

4.4   Integration of EM Methods and Tools

All interviewees agreed that neglecting integration is one of the key causes for poor practical performance of EM methods or tools. Integration is vital since an EM method and tool aims to elucidate and describe the different aspects of an enterprise through the creation of a shared model. As citation 17 shows, supporting integration is crucial since it affects numerous components that relates to the problem matter.

> *Citation 17: "I am responsible for an area and all these products that are related to that area. So, I've been responsible for Big Data and Analytics, so, in there I am supposed to brand that category. But I also have products in that category that support each other. I mean you can't just say Big Data. You need a database, you need some analyzing tools, and somewhere to store it, and you need to handle it and so on... So, there are so many components." [i7]*

Integration is needed for the creation and management of products in general. Consequently, a lack of integration with the business results in difficulties in viewing EM methods or tools as products.

Another factor leading to difficulties in regarding EM methods or tools as products is the separation of a method and tool. Integration of them as package is preferred. Without it the parts will not be perceived as products, as interviewee 2 states it below.

Citation 19: "… if you just have a method then it is difficult to present it as a product of anything more than just of "this is my consulting service and we're using this method". If you have a tool then you have a stronger selling point because you can give something to the customer and there is something to license and something to support. So, a method plus tool always puts one in a stronger position than just having a method." [i2]

On the contrary, some interviewees argued that we do not always have to develop a supporting tool whenever creating a new EM method because many methods can be used with existing tools. Moreover, it is less complex to develop a method than a tool because tool development requires software development. Interviewee 6 stated the relevant business concerns in this respect.

Citation 21: "You have to be aware of that there is a tool that can be used, and there are many tools around, so we do not have to develop our own. And it takes a lot of effort to develop a tool, so the market for a tool that is developed cannot be as small as our method it's used only in certain places." [i6]

The interviewees also stated that integration with other development activities within an organization is crucial for the usefulness of EM, e.g. see below. An aspect of this is being able to technically integrate with other methods and tools.

Citation 22: "The integration between EM and other development activities, like software development, business development, particularly the software development…if you can't translate those models into what's normally used for software development then the models are not useful. So, the integration with that kind of development and tools and development situations I think is an extremely important factor to think about." [i2]

In summary, successful productization is influenced by integration – an EM method or tool must be able to integrate with business and other organizational activities.

4.5   Marketing and Sales Aspects of EM Methods and Tools

An EM method or tool must provide value to be successful. The interviewees argued that without value to be gained from using the method or tool it will be difficult to attract users. Interviewee 7 exemplified value creation by stating the following.

Citation 26: "You kind of need to show the value for them. Like, what is the business value? How are the results going to improve by buying this tool? How are you being optimized? How is it going to affect your day?" [i7]

The interview analysis show that the value is affected by what can be called soft attributes, such as, positive psychological qualities experienced from a product such as, e.g., appreciation, positive user experience, emotional satisfaction, and fulfillment.

Citation 27: "…you need to add the soft values, that's what's gonna sell a product, because the product won't sell itself and you can't rely on product features and functions to be cool. That only works depending on what kind of brand image you already have…" [i7]

Citation 29: "…more and more we need to think about the psychology of it… Humans are humans and we are gonna interact in a certain ways and react in a certain ways. And we like to feel different things so if you manage to push on those things and also have a product that is complementing them then I think you have a success." [i7]

One must therefore sell the usage of EM in a manner that focuses on the desired effect, by understanding customers' business and how the use of EM would improve it. Hence, interaction with customers is needed. Yet, the interviews show that in reality there is little focus on customers. This is especially the case when an EM method or tool has been developed by researchers. Interviewee 1 stated as follows.

Citation 30: "The strategy is always "we want this cool tool" and there is somebody that wants it; there is usually a project in which you use it for a specific business problem in some company, that needs to be solved. This is how all these 'A', 'B', and 'C' projects started.... But this is not your customer; it's your partner. So, there is no notion of customer. There is a notion of a business partner, who can later become a customer but seldom does." [i1]

One of the causes for the lack of clear focus on customers may stem from the fact that consultants are seen as the primary users for EM methods and tools. A belief is that consultants easily grasp how a method or tool is to be used due to their expertise and hence no focus is put on how to address them from a marketing and sales perspective. This mindset is inadequate and the interviewees agreed that it is vital to involve the customers and interact with them on the basis of their needs and preferences. i.e. customer centric marketing and sales processes should be established. It is influenced by how one builds a story, which allows customers to envision how a specific method or tool will satisfy an existing need in a better way than what is currently used or being offered by the competitors.

In summary, productization should include attributes related to an extended product that delivers customer value and complimentary assets. EM marketing and sales must be carefully thought through as well as value must be provided including soft attributes. These are the factors that include the characteristics needed to constitute an extended product. This leads to achieving outbound productization, i.e. the ability to sell. From an EM marketing and sales perspective the following is needed – (a) an EM method or tool must provide value to customers, and (b) it should address real business problems.

4.6 EM Methods and Tools as Products

The empirical results show that there are various factors influencing the view of an EM method or a tool as a product. One of the key findings is that it must consist of a full package. Thus, in addition to the actual EM method or tool itself, all activities and tasks that are related to it must cover the integration aspects (see Sect. 4.4). This regards everything from the language used in the method or tool to the training and intro-duction of EM in the company. Interviewee 2 described it as follows.

Citation 35: "... if it is supposed to be a product, it should be the full package. It should be a language, it should have guidance for the process when you model how to do that, there should be a tool, and there should be a good link to other methodologies. So, there should be a good integration with it, there should be very clear, which roles are involved in using the methods. There should be some idea of how to train people to use these methods. If you have all these things, I am sure there are more things that could be added, then I think you have a product. You have an EM product that should be marketed. But coming just with a language or just with a tool is not going to work." [i2]

Thus, it is of high importance that a product is extendable so that it can adapt to the changing needs of the environment as discussed in Sect. 4.3. Yet, our investigation also uncovered that customers and consultants do not generally perceive EM methods and tools as products. The three main causes for this is the lack of management, the lack of consideration of soft attributes (see Sect. 4.5), and the fact that an EM product is usually regarded as what is being produced by using the tool or method (models) and not the actual method or tool itself, as the citation below shows.

> Citation 38: *"The problem with EM is that... the product isn't the EM, it is not really...the product isn't the EM, the product is the models you produce with the EM. That's the only thing the customer is interested in. It's like trying to sell someone a hammer when they're really interested in getting a house. They want the house; they do not care how the house is built. So, they are products but it is hard to get customers to view them as products."* [i4]

In regard to management, many participants said that emphasis is rarely laid on it in terms of product management, as interviewees 2 and 4 exemplified below.

> Citation 36: *"I would say that there is no focus on managing this as a product."* [i2]

> Citation 37: *"It is very rare actually that you have someone who is responsible for the tools and methods and that stuff, it is very rare. It is not very common because people in organizations focus on the business not on improving the business, and this is a problem."* [i4]

Some interviewees suggested that using some sort of standardization could make the perception of EM method and tools as products more complete. This suggestion follows the common principle of IT product alignment and integration with standards. Interviewee 1 compared it to OMG below.

> Citation 38: *"... in system analysis or system design there is UML. For business process there is BPMN. These are OMG standards. So, this is another angle where modeling methods should work, is towards standardization. Because similarly to BPMN there are standards and there are tools supporting it. For EM there is none, although there are some attempts; there is the business motivation model that is also part of OMG.... But there are no integrated sets. So, promoting EM through standardization and professional bodies is one way."* [i1]

On a somewhat contrary note, the participants stressed the importance of not trying to make something general initially and to focus on specific domain or problem area, as interviewee 5 stated.

> Citation 39: *"...never try building a general solution that can solve any problem. Instead try focusing on specific problems that you've actually observed if it's in the organization or amongst your customers or whatever your domain is. And solve those first. Once that is done then you can look for how to extend this, How to make it more general. But never try to be general from the beginning because then you will end up with a monster like [method X] or one of these really, really big frameworks that don't work in reality."* [i5]

It can therefore be concluded that factors contributing to a successful EM method or tool are (a) a complete method and tool package, (b) alignment with standards, and (c) focus of a specific market.

5 Conclusions and Future Work

We have analyzed what factors influence productization of EM methods and tools. The primary focus has been on developing products rather than just method and tool artifacts. Hence, we have primarily focused on NPD and aspects of outbound productization. Figure 3 shows an overview of how the different factors discussed in Sect. 4 are related to productization; the links are used to show positive influence. Due to lack of space we have not analyzed dependencies among the factors.

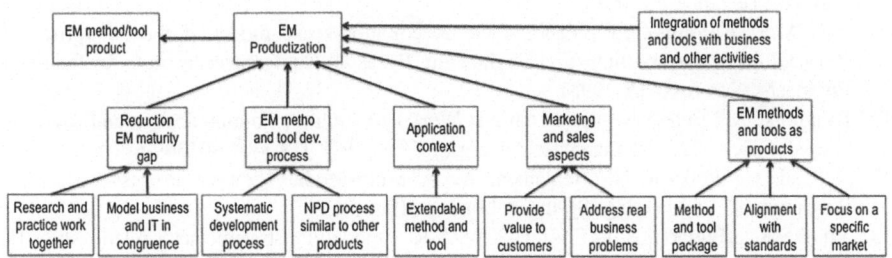

Fig. 3. Overview of factors influencing EM productization.

We have concentrated on the Scandinavian strand of EM but in principle our findings seem relevant to other EM methods and tools as well although more analysis of productization of other methods and tools is needed. This investigation should merely be seen in an initial attempt to identify the potential areas to which the EM community should pay closer attention. More in depth analysis of the existing findings is needed. Among the issues for future work we envision the need to develop NPD and productization approaches that are specific to EM and based on the best practices that exist in the field, to further investigate the process of method and tool acquisition and adoption in organizations, as well as to support the integration of EM with other areas of organizational development and management beyond what is traditionally seen as topics of Computer Science and Information Systems.

References

1. Stirna, J., Persson, A.: Purpose driven competency planning for enterprise modeling projects. In: Ralyté, J., Franch, X., Brinkkemper, S., Wrycza, S. (eds.) CAiSE 2012. LNCS, vol. 7328, pp. 662–677. Springer, Heidelberg (2012)
2. Willars, H.: Handbok i ABC-metoden. Plandata Strategi, Sweden (1988)
3. Bubenko, J.A.J., Persson, A., Stirna, J.: User guide of the knowledge management approach using enterprise knowledge patterns, deliverable D3, IST Programme project no. IST-2000-28401. Royal Institute of Technology, Sweden (2001)
4. Loucopoulos, P., Kavakli, V., Prekas, N., Rolland, C., Grosz, G., Nurcan, S.: Using the EKD Approach: The Modelling Component. UMIST, Manchester (1997)

5. Sandkuhl, K., Stirna, J., Persson, A., Wißotzki, M.: Enterprise Modeling – Tackling Business Challenges with the 4EM Method. Springer, Heidelberg (2014). ISBN 978-3-662-43724-7

6. Nilsson, A.G., Tolis, C., Nellborn, C. (eds.): Perspectives on Business Modelling: Understanding and Changing Organisations. Springer, Heidelberg (1999)

7. Lillehagen, F., Krogstie, J.: Active Knowledge Modeling of Enterprises. Springer, Heidelberg (2008). ISBN 978-3-540-79415-8

8. Bajec, M., Krisper, M.: A methodology and tool support for managing business rules in organisations. Inf. Syst. **30**(6), 423–443 (2005)

9. Castro, J., Kolp, M., Mylopoulos, J.: A Requirements-driven development methodology. In: Dittrich, K.R., Geppert, A., Norrie, M. (eds.) CAiSE 2001. LNCS, vol. 2068, p. 108. Springer, Heidelberg (2001)

10. Fox, M.S., Chionglo, J.F., Fadel, F.G.: A common-sense model of the enterprise. In: Proceedings of the 2nd Industrial Engineering Research Conference. Institute for Industrial Engineers, Norcross/GA(1993)

11. Lankhorst, M.: Enterprise Architecture at Work - Modelling, Communication and Analysis, 2nd edn, pp. 1–325. Springer, Heidelberg (2009). ISBN 978-3-642-01309-6

12. Rolland, C., Prakash, N., Benjamen, A.: A Multi-Model View of Process Modelling. Requirements Engineering. Springer, London (1999)

13. Yu, E.S.K., Mylopoulos, J.: From E-R to "A-R" - modelling strategic actor relationships for business process reengineering. In: Proceedings of the 13th International Conference on the Entity-Relationship Approach, Manchester (1994)

14. Stirna, J.: The Influence of Intentional and Situational Factors on EM Tool Acquisition in Organisations. Ph.D. thesis, Royal Institute of Technology, Sweden (2001)

15. Booz, Allen, Hamilton: New product Management for the 1980's. Booz, Allen & Hamilton Inc., New York (1982)

16. Bhuiyan, N.: A framework for successful new product development. J. Ind. Eng. Manag. **4**(4), 746–770 (2011)

17. Lester, D.H.: Critical success factors for new product development. Res. Technol. Manag. **41**(1), 36 (1998)

18. Brown, S., Eisenhardt, K.: Product development: past research, present findings, and future directions. Acad. Manag. Rev. **20**(2), 343–378 (1995)

19. PMI: A Guide to the Project Management Body of Knowledge (PMBOK Guide), Project Management Institute, ISBN 978-1-935589-67-9 (2012)

20. Hietala, J., Kontio, J., Jokinen, J., Pyysiäinen, J.: Challenges of software product companies: results of a national survey in Finland. In: IEEE METRICS, pp. 232–243 (2004)

21. Artz, P., van de Weerd, I., Brinkkemper, S., Fieggen, J.: Productization: transforming from developing customer-specific software to product software. In: Tyrväinen, P., Jansen, S., Cusumano, M.A. (eds.) ICSOB 2010. LNBIP, vol. 51, pp. 90–102. Springer, Heidelberg (2010)

22. Simula, H., Lethtimäki, T., Salo, J.: Re-thinking the product: from innovative technology to productized offering. In: Proceedings. of the 19th International Society for Professional Innovation Management Conference, Tours, France (2008)

23. Henderson-Sellers, B., Ralyté, J., Ågerfalk, P.J., Rossi, M.: Situational Method Engineering, pp. 1–274. Springer, Heidelberg (2014). ISBN 978-3-642-41466-4

24. Glaser, B., Strauss, A.: The Discovery of Grounded Theory. Aldine, Chicago (1967)

Methods in Designing and Developing Capabilities: A Systematic Mapping Study

Hasan Koç[✉]

Institute of Computer Science, University of Rostock, 18051 Rostock, Germany
hasan.koc@uni-rostock.de

Abstract. Enterprises operate in dynamically changing environments that have an influence on both business and IT areas. Capabilities have been proposed as instruments to align business and IT in such environments. One aim of enterprise modelling is a better communication between the stakeholders of an enterprise at various levels. Thus, the alignment can be facilitated by the exploitation of enterprise models as an abstraction instrument. In this respective the paper analyses the methods for capability design and development from the enterprise modelling perspective by conducting a mapping study, i.e. the level of methodological support for capability modelling is investigated. For this purpose 112 journals and 24 conference proceedings were analysed. The most important findings are that the research in capability design (i) adopts empirical research, mostly in form of case studies and surveys (ii) is mainly motivated by Resource Based View (RBV) and changing environments (iii) proposes development approaches and frameworks as solution artefacts, (iv) lately receives attention in the Information Systems Development & Tools of MIS subject classification lately, (v) provides a scarce methodological support that is mostly represented as procedures and most importantly (vi) only to some extent exploit enterprise models that could enhance stakeholder communication at various abstraction levels.

Keywords: Capability modelling · Capability development · Method · Systematic literature review · Mapping study

1 Introduction

The organizations are operating in an ever-shifting environment. Due to the rapid changes in regulations, globalization, time-to-market pressures and technological advances, the alignment of business and information technology (IT) becomes a serious challenge. Enterprises thus require the agility to adjust their offerings for a sustainable competitive advantage. One way to tackle these challenges is the design and development of the capabilities. As fundamental abstraction instruments in the stakeholder communication at various levels, modelling of capabilities can establish the required alignment [1].

Research in the field of capability management steadily rose during the last decade. However, there is a paucity of articles that systematically investigate methods, approaches and procedures in identifying, developing and designing an organization's core capabilities. In terms of the systematic literature reviews the contributions focus on the capability

© IFIP International Federation for Information Processing 2015
J. Ralyté et al. (Eds.): PoEM 2015, LNBIP 235, pp. 209–222, 2015.
DOI: 10.1007/978-3-319-25897-3_14

maturity models [7]. This paper presents a systematic mapping study in the methods of the capability design and development by analysing the research topics, research methods and research activities. The findings show that the research in capability design methods (i) adopts empirical research, mostly in form of case studies and surveys (ii) is mainly motivated by Resource Based View (RBV) and changing environments (iii) proposes development approaches and frameworks, (iv) receives attention in the Information Systems Development & Tools of MIS subject classification lately [9], (v) provides a scarce methodological support and (vi) only to some extent exploit enterprise models that could enhance stakeholder communication at various abstraction levels.

In line with [11] we define a method as a systematic way of problem solving consisting of *concepts*, *activities* and *notations*. The concepts specify what should be captured in a model. The activities describe in concrete terms how to identify the relevant concepts in a method component and the notation specifies how the result of the proce-dure should be documented. In this respect our findings show that the methodological support in capability development does hardly fit into the aforementioned method framework. The analysed articles propose steps, procedures or guidelines to design capabilities, which only to a weak extent expose the concept-activity-notation structure. This is investigated in Sect. 4 in detail.

The remainder of the paper is structured as follows. Section 2 describes the research approach, which is a mapping study, a specific type of systematic literature review (SLR). Then Sect. 3 presents the research design, i.e. which literature sources are included in the analysis. Following that, Sect. 4 analyses the findings and Sect. 5 concludes the work.

2   Research Approach

The research approach used in this work is a mapping study, which is a specific type of systematic literature review (SLR). A SLR is a review process of prior studies with a structured and comprehensible procedure that aims to accumulate all "existing evidence concerning a treatment or technology" and "identify gaps in current research". Mapping studies are characterized by their wider scope of the study and the generalization of research questions in a broader field [13]. After getting an overview of the research area by for instance defining the research methods, research design and research topics, detailed information can be extracted from a set of publications.

This work conducted a mapping study and developed a scheme to classify the find-ings thoroughly. Thus the guidelines of Kitchenham [1] were extended by the *develop/classify/refine* steps, as illustrated in Fig. 1. The selection process of the journals and conferences during scope definition was exhibited (Sect. 3.1) to provide transparency for researchers who might repeat the analysis by extending the sources or changing the inclusion criteria of journals, conferences or books. After defining the scope (Sect. 1) and data sources (Sect. 3), four research questions (RQ) are formulated, which are answered subsequently in Sect. 4.

- RQ1: Which research methods and research design are used in the capability develop-ment field?

- RQ2: Which topics are under investigation in the field of capability design methods? Is it possible to identify a trend in these topics?
- RQ3: Which countries and institutes are active in the field of capability design methods?
- RQ4: Which methods, steps or approaches are proposed to develop and design capabilities?

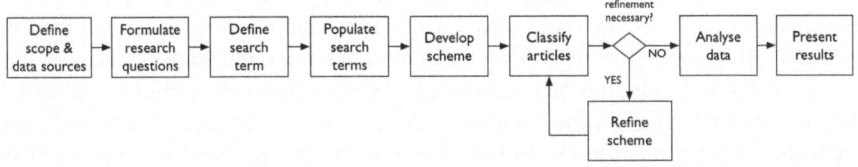

Fig. 1. Steps of the systematic literature analysis

3 Review Design

This chapter introduces the literature sources that are included in the analysis as well as the process of classification scheme development.

3.1 Selecting Literature Sources and Papers

Conducting a SLR requires a thorough selection of the data sources that serve as a starting point. To select the literature sources, we first identified A + and A Journals based on the rankings from [3]. Next, we complemented this list with B Journals from the Business Information Systems sub-discipline. To stabilize the journal selection we crosschecked our results with the rankings from [4] and finalized the journal selection part. After that we populated the list of journals with A and B ranked conferences from [5], with "A" being the highest ranking. As a result we identified a total of 112 journals and 24 conferences.

The main terms used for the initial search were "capability" (in abstract) and "method OR design OR proc*" (in keywords). The keyword terms were populated with the additional terms "practice OR step OR modeling OR modelling". Consequently we searched in the selected sources that included the term {capability} in abstract and one of the following terms {method, modeling, modelling, proc*, design, step, practice} in keywords. After removing the duplicates and inaccessible articles, the search resulted in a total of 362 journal articles and 178 conference papers.

The selection of the papers was based on a set of criteria, which is applied during abstract reading. In cases where the exclusion or inclusion was unclear, an additional full-text reading is conducted. First of all, the articles are eliminated that did not explicitly address "design and development of capabilities" as their research scope. For instance, if capabilities were proposed only as means to leverage the value of a firm's knowledge or mentioned as enablers of enhanced outsourcing arrangements, then it was excluded. Furthermore we eliminated an article when the term capability was used as a synonym for "ability" or "future", i.e. unrelated to its application in the Information Systems. Also the articles were excluded, which use the term capability in the abstract and do not mention it in the narrative text or mention dynamic capabilities to position their proposals as means to gain competitive advantage.

The main purpose in line with the research questions was analysing the state of the research in fields of capability modelling as a subset of enterprise modelling, in particular where processes, procedures, steps or methods are proposed to develop or design business capabilities. Hence the articles are included that address this aspect in a narrower context, i.e. the articles that investigate steps, best practices, guidelines, concepts, notations and roles in developing such capabilities. Most of the journal articles explored the relation between the capabilities of an enterprise as well as its environment and lacked establishing a clear relationship to the enterprise modelling. For the purposes of this paper, this is an interpretation of capability design in a broader context. Still, if the article contributed to capability development method area, then it was included. On the other hand the publications were excluded that investigate how for instance the IT capabilities are interlinked with the provision of e-government services by applying statistical methods and developing hypothesis. After the application of those criteria, a total of 22 journal articles and 23 conference papers resulted for further analysis[1].

3.2 Developing the Classification Scheme

A classification scheme provides a way to organise and structure the selected papers. The scheme included three main categories, research methods, research design and research topics, which are elaborated in this section.

The starting point for the classification in the category *research design* was the framework of Alavi and Carlson [12] that on the highest level distinguishes between empirical and non-empirical research. Articles carrying out empirical research capture the essence of research by relying on observation that are supported by data, which is acquired via qualitative (case study, interviews) or quantitative (experiments, surveys) techniques. The research design types are extended with "conceptual articles" and "design science research" articles [7]. Conceptual articles are primarily based on the ideas, frameworks, and suggestions rather than the systematic observation. Design science research articles answer questions relevant to human problems via the creation of innovative artefacts, thereby producing new knowledge and contributing to the body of scientific evidence. Design science research is fundamentally a problem-solving paradigm whose end goal is to produce a useful solution by creating and evaluating an artefact relevant to an IS problem. To be classified as design-oriented, the articles should follow the guidelines provided by [8].

The category *research methods* is created based on the article of Palvia et al. [9], which examined the mainstream journals in MIS research in terms of employed methodologies. The structure is expanded in order to fit our research purpose. We first defined

---

[1] The list of the investigated journals, conferences and selected papers can be accessed from http://bit.ly/1O5sS18.

"qualitative & quantitative research" as two main classes of research methods. Then we specified the two method types, *systematic literature reviews* and *experiments*. Finally *grounded theory* was added as an additional research method, which seeks to develop a theory by analysing gathered data systematically [10].

To structure the research topics the "concept matrix" approach was adapted from Webster and Watson [5], where the articles are structured according to their contribution areas. As illustrated in Fig. 1, these research topics were refined whenever necessary. Here three main contribution classes were observed. *Motivation* analysed the starting point of the articles, which is mostly reflected in the abstracts and state of the art sections. *Investigation* analysed the topics that the papers explore and contribute in, mostly stated in the conclusion parts. In line with [9] *subject classification* structured the research endeavour to more general research subjects in the Information Systems discipline. Figure 2 shows the classification scheme, including the research design, research method and research topics as the main categories.

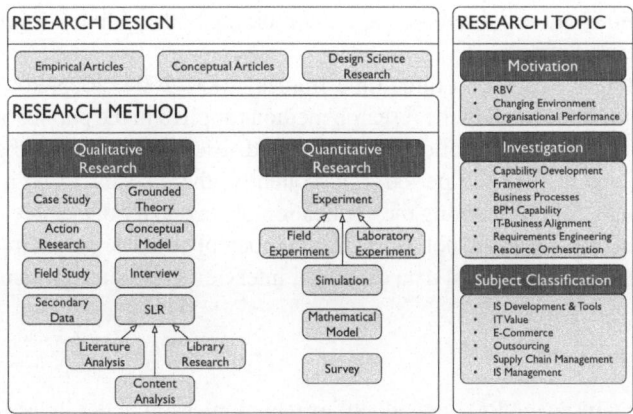

Fig. 2. The classification scheme

4 Data Analysis

4.1 Research Methods and Research Design

This section classifies the articles in line with their research approach (Fig. 2). The "research design" category is mutually exclusive, i.e. an article can apply only empirical, conceptual or design science research paradigm. On the other hand in the "research method" category the articles may be related to more than one method. To exemplify, an article can conduct a case study after a survey and thus use two different research methods. The analysis of all articles has shown that empirical design is used at most in the design of capabilities (76 % of all articles). A remarkable result was the application rate of design science research, which only took place in 4 % of all articles.

When conducting empirical research, 2 of 3 articles based their findings on qualitative research methods by applying case studies (38 %), interviews (26 %) and conceptual models (21 %). The articles adopting quantitative research methods use surveys extensively (55 %). The structure that these articles follow is (i) developing hypotheses to investigate the factors, phenomena, abilities, roles influencing design and development of capabilities, (ii) conducting a survey and (iii) statistically evaluating if the hypotheses hold. The results of such articles might be quite beneficial when constructing methods for capability design. Surveys are followed by secondary data (36 %), where the authors collect business data such as financial reports, documentations, archival materials and published documents.

The conference papers extensively use qualitative research methods (75 %). In fact, only 2 % of relevant articles apply quantitative methods solely. On the contrary the allocation in journal publications seems to be balanced, i.e. 44 % of all articles conduct quantitative and 56 % qualitative method techniques. In the set of 45 papers, 15 publications combined qualitative and quantitative methods (the exact allocation is 10 journal articles and 5 conference papers). Interestingly 8 of these 15 publications adopt case studies, interviews and analysis of secondary data, which seems to be a research method pattern. Also 80 % of the conference papers combining both qualitative and quantitative methods adopt this pattern.

By allocating 45 papers to three time frames; 2000–2004, 2005–2009 and 2010–2014, we analysed the trend in the research methods applied in the publications. In order to do so, we observed the relation of the selected research method to the sum of the published articles in the time period. Subsequently, there seems to be a trend in the capability design field concerning the application of secondary data and case studies as a research method. Last but not least, the number of articles producing conceptual models based on non-empirical data diminish, interviews and surveys remain stable.

4.2 Research Topics

This section analyses the RQ2 and identifies what topics are under investigation in the field of capability design methods and which terms are used most often. To determine the research topics we first analysed the title, abstract and keyword of the publication and summarized the mentioned terms. Next, a full text reading of 45 papers was conducted to limit the number of terms and include only the main focus and contribution of the work at hand. After this we clustered the final terms and classified them into the research topics in line with the developed scheme (Fig. 2), where an article can be related to multiple topics. The clustered topics include following terms:

Resource Based View. Articles motivating their work based on "Resource Based View, Dynamic Capability or Competitive Advantage" are categorized here. This topic is used for nearly half of the total works (45 %). Obviously these topics address the inspiration in the field of capability design and development methods (Fig. 3).

IT Value. Includes the terms "IT Capability, Information Communication Technology (ICT), ICT Capability" or "Leveraging IT". This topic is analysed in 38 % of the relevant articles and exposes the importance of IT in capability design.

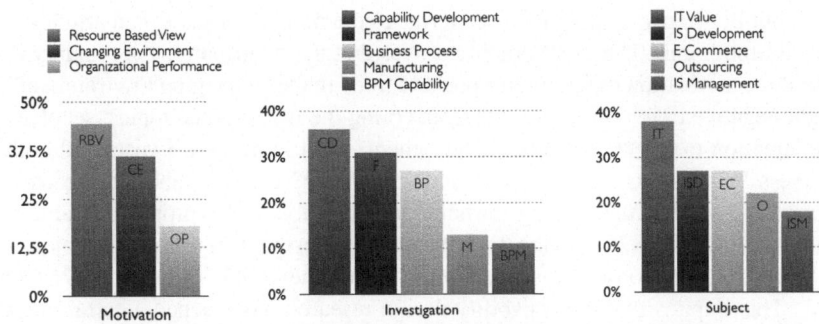

Fig. 3. Research topics in capability design (Color figure online)

Changing Environment. Includes articles with the terms "Change in Business, Change Management, Growing Enterprises, Business Model Transformation, Evolving Needs, Different Contexts, Unanticipated Changes, Dynamic Business Environment, Developing Countries, Emerging Economies". 36 % of articles motivate their work based on this topic. This is an indicator that capabilities are used as instruments to deal with agility and flexibility issues based on changing requirements.

E-Commerce. Includes the subject terms "E-Service, Electronic Service Delivery, Cloud Computing, Cloud Service, E-Business Strategy, E-Government, E-Business". %27 of the relevant articles deals with E-commerce topic.

IS Development & Tools. Includes subject terms "Enterprise Modelling, Goal Modelling, Pattern Modelling, BPM, Business Process Design, Business Models, Context Modelling". %27 of the relevant articles deals with this topic, all of which are published in conference proceedings. This finding addresses that the capabilities are important abstraction instruments for business and IT alignment and their modelling is closely related to the enterprise modelling area.

IS Management. Includes subject terms "Strategic Management, Strategy Process, Internationalisation Strategy, Strategy Optimisation, Business Strategy Development, Strategic Business".

Outsourcing. Includes subject terms "IT Outsourcing, Business Process Outsourcing, Service Level Agreement, Interorganizational Relations".

In addition to these topics, specific concepts were identified that cannot be structured in the above-mentioned groups, such as "Framework, Capability Development, Business Process, and BPM Capability". Figure 3 illustrates the results of the research topic classification including both clustered terms as well as specific topics. For brevity reasons, the topics were omitted which were motivated or investigated in less than 10 % of all articles. No trend analysis was conducted for such topics.

The analysis shows that concerning some of the aforementioned research topics it is possible to speak of a trend. Here it should be noted that all three classes (motivation, investigation and subject) are observed together as illustrated in Fig. 4. The analysis was

216   H. Koç

carried out by simply relating the used terms to the number of published articles in the selected time frame. The trend graphic proves that the contributions are mainly based on the three motivation topics, with a positive trend in the "Changing Environment" and a slight negative trend in the "RBV". Concerning the investigated topics, scholars pay more attention to the "Capability Development" field in the last 5 years and both the "Business Process" as well as the "BPM Capability" have a stable course over the observed 15 years. On the contrary the number of the publications proposing frameworks diminish from 2010 to 2014 in the field of capability design. In terms of the subject areas a negative trend was observed in the topics "E-Commerce, IT Value" and IS Management". This implies that the capability design research has reached a certain level of maturity in these subject areas. Conversely, the topic "IS Development and Tools" gains a recognizable attention, for which we did not find an article between 2000 and 2004. As all the articles covering this topic were published in conference proceedings, we argue that the research trend in the capability design and development is moving lately towards methods, ways, steps, procedures in capability modelling, capability construction as well as relation of capabilities to enterprise models. This view is also in line with our findings from two other topic classes, the *motivation* (trend in the topic "Changing Environment") and the *investigation* (trends in the topics "Business Processes, Capability Development, BPM Capability"). Conclusively there seems to be a correlation between "modelling capabilities in the changing environments of the enterprises and their business processes". In other words, the focus in enterprise modelling in changing environments is shifting towards adding an abstraction level with capabilities rather than creating adaptable business process models, which are complex to understand and hard to manage. This hypothesis should be falsified or confirmed in the future work.

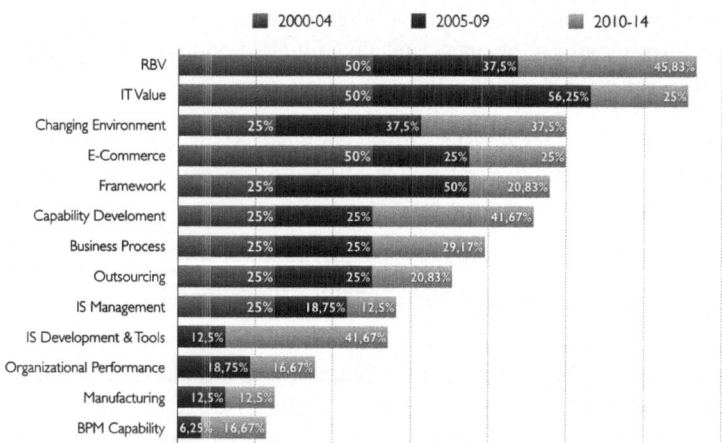

Fig. 4. Trends in topics (Color figure online)

4.3 Activity in Capability Design and Development Methods

[14] addressed a new thinking about the organization of IT activities amongst which *identifying and developing an organization's core IT capabilities* had a significant role. Before this article, we did not encounter any publications focusing on capability design and development; our set included only one article before 2000, which was published in 1988. The analysis of activities shows that the scholars have followed the advice of [14], since the findings expose the growing interest in developing capabilities over the years.

To observe the activities in design and development of capabilities, three time frames were applied from 2000–2004, 2005–2009 and 2010–2014. The number of the published articles in this field rose steadily in the conferences. In this context conferences and workshops of International Conference on Advanced Information Systems Engineering (CAiSE) focus most on the design and development of capabilities (30 % of all conference papers) followed by European Conference on Information Systems (ECIS), with 17 %. Please note that the workshops are assigned to the conferences in which they were held. In terms of journals, the scholars are engaged in this field after 2005 and no journal article particularly focuses on capability design and development methods. Although the interest does not increase regularly, the amount of published articles in 2010–2014 shows that capability development is still in the focus. This is illustrated in Table 1.

Table 1. Classification of articles per time frame and publication source

	2000–2004	2005–2009	2010–2014
Journal	3	11	7
Conference	1	5	17

A high amount of contributions to the capability design and development field originates from the institutes in USA (30 %), which are to a very large extent published in journals (1 conference and 13 journal papers). On the contrary, Germany, the second country with most contributions (22 %) has provided only 1 journal article and 9 conference papers. The allocation of relevant articles to countries is illustrated in Fig. 5. Here the authors are classified to the nations in accordance with their institutes defined in the publications. Furthermore, a country was not included in the graphic for brevity reasons, if the researchers contributed only once to the field. In this context, three main universities were identified that have contributed mostly to this area, namely Münster University (Germany), Stockholm University (Sweden) and Riga Technical University (Latvia).

Although USA contributes most the field under study, 55 % of all articles originate from Europe, where conferences play a predominant role (70 % of all European publications). Europe is followed by America (25 %) and Asia (15 %), whereas in America the scholars contribute to this field primarily with journal publications (84 % of all American contributions). The findings can be exploited for practical purposes. In that respective an initial list of researchers and practitioners can be established, for instance when sharing experiences during the engineering of a capability modelling method or when applying it in a real world setting and validating it against a set of requirements.

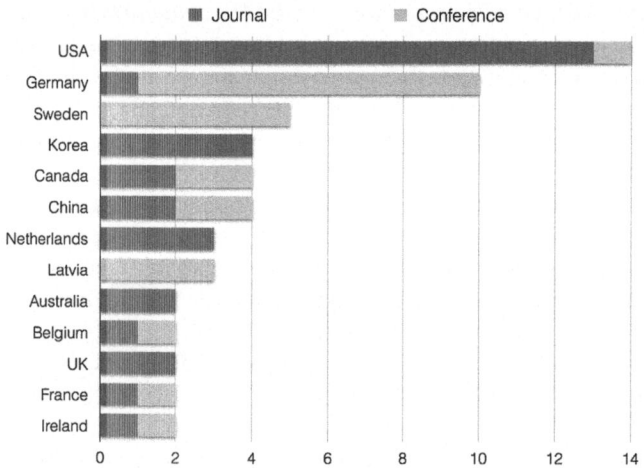

Fig. 5. Articles per countries

4.4   Methods for Designing and Developing Capabilities

In line with the method framework presented in Sect. 1 shortly, this section analyses which methods exist to design capabilities and how they are related to the research topics provided in Sect. 4.2.

IS Development. The articles providing methods for capability design based on a novel approach in the capability modelling field, Capability-driven Development (CDD), proposed in [15] are classified here. The CDD approach integrates organisational development with IS development by considering the application context and adjusting the solution in line with the dynamic changes. In this connection [16] presents an approach to design capabilities and establishes first cornerstones of capability development method. [18] addresses the stakeholder concerns to be taken into account when developing capabilities and presents a process for specifying requirements. [19] provides an overview of CDD method components, including context modelling, patterns modelling and enterprise modelling parts. Finally [2] uses the CDD approach on a case study and reports feedbacks for the improvement of CDD methodology.

E-Commerce. The capability design methods for adjustable service provision received attention in the e-commerce field between 2005 and 2009. To exemplify, [20] indicates the need for developing focal capabilities to achieve an e-commerce adoption and presents a process model to orchestrate the organizational resources in line with the changing business delivery context. However no steps, activities and tasks are defined and the approach lacks notation to model the outputs of the phases. [21] suggests strategies for practitioners how to develop organisational capabilities in e-commerce field and provides a process model including the key actions to be carried out.

Business Process Management (BPM). Notably in the last third of the analysed time frame, works in the BPM field relate to the methods in capability design. [22, 23] investigate BPM topic from the Dynamic Capability point of view and present a framework, which supports the design of BPM capabilities. The framework consists of three activities, namely sensing, seizing and transformation, which are further elaborated in subcapabilities. Last but not least [24] offers a method for IT capability based business process design, which consists of 8 steps. The work describes roles and notations loosely, whereas the important concepts, outputs of the activities are not mentioned at all.

In addition to the above-mentioned topics, [25] proposes a process model for the development of capabilities to meet fast growing business demands. [26] develops a theoretical model for conceptualizing the internationalization strategies of IT vendors, which consists amongst others a capability-building process. Regarding both articles however, the processes cannot be applied solely as a capability design method since the roles, goals, concepts and notation is not defined. Besides, the latter contribution analyses the capabilities of IT service vendors in emerging economies, which remains too specific.

To sum up our findings, the CDD approach provides amongst the investigated publications the most comprehensive methodological support to design enterprise-grade capabilities. This is based on the following reasons. First, the method exploits enterprise models to develop capabilities by explicitly defining the important concepts and notations to represent them. Second, the CDD approach assumes different starting points to develop capabilities, such as business process models, goal models or concept models, which should support different ways of working. Last but not least, the method takes the contextual factors into account, i.e. the realization of enterprise goals can be adapted to changing situations. This is a significant contribution towards the business and IT alignment, since the business-centric concerns can be represented in goal models whereas their actual implementation can be addressed in context models. Apart from the CDD, the analysed articles (i) address which factors should be taken into account when designing capabilities, (ii) show how they relate to subject under study, (iii) provide means for capability evaluation, such as maturity models, (iv) focus on capabilities that are decoupled from enterprise goals and (v) propose steps, procedures, guidelines to design capabilities, which cannot be developed by analysing the existing enterprise models and stakeholder goals.

5   Discussion and Conclusions

This paper contributes to the research field in capability design and development methods by conducting a mapping study as shown in [1, 6]. In line with the rankings in [3–5] a search term was applied to 112 journals and 24 conference proceedings. A number of criteria were defined to include and exclude the articles in the final set. As a result a total of 45 articles were classified into a scheme, i.e. applied research design, used research methods and investigated research topics. To analyse the results and to identify trends we defined three time frames, namely 2000–2004, 2005–2009 and 2010–2014. The trend calculation was done by relating the used terms to the number of published articles in the selected time frame. For instance, the topic business process was investigated in 25 % of the papers that are published between 2000 and 2004. In doing so, we aimed to hinder the effect of the increase on the number of the articles through the years. Following summarizes the findings of the work.

Research Method & Design. Empirical research is used extensively in developing and designing capabilities. More than a half of the articles adopting quantitative research conduct surveys and follow a structure consisting of three steps (see Sect. 4.1). Their results can be used when engineering a method for developing and designing capabilities. There seems to be a trend in the capability design field concerning the application of secondary data and case studies as a research method. On the other hand DSR is applied scarcely, which is a certain motivation for further research. In addition to that, if an article combines both qualitative and quantitative research methods, then it more likely adopts a research method pattern, i.e. case studies, interviews and analysis of secondary data are engaged.

Research Topics. The topics related to the enterprise modelling, BPM, Business Models are only analysed in conference proceedings. The articles investigating capabilities are motivated by RBV, however the focus moves towards "changing environment" lately. There might be a correlation between 3 topics, namely capability development, enterprise models and changing environment, which should be falsified or confirmed in the future work.

Activity. Over the years there is a growing interest in developing capabilities. The number of the published articles in this field rose steadily in the conferences. Among the investigated conference proceedings, CAiSE focus most on the design and development of capabilities. The journal articles investigate the frameworks, attributes and the organizational characteristics when designing the capabilities, though the aspects including the methodological support are neglected. Finally, a list of the active countries and research institutes in this field are provided, which might serve practical purposes such as collaboration in the capability development methods area.

Methods. The term "method" is used synonymously with "process, procedure" or "step". Except for the CDD approach we were not able to identify a comprehensive method including stakeholder goals, actors, notations, important concepts and activities to be executed when designing capabilities. Moreover, most of the articles present evidence on how capabilities interact with the subjects under study, such as service quality, customer satisfaction, success factors and knowledge management, but they do not provide further information on how to design such capabilities.

Acknowledgements. This work has been performed as part of the EU-FP7 funded project no: 611351 CaaS – Capability as a Service in Digital Enterprises.

References

1. Ulrich, W., Rosen, M.: The Business Capability Map: Building a Foundation for Business/IT Alignment (2011). http://www.cutter.com/content-and-analysis/resource-centers/enterprise-architecture/sample-our-research/ea110504.html. Accessed February 2014
2. Kitchenham, B.: Procedures for performing systematic reviews. Technical report TR/SE-0401, Keele University, July 2004. ISSN:1353-7776
3. Schrader, U., Hennig-Thurau, T.: VHB-JOURQUAL2: method, results, and implications of the German academic association for business research's journal ranking. BuR-Business Res. 2(2), 180–204 (2009)
4. Peffers, K., Ya, T.: Identifying and evaluating the universe of outlets for information systems research: ranking the journals. J. Inf. Technol. Theor. Appl. (JITTA) 5(1), 6 (2003)
5. WI-Orientierungslisten. WIRTSCHAFTSINFORMATIK. 50, 155–163 (2008)
6. Webster, J., Watson, R.T.: Analyzing past to prepare for future: writing a literature review. MIS Q. 26, xiii–xxiii (2002)
7. Wendler, R.: The maturity of maturity model research: a systematic mapping study. Inf. Softw. Technol. 54(12), 1317–1339 (2012)
8. Hevner, A.R., March, S.T., Park, J., Ram, S.: Design science in information systems research. MIS Q. 28(1), 75–105 (2004)
9. Palvia, P., Leary, D., Mao, E., Midha, V., Pinjani, P., Salam, A.F.: Research methodologies in MIS: an update. Commun. Assoc. Inf. Syst. 14, 24 pp. (2004)
10. Myers, M.D.: Qualitative research in information systems. MIS Q. 21(2), 241–242 (1997). http://www.qual.auckland.ac.nz. Accessed 3 Feb 2015
11. Goldkuhl, G., Lind, M., Seigerroth, U.: Method integration: the need for a learning perspective. IEE Proc. Softw. (Special issue on Information System Methodologies) 145(4), 113–118 (1998)
12. Alavi, M., Carlson, A.: Review of MIS research and disciplinary development. J. Manag. Inf. Syst. 8, 45–62 (1992)
13. Budgen, D., Turner, M., Brereton, P., Kitchenham, B.: Using mapping studies in software engineering. In: Proceedings of PPIG 2008, pp. 195–204 (2008)
14. Sambamurthy, V., Zmud, R.W.: Research commentary: the organizing logic for an enterprise's IT activities in the digital era—a prognosis of practice and a call for research. Inf. Syst. Res. 11(2), 105–114 (2000)
15. Stirna, J., Grabis, J., Henkel, M., Zdravkovic, J.: Capability driven development – an approach to support evolving organizations. In: Sandkuhl, K., Seigerroth, U., Stirna, J. (eds.) PoEM 2012. LNBIP, vol. 134, pp. 117–131. Springer, Heidelberg (2012)
16. Zdravkovic, J., Stirna, J., Henkel, M., Grabis, J.: Modeling business capabilities and context dependent delivery by cloud services. In: Salinesi, C., Norrie, M.C., Pastor, Ó. (eds.) CAiSE 2013. LNCS, vol. 7908, pp. 369–383. Springer, Heidelberg (2013)
17. España, S., González, T., Grabis, J., Jokste, L., Juanes, R., Valverde, F.: Capability-driven development of a SOA platform: a case study. In: Iliadis, L., Papazoglou, M., Pohl, K. (eds.) CAiSE Workshops 2014. LNBIP, vol. 178, pp. 100–111. Springer, Heidelberg (2014)
18. Zdravkovic, J., Stirna, J., Kuhr, J.-C., Koç, H.: Requirements Engineering for Capability Driven Development. In: Frank, U., Loucopoulos, P., Pastor, Ó., Petrounias, I. (eds.) PoEM 2014. LNBIP, vol. 197, pp. 193–207. Springer, Heidelberg (2014)
19. Sandkuhl, K., Koç, H., Stirna, J.: Context-aware business services: technological support for business and IT-alignment. In: Abramowicz, W., Kokkinaki, A. (eds.) BIS 2014 Workshops. LNBIP, vol. 183, pp. 190–201. Springer, Heidelberg (2014)

20. Cui, M., Pan, S.: Developing focal capabilities for E-Commerce adoption: a resource orchestration perspective. Inf. Manag. **52**, 200 (2015)
21. Montealegre, R.: A process model of capability development: lessons from the electronic commerce strategy at Bolsa de Valores de Guayaquil. Organ. Sci. **13**(5), 514–553 (2002)
22. Niehaves, B., Plattfaut, R., Sarker, S.: Understanding dynamic IS capabilities for effective process change: a theoretical framework and an empirical application. In: Proceedings of ICIS 2011, Paper 11 (2011)
23. Ortbach, K., Plattfaut, R., Poppelbuss, J., Niehaves, B.: A dynamic capability-based framework for business process management: theorizing and empirical application. In: 45th Hawaii International Conference System Science (HICSS), pp. 4287–4296 (2012)
24. Adam, S., Ünalan, Ö., Riegel, N., Kerkow, D.: IT capability-based business process design through service-oriented requirements engineering. In: Halpin, T., Krogstie, J., Nurcan, S., Proper, E., Schmidt, R., Soffer, P., Ukor, R. (eds.) Enterprise, Business-Process and Information Systems Modeling. LNBIP, vol. 29, pp. 113–125. Springer, Heidelberg (2009)
25. Zhou, J., Zuo, M., Li, Q., Xu, W.: Developing an agile it capability accompanying business's fast growing:a case study on a chinese E-Commerce company. In: Proceedings of PACIS 2012, Paper 24 (2012)
26. Ning, S.: Internationalization strategies of IT vendors from emerging economies: the case of China. In: Proceedings of ICIS 2008, Paper 96 (2008)

Benefits of Enterprise Architecture Management – Insights from European Experts

Rainer Schmidt[1(✉)], Michael Möhring[2], Ralf-Christian Härting[2],
Christopher Reichstein[2], Alfred Zimmermann[3], and Sandro Luceri[2]

[1] Computer Science and Mathematics,
Munich University of Applied Sciences, Munich, Germany
Rainer.Schmidt@hm.edu
[2] Business Administration, Aalen University of Applied Sciences,
Aalen, Germany
[3] Computer Science, Reutlingen University,
Reutlingen, Germany

Abstract. Excellence in IT is a key enabler for the digital transformation of enterprises. To realize the vision of Digital Enterprises it is necessary to cope with changing business requirements and to align business and IT. In order to evaluate the contribution of Enterprise Architecture Management to these goals, our paper explores the impact of various factors to the perceived benefit of EAM in enterprises. Based on literature, we build an empirical research model. It is tested with empirical data of European EAM experts using a structural equation modelling approach. It is shown that changing business requirements, IT Business Alignment, the complexity of Information Technology infrastructure as well as enterprise architecture knowledge of Information Technology employees are crucial impact factors to the perceived benefit of EAM in enterprises.

Keywords: EAM · Empirical research · Benefit of EAM · Use of EAM · Enterprise architecture management · Study · European experts · IT business alignment

1 Introduction

Enterprise Architecture is the organizing logic for business processes and IT infrastructure [1]. It reflects the integration and standardization necessary for delivering goods and services [1]. Enterprise Architecture Management [2] aims at aligning business and IT. Service-oriented Enterprise Architecture Management and engineering [3] target innovative enterprise architectures based on services and cloud-computing.

One of the challenges to Enterprise Architecture Management is digitization. Digitization embraces the digital representation of data, the automation of processes, and the enrichment of products by services [4]. E.g, the majority (63 %) of executives in a study from MIT Sloan Management Review said that the pace of digitization, the transformation to digital processes in their organization is too slow [5].

© IFIP International Federation for Information Processing 2015
J. Ralyté et al. (Eds.): PoEM 2015, LNBIP 235, pp. 223–236, 2015.
DOI: 10.1007/978-3-319-25897-3_15

To overcome such challenges, a number of frameworks have been developed such as TOGAF [6], Archimate [7], SEAM [8] and ARIS [9]. They are supported by a plethora of tools [10]. Using them, different stages of maturity can be achieved. To formalize these stages, models as described in [1, 11] have been developed.

Despite the ongoing research in academia, the benefits and the use of Enterprise Architecture Management are still a topic of lively discussions (cf. related work section). According to the current literature, there is a gap of research on different influencing factors on the perceived benefit of Enterprise Architecture Management in enterprises as well as a multivariate analysis of it. Therefore, this paper will present insights on the contribution of the perceived benefit of Enterprise Architecture Management that are collected from 126 experts via an empirical model driven research approach and multi-variate data analysis based on a structural equation model.

The paper proceeds as follows. In the following section, the research model and the background are described. Then, the research methods and data collection are defined. Finally, we present and discuss the insights obtained from the data collected as well as a section for related work.

2   Research Model and Background

According to the current topic and challenge of the use and benefit of EAM [12], we explore the impact of different influencing factors regarding the perceived benefit of EAM. In general, the perceived benefit of EAM can be defined as the individual observed benefit of Enterprise Architecture Management in companies (or organizations) from the viewpoint of an EAM expert. Therefore, we develop in this section a theoretical research model with testable hypotheses according to general empirical research guidelines [13, 14] regarding the current literature [15].

2.1   Changing Business Requirements

Business requirements often change because most organizations compete in dynamic and rapidly altering environments (e.g. need for modification of strategies, business models as well as business processes, etc.) [16]. The question how to assure the ability of IT to cope with changing business requirements is a topic that received attention in research and practice [8, 17]. Therefore the question, whether Enterprise Architecture Management contributes to the ability of IT to cope with changing business requirements is a subject of high relevance. In consequence, we created hypothesis 1:

> **Hypothesis 1: Frequent changes of business requirements positively influence the perceived benefits of EAM.**

2.2   IT Business Alignment

IT Business Alignment is the application of Information Technology in an appropriate and timely way [18, 19]. IT Business Alignment is a crucial topic for IT-management [20].

The use of Enterprise Architecture Management for the alignment of business IT has been proposed by a number of authors such as [21–23]. The alignment of business and IT is considered mature, if IT and other business functions adapt their strategies to each other [19]. The question how organizations improve and achieve a mature alignment of business and IT has been identified as a key subject in management [19]. Yet, it is not discovered how IT Business Alignment influences the perceived benefit of EAM (from the point of view of European experts). Based on this finding, we created hypothesis 2:

Hypothesis 2: The alignment of Business and IT positively influences the perceived benefits of EAM.

2.3 EAM Frameworks

Enterprise Architecture Frameworks [24] provide both means for the specification of architecture components and tools for planning and solving problems [25]. Therefore, Enterprise Architecture Frameworks [25–27] are an important concept of Enterprise Architecture Management. Their support for the concerns of CIO's has been already investigated in [28]. In [12], two questions are discussed: first how governance impacts the use of EA standards and how EA standards support the integration and sharing of IT. Nevertheless, an empirical investigation of this interesting research question did not take place so far. Therefore, we created hypothesis 3:

Hypothesis 3: The use of EAM frameworks has a positive impact on the perceived benefits of EAM.

2.4 IT Landscape Complexity

IT landscapes [29] are proposed as a mean for Enterprise Architecture Management in order to create integrated IT governance platforms [29]. Their visualization is thus a current theme of research [30, 31]. Tackling IT landscape, complexity is an important means for the reduction of IT cost [32]. According to systems science, complexity can be defined by the number of components and relations as well as the heterogeneity of relations and components [33–36]. Complexity in general can be measured by different indicators (e.g. Entropy Measure, McCabe, LOC, Average Service Cyclomatic Complexity etc.) [37–39]. Depicting the IT landscape using enterprise architecture may consequently help to identify areas that are driving cost due to their high complexity [40]. To discover the influence on the perceived benefit of EAM, we created the hypothesis 4:

Hypothesis 4: The complexity of the IT landscape positively influences the perceived benefit of EAM.

2.5 EAM Knowledge of IT Employees

The role of IT employees within Enterprise Architecture Management has been addressed by [41]. The communication of enterprise architectures has been identified as an important theme of research in [42]. In general information systems knowledge is very crucial for developing competitive, successful enterprises [43]. To explore the impact of enterprise architecture knowledge of Information Technology employees to the perceived benefit of EAM, we created hypothesis 5:

Hypothesis 5: EAM Knowledge of IT employees influences the perceived benefit of EAM.

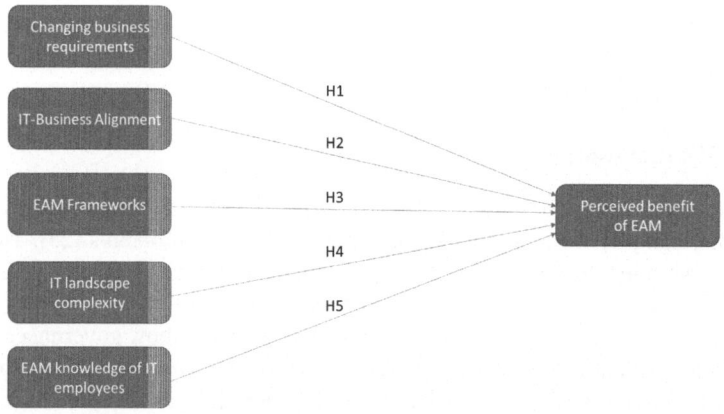

Fig. 1. Research model

In order to examine the impact of the specified factors on the perceived benefit of Enterprise Architecture Management, participants had to respond to our questions related to the hypothesis in our model (see also Fig. 1) within the online-based survey on a one to five Likert scale (5: very important; 4: important; 3: neither... nor; 2: unimportant; 1: very unimportant) [44]. The questions related to the hypotheses are listed in the Table 1.

Table 1. Applied questions according to the hypotheses

Perceived benefit of EAM *(How high is the benefit of Enterprise Architecture Management for enterprises?)*
IT Business Alignment *(How important are IT Business Alignments (balancing business and IT goals) for EAM?)*
EAM Frameworks *(How important are EAM frameworks to implement EAM in general?)*
IT landscape complexity *(How important is EAM to manage the IT landscape complexity?)*
EAM knowledge of IT employees *(How important is EAM knowledge of IT employees?)*
Changing business requirements *(How important is EAM to react to changing business requirements?)*

In addition, there are further questions related to the descriptive analysis as well as check questions to ensure a high quality of the study (cf. data collection section).

3   Research Methods

To investigate our research model, we used a quantitative research approach [45]. In general a quantitative research approach is applied to test the confirmation or disconfirmation of hypotheses [45]. Based on empirical data we want to confirm or disconfirm our hypotheses defined in the last section. A web-based survey is one method to collect quantitative empirical data [46]. According to the next section, we collect these data via the internet from leading European experts.

For analyzing a theoretical model, different approaches like correlation and variance analysis as well as structural equation modeling etc. can be used. To test our hypotheses (theoretical causal model) with the data sample of the web-based survey (empirical data), we chose a structural equation modelling approach (SEM). SEM is a further development of multivariate analyses according to get more details about the analysis of different relations [47, 48]. In general, there are two parts of an SEM [48, 49]. First, the measurement model validates the latent variables. Second, the structural model analyses the relationships between the variables and the model. To visualize the relations between different impact factors (variables), a SEM can be built via several approaches (e.g. AMOS, Lisrel, SmartPLS) [50]. Because of special requirements through EAM experts (limited data set), we chose SmartPLS. Single item sets are allowed and often used by SmartPLS [51]. Furthermore, path significances are calculated via Bootstrapping [50, 52, 53] based on our empirical sample.

4   Data Collection

To test our developed hypotheses, we conducted a quantitative research model using a web-based online survey [54]. Before implementing the online survey in the German language via the open source software LimeSurvey [55], we pretested our questionnaire to ensure a high quality of research standard by removing potential ambiguities.

The revised survey finally started in December 2014 and finished in March 2015. During the period of 4 months, we received a sample of n = 263 different IT experts from Central Europe. Regarding the different participants, we only addressed IT experts with knowledge and experience in Enterprise Architecture Management by contacting them partly formal via email, phone, or letter and partly informal using personal networks. In addition, the first question in our survey proved the expertise of the respondents in EAM by asking whether the respondent has knowledge and/or experience in EAM or not. Experts that stated to have no knowledge and/or experience in EAM were selected and were no longer taken into consideration. We only asked IT experts, because a previous pre-study in 2014 showed that other experts from outside the Information Technology field cannot well answer to our specific EAM questions. Furthermore, expert surveys are very often used in information systems research (e.g. [56–58]) and can control bias e.g. via cross-checking [59].

After data cleaning, we obtained a final sample of n = 126 IT experts having a special expertise in EAM of about 7.56 years on average. Only 1 participant has a work experience with less than 1 year while most of the experts have an EAM work experience of far more than 5 years (see Fig. 2).

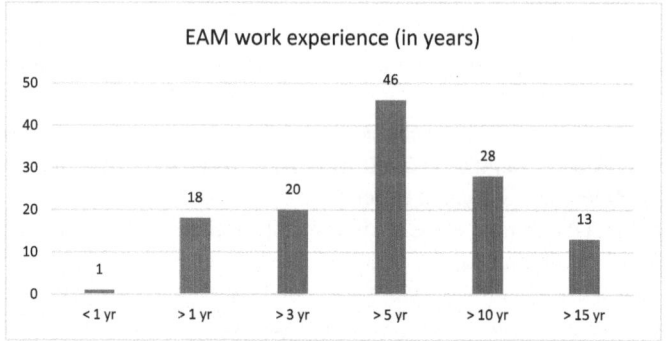

Fig. 2. EAM work experience

Circa 84.2 % of the experts are male, only 15.8 % are female. The average age of our EAM experts is 42.54 years. The majority of the experts are from the industry (ca. 90 %). Only ca. 10 % (n = 13) are researchers in the field of EAM. According to the following figure, the benefit of EAM is important (>90 %) for most of the experts asked (Fig. 3).

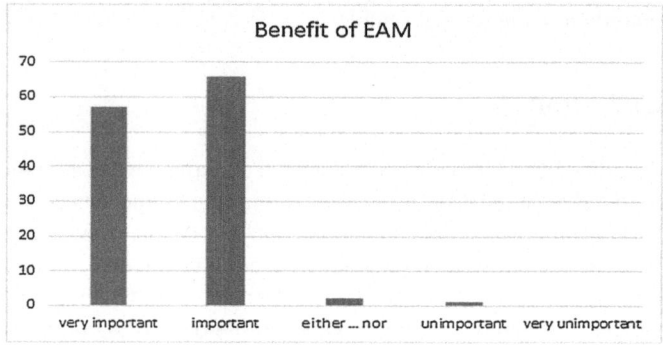

Fig. 3. Benefit of EAM

Furthermore, for 44 % of the experts (n = 56) the size of the enterprise is not decisive for the use of EAM. In contrast to this, 56 % (n = 70) define that the size of the enterprise is very important for the use and implementation of EAM.

For the majority of the experts (n = 124, 98 %) EAM is not only useful for a special industry sector but can be implemented in various industries.

After this descriptive analysis, our hypotheses (cf. Sect. 2.) are tested in the next section via multivariate analysis.

5   Results

We tested our empirical data with our research model via structural equation modelling (SEM). Therefore, we used SmartPLS 3.1 [52]. According to the research method section, we followed the guidelines of SEM to calculate and analyze our model. After SEM modelling and analyzing, we got the following results (Fig. 4).

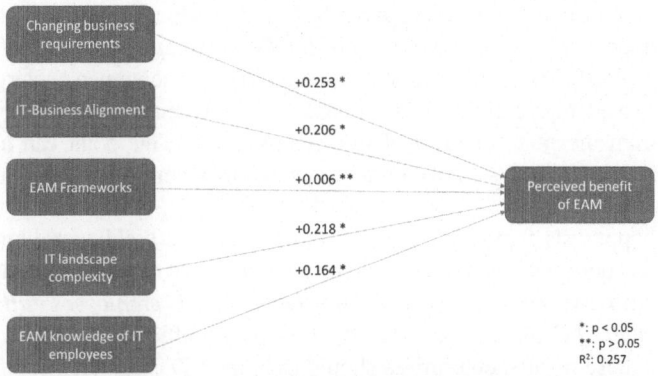

Fig. 4. Results of our research model and empirical data via SEM

According to hypothesis 1 (*Frequent changes of business requirements positively influence the perceived benefit of EAM*) the frequent change of business requirements has a positive impact on the perceived benefit of Enterprise Architecture Management, because of a positive path coefficient (+0.253) of our SEM. Therefore, hypothesis 1 can be confirmed. Based on these results, enterprises have a higher benefit of EAM if they are placed in a dynamic environment with frequent changes of business requirements. The positive impact can be explained also by the theory of transaction costs [60]. Studies based on this approach indicate, that information systems, which are aligned with the enterprise strategy, are able to raise business processes to a higher level of efficiency and to generate economies of scale [61]. In that context EAM can help to manage this complexity.

IT Business Alignment is a very important challenge in many enterprises or other organizations [20]. Our study explores the influence of IT Business Alignment to the perceived benefit of EAM via hypothesis 2. Regarding the results of our structural equation model, we can support hypothesis 2 (*The alignment of Business and IT positively influences the perceived benefit of EAM.*). The path coefficient (+0.206) shows a positive significant influence. Therefore, the benefit of EAM is very huge by implementing a high degree of IT Business Alignment. According to the literature, a high degree of IT Business Alignment is recommended [62]. Thus, EAM should be very important for enterprises.

The impact of enterprise architecture frameworks to the perceived benefit of EAM is discovered in hypothesis 3. Unfortunately, the results are not significant according to Table 2 ($p > 0.05$). Therefore, hypothesis 3 (*The use of EAM frameworks has a positive impact on the perceived benefit of EAM.*) cannot be confirmed. One reason of this result could be the variance of the data generated by the disagreement of the different experts asked according to this question about EAM frameworks. Another explanation could be various foci of numerous frameworks. That causes a different understanding of EAM frameworks.

The growing Information Technology infrastructure complexity in organizations and enterprises is a very important topic to the daily business of many CIO's [63]. Our research tries to find out, if there is a positive link between the IT landscape complexity and the perceived benefit of EAM. According to our SEM analysis (path coefficient: + 0.218), we can support hypothesis 4 *(The complexity of the IT landscape positively influences the perceived benefit of EAM.)*. In relation to our analysis, we recommend enterprises to use EAM if they have a high complex IT landscape. Therefore, enterprises can better manage complexity from the point of view of the experts asked. This point can also help by acquiring (e.g. Merger and Acquisition transactions) new companies (and their IT landscape) [64].

Finally, hypothesis 5 explores the impact of enterprise architecture knowledge of Information Technology employees to the perceived benefit of EAM. Based on our data we can confirm hypothesis 5 *(EAM Knowledge of IT employees influences the perceived benefit of EAM.)*, because of a positive path coefficient (+0.164) of the SEM. According to these results, enterprises should train their IT staff with EAM basics and fundamental skills to get a higher benefit of EAM. This could be a sustainable way to ensure a good EAM implementation.

All values of our structural equation modelling analysis are described in the following table.

Table 2. SEM Coefficients, Significance

SEM Path	Path coefficient	T statistics	P values (Significance)
EAM-frameworks → perceived benefit of EAM	0.006	0.080	0.936
Enterprise architecture knowledge of Information Technology employees → perceived benefit of EAM	0.164	2.017	0.044
IT Business Alignment → perceived benefit of EAM	0.206	2.157	0.032
Information Technology landscape complexity → perceived benefit of EAM	0.218	2.719	0.007
changing business requirements → perceived benefit of EAM	0.253	3.170	0.002

Furthermore the coefficient of the determination (R^2) is in a good range $(0.257 > 0.19)$ according to literature [53]. The path coefficients of hypotheses 1,2,4,5 are significant $(p < 0.05$ according to Table 2). Only the path coefficient of hypothesis 3 is not significant $(0.936 > 0.05)$. Furthermore, single item sets are allowed by using the SmartPLS SEM approach as well as often used in research [51]. For single item sets there is no need to calculate metrics like Cronbachs Alpha [51].

6   Related Work

Enterprise Architecture Management has been the theme research in a number of areas. A very broad view on the state of the art in Enterprise Architecture Management can be found in [65]. A broad and thorough overview on enterprise architecture concepts and principles presented in [66, 67]. To provide a formal foundation for Enterprise Architecture Management, a meta-model is used in [68]. In [69] the context of Enterprise Architecture Management is described and challenges for it are identified.

Directly related to our work are the following papers. A literature review is conducted in [70] to identify the benefits of Enterprise Architecture. It is supplemented by interviews with seven practitioners from five organizations. Factors for the success of Enterprise Architecture Management in the financial industry are investigated in the empirical analysis in [71]. The impact of Enterprise Architecture standards on the sharing and the integration of IT resources is investigated in [12].

Digitization and enterprise architecture is the theme of the following papers. In [72] the impact of digitization on enterprise IT is analyzed and shifts from efficiency to speed in implementing change is identified as central requirement. In [5] three areas of transformative effects of digitization are identified: improvement of customer experience, operational improvements and business model change. In [73] the phases of transformation by digitization are analyzed and drivers for digitization are identified.

Beneath these approaches, a number of other researches exist in relation to the investigation presented here. An empirical analysis on the design of Enterprise Architecture Management is presented in [74]. The relationship of changes in enterprise architecture and business models is investigated in [75]. A relation between Archimate [7] and the business model canvas [76] is established. Kluge et al., design a value realization model for Enterprise Architecture in [77]. They identify service quality and actual use as factors for Enterprise Architecture success. The question whether enterprise architecture frameworks give support on managing IT, is discussed in [28]. The use of a scorecard to depict the strengths and weaknesses in the EA realization is developed in [78]. A comparative study of methods to measure the effectiveness of enterprise architecture is given in [79]. An examination of the organizational factors influencing EAM Challenges is described in [57]. A catalog of capabilities in Enterprise Architecture Management is developed in [24].

Challenges of Enterprise Architecture Management are identified in [80]. A framework for the support of Enterprise Architecture Management with Advanced Analytics is introduced. In [10] a number of tools for the support of Enterprise Architecture Management are compared. The visualization of Enterprise Architecture Management models is discussed in [81].

7   Conclusion and Discussion

Enterprise Architecture Management is a widely discussed topic and a challenge for practice and research. It plays a crucial role in implementing the vision of digital enterprises. Our paper explores the impact of different important impact factors regarding the perceived benefit of EAM in enterprises. Therefore, we build an empirical research model based on the literature and test it with empirical data of European EAM experts via a structural equation modelling approach.

According to our research, we got interesting insights of different impact factors to the perceived benefit of EAM in enterprises. Changing business requirements, IT Business Alignment, Information Technology infrastructure complexity, as well as enterprise architecture knowledge of Information Technology employees are very important impact factors to the perceived benefit of EAM in enterprises. Nevertheless, one impact factor (EAM Frameworks) could not be significantly explored.

There are different implications according to our research results. First, we contribute to the current information systems research by constructing and testing a new model of the perceived benefit of Enterprise Architecture Management. Our model can help researchers to get a deeper understanding in the benefit of Enterprise Architecture Management in enterprises. Therefore, current approaches of the benefit of information systems can be adapted based on our results. Second, important impact factors, how the perceived benefit of EAM can be explained and influenced, are defined and validated.

Practical users and managers are able to work with our model to prepare EAM decisions by checking their individual instance of the different impact factors to get a recommendation of the perceived benefit of EAM according to their individual enterprise. Employee EAM trainings, good IT Business Alignment etc. can be a good chance for well implementing EAM in enterprises. Therefore, enterprises can go a sustainable as well as very competitive way.

There are some limitations according to our research. First, we only asked experts from Central Europe. There could be other results according to other countries with a different Information Technology use and structure (e.g. BRIC states). Furthermore, there might be some more influencing factors which were not taken into consideration within our quantitative approach. In addition, there are general limitations of a quantitative research method via a web-based survey, according to the literature [45, 82]. A qualitative research approach might probably investigate more influencing factors. Finally, one of our paths is not significant (refer to EAM Frameworks – hypothesis 3).

Therefore, future research should enlarge the sample according to the experts asked and involved countries. Furthermore, more domain-specific factors (e.g. in highly complained environments) should be discovered. Current models of the use of information systems can be adopted and qualitative research approaches can be implemented to get a deeper insight. Future research should use our model to improve and communicate the current understanding of the use of EAM in organizations.

References

1. Ross, J.W., Weill, P., Robertson, D.C.: Enterprise Architecture as Strategy, vol. 1. Havard Business School Press, Cambridge (2006)
2. Buckl, S., Ernst, A.M., Lankes, J., Matthes, F., Schweda, C.M.: Enterprise architecture management patterns–exemplifying the approach. In: 12th International IEEE Enterprise Distributed Object Computing Conference, 2008. EDOC 2008, pp. 393–402 (2008)
3. Nurcan, S., Schmidt, R., and others: Introduction to the second international workshop service-oriented enterprise architecture for enterprise engineering. In: Proceedings of Service-oriented Enterprise Architecture for Enterprise Engineering (2010)
4. Schmidt, R., Zimmermann, A., Nurcan, S., Möhring, M., Bär, F., Keller, B.: Digitization – Perspectives for Conceptualization (2015, to appear)
5. Fitzgerald, M., Kruschwitz, N., Bonnet, D., Welch, M.: Embracing digital technology. MIT Sloan Manag. Rev., 1–12 (2013)
6. Blevins, T., Harrison, R., Homan, P., Josey, A., Rouse, M.F., van Sante, T.: TOGAF Version 8.1. 1 Enterprise Edition: A Pocket Guide. Van Haren Publishing, Zaltbommel (2007)
7. Lankhorst, M.M., Proper, H.A., Jonkers, H.: The architecture of the ArchiMate language. In: Halpin, T., Krogstie, J., Nurcan, S., Proper, E., Schmidt, R., Soffer, P., Ukor, R. (eds.) Enterprise, Business-Process and Information Systems Modeling. LNBIP, vol. 29, pp. 367–380. Springer, Heidelberg (2009)
8. Wegmann, A.: Systemic enterprise architecture methodology (SEAM), in *SEAM*. In: International Conference on Enterprise Information Systems 2003 (ICEIS 2003), pp. 483–490 (2003)
9. Scheer, A.W.: ARIS-Business Process Modeling. Springer, Berlin (2000)
10. Matthes, F., Buckl, S., Leitel, J., Schweda, C.M.: *Enterprise Architecture Management Tool Survey 2008*. Techn. Univ, München (2008)
11. Schekkerman, J.: Extended enterprise architecture maturity model support guide (Version 2.0), Institute for Enterprise Architecture Developments (2006). http://www.enterprise-architecture.info/Images/E2AF/Extended%20Enterprise%20Architecture%20Maturity %20Model%20Guide%20v2.pdf. Accessed 20 July 2011
12. Boh, W.F., Yellin, D.: Using enterprise architecture standards in managing information technology. J. Manag. Inf. Syst. **23**(3), 163–207 (2006)
13. Ang, S.H.: Research Design for Business & Management. SAGE Publications Ltd, Thousand Oaks (2014)
14. McBurney, D.H., White, T.L.: Research Methods, 7th edn. Wadsworth Publishing, Belmont (2006)
15. Cooper, H.M.: Synthesizing Research: A Guide for Literature Reviews, vol. 2. Sage, Beverly Hills (1998)
16. Kennerley, M., Neely, A.: Measuring performance in a changing business environment. Int. J. Oper. Prod. Manag. **23**(2), 213–229 (2003)
17. Winter, R., Fischer, R.: Essential layers, artifacts, and dependencies of enterprise architecture. In: 10th IEEE International Enterprise Distributed Object Computing Conference Workshops, 2006. EDOCW 2006, pp. 30–30 (2006)
18. Pereira, C.M., Sousa, P.: Enterprise architecture: business and IT alignment. In: Proceedings of the 2005 ACM Symposium on Applied Computing, pp. 1344–1345 (2005)
19. Luftman, J.: Assessing business-IT alignment maturity. Strateg. Inf. Technol. Governance **4**, 99 (2004)
20. Wegmann, A.: The systemic enterprise architecture methodology (SEAM). Business and IT alignment for competitiveness. In: EPFL I&C, 200265 (2002)

21. Wang, X., Zhou, X., Jiang, L.: A method of business and IT alignment based on enterprise architecture. In: IEEE International Conference on Service Operations and Logistics, and Informatics, 2008. IEEE/SOLI 2008, vol. 1, pp. 740–745 (2008)

22. Cuenca, L., Boza, A., Ortiz, A.: An enterprise engineering approach for the alignment of business and information technology strategy. Int. J. Comput. Integr. Manuf. 24(11), 974–992 (2011)

23. Boucharas, V., van Steenbergen, M., Jansen, S., Brinkkemper, S.: The contribution of enterprise architecture to the achievement of organizational goals: establishing the enterprise architecture benefits framework. Department of Information and Computing Sciences, Utrecht University, Utrecht (2010)

24. Lankhorst, M.: State of the Art. Enterprise Architecture at Work, pp. 11–41. Springer, Berlin (2013)

25. Shah, H., Kourdi, M.E.: Frameworks for enterprise architecture. IT Prof. 9(5), 36–41 (2007)

26. Schekkerman, J.: How to Survive in the Jungle of Enterprise Architecture Frameworks: Creating or Choosing an Enterprise Architecture Framework. Trafford Publishing, Bloomington (2004)

27. Urbaczewski, L., Mrdalj, S.: A comparison of enterprise architecture frameworks. Issues Inf. Syst. 7(2), 18–23 (2006)

28. Lindström, A., Johnson, P., Johansson, E., Ekstedt, M., Simonsson, M.: A survey on CIO concerns-do enterprise architecture frameworks support them? Inf. Syst. Front. 8(2), 81–90 (2006)

29. Wittenburg, A., Matthes, F., Fischer, F., Hallermeier, T.: Building an integrated IT governance platform at the BMW Group. Int. J. Bus. Process Integr. Manag. 2(4), 327–337 (2007)

30. Buckl, S., Ernst, A.M., Lankes, J., Schweda, C.M., Wittenburg, A.: Generating visualizations of enterprise architectures using model transformations. EMISA 2007, 33–46 (2007)

31. Lankhorst, M.: Viewpoints and visualisation. Enterprise Architecture at Work, pp. 153–197. Springer, Berlin (2009)

32. Mattern, F., Schönwälder, S., Stein, W.: Fighting complexity in IT. McKinsey Q. 1, 57–65 (2003)

33. Simon, H.A.: The architecture of complexity. Gen. Syst. 10(1965), 63–76 (1965)

34. Ashby, W.R., et al.: An introduction to cybernetics. An introduction to cybernetics. Chapman and Hail Ltd, London (1956)

35. Flood, R.L.: Dealing with Complexity: an Introduction to the Theory and Application of Systems Science. Springer Science & Business Media, Berlin (1993)

36. Klir, G.: Facets of Systems Science, vol. 15. Springer Science & Business Media, Berlin (2001)

37. Banker, R.D., Datar, S.M., Kemerer, C.F., Zweig, D.: Software complexity and maintenance costs. Commun. ACM 36(11), 81–94 (1993)

38. Vasconcelos, A., Sousa, P., Tribolet, J.: Information system architecture metrics: an enterprise engineering evaluation approach. Electron. J. Inf. Syst. Eval. 10(1), 91–122 (2007)

39. Widjaja, T., Kaiser, J., Tepel, D., Buxmann, P.: Heterogeneity in IT landscapes and monopoly power of firms: a model to quantify heterogeneity (2012)

40. Akella, J., Buckow, H., Rey, S.: IT architecture: cutting costs and complexity. McKinsey Q., 4 (2009)

41. Hoogervorst, J.: Enterprise architecture: Enabling integration, agility and change. Int. J. Coop. Inf. Syst. 13(03), 213–233 (2004)

42. Lankhorst, M.: Communication of enterprise architectures. Enterprise Architecture at Work, pp. 69–84. Springer, Berlin (2009)

43. Laudon, K.C.: Managing Information Systems: Managing the Digital Firm, 13th edn. Prentice Hall, Englewood Cliffs (2013)
44. Allen, I.E., Seaman, C.A.: Likert scales and data analyses. Qual. Prog. **40**(7), 64–65 (2007)
45. Newman, I.: Qualitative-Quantitative Research Methodology: Exploring the Interactive Continuum. SIU Press, Carbondale (1998)
46. Lee A.S., DeGross II, J.: Information systems and qualitative research. In: Proceedings of the IFIP TC8 WG, vol. 8 (1997)
47. Samoilenko, S., Osei-Bryson, K.M.: Linking investments in telecoms and productivity growth in the context of transition economies within the framework of neoclassical growth accounting: solving endogeneity problem with structural equation modeling. In: Proceedings of 18th European Conference on Information Systems, Pretoria, South Africa (2010)
48. Fornell, C., Larcker, D.F.: Evaluating structural equation models with unobservable variables and measurement error. J. Mark. Res. **18**, 39–50 (1981)
49. Markus, K.A.: Principles and practice of structural equation modeling by Rex B. Kline. Struct. Eqn. Model. Multi. J. **19**(3), 509–512 (2012)
50. Wong, K.K.-K.: Partial least squares structural equation modeling (PLS-SEM) techniques using SmartPLS. Mark. Bull. **24**, 1–32 (2013)
51. Ringle, C.M., Sarstedt, M., Straub, D.: A critical look at the use of PLS-SEM in MIS Quarterly. MIS Q. (MISQ) **36**(1), 3–14 (2012)
52. Ringle, C.M., Wende, S., Will, A.: SmartPLS 2.0 (beta). Hamburg, Germany (2005)
53. Chin, W.W.: The partial least squares approach to structural equation modeling. Mod. Methods Bus. Res. **295**(2), 295–336 (1998)
54. Rea, L.M., Parker, R.A.: Designing and Conducting Survey Research: A Comprehensive Guide. Wiley, New York (2012)
55. LimeSurvey - the free and open source survey software tool! (24 April 2011). http://www.limesurvey.org/de/start. Accessed 23 November 2014
56. Friedrich, I., Sprenger, J., Breitner, M.H.: Discussion and validation of a CRM system selection approach with experts. In: AMCIS (2011)
57. Hauder, M., Roth, S., Schulz, C., Matthes, F.: An examination of organizational factors influencing enterprise architecture management challenges. In: ECIS, p. 175 (2013)
58. Schmidt, R., Möhring, M., Maier, S., Pietsch, J., Härting, R.-C.: Big data as strategic enabler - insights from Central European enterprises. In: Abramowicz, W., Kokkinaki, A. (eds.) BIS 2014. LNBIP, vol. 176, pp. 50–60. Springer, Heidelberg (2014)
59. O'Keefe, R.M., Balci, O., Smith, E.P.: Validation of expert system performance. Department of Computer Science, Virginia Polytechnic Institute and State University (1986)
60. Williamson, O.E.: Transaction-cost economics: the governance of contractual relations. J. Law Econ. **22**(2), 233–261 (1979)
61. Wigand, R.T., Picot, A., Reichwald, R.: Information, Organization and Management: Expanding Markets and Corporate Boundaries. Wiley, Chichester (1997)
62. Luftman, J., Brier, T.: Achieving and sustaining business-IT alignment. Calif. Manag. Rev. **42**, 109–122 (1999)
63. Weill, P., Ross, J.W.: IT Savvy: What Top Executives Must Know to go from Pain to Gain. Harvard Business Press, Cambridge (2009)
64. Giacomazzi, F., Panella, C., Pernici, B., Sansoni, M.: Information systems integration in mergers and acquisitions: a normative model. Inf. Manag. **32**(6), 289–302 (1997)
65. Winter, K., Buckl, S., Matthes, F., Schweda, C.M.: Investigating the state-of-the-art in enterprise architecture management methods in literature and practice. In: MCIS, vol. 90 (2010)

66. Stelzer, D.: Enterprise architecture principles: literature review and research directions. In: Dan, A., Gittler, F., Toumani, F. (eds.) ICSOC/ServiceWave 2009. LNCS, vol. 6275, pp. 12–21. Springer, Heidelberg (2010)

67. Bernard, S.A.: An Introduction to Enterprise Architecture. AuthorHouse, Bloomington (2012)

68. Braun, C., Winter, R.: A comprehensive enterprise architecture metamodel and its implementation using a metamodeling platform. In: Proceedings of Enterprise Modelling and Information Systems Architectures, Proceedings of the Workshop in Klagenfurt, pp. 64–79 (2005)

69. Wißotzki, M., Koç, H., Weichert, T., Sandkuhl, K.: Development of an enterprise architecture management capability catalog. In: Kobyliński, A., Sobczak, A. (eds.) BIR 2013. LNBIP, vol. 158, pp. 112–126. Springer, Heidelberg (2013)

70. Niemi, E.: Enterprise architecture benefits: perceptions from literature and practice, *evaluation of enterprise and software architectures: critical issues, metrics and practices: [AISA Project 2005-2008]/Eetu Niemi, Tanja Ylimäki & Niina Hämäläinen (eds.). Jyväskylä: University of Jyväskylä, Information Technology Research Institute, 2008.-(Tietotekniikan tutkimusinstituutin julkaisuja, ISSN 1236-1615; 18). ISBN 978-951-39-3108-7 (CD-ROM).* (2008)

71. Schmidt, C., Buxmann, P.: Outcomes and success factors of enterprise IT architecture management: empirical insight from the international financial services industry. Eur. J. Inf. Syst. **20**(2), 168–185 (2011)

72. H. Andersson and P. Tuddenham, *Reinventing IT to support digitization.* McKinsey, 2014

73. Hirt, M., Willmott, P.: Strategic principles for competing in the digital age. McKinsey Quarterly (May 2014)

74. Aier, S., Gleichauf, B., Winter, R.: Understanding enterprise architecture management design-an empirical analysis. In: Wirtschaftsinformatik, p. 50 (2011)

75. Iacob, M.E., Meertens, L.O., Jonkers, H., Quartel, D.A.C., Nieuwenhuis, L.J.M., Van Sinderen, M.J.: From enterprise architecture to business models and back. Softw. Syst. Model. **13**(3), 1059–1083 (2014)

76. Osterwalder, A., Pigneur, Y., Tucci, C.L.: Clarifying business models: origins, present, and future of the concept. Commun. Assoc. Inf. Syst. **16**(1), 1–25 (2005)

77. Kluge, C., Dietzsch, A., Rosemann, M.: How to realise corporate value from enterprise architecture. In: ECIS, pp. 1572–1581 (2006)

78. Pruijt, L., Slot, R., Plessius, H., Bos, R., Brinkkemper, S.: The enterprise architecture realization scorecard: a result oriented assessment instrument. In: Aier, S., Ekstedt, M., Matthes, F., Proper, E., Sanz, J.L. (eds.) PRET 2012 and TEAR 2012. LNBIP, vol. 131, pp. 300–318. Springer, Heidelberg (2012)

79. Morganwalp, J.M., Sage, A.P.: Enterprise architecture measures of effectiveness. Int. J. Technol. Policy Manag. **4**(1), 81–94 (2004)

80. Schmidt, R., Möhring, M., Zimmermann, A., Wissotzki, M., Sandkuhl, K., Jugel, D.: Towards a framework for enterprise architecture analytics. In: Proceedings of the 18th IEEE International Enterprise Distributed Object Computing Conference Workshops (EDOCW), Ulm, Germany (2014, in press)

81. Schaub, M., Matthes, F., Roth, S.: Towards a conceptual framework for interactive enterprise architecture management visualizations. In: Modellierung, pp. 75–90 (2012)

82. Taylor, G.R.: Integrating Quantitative and Qualitative Methods in Research. University Press of America, Maryland (2005)

Managing Risks and Threats

Using Value Models for Business Risk Analysis in e-Service Networks

Dan Ionita[1]([✉]), Roel J. Wieringa[1], Lars Wolos[2], Jaap Gordijn[3], and Wolter Pieters[1,4]

[1] University of Twente, Drienerlolaan 5, 7522 NB Enschede, The Netherlands
{d.ionita,r.j.wieringa}@utwente.nl
[2] Goethe University Frankfurt, Frankfurt, Germany
lars.wolos@m-chair.de
[3] Vrije Universiteit Amsterdam,
De Boelelaan 1105, 1081 HV Amsterdam, The Netherlands
gordijn@cs.vu.nl
[4] TU Delft, Mekelweg 5, 2628 CC Delft, The Netherlands
w.pieters@tudelft.nl

Abstract. Commercially provided electronic services commonly operate on top of a complex, highly-interconnected infrastructure, which provides a multitude of entry points for attackers. Providers of e-services also operate in dynamic, highly competitive markets, which provides fertile ground for fraud. Before a business idea to provide commercial e-services is implemented in practice, it should therefore be analysed on its fraud potential.

This analysis is a risk assessment process, in which risks are ordered on severity and the unacceptable ones are mitigated. Mitigations may consist of changes in the e-service network to reduce the attractiveness of fraud for the fraudster, or changes in coordination process steps or IT architecture elements to make fraud harder or better detectable.

We propose to use e^3 *value* business value models for the identification and quantification of risks associated with e-service packages. This allows for impact estimation as well as understanding the attacker's business cases. We show how the e^3 *value* ontology — with minimal extensions – can be used to analyse known telecommunication fraud scenarios. We also show how the approach can be used to quantify infrastructure risks. Based on the results, as well as feedback from practitioners, we discuss the scope and limits of generalizability of our approach.

Keywords: e-services · Fraud · Risk · Governance and control · Value modelling

1 Introduction

e-Services, commercial services delivered electronically [12], are of vital and increasing importance to society. Examples are internet provision services, telephony services, email services, on-line delivery of music or other content,

© IFIP International Federation for Information Processing 2015
J. Ralyté et al. (Eds.): PoEM 2015, LNBIP 235, pp. 239–253, 2015.
DOI: 10.1007/978-3-319-25897-3_16

e-banking, on-line booking, etc. These services are delivered fully electronically, as opposed to many other 'physical' services such as a haircut at a barber. In this paper we will use telephony services as running examples.

The delivery of e-services is done via an *Information and Communication Technology (ICT)* infrastructure. For instance, modern telephony connections are handled by a complex technical architecture and rely on several information systems, e.g. for billing or call management. Technical vulnerabilities in such infrastructures may cause great concern [2].

However, since e-services are commercial offerings, they have *commercial* vulnerabilities in addition to technical ones. For instance, it is possible to register a telephony subscription using the identity of someone else (e.g. by providing a false proof of identity in the subscription process), resulting in calling for free.

These problems are exacerbated in highly competitive e-service markets such as telecom and on-line content provision, where service providers struggle to increase their market share by pushing new, increasingly flexible service packages with low and sometimes even negative margins. In an effort to reduce time to market, service providers might not have the time or resources to fully assess the potential for loss of each new service package. However, due to the increasingly complex and inter-connected nature of e-service provision, these plans often contain loopholes which malicious customers might abuse in order to reduce their costs or even turn a profit. Traditional heavy-weight GRC[1] frameworks are therefore of little use to analyse fraud potential: their models are focused on the socio-technical layout while established methods are mostly concerned with confidentiality, integrity and availability issues and may take days or weeks to apply [7].

We propose $e^3 fraud$ for risk analysis in e-service networks. $e^3 fraud$ is based on the $e^3 value$ ontology [3] for exploring new e-business ideas. $e^3 fraud$ conceptualizes risks in a *model*-based way, using a business oriented terminology. This ensures that the approach is usable by IT-oriented stakeholders, while keeping business concerns in mind. We present examples of fraudulent behaviour in the telecom industry, and show how to analyse them using $e^3 fraud$. Furthermore, we show how the approach could be used to model the commercial aspects of infrastructure risks.

Our methodology explicitly recognizes the notion of a *value constellation* [13]. Many e-services in fact are value constellations because they require multiple profit-loss responsible actors to collaborate in order to produce value for the customer. For example, in the telephone domain there is a caller, a callee, one or more telecommunication companies (e.g. for transit traffic), parties for billing and selling of prepaid cards, etc.

This paper is structured as follows: In Sect. 2 we summarize the steps taken to produce the results presented in this paper. In Sect. 3 we outline the $e^3 fraud$ approach to analyse *commercial* risks in networks of e-services using two cases provided by a telecommunication operator. In Sect. 4 we show how the $e^3 fraud$

---

[1] Governance, Risk and Compliance.

approach could be used to quantify known *infrastructure* risks. Section 5 tackles some of the issues encountered by the authors.

2   Research Methodology

The approach undertaken follows the traditional Design Cycle [18]. Partners from the telecom industry put forth the need for an approach to conducting lightwieght risk analysis of new service packages before they hit the market and provided several fraud scenarios for analysis. Investigation of these scenarios revealed that they could be commonly described solely in terms of value exchanges amongst the actors.

Based on previous experience in creating value models and doing profitability analyses of a value constellation, we selected the e^3value framework as a starting point. The e^3value approach models a network of end users and enterprises who exchange things of economic value with each other. However, e^3value is designed for mutually beneficial value models. So we iteratively extended the e^3value ontology and toolkit so as to accommodate the scenarios in questions (see Sect. 3.3) and provide meaningful output (see Sect. 3.4), respectively.

The long term goal of this research is to facilitate automatic identification, modelling and analysis of business risks related to e-service provision by software tool support. In this paper, we present two real life case studies demonstrating our modelling conventions and analysis approach. Most of the results shown were produced using software tools: for the creation of the initial models, tool support is available (see e3value.few.vu.nl) and for running the analysis a custom Java extension was created.

For initial validation, we obtained feedback from a telecom provider about their perception of the potential usability and utility of our approach in practice, which we discuss in Sect. 5.1.

3   The e^3fraud Approach to Analysing Business Risks in Networks of e-Services

The e^3fraud approach takes as input an ideal business model and produces a set of sub-ideal business models. Each sub-ideal business model represents a business risk, for which graphs can be generated showing the loss/gain of each Risk.

The e^3fraud approach consists of three steps:

1. Construct the ideal business value model in e^3value, showing the e-service at hand in terms of expected economic value creation and distribution
2. Construct/generate one or more sub-ideal models in e^3fraud, showing possible fraud scenarios in terms of economic value
3. Analyse financial feasibility and financial impact of the fraud.

Steps 1 and 2 are also proposed by Kartseva et al. [10]. However, where Kartseva et al. continue with proposing solutions to possibilities to prevent committing a fraud, the e^3fraud analyses in step 3 the financial feasibility of the fraud for the fraudster, and the financial impact of the fraud on the ToA. In other words: the attack should be profitable for the attacker; otherwise the attack is not financially feasible. In addition, the attack should be costly for the ToA; otherwise countermeasures are not financially feasible. This allows stakeholders to assess the severity of a fraud scenario represented by the sub-ideal model, and helps decision makers choose which scenarios need to be mitigated.

Furthermore, in Kartseva models [9], sub ideal model behaviour is represented by value transfers that do not occur (e.g. a customer not paying for a product), or occur wrongly (e.g. paying an insufficient amount of money). e^3fraud adds the notion of *hidden* transfers: fraudulent behaviour might involve value transfers that some (honest) parties do not expect or cannot observe, but of which they later experience the financial effects. This implies that an e^3fraud model now takes the *perspective* of an individual enterprise or customer.

Currently, as a proof of concept, sub-ideal models are constructed manually, but we plan to provide tool support for automatic generation and ranking of sub-ideal models.

3.1   Scenario Description

In this section we explain the e^3fraud approach by means of an easy to understand example, from the field of telecommunication/telephony.

A simple example of fraud in the telephony sector is Revenue Share Fraud (RSF), and involves setting up revenue sharing agreement with one provider, and a flat-rate (unlimited) subscription with another, and then calling yourself. This triggers the payment of interconnection fees from one provider to the other, thus resulting in a transfer of economic value between the providers. Depending on the scale of the operation and the detection capabilities of the provider, fraudsters could pull in up to several million dollars over a weekend [1]. We define Telecom misuse as the contracting or consumption of telecommunication services in a manner that is not in line with the service provider's expectations. Fraud is then any instance of misuse as previously defined with the explicit goal of obtaining financial rewards.

3.2   Construction of an Ideal Business Value Model

We develop first an ideal business value model. Such a model shows what actors transfer in terms of economic value if all actors behave *honestly*. We explain e^3value as we go along.

Figure 1 presents the ideal business value model for a flat-rate mobile phone subscription. The e^3value language supports the notion of *actors*. Actors are profit-and-loss responsible enterprises, non-profit organizations, or end-users. In this specific example, actors are telecommunication providers (provider A and B) and end users (user A and B).

The e^3value language also has the construct of *market segment*. A market segment groups actors that assign economic value to received or provided objects

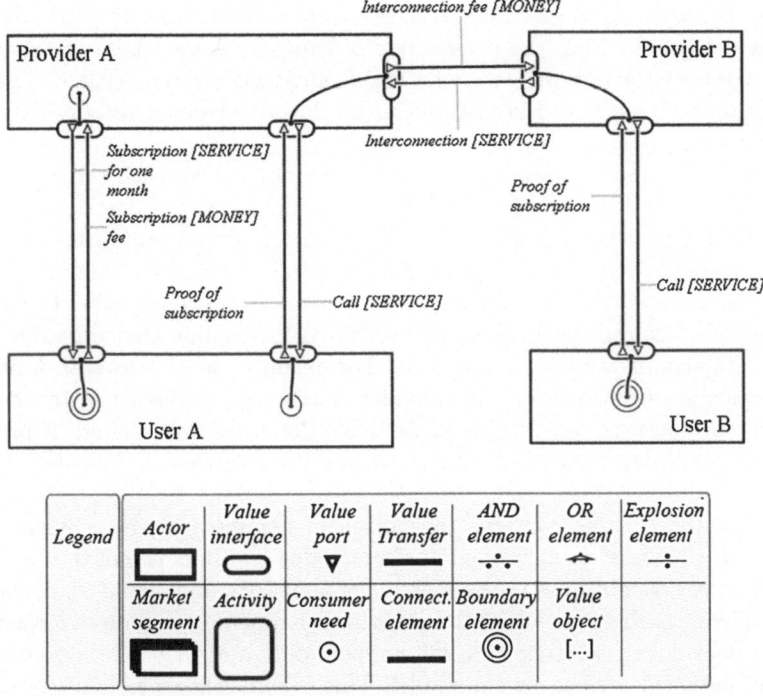

Fig. 1. Ideal model: User A calls user B

in the same way. For explanatory reasons, we do not use the notion of market segment yet.

Actors exchange things of economic value with each other, called *value objects*, via *value transfers* (visualized as straight line *between* actors). Value objects are physical objects or outcomes of services that are experienced by at least one actor in the model as of economic value.

In Fig. 1 user A obtains a monthly flat-rate subscription ("Subscription for one month") with Provider A and in return for this, the users pays Provider A an amount of money on a monthly basis ("Subscription fee"). The flat-rate subscription entitles the users to perform unlimited telephone calls to any other number. In return for presenting proof of this subscription to the provider, the provider delivers its service, which is a telephone call.

In many cases, the caller and the callee do not have a subscription with the same provider, but rather with two providers, in Fig. 1 provider A and B. So, to create a telephone connection initiated by user A to user B, provider A has to interconnect with provider B, since provider B is the operator user B has a subscription with. In other words, provider B delivers an interconnection service to provider A, and this service of value to provider A, because otherwise provider A could not create telephone connection outside its own network.

User B has his own contractual agreement with Provider B. However, this ideal model is built from the perspective of Provider A for whom the structure of this agreement is not know nor observable and thus not represented. The only transaction between User B and Provider B which Provider A can observe is the telephone call.

An e^3value model shows how actors do business which each other in a *contract period*. This is a period described by the contracts that describe the value transfers among actors shown in the diagram. An important property of an e^3value model is *economic reciprocity*. Figure 1 shows various *value interfaces*, containing *value ports*, transferring value objects (see the legend). The notion of value interface represents economic reciprocity, meaning that *all* value ports transfer objects of value, or *none at all*. For example, when provider A obtains interconnection from provider B, provider A will pay, as described by the contract, in the contract period. The same holds the other way around: If provider B is paid, provider B provides the interconnection service as described by the contract.

Finally, the e^3value contains the notion of *dependency paths*. Such a path consists of *consumer needs*, value interfaces, value transfers *connection elements* (visualized as straight lines in the *interior* of an actor), and *boundary elements*[2]. A dependency path shows which transfers must happen, as a result of a consumer need. It does not show *when* they will happen, only *that* they will happen in the contract period described by the model. This is sufficient to estimate economic profitability in the contract period.

The technical and business processes by which these transactions are implemented contain a lot more detail and are not shown [4]. It is even possible that the coordination processes that implement the commercial transactions implement a value transfer between actors A and B by means of a coordination process involving actors A, B and C. An e^3value model abstracts from these operational details and shows commercial transactions only.

In Fig. 1, user A needs to make a call to User B. In exchange for the call, User A pays a sum of money. By following the dependency path, we can see that provider A should obtain interconnection to provide the telephone call, and should pay for this interconnection. Finally, provider B delivers a telephone call service to user B.

For now, it is important to understand that in this e^3value model *all* transfers on a dependency path are assumed to occur. In other words, the model shows what happens in reality, only all actors behave as agreed and expected. So, actors are always paying, and services are always provisioned. That is why we call such a model an *ideal* model; all actors operate honestly.

---

[2] A dependency path also may contain *AND, OR*, and *explosion/implosion* elements to represent dependency splits and joins, but for explanatory purposes, these are not used in Fig. 1.

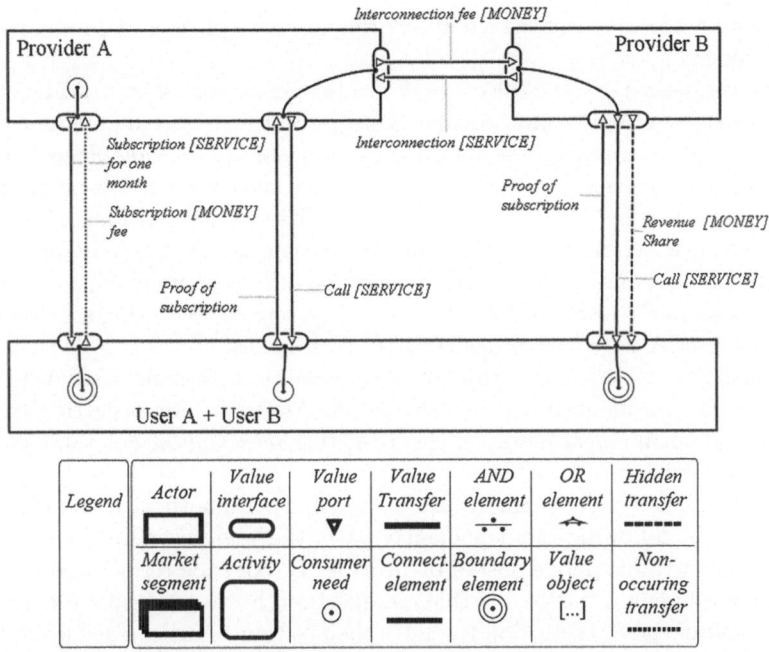

Fig. 2. Sub-ideal model: User A calls himself and earns money

3.3   Construction of Sub-ideal Business Value Models

In real-life, actors do not always behave as agreed and expected. They can perform intentionally or unintentionally in a different way. For example, an actor may not pay, or pay a wrong amount of money. Currently, in $e^3 fraud$, we consider two types of *intended* misbehaviours:

1. Transfers which should happen in the ideal model, do not happen at all in reality;
2. Transfers that happen in reality are not supposed to happen in the ideal model.

Furthermore, actors assumed to be independent in the ideal model may collude.

We construct sub-ideal value models from the point of view of the same actor, in this example provider A, who is the ToA. A sub-ideal model represents the business value model as seen by the attacker and is created by changing the ideal model to represent misbehaviour.

Figure 2 shows an example of revenue sharing fraud, exhibiting both types of misbehaviours described above, as well as collusion. Rather than two end-users, as shown in Fig. 1, we have now a single end-user A, who is exhibiting unwanted behaviour. This end-user has the same monthly subscription with Provider A as outlined in Fig. 1. It is important to understand that this monthly subscription is based on a flat-fee tariff, which allows the user a to place a unlimited number of calls for free.

However, user A *also* has also access to a telephone hosted by provider B. The contract between user A and provider B states that for *received* call, user B gets part of the interconnection fee obtained by provider B (*Revenue Share*). This is a common arrangement for 0900 numbers. Again, since we take the point of view of Provider A, we have no information on how User A obtained a contract with provider B or what the structure of their agreement is. For the fraud analysis, it is sufficient to assume such a bonus is being paid. Furthermore, since the bonus pay-out is hidden to Provider A (the ToA), it is represented using a *dashed* line. Note that user A only uses provider B to *receive* calls.

To make matters worse, in this sub-ideal scenario we assume User A does not intend to pay his monthly fee to Provider A. As it is a non-occurring transfer with respect to the ideal model of the ToA, the *Subscription Fee* value transfer is represented using a *dotted* line.

User A will now place as many calls as possible per month with provider B. As can be seen by following the dependency path, the *same* user A also terminates the call, but with his phone hosted by provider B. For each terminated call, user A receives a bonus. Considering that, in addition, he also intends to default on his payment of the Subscription fee, he is the position to make a generous profit.

3.4 Financial Analysis of the Attack

The most important financial factors of Telecom fraud, with regard to Risk Assessment are: (1) losses incurred by the provider and (2) motivation (in terms of potential gain) of the attacker. The former allows for estimating the impact of each type of fraud, while the latter is a critical part in estimating the likelihood of such a scenario taking place. The likelihood and impact of a fraud scenario can be used to compute the overall Risk associated with each particular scenario.

To estimate these factors, we need to analyse a pair of models: an ideal model showing the e^3value model of normal usage and a sub-ideal one showing the e^3fraud model of fraudulent usage. Furthermore, in pay-per-usage environments, such as telecom, the magnitude of the risk is dependent on the scale of usage (e.g. minutes called).

A custom software tool was developed that takes as input two models and generates profitability graphs for both the ideal and sub-ideal case(s) showing the dependency of the profitability with regard to usage. This allows for a visual comparison of ideal vs. non-ideal business cases of the provider as well as regular vs. fraudulent business case for the customers (and potential fraudsters) across a given range of occurrence rates.

The two graphs in Fig. 3 are generated by this tool from the models shown in Figs. 1 and 2. Realistic and, where available, real, values were used to instantiate the models. The chosen values are based on tariffs charge by Dutch Telecom providers in 2014. For simplicity, we only show the financial result of user A and Provider A (vertical axes), relative to the number of calls made (horizontal axis).

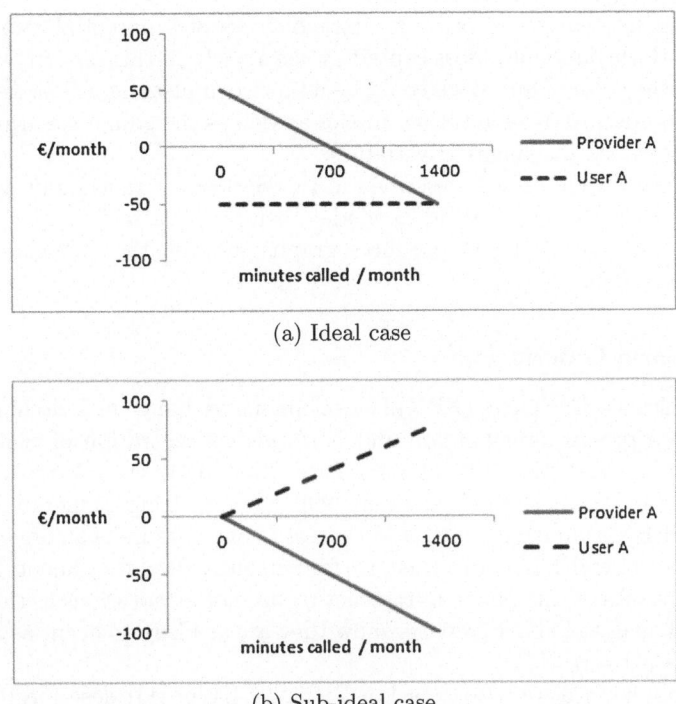

(a) Ideal case

(b) Sub-ideal case

Fig. 3. Profitability graphs of the RSF scenario

The financial outcome expected by the Telecom provider, in normal usage conditions, is visible in Fig. 3a. Here, the user has a fixed cost, the monthly cost of the subscription. The costs of Provider A increase with each call, due to the termination bonus paid to Provider B for the interconnection. Operating costs are not represented here as they are unknown and assumed to be negligible for an individual user, but could be easily included in the model. The sub-ideal case (Fig. 3b) is significantly different. Besides the clear loss for the provider, the fraudster's financial motivation is now clearly visible.

While the value model(s) alone do not contain sufficient information to reliably elicit procedural or technical countermeasures on it's own, these financial results can be used to discuss checks on the non-occurring transactions or infer thresholds based on break-even points so as to mitigate the Risks.

4   Using the e^3fraud Approach to Analyse Technical Risks

Real-world security risk assessments typically result in the identification of a list of risks that is too long to be mitigated completely. The assessors must therefore prioritize the risks and mitigate only the most "important" ones. Importance is usually estimated by factoring in attractiveness of a potential attack to the attacker with the amount of loss caused by the attack. In this section, we demonstrate how the e^3fraud approach could be used to complement a Risk Assessment of the infrastructure by facilitating impact as well as the gain estimation of individual risks, based on ranges of variables.

The alternative approach described in this Section takes as input a technical risk described in terms of an ideal model (before the attack) and a sub-ideal model (after the attack) and produces graphs showing the financial loss/gain related to the Risk.

4.1   Scenario Description

A Private Branch Exchange (PBX) is a telephone exchange or switching system that serves a private organization and performs concentration of central office lines or trunks and provides intercommunication between a large number of telephone stations in the organization [20]. By exploiting vulnerabilities in a company's PBX, fraudsters may obtain access to one or more of an organization's phone numbers, which they can then use for personal, often fraudulent, purposes. Although attacks on the phone infrastructure are not as notorious as the revenue share fraud analysed above, reports show they are as likely to occur as an attack on the data network [17].

There are several ways to attack a PBX. As Kuhn [11] describes, the most vulnerable is the remote access feature. Through this feature, for example, a fraudster can create a special mailbox which redirects him to a phone number of his choice. This number could be either a premium-rate (0900) number owned by a criminal organisation the fraudster is part of or a number that provides the callee with a revenue share for every received call.

Another option would of course be to obtain possession of a telephone within the company and start calling his number from there [15]. One way to do this is to blackmail or bribe a company employee. In e^3fraud, we abstract from the technical or social means to access a company's phone number, and concentrate on the business model for the attacker.

4.2   Construction of Ideal and Sub-ideal Business Value Models

We want to estimate the potential loss the company would face in case of unauthorized access to it's PBX, as well as the potential gain a malicious actor with such access could obtain.

To start, we create an ideal model of the value exchanges as perceived and expected by the Target of Assessment, whose perspective we take. In this case, we take the perspective of the Company who owns the PBX. We want to estimate the potential loss the company would face in case of unauthorized access to it's PBX, as well as the potential gain a malicious actor with such access could obtain. Figure 4a shows the ideal model: Employees (Company A employee) may call through the company PBX to external Users (User B). This is the normal usage the company expects, given honest actors.

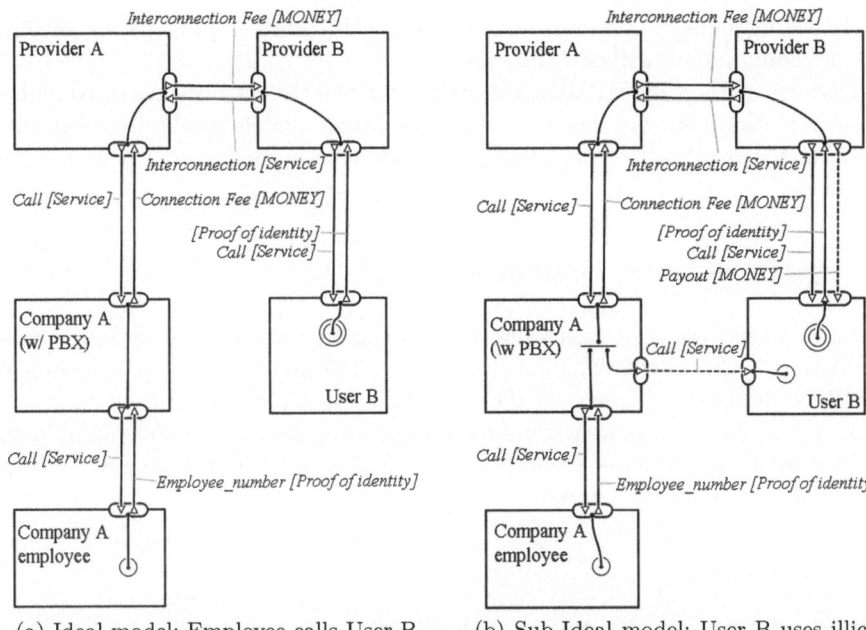

(a) Ideal model: Employee calls User B

(b) Sub-Ideal model: User B uses illicit access to PBX to call himself

Fig. 4. Models used to analyse the Risk of PBX hacking

Next, we tweak the model to show the commercial traces of the risk we want to analyse. For example, Fig. 4b shows a sub-ideal model where User B is an attacker. He obtains access to the PBX (dashed line) and exploits this (illicit) access order to make calls to through a provider that pays out a reward for every call received.

It is interesting to note that the value model abstracts away from the actual vulnerability being exploited and the process by which access is gained. In order to fully describe the attack, a coordination model such as an attack tree is needed.

To do a financial analysis of the risk, we instantiate both models with known or realistic values and use the $e^3 fraud$ computation engine to generate profitability graphs showing the financial result of all actors involved for both the ideal and sub-ideal case, similar to the ones shown in Fig. 3.

By contrasting the financial result of *Company A* in the ideal model with its financial results in the sub-ideal model, we can quantitatively estimate the *impact* associated with a technical risk. Furthermore, by computing the financial result of the attacker in each sub-ideal case, we can estimate the expected *gain* of each attack. It is worth noting that the costs of setting up the attack are not taken into account and thus we cannot claim to estimate the attack's *profitability* (as *costs-gain*).

Using the software tool described in Sect. 3.4, we can generate a multitude graphs, for various ranges of malicious calls.

Tweaking model parameters and re-running the tool also provides an efficient way of conducting sensitivity analyses.

Because e^3fraud models abstract away from the technical means of conducting an attack, there is reason to believe e^3fraud models might be re-usable, meaning the overhead of creating such a model for each Risk would not be significant.

5   Discussion and Conclusions

We have shown how business value models can be used to identify and quantify risks of fraud in e-service networks, where information about the technical infrastructure of the partners in the network is incomplete or even absent.

In particular, e^3fraud, a proof-of-concept extension of e^3value, is able to identify, model and analyse business risks, as well as quantify the business impact of technical or procedural risks.

5.1   Validity

The approach presented in this paper has been successfully applied to four Telecom fraud scenarios, containing a variety of business as well as technical risks. The models were validated with the help of the scenario owners. Results matched existing estimations and by using real values we were able to show that at least one instance Revenue Sharing Fraud is still possible today.

The approach was also demonstrated to domain experts working for the fraud department of a leading Telecom provider and received positive feedback. The method was generally perceived as useful, especially for quickly assessing the financial fitness of new plans before they are launched and estimating the impact of new types of fraud on existing plans. Furthermore, the experts saw the profitability graphs as an expressive means of communicating risks to product managers.

However, experts envisage several functional improvements before the e^3fraud method and toolkit would be usable in practice: the ability to model a larger variety of sub-ideal models (such as ones containing hidden actors) and the possibility of automatically generating and ranking sub-ideal models based on a given ideal model. Finally, a library of model patterns was mentioned as a way to promote (re)usage.

5.2   Limitations

While e^3fraud can be used to help reduce possibilities of fraud on the service level, as well as to quantify some known infrastructure risks, it does not necessarily help to identify attack on the technical infrastructure, such as a DDOS attack. e^3fraud is especially applicable in cases where the economics of risk are of particular importance, such as for analysing fraud that takes place on the service level rather than the technology level.

The biggest strength of e^3fraud models - similar to the e^3value models they build upon - is also their biggest weakness: they abstract away from any and all procedural and architectural information. But in some cases the order in which the transactions happen is important. For example, its impossible to make a call with a SIM card that hasn't been bought yet. The how question (critical to process models) does not concern us, but the order in which certain transactions are executed does matter.

Even though the order of execution is not important for the business model, to discuss countermeasures, we need to be able to reason about the coordination processes and IT architectures that can mitigate risks. In general, transformation to or generation of any sort of architecture or coordination model from an e^3value model is not feasible [4]. There exists previous work discussing these relationships for [5,6,8,14,16,19]. However, none of these papers are about (in-)security or fraud and mostly assume ideal business environments. This motivates a closer study of the relation between e^3fraud models, coordination models, and enterprise architecture which are relevant or useful in the context of Risk Assessment.

Finally, this work is still in its initial stages. As the methodology and tool have been developed and tested on a limited number of telecom fraud scenarios, the approach is somewhat example-driven. Thus, an obvious next step is to model and analyse a larger variety of scenarios so as to further develop and validate the idea.

5.3   Generalisability

We have developed and illustrated the e^3fraud approach on a number of cases from telecom service provision. To which extent is this generalizable to other kinds of e-service provision? At the moment we can only speculate about this, but the true test of generalizability is the application of e^3fraud to other kinds of e-service provision networks. We plan to do this in future work. In the absence of any such empirical evidence, we analyse the features of the studied telecom service networks that make e^3value and e^3fraud suitable to identify and analyse business risks.

In the telecommunications sector, information on the technical infrastructure of competitors is unobtainable, which makes e^3value and e^3fraud well-suited to model business risks. Describing the money flows and their triggers is necessary and sufficient to understand such scenarios and not only derive estimates of both impact for the provider and gain for the fraudsters, but also identify countermeasures.

A second characteristic of the telecom sector is the importance of a short time-to-market. The marketing department of a Telecom provider typically wants to launch new services without delay and so any kind of initial analysis of prospective risks arising from proposed products will need to be comprehensive enough to be meaningful and yet quick enough to be acceptable. Once the product is launched, it will be important to identify any unacceptable activity at the earliest opportunity, to minimise the losses associated with this. Our initial evidence shows that e^3fraud offers the promise to offer efficient support in risk identification and mitigation. To further improve this efficiency, we are currently working on automatically generating and ranking the sub-ideal models.

Based on this brief analysis of the factors that contribute to the usability and usefulness of $e^3 fraud$ in the identification and analysis of risks of fraud in telecom service provision, we speculate that $e^3 fraud$ will be equally useful in other cases of e-service provision where information about the technical infrastructure of competitors is unobtainable, time-to-market of new services must be short, and losses created by instances of fraud must be kept within acceptable bounds. We plan to do case studies that provide evidence for this speculation in future research.

Acknowledgements. The ideas and models presented here were developed with the support of S. Koenen and Dr. M. Daneva of the University of Twente. This research has received funding from the European Union Seventh Framework Programme (FP7/2007-2013) under grant agreement no. 318003 (TREs- PASS). This publication reflects only the author's views and the Union is not liable for any use that may be made of the information contained herein.

References

1. Baker, D.: International revenue share fraud: are we winning the battle against telecom pirates? Black Swan Telecom J., November 2012
2. Freedman, D.: The phone hacking scandal: implications for regulation. Telev. New Media **13**(1), 17–20 (2012)
3. Gordijn, J., Akkermans, H.: Value based requirements engineering: exploring innovative e-commerce idea. Requirements Eng. J. **8**(2), 114–134 (2003)
4. Gordijn, J., Akkermans, H., van Vliet, H.: Business modelling is not process modelling. In: Mayr, H.C., Liddle, S.W., Thalheim, B. (eds.) ER Workshops 2000. LNCS, vol. 1921, pp. 40–51. Springer, Heidelberg (2000)
5. Gordijn, J., Van Vliet, H.: On the interaction between business models and software architecture in electronic commerce. In: Addendum to the Proceedings of the 7th European Software Engineering Conference/Foundations of Software Engineering/ESEC 1999 (1999)
6. Gordijn, J., Wieringa, R.J.: A value-oriented approach to e-business process design. In: Eder, J., Missikoff, M. (eds.) CAiSE 2003. LNCS, vol. 2681, pp. 390–403. Springer, Heidelberg (2003)
7. Ionita, D., Hartel, P., Pieters, W., Wieringa, R.: Current established risk assessment methodologies and tools, September 2013
8. Janssen, W., van Buuren, R., Gordijn, J.: Business case modelling for e-services. In: Vogel, D.R., Walden, P., Gricar, J., Lenart, G. (eds.) Proceedings of the 18th BLED Conference (e-Integration in Action), pages cdrom, Maribor, SL. University of Maribor (2005)
9. Kartseva, V.: Designing Controls for Network Organization: A Value-Based Approach. Ph.D. thesis, Vrije Universiteit Amsterdam (2008)
10. Kartseva, V., Gordijn, J., Tan, Y.-H.: Designing value-based inter-organizational controls using patterns. In: Lyytinen, K., Loucopoulos, P., Mylopoulos, J., Robinson, B. (eds.) Design Requirements Engineering. LNBIP, vol. 14, pp. 276–301. Springer, Heidelberg (2009)

11. Kuhn, D.R.: National Institute of Standards and Technology (U.S.). PBX vulnerability analysis [microform] : finding holes in your PBX before someone else does/D. Richard Kuhn. U.S. Dept. of Commerce, Technology Administration, National Institute of Standards and Technology; For sale by the Supt. of Docs., U.S. G.P.O Gaithersburg, Md.: Washington, D.C. (2001)

12. Mohan, K., Ramesh, B.: Ontology-based support for variability management in product and service families. In: Proceedings of the 36th Hawaii International Conference on System Sciences, Hawaii (2003)

13. Normann, R., Ramírez, R.: Designing Interactive Strategy - From Value Chain to Value Constellation. Wiley, Chichester (1994)

14. Pijpers, V., Gordijn, J.: Bridging business value models and business process models in aviation value webs via possession rights. In: Proceedings of the 20th Annual Hawaii International Conference on System Sciences, page cdrom. Computer Society Press (2007)

15. Regan, T.: Pbx security in the voip environment, March 2013. http://www.spitfire.co.uk/pdf/05_PBX_Security_in_the_VoIP_environment-white_paper_140313_2.pdf. Accessed November 2014

16. Singh, P.M.: Integrating business value in enterprise architecture modeling and analysis, August 2013

17. SMARTVOX. How secure is your asterisk pbx? (2014). http://kb.smartvox.co.uk/asterisk/secure-asterisk-pbx-part-1/. Accessed November 2014

18. Wieringa, R.: Design Science Methodology for Information Systems and Software Engineering. Springer, Heidelberg (2014)

19. Wieringa, R., Gordijn, J.: Value-oriented design of correct service coordination protocols. In: Proceedings of the 20th ACM Symposium on Applied Computing, pp. 1320–1327. ACM Press (2005)

20. Wikipedia. Business telephone system – Wikipedia, the free encyclopedia (2014)

Analyzing Trust Requirements in Socio-Technical Systems: A Belief-Based Approach

Mohamad Gharib[✉] and Paolo Giorgini

University of Trento - DISI, Povo, 38123 Trento, Italy
{gharib,paolo.giorgini}@disi.unitn.it

Abstract. The Requirements Engineering (RE) community recognizes the importance of trust proposing several approaches to model and analyze trust requirements. However, such approaches mainly focus on trust as social relations without relating them to the requirements of the system's components. We propose a belief-based trust approach based on an extended version of Secure Tropos, where social relations are modeled and analyzed along with beliefs concerning capabilities and motivations of system's components. An example concerning US stock market crash (the Flash Crash) is used to illustrate our approach.

Keywords: Trust analysis · Beliefs · Requirements engineering

1 Introduction

Trust is very important in human societies [19], so it is in Socio-Technical Systems (STS) [7], where organizations and humans are an integral part of the system. Vulnerabilities of a STS are not only originated by technical issues, but they can be directly related to the social interactions of its components (both social and technical actors). For example, the Flash Crash was not caused by a mere technical failure, but it was due to undetected vulnerabilities in the interactions of the STS [21]. In [9], we showed how STS vulnerabilities can be avoided when trust requirements are considered properly during the system design.

The RE community recognizes the importance of trust, proposing several approaches for modeling trust requirements (e.g., Secure Tropos [17], SI* [24], etc.). However, none of them proposes to analyze trust starting from the perspective of socio-technical components of the system. More specifically, local objectives, competencies, motivations, etc. should be considered as main drivers for the definition of the trust requirements. One main contribution of this paper is enriching trust requirements analysis during the early phase of the system development by acquiring information about each socio-technical component (actor) and using such information to derive trust requirements.

To this end, we propose a belief-based trust approach built on an extended version of Secure Tropos [10], where a set of beliefs related to actors' competencies (can do) and motivations (will do) are used to clearly identify "why"

© IFIP International Federation for Information Processing 2015
J. Ralyté et al. (Eds.): PoEM 2015, LNBIP 235, pp. 254–270, 2015.
DOI: 10.1007/978-3-319-25897-3_17

an actor may trust/distrust another one. The proposed framework is fully supported by a CASE Tool, and it offers a methodological process to assist analysts during the different phases of the system analysis, along with several reasoning techniques that support the verification of the correctness and consistency of the requirements model. The rest of the paper is organized as follows; Sect. 2 describes the research baseline, and we discuss an example concerning the stock market system in Sect. 3. We detail our approach in Sect. 4, and we implement and evaluate it in Sect. 5. Related work is presented in Sect. 6, and we conclude the paper and discuss the future work in Sect. 7.

2   Research Baseline

Our research baseline is founded on three main research areas:

(1) **Goal Oriented Requirement Engineering (GORE)**: GORE is used to express the system requirements in terms of the actors of the system along with their objectives, entitlements, and capabilities. Among the existing GORE approaches (e.g., SI* [17], Secure Tropos [24], etc.), we adopt an extended version of Secure Tropos [10] as a baseline for our approach. In which, an actor covers two concepts a role and an agent, where roles can be specialized from one another (is_a), and an agent can play a role or more. Goals can be refined through And/Or decomposition of a root goal into sub-goals, where a goal is achieved if all of its (And-decomposition) or any of its (Or-decomposition) sub-goals are/is achieved. Goals may produce and read information. Finally, it provides concepts for modeling information provision and goals delegation among actors, and it adopts the notion of trust to capture the expectation of actors in one another.

(2) **Belief-Desire-Intention (BDI)**: The BDI paradigm [18] enables for analyzing actors of the system in terms of their beliefs, desires, and intentions. In BDI an agent has a set of beliefs representing its knowledge about the world, desires (goals) it aims to achieve, and intentions (plans) that play an important role in determining their behavior to achieve their desires. The main reason for considering BDI paradigm is our need to capture beliefs about the actors' capabilities and motivations.

(3) **Trust Management**: There is general consensus that trust is complex and multidimensional concept [6], which motivates several researchers to answer the challenging question "how can trust be constructed (built)?". However, Esfandiari and Chandrasekharan [8] argued that constructing trust can be broadly classified under two main types: cognitive and mathematical, where in the first trust is made up of underlying beliefs (e.g., [1,4]), while in the last trust can be constructed based on some trust metrics (e.g., [8,20,22]).

In particular, our approach adopts concepts from extended Secure Tropos [10] to model the system requirements in terms of the actors of the system along with their objectives, entitlements, and capabilities. However, this framework does not propose techniques for modeling nor analyzing trust requirements based on actors' capabilities and motivations. Thus, we rely on the BDI paradigm to capture actors' capabilities and motivations through their related beliefs. While, we depend on trust management to understand how different scholars have analyzed/constructed trust.

3   A Stock Market System Example

Our example concerns the Flash Crash, in which the Dow Jones Industrial Average (DJIA) dropped about 1000 points (about 9 % of its value). Several stakeholders of the stock market system can be identified based on [15], including: *stock investors* are individuals or companies, who have a main goal "Make profit from trading securities".

Stock traders are individuals or companies involved in trading securities in *stock markets* either for their own sake or on behalf of their *investors* with a main goal "Make profit by trading securities". *Stock traders* can be broadly classified under: *Market makers*: traders who facilitate trading on particular security and they have the capability of trading large amount of securities; *High-Frequency Traders (HFTs)*: traders who have the capability to trade large amount of securities with very high frequency; and *small traders*: traders who trade small amount of securities with low trading frequency.

Stock markets are places where *traders* gather and trade securities (e.g., NASDAQ, CME, NYSE, etc.), and they have a main goal "Make profit by facilitate security trading". Furthermore, *accounting firms* are specialized for providing companies with reliable information about their economic activities and the status of their assets. Moreover, *auditing firms* are specialized for monitoring the quality of the financial statements produced by companies. *Consulting firms* are specialized for providing professional advices for a fee about securities to *traders* and *investors*. Finally, *credit assessment ratings firms* are specialized for assessing of the credit worthiness of companies' securities.

Figure 1 shows a partial goal model of the stock market to clarify the modeling language main constructs, in which Fast trading is an agent that plays the HFT role, which is specialized from the stock trader role. A stock trader has a main goal Make profit by trading security that is And-decomposed into Analyze the market for targeted securities and Make profit by producing the right orders, which reads Investor's orders and produces Trader's orders. A market depends on trader for the provision of Trader's orders, and a trust relation concerning such provision exist. *Space Co* delegates Manage company's auditing operations to *Account and audit Co*, and a trust relation concerning such delegation exist.

Extended Secure Tropos [10] is able to capture the functional and trust requirements of the system in their organizational context. However, unlike functional requirements, which are supported with various kinds of analysis mechanisms that enable for deciding whether they can be achieved or not, trust analysis did not receive such an attention. For example, in order to ensure stable trading environment, a trust relation should hold between the *stock market* and *stock*

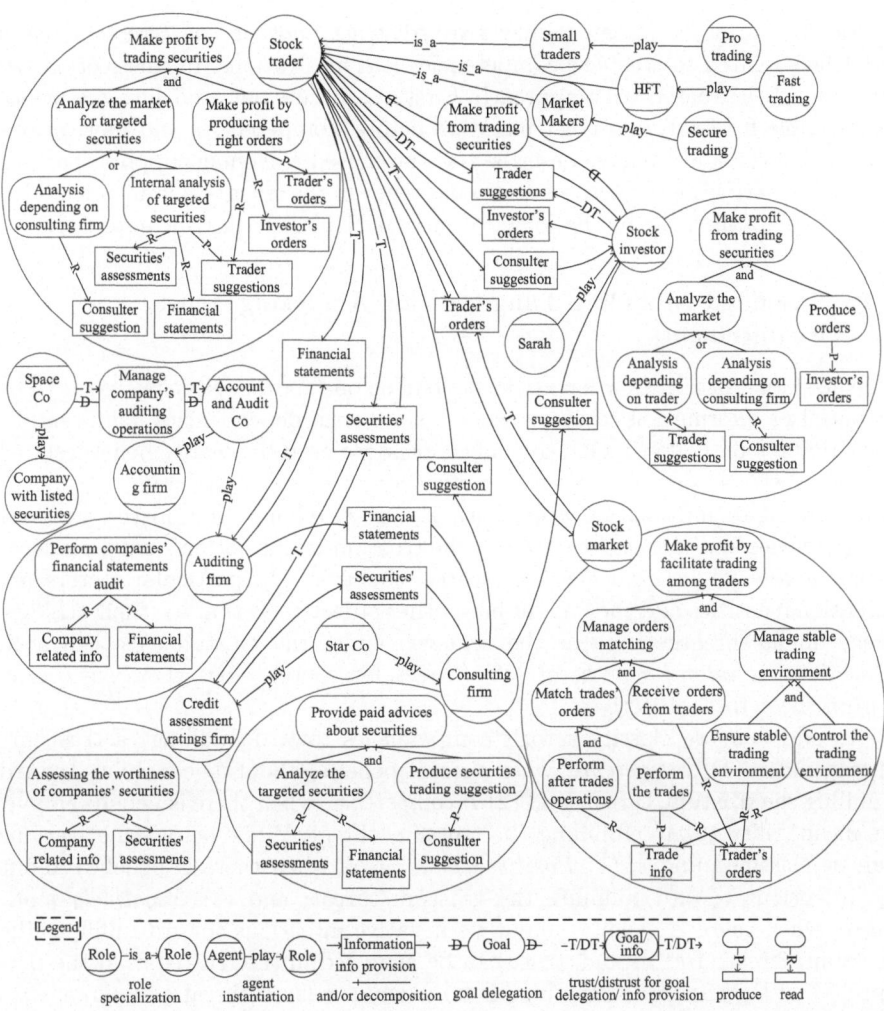

Fig. 1. A partial goal model concerning the U.S stock market structure

traders concerning the trading orders they provide. However, there is no existing technique that enables for analyzing trust relations based on the *traders'* capabilities and motivations, which form the bases of such trust, i.e., we cannot decide if such trust requirement is not conflicting with the *traders'* goals, intentions, etc.

4   A Belief-Based Approach for Analyzing Trust

Our approach proposes to model and analyze trust requirements among actors strictly from sets of beliefs concerning their capabilities and motivations. In particular, an actor (trustor) may trust/distrust another one (trustee) based on beliefs related to trustee's competencies and motivations. In this section, we detail our belief-based trust approach. First, we discuss our modeling extensions that enable for analyzing trust based on actors' competencies and motivations related beliefs, and then we describe the automated reasoning support that can be used to verify the correctness and consistency of the trust requirements model. Finally, we outline the methodological process that underlies our approach.

4.1   Extended Modeling Language for Analyzing Trust Requirements

The need for trust arises when actors depend on one another either for goals to be achieved or information to be provided[1], since such dependencies might entails risk (threat) [6]. Following [4], to analyze trust we need to identify beliefs related to the trustee's competencies and motivations toward the trustum (e.g., goal achievement or information provision). However, relying only on the trustee's competencies and motivations toward the trustum might not be enough; indeed, other factors might influence the trustee's behavior. In particular, actors are intentional entities and they might have other objective(s) that its/their achievement might threaten/prevent the achievement of the trustum. We call such objectives as *intentional threat* [23] (*threat* for short), since they exists only within the actors' objectives.

In addition, we classify actor's competencies toward fulfilling[2] a trustum/threat under: (1) *Competence*, when there is belief(s) about its capability toward fulfilling the trustum/threat; and (2) *Incompetence*, when there is belief(s) about its incapability toward fulfilling the trustum/threat. While actor's motivations can be classified under: (1) *Positively motivated*, when there is belief(s) about its intentions toward fulfilling the trustum/threat; and (2) *Negatively motivated*, when there is belief(s) about its negative intentions toward fulfilling the trustum/threat. To this end, trust can be analyzed in the trustee from the perspective of the trustor, when there is no trustum related threat as follows:

Definition 1. *Let a and b be two actors, and s be a trustum (e.g., a goal g or information i) that a aims for. Moreover, C and M are two sets of beliefs that a has about the capabilities and motivations of b, respectively. We say that a trusts b for fulfilling s, IFF $\exists\, c_1 \in C$, $\exists\, m_1 \in M \mid$ competence(fulfill, a, b, s) $\wedge$ positively_motivated(fulfill, a, b, s), and $\nexists\, c_2 \in C$, $\nexists\, m_2 \in M \mid$ incompetence(fulfill, a, b, s) $\vee$ negatively_motivated(fulfill, a, b, s), i.e., a has only beliefs concerning the competency and positive motivation of b toward fulfilling s.*

For example, in Fig. 1 a trust relation between the *Space Co* and *Account and audit Co* for fulfilling "Manage company's auditing operations" holds, if *Space Co* has beliefs about the competency and positive motivations of the *Account*

---

[1] We focus on the trustworthiness of the provided information, not information availability, i.e., whether information is provided or not.

[2] Fulfilling is used to refer to achieving a goal/threat, or provision of information.

and audit Co, and there is no beliefs concerning neither its incompetency nor negative motivations toward fulfilling the goal.

While if there is a trustum related threat(s), an integrated analysis of trust and its related threat(s) is required, i.e., we also need to determine whether the trustee is competence and positively motivated toward fulfilling the related threat(s) or not, and consider such knowledge while analyzing trust. In what follows, first we define a threat to trustum, and then we show how trust in the trustee can be analyzed when there is a trustum related threat(s).

Definition 2. *Let s be a trustum and t is a threat, we say that t is a threat to s, IFF the fulfillment of t threaten the fulfillment of s.*

For example, the *Space Co* can define "Biasing the audit information" as a threat to the goal "Manage company's auditing operation", where fulfilling such threat can threaten the fulfillment of the goal. Similarly, a *stock market* can define "Manipulate the market by providing falsified/fraud orders" as a threat to "trader's orders" information. After defining trustum related threat, we can enrich the trust analysis by considering the effect of such threat(s) over the trust relation as follows:

Definition 3. *Let a and b be actors, s is a trustum that a aims for, t is a threat of s, and a depends on b for fulfilling s. We say that a distrust b for fulfilling s, IF a has beliefs concerning the competencies and positive motivations of b toward fulfilling t.*

For example, in Fig. 1 *Space Co* distrusts *Account and audit Co* for fulfilling "Manage company's auditing operations", if it has beliefs concerning the competencies and positive motivations of *Account and audit Co* toward achieving the trustum related threat "Biasing the audit information". Similarly, the *stock market* distrusts a *stock trader* for providing "trader's orders", if it has beliefs concerning the competencies and positive motivations of the *trader* toward fulfilling the trustum related threat "Manipulate the market by providing falsified/fraud orders". Threat and threaten constructs are shown in Fig. 2.

Capture Actors' Competencies and Motivations Beliefs. Several belief sources can be used, Sabater and Sierra [19] identify three main sources of beliefs, namely: direct experiences, witness information, and sociological information. We mainly rely on *sociological information* that is information describes the social relations between agents and the roles they are playing in the society [19]. In particular, agents' capabilities can be derived from the role(s) they play, where roles' capabilities are predefined based on their different characterization in the society. Formally, this can be defined as follows:

Definition 4. *Let a be an agent, r is a role, s is a trustum, and t is a threat. We say that a is capable of fulfilling s/t, IFF a plays a role r that has the capability of fulfilling s/t. Otherwise, we say a is incapable of fulfilling s/t.*

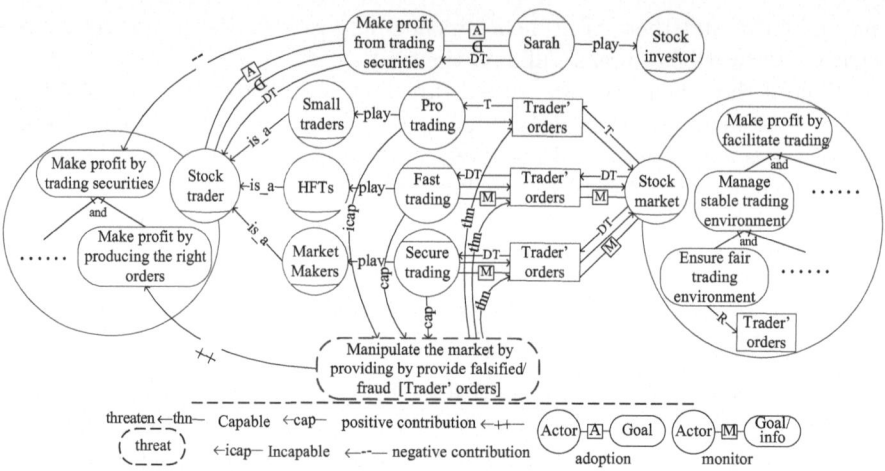

Fig. 2. A partial goal model of the stock market extended with belief-based constructs

Based on [15], in order to fulfill the threat "Manipulate the market by providing falsified/fraud orders", a *stock trader* has to be capable of trading with very high frequency (e.g., *HFT*), or it has to be capable of trading very large amount of securities (e.g., *Market Maker*), where such activities of *HFTs* and *Market Makers* were considered as a main reason of the Flash Crash. Actor's capability/incapability toward fulfilling a threat is modeled as edges between actors and threats labeled with cap/icap respectively (Fig. 2).

At the other hand, actors' motivations toward fulfilling a trustum/threat can be derived from the different interrelations among the actors own objectives and the trustum/threat, which can be captured by relying on the qualitative goal relationships [13], in which a goal can contribute positively or negatively towards the achievement of another one. In particular, an actor is positively motivated to fulfill a trustum/threat, if such trustum/threat contributes positively to at least one of its own goals. Similarly, an actor is negatively motivated to fulfill a trustum/threat, if such trustum/threat contributes negatively to at least one of its goals. Formally, this can be defined as follows:

Definition 5. *Let a, b be actors, s is a trustum, t is a threat, and g is a goal that b aims to achieve. We say that a beliefs that b is positively motivated to fulfill s/t, IFF s/t contributes positively to g. And we say that a beliefs that b is negatively motivated to fulfill s/t, IFF s/t contributes negatively to g.*

For example, *Space Co* delegates its goal "Manage company's auditing operations" to *Account and audit Co* that plays an *auditing firm*, which is capable of fulfilling the threat ("Biasing the audit information"), yet it does not have positive motivation towards fulfilling it. However, *Account and audit Co* plays another role that is *accounting firm*, which makes it positively motivated to fulfill the trustum related threat by several reasons (e.g., provides accounting services

Table 1. Analyzing trust based on the related beliefs

	Trustum beliefs				Threat beliefs			
	Competence		Motivation		Competence		Motivation	
	Comp	Incomp	Positive	Negative	Comp	Incomp	Positive	Negative
Trust	✓	X	✓	X	X	✓	-	-
Distrust	X	✓	-	-	-	-	-	-
	-	-	X	✓	-	-	-	-
	-	-	-	-	✓	X	✓	X

to a competing company, etc.). Positive and negative contribution among goals is modeled as edges labeled with ++ and -- respectively (Fig. 2).

Trust and Distrust Analysis. Previously, we have discussed how actors' competencies and motivations beliefs can be derived. Here, we show how these beliefs can be used to support trust analysis (shown in Table 1).

Trust: An actor *trusts* another one for a specific trustum, if it has belief(s) about the trustee's *competency* and *positive motivations* toward fulfilling the trustum, and it does not have belief(s) about the trustee's *incompetency* neither *negative motivations* toward fulfilling the trustum. Moreover, a trustor should have belief(s) about the trustee's *incompetence* to fulfill the trustum related threat (if any). For example in Fig. 2, a *stock market* trusts *Pro trading* for "trader's orders", since *Pro trading* has the competencies and it is positively motivated to provide them, and it is incompetent for fulfilling the related threat.

Distrust: An actor *distrusts* another one for a specific trustum, (1) if it does not have belief(s) about the trustee's *competency* toward the trustum, and has belief(s) about the trustee's *incompetency*; (2) if it does not have belief(s) about the *positive motivations* of the trustee toward the trustum, and it has belief(s) about its *negative motivations*; and (3) if it has belief(s) about the trustee's *competency* and *positive motivations* toward fulfilling the trustum related threat, and it does not have belief(s) about the trustee's *incompetency* and *negative motivations* toward fulfilling the threat. For example, in Fig. 2 *Sarah* distrusts the *stock trader* for fulfilling "Make profit from trading securities", since the *trader* might be *negatively motivated* to fulfill a goal that contributes negatively to one of its own goals. While a *stock market* distrusts both *Fast trading* and *Secure trading* for "trader's orders", since both of them have the *capability* and they are *positively motivated* toward fulfilling the trustum related threat "Manipulate the market by providing falsified/fraud orders".

Compensating the Lack of Trust. We propose two techniques to compensate the lack of trust (distrust):

Adopting can be defined as a commitment from the trustee toward the trustor that the first will behave as expected from the last toward the trustum [4]. We use *adopting* when the lacks of trust is due to belief(s) about the trustee's *negative motivations* toward fulfilling the trustum. For example, *Sarah* can compensate the lacks of trust in a *stock trader* concerning the goal "Make profit from trading securities" by *adoption*, i.e., *stock trader* commits to *Sarah* to fulfill the goal as expected. Adopting is modeled as an edge labeled with A between the trustor and trustee at one hand, and the trustum at the other (Fig. 2).

Monitoring can be defined as the process of observing and analyzing the performance of an actor in order to detect any undesirable performance [24]. We use *monitoring* when the lacks of trust is due to belief(s) about the trustee's *competencies* and *positive motivations* toward fulfilling the trusum related threat. For example, a *stock market* should monitor the "trader's orders" that are provided by both *Fast trading* and *Secure trading* to compensate the distrust in them concerning the orders they provide. Monitoring is modeled as an edge labeled with M between the trustor and trustee at one hand, and the trustum at the other (Fig. 2).

4.2   Model Analysis and Verification

In order to enable the automated reasoning support, we used disjunctive Datalog [2] to formalize all the concepts that have been introduced in the paper, along with the required reasoning axioms[3]. Moreover, we defined a set of properties (shown in Table 2) that can be used to verify the trust requirements model, i.e., the model is correct and consistent, if all of these proprieties hold.

Pro1: states that the model should not include any goal that is not achieved from the perspective of the actor, who aims for it. We rely on this property to quickly verify the requirements model, i.e., if this property holds for all goals, we can conclude that the model is correctness and consistency.

Pro2 states that the model should not include any goal delegation/delegation chain, if there is no trust/trust chain between the delegator and the delegatee, or there is at least a compensation of the lack of trust among them. This property aims to detect any delegation with no trust, since such delegation leaves the delegator with no guarantee that its goal will be achieved. For example, in Fig. 1 if the trust relation did not hold between the *Space Co* and *Account and Audit Co* concerning the goal "Manage company's auditing operations", *Pro2* will be able to detect such violation.

Pro3 states that goals should be delegated only to actors, who have the capability to achieve them either by themselves or they have valid delegation to an actor who has such capability. For example, in Fig. 1 if *Space Co* delegates the goal "Manage company's auditing operations" to *Star Co*, which does not play the role of "Auditing firm", and it does not has a valid delegation to an actor that plays such role, *Pro3* is able to detect such false delegation.

Pro4 states that actors should have all information that is required for the achievement of the goals they are responsible of, i.e., this property is specialized for detecting information unavailability related issues. Capturing information

---

[3] The formalization of the concepts and axioms is omitted due to space limitation, yet it can be found at https://mohamadgharib.wordpress.com/bbta/.

Table 2. Properties of the design

Pro1	:- aims(A,G), not achieved(A,G)
Pro2	:- deleChain(A,B,G), not trustChain(trust,A,B,achieve,G)
Pro3	:- deleChain(_,A,G), can_achieve(B,G), not can_achieve(A,G), not deleChain(A,B,G)
Pro4	:- needs(A,I), not has(A,I)
Pro5	:- prvChain(_,A,I), needs(B,I), not needs(A,I), not prvChain(A,B,I)
Pro6	:- need(G,I), is_responsible(A,G), not trusted(A,I)
Pro7	:- trustReq(Type,A,B,O,S), not trust(Type,A,B,O,S)
Pro8	:- motivation_belief(pos,A,B,achieve,G), motivation_belief(neg,A,B,achieve,G)
Pro9	:- motivation_belief(pos,A,B,achieve,G), adopt(A,B,achieve,G)
Pro10	:- monitor(A,B,S,O), not trust_threat(A,B,S,O)

availability is not always an easy task, since goals might be interdependent on one another for information, and if a goal that produces information was not achieved (prevented), all goals that depend on its information will be prevented as well. For example, in Fig. 1 if the *stock trader's* goal "Internal analysis of targeted securities" was not achieved due to unavailability of "securities' assessments" or "financial statements" information, it will not produce "trader suggestions" that is required by both goals "Make profit by producing the right orders" and "Analysis depending on trader", i.e., both of them will not be achieved as well.

Pro5 states that information should be only provided to actors, who require them either for achieving their goals, or they have valid provision chain to an actor who requires them. For example, in Fig. 1 if "consulter suggestion" was provided to any actor but the *stock trader* or *stock investor* (e.g., stock market), *Pro5* will detect such violation and notify the analyst about it.

Pro6 states that the model should not include any untrusted information provision from the perspective of its reader. In other words, there is no guarantee that information is trusted for read if no trust/trust chain holds between information reader and producer or there is a compensation of the lack of trust among them. For example, in Fig. 2 trust will not hold between *Fast trading* and *Secure trading* at one hand and the *stock market* at the other concerning the provision of "Trader's orders". If such provision was not accompanied with a trust compensation mechanism (monitoring), *Pro6* will be able to detect such situation and notify the analyst about it.

Pro7 states that the model should not include any trust/distrust relation that conflicts with the trustee's competencies and motivations. For example, in Fig. 2 if the provision of "Trader's orders" between *Fast trading* and *stock market* was modeled as trust, *Pro7* will notify the analyst that such trust relation is conflicting with the competencies and motivations of *Fast trading* toward the trustum and its related threat, i.e., it should be modeled as distrust. Similarly,

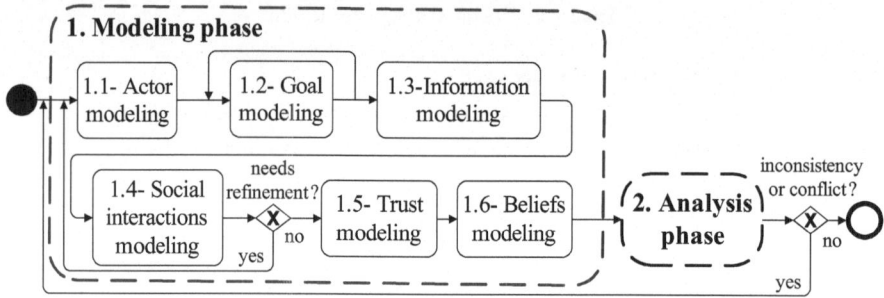

Fig. 3. Methodological process for analyzing trust requirements

if the provision of "Trader's orders" between *Pro trading* and *stock market* was modeled as distrust, *Pro7* will detect such situation and notify the analyst that it should be modeled as trust, since such distrust is conflicting with the capabilities and motivations of *Pro trading* toward the trustum and its related threat.

Pro8 states that the model should not include actors with conflicting motivational beliefs (positively and negatively motivated) toward the same trustum/ threat. We avoid having such situation, since our reasoning do not provide techniques for motivations conflict resolution yet.

Pro9 states that the model should not include an adoption relation between a trustor and a trustee, if the first beliefs that the last is positively motivated to fulfill the trustum. For example, if *Space Co* delegates its goal "Manage company's auditing operations" to an *auditing firms*, and there is also an adopting relation concerning the delegation, *Pro9* will notify the analyst that such adoption relation is not required, since there is no beliefs concerning the negative motivations of the *auditing firms* toward fulfilling the delegated goal.

Pro10 states that the model should not include a monitoring relation between a trustor and a trustee, if the last cannot be considered as a possible threat source for the trustum. For example, if the model has a monitoring relation concerning "trader's orders" that are provided from a *small trader* to *stock market*, *Pro10* is able to detect such situation and notify the analyst that such monitoring relation is not required.

4.3 Methodological Process for Analyzing Trust Requirements

Our approach is equipped with an engineering methodological process (shown in Fig. 3) that is specialized for modeling and analyzing trust requirements. The process consists of two main phases; we describe them as follows:

(1) **Modeling Phase**: This phase aims to model the requirements of the system with special emphasis on the trust requirements; and it is composed of six steps: (1.1) *Actors modeling*: in which the stakeholders of the system are identified and modeled in terms of agents and roles along with their objectives, entitlements and capabilities; (1.2) *Goals modeling*: the

stockholders' top-level goals are modeled and refined (if needed) through And/Or-decomposition until reaching their leaf goals, which might leads to new iteration of this step; (1.3) *Information modeling*: in which the different relations between goals and information are modeled (e.g., produce, read, etc.); and (1.4) *Social interactions modeling*: aims to model the different social dependencies among actors concerning information provisions and goal delegation. In other words, based on actors' capabilities some goals might be delegated to actors, who have the capabilities to achieve them; and based on actors' needs, information is provided to them.

After step 4, the model is checked and if it needs to be refined (e.g., adding new actors, refining some goal, etc.), we restart the modeling phase again; otherwise we proceed to the next step. (1.5) *Trust modeling*: trust requirements among actors concerning both goal delegation and information provisions are modeled at this step; (1.6) *Beliefs modeling*: aims to model threats, goals contributions, and the actors' competencies and motivations beliefs toward such threats. After finishing this step, the designer proceeds to the analysis phase.

(2) **Analysis Phase**: The aim of this phase is to support the verification of correctness and consistency of the requirements model. In particular, we define a set of properties of the design that helps in identifying any inconsistency or conflict in the model and notify the designer about them to find proper solutions. After the analysis phase the model is check, and the process reaches its end if the model is verified, otherwise the process restart again from the beginning to address the conflicts/inconsistencies in the model that have been identified (detected) during the analysis phase.

5   Implementation and Evaluation

Evaluation is an important aspect of any research proposal, and it aims to demonstrate the utility and efficacy of a design artifact. To this end, we evaluated our approach on a simulation basis following [14], by developing a prototype tool and test its applicability with artificial data. In particular, we developed IQ-Tool[4] (a screenshot of IQ-Tool is shown in Fig. 4) that is a prototype tool of our framework to test its applicability and effectiveness for modeling and analyzing trust requirements. In what follows, we briefly describe the tool, discuss its applicability and effectiveness over the Flash Crash case study, and then we discuss the scalability experiments we performed. Finally, we theoretically evaluate our proposed modeling language based on the semiotic clarity principle.

Implementation: The tool consist of three main parts: (1) A Graphical User Interface (GUI) that enables for drawing the requirements model by drag-and-drop modeling elements from different palettes; (2) Model-to-text transformation mechanism that supports the translating of the graphical models into disjunctive Datalog formal specifications; and (3) automated reasoning support (DLV

---

[4] https://mohamadgharib.wordpress.com/bbta/.

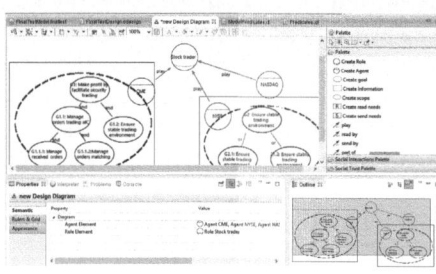

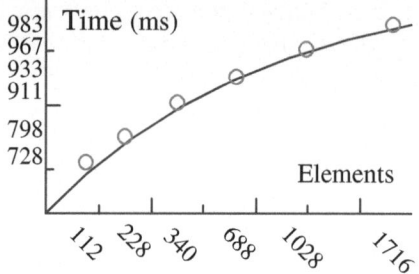

Fig. 4. Screenshot of the IQ-Tool   **Fig. 5.** Scalability experiment result

system[5]) takes the disjunctive Datalog specifications along with already defined reasoning axioms as an input, and then perform the required analysis to verify the trust requirements model against the properties of the design.

Applicability: To test the framework applicability, we modeled the Flash Crash case study, transformed it into disjunctive Datalog specifications, and then we run the automated analysis to test its ability in discovering violations to the properties of the design. The analysis returned several violations, including: a *stock market* considers orders received from any agent that plays either *HFTs* or *Market makers* roles as untrusted information, which we solved by monitoring the trustee. *Space Co* distrusts *Account and audit Co* for achieving the goal "manage company's auditing operation", which we solved by compensating the lack of trust by adopting. Moreover, the analysis detects all situations where agents became negatively motivated to fulfill a trustum, and when they became positively motivated to fulfill a threat when they play several roles that may conflict. For example, *Star Co* plays both *Credit assessment rating firms* and *Consulting firm* roles, which influences the trust in it concerning information it produces (e.g., consulter suggestions and securities assessments). In particular, the proposed analysis techniques were able to capture all the violations to the properties of the design that we consider in this paper, which enable in turn to avoid the different vulnerabilities in the system design that led or contributed to the Flash Crash and resolve them during the early requirements phase.

Experiments on Scalability: To test the scalability of the reasoning technique, we expanded the model shown in Fig. 1 by increasing the number of its modeling elements from 122 to 1716 through six steps, and we investigated the reasoning execution time at each step by repeating the reasoning execution seven times, discarding the fastest and slowest ones, and then computed the average execution time of the rest. The result is shown in Fig. 5, and it is clear that the relation between the size of the model and execution time is not exponential. We have performed the experiment on laptop computer, Intel(R) core(TM) i3-3227U CPU@ 190 GHz, 4 GB RAM, OS Window 8, 64-bit.

---

[5] http://www.dlvsystem.com/dlv/.

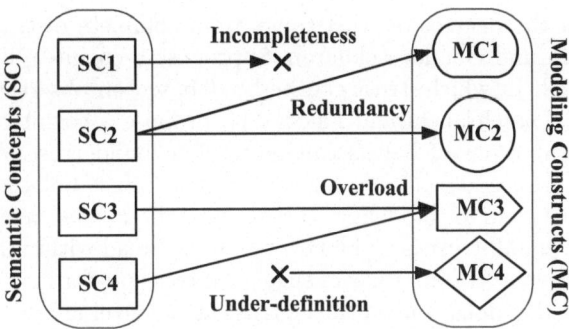

Fig. 6. Principle of semiotic clarity

Theoretical Evaluation: We evaluated our modeling language according to the principle of semiotic clarity [16], which helps in increasing the expressiveness and precision of the language. In this principle there should be a one-to-one mapping between semantic concepts and their corresponding constructs (Fig. 6), i.e., there should be no incompleteness, overload, redundancy, or under-definition between the semantic concepts and their corresponding language constructs.

Incompleteness: Occurs when a semantic concept is not represented by any modeling construct. We have only one case, we did not model the actor capability/incapability toward goals as we did for threats. However, symbol incompleteness is not necessarily a bad thing, since representing only the required concepts helps in keeping the language complexity manageable [16].

Redundancy: Occurs when multiple modeling constructs represent a single semantic concept. We did not observe any symbol redundancy in the language.

Overload: Occurs when a single modeling construct is used to represent multiple semantic concepts. We have the positive/negative contributions among goals and goals/threats, which can be considered as an overload. However, actors can differentiate between them easily based on the context. Moreover, we only represented actor's capability toward threats, and omitted representing its capability toward goals in order to avoid an overload.

Under-definition: Occurs when a modeling construct does not represent any semantic concept. There are no under-definition issues in the language.

6 Related Work

A large body of literature has focused on how trust can be constructed (built). For instance, Marsh [22] proposes one of the earliest trust models that consider direct interaction as a main source of trust related beliefs. Schillo et al. [20] introduce a trust model based on probability theory, which can be used when trust among agents has a Boolean value (good or bad). While in [1], trust can be build based on agents' beliefs in one another concerning their experience and reputation, and the degrees of trust range from complete distrust to complete trust. Esfandiary and Chandrasekharan [8] propose a cognitive based trust and reputation model. In which, trust can be built based on observation and interaction. Finally, Castelfranchi and Falcone [4] propose a cognitive trust model, in which different types of beliefs can be used to build trust. Although most of these works propose techniques for constructing trust, but they do not offer concepts or constructs for modeling or reasoning about trust requirements.

At the other hand, trust is still a new research thread within the RE community. However, several RE approaches suggested concepts for modeling trust. For instance, in [11] they focus on capturing trust at the level of roles. While in [12], they capture trust at two different levels (roles and agents), and they highlighted the problem that may arise when a trusted role is played by an untrusted individual (agent). In [24] trust was introduced as a fundamental aspect for making decisions on security. While Asnar et al. [3] introduce the notion of trust for assessing risk. Finally, Chopra et al. [5] introduce architectural trust that can be used to assist the trustworthiness of the overall STS. Although, most of these works propose constructs for modeling trust requirements, but none of them consider actors' competencies (capabilities), motivations, etc. as main drivers while analyzing trust requirements, i.e., they do not provide a specialized concepts nor constructs for modeling and analyzing trust requirements based on actors' competencies and motivations.

7   Conclusion and Future Work

We have proposed a belief-based trust approach that combines both cognitive and mathematical trust approaches, introducing concepts and constructs for modeling and analyzing trust based on sets of beliefs related to the actors' competencies and motivations toward the trustum and its related threat(s) (if any). Moreover, we have discussed the automated reasoning techniques our framework offers, and how they can be used to verify the correctness and consistency of the trust requirements model. In addition, we described the methodological process underlies our approach should be followed by designers/analysts during the system design. We evaluated our approach on a simulation basis by developing a prototype tool and test its applicability and effectiveness for modeling and analyzing trust requirements. Finally, we theoretically evaluated our proposed modeling language based on the semiotic clarity principle.

For the future work, we are exploring how to extend our approach by adding new types of beliefs that might influence the trust among actors. Moreover, we aim to enrich our approach with mechanisms to combine different kinds of beliefs while analyzing trust, and also with mechanisms for conflict resolution among different kinds of beliefs. Furthermore, we are planning to evaluate our approach with end users (e.g., designers, analysts, experts, etc.) to assess its adequacy for modeling and reasoning about trust requirements. Finally, we aim to better validate the approach by applying it to several complex case studies that belong to different domains.

Acknowledgments. This research has received funding from the ERC advanced grant 267856, "Lucretius: Foundations for Software Evolution", http://www.lucretius.eu/, and the European Unions Horizon 2020 research and innovation programme under grant agreement No 653642 - VisiOn.

References

1. Abdul-Rahman, A., Hailes. S.: Supporting trust in virtual communities. In: Proceedings of the 33rd Annual Hawaii International Conference on System Sciences, 2000, p. 9. IEEE (2000)
2. Alviano, M., Faber, W., Leone, N., Perri, S., Pfeifer, G., Terracina, G.: The disjunctive datalog system DLV. In: de Moor, O., Gottlob, G., Furche, T., Sellers, A. (eds.) Datalog 2010. LNCS, vol. 6702, pp. 282–301. Springer, Heidelberg (2011)
3. Asnar, Y., Giorgini, P., Massacci, F., Zannone, N.: From trust to dependability through risk analysis (2007)
4. Castelfranchi, C., Falcone, R.: Social trust: a cognitive approach. In: Castelfranchi, C., Tan, Y.-H. (eds.) Trust and Deception in Virtual Societies, pp. 55–90. Springer, Netherlands (2001)
5. Chopra, A.K., Paja, E., Giorgini, P.: Sociotechnical trust: an architectural approach. In: Jeusfeld, M., Delcambre, L., Ling, T.-W. (eds.) ER 2011. LNCS, vol. 6998, pp. 104–117. Springer, Heidelberg (2011)
6. Chopra, K., Wallace, W.A.: Trust in electronic environments. In: Proceedings of the 36th Annual Hawaii International Conference on System Sciences, 2003, p. 10. IEEE (2003)
7. Emery, F.E., Trist, E.L.: Socio-technical systems. In: Churchman, C.W. (eds.) Management sciences, models and techniques (1960)
8. Esfandiari, B., Chandrasekharan, S.: On how agents make friends: mechanisms for trust acquisition. In: Proceedings of the Fourth Workshop on Deception, Fraud and Trust in Agent Societies, Montreal, Canada, pp. 27–34 (2001)
9. Gharib, M., Giorgini, P.: Detecting conflicts in information quality requirements: the May 6, 2010 flash crash. Technical report, Universitá degli studi di Trento (2014)
10. Gharib, M., Giorgini, P.: Modeling and reasoning about information quality requirements. In: Fricker, S.A., Schneider, K. (eds.) REFSQ 2015. LNCS, vol. 9013, pp. 49–64. Springer, Heidelberg (2015)
11. Giorgini, P., Massacci, F., Mylopoulos, J., Zannone, N.: Filling the gap between requirements engineering and public key/trust management infrastructures. In: Katsikas, S.K., Gritzalis, S., López, J. (eds.) EuroPKI 2004. LNCS, vol. 3093, pp. 98–111. Springer, Heidelberg (2004)
12. Giorgini, P., Massacci, F., Mylopoulos, J., Zannone, N.: Modeling social and individual trust in requirements engineering methodologies. In: Herrmann, P., Issarny, V., Shiu, S.C.K. (eds.) iTrust 2005. LNCS, vol. 3477, pp. 161–176. Springer, Heidelberg (2005)
13. Giorgini, P., Mylopoulos, J., Nicchiarelli, E., Sebastiani, R.: Reasoning with goal models. Conceptual Model. ER **2002**, 167–181 (2003)
14. Hevner, A.R., March, S.T., Park, J., Ram, S.: Design science in information systems research. MIS Quart. **28**(1), 75–105 (2004)
15. Kirilenko, A., Kyle, A.S., Samadi, M., Tuzun, T.: The Flash Crash: The impact of high frequency trading on an electronic market. Manuscript, University of Maryland (2011)

16. Moody, D.L.: The physics of notations: toward a scientific basis for constructing visual notations in software engineering. IEEE Trans. Softw. Eng. **35**(6), 756–779 (2009)
17. Mouratidis, H., Giorgini, P.: Secure tropos: a security-oriented extension of the tropos methodology. Int. J. Softw. Eng. Knowl. Eng. **17**(2), 285–309 (2007)
18. Rao, A.S., Georgeff, M.P.: Modeling rational agents within a BDI-architecture, pp. 473–484. Kaufmann publishers, San Mateo (1991)
19. Sabater, J., Sierra, C.: Review on computational trust and reputation models. Artif. Intell. Rev. **24**(1), 33–60 (2005)
20. Schillo, M., Funk, P., Rovatsos, M.: Using trust for detecting deceitful agents in artificial societies. Appl. Artif. Intell. **14**(8), 825–848 (2000)
21. Sommerville, I., Cliff, D., Calinescu, R., Keen, J., Kelly, T., Kwiatkowska, M., Mcdermid, J., Paige, R.: Large-scale complex IT systems. Commun. ACM **55**(7), 71–77 (2012)
22. Stephen, M.: Formalising trust as a computational concept. Ph.D. dissertation. University of Stirling, Scotland (1994)
23. Van Lamsweerde, A.: Elaborating security requirements by construction of intentional anti-models. In: Proceedings of the 26th International Conference on Software Engineering, pp. 148–157. IEEE Computer Society (2004)
24. Zannone, N.: A requirements engineering methodology for trust, security, and privacy. Ph.D. thesis, University of Trento (2006)

An Experience Report of Improving Business Process Compliance Using Security Risk-Oriented Patterns

Mari-Liis Alaküla[1,2] and Raimundas Matulevičius[2(✉)]

[1] INSLY OÜ, Tallinn, Estonia
mariliis@gmx.com
[2] Institute of Computer Science, University of Tartu, Tartu, Estonia
rma@ut.ee

Abstract. Nowadays enterprises are searching the efficient compliance management method. Being compliant could potentially help capturing the most important information, using practice and existing process solutions; thus reducing the management effort and cost. When it comes to the security compliance management, it means treating and reducing the security risks to the acceptable level and employing the validated and cost effective security countermeasures. However, the typical question that small and medium enterprises face, is on how to achieve the security compliance in the efficient way. In this paper we report on our experience to use the security risk-oriented patterns to improve business processes of the insurance brokerage. The analysed case showed the major steps to apply the regulatory standard to check compliance, as well as the major procedures needed to improve the business process compliance. The lessons learnt highlight some method guidelines toward compliance management and suggest needed improvement directions for the application of the security risk-oriented patterns.

Keywords: Business process models and notations · Standards and regulations · Security modelling · Security patterns

1 Introduction

Business process management (BPM) is an instrument for enterprises to manage their activities in a holistic manner and to ensure consistent business outcomes that add value both to the enterprise and its customers [7]. This also means that the availability, integrity and confidentiality of valuable business assets (including data, processes, policies, etc.) need to be protected from intentional risks.

One way to achieve a certain security level within business processes is through compliance management. "*Compliance is a set of activities an enterprise does to ensure that its core business does not violate relevant regulations*" [10]. There exist a number of security regulations in terms of international and national standards (e.g., ISO/IEC 27001 [11], NIST SP 800-39 [15], Base III [4], IT-Grundschutz [12] and etc.); however the way to achieve business process compliance with the regulations remains rather labour intensive activity.

© IFIP International Federation for Information Processing 2015
J. Ralyté et al. (Eds.): PoEM 2015, LNBIP 235, pp. 271–285, 2015.
DOI: 10.1007/978-3-319-25897-3_18

In this paper we analyse *how security patterns could help achieving business process compliance*. More specifically we consider how business processes (represented in business process model and notation, a.k.a. BPMN) of some insurance company comply with the ISO/IEC 27001:2013 [11], standard before and after the security risk-oriented patterns (SRPs) [1] are applied and security constraints introduced to the business process. On one hand we have selected the ISO/IEC 27001:2013 standard because of its simplicity and popularity among enterprises; but we believe that other regulations or standards could be used instead. On the other hand we use the SRPs because they are expressed in BPMN and explicitly differentiate between the valuable assets, security risks, and risk countermeasures.

The lessons learnt are threefold. Firstly, we have observed that SRPs could contribute to the business process compliance. Secondly, we have learnt about the steps needed to pre-process business process models before applying SRPs. Finally, we have observed few SRP limitations, thus this results in the potential improvements to the SRP application process.

The remaining of the paper is structured as follows: in Sect. 2 we present the prerequisites of the case study. Section 3 discusses how compliance of the business process and application of the security risk-oriented patterns was performed. In Sect. 4 we survey a related work. Finally, in Sect. 5 we discuss the lessons learnt and present some future work.

2   Prerequisites

2.1   ISO/IEC 27001:2013

The ISO/IEC 27001:2013 standard is a specification for an information security management system [11]. It presents requirements for managing sensitive organisation's information by applying risk management, risk assessment and risk treatment means. The major parts of the standard include guidance on understanding context of organisation, leadership, planning, support, operation performance evaluation and improvement activities. Important part of the standard is its appendix, which provides a checklist of objectives and controls (although organisation could also choose other controls according to its preferences). The objectives and controls could be potentially combined to develop organisation's treatment plan to respond to security risks.

In this paper we consider how organisation's business processes could be estimated and improved to become compliant to the ISO/IEC objectives and controls listed in its appendix.

2.2   Security Risk-Oriented Patterns

"A *security pattern* describes a particular *recurring security problem* that arises in a *specific security context* and presents a well-proven generic scheme for a *security solution*" [23]. Table 1 presents a list of security risk-oriented patterns (SRP) [1], developed using domain model [6] for information system security risk management (ISSRM). This domain model differentiates between three major concept groups –

asset-related concepts, *risk-related concepts* and *risk treatment-related concepts*. Thus, based on this structure each security risk-oriented pattern consists of the specific security context (expressed using the asset-related concepts), recurring security problem (analysed in terms of the security risk-related concepts) and suggests the security countermeasures (presented through the security risk-treatment concepts).

Table 1. Security risk-oriented patterns

Security risk-oriented pattern	Description
SRP.1 Securing data from unauthorized access	This pattern describes how to secure confidential data from unauthorized access by people or devices. The pattern is based on implementation of access control where (stakeholder or device) roles and data are classified to levels of trust and sensitivity
SRP.2 Securing data that flow between the business entities	This pattern addresses the electronic transmission of data between two entities, i.e., client (where data is submitted) and business (where data is used)
SRP.3 Securing business activity after data is submitted	This pattern secures the business activity, which is carried out after data has been submitted, and where integrity and availability have to be ensured.
SRP.4 Securing business services against DoS attacks	This pattern addresses the Denial of Service (DoS) attacks and their protection strategies. It helps to protect the business assets in order to guarantee its availability
SRP.5 Securing data stored in/retrieved from the data store	The main goal of this pattern is to prevent the leaking of confidential data from the enterprise's data store

For example, *SRP.1 Securing data from unauthorized access* describes how to secure confidential data from access by unauthorised people or devices. In Fig. 1, a client requests data (a confidential business asset). In response to this request the data are retrieved (using the retrieval interface characterized as the IS asset) and provided to the user. The problem arises if the retrieval of the confidential data is allowed to any user (independently whether s/he is malicious or not) without checking his or her access permissions to the data. Such a risk event would lead to the disclosure of the confidential data; it might provoke that these data would be sent to the business competitors, thus, compromising the business itself. To reduce such risk, countermeasures to *check for the access rights* should be implemented.

Another example is *SRP.5 Securing data stored in/retrieved from the data store* (see Fig. 1). It ensures the data confidentiality stored at the data-store against insiders' attack (i.e., malicious administrators or malware that infects data-store). There exists a retrieval interface (i.e., IS asset), which helps clients (*i*) to store the client's confidential data (i.e., business asset) in the data-store and (*ii*) to retrieve them when needed. An attacker characterised as malicious insider is able to access the data-store and also retrieve data directly from it. If the retrieval interface (also including the queries to the database) is designed in a way that data are saved/retrieved in a plain-text format, the attacker could view the data, thus negating the data confidentiality. To reduce this security risk, one of the possible mechanisms is access control at the data-store level.

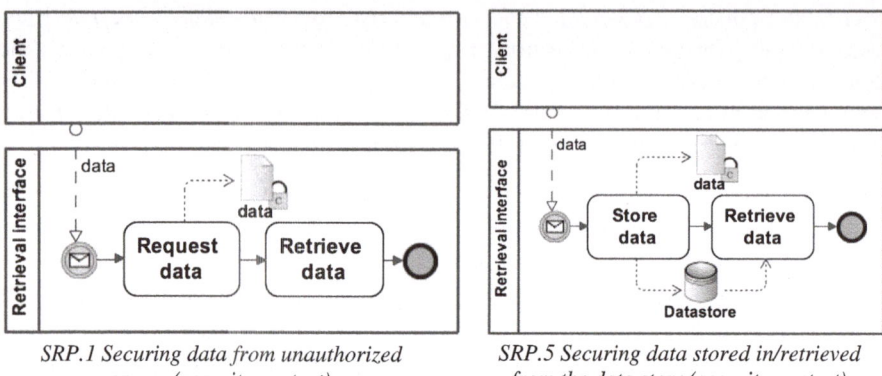

SRP.1 Securing data from unauthorized   SRP.5 Securing data stored in/retrieved
access (security context)   from the data store (security context)

Fig. 1. Security risk-oriented patterns (illustrated in the latter discussion)

We will illustrate how *SRP.1* and *SRP.5* are applied to analyse some business process model in Sect. 3.

2.3   Description of Business Process Model

An information system, used in our context, was developed two years ago with the aim to cut labour costs of insurance brokerage by automating the business processes. By beginning of this study the system was already developed as the real-life application. But our first task was to model explicitly the business processes supported by the application. The created models were briefly reviewed by the project managers who confirmed the logics of the modelled processes.

In Fig. 2 we present an extract of the value chain where the main value, *offer*, is created as a result of consecutive steps. The process begins with *adding customer data* to the offer form, after which the *product* and *offer object* data are added, too. Product data describes the coverage information of various insurance services types (e.g., travel insurance or health insurance related excess amounts and deductibles), while object data defines the characteristics of the insurable body (e.g., a person or a vehicle). Next, *offer quotes* from different insurers are added to the offer form according to the product and object data. The last step is *acceptance of the offer*. The offer form is sent to the customer to his acceptance or decline. In case of acceptance, the customer chooses the relevant quote to purchase.

In Fig. 3 we expand process of *Accept offer process*. The diagram includes three pools, presenting *Broker*, *Customer* (both human participants) and the *Insurance brokerage system* (a software system used by *Broker* and *Customer*). This insurance

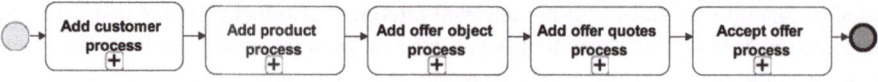

Fig. 2. Value chain

brokerage *system* is used to manage the *Offer* information in this example. Here the *Offer* is not described in detail in Fig. 3, but is characterized by *customer data, relevant quotes, offer status* and the *selected quote*. In order for this business process to be completed both *Broker* and *Customer* must collaborate while performing various tasks: e.g., *Broker* prepares of the offer. After, the *Offer* is e-mailed to the *Customer*, *Broker* is able to checks Offer status (e.g., to be sure that *Offer* is emailed). The *Customer* could initiate the response, which indicates acceptance or rejection of the *Offer*. If response is not sent after some time, the *Offer* is cancelled.

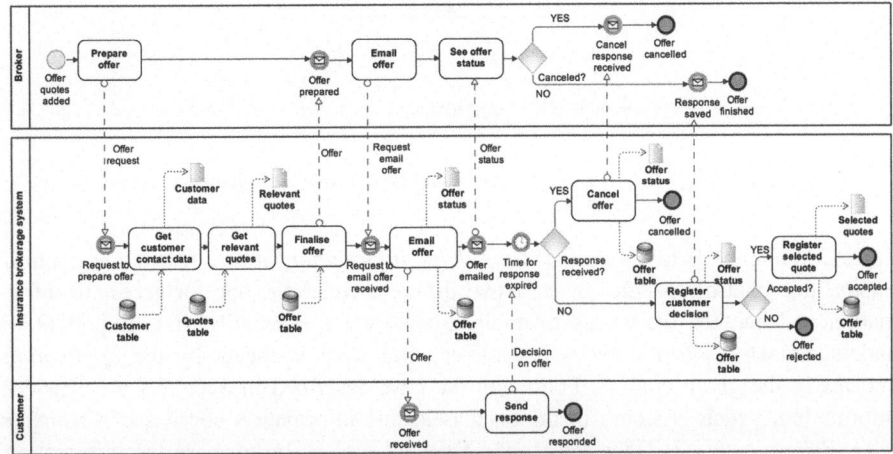

Fig. 3. Business process model of *Accept Offer Process*

3 Checking and Improving Business Process Compliance

The approach to check and improve business process compliance to the ISO 27001 standard is illustrated in Fig. 4. Firstly, we evaluated the level of compliance of the considered business process. We confronted the model to the ISO 27001:2013 standard. In Step 2 the security risk-oriented patterns are applied to derive security requirements and to introduce security constraints to the business process model. In the third step the business process compliance is checked again. Finally, in Step 4 we compare the compliance results of both compliance checks (Step 1 and Step 2) and draw conclusion on compliance change.

3.1 Evaluate Initial Model Compliance

Evaluation of the initial business process compliance consists of two steps: (*i*) instantiation of the standard to the considered problem, and (*ii*) checking how the business process visualised in Fig. 3 model complies the requirements described in the standard.

Instantiate Standard. The ISO/IEC 27001:2013 standard describes a generic situation [14], which potentially could be adapted to various specific cases. For example, in

Fig. 4. Approach to check and to improve compliance

Table 2 (columns 0 to 2) we list the *A.9.4.1 Information access restriction* control. Firstly, this control specifies at least two different concerns: one for access to information and another for access to application systems. Secondly, it is important to understand what *information* is considered, and what is meant by the *application systems* in the given context. Following the case described in Sect. 2.3 we consider information, which is stored in the databases; this information consists of *Customer data*, *Relevant quotes*, *Offer status*, and *Selected quotes*. In our case the information system is *Insurance brokerage system*, which includes functions to manage the information; thus we need to consider the access to business processes such as *Get customer contact data*, *Get relevant quotes*, *Email offer*, *Cancel offer*, *Register customer decision*, and *Register selected quotes*. The refinement of the *A.9.4.1* control is presented in Table 2 as listed in columns 3 and 4.

Similarly, all standard controls need to be refined. For instance, *A.13.2.1* is another example. As illustrated in Table 2 it is refined to three requirements – regarding *policies*, *procedures* and *controls*.

Check Compliance. Once the standard is initialised to the considered case, it becomes possible to analyse the business process compliance to the instantiated requirements. In our case we use a simple three-measure scale: "*Yes*" stands to indicate compliance; "*No*" – there is no compliance; and "*NR*" – the standard requirement is not relevant (NR) in the analysed case.

In Table 2, column 5, we present compliance assessment of business process. The business process model does not imply any access control policy; therefore requirements *A.9.4.1.i* and *A.9.4.1.ii* are given "No" score. Similarly, the model does not indicate any transfer policies or procedures, so *A.13.2.1.i* and *A.13.2.1.ii* also result in "No" score. Finally, as indicated in [3], the language used to visualise business process (namely, BPMN – business process model and notation) does not contain means to present controls; therefore *A.13.2.1.iii* is graded as "NR".

Table 2. Instantiating the ISO27001 standard

Name of the control	Original standard		Instantiated standard		Compliance
	Number	Description	Number	Description	
0	1	2	3	4	5
Information access restriction	A.9.4.1	Access to *information* and *application system functions* shall be restricted in accordance with the access control policy	A.9.4.1.i	Access to *Customer data, Relevant quotes, Offer status,* and *Selected quotes* shall be restricted in accordance with the access control policy	No
			A.9.4.1. ii	Access to *Get customer contact data, Get relevant quotes, Email offer, Cancel offer, Register customer decision,* and *Register selected quotes* shall be restricted in accordance with the access control policy	No
Information transfer policies and procedures	A.13.2.1	Formal transfer *policies, procedures* and *controls* shall be in place to protect the transfer of information through the use of all types of communication facilities	A.13.2.1. i	Formal transfer *policies* shall be in place to protect the transfer of *Offer request, Offer, Request email offer, Offer status,* and *Decision on offer* through the use of all types of communication facilities	No
			A.13.2.1. ii	Formal transfer *procedures* shall be in place to protect the transfer of *Offer request, Offer, Request email offer, Offer status,* and *Decision on offer* through the use of all types of communication facilities	No
			A.13.2.1. iii	Formal transfer *controls* shall be in place to protect the transfer of *Offer request, Offer, Request email offer, Offer status,* and *Decision on offer* through the use of all types of communication facilities	NR

3.2   Apply Security Risk-Oriented Patterns

Application of security risk-oriented patterns consists of two steps: (*i*) security requirements derivation, and (*ii*) introduction of the security constraints to the business process model.

Security Requirements Derivation. as illustrated in [2, 13], consists of three steps. Firstly, one needs to *identify pattern occurrences*. The security context presentation of the security risk-oriented pattern (see Fig. 1) is used to analyse business process model and to identify potential occurrences of the pattern. We observe six occurrences of *SRP.1* and seven occurrences of *SRP.5* in Fig. 3.

Secondly, one needs to *extract security model* from the business process model. For instance, security model created when applying *SRP.1* is given in Fig. 5, and *SRP.5* - in Fig. 6. Extraction of security models for each pattern is performed followed pattern specific guidelines [2].

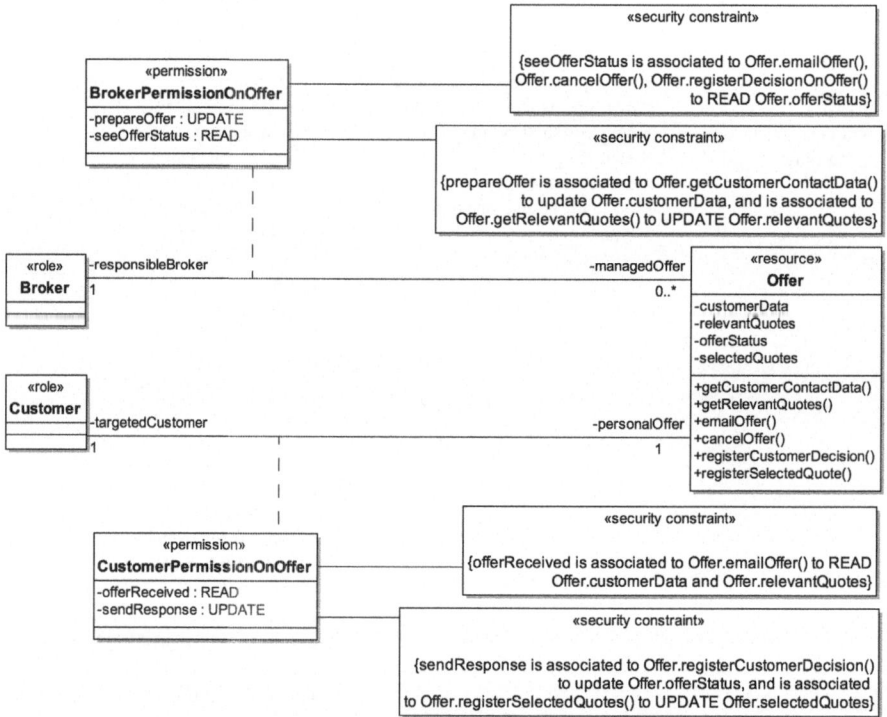

Fig. 5. Security model derived using *SRP.1*

For example, when applying *SRP.1*, one needs to (*i*) identify secured resource (e.g., *Offer*, determined by analysing the value chain, i.e., Figure 2); (*ii*) identify roles (e.g., *Broker* and *Customer*); (*iii*) assign users (e.g., organisation's employees who play the identified roles); (*iv*) identify secured operations (e.g., *Get customer contact data*, *Get relevant quotes*, *Email offer*, *Cancel offer*, *Register customer decision*, and *Register*

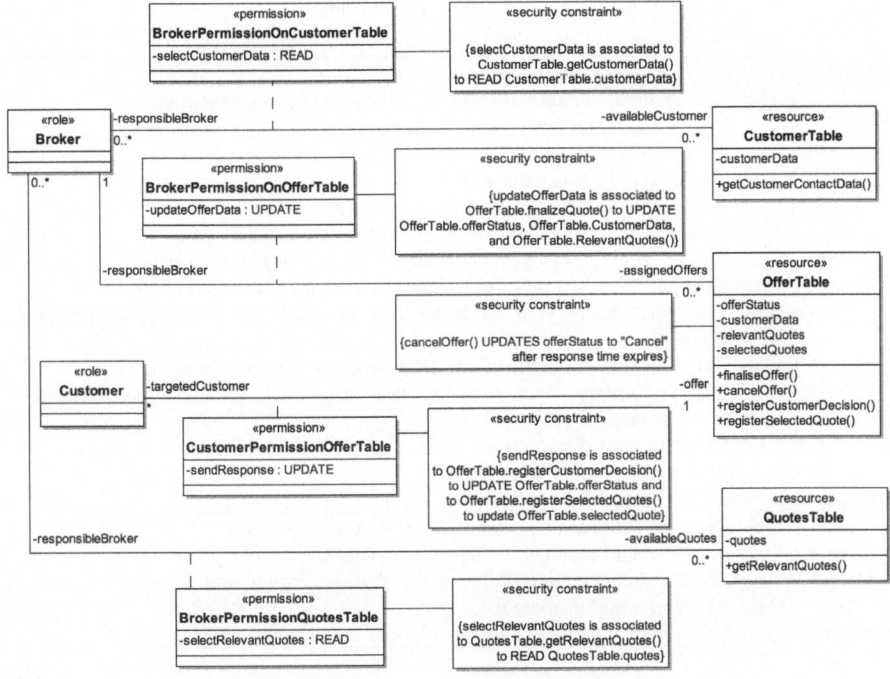

Fig. 6. Security model derived using *SRP.5*

selected quotes); and (*v*) assign permissions (e.g., *Broker permissions on Offer* and *Customer permissions on Offer*). These extracted data is used to create the security model (i.e., Figure 5), which typically is graphical structure assigned to each pattern.

Finally, security requirements are derived from security models and explicitly documented. In Table 3 we list security requirements derived when applying *SRP.1* and *SRP.5*. These security requirements indicate that *Broker* and *Customer* have different permissions to the functionality of *Insurance brokerage system*, as well as different permissions to update and retrieve information to/from the data-stores (i.e., tables) used in the *Insurance brokerage system*.

Introduction of the Security Constraints to the Business Process Model. Figure 7 presents an extract of the business process model from Fig. 3. The security require-ments derived in the previous steps are introduced as the security constraints to the business activities. This means that in order to execute the activity (e.g., *Get customer contact data*), it should be checked (*i*) whether the user assigned to the role *Broker* is trying to execute this activity (i.e., SReq.1.1.1) and guarantee that his role is *Broker* and is allowed to read *Customer data* from the *Customer table* (i.e., SReq5.1).

It is also important to note that both SReq.1.1.1 and SReq.5.1 should be respected in the given situation. This could be explained by the case, for example, to avoid the unauthorised access of the *Customer table* (by the user or software, which does not have the role of *Broker*, i.e., violation of SReq5.1) while *Broker* is performing task *Get customer contact data*. In other words, the security requirements are introduced to the

Table 3. Derived security requirements

Requirement resulting from *SRP.1* application

SReq.1.1: Only *Broker* should ***update*** offer's *Customer data* and *Relevant quotes*.
    SReq.1.1.1: *Broker* should perform *Get customer contact data*.
    SReq.1.1.2: *Broker* should perform *Get relevant quotes*.
SReq.1.2: Only *Broker* should ***read*** offer's *Offer status*.
    SReq.1.2.1: *Broker* should view *Offer status* after operation *Email offer*.
    SReq.1.2.2: *Broker* should view *Offer status* after operation *Cancel offer*.
    SReq.1.2.3: *Broker* should view *Offer status* after operation *Register customer decision*.
SReq.1.3: Only *Customer* should ***read*** offer's *Customer data* and *Relevant quotes*.
    SReq.1.3.1: *Customer* should view *Customer data* and *Relevant quotes* after operation *Email offer*.
SReq.1.4: Only *Customer* should ***update*** offer's *Offer status* and *Selected quotes*.
    SReq.1.4.1: By performing *Send response* task, *Customer* should invoke *Register customer decision*.
    SReq.1.4.2: By performing *Send response* task, *Customer* should invoke *Register selected quote* if *Offer status* is "Accepted".

Requirement resulting from *SRP.5* application
SReq.5.1: Only *Broker* should ***read*** *Customer data* from *Customer table*. SReq.5.2: Only *Broker* should ***read*** *Quotes* from *Quotes table*. SReq.5.3: Only *Broker* should ***update*** *Offer status*, *Customer data*, and *Relevant quotes* in *Offer table* with a single operation. SReq.5.4: Only *Customer* should invoke ***update*** of *Offer status* in *Offer table*.

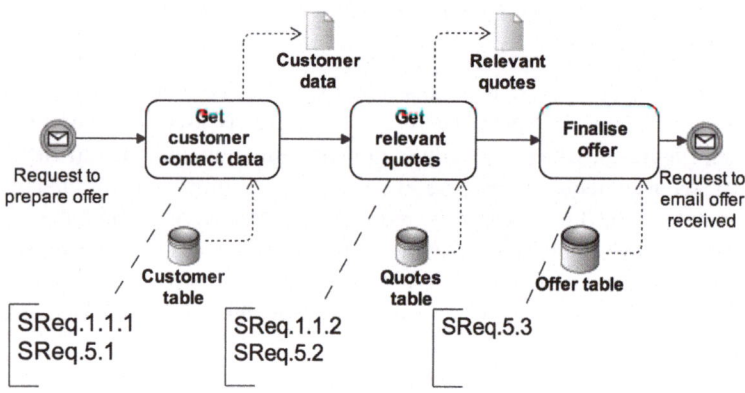

Fig. 7. Introduction of security constraints

business process model and the *runtime* constraints, which must be respected when executing the business process.

3.3 Evaluate Secured Model Compliance and Compare Compliance Results

The instantiated standard and its requirements (see Sect. 3.1) are used to evaluate the secured business process. The evaluation is presented in Table 4, column 6. Hence, after applying the *SRP.1* and *SRP.5* we could observe that access control policy (in terms of the security models, security requirements, and security constraints introduced to the business process model) is defined both (*i*) to restrict access to the business tasks (in terms of standard – application system functions) and (*ii*) to restrict access to data/information kept in data-stores (in terms of standard – information). Thus we assign to *A.9.4.1.i* and *A.9.4.1.ii* "Yes" score.

Table 4. Comparison of two compliance assessment results

Instantiated standard		Initial model compliance	Secured model compliance
Number	Description		
3	4	5	6
A.9.4.1.i	Access to *Customer data*, *Relevant quotes*, *Offer status*, and *Selected quotes* shall be restricted in accordance with the access control policy	No	**Yes**
A.9.4.1.ii	Access to *Get customer contact data*, *Get relevant quotes*, *Email offer*, *Cancel offer*, *Register customer decision*, and *Register selected quotes* shall be restricted in accordance with the access control policy	No	**Yes**
A.13.2.1.i	Formal transfer *policies* shall be in place to protect the transfer of *Offer request*, *Offer*, *Request email offer*, *Offer status*, and *Decision on offer* through the use of all types of communication facilities	No	No
A.13.2.1.ii	Formal transfer *procedures* shall be in place to protect the transfer of *Offer request*, *Offer*, *Request email offer*, *Offer status*, and *Decision on offer* through the use of all types of communication facilities	No	No
A.13.2.1.iii	Formal transfer *controls* shall be in place to protect the transfer of *Offer request*, *Offer*, *Request email offer*, *Offer status*, and *Decision on offer* through the use of all types of communication facilities	NR	NR

Business model compliance to other standard requirement (e.g., *A.13.2.1*) remains the same as in the in initial assessment. However, it could be noted that application of *SRP.2* would potentially result in business process compliance to *A.13.2.1.i* and *A.13.2.1.ii* requirements. This illustration did not take the *SRP.2* application into account, but in our actual analysis we have performed the *SRP.2* (and other pattern) application to reach the business process compliance.

4   Related Work

Different aspects of business process compliance management are rather extensively reported in literature. For instance, Papazoglou in [16] and El Kharbili *et al.* in [8] propose some business process compliance management frameworks. Ramezani *et al.* considers how to separate compliance management and business process management activities [17]. Elsewhere in [18] some means to organize and select compliance rules are presented. Schumm *et al.* propose to achieve process compliance through reusable units of compliant processes [24]. This at some extend resembles to the use of the (security risk-oriented) patterns to identify process fragments where the needed compliance regulations are determined.

In [19], Sadiq and Governatory propose a methodology for business process compliance management by process design. The major steps include control directory management, where regulations and directives are interpreted following the considered domain (we perform similar activities described in Sect. 3.1). Another important step is control modelling and process model enrichment (which highly correspond to security requirements derivation and security constraint introduction as discussed in Sect. 3.2).

There exist few studies that concern the business process compliance with respect to the access control regulations. For instance, an approach for compliance validation of secure service composition is described in [5]. Here validation of the access control and separation of duty concerns is managed using some automated tool support. In [22], application controls are used to enrich business process models. The work specifically focuses on preventive controls patterns, detective control patterns and required activity patterns. In our study we not only consider the access control (e.g., *SRP.1* and *SRP.5*), but we extent the analysis to other concerns, like secure communication (e.g., *SRP.2*), secure data input (e.g., *SRP.3*), and secure operation after data input (e.g., *SRP.4*).

An approach to extract security requirements and introduce security policies is reported in [20]. Authors are using actor-goal modelling approach to understand the stakeholder requirements through their goals, interactions, information and authorisations. The extracted requirements are introduced as security annotations (i.e., in terms of security countermeasures) to the business process model. In comparison to [20] we use the security risk-oriented patterns represented in the same modelling language as the business model. In [20] model compliance is performed at the model (i.e., graphical) level; in our case this still remains a future work.

5   Discussion and Future Work

In the paper we report on our experience to apply the SRPs to the insurance business processes in order to determine security requirements and improve process compliance with the selected security regulations. In this section we discuss observed limitations and lessons learnt. We also highlight some future work.

5.1   Limitations

Our work contains few limitations and threats to validity. We acknowledge that it includes some degree of subjectivity regarding (*i*) selecting regulation standard; (*ii*) created business process models and (*iii*) application and interpretation of the security risk-oriented patterns.

Firstly, ISO/IEC 27001:2013 is rather popular standard to which many enterprises tend to certify to. We do not believe that the process (e.g., see Fig. 2) would change much or result in too much different outcome if we had selected another regulation standard. However, applying other regulation standards could potentially be a future work of this study. Secondly, the first author of the paper is directly involved in the development of the system and supported processes. This helped us explicitly to identify the problem, to understand the particularities of the business process and to determine business activities, which should be automated using software systems. Thirdly, the second author of the paper is a co-author of SRPs [1], thus this helped us to apply the SRPs in the intended manner.

Another limitation is that we do not perform the formal compliance checking (i.e., "*a relationship between the formal representation of a business model and the formal representation of a relevant regulation*" [10]). We also did not have the goal to enrich the business process model with security-related activities (e.g., as discussed in [19]). Annotating business process model (e.g., Fig. 7) leaves the core business process representation separated from the security (i.e., compliance) details. However we acknowledge the importance of the formal compliance management and consider it as the future work.

The current report is limited to the application of two SRPs (namely *SPR.1* and *SRP.5*). However, other SRPs were also applied in the actual case (as mentioned in Sect. 3.3 discussing *SRP.2*) and showed their usefulness to contribute to the compliance of the business process.

5.2   Lessons Learnt

Firstly, the current work serves as a proof-of-concept showing that SRPs could systematically guide the compliance manager to achieve business process compliance with the selected regulations.

Secondly, we have learnt that the current security risk-oriented patterns [1] are rather limited to cover the complete list of security regulations. For instance, ISO/IEC 27001:2013 (and other standards) does not only concern the computerised information management (i.e., access control, cryptology, or information classification). It also deals with (physical) human resource security, media handling, physical and environmental security, equipment and other. Thus this leads to the necessity to develop new security risk, which potentially could be applied to compliance management at different enterprise level.

Thirdly, we have experienced that the heuristics of the SRP application should be improved. For instance, we have observed that it is important to perform some model pre-processing (by introducing *data stores*, *data object*, by explicitly clarifying *data flows* between the pools, etc.) before the SRPs could actually be used in the business process models. One possible way to improve the SRP application is its specification using method engineering principles [9]. This work is already started in [21], however further validation is still needed.

Acknowledgements. This research is supported by the Estonian Research Council.

The paper of the Baltic-German University Liaison Office is also supported by the German Academic Exchange Service (DAAD) with funds from the Foreign Office of the Federal Republic Germany.

References

1. Ahmed, N., Matulevičius, R.: Securing business processes using security risk-oriented patterns. Comput. Stand. Interfaces **36**(4), 723–733 (2014)
2. Ahmed, N., Matulevičius, R.: Presentation and validation of method for security requirements elicitation from business processes. In: Nurcan, S., Pimenidis, E. (eds.) CAiSE Forum 2014. LNBIP, vol. 204, pp. 20–35. Springer, Heidelberg (2015)
3. Altuhhova, O., Matulevičius, R., Ahmed, N.: An extension of business process model and notification for security risk management. Int. J. IS Model. Des. (IJISMD) **4**, 93–113 (2013)
4. Basel Committee on Banking Supervision, Basel III: A Global Regulatory Framework for More Resilient Banks and Banking Systems, revised 2011, Bank for International Settlements Communications
5. Brucker, A.D., Compagna, L., Guilleminot, P.: Compliance validation of secure service compositions. In: Brucker, A.D., Dalpiaz, F., Giorgini, P., Meland, P.H., Rios, E. (eds.) Secure and Trustworthy Service Composition. LNCS, vol. 8900, pp. 136–149. Springer, Heidelberg (2014)
6. Dubois, E., Heymans, P., Mayer, N., Matulevičius, R.: A systematic approach to define the domain of information system security risk management. In: Nurcan, S., Salinesi, C., Souveyrt, C., Ralyté, J. (eds.) Intentional Perspectives on Information Systems Engineering, pp. 289–306. Springer, Heidelberg (2010)
7. Dumas, M., La Rosa, M., Mendling, J., Reijers, H.A.: Fundamentals of Business Process Management, p. 1. Springer, Heidelberg (2013)
8. El Kharbili, M., Stein, S., Markovic, I., Pulvermuller, E.: Towards a framework for semantic business process compliance management. In: Proceedings of GRCIS 2008, pp 1–15 (2008)
9. Goldkuhl, G., Lind, M., Seigerroth, U.: Method integration: the need for a learning Perspective. IEE Proc. Softw. **145**(4), 113–118 (1998). (Special issue on Information System Methodologies)
10. Governatori, G., Shek, S.: Rule based business process compliance. In: Proceedings of the RuleML2012@ECAI Challenge (2012)
11. ISO/IEC 27001:2013: Information Technology – Security Techniques – Information Security Management Systems – Requirements. International Organization for Standardization, Geneva (2013)
12. IT-Grundschutz Catalogues. Bundesamt für Sicherheit in der Informationstechnik (BSI), Bonn (2013)
13. Matulevičius, R., Ahmed, N.: Eliciting security requirements from the business processes using security risk- oriented patterns. IT Inf. Technol. **55**(6), 225–230 (2013)

14. Neubauer, T., Ekelhart, A., Fenz, S.: Interactive selection of ISO 27001 controls under multiple objectives. In: Jajodia, S., Samarati, P., Climato, S. (eds.) Proceedings of The Ifip Tc 11 23rd International Information Security Conference. IFIP, vol. 287, pp. 477–492. Springer, Heidelberg (2008)
15. NIST Special Publication 800-39: Managing Information Security Risk – Organization, Mission, and Information System View. National Institute of Standards and Technology, Gaithersburg (2011)
16. Papazoglou, M.P.: Making business processes compliant to standards and regulations. In: 15th IEEE International Enterprise Distributed Object Computing Conference (EDOC), pp. 3–13 (2011)
17. Ramezani, E., Fahland, D., van der Werf, J.M., Mattheis, P.: Separating compliance management and business process management. In: Daniel, F., Barkaoui, K., Dustdar, S. (eds.) BPM Workshops 2011, Part II. LNBIP, vol. 100, pp. 459–464. Springer, Heidelberg (2012)
18. Ramezani, E., Fahland, D., van der Aalst, W.M.P.: Supporting domain experts to select and configure precise compliance rules. In: Lohmann, N., Song, M., Wohed, P. (eds.) BPM 2013 Workshops. LNBIP, vol. 171, pp. 498–512. Springer, Heidelberg (2014)
19. Sadiq, S., Governatori, G.: Managing regulatory compliance in business processes. In: vom Brocke, J., Rosemann, M. (eds.) Handbook on Business Process Management 2. International Handbooks on Information Systems, pp. 265–288. Springer, Heidelberg (2015)
20. Salnitri, M., Paja, E., Giorgini, P.: Preserving compliance with security requirements in socio-technical systems. In: Cleary, F., Felici, M. (eds.) CSP Forum 2014. CCIS, vol. 470, pp. 49–62. Springer, Heidelberg (2014)
21. Sandkuhl, K., Matulevičius, R., Ahmed, N., Kirikova, M.: Refining security requirement elicitation from business processes using method engineering. Accepted at the Workshop on Security and Compliance in Business Processes (2015)
22. Schultz, M.: Enriching process models for business process compliance checking in ERP environments. In: vom Brocke, J., Hekkala, R., Ram, S., Rossi, M. (eds.) DESRIST 2013. LNCS, vol. 7939, pp. 120–135. Springer, Heidelberg (2013)
23. Schumacher, M., Fernandez, B.E., Hybertson, D., Buschmann, F., Sommerlad, P.: Security Patterns: Integrating Security and Systems Engineering. Wiley, New York (2006)
24. Schumm, D., Turetken, O., Kokash, N., Elgammal, A., Leymann, F., van den Heuvel, W.-J.: Business process compliance through reusable units of compliant processes. In: Daniel, F., Facca, F.M. (eds.) ICWE 2010. LNCS, vol. 6385, pp. 325–337. Springer, Heidelberg (2010)

Making Decisions in Enterprises

Towards an OSS Adoption Business Impact Assessment

Lucía Méndez Tapia[1,2(✉)], Lidia López[1], Claudia P. Ayala[1],
and María Carmela Annosi[3]

[1] Universitat Politècnica de Catalunya (UPC),
c/Jordi Girona, 1-3, 08034 Barcelona, Spain
emendez@lsi.upc.edu, lmendez@uazuay.edu.ec,
{llopez,cayala}@essi.upc.edu
[2] Universidad del Azuay (UDA), Av. 24 de Mayo 7-77 y Francisco Moscoso,
Cuenca, Ecuador
[3] Ericsson Research – Ericsson AB, 84016 Pagani, Italy
mariacarmela.annosi@ericsson.com

Abstract. Nowadays, the adoption of Open Source Software (OSS) by organizations is becoming a strategic need in a wide variety of application areas. Organizations adopt OSS in very diverse ways. The way in which they adopt OSS affects and shapes their businesses. Therefore, knowing the impact of different OSS adoption strategies in the context of an organization may help improving the processes undertaken inside this organization and ultimately pave the road to strategic moves. However, there is a lack of support for assessing the impact of the OSS adoption over the business of the adopter organizations. Based on the goal-oriented characterization of some OSS adoption strategies, in this paper, we propose a preliminary approach to assess the business impact of the OSS adoption strategies over the adopter organizations. The proposal is based on the Business Model Canvas and graph theory notions to support the elicitation and assessment of the impact of each goal over the adopter organization. We illustrate the application of the approach in the context of a telecommunications company.

Keywords: Open Source Software · Goal-oriented · OSS adoption strategies · Business model canvas

1 Introduction

Open Source Software (OSS) has become a strategic asset for a number of reasons, such as short time-to-market software delivery, reduced development and maintenance costs, and its customization capabilities [1]. Therefore, organizations are increasingly becoming OSS adopters, either as a result of a strategic decision or because it is almost unavoidable nowadays, given the fact that most commercial software also relies at some extent in OSS infrastructure [2]. Organizations might adopt OSS in very diverse ways [3]. The way in which organizations adopt OSS affects and shapes their businesses [4]. Leveraging OSS adoption strategies with the organization context is a challenging task per se, as it implies reconciling them from very different perspectives

© IFIP International Federation for Information Processing 2015
J. Ralyté et al. (Eds.): PoEM 2015, LNBIP 235, pp. 289–305, 2015.
DOI: 10.1007/978-3-319-25897-3_19

[5]. However, there is a lack of support to help organizations to assess the impact of OSS adoption [6]. Organizational modelling can provide a way to define the organization's goals and to serve as the context in which processes operate and business is done. In line with this idea, López et al. [7] model diverse OSS adoption strategies as dependency goals between OSS communities and the adopter organizations. These models describe the consequences of adopting one such strategy or another: which are the strategic and operational goals that are supported, which are the resources that emerge. In order to assess which is the OSS adoption strategy that better fits the organization needs, they introduce the notion of model coverage, which allows to measure the degree of concordance among every strategy with the model of the organization by comparing the respective models. However, the approach taken in [7] does not focus on a crucial aspect that need to be taken into account: OSS-based solutions are not developed, and do not exist, in isolation, instead, they exist in the wider context of an organization or a community, in larger OSS-based business ecosystems, which include groups of projects, companies that may be competitors, OSS communities, regulatory bodies, customers, etc. Thus, in this paper, we complement the work done in [7] by considering a further business assessment of the OSS adopter ecosystem when approaching a specific OSS adoption strategy. Hence, the research question that guide this work is:

RQ1: How to assess the impact of the OSS adoption strategies presented in [7] over the business of an organization?

This research question explores how the goals stated by the OSS adoption strategies stated in [7], further affect the business of an organization. The resulting approach uses the Business Model Canvas approach [8] to organize and link the diverse kinds of goals of an organization; as well as graph theory notions to realize the impact of each goal over the whole organization. This paper aims to detail the preliminary elements of this approach and its application to a real case.

The rest of the paper is structured as follows: Sect. 2 introduces the background required to envisage the resulting approach. Section 3 details the foundations and elements of the proposal. To illustrate the application of the proposal, Sect. 4 details its application in a big telecommunications company: Ericsson Telecomunicazioni (Italy), one of the RISCOSS EU-funded project industrial partners (www.riscoss.eu). Finally, Sect. 5 presents the conclusions and the future work.

2   Background

This section briefly characterizes the goal-oriented OSS adoption strategies [7] used as the basis of this paper; and describes the basic elements of the Business Model Canvas [8] used to articulate the elicitation and assessment of the impact of the different OSS adoption strategies over the adopter organizations.

2.1 OSS Adoption Strategies

The concept of strategy comes from the Greek 'strategos' to denote 'leadership'. For organizations, the strategy denotes a set of actions taken to achieve their business goals [9]. In terms of OSS adoption, each adopter organization should define its own OSS adoption goals and determine the actions involved to achieve these goals (i.e., to define the strategy to be followed to fulfill its business model).

López et al. [7] describe six different OSS adoption strategies in terms of models that can be used as a reference for understanding and assessing the impact of the OSS adoption strategies on the OSS adopter organization, as well as complementing the OSS adopter organizational model. These strategies were characterized using $i*$ modeling language, a goal and agent oriented framework formulated for representing, modelling and reasoning about socio-technical systems [10]. We use these OSS adoption strategies as the basis of the approach presented in this paper. A textual description of each OSS adoption strategy is provided below:

- **OSS Acquisition:** refers to use existing OSS code without contributing to its OSS project/community.
- **OSS Integration:** involves the active participation of an organization in an OSS community in order to share and co-create OSS.
- **OSS Initiative:** is oriented to initiate an OSS project and to establish a community around it.
- **OSS Takeover:** is focused on investing some resources to lead an existing OSS project/community.
- **OSS Fork:** means to create an own independent version of the software that is available from an existing OSS project/community.
- **OSS Release:** implies that the organization releases software as OSS but does not care whether an OSS community takes it up or forms around it.

2.2 The Business Model Canvas

In order to enable the elicitation and assessment of goals related to the OSS adopter ecosystem and those related to the different OSS adoption strategies, we used the Business Model Canvas [8]. We chose it as it is a well-known tool that covered a wide spectrum of operational and strategic elements of a business model and successfully helped us as the basis to articulate the elicitation and assessment of the different goals involved in OSS adoption.

The Business Model Canvas has nine business model building blocks that describe the organization and how it works [9]. These blocks are:

- **Value propositions:** the bundle of products and services that create value for a specific Customer Segment.
- **Customer segments:** groups of people or organizations an enterprise aims to reach and serve.
- **Channels:** describes how a company communicates with and reaches its Customer Segments to deliver a Value Proposition.

- **Customer relationships:** describes the types of relationships a company establishes with specific Customer Segments.
- **Key resources:** describes the most important assets required to make a business model work. Key resources can be physical, financial, intellectual, or human.
- **Key activities:** describes the most important things a company must do to make its business model work.
- **Key partnerships:** describes the network of suppliers and partners that make the business model work.
- **Cost Structure:** describes all costs incurred to operate a business model.
- **Revenue streams:** represents the cash a company generates from each Customer Segment.

3   A Goal-Oriented Approach to OSS Adoption Business Impact Assessment

This section describes the foundations of the main elements of the proposed approach to assess the business impact of the OSS adoption strategies stated in [7] over the OSS adopter organizations.

To answer our research question and conceive the resulting approach, we needed to deal with three essential issues:

(1) *Elicitation of relevant goals:* how to discover and refine business and ecosystem related goals that are relevant in OSS adoption processes?
(2) *Goal Alignment:* how to align each OSS adoption strategy' goals from [7] to the OSS adopter business and ecosystem related goals?
(3) *Goal Impact Assessment:* how to assess and estimate the impact of the OSS related goals over the whole organization?

Sections 3.1, 3.2 and 3.3 focus on explaining how we dealt with the elicitation of relevant goals, goal alignment and goal impact assessment respectively.

3.1   Elicitation of Relevant Goals

OSS adoption might deeply affects the business of an organization, mainly because OSS-based solutions are not developed, and do not exist, in isolation, instead, they exist in the wider context of an organization or a community, in larger OSS-based business ecosystems, which include groups of projects, companies that may be competitors, OSS communities, regulatory bodies, customers, etc. As mentioned above, there is a lack of support for assessing this complex situation. Thus, to support the elicitation and assessment of relevant goals in OSS adoption processes, we suggest to classify them into:

- **Generic Business Goals:** related to the external environment and the strategic organizational components.
- **Generic OSS Goals:** related to OSS adoption goals that any organization might want to achieve independently from the adoption strategy chosen.

- **OSS Adoption Strategy Goals:** related to those goals that depend directly to the adoption strategy, as assumed in [7].

On the other hand, we also suggest to characterize goals using a common goal level classification from [11] that characterize them as: strategic, tactical and operational to denote another important aspect of the nature of the goals. Table 1 presents the main characteristics of each goal level.

Table 1. Characterization of goal levels

Goal level	Characteristics			
	Scope	Impact	Related to	Period
Strategic	Broad	High	Organizational environment	Long term
Tactical	Middle	Middle	Transform the strategy in actions	Medium term
Operational	Limited	Low	Implement the strategy	Short term

Next subsections describe how these set of goals were elicited and might serve as reference catalogues to help organizations to elicit their own specific goals. We used the Business Model Canvas [8] as an umbrella to elicit and articulate the goal alignment.

3.1.1 Generic Business Goals

These goal were identified considering the following factors:

- **Macro-environment:** external factors that impact in the business and on which the OSS adopter has a little or none influences. Concretely related to: political, economic, social, technological, environmental, legal, demographic and regulatory issues [12, 13]. For instance, some public organizations are affected by the governmental policy of using OSS whenever possible [3].
- **Micro-environment:** it refers to factors that have a direct contact to the organization itself and to all the challenges that come from inside the organization [14]. For instance, assessing the micro-environment, we should realize the existence of co-opetitors (i.e., entities that collaborate with the organization and at the same time are competitors in other lines or products [15]), thus shaping the corresponding goals.
- **Strategic Elements of the Organization:** this embraces issues such as the mission, vision, and business strategy of the organization [16], as well as the competitive strategies [17] and business models [4, 8] put in place in the organization.

Table 2 shows the resulting list of generic business goals, which can be applied regardless of the nature or economic activity of the OSS adopter. These goals were codified and mapped to the corresponding Business Model Canvas building block, and assigned to the hierarchical level (S for strategic, T for tactical, and O for operational).

3.1.2 Generic OSS Goals

Generic OSS goals are related with adopting OSS in general, independently of the adoption way. The list of generic goals presented in Table 3 was based on literature

Table 2. Generic Business Goals

Canvas building block	Code	Generic business goals	Level
Customer segments	BG01	To consolidate/improve market position	S
	BG02	To expand coverage of supply to new markets with existing services and/or new	S
Value proposition	BG03	To offer brand/status	S
	BG04	To offer a product/service with high quality	S/T
	BG05	To offer an innovative product/service	S/T
Channels	BG06	To deliver the product or service to customers	S
	BG07	To enable the after sales service	S
	BG08	To enable customers to multichannel purchase of products or services	S
	BG09	To build customer loyalty (to establish long-term relationships)	S
Customer relationships	BG10	To establish, maintain and expand customer relationships	S
	BG11	To know the customer's profile for personalization purposes	T
	BG12	To provide quality customer care	S
	BG13	To improve revenues resulting from one-time customer payments	S
Revenue streams	BG14	To improve revenues resulting from ongoing payments	S
	BG15	To implement a strategy to obtain a source of differentiation	S
Key resources	BG16	To maintain/innovate the infrastructure	S
	BG17	To develop a capacitation plan	S
	BG18	To achieve and maintain a differentiation factor	
Key activities	BG19	To achieve and maintain competitive advantage	S
	BG20	To establish barriers to entry for potential new competitors	S
	BG21	To approval of any use/licensing in or licensing out of software	T
	BG22	To ensure quality IT services	S
	BG23	To implement and distribute software product and licenses to customers according to corporate policies	O
	BG24	To optimize the production processes	T
	BG25	To strengthen Research, Development and innovation (R&D&i)	T
	BG26	To establish/consolidate software as (part of) a competitive advantage	S
	BG27	To ensure the quality level of software adopted	S
	BG28	To establish strategic alliances for ensuring provisions	S

(Continued)

Table 2. *(Continued)*

Canvas building block	Code	Generic business goals	Level
Key partnerships	BG29	To establish strategic alliances for ensuring input logistics (supply chain)	S
	BG30	To guarantee the data confidentiality level among the cooperator and competitor roles when they are played with the same organization	S
	BG31	To ensure the law's accomplishment (licensing, intellectual property ownerships, patents, and others)	S
	BG32	To obtain (long term) agreements with external services	T
	BG33	To have a licensing schema for operating/distributing/selling software	T
	BG34	To achieve cost advantages through economies of scale and economies of scope (according to the good or service and customer segment)	S
Cost structure	BG35	To implement a strategy to reduce costs	S

related to the business role of OSS [1, 4, 18], and innovation [19]. These goals were also codified and mapped to the corresponding Canvas building block, and assigned to the hierarchical level (S for strategic, T for tactical, and O for operational).

3.1.3 OSS Adoption Strategy Goals

Each OSS adoption strategy (fully described in [7]) taken as a basis in this work, has a set of relationships between the OSS adopter and the OSS community that provide the OSS. However, these relationships need to be further assessed to elicit business and ecosystem related goals. Therefore, we defined a process to elicit these goals from each OSS adoption strategy.

A process for eliciting goals from the OSS adoption strategy models. The *i** language used to model the OSS strategies is composed of a set of constructs, which can be used in two types of models. The Strategic Dependency (SD) Model allows the representation of organizational actors and the strategic dependencies among them. A Dependency is a relationship between two actors: one of them, named depender, depends for the accomplishment of some internal intention on a second actor, named dependee. The dependency is characterized by an intentional element (Dependum). The main Intentional Elements are: Resource, Task, Goal and Softgoal. A softgoal represents a goal that can be partially satisfied, or a goal that requires additional agreement about how it is satisfied. The Strategic Rationale (SR) Model represents the internal actor's rationale, allowing the representation of the actor's goals and their decomposition [20].

Figure 1 shows an excerpt of the OSS Integration strategy model from [7]. In order to improve the understandability of the model, in Fig. 1, the elements' names correspond to descriptions instead of the identifiers originally used in [7]. We use this model as a basis to explain the process followed for extracting goals from each OSS adoption strategy models.

Table 3. Generic OSS goals

Canvas building block	Code	Generic OSS goals	Level
Customer segments	OG01	To change customer and market perceptions	S
	OG02	To create a new markets	S
Value proposition	OG03	To ensure availability	T
	OG04	To ensure robustness	T
	OG05	To ensure security	T
	OG06	To facilitate the adaptation of software systems to business dynamic	S
	OG07	To improve the corporate/enterprise image or brand	S
	OG08	To incorporate the best practices in the business area for primary processes	S
	OG09	To work in concordance to specific ethical, moral, and political statements	S
	OG10	To achieve ubiquity for the product or product platform	S
	OG11	To incorporate the innovation in products/services	S
Customer relationships	OG12	To involve to end-users with the obtain feedback information process	T
Revenue streams	OG13	To establish the revenues resulting from OSS component support	S
Key resources	OG14	To incorporate technical personnel to deal with OSS internal support	S
Key activities	OG15	To improve security control	T
	OG16	To improve quality (performance, security, flexibility and interoperability	S
	OG17	To reduce the time to market	S
	OG18	To avoid vendor/consultant lock/in	S
	OG19	To incorporate best software development practices	T
	OG20	To change the pricing practices	T
	OG21	To have a licensing schema for operate/distribute/sell OSS	S
Key partnerships	OG22	To achieving a degree of interaction with the community for a continued support to OSS component	S
Cost structure	OG23	To reduce costs/make savings	S

For each OSS adoption strategy model, we produce the set of specific OSS goals following the process detailed below:

(1) Identifying what the OSS adopter organization needs from the OSS community. For this purpose, we derived the goals from the dependencies where the OSS adopter is the depender. As we are interested on goals, there are two cases, according to the kind of intentional element characterizing the dependum:

(a) The dependum is a goal or softgoal, the dependum is an OSS specific goal. The goals and softgoals associated to this dependency inside the OSS adopter rationale are also considered as OSS specific goals. For example dependencies "Acceptance as contributor" and "Help obtained".

(b) The dependum is a task or resource. In this case, the specific goals are only the goals and softgoals associated to this dependency inside the OSS adopter rationale. For example, "Technical Quality", connected to the dependency with resource "User documentation".

(2) Identifying the goals that the OSS adopter must achieve to satisfy the OSS community needs. In this case, the dependency considered are the ones where the OSS adopter is thee dependee and the dependum is characterized by a goal or softgoal:

(c) The specific goals are the goals and softgoals associated to this dependency inside the OSS adopter rationale. As example, the community has the goal "Supporting activities held", that impacts over the internal task "Give support to activities" (i.e. "to provide any kind of support to the community not related to reporting bugs and providing patches"), which enables us to find the goal "OSS Community Contributed".

(3) Identifying the internal strategic goals that are not directly related to the dependencies with the OSS community. The OSS adoption strategy models presented in [7] contains two types of information: the high-level goals attained by the strategy and the low-level task and resources that are requirements for an adequate application of the OSS adoption strategy. We only include the high-level goals in the process. In the particular case of OSS Integration adoption strategy, there are no additional goals to find because all explored dependencies in the steps 1 and 2 are related with the high-level strategy goals.

Table 4 shows the result of applying the process previously detailed to the OSS adoption integration strategy partially shown in Fig. 1.

3.2   Goal Alignment

To reconcile and map the diverse elicited goals from the previous stage, we : (a) defined a process of goal mapping aimed to assess all potential relationships among goals and; (b) define the influence paths from the relevant relationships found in the goal mapping matrix in order to visualize and process the potential impact of the goals.

3.2.1   Goal Mapping Process
The type of goal relationships in each Business Model Canvas building block is many-to-many: one *generic OSS goal* may contribute to one or more *generic business goals*, and one *generic business goal* can be supported by one or more *generic OSS goal*; a similar relationship exists among *OSS adoption strategy goals* and *generic OSS goals*.

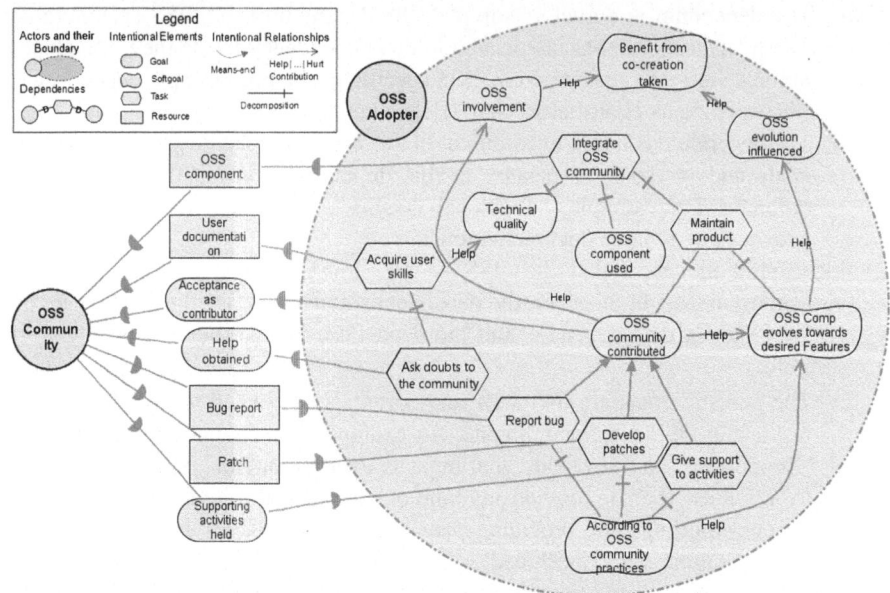

Fig. 1. Excerpt for the OSS Integration strategy model.

Table 4. OSS specific goals of integration OSS adoption strategy

OSS adoption strategy specific goals		Step
IG01	Benefit from co-creation taken	b
IG04	Technical quality	b
IG05	OSS component used	b
IG11	Help obtained	a
IG12	Acceptance as contributor	a
IG08	OSS community contributed	b, c
IG09	According OSS community practices	b
IG02	OSS involvement	b
IG07	OSS component evolves towards desired features	a, c
IG06	Quality of the evolved OSS component	a, c
IG03	OSS evolution influenced	a, c

Therefore, the goal mapping process consist on relating the whole set of goals from (i.e., the generic business goal, OSS generic goals, and OSS adoption strategy goals) to assess their implications for each Business Model Canvas building block. Meaningful relationships are marked to proceed to their further assessment while non-meaningful ones are just discarded (see example in Sect. 4.2.1). The goal mapping matrix help to identify meaningful relationships that need to be further assessed by the organization.

3.2.2 Influence Path

To understand and process the relationships found through the goal mapping matrix, we built a graph where the nodes are the goals and the edges are the dependency/contribution links. Thus, we identify a set of influence paths that help us to trace the impact of relevant goals (see example in Sect. 4.2.2) and to apply graph theory notions for the subsequent goal impact assessment.

3.3 Goal Impact Assessment

Last, to assess the impact of the elicited goals over the organizations we apply some concepts from the graph theory [21]. The objective is to quantify the importance of a goal (represented as a node) based on the support that it provides to other goals, as well as the support needed from other goals.

The goal influence is the relation between goals that indicates that one goal is supporting the achievement of another goal. From the organization's point of view, the importance of a goal is given, among other factors, by the number of goals that it influences. The influence level depends on the levels of the supported goals (Strategic, Tactical or Operational): higher level goals are more important than lower ones. If we represent the goals as nodes, and the influence of a goal over another goal as a directed edge, the importance of a node can be calculated in terms of degree centrality [21].

There are two ways to know the goal importance of a given goal: the first one depends on the number of goals it is supporting (here the goal acts like a support provider), and the second one depends on the number of goals supporting it (here the goal acts like a support consumer).

To assess the importance of goals acting as support providers, we propose the calculation of the *Goal Impact Factor (GIF)* to quantify the importance of a specific goal, based on the number and level of goals to which it influences. We assign for example, the weight factor of 1 (the maximum value) to the impact over a strategic business goal; 0.75 to the impact over a tactical business goal; and 0.5 (the minimum value) to the impact over an operational business goal. These values can be modified according to the specific criteria of the organizations. The GIF for any node i, through its influence path, is calculated as follows:

$$GIF(i) = 1 * SGI + 0.75 * TGI + 0.5 * OGI \tag{1}$$

Where *SGI* is the total number of Strategic Goals Impacted, *TGI* is the total number of Tactical Goals Impacted, and *OGI* is the total number of Operational Goals Impacted. Taking any goal (i) in the directed influence path, the *SGI*, *TGI* and *OGI* are calculated as the number of nodes from node i (itself included), to the goals at the end of each influence path; each node is counted only one time. The results are normalized in relation to the total number of nodes in the graph.

To assess the importance of goals acting as support consumers, we applied the Goal Grouping Factor (*GGF*) to quantify the importance of a specific goal based on the number and level of goals that support it. The weight factor is applied in the same way than in *GIF*. The *GGF* for any node *i*, through its influenced path, is calculated as follows:

$$GGF(i) = 1 * SGG + 0.75 * TGG + 0.5 * OGG \qquad (2)$$

Where *SGG* is the Strategic Goal Grouped, *TGG* the Tactical Goal Grouped, and *OGG* the Operational Goal Grouped. Taking any goal (*i*) in the directed influence path, the *SGG*, *TGG* and *OGG* are calculated as the number of nodes from *i* (itself excluded), through each influence path, to the goals that are not supported by others (self-sufficient goals); each node is counted only one time. The results are normalized in relation to the total number of nodes in the graph.

The quantification of the goal importance using *GIF* can help to:

(a) identify the goals with higher impact over the business, helping to establish priorities in the resources assigned to the related tasks;
(b) compare the impact of one OSS adoption strategy over another, comparing the sum of *GIF* of all self-sufficient goals of each strategy; this comparison can support the OSS strategy selection.

On the other hand, when we use *GGF*, the obtained value reveals the number and level of goals that are its contributors; in this sense, the *GGF* can help to establish the general schedule for the goals achievement, as part of the business plan.

4   An Example of Application of the Approach: The TEI Case

This section details the application of the approach described above, in the context of TEI (Ericsson Italy at Pagani, TEI), one of the RISCOSS project industrial partners.

TEI is part of Ericsson, one of the world's leading telecommunication corporations. Ericsson produces hardware (telecommunications infrastructure and devices) as well as the software to run it. The company's mission is to empower people, business and society at large, guided by a vision of a sustainable networked society. One of TEI's roles within the Ericsson ecosystem is to provide OSS alternatives to support efficient third party products handling. Therefore, it is important for TEI to adopt OSS components following the adoption strategy that is most suitable to the organization needs.

Based on a preliminary assessment of TEI, the most suitable strategy for them was OSS adoption integration strategy [7]. The example presented in this section refers to this specific strategy, and focus on a specific Business Model Canvas building block, named Value Proposition area.

4.1   Elicitation of Relevant Goals for TEI

The elicitation of relevant goals was supported by the list of Generic Business Goals (Table 2), Generic OSS Goals (Table 3), and OSS Strategy Goals (Table 4), that acted as catalogues of goals that were customized to the specific circumstances, needs and expectations of TEI.

Table 5 shows an excerpt of the resulting TEI's Business Model Canvas-based elicited goals.

It can be observed that some of the customizations over the catalogues to satisfy TEI's needs were:

- The generic business goal BG03 "To offer brand /status" was modified to "To offer reputation", to better accommodate it to the TEI context.
- The level of generic business goals BG04 "To offer a product/service with high quality" and BG05 "To offer an innovative product/service" were taken to strategic (i.e., level S) due the higher importance to the TEI's business performance.
- The level of OSS specific goals of Integration OSS adoption strategy IG02 "OSS Involvement" and IG03 "OSS evolution influenced" were decided to be strategic (i.e., level S) due the higher importance of the OSS community for TEI.

Table 5. Canvas-based elicited goals for TEI (Value proposition area)

Code	Business goal	Level
BG03	To offer reputation	S
BG04	To offer a product/service with high quality	S
BG05	To offer an innovative product/service	S
Code	OSS goal	Level
OG03	To ensure availability	T
OG04	To ensure robustness	T
OG05	To ensure security	T
OG06	To facilitate the adaptation of software systems to business dynamic	S
OG07	To improve the corporate/enterprise image or brand	S
OG08	To incorporate the best practices in the business area for primary processes	S
OG09	To work in concordance to specific ethical, moral, and political statements	S
OG10	To achieve ubiquity for the product or product platform	S
OG11	To incorporate the innovation in products/services	S
Code	OSS integration strategy goal	Level
IG01	Benefit from co-creation taken	S
IG04	Technical quality	T
IG05	OSS component used	T
IG11	Help obtained	T
IG12	Acceptance as contributor	S
IG08	OSS community contributed	T
IG09	According OSS community practices	O
IG02	OSS involvement	S
IG07	OSS component evolves towards desired features	T
IG06	Quality of the evolved OSS component	T
IG03	OSS evolution influenced	S

4.2   Goal Alignment

To perform the goal alignment, we built the goal mapping matrix followed by the influence paths. Next subsections summarize the results.

4.2.1   Goal Mapping Process

We obtain the goal mapping matrix in Table 6 by applying the Cartesian product of all TEI's relevant goals (see Table 5) related to the Value Proposition area. Due to space restrictions, the table only includes the goals related to the quality of code, one of the tactical goals for TEI. Only meaningful relationships are marked with an arrow. Please note that those cells in grey color just denote reflexive relations that are not applicable.

Table 6. Goal Mapping Matrix

	Code	BG03	BG04	OG03	OG04	OG05	OG07	IG01	IG04	IG011	IG06
Code	**Level**	S	S	T	T	T	S	S	T	T	T
BG03	S										
BG04	S	↑									
...											
OG03	T		↑								
OG04	T		↑								
OG05	T		↑								
OG07	S	↑	↑								
...											
IG01	S			↑	↑	↑	↑				
IG04	T							↑			
IG11	T								↑		
IG06	T							↑			

4.2.2   Influence Paths

Based on the relevant relationships assessed from Table 6, we built the corresponding influence path, as shown in Fig. 2. This figure graphically shows the potential influence of goals over the diverse levels of the organization.

4.3   Goal Impact Assessment

In the case of TEI, assuming that the influence path of the Fig. 2 was the entire graph, the total number of nodes should be 10. Applying the formula (1), *GIF (IG11)* "Help

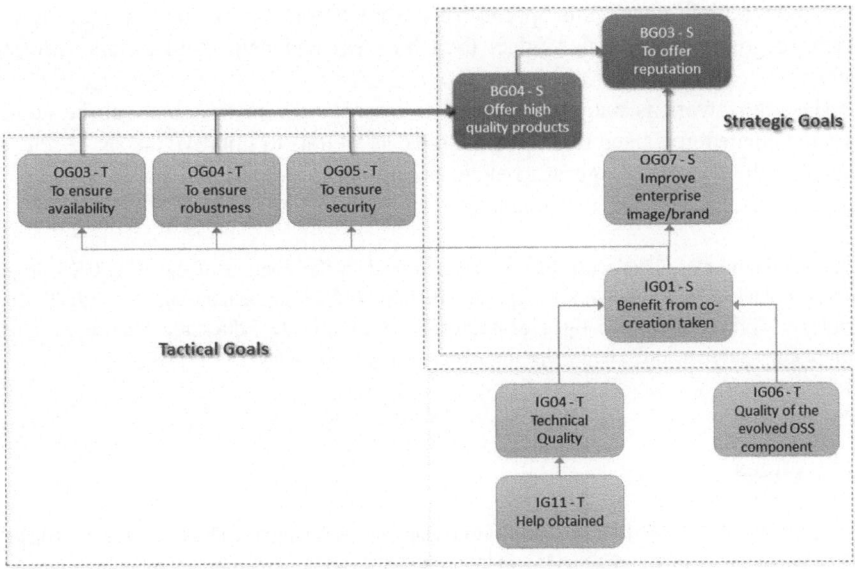

Fig. 2. Influence path

Obtained" is 7.75 normalized as 77.5 %; and *GIF(IG01)* "Benefit from co-creation taken" is 6.25, normalized as 62.5 per cent. Therefore, IG11 has more impact than IG01 in the organization business goals.

Working in the same way with the influence path of the Fig. 2 and the total number of nodes, we can apply the formula (2) to obtain *GGF(BG04)* "Offer high quality products" is 5.5 normalized as 55 %; and *GGF(IG01)* "Benefit from co-creation taken" is 2.25 normalized as 22.5 %. This meaning that BG04 requires more support (that is, the contribution of more goals) than IG01.

5 Conclusions and Future Work

In this paper, we propose a complementary approach to [7], aimed to assess the business impact of a specific OSS adoption strategy over the OSS adopter organization. In order to give an answer to our research question, we:

1. use the Business Model Canvas as an umbrella to organize and elicit goals for enabling their subsequent analysis.
2. manage the many-to-many relationships, among business and OSS-related goals, using a mapping goal matrix and influence path (a directed graph) that allow us to adopt some concepts from the graph theory to assess the resulting goal relationships.
3. define some preliminary metrics (*GIF* and *GGF*) for supporting the estimation of the goal influence and goal relevance.

Although preliminary, this approach has shown potential to support organizations to realize goal influences that affect their business and help them to take informed decisions.

The future work is mainly addressed to improve the metrics that can be applied from the elicited goals and their relationships, as well as to improve the set of relevant goals that the approach suggest to elicit, taking into account risks that might have an impact on the business of the organizations.

Acknowledgements. This work has been performed in the context of the RISCOSS project, funded by the EC 7th Framework Programme FP7/2007-2013, agreement number 318249. Lucía Méndez's work is supported by a SENESCYT (Secretaría de Educación Superior, Ciencia, Tecnología e Innovación) grant from the Ecuatorian government.

References

1. Goldman, R., Gabriel, R.P.: Innovation Happens Elsewhere - Open Source as Business Strategy. Morgan Kaufmann, Los Altos (2005)
2. BlackDuck: The 2015 Future of Open Source Survey. www.blackducksoftware.com/future-of-open-source. Accessed July 2015
3. Hauge, O., Ayala, C., Conradi, R.: Adoption of open source software in software-intensive organizations – a systematic literature review. Inf. Softw. Technol. **52**(11), 1133–1154 (2010)
4. Chesbrough, H.W.: Open Business Models – How to Thrive in the New Innovation Landscape. Harvard Business School Press, Cambridge (2006)
5. Osterwalder, A.: The Business Model Ontology - A Proposition in a Design Science Approach. Université de Lausanne. Ecole des Hautes Etudes Commerciales (2004)
6. Franch, X., Susi, A., Annosi, M.C., Ayala, C.P., Glott, R., Gross, D., Kenett, R.S., Mancinelli, F., Ramsamy, P., Thomas, C., Ameller, D., Bannier, S., Bergida, N., Blumenfeld, Y., Bouzereau, O., Costal, D., Dominguez, M., Haaland, K., López, L., Morandini, M., Siena, A.: Managing risk in open source software adoption. In: Proceedings of International Joint Conference on Software Technologies (ICSOFT), pp. 258–264 (2013)
7. López, L., Costal, D., Ayala, C., Franch, X., Annosi, M., Glott, R., Haaland, R.: Adoption of OSS components: a goal-oriented approach. Data & Knowledge Engineering. Elsevier, Amsterdam (2015)
8. Osterwalder, A., Pigneur, Y.: Business Model Generation. Wiley, New York (2010)
9. Mintzberg, H., Ahlstrand, B., Lampel, J.: Strategy Safari: A Guided Tour Through the Wilds of Strategic Management. The Free Press, New York (1998)
10. Yu, E.: Modelling strategic relationships for process reengineering. PhD. Thesis, Toronto (1995)
11. Kotler, P., Berger, R., Bickhoff, N.: The Quintessence of Strategic Management – What You Really Need to Know to Survive in Business. Springer, Berlin (2010)
12. Dess, G.G., Lumpkin, G.T., Eisner, A.B.: Strategic Management - Creating Competitive Advantages, 5th edn. McGraw-Hill/Irwin, New York (2010)
13. Team FME: PESTLE Analysis, strategy skills (2013)
14. Porter, M.: Competitive Advantage. Free Press, New York (1985)
15. Brandenburger, A.M., Nalebuff, B.J.: Co-opetition. Bantam Doubleday Dell, New York (1996)

16. Kaplan, R.S., Norton, D.P.: Strategy Maps. Harvard Business School Press, Cambridge (2004)
17. Porter, M.: Competitive Strategy. Techniques for Analyzing Industries and Competitors. The Free Press, New York (1980)
18. Lundell, B., Lings, B., Syberfeldt, A.: Practitioner perceptions of open source software in the embedded systems area. J. Syst. Softw. **84**, 1540–1549 (2011)
19. Morgan, L., Finnegan, P.: Open innovation in secondary software firms: an exploration of managers' perceptions of open source software. Database Adv. Inf. Syst. **41**(1), 76–95 (2010)
20. Yu, E.: Social modeling and i*. In: Conceptual Modeling: Foundations and Applications. Lecture Notes in Computer Science, vol. 5600, pp 99–121 (2009)
21. Newman, M.E.J.: Networks – An introduction. University of Michigan and Santa Fe Institute, Oxford University Press, Oxford (2010)

The Concepts of Decision Making: An Analysis of Classical Approaches and Avenues for the Field of Enterprise Modeling

Alexander Bock$^{(\boxtimes)}$

Information Systems and Enterprise Modeling Research Group,
University of Duisburg-Essen, Essen, Germany
alexander.bock@uni-due.de

Abstract. The field of enterprise modeling seeks to help make organizational decisions that take place under conditions of complexity, ambiguity, and conflicting views. But available concepts to describe decision situations are still in their infancy. A variety of existing model-based approaches to aid decision making have been developed in adjacent research fields. The paper investigates a selection of these approaches and reconstructs central concepts in the form of meta models. Implications and ways of integrating decision concepts with existing enterprise modeling methods are considered, and possible avenues for the field of enterprise modeling are discussed.

Keywords: Organizational decision making · Enterprise modeling · Decision model · Decision analysis · Problem construction

1 Introduction

The conditions within which organizational decisions must be made are complex, ambiguous, and conflict-laden [1]. Decisions in organizations happen in view of conflicting goals [2], contradictory problem definitions [3], and increasingly volatile markets and environments. In consequence, it is long apparent that decision makers in organizations can profit from support (e.g., [2,4]).

The field of enterprise modeling (EM) seeks to offer conceptual means to describe, integrate, and analyze multidisciplinary views of an organization [5, pp. 942–943] [6, pp. 18–20]. It is conventionally argued that enterprise modeling can aid decision making. Help is supposed to be offered by virtue of explicating links between different areas of an enterprise, stimulating multidisciplinary discussions, and enabling various domain-specific analyses (see, e.g., [5, pp. 943–944] [6, pp. 9–20]). But although this sort of decision support is implicit in the notion of enterprise modeling, common methods such as For Enterprise Modeling (4EM) [6], ArchiMate [7], or Multi-Perspective Enterprise Modeling (MEMO) [5] offer few, if any, specific concepts to describe decision situations.

The lack of decision-related concepts in enterprise modeling has already been recognized, and some suggestions have been made as to the extension of existing

© IFIP International Federation for Information Processing 2015
J. Ralyté et al. (Eds.): PoEM 2015, LNBIP 235, pp. 306–321, 2015.
DOI: 10.1007/978-3-319-25897-3_20

methods with decision concepts (see, e.g., [8–10]). Incorporating decision models in enterprise models may be useful in several ways. For example, integrated models could help document and evaluate the determinants considered in certain *types* of recurring decision processes (see [8]). This could contribute to a continuous (re-)assessment of decision practices in the organization—an effort whose practical relevance has come to recognition (see [4,11]). It would also be possible to model and analyze *particular* decision situations. This would address aims similar to those of known kinds of decision models (see, e.g., [12, pp. 105–112]) but with an enhanced account of the organizational context. Furthermore, the models could be used to document particular *past* decisions (see [9]). But while previous research has indicated these and other benefits, most existing contributions are still in an early stage of development.

Meanwhile, using models to support decision making has a long tradition. Different research fields have long been developing and putting to use model-based approaches to analyze decision situations. That includes research fields such as decision theory and analysis [2,13–15], systems thinking research [16, 17], management and consulting studies [3,12], and more remote fields such as political studies [18]. Example approaches include decision trees, influence diagrams, cognitive mapping, and Soft Systems Methodology (SSM) [16,17]. In view of their different backgrounds, it can be assumed that these existing approaches, when taken together, offer a wide variety of different concepts to make sense of decision situations.

In order to advance research on incorporating decision concepts in enterprise modeling, this paper seeks to contribute to the development of a broader perspective on possible concepts to describe decision situations. The paper makes two contributions. One is to obtain a set of decision-related concepts which have been discussed extensively in a rich body of existing research. This is done by reviewing a selection of classical decision modeling approaches and reconstructing their concepts in the form of meta models. Second, implications and prospects for the field of enterprise modeling are formulated and discussed to indicate research avenues for the development of decision modeling extensions.

The paper proceeds as follows. In Sect. 2, selected theoretical lines of decision research are summarized. The current state of decision concepts in the field of EM is assessed in Sect. 3. Classical decision modeling approaches are analyzed in Sect. 4. Implications and possible avenues are discussed in Sect. 5. The paper closes with a call for further research in Sect. 6.

2 Theoretical Views on Decisions

Human decision making and problem solving processes are investigated in many disciplines. To prepare the discussion in Sect. 4, selected insights of descriptive decision research are briefly visited. What is a decision? Ordinary definitions in many research fields state that it is a *choice* among a set of alternatives [1, pp. 10–11] [19, p. 11]. An individual who must make a decision is thought to have to choose between a set of alternative courses of action. A good or "optimal" choice, according to this view, is seen as one that maximizes the presumed attainment of pursued goals [1, p. 11]. This view is shared in wide parts of various research fields, including psychology (see, e.g., [20, pp. 656–657] [21, pp. 568–572]) and decision analysis (see, e.g., [2, pp. 806–807]). The choice view directs attention at some aspects of decision making and neglects others. What it neglects is that neither the full context of a decision situation, let alone all possible courses of action [22, p. 81], may be readily apparent to an individual as soon as a need to make a decision is perceived. Rather, these aspects have to be explored and constructed gradually [20, p. 658]. In consequence, decisions have been recognized to emerge from perhaps lengthy *processes* [23, pp. 39–40] [24, p. 246].

How does a decision process unfold? Many theories exist. It has been argued that a decision process is initiated as soon as an individual perceives that a situation warrants action but it is not obvious what kind of action may be adequate (cf. [19, p. 127] [23, p. 102]). In this connection, it is often distinguished between situations that are more routinized or rule-driven and situations that require conscious deliberation and reflection (e.g., coined 'programmed' and 'non-programmed' decisions by [23, p. 46]). Situations of the latter kind are commonly referred to as *'problems'* (see, e.g., [17,25,26]). However, it has been contended that a situation may be seen as a 'problem' only inasmuch as an individual construes it as one [3, p. 8] [19, p. 127]. In this sense, problems have become understood as human *constructions* rather than as objective entities [27, pp. 326–330] [3, p. 8] [26, p. 35]. The argument may also be relevant when considering common distinctions between 'well-structured' and 'unstructured' problems, where the determinants of the former are thought to be clear in advance, while those of the latter require investigation (cf. [27, pp. 321–330]; see also [25, pp. 4–9]). As has been pointed out, even the structure of 'structured' problems is not a property of an objective situation, but the result of a human interpretation [27, pp. 321–332] [26, p. 35]. Once a decision process is initiated, a plethora of modes of behavior and cognitive processes have been hypothesized to be functional, including information search, solution generation, and various evaluation and choice heuristics and strategies (see, e.g., [21, pp. 581–601] [20, pp. 658–674]). In case an acceptable course of action is identified, a decision process may result in a decision—not necessarily in the sense of choice, but as a *commitment* to this course of action [4, p. 24] [24, p. 246]. Finally, matters become more complicated when considering collective decision processes. Individuals in organizations are working in a social context. In consequence, it has also been argued that problems, in the process of being analyzed and discussed, are *socially* constructed (see, e.g., [3,25]). But aside from a collaboration-centric dimension, the social context is also recognized to add modes of behavior such as power exertion, manipulation, and bargaining (e.g., [1,3]).

3   Decisions in EM: Current State and Related Work

Enterprise models are intended to describe both sociological-organizational and informational-technological facets of an enterprise in a manner which points out the interleaving between them [5, pp. 942–943] [6, p. 29]. It would therefore seem plausible to expect that EM approaches offer concepts to describe decision processes and problem situations in the organizational context. In this section, it is reviewed whether this is so. First, existing EM methods are reviewed. Second, attention is directed at specific decision modeling extensions.

General Enterprise Modeling Methods. A variety of EM methods exists (for recent overviews, see [6, pp. 233–272] [28]). Three common example methods that specifically aim to cover different areas of an enterprise are For Enterprise Modeling (4EM) [6], ArchiMate [7], and Multi-Perspective Enterprise Modeling (MEMO) [5]. These are briefly reviewed to indicate conventional concepts in the field. *4EM* does not provide a specific decision concept. But concepts are offered to create 'goals models', which most importantly encompass the concept of a 'goal' [6, p. 88]. In addition, 'goals models' may include the related concepts 'problem', 'cause', 'constraint', and 'opportunity' [6, p. 88]. In the context of business process models, an 'OR' split concept can be found which can be construed as a decision concept in the sense of a choice [6, p. 121]. *ArchiMate* [7] also does not offer a 'decision' concept. Decision-related concepts can be found in the motivation extension [7, pp. 141–152]. These are essentially normative in nature, including the concept of a 'goal' plus the related concepts 'driver' and 'requirement' [7, pp. 143–148]. There are also the concepts 'constraint' and 'principle' [7, pp. 149–151]. *MEMO* is an enterprise modeling method that comprises a set of integrated modeling languages to describe different views on an enterprise [5, p. 946]. The goal concepts 'EngagementGoal' and 'SymbolicGoal' can be found in a comprehensive goal modeling language [29, pp. 10–12]. Further, in the context of a business process modeling language, the concept 'branching' is defined to describe branching points in processes [30, p. 56]. Its attribute 'decision' can be used to indicate whether that path choice is rule-driven or requires human expertise [30, p. 54]. Decision-related aspects are also implicit in various attributes such as 'justification' (see, e.g., [29, p. 11]). Recently, an extension to describe decision processes has been suggested [8], which is mentioned below.

In sum, common EM methods mainly offer decision concepts in four respects (although the level of detail and elaborateness varies significantly). (1) They offer goal and other *teleological concepts*; (2) they offer exclusive *path choice* concepts for business processes; (3) they offer coarse concepts related to *problems*; and (4) they can *document* various kinds of decisions implicitly by means of justificatory or explanatory attributes. What is missing, however, are dedicated concepts to describe decision situations or decision processes in detail.

Specific Decision Modeling Approaches. In view of the situation indicated above, some extensions to model decisions in the context of enterprise models have been suggested. An approach to document the rationales for design decisions in enterprise architecture (EA) management is developed by [9]. The approach mainly takes an ex-post view of decisions. Its main concepts include 'EA Decision', 'EA Issue', 'Decision-Making Strategy', 'Strategy Rationale', 'Criterion', and various relationships including 'Decomposition' and 'Alternative' [9, pp. 135–137]. Instances of these concepts can be linked to elements in EA models to explain how they have been arrived at [9, pp. 135–137]. A domain-specific modeling language as an extension to EM methods (in particular, MEMO) has been proposed in [8]. It aims to permit modeling organizational decision process types plus their context from various perspectives [8, pp. 183–186]. Its main concepts to describe problem situations include 'DecisionPremise', 'ValueDecisionPremise', 'AbstracGoal' (resued from [29]), 'FactualDecisionPremise', 'ActionVariable', 'SituationalAspect', 'EnvironmentalFactor', and relationships such as 'RelevanceRelation' and 'PresumedInfluenceRelation' [8, pp. 187–189]. The approach intends to support continuous reflections about the premises as well as the organizational-regulatory and information-technological conditions of decision processes [8, pp. 183–186]. As an industry-driven initiative, the Decision Model and Notation (DMN) has been suggested by the Object Management Group (OMG) [10]. It permits to describe the logic and rationale of decisions and link them to business processes and organizational units [10, pp. 23–53]. Its underlying definition of a decision as an "act of determining an output value [...], from a number of input values, using logic" [10, p. 23] makes it clear that the focus of DMN is placed on more routine operational decisions (cf. [7, p. 27]). The provided concepts include 'Decision', 'InformationRequirement', 'KnowledgeSource', 'InputData', and various relationships [10, pp. 37–53]. Comprehensive mechanisms are provided to specify the rules for choosing among given input values, including decision tables and an expression language [7, pp. 70–141].

Wrapping up the discussion, it can be summarized that work is in progress to augment enterprise modeling approaches with decision concepts. Even in this early stage, the existing contributions indicate a considerable range of possible uses for such concepts. However, as the development of each approach sets out from an individual starting premise, the respective publications do not discuss markedly different concepts to describe decision situations. In particular, while there seems to be a minimal consensus on concepts to describe more clear decision situations (e.g., alternatives and criteria), only a few broader concepts (e.g., 'SituationalAspect'; [8]) are available to describe decision situations that might be interpreted as less structured. In the following section, this paper seeks to contribute to advancing research in this direction by intending to unveil long-standing, yet varied decision concepts developed in different research fields.

4   Classical Decision Modeling Approaches

Different model-based approaches to facilitate decision making and problem solving have been proposed in the literature and advanced in practice. A selection of such tools are reviewed and discussed below. The approaches have been selected in view of two criteria. First, focus is placed on tools which have found considerable use and reception practice and academia. Second, as a contrast to the first criterion, the tools were selected such as to be deliberately distinct and varied, in terms of the scientific background, the underlying assumptions, and the specific concepts used. In particular, the tools have been taken from traditional decision analysis as well as from skeptical movements in other fields (for comparative discussions, see [12, pp. 105–111] [25]). The discussion centers around concepts to describe decision situations or problems *as such*. Other relevant aspects, such as organizational regulations or psychological phenomena, are not considered. The central concepts of the approaches are reconstructed in the form of meta models (at level M_2) using the MEMO meta modeling language (MML) [31]. The main purpose of the meta models is to point out central concepts; the meta models do not suffice to specify fully correct models of the respective approaches (additional constraints are omitted as well). Furthermore, as classical modeling approaches do not follow the exact same abstraction patterns as are common in the field of EM, the abstraction levels are not determined unambiguously.

4.1   Concepts in Classical Decision Analysis

There is an abundance of work on decision models in the fields of decision theory and analysis (for overviews, see, e.g., [2,13–15]). But although advanced mathematical and probability theory is applied, it is commonly asserted that decision situations are essentially apprehended through the lens of a basic framework (see, e.g., [14, pp. xxii–xxiii] [15, pp. 13–22]). The elements of this framework resemble the choice view mentioned in Sect. 2 and can be identified as follows. (1) There is a set of *alternatives* among which a decision maker must choose (see, e.g., [2, p. 807] [13, pp. 1–2] [15, pp. 15–18]). It is often distinguished between discrete (e.g., different products to be purchased) and continuous alternatives (e.g., the amount of financial budgets) [13, p. 1]. In case different aspects can be varied the full alternative space is the set of all combinations of decision variable values. (2) Perhaps, there are *environmental factors* which can take different states in the future [14, pp. xxii–xxiii]. This is sometimes referred to as uncertainty or risk in general (cf. [2, p. 807]). (3) There is a set of *outcomes* (or *consequences*), each of which is linked to a combination of an alternative and an environmental state (see, e.g., [2, p. 807]). (4) To evaluate outcomes, it is assumed that there is at least one and perhaps several *goals* (or *objectives* or *criteria*) (see, e.g., [2, p. 807] [13, p. 2]). To be able to quantitatively evaluate outcomes with respect to goals, goal fulfillment values have to be defined. Sometimes the outcome itself is already taken to represent the extent of goal fulfillment (e.g., in the case of profit figures which are the better the greater they are). To represent formal models, specific representational forms have been developed. A selection of common examples is discussed below.

Decision matrices (or tables) are one of the most common and elementary representational form used in the field of multi-criteria decision analysis (see, e.g., [13, pp. 2–3]). Different variants exist. One customary variant assigns outcome values to particular combinations of an alternative, environmental state and/or goal (cf. [15, p. 27]). An example is shown in Fig. 1. It is apparent that a decision matrix displays concrete values for the concepts 'goal', 'environmental state', 'alternative', and 'outcome'. Note that the alternative values must be fully disjunctive. Figure 2 shows a reconstructed meta model for decision matrices.

Decision trees are another ordinary representational form used in decision analysis (see, e.g., [14, pp. 10–17] [15, pp. 242–243]). The basic purpose of

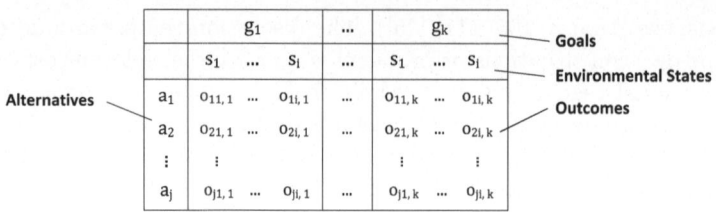

Fig. 1. Example decision matrix

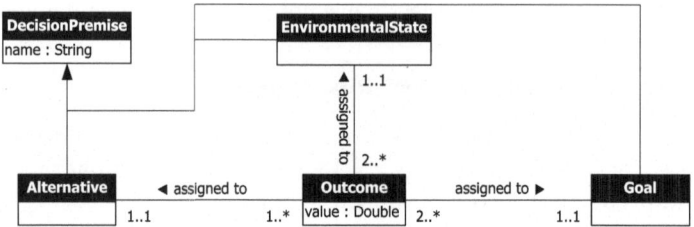

Fig. 2. Reconstructed meta model of decision matrices

decision trees, again, is to assign outcome values to all combinations of alternative and environmental states. Contrary to decision matrices, however, it is possible to divide one fully disjunctive alternative space into alternatives for several sequential decisions [15, p. 242]. Decision trees are tree-like graphs that consist of three kind of nodes: Decision nodes, chance nodes, and outcome nodes. Figure 4 shows a reconstructed meta model for decision trees (Fig. 3).

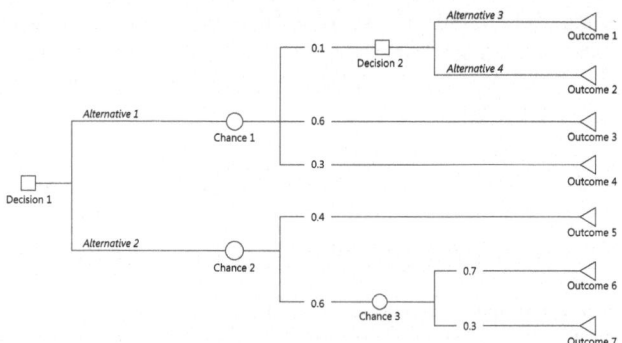

Fig. 3. Example decision tree

Influence diagrams were first suggested during the 1970s [32, p. 5] [33, p. 144]. They were developed to enable formal reasoning on probabilistic relations [34, p. 127], while also being able to support communication with non-mathematically

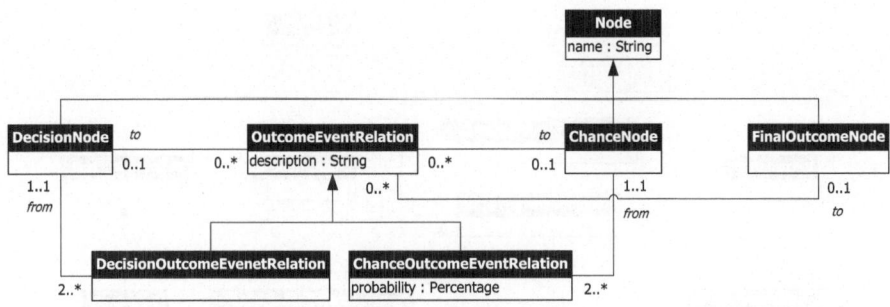

Fig. 4. Reconstructed meta model of decision trees

trained people [34, p. 127]. Influence diagrams are significantly more compact than decision trees [33, p. 144], and they especially support probabilistic operations which are hard to do using decision trees [34, pp. 129–130]. Influence diagrams consist of two basic kind of nodes: *Decision nodes* and *chance nodes* [34, p. 133]. Decision nodes describe mathematical variables whose value can be chosen. Chance nodes describe stochastic variables [34, p. 133] whose value cannot be controlled. There are two special cases of chance nodes. A *deterministic node* is a chance node whose conditional probability has a value of one [32, p. 5]. A *value node*, in turn, is a deterministic node whose value is to be optimized [32, p. 6]. Arrows that point to chance nodes state that the stochastic variable is conditionally dependent on the result of the preceding chance or decision node [34, p. 133]. Arrows heading into decision nodes mean that the outcome of the preceding variable is known [34, p. 133]. Importantly, the absence of a link means that there is probabilistic independence or ignorance of a given outcome [34, pp. 130–131]. An example of an influence diagram is shown in Fig. 5. Because influence diagram describe probabilistic dependencies, they can be used for advanced calculations (see [34]). In general, it is evident that influence diagrams are more abstract than decision trees and matrices. They abstract from concrete values of variables (e.g., alternatives), essentially offering a way of specifying relations among choice and random variables. Figure 6 shows a reconstructed meta model for influence diagrams.

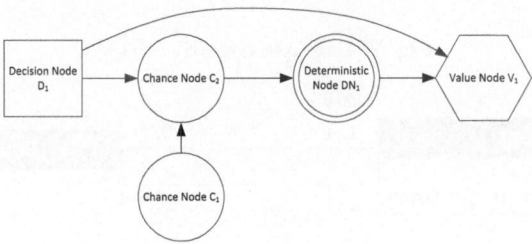

Fig. 5. Example influence diagram

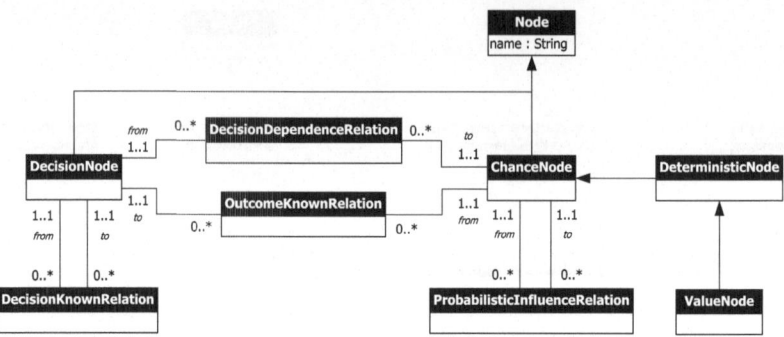

Fig. 6. Reconstructed meta model of influence diagrams

4.2 Concepts in Problem Structuring Approaches

As the traditional instruments of decision analysis have received a substantial share of criticism [12, 25, 26], other roads to aid decision making have been assessed. One stream of research placed emphasis on developing means to support the elicitation of different problem interpretations, communication among all stakeholders, and collaborative model-building [25, pp. 9–17] [12, pp. 106–110]. Methods from this field have become known as 'problem structuring methods' [25, pp. 9–10], and they are sometimes opposed to 'hard' approaches as 'soft' ones [12, p. 107]. Two common examples are visited below.

Cognitive mapping is a modeling approach that has been used in quite distinct fields of research, including cognitive psychology, practical business consulting (see, e.g., [3, 12]), and political studies (see, e.g., [18]). It is also a part of more comprehensive methods (see [12, pp. 138–168]). Conceptually, cognitive mapping is a minimalist approach. It consists of a single concept, whose name is

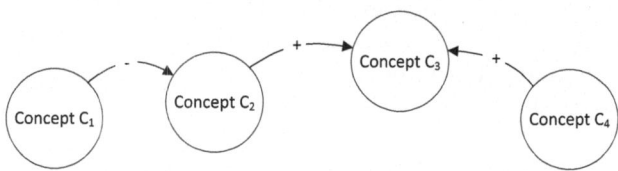

Fig. 7. Example cognitive map

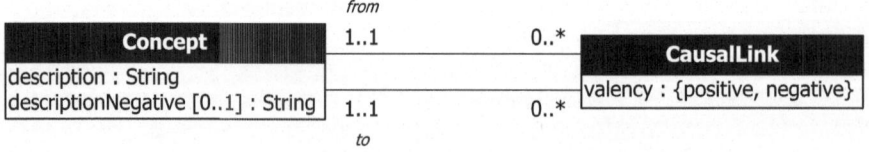

Fig. 8. Reconstructed meta model of cognitive maps

in fact 'concept' [12, pp. 142–143], and one relation, usually called arrow or arc [12, pp. 142–143]. A 'concept' in cognitive mapping has been defined as "an idea, issue or concern that has been expressed by someone or agreed by a group" [12, p. 142]. The arrow, in turn, expresses a *causal* relationship [3, p. 41] [18, pp. 5–8]. An increase (or decrease) in what is expressed by a given concept is supposed to also increase (or decrease) what is expressed by a successor. Figure 7 shows an example. It is apparent that the construct of a 'concept' is a loaded one. It is excessively broad and abstract. In consequence, quite varied aspects can be indicated by means of a cognitive map. But it is interesting to note how different the general idea is from decision analysis. Rather that selecting an "optimal" alternative, the aim is to "articulate thinking, and see it reflexively in a model [as a] representation of a part of the world as a particular person sees it" [3, pp. 43–44]. Figure 8 shows a reconstructed meta model.

Soft Systems Methodology was initially conceived in the 1970s, and it has since then been advanced and modified over time [16, p. 12]. The motivation for its inception was the observation that some assumptions of methods from the fields of decision analysis and operations research proved inadequate for the treatment of real-world problems [17, pp. 195–200]. For example, a point of criticism was directed at the assumption that all possible alternatives and consistent goal systems are already given [25, p. 6] (cf. Sect. 4.1). One of the seminal ideas of SSM is to apply a "soft" notion of systems to look at problematic situations [16, p. 14]. For that purpose, the concept of a 'human activity systems' was set forth [16, p. 14]. It is seen as a set "of linked activities which together could exhibit the emergent property of purposefulness" [16, p. 14]. To guide the use of this idea, SSM offers a comprehensive framework for thinking. Its different components cannot be discussed fully here (for overviews, see [16,17]). What is central from a modeling perspective is that SSM advises to create *conceptual models* of problem situations as interlinked human activity systems [17, pp. 218–225]. An example is provided in Fig. 9. What are the concepts of such models? Besides the concept of an 'activity system' (see above), the second main concept is a 'purposeful *activity*' that describes "a transformation process, one in which some entity [...] is transformed into a different state" [17, p. 219]. Further, activities may be linked to "indicate the dependency of one activity upon another" [17, p. 223]. A reconstruction of these concepts is shown in Fig. 10. When it comes to using conceptual models of activity systems, the models, again, are not intended to imply "optimal" solutions. Instead, it is emphasized that each model will be based on a particular worldview so that it will present a subjective way of seeing the problem [17, pp. 204–205]. The essential aim, then, is to support "discussion [...] to find changes which are both arguably desirable and also culturally feasible in this particular situation" [17, p. 207].

Taken together, it is apparent that SSM, like cognitive mapping, uses a rather small set of concepts to incite reflections on problem situations. The modeling concepts are generic in nature and do not even include include concepts to describe possible solutions. The potential usefulness of the approach for tackling ambiguous problems in social settings has been indicated in a variety of practical

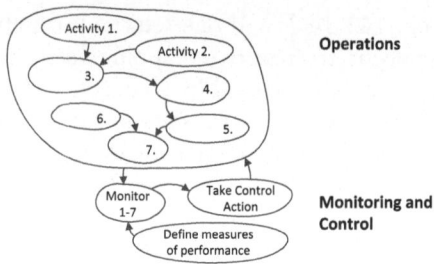

Fig. 9. Example activity system model (based on [17, p. 204])

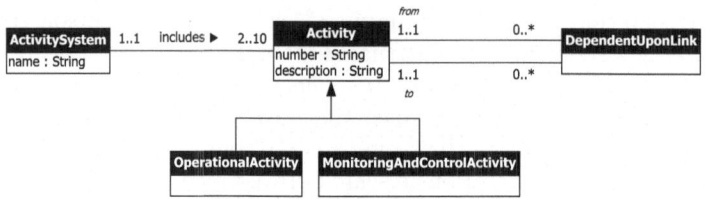

Fig. 10. Reconstructed meta model of activity systems as part of SSM

use cases (cf. [16, pp. 11–13]). At the same time, from a modeling perspective, SSM has been criticized for being simplistic and minimalist [35, pp. 127–128]. This, however, may be a starting point for assessing integration potentials with enterprise modeling, to which the discussion will now turn.

5   Implications and Prospects

The analysis indicated that a considerable spectrum of concepts can be used to make sense of problem situations. In this section, implications and integration points for the field of EM are discussed (Sect. 5.1) and illustrated (Sect. 5.2).

5.1   General Discussion

Key Aims and Integration Points. As has become apparent, the aim of decision support can be taken in different ways. At one end of the spectrum, it can mean reasoning on concrete courses of action (see Subsect. 4.1). At the other end of the spectrum, it can mean aiding discussions on how to structure, understand, and reconcile different views of a problem (see Subsect. 4.2). While the former aim may be primarily associated with situations that are more routinized or pre-analyzed, the latter may be preferable for dealing with more ambiguous, complex, or novel problems (see [25, pp. 9–12]). In principle, either sort of decision support could be usefully advanced by incorporating decision concepts in enterprise models. Generally speaking, such an integration could mean to prepare models of certain kinds of decision situations, to link them to the location of an enterprise model where they may typically occur, and to critically reassess and adjust them periodically. This could contribute to improving organizational decision making practices over time. Furthermore, the use and interpretation of the decision models may profit from the domain-specific knowledge in the enterprise model (see below). Organizational areas where rule-driven or pre-analyzable decision situations may naturally occur include operational business processes (see, e.g., [30, pp. 19–20]) and other operational areas of responsibility. Consequentially, models based on choice-centric concepts (e.g., those of decision matrices or influence diagrams) could be attached to branching points, activities, or task concepts in an EM modeling language. The practical use of these models might consist in analyzing recurring choice situations during operational processes. Steps in this direction have already been made, although the focus so far has been placed on prescribing rather than aiding decision making (cf. [10, pp. 19–21]). With respect to decision processes that deal with more complex and ambiguous problems, EM languages could be augmented with broader concepts such as those identified in Sect. 4.2. Model use would then shift to aiding discussions and explorations into the unclear situations in question. However, in contrast to operational decisions, it is not obvious how these models could be integrated with EM methods, as there are few concepts to describe non-routine decision processes (but see Sect. 3 and [8] for a suggestion in this direction). In other words, adequate abstractions are needed.

Adequate Abstractions. To develop time-stable models of non-routine decision situations or decision processes at level M_1, it is necessary to develop abstractions of similar past, present, and future occurrences of these situations or processes (see also [8, pp. 184, 187]). However, non-routine decision situations are precisely characterized by novelty or ambiguity. This is a challenge for future research.

Domain-Specificity. The analysis has shown that the concepts which are used in traditional decision tools are essentially *generic* in nature (e.g., 'alternative', 'concept', and 'activity'). They can be used to describe choices in almost any domain. Using highly abstract and generic concepts to understand decision making, in fact, has a long tradition in decision research, as is demonstrated by the widely shared choice view (see [21, pp. 568–572]). Contrary to this position, however, results in psychological research indicate that people who deal with decision situations draw on, and require, *domain-specific* knowledge, expertise, and concepts [21, pp. 581–601]. Therefore, an immediate value of enterprise modeling can be seen in the fact that it offers a rich source of domain specific knowledge, from the instance level M_0 (i.e., knowledge about particular occurrences) to the (meta) level M_2 or higher (i.e., conceptual knowledge). A first step of utilizing this prospect may consist in integrating decision models in enterprise models at level M_1 (as noted above). But beyond such a straightforward integration, it would also seem promising to investigate how the domain-specific knowledge captured in an enterprise model and its linguistic structure at level M_2 or above could be exploited to facilitate more sophisticated deliberation processes.

Ways of Seeing. Finally, the analysis revealed that different decision modeling approaches present fundamentally different ways of seeing a problem situation (cf. [12, p. 106]). The approaches from the field of decision analysis essentially take an instrumental *means-end* perspective (cf. [25, pp. 6–7] [27, p. 321]). A choice must be made among given means (alternatives) such as to achieve given ends (goals) [25, p. 7]. Cognitive maps, in turn, consider problem situations solely in terms of *causal* relations. This permits to describe aspects other than those captured by the choice framework—but only in causal terms, which itself excludes other aspects (e.g., teleological ones). The perspective of SSM, in turn, gives weight to the *purposefulness* of human activities in problem situations [17, p. 192]. In contrast to the first perspective, this does not presuppose a solution space of possible means. As a general conclusion, it may be stated that any set of decision modeling concepts can bring about a specific way of seeing problem situations that highlights some aspects and forgoes others. "The language we used is not neutral and can even become a trap, confusing [...] the way [of] talking about unsatisfactory situations with reality itself" [27, p. 339]. That seems important, too, when thinking about modeling languages.

5.2   Illustration of an Example Integration

It has been indicated that enterprise modeling could possibly provide a helpful basis for decision support. Finally, in order to indicate how an augmentation of existing EM methods with classical concepts could look like, a simple scenario is illustrated in Fig. 11. The figure displays four partial diagrams of the enterprise model of a production company. The model is created using various MEMO languages [5, 29, 30]. It consists of (1) a partial goal model, (2) a model of the organizational structure, (3) a model of organizational decision processes, (4) and a model of a business process. The preliminary concept and notation of a decision process type (the blue hexagons) are adopted from [8]. Two decision process types can be found: One is concerned with routine decisions in the business process (automatic vs. manual production), whereas the other is dealing with a more complex problem (reconsidering and possibly restructuring the entire production process). The key point is that these decision process types are linked to partial *classical decision models*. In line with the nature of the decision processes, the more routinized one is detailed by means of a decision matrix. For the less structured and predetermined one, an excerpt of a cognitive map is attached, which could be used to reflect on the assumed causal relations.

What are the prospects of such an integration? First, and most importantly, embedding the classical models with enterprise models enriches them with information on the relevant context. This is indicated by the violet dotted lines. For example, the goals which are considered in the decision matrix in fact correspond to goals specified in the organizational goal system (see partial diagram 1). As another example, the different concepts in the cognitive map are linked to different elements of the enterprise model, such as units of the organizational structure (partial diagram 3), or activities in the business process (partial diagram 4). This

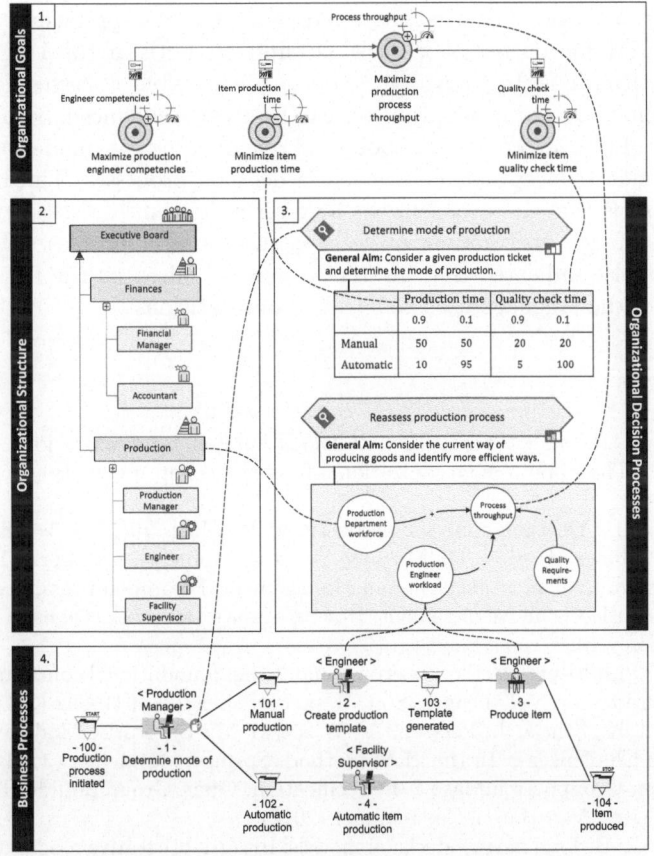

Fig. 11. Illustration of an example integration

can be assumed to foster interpretation of the decision situation, while also offering connection points for further analyses in the enterprise model. Furthermore, it would be possible to augment the links with additional attributes that could be used to make explicit the underlying assumptions, or to note estimations regarding their validity. Finally, in case such integrated models would be maintained over time, they could be used as part of continuous management processes to reassess, and perhaps improve decision making practices.

6   Conclusions and Outlook

Decision making is at the heart of human action. An analysis of classical model-based approaches has brought to the fore quite distinct conceptual ways of dissecting decision situations. Apparent linking points and complementary benefits, as well as general prospects and challenges of enriching the field of enterprise modeling with decision concepts have been discussed. Various paths for future research can be suggested. First, it would generally seem promising to advance the use of EM for purposes of decision support, both in the long term and for specific situations. In particular, support for decision processes dealing with complex, ambiguous, or novel problems can be greatly enhanced. Second, further attention could be directed at the potential role of enterprise models as stocks of domain-specific (conceptual) knowledge in decision processes. Third, to realize decision models that are useful in the long term, it seems necessary to advance conceptions of *type* abstractions of decision situations or processes. Finally, the analysis has also indicated that awareness may be raised on the possible limits and biases of the language used to speak about decisions.

References

1. March, J.G.: Understanding how decisions happen in organizations. In: March, J.G. (ed.) The Pursuit of Organizational Intelligence, pp. 13–38. Blackwell, Malden (1999)
2. Keeney, R.L.: Decision analysis: an overview. Op. Res. **30**(5), 803–838 (1982)
3. Eden, C., Jones, S., Sims, D.: Messing About in Problems: An Informal Structured Approach to their Identification and Management. Pergamon Press, Oxford (1983)
4. Yates, J.F.: Decision Management: How to Assure Better Decisions in Your Company. Jossey-Bass, San Francisco (2003)
5. Frank, U.: Multi-perspective enterprise modeling: foundational concepts, prospects and future research challenges. Soft. Syst. Model. **13**(3), 941–962 (2014)
6. Sandkuhl, K., Stirna, J., Persson, A., Wißotzki, M.: Enterprise Modeling: Tackling Business Challenges with the 4EM Method. Springer, Heidelberg (2014)
7. The Open Group: ArchiMate 2.0 Specification: Open Group Standard. The Open Group Series. Van Haren, Zaltbommel (2012)
8. Bock, A.C.: Beyond narrow decision models: toward integrative models of organizational decision processes. In: Proceedings of the 17th IEEE Conference on Business Informatics (CBI 2015), pp. 181–190. IEEE Computer Society (2015)
9. Plataniotis, G., de Kinderen, S., Proper, H.A.: Capturing design rationales in enterprise architecture: a case study. In: Frank, U., Loucopoulos, P., Pastor, Ó., Petrounias, I. (eds.) PoEM 2014. LNBIP, vol. 197, pp. 133–147. Springer, Heidelberg (2014)
10. Object Management Group: Decision Model and Notation: Beta 1 (2014)
11. Davenport, T.H.: Make better decisions. HBR **87**(11), 117–123 (2009)
12. Pidd, M.: Tools for Thinking: Modelling in Management Science, 2nd edn. Wiley, Chichester and Hoboken (2003)
13. Triantaphyllou, E.: Multi-Criteria Decision Making Methods: A Comparative Study. Kluwer, Dordrecht (2000)
14. Raiffa, H.: Decision Analysis: Introductory Lectures on Choices under Uncertainty. Addison-Wesley, Reading (1970)
15. Bamberg, G., Coenenberg, A.G., Krapp, M.: Betriebswirtschaftliche Entscheidungslehre, 14th edn. Vahlen, München (2008)
16. Checkland, P.: Soft systems methodology: a thirty year retrospective. Syst. Res. Behav. Sci. **17**(1), S11–S58 (2000)
17. Checkland, P., Poulter, J.: Soft systems methodology. In: Reynolds, M., Holwell, S. (eds.) Systems Approaches to Managing Change, pp. 191–242. Springer, London (2010)

18. Axelrod, R.: The cognitive mapping approach to decision making. In: Axelrod, R. (ed.) Structure of Decision, pp. 3–17. Princeton University Press, Princeton (1976)
19. Elbing, A.O.: Behavioral Decisions in Organizations. Scott, Foresman and Company, Glenview (1970)
20. Hastie, R.: Problems for judgment and decision making. Annu. Rev. Psychol. **52**, 653–683 (2001)
21. Goldstein, W.M., Weber, E.U.: Content and discontent: Indications and implications of domain specificity in preferential decision making. In: Goldstein, W.M., Hogarth, R.M. (eds.) Research on Judgment and Decision Making, pp. 566–617. Cambridge University Press, Cambridge (1997)
22. Simon, H.A.: Administrative Behavior: A Study of Decision-Making Processes in Administrative Organization, 3rd edn. Free Press, New York (1976)
23. Simon, H.A.: The New Science of Management Decision. Harper, New York (1960)
24. Mintzberg, H., Raisinghani, D., Théorêt, A.: The structure of unstructured decision processes. Adm. Sci. Q. **21**(2), 246–275 (1976)
25. Rosenhead, J., Mingers, J.: A new paradigm of analysis. In: Rosenhead, J., Mingers, J. (eds.) Rational Analysis for a Problematic World Revisited, pp. 1–19. Wiley, Chichester (2001)
26. Bretzke, W.R.: Der Problembezug von Entscheidungsmodellen. Mohr, Tübingen (1980)
27. Landry, M.: A note on the concept of 'Problem'. Organ. Stud. **16**(2), 315–343 (1995)
28. Bock, A., Kaczmarek, M., Overbeek, S., Heß, M.: A comparative analysis of selected enterprise modeling approaches. In: Frank, U., Loucopoulos, P., Pastor, Ó., Petrounias, I. (eds.) PoEM 2014. LNBIP, vol. 197, pp. 148–163. Springer, Heidelberg (2014)
29. Overbeek, S., Frank, U., Köhling, C.: A language for multi-perspective goal modelling: challenges, requirements and solutions. Comput. Stand. Interfaces **38**, 1–16 (2015)
30. Frank, U.: MEMO Organisation Modelling Language (2) - Focus on Business Processes. ICB Research Report 49. University of Duisburg-Essen, Essen (2011)
31. Frank, U.: The MEMO Meta Modelling Language (MML) and Language Architecture. ICB Research Report 43. University of Duisburg-Essen, Essen (2011)
32. Howard, R.A.: From influence to relevance to knowledge. In: Oliver, R.M., Smith, J.Q. (eds.) Influence Diagrams, Belief Nets and Decision Analysis, pp. 3–23. Wiley, Chichester (1990)
33. Howard, R.A., Matheson, J.E.: Influence diagram retrospective. Decis. Anal. **2**(3), 144–147 (2005)
34. Howard, R.A., Matheson, J.E.: Influence diagrams. Decis. Anal. **2**(3), 127–143 (2005)
35. Hirschheim, R., Klein, H.K., Lyytinen, K.: Information Systems Development and Data Modeling: Conceptual and Philosophical Foundations. Cambridge University Press, Cambridge (1995)

Modeling DevOps Deployment Choices Using Process Architecture Design Dimensions

Zia Babar[1(✉)], Alexei Lapouchnian[2], and Eric Yu[1,2]

[1] Faculty of Information, University of Toronto, Toronto, Canada
zia.babar@mail.utoronto.ca, eric.yu@utoronto.ca
[2] Department of Computer Science, University of Toronto, Toronto, Canada
alexei@cs.toronto.edu

Abstract. DevOps is a software development approach that enables enterprises to rapidly deliver software product features through process automation, greater inter-team collaboration and increased efficiency introduced through monitoring and measuring activities. No two enterprise-adopted DevOps approaches would be similar as each enterprise has unique characteristics and requirements. At present, there is no structured method in enterprise architecture modeling that would enable enterprises to devise a DevOps approach suitable for their requirements while considering possible process reconfigurations. Any DevOps implementation can have variations at different points across development and operational processes and enterprises need to be able to systematically map these variation points and understand the trade-offs involved in selecting one alternative over another. In this paper, we use our previously proposed Business Process Architecture modeling technique to express and analyze DevOps alternatives and help enterprises select customized DevOps processes that match their contexts and requirements.

Keywords: Enterprise modeling · Software processes · Business process modeling · Devops · Goal modeling · Adaptive enterprise

1 Introduction

Enterprises are expected to continuously respond to ongoing changes and evolving environmental factors. Increasing competition and emergence of new market players from non-traditional sectors require enterprises to react and adapt to change more quickly than ever before [1, 2]. To this end, more and more enterprises are relying on software for the development and delivery of appropriate products and services. As a result, software processes are becoming an integral part of enterprise processes. Just like business processes (BPs), software development processes can vary significantly from organization to organization due to unique enterprise characteristics; these processes can be reconfigured in multiple ways to take account of enterprise variations and behavioral peculiarities so as to fulfill high-level enterprise requirements. However, current methods of modeling software process reconfigurations are limited in their ability to consider multiple enterprise perspectives and help choose

J. Ralyté et al. (Eds.): PoEM 2015, LNBIP 235, pp. 322–337, 2015.
DOI: 10.1007/978-3-319-25897-3_21

among alternate configurations. In this paper, we elaborate on the software process reconfigurations that are possible in the DevOps approach for the purpose of describing a Business Process Architecture (BPA) modeling technique, which allows the depiction and analysis of BP reconfigurations along multiple dimensions.

The term "DevOps" is a combination of two words "Development" and "Operations" and has been described and referred to as a phenomenon, a philosophy, a mindset, a set of techniques, a methodology, etc. DevOps is not a software tool or methodology per se, but rather an approach for rapidly and frequently delivering new software product features and service innovation. A recent Gartner news release predicted that "DevOps will evolve from a niche strategy employed by large cloud providers to a mainstream strategy employed by 25 % of Global 2000 organizations" [3]. Broadly speaking, DevOps attempts to introduce rapid delivery of product features, services and bug fixes to end-users through frequent release cycles, each containing a small feature set. Rapid delivery enables an enterprise to reduce the time-to-market for new products and features, provides greater customer centricity by introducing new features based on evolving customer needs, quickly resolves operational and support issues, and shows greater responsiveness to changing (internal and external) environment situations. DevOps enables the above by [4–6]:

- Automating activities in the overall software development process through the introduction of software tools and custom development of scripts, thus shortening the time required for new feature development and bug fixes through reduction of manual effort. This enables software teams to deliver more frequent releases to customers and the user base.
- Using feedback loops for continuously improving software development processes and development of product features through the monitoring and measurement of various software process and technical metrics. These metrics are then interpreted and utilized for overall process improvement.
- Promoting a culture of collaboration and information sharing between multiple teams. The traditional approach of having organization silos with defined boundaries and handover points is discouraged, and team members are expected to collectively collaborate towards the attainment of enterprise objectives.

The above characteristics are not unique to DevOps, and indeed, are generally applicable to enterprises with respect to enterprise agility and enterprise digital transformation [7]. Looking at software processes can provide insights into a broader context, such as the development and evolution of new products and services, many of which are digitally enabled. A BPA needs to be understood through a combination of these ideas and concepts, particularly in light of enterprise requirement for greater responsiveness and adaptability, with DevOps being a suitable example for such a study.

This paper is organized as follows. In Sect. 2, we introduce a DevOps-based motivating example that allows us to discuss the core concepts of this paper. In Sect. 3, we model a typical DevOps implementation using the BPA modeling technique and indicate possible areas and dimensions of software process variability. In Sect. 4, we refer to the related work, while in Sect. 5 we outline future directions of this research. Section 6 concludes this paper.

2 Motivating Example

DevOps is an interesting challenge for enterprise modeling for a number of reasons. As described above, DevOps involves diverse considerations from the viewpoints of process design, systems and tools development and deployment, and social and organizational issues. Continuous Integration (CI) and Continuous Deployment (CD) of product functionality and infrastructure setup are outcomes of DevOps [6]. The general area of continuous software engineering, CI and CD has been covered in both academic and industry literature with numerous published case studies [8]. Through CD, "companies could benefit from even shorter feedback loops, more frequent customer feedback, and the ability to more accurately validate whether the functionality that is developed corresponds to customer needs and behaviors" [8]. Studying all facets of the DevOps approach is thus best done through the enterprise modeling lens enabling a multi-perspective understanding of the various considerations.

Analyzing and deciding between various DevOps process reconfigurations can be done by considering enterprise objectives and benefits, which can be interpreted as functional requirements (FRs) and non-functional requirements (NFRs) from a process design perspective. The use of NFRs (represented by softgoals) in the requirements engineering discipline to evaluate and decide between variations and reconfigurations is well established [9]. Some of the NFRs, as present in a typical DevOps adoption, would be:

- **Agility and Adaptability:** Rapidly adapting to changing circumstances such as evolving customer behavior, regulatory environment, emerging technologies, etc.
- **Responsiveness:** Quickly responding to user feedback and change requests in the form of new product features and bug fixes.
- **Speed and Frequency:** Delivering new product features and bug fixes faster as well as having a high deployment frequency.
- **Efficiency:** Improvement in software process execution by automating key process segments and increasing collaboration between team members for greater information flow.
- **Customizability:** Being able to customize the behavior of the software development lifecycle based on changing contextual and situational needs.

Figure 1 shows a simple BPMN [10] process model indicating the primary participants and the major activities in a typical DevOps-inspired software process. We have developed this context by referencing published literature from multiple sources, such as [8, 11–14], with the intention of highlighting how the various process activities in DevOps can be better configured to serve a variety of enterprise FRs and NFRs.

In DevOps, the development of product features can be done using different development methodologies while adhering to different practices and policies specific to an enterprise adoption; in this context we assume the use of the Scrum project management methodology [14]. However, this general DevOps context is not intended to be an exhaustive depiction of variations in DevOps adoption in an enterprise setting, but rather is meant to illustrate variability in software process configurations. We consider four scenarios of variable behavior in this contextual setting, which correspond to the numbered annotations in the BPMN diagram:

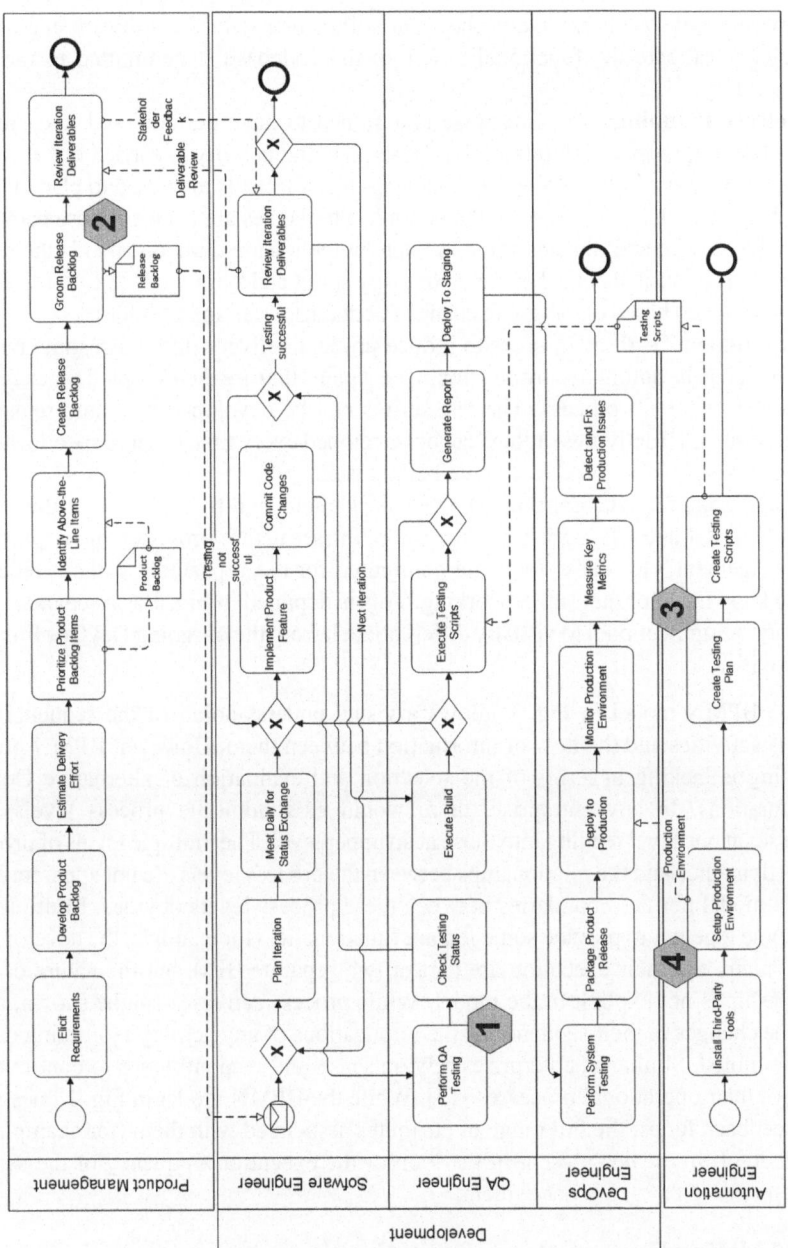

Fig. 1. A simple BPMN model representing a typical DevOps approach

1. **QA Testing:** Any developed feature has to be functional tested before it goes through the CD process. This testing can be carried out by QA engineers in at least two ways: they can retrieve the committed code from the code repository and test it on a test

environment, or alternatively, they can collaborate with the software engineer to quickly validate the functionality before the codebase is committed to the code repository.

2. **Release Planning:** The enterprise is assumed to have periodic and fixed release cycles of appropriate duration. A release planning activity is carried out at release initiation that results in a *release backlog*; this artifact is then used to plan out individual sprint iterations. Two of the possible alternatives are (1) the release backlog is produced once and remains static throughout the release duration and (2) the release backlog is revisited at the beginning of every sprint and "groomed" (i.e. reordered and re-estimated) based on on-going change in circumstances and priorities.

3. **Automated Testing:** In order to reduce product delivery durations, some product testing can be automated by developing test plans that are then scripted for execution as part of the CI process. The test scripts can be developed once and reused for subsequent CI activities or they can be developed every time to serve specific testing needs based on the product feature being tested.

4. **Tool Usage for Automation:** DevOps is characterized by the usage of third-party tools for CI and CD, server configuration, infrastructure provisioning, deployment management, etc. These tools are configured for use repeatedly without requiring the knowledge of their inner working. This is depicted in Fig. 1 as a separate Automation Engineer pool to visually differentiate it from the on-going DevOps Engineer activities.

The BPMN model in Fig. 1 allows a visual understanding of the sequencing of process activities and the flow of information between them. However, BPMN process modeling is lacking in terms of the selection and evaluation of alternative DevOps configurations. In any enterprise, there would exist multiple process levels, with processes at one level feeding into those at an upper level. The multiple levels of process-driven dynamics and the relationships between the process levels are not apparent in the BPMN model nor are boundaries between these process levels obvious. Multiple BPs may come together to provide some feature functionality (for example, the development of test plans and their execution are part of two separate BPs), but the nature of their relationship is not explicit in the model. While process activities can be shown, along with the changes in their sequencing, the implications of any activity reordering cannot be determined. Similarly, enterprises rely on sense-and-respond loops to continuously improve their operational processes [15]. While the BPMN model in Fig. 1 does show such feedback loops, the full range of attributes associated with them (for example, the multitude of timescales present in the loop or the execution frequency of the sensing and responding parts) are not evident.

3   Modeling Process Reconfigurations

The BPA modeling framework was introduced in [16, 17] for assisting with the modeling of BPs, their relationships, and the flexibility afforded by various BPA configurations. We use this framework to evaluate various DevOps reconfigurations and to choose among them. Fundamental concepts in the BPA framework are that of *Process Element* (PE), *Variation Point* (VP), *Stage* and *Phase* [16].

- A PE is defined as "an activity that produces some output or outcome. It may also include the act of making decisions".
- A VP is referred to "the point in a process where multiple options exist. Variation points may appear anywhere in a process".
- PEs are grouped together in process Stages if they are executed together as part of the same execution cycle. A *stage boundary* exists between two stages and PEs can be moved across stage boundaries as required while considering different trade-offs.
- A stage may contain one or more Phases, which are sections of a stage that are the "portions of a process such that placing a PE under consideration anywhere within a phase produces the same result...However, moving PEs across *phase boundaries* may affect the quality of decisions and the outcome of actions".

A PE can be repositioned along four dimensions in any process architecture. These four dimensions include, (1) *the temporal dimension* – positioning a PE either before or after other PEs (with respect to sequence of execution), (2) *the recurrence dimension* – positioning a PE in a stage that is executed more frequently or less frequently compared to other stages, (3) *the plan-execution dimension* – positioning a PE in a stage that either is responsible for planning or responsible for the execution of that plan, (4) *the design-use dimension* – positioning a PE in a stage that either is responsible for designing a tool, capability or artifact, or responsible for using the output of that design stage. These dimensions are discussed in more detail in the subsequent sub-sections.

Figure 2 shows a BPA model for the DevOps approach with multitudes of process elements, stages, phases and the relationships among them. The model visualizes the key aspects of software development and operational support processes that are commonly present in the DevOps approach starting from the Product Management stage to the Operational Support stage. For the sake of comprehension and understandability, we conceptually divide the model into multiple sections and consider them individually with regards to the overall DevOps approach as follows:

- **Product Management:** Product FRs and NFRs are elicited and gathered from a variety of sources (such as User Input and Business Need) and consolidated together. This is then used to develop a Product Backlog, which is frequently groomed for estimating and prioritizing individual Product Backlog Items (PBIs). The grooming exercise is a periodic process that runs at a higher recurrence than the requirements elicitation activity, which is denoted by the recurrence relationship between the two stages.
- **Development:** The model depicts the Scrum project management methodology with the various rituals and iterations shown as part of the Release Planning and Sprint Cycle stages. Evidence of recurrence is apparent in the usage of the Product Backlog over multiple Release Planning iterations. The Perform QA Testing process element can be used to demonstrate the temporal dimension as the testing can be done either before the code is committed to the source repository or after. Both options have different consequences as shall be seen in the Sect. 3.1.
- **Automated Testing:** The DevOps approach promotes the usage of tools and scripts for automating the testing of product features. For this, test plans and test scripts are created and are then used to automate the testing effort, whereas test plans are

implemented through test scripts. The test plans and test scripts are created in the Testing Plan stage and the test scripts are executed through the Execute Test Scripts PE (part of the Continuous Integration stage); these are illustrative of the plan-execute dimension.

- **Ongoing Deployment:** As with testing, the deployment of the developed product feature is ongoing, immediate and automated while factoring in the variable and multiple environments that the product would have to run on. The software deployment is automated through deployment scripts that are executed by various deployment tools; these scripts are developed by the DevOps engineers and executed as part of the Continuous Deployment stage that gets triggered on the successful completion of the Automated Testing and Continuous Integration stages.

- **Operational Support:** A major contribution of DevOps to software development is the breaking down of silos between the development and operational teams, thus fostering a culture of collaboration. The BPA models do not show process participants, so the collaborative aspect of DevOps is not visible. However, the Operational Support stage (along with the monitoring and measurement of operational metrics) is visually apparent, including the incorporation of software metrics into the product backlog (through a feedback loop) for ongoing software process lifecycle improvement.

The positioning of certain PEs in the DevOps approach are described in subsequent subsections along with the criteria for deciding among the options. Enterprises may want to analyze alternate positioning of PEs based on their FRs and NFRs. For this purpose, goal modeling can be used for representing the variations and helping select the appropriate alternative. NFRs are represented as softgoals and alternate methods of achieving a goal are represented as OR decompositions. Selection of a suitable alternative is made based on the positive and/or negative contribution(s) that the alternative would have on the NFRs (softgoals). The four scenarios described in the previous section (which also correspond to each of the four process architecture dimensions) are presented, with goal models shown alongside the BPA model snippets. In all goal model examples, the root goal can be achieved through two alternate sub-goals. The choices are limited to just two for brevity and space reasons. A real-world situation could contain many possible choices, as well as many competing and complementary NFRs. Also, the goals are shown at a PE level and decomposed down to just one level. In the general case, the goal model would start from enterprise-level goals, with multiple levels of goal refinement and alternatives until PE level sub-goals are reached [9].

3.1 The Temporal Dimension

The particular temporal placement of a PE can bring about certain benefits. A PE can either be advanced (and be executed) before other PEs or postponed after those PEs. Postponing a PE provides the benefit of executing it with the latest context and information available, thus reducing the risk and uncertainty that are inherent in any BP. The alternative is to advance the PE relative to other PEs, which reduces the complexity and cost as less effort is required to process the limited contextual information available at that instant. Uncertainty is also reduced. Therefore, the placement of any PE should be carefully considered with regards to various NFRs, subject to inherent temporal constraints among the PEs. The

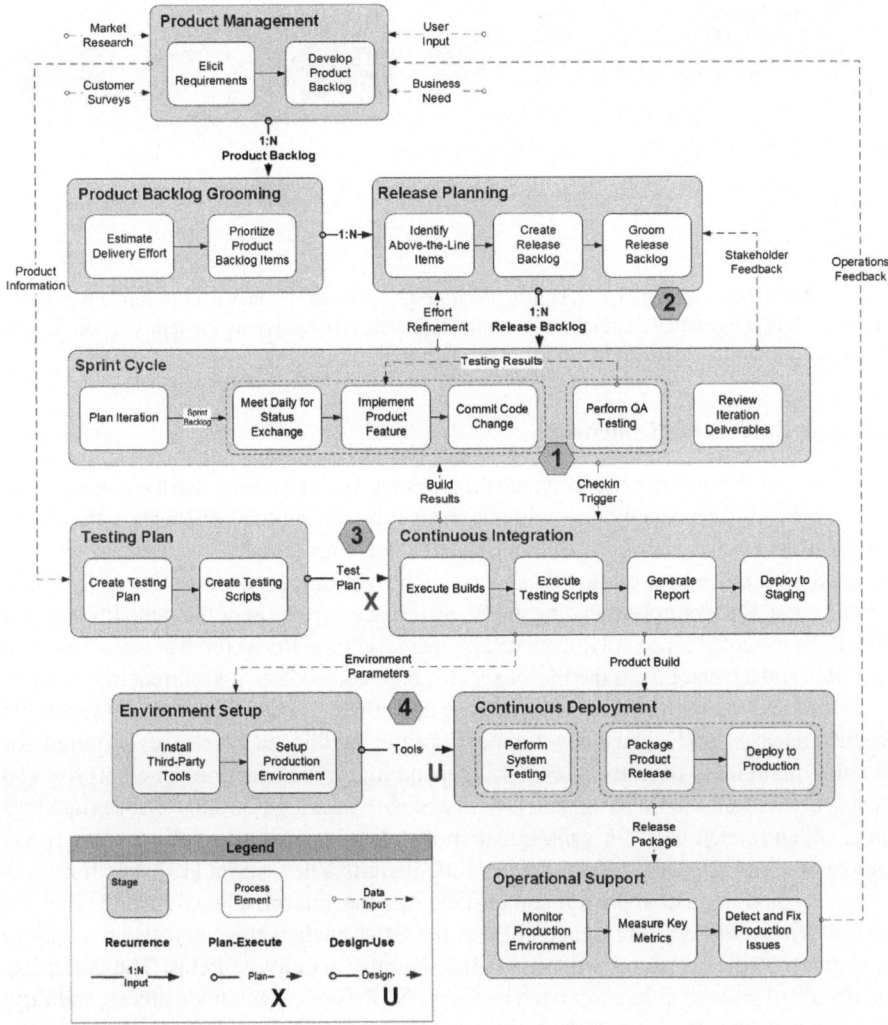

Fig. 2. Business process architecture (BPA) for a DevOps approach

testing of a product feature by a QA engineer illustrates the trade-offs between advancing and postponing a PE (Fig. 3). The QA engineer can verify the developed feature (Perform QA Testing) after the software engineer checks in the code to the code repository (Commit Code Changes) or before the code is checked in by working directly with the software engineer. As shown by the goal model, the latter approach has the benefit of being collaborative in nature and encouraging both the software engineer and QA engineer to work together to solve the problem quickly. The former approach is more methodological and allows for the proper (and independent) validation of the feature and the tracking of testing issues. The appropriate order of the Perform QA Testing PE is determined based on the organization's prioritization between the softgoals.

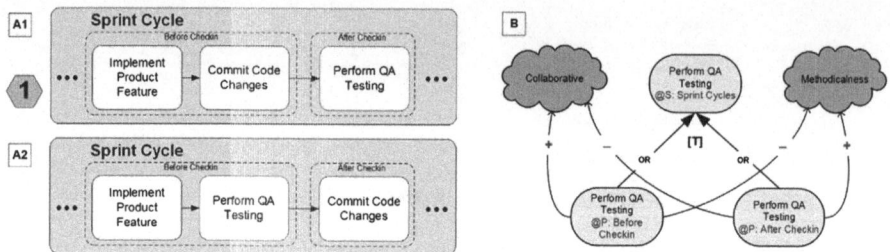

Fig. 3. QA testing alternatives (A1) as a separate phase from product feature implementation, (A2) as part of the product feature implementation phase. (B) Analyzing the temporal placement of QA testing process element based on NFRs.

3.2   The Recurrence Dimension

A recurrence relationship exists between the two stages of a process when the output of one stage can be used repeatedly (and without change) by the subsequent stage. A PE can be moved from a stage with a lower recurrence to one with a higher recurrence (and vice versa). Such a movement of the PE can change the non-functional properties of the BP in various ways. For example, reducing the PE recurrence saves cost as the same PE does not have to be executed repeatedly. Conversely, increasing the PE recurrence can assist with flexibility and adaptability as the PE is executed based on updated and current information.

In the DevOps approach, a product can be developed by having periodic and multiple product releases with many development sprints (within each release) required for attaining the release objectives (Fig. 4). Depending on the situation, an enterprise can create (Create Release Backlog) and groom a release backlog (Groom Release Backlog) once, which is then used for subsequent sprint planning. Alternatively, the enterprise can reassess the release objectives every time it starts a new sprint [13]. The former is a more methodological approach and ensures that the enterprise is aligned to what the release deliverable is going to be, whereas the latter enables the enterprise to adapt to changing priorities by constantly reviewing the release delivery items. The enterprise can decide to go with either approach based on NFRs such as methodicalness, stability, cost, adaptability, flexibility, etc., by moving the Groom Release Backlog between the Sprint Cycle and Release Planning stages.

3.3   The Plan-Execute Dimension

A BP can be considered to have two distinct segments, where one segment is responsible for creating a plan, which the other segment would then execute one or many times. Here, a plan-execute relationship exists between the two segments of the process. In the BPA modeling technique, each segment is modeled as a stage, with the stage producing the plan being the *planning stage* and the stage executing it being the *execution stage*. PEs can also be moved from an execution stage to a planning stage (and vice versa) based on the goal-driven analysis of their contribution to the relevant NFRs. Such movements create variations in the plan-execute behavior and allow either increased

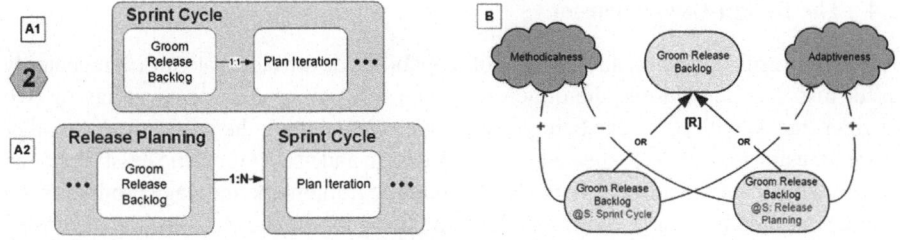

Fig. 4. Release backlog grooming alternatives (A1) as part of the sprint cycle stage with no recurrence, (A2) moved to the release planning stage with a multi-recurrence dimension between both stages. (B) Analyzing the recurrence arrangement of the release backlog grooming and sprint planning stages based on NFRs.

pre-planning (by moving a PE to the planning stage) or shifting more responsibility to the execution side (by moving a PE to the execution stage).

Typically, testing plans are created (Create Testing Plan) for enabling automated testing. They are then coded up (Create Testing Scripts) in the form of testing scripts by the DevOps engineer and repeatedly executed (Execute Testing Scripts). As shown in Fig. 5, there are two possibilities with respect to the creation of the testing scripts. One is to create the testing scripts for every instance of automated testing so that the scripts are customized to the particular feature being tested (Create Testing Scripts PE is part of the Continuous Integration stage), whereas the other is to have a consistent and standard set of testing scripts that would allow testing coverage irrespective of particular product features being developed (Create Testing Scripts PE is part of the Testing Plan stage). The trade-offs would be between customized behavior and efficiency; on the one hand, the repeated creation of testing scripts would allow specific and customized testing, while in the other case, the development lifecycle automation would be higher. Enterprises would have to choose the appropriate configuration based on their situational and contextual needs.

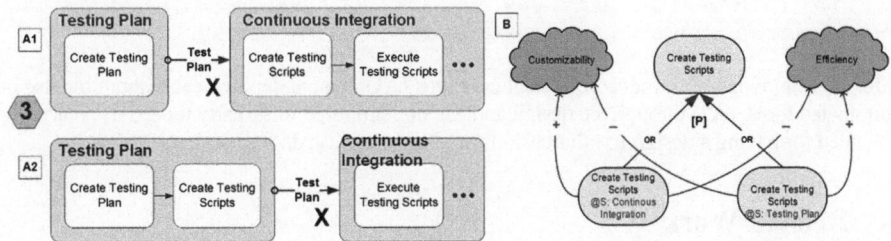

Fig. 5. Test scripts creation placement alternatives (A1) as part of the continuous integration stage with increase customizability of testing, (A2) as part of the testing plan stage leading to greater efficiency and reuse. (B) Analyzing the placement of test script creation along the plan-execute dimension while considering trade-offs for NFRs.

3.4 The Design-Use Dimension

A BP can result in the creation of a tool, capability or artifact that can be repeatedly used. Just like the plan-execute dimension, such BPs can be considered as having two distinct stages, with one stage being responsible for designing the artifact and the other stage for using that artifact repeatedly. Thus, a design and use relationship exists between these segments of the process. In the BPA modeling framework, the stage producing the artifact is called the *design stage* and the stage using the artifact is called the *use stage*. The use stage uses the artifact repeatedly without necessarily being aware of the inner working of that artifact. PEs can also be moved from a design stage to a use stage (and vice versa), with such a repositioning either leading to an increased design/artifact sophistication/automation or to trading the design effort for run-time usage control/customizability.

The DevOps approach emphasizes greater automation of the software development lifecycle through the use of tools. A number of third-party tools are available (e.g., Jenkins[1] for CI, Chef[2] for deployment management, Github[3] for source repository and Splunk[4] for application monitoring etc.), which provide such automation of process activities. These tools are configured (designed) for use in any particular DevOps implementation and thus enable a move from manual methods of product deployment (shown by the Manual Deployment stage in Fig. 6) to more automated and CD cycles (shown by the Environment Setup design stage and the Continuous Deployment use stage). However, the introduction of any artifact in the design-use dimension should be evaluated against the NFRs (as shown by the goal model).

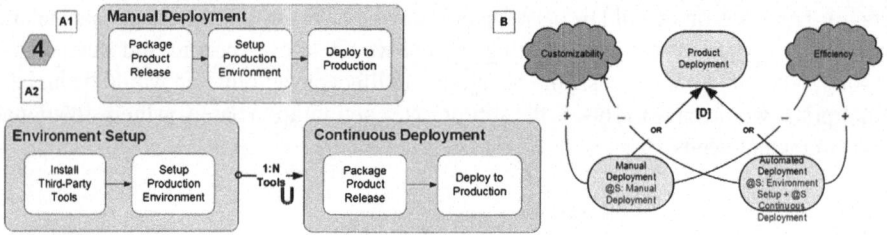

Fig. 6. Deployment of product release alternatives (A1) manual deployment without the use of automated tools, (A2) through the design and use of configured third-party tools. (B) Analyzing the need for having a design-use dimension for product release deployment.

4   Related Work

CI and CD are well understood concepts in continuous software engineering where the objective is to deliver ongoing software product improvement and enhancements in less

---

[1] https://jenkins-ci.org/.

[2] https://www.chef.io/.

[3] https://github.com/.

[4] http://www.splunk.com/.

time and greater frequency through improved process automation and introduction of suitable software tools [8]. Generally, any organization would have multitudes of software processes to handle different project development situations; appropriate software processes are selected based on situational needs and business context [18]. Software process tailoring refers to the customization of standard software planning, development and operational processes [19] in situations where organizations need an enterprise-level assessment on how environmental factors, product and project goals, and other organizational aspects influence software process configurations. Commonalities and variabilities exist between these software processes and, as such, these software processes can be tailored to meet specific enterprise business and operational goals and objectives using different techniques for decision making [20, 21].

Several software process modeling techniques exist and are primarily based on process modeling languages (such as BPMN), Unified Modeling Language (UML) or Software & Systems Engineering Metamodel (SPEM) [22]. Apart from a few (such as [23, 24]), most of the software process modeling frameworks do not provide support for modeling variability in software process configurations and the ability to reason about them while taking enterprise- and process-level NFRs into consideration.

Enterprises attempt to reduce development effort and increase the range of product features offered through software product lines (SPLs). SPLs can be used to support multiple software products through the development of common software architecture(s) and code components. SPLs rely on variation points to support software product variability [25]. Delaying decisions during the development cycles of these SPLs provides the benefit of allowing the optimization of technical and business goals (e.g., increased code reuse) across multiple products, possibly at the expense of other goals (e.g., simpler architecture). Extending the idea of SPLs to processes results in the notion of Software *Process* Lines (SPrL) [26], which is based on a similar premise: similarities and differences between a set of software processes could be scoped for determining customized software process configurations as per unique software project conditions. In [27], the idea of (software) Process Line Architectures (PLA) is introduced. A PLA is described as "a process structure which reflects the commonality and variability in a collection of processes that make up a process line from the perspective of overall optimization". Like a BPA, a PLA also represents the existence of VPs in (software) processes. However, it does not support the placement of a process element along the four dimensions as described in this paper.

Previous research on BPAs largely focused on the nature of the relationships among their BPs. Various relationship types were proposed (e.g., [28, 29]), such as sequence, reference, composition, etc. Unlike most BPA approaches, we focus on systematically analyzing multiple BPA alternatives along the four variability dimensions with the aim at finding the one that best matches the properties of the domain.

Another relevant domain is BP variability modeling that focuses on representing customizable BP models and deriving custom variants from them (see [30] for an overview), with the key element being a VP, which is used to represent and bind variability. Overall, these approaches deliberate about variability only at the process level (within a single process) and do not support reasoning about BPAs. In dealing with BP flexibility, Weber et al. [31] propose four dimensions of change, including the one focusing on the recurrence of activity execution. While somewhat similar to our approach, it neglects trade-offs among the various options and does not cover flexibility in BPAs. Feature models [32] are sometimes employed as a useful abstraction to help guide BP customization (i.e., selecting or deriving a BP variant from a customizable process model). While a viable option, feature models (unlike goal models used here) lack the ability to represent selection criteria and support trade-off analysis among configuration alternatives.

5 Future Work

In future iterations of this work we plan to study the following:

- Many enterprises are becoming critically dependent on software and software processes to create and deliver value to their stakeholders in the form of products and services. Successfully introducing software process reconfigurations in response to changing business models or strategic direction may impact the ongoing delivery of value, product and services [33]. We aim to link the impact of software process reconfigurations to business goals and value in order to exploit synergies and mitigate negative consequences.
- We wish to understand the possible forms of software process reconfigurations with the intention of identifying key points of process variations and the influencing factors that contribute towards these process reconfigurations. Requirements for software process reconfiguration are usually developed in response to shifting enterprise objectives, adaptability requirements and emerging digital technologies in the enterprise context. The relationship between these requirements and their influence on variation points for software processes would need to be understood.
- Processes are executed by participants or actors in any enterprise. Changes in organizational structure and team dynamics would invariably influence process configurations (and vice versa). For example, any process reconfiguration would possibly shift the boundaries of actor influence with some actors gaining responsibility and other actors losing responsibility or power. Conversely, changing an actor's boundary of influence may also require the selection of an alternate process configuration to successfully attain the same set of goals. The association of operational process level concerns and social organizational considerations needs to be studied and developed by combining the BPA technique (for process representation) with a social actor modeling framework, such as $i*$ [34].
- Enterprises take advantage of software metrics to routinely and incrementally improve on software processes. While software metrics are well documented [35], illustrating and analyzing the integration and usage of these software metrics for ongoing software process improvements, through the use of enterprise modeling techniques, is not well covered. The BPA can be continuously refined through use of software metrics and data analytics in all stages of the feedback loop – i.e., sensing, interpreting, deciding and acting.

We are exploring methods and techniques from diverse areas, including software engineering, requirements engineering, system dynamics, and management literature, to contribute towards a framework for the management of enterprise software process variability. We are developing a meta-model and an ontology to understand the nature of software process variability and to extend existing enterprise modeling techniques to incorporate attributes and constructs for denoting variability and flexibility in software processes. Finally, we aim to validate such a proposed framework by conducting case studies for various types of enterprises.

6   Conclusions

Every enterprise relies on various BPs for proper functioning, which can take many forms and can include operational, transactional, strategic, recurring, design processes, etc. Having uniform and static processes is no longer an option for enterprises dealing with a multitude of dynamically changing situations that require periodic adjustment of process configurations [36, 37]. A recent report from Gartner mentions that "by 2017, 70 % of successful digital business models will rely on deliberately unstable processes designed to shift as customer needs shift" [38]. In this paper, we considered the possible dimensions of software process reconfigurability using the DevOps approach as a motivating example. Limitations of current process modeling languages, such as BPMN, in illustrating multiple aspects of process architecture were discussed, with the BPA modeling technique being used to describe four dimensions of PE positioning, namely, temporal, recurrence, plan-execute, and design-use, in a typical DevOps implementation. Goal models were used for evaluating alternate software process reconfigurations by assessing the satisfaction of enterprise NFRs.

References

1. Wilkinson, M.: Designing an "adaptive" enterprise architecture. BT Technol. J. **24**(4), 81–92 (2006)
2. The Economist: Organisational agility: how business can survive and thrive in turbulent times. A report from The Economist Intelligence Unit (2009)
3. Gartner Research: Gartner says by 2016, DevOps will evolve from a niche to a mainstream strategy employed by 25 percent of global 2000 organizations. http://www.gartner.com/newsroom/id/2999017. Accessed 5 March 2015
4. Erich, F., Amrit, C., Daneva, M.: A mapping study on cooperation between information system development and operations. In: Jedlitschka, A., Kuvaja, P., Kuhrmann, M., Männistö, T., Münch, J., Raatikainen, M. (eds.) PROFES 2014. LNCS, vol. 8892, pp. 277–280. Springer, Heidelberg (2014)
5. Bang, S.K., Chung, S., Choh, Y., Dupuis, M.: A grounded theory analysis of modern web applications: knowledge, skills, and abilities for DevOps. In: Proceedings of the 2nd Annual Conference on Research in Information Technology, pp. 61–62. ACM (2013)
6. Lwakatare, L.E., Kuvaja, P., Oivo, M.: Dimensions of DevOps. In: Lassenius, C., Dingsøyr, T., Paasivaara, M. (eds.) XP 2015. LNBIP, vol. 212, pp. 212–217. Springer, Heidelberg (2015)

7. Smeds, J., Nybom, K., Porres, I.: DevOps: a definition and perceived adoption impediments. In: Lassenius, C., Dingsøyr, T., Paasivaara, M. (eds.) XP 2015. LNBIP, vol. 212, pp. 166–177. Springer, Heidelberg (2015)

8. Bosch, J. (Ed.): Continuous Software Engineering. Springer (2014)

9. Lapouchnian, A., Yu, Y., Mylopoulos, J.: Requirements-driven design and configuration management of business processes. In: Alonso, G., Dadam, P., Rosemann, M. (eds.) BPM 2007. LNCS, vol. 4714, pp. 246–261. Springer, Heidelberg (2007)

10. Business Process Model and Notation, v2.0. http://www.omg.org/spec/BPMN/2.0/PDF/

11. Ståhl, D., Bosch, J.: Modeling continuous integration practice differences in industry software development. J. Syst. Softw. **87**, 48–59 (2014)

12. Paasivaara, M., Durasiewicz, S., Lassenius, C.: Using scrum in distributed agile development: a multiple case study. In: Fourth IEEE International Conference on Global Software Engineering, ICGSE 2009, pp. 195–204. IEEE (2009)

13. Fitzgerald, B., Stol, K.J.: Continuous software engineering and beyond: trends and challenges. In: Proceedings of the 1st International Workshop on Rapid Continuous Software Engineering, pp. 1–9. ACM (2014)

14. Schwaber, K., Beedle, M.: Agile Software Development with Scrum. Prentice Hall, Upper Saddle River (2002)

15. Haeckel, S.H.: Adaptive Enterprise: Creating and Leading Sense-And-Respond Organizations. Harvard Business Press, Boston (1999)

16. Lapouchnian, A., Yu, E., Sturm, A.: Re-designing process architectures towards a framework of design dimensions. In: 2015 IEEE 9th International Conference on Research Challenges in Information Science (RCIS), pp. 205–210. IEEE, Chicago (2015)

17. Lapouchnian, A., Yu, E., Sturm, A.: Towards variability design for business process architecture. In: 34th International Conference on Conceptual Modeling (2015) (Accepted)

18. Alegría, J.A.H., Bastarrica, M.C.: Building software process lines with CASPER. In: 2012 International Conference on Software and System Process (ICSSP), pp. 170–179. IEEE (2012)

19. Pedreira, O., Piattini, M., Luaces, M.R., Brisaboa, N.R.: A systematic review of software process tailoring. ACM SIGSOFT Softw. Eng. Notes **32**(3), 1–6 (2007)

20. Martinez-Ruiz, T., Garcia, F., Piattini, M., Munch, J.: Modelling software process variability: an empirical study. Softw. IET **5**(2), 172–187 (2011)

21. Martínez-Ruiz, T., García, F., Piattini, M.: Managing process diversity by applying rationale management in variant rich processes. In: Caivano, D., Oivo, M., Baldassarre, M.T., Visaggio, G. (eds.) PROFES 2011. LNCS, vol. 6759, pp. 128–142. Springer, Heidelberg (2011)

22. García-Borgoñon, L., Barcelona, M.A., García-García, J.A., Alba, M., Escalona, M.J.: Software process modeling languages: a systematic literature review. Inf. Softw. Technol. **56**(2), 103–116 (2014)

23. Cares, C., Mayol, E., Franch, X., Alvarez, E., Goal-driven agent-oriented software processes. In: Proceedings of the 32nd Euromicro Conference on Software Engineering and Advanced Applications, SEAA, Cavtat/Dubrovnik, Croatia, pp. 336–343 (2006)

24. Washizaki, H.: Deriving project-specific processes from process line architecture with commonality and variability. In: Proceedings of the IEEE International Conference on Industrial Informatics (INDIN 2006), Singapore, pp. 1301–1306 (2007)

25. Van Gurp, J., Bosch, J., Svahnberg, M.: On the notion of variability in software product lines. In: Working IEEE/IFIP Conference on Software Architecture. Proceedings, pp. 45–54. IEEE (2001)

26. Rombach, H.D.: Integrated software process and product lines. In: Li, M., Boehm, B., Osterweil, L.J. (eds.) SPW 2005. LNCS, vol. 3840, pp. 83–90. Springer, Heidelberg (2006)
27. Washizaki, H.: Building software process line architectures from bottom up. In: Münch, J., Vierimaa, M. (eds.) PROFES 2006. LNCS, vol. 4034, pp. 415–421. Springer, Heidelberg (2006)
28. Dumas, M., La Rosa, M., Mendling, J., Reijers, H.: Fundamentals of Business Process Management, Chap. 2. Springer, Heidelberg (2013)
29. Eid-Sabbagh, R.-H., Dijkman, R., Weske, M.: Business process architecture: use and correctness. In: Barros, A., Gal, A., Kindler, E. (eds.) BPM 2012. LNCS, vol. 7481, pp. 65–81. Springer, Heidelberg (2012)
30. La Rosa, M., Aalst, W.M.P. van der, Dumas, M., Milani, F.P.: Business process variability modeling: a survey. ACM Computing Surveys (2013)
31. Weber, B., Reichert, M., Rinderle-Ma, S.: Change patterns and change support features – enhancing flexibility in process-aware information systems. Data Knowl. Eng. **66**(3), 438–466 (2008)
32. Kang, K., Cohen, S., Hess, J., Novak, W., Peterson, A.: Feature-oriented domain analysis (FODA) feasibility study. Technical Report CMU/SEI-90-TR-21, SEI, Carnegie Mellon University (1990)
33. Esfahani, H.C., Yu, E., Annosi, M.C.: Strategically balanced process adoption. In: Proceedings of the 2011 International Conference on Software and Systems Process, pp. 169–178. ACM (2011)
34. Yu, E., Giorgini, P., Maiden, N., Mylopoulos, J.: Social Modeling for Requirements Engineering. MIT Press, Cambridge (2011)
35. Fenton, N., Bieman, J.: Software Metrics: Rigorous and Practical Approach. CRC Press, Boca Raton (2014)
36. Yu, E., Deng, S., Sasmal, D.: Enterprise architecture for the adaptive enterprise – a vision paper. In: Aier, S., Ekstedt, M., Matthes, F., Proper, E., Sanz, J.L. (eds.) PRET 2012 and TEAR 2012. LNBIP, vol. 131, pp. 146–161. Springer, Heidelberg (2012)
37. Yu, E., Lapouchnian, A.: Architecting the enterprise to leverage a confluence of emerging technologies. In: Proceedings of the 2013 CASCON. IBM Corporation (2013)
38. Spender, A.: Top 10 strategic technology predictions for 2015 and beyond, gartner research. http://www.gartner.com/smarterwithgartner/top-10-strategic-technology-predictions-for-2015-and-beyond/. Accessed 18 February 2015

Engineering Methods

Simplicity is not Simple: How Business Architecture in One of Belgium's Biggest Companies Can Be Simple and Easy-to-Use

Dave De Clercq, Maxime Bernaert, Ben Roelens[(⊠)], and Geert Poels

Department of Business Informatics and Operations Management,
Faculty of Economics and Business Administration, Ghent University,
Tweekerkenstraat 2, 9000 Ghent, Belgium
{Dave.DeClercq,Maxime.Bernaert,Ben.Roelens,
Geert.Poels}@UGent.be

Abstract. As organizations are becoming more complex, Enterprise Architecture (EA) serves as an important means to align the strategy with the operations and to achieve business/IT (i.e., Information Technology) alignment. Although numerous approaches have been designed for large enterprises, little EA research was oriented towards small- and medium-sized enterprises (SMEs). However, both organizational types are fundamentally different and require a tailored approach. Therefore, CHOOSE was designed as an EA approach that is in accordance with the needs of SMEs. By performing a case study in the department of a large enterprise, this paper aims to investigate how CHOOSE can be used outside its original context. More specifically, it will be examined how the metamodel and modeling method could be extended to deliver an overview and valuable insights about a complex business reality. To realize this, potential solutions for the encountered issues are formulated and evaluated by the involved business stakeholders.

Keywords: Enterprise architecture · Small- and medium-sized enterprise · CHOOSE approach · Case study

1 Introduction

EA is a crucial aspect to manage the complexity of an organization by using a coherent whole of principles, methods, and models that offer a holistic view on the design and realization of the enterprise's organizational structure, business processes, information systems, and infrastructure [1, 2]. This holistic view of the enterprise is considered as the (end) product of an EA approach, which could be used as a communication device among the various stakeholders of a company [2]. Furthermore, EA facilitates the realization of business/IT alignment as it provides insights in how to derive value by keeping information system requirements in line with the business needs [3, 4].

EA has become a fairly mature domain when it comes to large enterprises, but it neglected SMEs for a long time [5]. As a result, SMEs perceive most existing EA techniques as being complex and over-engineered [6]. Consequently, EA models are hard to understand and thus are inefficient as a communication instrument or as a

© IFIP International Federation for Information Processing 2015
J. Ralyté et al. (Eds.): PoEM 2015, LNBIP 235, pp. 341–355, 2015.
DOI: 10.1007/978-3-319-25897-3_22

support for the strategic reasoning process. This difference in perception is not surprising as SMEs and large enterprises conduct business in a fundamentally different fashion [7]. Indeed, SMEs are confronted with problems concerning lack of structure and overview [8]. In contrast, most large enterprises have elaborate organizational structures, documented in the form of an organigram. However, large enterprises cope with problems concerning complexity, which is the result of increasingly complex IT systems and of the globalization in the expanding market space. Moreover, knowledge is less centralized within large enterprises as they have resources for consulting aid in a full scale implementation [9]. Consequently, SMEs require a different approach than the existing EA techniques. Therefore, the CHOOSE approach was specifically designed to bring EA towards SMEs [8].

Nevertheless, the operations department of KBC Asset Management (KBC AM), a Belgian bank, showed interest in CHOOSE for a strategy-operations alignment process. As KBC AM does not qualify as an SME, CHOOSE may not be suitable in this context. Furthermore, there is no such thing as a "one size fits all" technique. Initial tests with the CHOOSE approach in the operations department yielded a complex model, which was hard to understand and thus not ideal for communication. Therefore, adaptations were needed to make the complex matter clear and useful.

The goal of this research is to investigate how CHOOSE can be used in the operations department of KBC AM. Using CHOOSE out of its intended context can yield valuable insights to make the metamodel and modeling method more robust and to increase its potential for a wider applicability in large enterprises. This includes an analysis about how the metamodel can be extended to be usable in the search for alignment and communication and to deliver a clear overview in a complex matter for management. Furthermore, the supporting method is discussed and compared with the existing CHOOSE modeling method.

The paper is structured as follows. In Sect. 2, the EA approach CHOOSE is briefly explained. The research methodology (Sect. 3) guides the execution of the case study in Sect. 4. Section 5 presents the insights of this case study, which result in extensions to the metamodel and modeling method of the CHOOSE approach. Finally, Sect. 6 provides the conclusions and suggestions for future research.

2   CHOOSE Approach

CHOOSE is an acronym for 'keep Control, by means of a Holistic Overview, based on Objectives and kept Simple, of your Enterprise'. In other words, this EA approach wants to control the complexity of an SME by offering a holistic overview of its essential organizational elements, such as the corporate strategy, the business processes, the information systems, and IT systems [10]. Furthermore, this approach takes into account the specific characteristics and attributes of SMEs by adhering to six requirements for the adoption and successful use of IT in SMEs [10]: (i) the approach should enable SMEs to work in a time-efficient manner on strategic issues, (ii) a person with limited IT skills should be able to apply the approach, (iii) it should be possible to apply the approach with little assistance of external experts, (iv) the approach should enable to make descriptions of the processes in the company, (v) the CEO must be involved in the approach, and (vi) the expected revenues of the approach must exceed the expected costs and risks. Consequently, the application of the CHOOSE approach will result in an EA model, which is understandable and adaptable by non-experts in an SME. Therefore, the approach was explicitly designed based on simplicity, which supports the communication between the various stakeholders [1] and is key in controlling the complexity of an organization [10].

The CHOOSE approach consists of a metamodel, a modeling method and tool support. The metamodel development was guided by requirements to enable SMEs to create simple, but comprehensive models of their enterprise [8]. The model presents a holistic overview of the organization by using elements of the business, information, and technology EA perspectives [11]. The metamodel (see Fig. 1) consists of elements that address four dimensions: (i) strategic goals (i.e., yellow color), (ii) actors (i.e., red color), (iii) operations (i.e., purple color) and (iv) objects (i.e., green color).

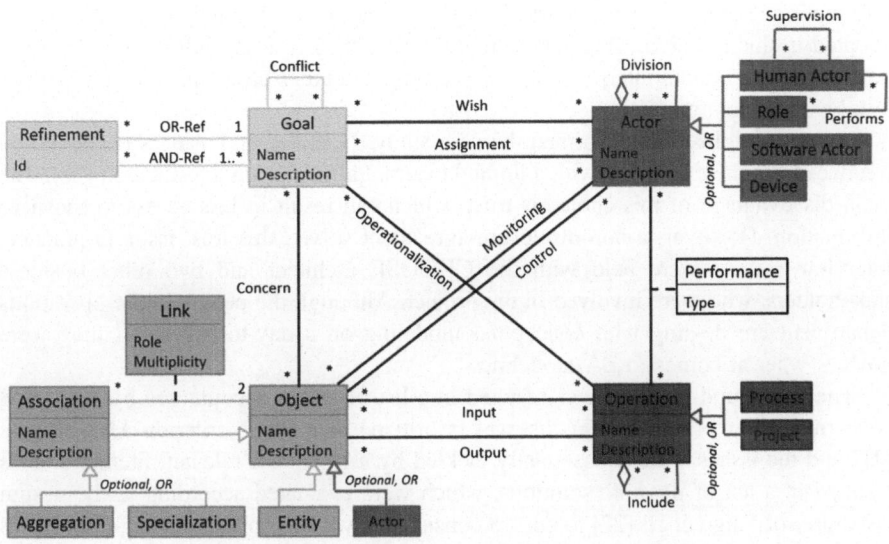

Fig. 1. CHOOSE metamodel [8] (Color figure online)

The CHOOSE modeling method consists of a six-stage roadmap, supported by a three-step interview-method and two-fold stop criteria for each dimension [12]. The roadmap guides the construction of a CHOOSE model and is built around two frameworks: (i) the Balanced ScoreCard (BSC) [13] and (ii) Porter's value chain [14]. It starts with defining high-level goals for each of the four BSC dimensions. In a second step, these goals are broke down to lower-level objectives by using why-how questioning [7]. Thereafter, the actor, operation and object dimensions are added to the model. The interview-method describes best practices to structure interviews with stakeholders, while the stop criteria delineate when a model is complete. Tool support is the last element of the CHOOSE approach, which has already been developed for different platforms (e.g., see [15–17]). These software tools are a crucial element in the process of bringing EA towards SMEs, as it lowers the threshold and increases the rate of adoption [12].

3   Methodology

This research is situated in the field of Information Systems, which is concerned with the interaction between social and technical issues. In other words, the emphasis is put on the link between human and social aspects within an organizational setting and the hardware and data aspects of IT [18]. Qualitative case study research was used as Information Systems research strategy to describe the organizational phenomena in its natural setting and to grasp the complexity of this setting. This included the use of interviews as the main method for obtaining information. Nevertheless, other data collection methods were used to increase the reliability of the data (i.e., physical artifacts, documentation and archival records) [19]. As the only way to access this information is trough social constructs (e.g., language), an interpretive perspective was adopted in this research. This perspective is often chosen in the Information Systems field to capture human interpretations concerning computer-based information systems in a business context [20].

An outside observer performed the case study. In this way, business people could freely express their opinions with a limited external influence on the situation [20]. The main disadvantage of this choice is trust, which can result in less access to sensitive information. However, a non-disclosure-agreement solved this trust issue in practice. Interview rounds were held with the CHOOSE architect and two other business stakeholders, who were involved in the project. Although the people in the operations department are dealing with conceptual modeling on a day-to-day basis, they were novices when it comes to EA modeling.

The first round of interviews resulted in a list of issues encountered by KBC AM concerning the metamodel. This list was prioritized by a single-criterion AHP process [21] and the issues were subsequently tackled by a review of relevant literature. This resulted in a list of possible solutions, which were evaluated according to the design principles of Paige et al. [22] to ensure consistency with the original design principles of the CHOOSE modeling language. In this respect, the relevant criteria are simplicity (i.e., no unnecessary complexity is introduced), uniqueness (i.e., no redundant or overlapping features), and consistency (i.e., language features meet design goals). This provided input for a second interview round, during which the involved business people qualitatively evaluated the proposed improvements. This evaluation was performed based on two criteria, which were considered as important by the stakeholders in the business context: (i) 'added value' and (ii) 'time efficiency'.

In the first interview, the method that was used in practice was also explained. This ad-hoc method stands far from the existing CHOOSE modeling method, but enabled us to derive some shortcomings and promising elements. Although not explicitly evaluated, this analysis can provide a starting point to guide the further application of CHOOSE in large organizations.

4   Case Study

4.1   General

KBC Bank, which was founded in 1998, is a subsidiary of KBC group NV through a series of mergers and acquisitions since 2005 [23]. By 2015, the group is the 18th largest bank insurer in Europe with main markets in Belgium and Eastern Europe.

KBC AM is one of three subsidiaries of KBC group NV, which is mainly responsible for the management of the investment portfolios, giving investment advice and other general activities [23]. The activities are geographically dispersed in Belgium, Luxemburg, Ireland, Czech Republic and Slovakia. The office in Brussels houses the general activities, such as operations, database management and architecture. This operations department does not manage portfolios itself, which is the job of the competence centers. Each center is specialized in a certain type of product and disposes of the appropriate supporting technology. The office in Brussels employs approximately 300 people and qualifies as a large organization according to the European definition of SMEs [24]. In addition, the banking industry places some specific demands on the architecture, coming from the BASEL II norms [1].

4.2   Project Description

The project was conducted in the operations department of the KBC AM subsidiary to realize two main goals: (i) creating an entrepreneurial mindset and (ii) strategy-operations alignment. The first goal included motivating the personnel to be entrepreneurs and to undertake initiatives. This was considered difficult in a static operations environment as resistance to change could be expected. For the second objective, it was preferable that the undertaken initiatives are aligned with the defined corporate and operations strategy. Therefore, it was important to explain the workforce how their daily activities contribute to the fulfillment of the strategy. This objective is closely related to the main purpose of EA as proposed by Lankhorst [1]: "Translating the goals into concrete changes to the daily operations of the company is where EA comes into play". The choice for an appropriate EA approach was guided by the belief that simplicity was key in this project, in order to enable a clear communication with the workforce. Consequently, CHOOSE's focus on simplicity and easiness-to-use made it a suitable alternative [8].

The operations department had two distinct applications in mind for the CHOOSE approach:

- Gap analysis: the definition of a to-be model, starting from the as-is model. The to-be model is constructed by omitting existing elements and introducing new elements in the as-is model. Comparing these two versions should result in the identification of discrepancies or redundancies.
- Impact analysis: investigating the impact of changes (e.g., omitting an existing or adding a new goal) on the other elements in the EA (e.g., employees, IT systems, business processes, etc.). During the interviews, the impact analysis was focused on

'introducing a new product' because of the rapidly changing market conditions and the shortening life cycle of banking products.

5   CHOOSE Refinements

5.1   General

The initial CHOOSE modeling efforts yielded a complex model, which prevented to offer a clear overview of the enterprise. In this context, the main issue was the diagrammatic complexity (i.e., too many model elements and relations between them) [25], which reduces cognitive efficiency and the usability of the model as a tool for strategic reasoning.

To solve this problem, it was decided to use modularization (i.e., one model for each of the three departments) to decrease the number of elements displayed in a certain model. This should lead to an easier and faster understanding of the underlying content. This is particularly useful for novice users, who have more difficulties of coping with complexity than experts [26]. However, as this approach considers separate parts of the organization, the holistic overview may get lost. This is important as it is a major advantage of the CHOOSE approach [8]. Therefore, modularization is ideally included in the software tool to enable an easy switch between the complete model and specific departmental views.

Furthermore, it was not necessary to focus on all CHOOSE dimensions in the model. In this respect, viewpoints provide a means to focus on certain aspects of an architectural model [25]. The choice of these aspects is dependent on the stakeholder with whom communication takes place [1]. In the alignment project, the developed viewpoint focused on the goal dimension of the CHOOSE approach to support the communication with the employees. This allowed to illustrate how individual objectives contribute to the high-level goals and key performance indicators (KPIs). Due to confidentiality restrictions, it is however not possible to show this viewpoint here.

5.2   Metamodel

Issues and Solutions. During the interviews, we identified eight issues regarding the CHOOSE metamodel. In Table 1, these issues are ranked according to their importance, which was determined by using a single-criterion AHP procedure [21]. In the next paragraphs, solutions are formulated for each problem and an alternative is chosen according to the relevant design principles of Paige et al. [22] (i.e., simplicity, uniqueness, and consistency). Afterwards, these solutions are evaluated by the business stakeholders, who were involved in the case study.

Issue 1: Neutral for Positional Changes. The most important problem was expressed by the CHOOSE architect as: "In a large enterprise, people often change seats. The metamodel should be neutral for this, to guarantee maintainability". 'The seats'

Table 1. Prioritized list of issues regarding the CHOOSE metamodel.

Issue	Description	Issue	Description
1	Neutral for positional changes	5	Complex IT structures
2	Department dimension	6	Terminology
3	Gap analysis	7	National dimension
4	Capacity measures	8	Process flows

resemble functions, modeled as a *Role* construct that is performed by a *Human Actor* (see Fig. 1). People change functions quite often, but the content of these functions does not. Thus, the *Role* construct should be modeled independently from the *Human Actor* construct. Due to extra constraints, this was not possible when building CHOOSE models.

A potential solution is to use the *Role* construct, without specifying the *Human Actor* that performs this *Role*. In this way, the model content will not be affected when people are changing seats. Other solutions could be suggested, but this solution was preferred based on the uniqueness principle.

Issue 2: Department Dimension. It is possible to model business units in CHOOSE, but at KBC AM they felt the need to model actors on different levels of granularity to express their organizational structure (i.e., the different departments that are part the organization) in the model.

Potential solutions are:

- Introduce an extra metamodel element, *Department*, as specialization of the *Actor* class. Consequently, the different business units, which are defined in the *Division* relation, make up such a department.
- Introduce a *Department* attribute for the aggregation relation *Division*. By doing this, queries should be able to show the different departments.
- Make a model for each department separately.

In this case, the second option was chosen, as the explicit purpose of the *Division* relation is to model the organizational structure. This coincides with the uniqueness and simplicity principle.

Issue 3: Gap Analysis. As mentioned above (cfr., Sect. 4.2), a preferred application of the CHOOSE approach was the execution of a gap analysis between a to-be and an as-is model. For the goal dimension, this was realized by modeling the to-be goals as OR-refinements. All other elements, which are related to these goals, would represent the to-be model. Nevertheless, the application of a gap analysis should start from the as-is model and should include all CHOOSE dimensions.

Potential solutions are:

- Develop separate models for the as-is and to-be situation, starting from identical elements.
- Use AND-refinements and OR-refinements for all CHOOSE dimensions (as for the obstacles in the KAOS metamodel [27]).
- Use specific symbols for the to-be elements and relations.

- Introduce gap and plateau constructs as in the implementation & migration extension of ArchiMate [28]. While the first construct can be used to model to-be elements, the latter denotes stable as-is elements of the EA.

Developing a to-be model comes down to introducing a new element or deleting an existing element in the as-is model, which results in a new set of relations in the model. Thus, a specific symbol for these new elements and relations could solve the experienced issue. By introducing this symbol as an attribute to the elements and relations in the CHOOSE metamodel (e.g., an attribute: _Model_ = {as-is, to-be, as-is and to-be}, the to-be model can be constructed and saved starting from the as-is. Furthermore, the use of separate models is not desirable because this would lead to extensive time consumption. Moreover, option 2 and 4 would imply introducing new elements to the metamodel. Consequently, we have opted for the third solution based on the simplicity and consistency principles.

Issue 4: Capacity Measures. This issue is related to the impact analysis, during which the introduction of a new product was investigated (cfr., Sect. 4.2). In this case, the impact on the available capacity should become visible. However, capacity measures are missing in the current version of the CHOOSE metamodel. As this type of changes may impact the whole organization, a decision should be taken about where to introduce these capacity attributes (e.g., employee workload constraints).
Potential solutions are:

- Adding attributes to the _Role_ construct. A first attribute denotes the _Maximal Available Capacity_ and the second attribute expresses the _Remaining Free Capacity_ for a certain _Role_.
- To obtain a lower-level view, the attributes that are described above could be placed on the _Performance_ link between an _Actor_ and an _Operation_.
- _Operations_ may have capacity constraints, thus adding the relevant attributes to the _Input_ and _Output_ relations have to be considered.

The second and third option would result in a larger number of model elements, which increases the diagrammatic complexity. Based on the simplicity and uniqueness principle, the first alternative was proposed here.

Issue 5: Complex IT Structures. Doubts were raised about the ability of CHOOSE to model extensive and complex IT structures. Indeed, it should be able to model how the functionalities of different IT components in the organization are linked. As CHOOSE primarily focuses on the business layer, this aspect could be elaborated more.
Potential solutions are:

- Further elaborate the _Object_ construct to enable the modeling of complex IT structures.
- Establish a link with more specialized EA approaches (e.g., ArchiMate [28]).

Based on the separation of concerns, we have opted for the second alternative. This enables to restrict the complexity of the CHOOSE approach [29]. This integration was also suggested in [8].

Issue 6: Terminology. Although the involved business stakeholders are dealing with conceptual modeling on a day-to-day basis, they struggled with the CHOOSE terminology as the project was executed. Furthermore, the CHOOSE architect needed to develop extensive knowledge to develop the model, which was an unexpected hurdle to overcome when starting modeling.

Potential solutions are:

- Only include metamodel concepts that directly relate to the business.
- Develop the CHOOSE model with the external help of an expert/consultant.
- Build an entry-level approach by using a modeling language dialect especially designed for novice users
- Explain the definitions of the elements of CHOOSE as a first step in the modeling method.

Based on the consistency and simplicity principle, the last alternative was preferred here. This has also been discussed in [8]. Although the use of an expert/consultant conflicts with the original orientation towards SMEs [10], large enterprises are expected to have more resources available for EA. Therefore, option 2 could also be a solution.

Issue 7: National Dimension. Geographical dispersion is an aspect that is typically associated with large enterprises rather than with SMEs. This aspect was not yet present in the metamodel.

Potential solutions are:

- The introduction of a *Location* construct that is linked with the other metamodel constructs.
- Add optional *Location* attribute to *Actor*, *Operations* and/or *Objects*. For larger enterprises, *Goals* typically do not change over national boundaries.

Based on the simplicity principle, the second alternative was preferred. Indeed, this solution enables the modeler to decide which elements of the metamodel should have this attribute. For this specific case, the *Location* attribute was only used for *Actors* and *Objects*, as the relevant *Operations* differ across national boundaries.

Issue 8: Link with Process Flows. Modeling process flows is not possible in CHOOSE. This is a deliberate choice as this aspect is adopted by process modeling languages (e.g., BPMN [30]). This clear separation of concerns preserves the simplicity of the CHOOSE approach [29]. A possible solution for this issue includes a consistent naming of actors who perform the same activity in process and CHOOSE models. By using appropriate references, this enables to integrate the information about a certain element in both models.

Evaluation. The qualitative evaluation of the proposed solutions was done by the business stakeholders and is based on the criteria they valued important: (i) added value and (ii) time efficiency. This ensured an evaluation of the proposed solutions in the relevant case study context.

Issue 1: Neutral for Positional Changes. Modeling the names of the individual employees was not considered as relevant for this case study but was nevertheless imposed during the project. As this aspect created problems, only using the _Role_ construct could allow neutrality in the models.

Issue 2: Department Dimension. Being able to create a hierarchy of the different business units was perceived as an important aspect for the clarity of the organizational structure.

Issue 3: Gap Analysis. During the interview, the use of an extra symbol to identify the changes between as-is and to-be models was preferred. In addition, the suggestion of an extra highlighting functionality aroused enthusiasm (i.e., when selecting a certain element or relation in the model, this functionality highlights every connected element). The research in [31] shows that this functionality increases the perceived usefulness of a model, which could further facilitate the gap analysis.

Issue 4: Capacity Measures. The capacity measures were considered as relevant for the _Actor/Role_ construct, because capacity is measured in FTEs at KBC AM. Introducing more detail on the _Performance_ relation would ask more time and add less value as this level of detail is only consulted when capacity problems arise. Although it could be useful in a production environment, the measure on the _Input_ and _Output_ relation of the _Operation_ construct is not very useful in a service industry. This is mainly because these _Input_ and _Output_ relations are perceived as vaguer in the context of KBC and can vary according to the situation.

Issue 5: Complex IT Structures. Establishing a link with specialized EA approaches scored highest on both criteria as it allows the integration of both business and IT perspectives. During the project, it was noticed that there is a considerable gap between both worlds. IT employees were primarily oriented towards the object dimension of CHOOSE and experienced problems to implement their ideas about complex IT structures. Business-minded employees focused on the other dimensions and largely neglected IT structures. Consequently, the integration of CHOOSE with a more IT-oriented EA approach was considered as an indispensable aspect.

Issue 6: Terminology. The use of an entry-level metamodel was perceived as the best option with respect to the timesaving criterion. Besides this, it was believed that hiring a consultant would add the most value to the EA modeling. The suggestion of explaining the definitions was deemed interesting but time-consuming. Due to the higher availability of resources in contrast to SMEs, a combination of these options (e.g., the combined use of an expert and a supporting explanation of the definitions) was also seen as a feasible solution.

Issue 7: National dimension. As the location of most departments is included in their description (e.g., operations department Belgium), it was preferred to model the national dimension by means of an attribute to the relevant actors.

Issue 8: Process Flows. The functionality of developing references with related process models was conceived as a value-adding aspect. However, doubts were raised about the time that is needed to establish this integration.

5.3   Modeling Method

Ad-hoc Modeling Method. The project in the operations department was constructed in an ad-hoc fashion, without following the documented CHOOSE method. However, certain elements were applied similarly and other elements were added. Therefore, we first explain the alternative method that was applied during this project. Afterwards, possible additions to the existing CHOOSE method are presented. This contributes to the robustness of the CHOOSE method for a wider applicability in large organizations.

Step 1: Defining Strategy. The operations department of KBC AM was lacking a clear functional strategy to support the general strategy of KBC AM. However, conformity between both strategies is important to align all future initiatives with the overarching strategy. Therefore, the COO and the operations board, which consisted of the heads of the three departments (i.e., back-office, front-office, and architecture-processes-technology), defined a suitable strategy, vision, mission and KPIs (i.e., to make the goals measurable). A second aspect was adapting the employee mindset towards the entrepreneurial idea. This step lasted approximately six months to overcome the resistance to change.

Step 2: Model Building. After defining the operations strategy and its communication towards the employees, the EA model was designed. Each department head organized workshops with their team members to define the relevant actors, objects, and strategic goals. Afterwards, the goal tree was modeled and linked with the important KPIs defined in step 1. During this phase, differences in the interpretation of definitions by employees were noticed. This problem was resolved by a clarification of the keywords by the operations board. As the development of well-defined constructs is important for the success of the knowledge work of a team, the issue should be further elaborated in the future [32].

Step 3: Elaboration. The EA model of the previous step resulted in a tangle of relations, which prevented clear insights. Therefore, the decision was made to concentrate on the goal dimension of CHOOSE as this aspect was the most relevant for the project. Furthermore, additional steps were needed to make the complex matter useful and clear, which enables to think about strategy alignment. The biggest decrease in complexity was the result of breaking the single goal tree down into more manageable parts, one for each department. This significantly decreased the number of model elements and the resulting visual complexity [25].

Step 4: Analysis. Once the model was clearly understandable, the analysis could start. Most insights were generated by reasoning about strategic issues. More specifically, by linking the goal tree with the KPIs from step 1, it was noticed in the CHOOSE model that some *Goals* functioned as a crossroad with a considerable higher number of paths passing through. These were named 'gateways' and underlying managerial levers were defined to obtain more detailed insights. The second part of the analysis was done by the management team, who clustered the goals according to their relevance. It was remarkable that these clusters resembled the categories of the BSC. This was interpreted as a signal that the analysis was performed in the right way. A third aspect of the analysis was performed because the enterprise architect noticed that some activities did not link to the highest-level goals. These activities were mainly situated in the Legal and Reporting business and coincide with the BASEL II norms, which are specific for the banking industry.

Step 5: Implementation. Using the identified clusters of gateways as a starting point, the department heads organized workshops with their employees. During these workshops, plans for future actions were defined with matching KPIs. The importance of the communication aspect for EA arose in this phase. Indeed, communicating the model with the employees offered the possibility of coupling daily activities with goals and according KPIs, up until the high-level goals from step 1. In this context, the model had to offer a clear overview of the EA, which was achieved by the use of viewpoints (cfr., Sect. 5.1).

Step 6: Follow-up. The follow-up of this project is essential to keep the EA model a living document. This happens monthly at management level and yearly for the employees.

Additions to CHOOSE Method. In step 1, the operations board started with the definition of a strategy, vision, mission and the coinciding high-level goals. This step was performed as suggested by Kaplan and Norton, who argue that it is easier to start with the strategy/mission/vision of the organization, before formulating KPIs in the four areas of the BSC [13]. This could be a valuable addition to the roadmap of the CHOOSE Method.

In contrast with CHOOSE, building the goal tree in step 2 happened in a bottom-up manner, instead of the suggested top-down approach where the highest-level goals in each of the four BSC dimensions are further operationalized. The rationale behind this choice was to ensure a bigger involvement of the employees. A third remarkable aspect was the different interpretation of the definitions. These definitions should be aligned at the start of the project to ensure the development of a strong knowledge domain. The architect also mentioned that some terminology was complicated for novice users. As already suggested by Bernaert et al. [8], a first explanatory step to clarify the main CHOOSE concepts could be a useful addition to the modeling method. Moreover, the architect experienced the input phase as being very time consuming. To save time, it was suggested to automatically introduce existing models (e.g., organigrams) in the software tool. As this suggestion is related to the development of appropriate tool support, it only indirectly affects the CHOOSE modeling method.

In the analysis phase (i.e., step 4), the strategic thinking process lead to valuable insights in the form of gateways and managerial levers. Although the method was different, this process is still based on the original CHOOSE metamodel. However, finding the gateways in an automated fashion (e.g., by the formulation of appropriate queries), could increase the efficiency and usability of CHOOSE for this case study. Nevertheless, it is expected that this analysis is specific to the case study project. Consequently, adding these queries is not suggested as an extension to the existing method.

A final remark was that the process happened not strictly linear, but in an iterative manner. In other words, it is important to provide the flexibility to users to iteratively apply the different steps of the modeling method.

5.4 Summary

Possible extensions of the metamodel (see Fig. 1) are threefold: (i) special symbols to differentiate between as-is and to-be model elements, (ii) capacity measures on the *Actor* construct, and (iii) nationality attributes on the metamodel elements. Furthermore, the case study led to the suggestion of two extra functionalities (i.e., based on issue 3 and 8), which could be also included in the existing tool support. Concerning the modeling method, starting with the development of a mission, vision, and strategy and the upfront explanation of the CHOOSE concepts could be valuable additions.

6 Conclusion and Future Research

The CHOOSE approach, originally designed for SMEs, was applied in the KBC AM operations department for an operations-strategy alignment project. It can be concluded that by a minimal extension of the metamodel, we would be able to model the real-life business situation of this large organization. During the execution of the ad-hoc modeling method, the discovery of gateways illustrated the ability of CHOOSE to generate insights trough a strategic thinking process. In addition to this, the approach enabled to create an overview for the management about a complex matter. From the ad-hoc modeling method, two promising additional steps for the CHOOSE roadmap could be identified.

As CHOOSE was used out of its intended context, these extensions should not be seen as changes to the general metamodel and modeling procedure. Indeed, iterative adaptations could endanger the simplicity of the approach. However, they can be useful for the further application of CHOOSE in large-scale organizations. Therefore, it would be interesting to build a repository of user-defined elements, which could be added to the CHOOSE metamodel depending on the particular application domain.

A notion of caution needs to be introduced here. Making generalizations is very hard, especially as only one EA approach was applied, only one organization was the subject of study (i.e., single case study design [18]), and only few people within the organization were involved. On the other hand, our conclusions can be useful for the application of CHOOSE in other organizations and contexts. Therefore, certain details of the organization were made explicit to enable other researchers to interpret these results.

The result of this EA project within KBC AM is the execution of a follow-up project, in which the Target Application Architecture will be modeled by using the CHOOSE approach. In this follow-up project, it would be useful to test the proposed solutions, which will increase the generalizability of findings.

Future research concerning these case study results includes three major topics. First, the application of CHOOSE as a means for gap and impact analysis provides interesting opportunities, even within SMEs. Therefore, these applications are currently under further investigation. Moreover, the use of viewpoints within the CHOOSE approach should be further elaborated. As the case study has shown, this enables to reduce the diagrammatic complexity of the models and facilitates the generated insights. Finally, establishing a link with ArchiMate could be a valuable addition for the CHOOSE approach. This could be particularly useful for experienced SME users, who experience the need to model IT systems in more detail [8].

References

1. Lankhorst, M.: Enterprise Architecture at Work: Modelling, Communication and Analysis. Springer, New York (2013)
2. Jonkers, H., Lankhorst, M., ter Doest, H., Arbab, F., Bosma, H., Wieringa, R.: Enterprise architecture: management tool and blueprint for the organisation. Inf. Syst. Front. **8**(2), 63–66 (2006)
3. Maes, R.: An Integrative perspective on information management. In: Huizing, A., De Vries, E. (eds.) Information Management: Setting the Scene, pp. 11–28. Elsevier Science, Oxford (2007)
4. Sessions, R.: https://msdn.microsoft.com/en-us/library/bb466232.aspx
5. Bhagwat, R., Sharma, M.: Information system architecture: a framework for a cluster of small- and medium-sized enterprises (SMEs). Prod. Plann. Control **18**(4), 283–296 (2007)
6. Balabko, P., Wegmann, A.: Systemic classification of concern-based design methods in the context of enterprise architecture. Inf. Syst. Front. **8**(2), 115–131 (2006)
7. Bernaert, M., Poels, G.: The quest for know-how, know-why, know-what and know-who: using KAOS for enterprise modelling. In: Salinesi, C., Pastor, O. (eds.) CAiSE Workshops 2011. LNBIP, vol. 83, pp. 29–40. Springer, Heidelberg (2011)
8. Bernaert, M., Poels, G., Snoeck, M., De Backer, M.: CHOOSE: towards a metamodel for enterprise architecture in small and medium-sized enterprises. Inf. Syst. Front. 1–38 (2015)
9. Kroon, B., Van De Voorde, K., Timmers, J.: High performance work practices in small firms: a resource-poverty and strategic decision-making perspective. Small Bus. Econ. **41**(1), 71–91 (2013)
10. Bernaert, M., Poels, G., Snoeck, M., De Backer, M.: Enterprise architecture for small and medium-sized enterprises: a starting point for bringing EA to SMEs, based on adoption models. In: Devos, J., van Landeghem, H., Deschoolmeester, D. (eds.) State of Art of IS Research in SMEs, pp. 67–96. Springer, Heidelberg (2013)
11. Wagter, R., Van Den Berg, M., Luijpers, J., van Steenbergen, M.: Dynamic Enterprise Architecture: How to Make It Work. Wiley, Hoboken (2005)
12. Callaert, M.: Business Architectuur Modellering in KMO's: Case Study Onderzoek ter Verfijning en Validatie van de CHOOSE Methode en Metamodel. UGent, Gent, Belgium (2013)
13. Kaplan, R., Norton, D.: The balanced scorecard - measures that drive performance. Harvard Bus. Rev. 71–79 (1992)
14. Porter, M.: Competitive Advantage: Creating and Sustaining Superior Performance. The Free Press, New York (1985)
15. Bernaert, M., Maes, J., Poels, G.: An android tablet tool for enterprise architecture modeling in small and medium-sized enterprises. In: Grabis, J., Kirikova, M., Zdravkovic, J., Stirna, J. (eds.) PoEM 2013. LNBIP, vol. 165, pp. 145–160. Springer, Heidelberg (2013)
16. Dumeez, J., Bernaert, M., Poels, G.: Development of software tool support for enterprise architecture in small and medium-sized enterprises. In: Franch, X., Soffer, P. (eds.) CAiSE Workshops 2013. LNBIP, vol. 148, pp. 87–98. Springer, Heidelberg (2013)
17. Ingelbeen, D., Bernaert, M., Poels, G.: Enterprise architecture software tool support for small and medium-sized enterprises: EASE. In: AMCIS 2013, Chicago, Illinois (2013)

18. Berndtsson, M., Hansson, J., Olsson, B., Lundell, B.: Thesis Projects: a Guide for Students in Computer Science and Information Systems. Springer, London (2008)
19. Yin, R.: Case Study Research: Design and Methods. Sage publications Inc., London (2009)
20. Walsham, G.: Interpretive case studies in IS research: nature and method. Eur. J. Inf. Syst. **4** (2), 74–81 (1995)
21. Saaty, T.: How to make a decision: the analytic hierarchy process. Eur. J. Oper. Res. **48**(1), 9–26 (1990)
22. Paige, R., Ostroff, J., Brooke, P.: Principles for modeling language design. Inf. Softw. Technol. **42**(10), 665–675 (2000)
23. KBC. https://multimediafiles.kbcgroup.eu/ng/published/KBCCOM/PDF/COM_BDV_pdf_ GROEP_JVS_2014_nl.pdf?
24. European Commission: The New SME Definition: User Guide and Model Declaration (2005)
25. Moody, D.: The "physics" of notations: toward a scientific basis for constructing visual notations in software engineering. IEEE Trans. Softw. Eng. **35**(6), 756–779 (2009)
26. Sweller, J.: Cognitive load theory. Learn. Difficulty Instr. Des. Learn. Instr. **4**(4), 295–312 (1994)
27. Dardenne, A., Van Lamsweerde, A., Fickas, S.: Goal-directed requirements acquisition. Sci. Comput. Program. **20**(1–2), 3–50 (1993)
28. The Open Group: ArchiMate® 2.1 Specification (2013)
29. Frank, U.: Multi-perspective enterprise modeling: foundational concepts, prospects, and future research challenges. Softw. Syst. Model. **13**(3), 941–962 (2014)
30. OMG: Business Process Model and Notation (BPMN) (version 2.0) (2010)
31. Boone, S., Bernaert, M., Roelens, B., Mertens, S., Poels, G.: Evaluating and improving the visualisation of CHOOSE, an enterprise architecture approach for SMEs. In: Frank, U., Loucopoulos, P., Pastor, Ó., Petrounias, I. (eds.) PoEM 2014. LNBIP, vol. 197, pp. 87–102. Springer, Heidelberg (2014)
32. Boland, R., Tankasi, R.: Perspective making and perspective taking in communities of knowing. Organ. Sci. **6**(4), 350–372 (1995)

Agile Modelling Method Engineering: Lessons Learned in the ComVantage Research Project

Robert Andrei Buchmann[1(✉)] and Dimitris Karagiannis[2]

[1] Faculty of Economic Sciences and Business Administration,
Babes-Bolyai University, Cluj-Napoca, Romania
robert.buchmann@econ.ubbcluj.ro
[2] Faculty of Computer Science, University of Vienna, Vienna, Austria
dk@dke.univie.ac.at

Abstract. The paper reports on experiences accumulated during a EU research project where challenges pertaining to requirements-driven metamodelling agility have been analysed. Traditionally, modelling languages are perceived as stable artefacts – that is, if they address a sufficiently large community with fixed modelling requirements on a fixed layer of abstraction. However, the enterprise modelling community must also consider the case where evolving requirements emerge in a narrow domain, or even in a single enterprise, therefore reusability across domains will be sacrificed to the benefit of on-demand adaptation, specialization or integration. Under such conditions, an agile metamodelling approach was applied in the ComVantage project and this, in turn, raised specific requirements for conceptual and technological enablers, allowing us to derive conclusions that are generalized here beyond the project scope. The paper's concluding SWOT analysis highlights the need to stimulate the emergence of an agile metamodelling paradigm based on community-driven enablers.

Keywords: Agile modelling method engineering · Enterprise modelling · Metamodelling · Modelling requirements

1 Introduction

Diagrammatic conceptual modelling has been concerned with standardization even from its earliest days, when the first draft of "process chart" symbols [1] was presented to the American Society of Mechanical Engineers (ASME), with a subtitle suggesting optimality: "Process Charts – First Steps in Finding the One Best Way to Do Work". According to the authors, the process charts were "a device for visualizing a process as means for improving it" and, for this purpose, an initial set of quite arbitrarily chosen symbols was proposed. The set of symbols was further developed by ASME in a new set of flowcharting symbols whose key quality was that they could be drawn by engineers using crayon and "template rulers". Later, Von Neumann adopted these to describe the first programs in a control flow visualization style. Many years later, standards like UML and BPMN still inherit the rhombus shape for decision concepts

© IFIP International Federation for Information Processing 2015
J. Ralyté et al. (Eds.): PoEM 2015, LNBIP 235, pp. 356–373, 2015.
DOI: 10.1007/978-3-319-25897-3_23

(and other such "legacy symbols") as part of standardized notations. However, computer-aided diagrammatic modelling can now benefit from enriching notation with a variety of features, such as: *interactivity* (symbols acting as hyperlinks), *dynamics* (symbols changing based on some machine-readable properties or semantics), *visual semantics* (information communicated through ornamental aspects, or even animation). None of these had been possible in the days of crayon and template rulers, and the variety of available options in this respect is nowadays subject to **modelling requirements**, together with other customization needs of the targeted users (modellers) pertaining to (i) model-driven functionality, (ii) semantic coverage of models or (iii) the depth of domain-specificity.

As software engineering recognized the unstable nature of requirements and the competitive value of flexible response to evolving requirements, the Agile Manifesto [2] and community emerged to challenge the traditional rigid ways of building software. Similar challenges can be met with respect to modelling requirements in the practice of modelling method engineering, particularly in its application for enterprise modelling. Consequently, an Agile Modelling Method Engineering (AMME) approach and its enablers must be consolidated from experience reports such as the one to be provided in the work at hand.

The goal of this paper is to share metamodelling experiences from our research on modelling virtual enterprises in the ComVantage research project [3], consequently highlighting characteristics of AMME as a key methodological necessity. In order to establish the motivation, we will introduce the improvised term "ComVantage enterprise" and compile its characteristics and challenges that must be tackled with an AMME approach. A modelling method and prototype was developed for the mentioned project within the environment provided by the Open Model Initiative Laboratory [4], and the paper reflects back on this development experience.

The remainder of the paper is structured as follows: Sect. 2 provides a brief project overview and, as a generalized motivation, compiles the enterprise characteristics that require an AMME approach. Section 3 provides an overview on the emerging AMME approach and its key enablers. Section 4 reports on experiences with AMME in relation to examples extracted from the ComVantage modelling method. Section 5 positions the paper in the context of related works. The final section generalizes conclusions beyond the project scope.

2 Motivational Characteristics of a "ComVantage Enterprise"

In this section we will compile characteristics for a "ComVantage enterprise" from the project experience, as well as by instantiating features identified in research roadmaps provided by European research clusters where the project took part - e.g., *FInES* [5].

The ComVantage research project aimed to support collaborative business processes in virtual enterprises with adaptive mobile technology driven by models designed with the domain-specific "ComVantage modelling method". The modelling method had to be developed iteratively, as requirements evolved and the development of run-time systems also imposed an incremental iterative approach. Details on different snapshots of the evolving modelling method are available in deliverables [3] (deliverables D311, D312) and previous publications [6, 7]. In this paper we will only provide insight for a few modelling elements in order to derive key characteristics for AMME. In the following, we highlight the enterprise characteristics that must be tackled by the AMME approach:

A. Modelling is Employed as Knowledge Representation. Historically, model-driven software engineering employed models in different ways, as highlighted by Table 1. The "modelling is programming" paradigm [8] uses models for generation of executable code. This vision was later complemented by a "modelling is configuration" approach, having run-time systems parameterized with model information and models acting as "control panels" to influence run-time behaviour – e.g., in the context of process-aware information systems [9], with the help of XML model serializations such as BPEL [10]). As enterprise modelling expanded beyond the goals of business process management in order to build a holistic representation of the enterprise, diagrammatic models became means of capturing the knowledge of stakeholders on different enterprise aspects (e.g. processes, goals, capabilities).

Table 1. The different stages of model-driven software engineering

How models are employed	Relation to run-time systems	Pre-condition
Modelling is Programming	Run-time code is generated from model	All information necessary in the final code is available, explicitly or implicitly, in models
Modelling is Configuration	Run-time system is parameterized and its execution driven by model information	Model information can be serialized in some interoperable format, typically XML
Modelling is Knowledge representation	Run-time system functionality is influenced by properties, concepts and reasoning based on the semantics captured in models	Model information can be converted to some machine-readable knowledge base (that supports querying and reasoning)

Relevance to AMME: AMME is called to ensure that the necessary semantics is captured, in relation to modelling needs that may evolve as users become accustomed to modelling. On the side of stakeholders, inexperienced modellers will gradually raise requirements for deeper specialization of modelling concepts (deepening domain-specificity), while the modelling method engineer can be confronted with gradual understanding of the application domain.

B. Semantics-Awareness is Required for Run-Time Enterprise Systems. The functionality of enterprise systems can be, at execution time, sensitive to machine-readable semantics captured in various forms. Typically such semantic representations are nowadays available in a new type of semantic networks (the Linked Enterprise Data paradigm [11]), possibly enriched by ontologies and rules to enable reasoning over the

Web of Data. Alternatively, *information systems may also be sensitive to the semantics captured in diagrammatic form by enterprise models* (with the modelling language alphabet acting as a "terminological box") – that is, if relevant granularity is ensured, and a machine-readable model repository is provided.

Relevance to AMME: AMME is called to ensure that changes in requirements for the run-time enterprise system propagate accordingly to modelling requirements so that the necessary properties are assimilated in the modelling language (to become accessible at run-time).

C. Scenario-Driven Requirements for Run-Time Systems. Means that run-time requirements should be built around work processes and work capabilities rather than around disparate use cases. While traditional requirements elicitation practices used to advocate atomization of user stories, the increasing experience of stakeholders with business process management may be leveraged in order to capture requirements in control flow representations mapped on resource/capability requirements. Agile software engineering already recognized this by aggregating requirements in narrative units such as stories and epics.

Relevance to AMME: As [12] emphasizes, requirements elicitation does not produce requirements per se, but requirements representations, whose descriptions may involve domain-specific concepts and properties relative to the business context. AMME is called to provide agile modelling means for collecting enterprise system requirements that include domain-specific aspects, thus bridging the gap between stakeholders and system developers [7].

D. Complexity Management Challenges. Although modelling typically means abstraction and simplification, in enterprise modelling even the model is too complex to be comprehensive in a single diagrammatic representation. Enterprise models are partitioned in different facets/layers across different abstraction layers or viewpoints (see Archimate [13], Zachman [14]). Since diagrammatic enterprise models are subjected to human interpretation, an inherent decomposition requirement must ensure model understandability and should be satisfied both on the *meta level* (e.g., by partitioning a metamodel in multiple model types) and on the *model level* (e.g., decomposing a business process model in subprocesses).

Relevance to AMME: AMME is called to identify building blocks of manageable granularity for both modellers (to help with model comprehension) and metamodellers (to help defining backlog units). Such building blocks will make it possible to isolate evolving modelling requirements so that an agile response to changes does not affect the entire method and change propagations become traceable.

E. Domain-Specific Modelling Requirements. Enterprise models can be specialized and contextual, and it is plausible to have an enterprise modelling method adopted in a narrow community, or even for a single case/project, where the enterprise is interested in employing models for internal purposes (e.g., as input for a custom model-aware run-time system), with no desire for sharing and reusing them in the external environment.

Relevance to AMME: In domain-specific modelling, the level of concept special-ization is not necessarily fixed, as new properties and subtyping may be gradually required to achieve new capabilities and the proverbial "competitive advantage" of agile development. AMME is called to ensure that such evolving specialization is assimilated in the method in a timely manner.

3   The AMME Framework

3.1   Framework Overview

Without going point by point through the Agile Manifesto [2], we highlight the key characteristics of Agile development as compiled by [15]:

- *Iterative*: repeat activities and potentially revisit same work products;
- *Incremental*: each successive version is usable and builds upon previous versions;
- *Version control*: enable for other agile practices;
- *Team control*: small group of people assigned to the same project building block with shared accountability.

In order to achieve agility in Modelling Method Engineering, such principles must be grafted on the fundamentals of modelling method design, considering the building blocks defined in [16], described as follows:

(1) The *modelling language* describes the set of modelling constructs (their notation, grammar and semantics. To achieve manageable granularity and model compre-hensibility, the modelling language can be partitioned in model types addressing different facets or abstraction layers of the system under study. The partitioning can be perceived as a usability feature (a top-down decomposition approach to avoid visual cluttering) or a consequence of hybridization (a bottom-up strategy employed to interconnect modelling language fragments).

(2) The *modelling procedure* defines the steps that must be taken by modellers towards some goal (in the simplest case, it advises on the precedence in creating different types of models).

(3) The *mechanisms and algorithms* cover functionality that process model infor-mation for various purposes (visualization, transformation, evaluation etc.).

Agility relies on *iterative incremental cycles integrated in a high level framework* such as the one depicted in Fig. 1.

In the centre, the modelling method evolves in a *Produce-Use* metamodelling cycle (by analogy with the *Code-Test* cycle): (i) in the top phase, the modelling language is derived from so called "Models of Concepts" that capture the domain knowledge and structure it in modelling constructs (the language alphabet); (ii) in the lower phase, each iteration of the modelling method is implemented in a modelling tool that allows the creation and evaluation of enterprise models ("Models that Use Concepts") by instantiating the concepts designed in the previous phase/For this cycle, the Application Environment raises modelling requirements and provides domain knowledge, while in the backend a Knowledge and Resource Repository accumulates reusable resources

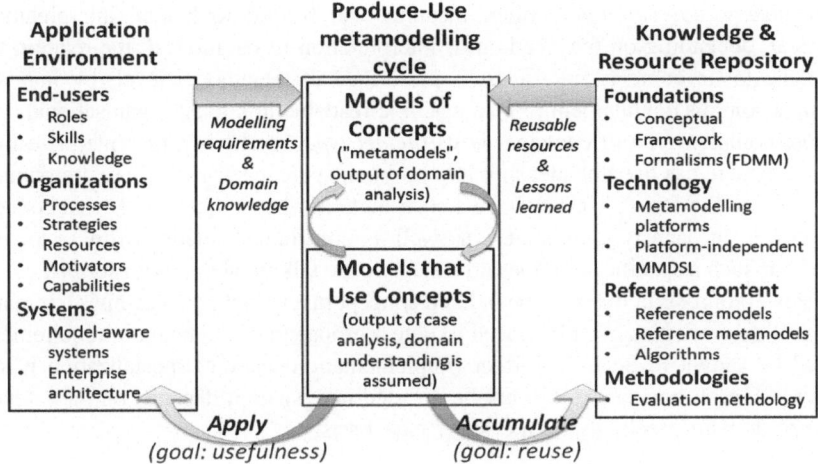

Fig. 1. The AMME Framework (adapted from [17])

and lessons learned. In our case the Knowledge and Resource Repository is accumulated through the Open Model Initiative Laboratory, a physical and virtual research environment that also hosts an implementation of the ComVantage modelling prototype [4] (which still evolves in follow-up projects).

3.2 Conceptual Enablers

During the *Produce* phase of the cycle depicted in Fig. 1, a knowledge acquisition effort will produce a "Model of Concepts" to describe the enterprise ontologically. A practical requirement for decomposition naturally emerges in order to ensure model comprehensibility and a usable separation of concerns. The solutions that fulfil the decomposition requirement are also the basis of establishing a manageable backlog granularity during AMME, beyond the building blocks suggested in Sect. 3.1. A generic classification scheme for different kinds of units (content containers) is provided in Fig. 2.

On the Top Layer: *Asemantic containers* provide a grouping of modelling constructs without assigning explicit machine-readable semantics to this grouping, unlike the *semantic containers* which have to their content a richer relation than the generic mereological one ("part-of"/"contains"). Depending on how containers are perceived, we may have *visual containers* (visual partitions sectioning the modelling canvas according to some criteria, e.g. business process swimlanes) or *functional containers* (an entire model). With respect to how the contents of a container are related to the exterior of that container, we may have *related content* (through machine-readable relations) or isolated content.

On the Lower Layer: The container types are further subsumed to more specialized building blocks: for example *swimlanes/pools* in business process models are typically *unspecified visual containers* (their meaning can be left to human interpretation). However, depending on the freedom of interpretation to be allowed, the relation of a swimlane to its contents may also be prescribed at metamodel level, by imposing semantics on this containment (e.g., a machine-readable link to an organisational unit). A more complex type of container is the *model type*, used when the enterprise modelling language has the alphabet split into problem-specific subsets. These are *semantic containers* in the sense that they have a clear meta-level specification of what concepts are allowed in each type of model, as well as constrained relations (links) to other models. If such a specification does not exist, we are talking about *unprescribed canvas* (e.g. Powerpoint-style free sketches). Each concept in a model type becomes a semantic unit, and its properties must be traced to detect propagation of changing requirements, as will be shown in Sect. 4. Further (implementation-specific) specialization is suggested in Fig. 2, however it will not be detailed here since it depends on the intended depth of domain-specificity on a case by case basis.

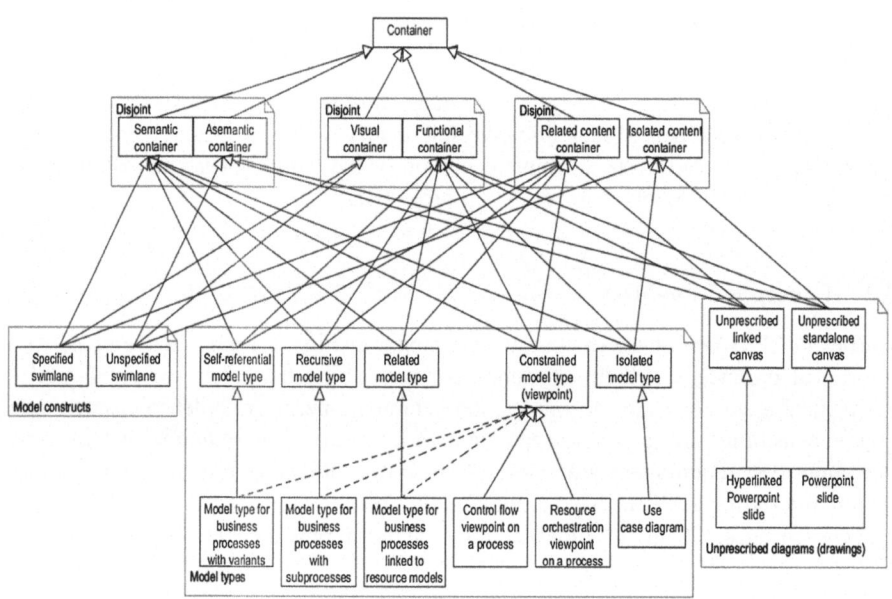

Fig. 2. A taxonomy of modelling units to tackle the decomposition requirement

3.3   Technological Enablers

Rapid prototyping is a key necessity for producing iterative prototypes that meet gradually refined requirements, even "throwaway prototypes" aimed to (i) familiarize inexperienced modellers with what they can expect from the final implementation and to (ii) stimulate their ability to formulate modelling requirements. The practice of metamodelling has answered such necessities and nowadays we see an increasing popularity of platforms that provide built-in functionality for productive development of modelling tools according to some existing conceptualisation (e.g., ADOxx [18],

MetaEdit+ [19]). Each available metamodelling platforms relies on a meta²model providing primitive built-in constructs (e.g., concept, connector) to create "Models of Concepts". As a complement to the available metamodelling platforms, specifically aimed to support rapid cross-platform prototyping, we have proposed in [20] an *additional abstraction layer* where a modelling method can be described in a declarative language (**MM-DSL**, Fig. 3) built on a common subset of primitives of the popular meta²models. A draft of the language grammar is openly available at [21]. Rapid prototyping is enabled by compilers that translate MM-DSL code to a platform-specific format for the metamodelling platform of choice in order to produce modelling prototypes in a highly automated way (a proof-of-concept compiler is currently available only for ADOxx deployment, with additional compilers expected to emerge from the OMILab community).

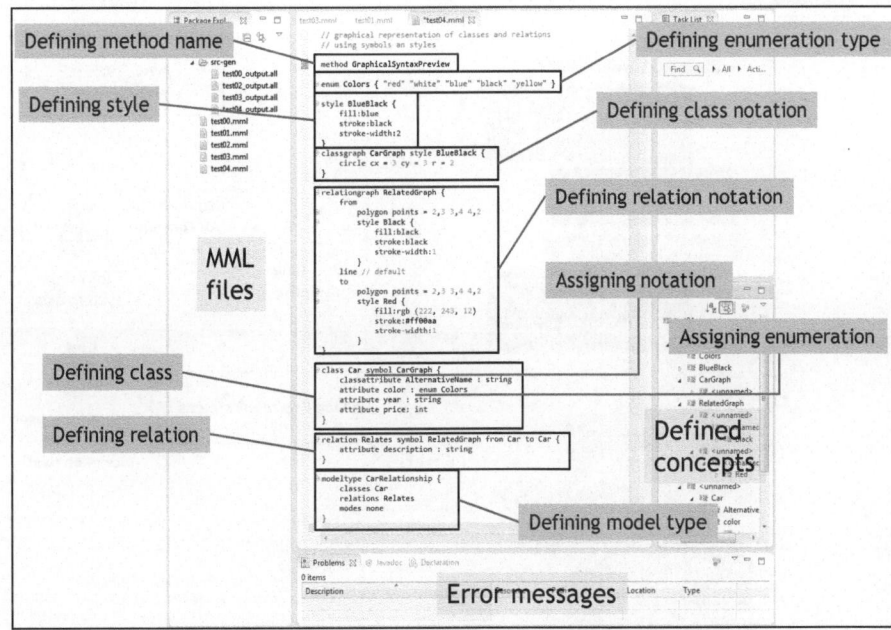

Fig. 3. The blocks of modelling method definition with MM-DSL (details on code snippets and grammar available in [20, 21])

4 AMME: The ComVantage Case

Enterprise modelling methods typically show a recurring frame of facets/layers/viewpoints and this was also adopted in the ComVantage modelling method, as its metamodel is split in various enterprise facets – the business model, business processes, app and data requirements (due to the project's technological specificity), models of domain-specific resources. Semantic relations are present in the form of hyperlinks that allow navigability across models and at the same time characterize the semantics of how the different facets (typically covered by different model types) are related one to another. We will not discuss here the entire metamodel layering (details available in public deliverables [3, D312]), only some fragments that illustrate the modelling requirements evolution and its propagation in the method building blocks.

Since decomposition is a key enabler for agility, the modelling method building blocks *must be mapped on backlog tasks and sprint responsibilities*. Metamodellers are typically confronted with requirements that propagate across these building blocks, with typical situations being reflected in Fig. 4 according to the following numbering (concrete project-based examples follow in the subsequent subsection):

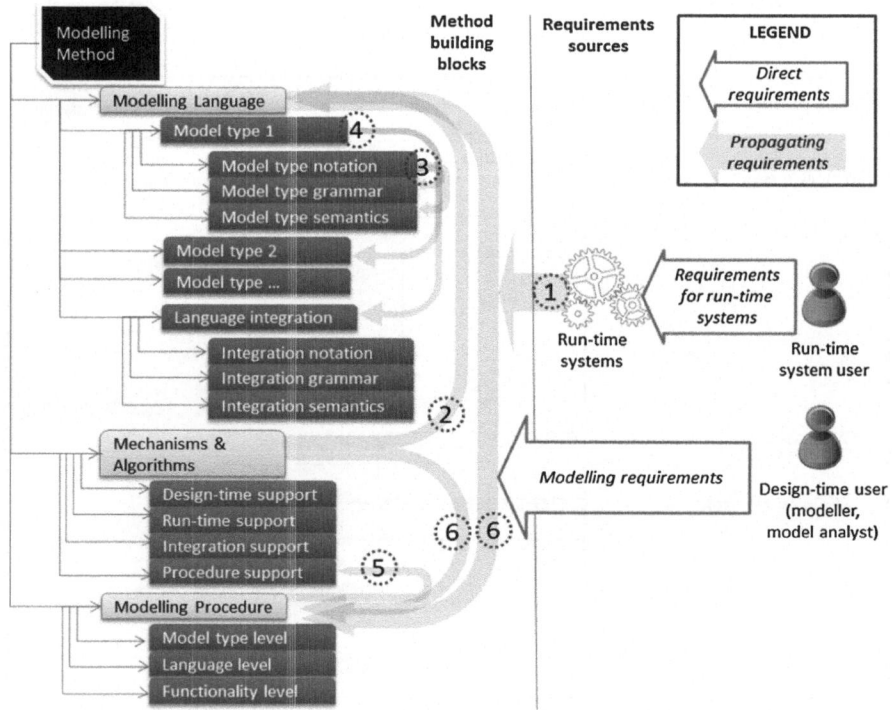

Fig. 4. Propagation of modelling requirements across method building blocks

1. Requirements for (semantics-aware) run-time systems will propagate in requirements for semantics available in models;
2. Requirements on mechanisms and algorithms typically propagate in requirements for new properties or concepts in the language (to provide additional input to functionality);
3. Requirements on notation change quite often, as most users perceive modelling primarily on a visual level. Change requests on notation level typically propagate in the other building blocks, e.g.: (i) dynamic or interactive notations will depend on

the presence of some property in the concept semantics; (ii) excessive visual cluttering will be solved by splitting a model type in multiple model types, also raising new integration needs (hyperlinks between models);

4. Requirements on a model type typically propagate in other related model types, as concepts are transferred among model types to reduce the linking effort, or new concepts are introduced;
5. The modelling procedure typically takes the form of modelling guidelines, therefore usually there are no direct requirements on the modelling procedure. However, users may impose requirements in the form of constraints, which are quite volatile in nature (e.g., "I don't want to have more than 5 model types"). More importantly, such constraints refer to usability and the automation of some procedure steps (e.g., "I don't want to create models of type X. Instead, they should be generated automatically") and this typically propagates towards additional functionality;
6. Any changes in the modelling language and functionality propagate in the modelling procedure guidelines.

A core concept of the method is the **App requirement** concept aiming to capture, at business process level, what kinds of mobile apps are required to support specific business activities. As an app-centred run-time architecture was being developed in the project, the modelling requirements on how the "required apps" should be described evolved. Table 2 illustrates this evolution along 5 phases, while the subsequent figures reflect how the concept evolved on a diagrammatic level.

Table 2. Evolving "required App" concept in relation to modelling requirements

	Modelling requirement	Solution	Propagations to backlog items
Phase 1	The business process activities should indicate when an activity must be supported by a mobile app	The concept of business process Activity gets some editable properties where the modeller (e.g., app requirements elicitator) captures descriptions of the app capabilities required to support that activity	The concept of Activity in the business process model type is extended with new properties. The modelling procedure guidelines must indicate how the app requirements are expressed (see a mockup in Fig. 5)
Phase 2	The mobile app requirement should be symbolised by its own concept with domain-specific properties to describe the required app	All semantics pertaining to the app requirements are isolated in a new app concept. Apps are visually connected to activities to indicate where a mobile app is required. Each app	The concept of Activity loses some properties. The App concept is added to the language alphabet (i.e., to the business process model type), with new editable properties. The modelling

(Continued)

Table 2. (*Continued*)

	Modelling requirement	Solution	Propagations to backlog items
		symbol is further described by its own property sheet capturing various non-functional requirements (e.g., device type, operating system)	procedure guidelines must reflect the new way of connecting app requirements to activities
Phase 3	To avoid visual cluttering, the mobile app symbols should be linked outside the business process modelling canvas and collected in a pool of reusable app requirements	A new model type is created to collect the app symbols in a single catalogue of "required apps". The notation in the business process activity provides a hyperlink to easily navigate to the app description linked to each activity. This is visible in Fig. 6 as an app icon in the top left corner of the app-supported activities	The business process model type is split, so that a new model type will include only the app symbols. The connector between activities and apps is replaced by a hyperlink between the two model types (on the Activity notation). The modelling procedure guidelines must be updated with the new way of linking app requirements, as well as with the prerequisite of having an app element available before a hyperlink is created for it
Phase 4	Each required mobile app should be further described by its features in the form of abstract user interaction elements of different types (e.g., buttons, labels etc.). This requirement aims to provide a basis for early mockup designs for the required app, thus making the elicitation of app requirements "bleed	A new model type is added to describe an abstract user interface (similar to the "abstract UI" concept in the Cameleon framework [22]). This expresses the key app features that must be available for user interaction in each required app	The metamodel is extended with a new model type, describing an app user interface in terms of some abstract types of UI controls (a taxonomy of such controls must be devised). A hyperlink is enabled between app symbols and such UI models. The modelling procedure guidelines must

(*Continued*)

Table 2. (Continued)

	Modelling requirement	Solution	Propagations to backlog items
	into" the app design phase		include explanations on the proposed taxonomy of UI controls and how the new type of model should be linked
Phase 5	An external app orchestration system will automatically deploy and execute mobile apps that are chained according to the workflow dictated by the business process model. The orchestration engine should be model-aware in the sense that the precedence of app chaining must be dictated by the precedence of the apps modelled for the business process (details in [23])	(a) A new model type depicts the app precedence; (b) Functionality for automated derivation of the app precedence from existing business process models; (c) Functionality for exporting the resulted diagrams in a serialization format that can be queried by the app orchestration engine responsible with app deployment (RDF [24] was the format of choice)	The metamodel is extended with a new model type (the "orchestration", describing the precedence of app usage for a business process. A mechanism is needed to derive such models from business process models, in order to ensure their consistency. Another mechanism is created to serialize the contents of models in some query-able format, to facilitate the extraction of semantics from the model information). Modelling procedure guidelines must be updated to (a) instruct the user in using these mechanisms; (b) instruct the run-time system developer on the RDF vocabulary that must be used to build model queries

Figure 5 shows how the app requirement description evolved between Phases 1 and 2, from an editable property of a process activity to a modelling symbol with its own domain-specific editable properties (the blue boxes are mock-ups of the property sheets).

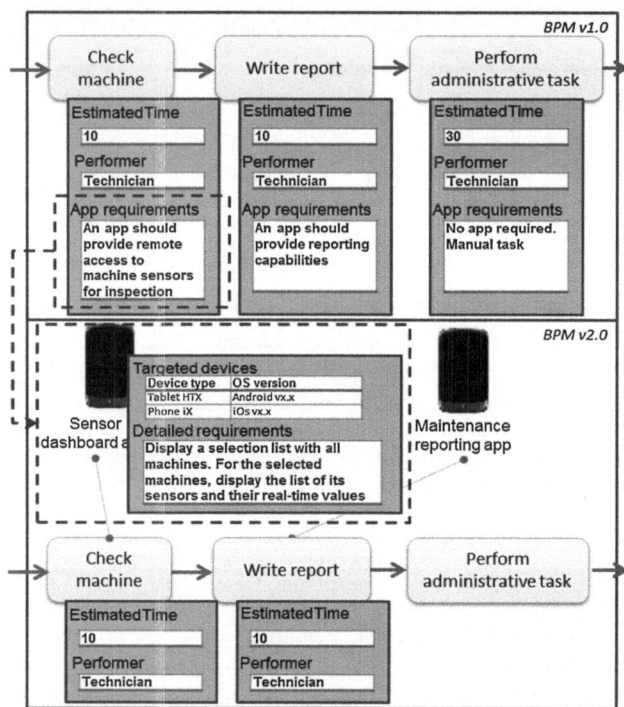

Fig. 5. Descriptive property evolves into modelling concept (Phase 1–2 requirements) (Color figure online)

Figure 6 shows the additional model types that emerged from Phases 3 and 4 (the pool of required apps isolated from the business process model, and the abstract UI model for each app), as well as the types of links that can be created between models (see the legend). Figure 7 shows the orchestration model type emerging in Phase 5 as a necessity for exposing the app usage precedence to the run-time system (run-time orchestrated apps [23]). The sample model in Fig. 7 is generated automatically via a graph rewriting rule set applied on the business process model example in Fig. 6 (details on the transformation are out of this paper's scope, being available in [7]).

5 Related Works

To the best of our knowledge, the framework of Agile Modelling Method Engineering was initially outlined on a generic level in some of our previous work - the published keynote [17] and the works of the NEMO (*Next Generation Enterprise Modelling*) Summer School [25], with some characteristics being suggested (in the context of fast prototyping) in [20]. This paper is distinguished from the mentioned works by (a) reporting on experiences from an application case of the generic AMME framework, with respect to challenges identified in the ComVantage research project (the case

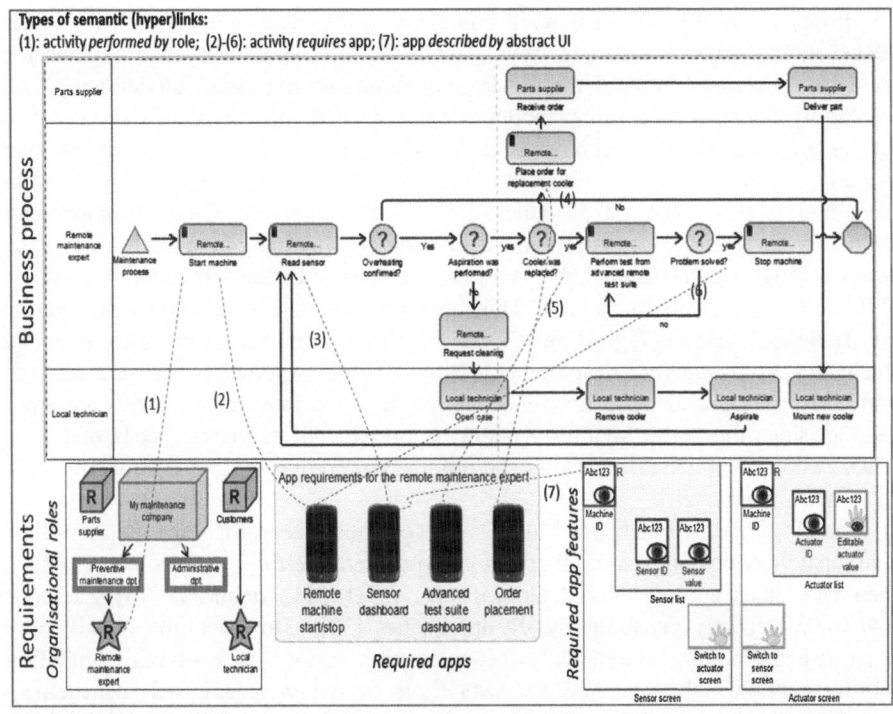

Fig. 6. Modelling concept evolves into linked model type (Phase 3–4 requirements)

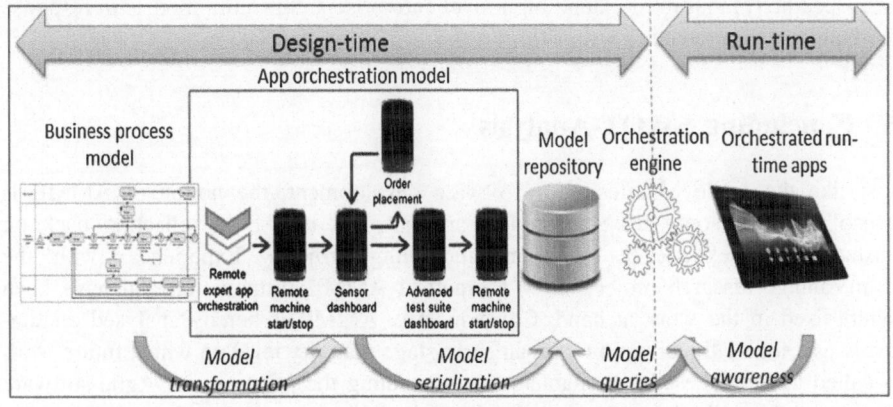

Fig. 7. Linked model types enriched with functionality (Phase 5 requirements)

discussed in Sect. 4); (b) refining the characteristics of a "Next Generation Enterprise" by anchoring them in characteristics of enterprises involved in the discussed project (Sect. 2); and (c) providing details on the conceptual and technological enablers (Sects. 3.2 and 3.3).

However, the AMME framework builds on agility challenges identified in other related works, since it emerged from a multi-disciplinary convergence of concerns previously discussed in the fields of Metamodelling and Enterprise Modelling:

Agility challenges, as well as model complexity challenges, have been discussed in the field of Metamodelling with respect to improving productivity for multi-perspective modelling [26], domain-specific multi-level modelling [27], as well as in a meta-modelling interpretation on Language-oriented Programming [28]. Metamodelling itself, as a discipline, emerged from the need to enable flexibility in modelling language design through a multi-layered abstraction architecture (e.g., the "powertype" approach [29], the MetaEdit+ approach [30]). This, however, has not been complemented yet by a fully-fledged methodological agile approach that mirrors the agility principles and challenges from software development. Project-based experiences are necessary to bring forth the kind of reflections that fuelled the agile movement in software engineering, since the Agile Manifesto mainly evolved from pragmatic needs of practitioners who questioned the obstacles and pitfalls of rigid management approaches (e.g., the waterfall approach).

The discipline of Enterprise Modelling recognizes a need for semantic as well as notational diversity, since a multitude of enterprise architectures and frameworks have been established and are widely adopted (e.g., EKD [31], ArchiMate [13], Zachman [14], more recently capability-driven approaches [32]). However, the paradigm of Enterprise Modelling traditionally obscures the notion of **evolving modelling requirements** which is central to AMME, as it requires dedicated management strategies. This is perhaps due to ambitions for standardization, which is in line with the original goal of ASME process charts on enabling "the best way to do work". The work at hand aims to stimulate the assimilation of "unstable" domain-specificity (or even case-specificity) that must extend high-level enterprise architecture models in response to changing requirements.

6 Concluding SWOT Analysis

Just like the Agile Manifesto for software development, the notion of AMME is consolidated not only from theoretical analysis, but also from reflecting back on obstacles and experiences with metamodelling projects. Experiences with the ComVantage research project show a practical AMME instantiation and have been synthesized in the work at hand. Consequently, AMME is hereby analysed qualitatively as a foundational notion with an early-stage maturity level on which future work is called to further establish enablers. By paralleling the principles of Agile software development, methodological or technological enablers are expected to emerge from community-driven efforts and shared experiences: management support tools, rapid prototyping enablers, validation methodologies, reports on agile best practices or agility pitfalls. Since we are not dealing yet with a wide adoption of AMME, it is too early to assess comparative experience reports. A SWOT analysis is hereby provided to evaluate the success of AMME for the instance experience:

Strengths: AMME was a necessity for enabling the evolution of Enterprise Modelling requirements and for dealing with their multi-faceted nature, as multiple types of stakeholders have been involved, from design-time decision makers (aiming for model analysis) to run-time system users (relying on machine-readable model semantics). Conceptual and technological enablers supported the agile approach and brought forward the need for a mature agile approach to metamodeling.

Weaknesses: The experience with applying AMME is still limited to OMILab projects. Its application to ComVantage emerged as a necessity driven by unstable requirements. The main identified pitfalls are (a) that synchronicity with the development of the run-time systems relying on model information is difficult to maintain if not planned from the very beginning; and (b) an evaluation methodology for user acceptance involves a training phase that can create bottlenecks, as stakeholders are called to frequently re-learn the modelling language. In addition, aspects pertaining to the management of human resources in agile teams have not been tackled in this paper. Future works must consider strategies to tackle such challenges.

Opportunities: The evolution of the Agile software development practices and tool support was fundamentally community-driven. Future work may be layered on the conceptual foundation established by the work at hand in order to enrich AMME as a community-driven framework, to raise its maturity level, to enrich tool support and to enable longitudinal studies for further refinement.

Threats: Standards typically defuse the problems raised in the work at hand by bringing all potential users on the same level of abstraction and encouraging universal adoption for the benefit of reusability across domains. Therefore, the generalized relevance of the work at hand depends on the desired trade-off between reusability and domain specialization, as well as on the uptake of semantics-aware information systems whose evolving requirements are an inherent cause for propagating modelling requirements.

Acknowledgment. The research leading to these results was funded by the European Community's Seventh Framework Programme under grant agreement no. FP7-284928 ComVantage.

References

1. Gilbreth, F.B., Gilbreth, L.M.: Process Charts. American Society of Mechanical Engineers (1921)
2. Manifesto for Agile Software Development. http://agilemanifesto.org/
3. ComVantage Consortium, ComVantage public deliverables. http://www.comvantage.eu/results-publications/public-deriverables/
4. Open Model Initiative Laboratory, ComVantage modelling prototype and resources. http://www.omilab.org/web/comvantage/home
5. Future Internet Enterprise Systems cluster, The FInES Research Roadmap 2025. http://cordis.europa.eu/fp7/ict/enet/documents/fines-research-roadmap-v30_en.pdf

6. Buchmann, R.: Conceptual modeling for mobile maintenance: the ComVantage case. In: Sprague, R.H. Jr. (ed.) Proceedings of HICSS 47, pp. 3390–3399. IEEE (2014)
7. Buchmann, R., Karagiannis, D.: Modelling mobile app requirements for semantic traceability. J. Requirements Eng. (2015, in press). doi:10.1007/s00766-015-0235-1
8. Aquino, N., Vanderdonckt, J., Panach, J.I., Pastor, O.: Conceptual modelling of interaction. In: Embley, D., Thalheim, B. (eds.) Handbook of Conceptual Modeling: Theory, Practice and Research Challenges, pp. 335–355. Springer, Berlin (2011)
9. van der Aalst, W.M.P.: Process-aware information systems: lessons to be learned from process mining. In: Jensen, K., van der Aalst, W.M.P. (eds.) Transactions on Petri Nets and Other Models of Concurrency II. LNCS, vol. 5460, pp. 1–26. Springer, Heidelberg (2009)
10. OASIS, BPEL - the official website. https://www.oasis-open.org/committees/tc_home.php?wg_abbrev=wsbpel
11. Wood, D. (ed.): Linking Enterprise Data. Springer, Berlin (2010)
12. Kaindl, H., Svetinovic, D.: On confusion between requirements and their representations. Requirements Eng. **15**, 307–311 (2010)
13. The Open Group, ArchiMate® 2.1 Specification. http://www.opengroup.org/archimate/
14. Zachman, J.A.: A framework for information systems architecture. IBM Syst. J. **26**(3), 276–292 (1987)
15. Agile Alliance. http://guide.agilealliance.org/subway.html
16. Karagiannis, D., Kühn, H.: Metamodelling platforms. In: Bauknecht, K., Min Tjoa, A., Quirchmayr, G. (eds.) EC-Web 2002. LNCS, vol. 2455, p. 182. Springer, Heidelberg (2002)
17. Karagiannis, D.: Agile modelling method engineering. In: Proceedings of the 19th Panhellenic Conference on Informatics. ACM (2015)
18. BOC-Group, ADOxx tool page. http://www.adoxx.org/live/
19. MetaCase, MetaEdit+ tool page. http://www.metacase.com/products.html
20. Visic, N., Fill, H.-G., Buchmann, R., Karagiannis, D.: A domain-specific language for modelling method definition: from requirements to grammar. In: Rolland, C., Anagnostopoulos, D., Loucopoulos, P., Gonzalez-Perez, C. (eds.) Proceedings of RCIS 2015, pp. 286–297. IEEE (2015)
21. The MM-DSL grammar specification. http://www.omilab.org/c/document_library/get_file?uuid=eb040aac-ea0d-4df7-a0a9-80b73f00c5f8&groupId=10122
22. Calvary, G., Coutaz, J., Thevenin, D., Limbourg, Q., Bouillon, L., Vanderdonckt, J.: A unifying reference framework for multi-target user interfaces. Interact. Comput. **15**(3), 289–308 (2003)
23. Ziegler, J., Graube, M., Pfeffer, J., Urbas, L.: Beyond app-chaining - mobile app orchestration for efficient model driven software generation. In: Proceedings of EFTA 2012, pp. 1–8. IEEE (2012)
24. W3C, RDF 1.1 Concepts and Abstract Syntax. http://www.w3.org/TR/rdf11-concepts/
25. Open Model Initiative Laboratory, NEMO 2015 Summer School materials. http://www.omilab.org/web/guest/camp2015/topics-and-program
26. Frank, U.: Multi-perspective enterprise modeling: conceptual framework and modeling languages. In: Sprague, R.H. Jr. (ed.) Proceedings of HICSS 2002, pp. 72–82. IEEE (2002)
27. Frank, U.: Multilevel modeling: toward a new paradigm of conceptual modeling and information systems design. Bus. Inf. Syst. Eng. **6**(6), 319–337 (2014)
28. Clark, T., Sammut, P., Willans, J.: Applied metamodelling: a foundation for language driven development. http://eprints.mdx.ac.uk/6060/
29. Gonzalez-Perez, C., Henderson-Sellers, B.: Metamodelling for Software Engineering. Wiley, London (2008)

30. Kelly, S., Lyytinen, K., Rossi, M.: MetaEdit+ a fully configurable multi-user and multi-tool CASE and CAME environment. In: Bubenko, J., Krogstie, J., Pastor, O., Pernici, B., Rolland, C., Solvberg, A. (eds.) Seminal Contributions to Information Systems Engineering, pp. 109–129. Springer, Berlin (2013)
31. Loucopoulos, P., Kavakli, V.: Enterprise knowledge management and conceptual modelling. In: Chen, P.P., Akoka, J., Kangassalu, H., Thalheim, B. (eds.) Conceptual Modeling. LNCS, vol. 1565, pp. 123–143. Springer, Heidelberg (1999)
32. Zdravkovic, J., Stirna, J., Kuhr, J.-C., Koç, H.: Requirements engineering for capability driven development. In: Frank, U., Loucopoulos, P., Pastor, Ó., Petrounias, I. (eds.) PoEM 2014. LNBIP, vol. 197, pp. 193–207. Springer, Heidelberg (2014)

Towards DW Support for Formulating Policies

Deepika Prakash[1(✉)] and Naveen Prakash[2]

[1] Delhi Technological University, Delhi 110042, India
dpka.prakash@gmail.com
[2] ITM University, Gurgaon, India
praknav@hotmail.com

Abstract. Data warehousing is largely directed towards "what to do next" type of decisions that essentially address operational decision-making needs. We argue for developing data warehouse support for deciding on organizational policies: policies evolve and therefore need continual decision-making support. We propose an RE approach for discovering information contents of a data warehouse for policy decision-making. Each policy is represented in an extended first order logic that can be converted into a policy hierarchy. Each node in this hierarchy can be selected, rejected, or modified. In order to take this decision, the relevant information is determined by using Ends Information Elicitation and Critical Success Factor Elicitation techniques for information elicitation. The elicited information is converted into an ER diagram from which star schemas are obtained.

Keywords: Policy · Policy formulation · Directive · Requirements engineering

1 Introduction

A Data Warehouse, DW, provides information in an appropriately processed form to decision makers who then use it for decision-making. Thus, data warehousing provides the decisional perspective of an enterprise in contrast to transaction orientation of conventional enterprise models. Modeling of the information needs of a decision maker is now required and not of operational tasks/transactions.

Decision-making is required to bridge the gap between the expected and actual results produced by an organization. Thus, DW systems emphasize the 'operational' aspects of organizations, that is, what should be done next in order to have a beneficial influence on the operations of an organization. Imhoff and White propose to address multiple levels of decision makers in an organization in their DSS 2.0 [7]. They propose three kinds of business intelligence, BI, needs: Strategic BI is for meeting long term goals and its users are executives and business analysts; Tactical for taking initiatives to meet strategic goals having users as business analysts and managers; Operational for monitoring and optimizing business processes to be used by managers and operational users.

Whereas DSS 2.0 is based on an analysis of operational BI needs, OMG in its Business Motivation Model, BMM [10], and Prakash et al. [14] propose that organizations need to look at non-operational decision making as well.

© IFIP International Federation for Information Processing 2015
J. Ralyté et al. (Eds.): PoEM 2015, LNBIP 235, pp. 374–388, 2015.
DOI: 10.1007/978-3-319-25897-3_24

1. BMM [10] proposes the notion of directives in its Means dimension. Directives may be policies and rules. BMM points out the need for formulating directives, that is on deciding what the policies and rules of an organization are. Thus decision making here is for formulating the environment within which operations of an organization shall be carried out.
2. Prakash et al. [14] see decision-making in an organization in three levels, formulation of policies, formulation of policy enforcement rules, and taking operation decisions that they call imperative decisions. The authors see these three levels as closely related to one another, policy level with policy enforcement level that, in turn, is related to the operational level.

Our analysis of policies brings out a number of properties of policies as follows:

a. **Policies evolve**: Policy evolution may occur due to (a) changing operational realities or (b) changing business realities like changes in the business environment or changes in regulations etc. This evolution implies periodic assessment and re-formulation of policies.
b. **Policies need specific information**: Policy formulation requires information so that both, the need for change is identified, and also the most appropriate policy is formulated. Thus, high attrition rates among doctors may indicate changes in Human Resource policies of a hospital. Notice also that a piece of information required for formulating a policy may not be of interest for operational decision making. Thus, for formulating policies, the attrition rates may be of interest whereas in the latter, the number of employees against the sanctioned employees only may be of interest. In general, we can say that policy formulation requires both operational as well as policy-specific data.

From the foregoing discussion we conclude that policy formulation is a good candidate for support through data warehouse technology because

1. Policy formulation is not a one-time task but is evolutionary in nature. It would therefore benefit from computer based decision-making support
2. A data warehouse is a good place to store both operational as well as policy specific information.

Since DW development starts off from the requirements engineering phase, **our research question is how can we do Requirements Engineering, RE, for a Policy Data Warehouse?**
We start by noting that a policy [10] governs strategies/tactics that are in turn, the means to obtain the desired results expressed as goals and objectives. This suggests goal orientation as a starting point. However, we believe that adopting goal-orientation data warehouse requirements engineering [1–4, 8, 12, 13] would make our requirements engineering process very heavy. This is because we would (a) determine goals, (b) arrive at the strategies/tactics for goals, (c) discover policies for strategies/tactics and, lastly, (d) elicit information relevant to each policy and structure it in multi-dimensional form. Evidently, the number of steps here is quite large and involved. On the other hand, we notice that a rich source of policies is often available:

- From regulatory bodies, organizations that lay down standards etc. For example restaurants and hotels are covered by municipal and hygienic norms, hospitals by health norms, educational institutions by accreditation standards and so on.
- Other organizations carrying out similar business have their own policies that constitute best practice.
- An organization may have its own legacy policies.

Since starting from policies directly, makes for a relatively lighter approach, we propose **a reuse-based requirements engineering technique** that exploits such 'given' policies. For each policy, we can accept, modify, or reject either the total policy itself or any component that constitutes it. Thus, we set up a choice set, {select policy component, modify policy component, delete policy component} and our decisional problem is the selection of an alternative from this set. As we have already seen, this selection requires information. Thus, **our problem is to elicit policy-specific information and then to structure it in multi-dimensional form**. We propose to address this problem in four steps as follows.

A. **Represent policies**: We propose to represent policies in first order logic. This is in accordance with the principle given in article 5.3 of the Business Rules Manifesto [15]: expressions in logic are fundamental to represent business rules as business people see them. From an operational point of view, the structuring of a statement in logic over simpler well defined formulae allows us to examine each sub-formula (recursively) for selection, deletion, modification as discussed above. As in SBVR [11] we can then develop a natural language capacity over the theoretical underpinning of the first order logic.

B. **Determine the nature of Information**: In order to elicit information, we need a model that identifies what information is to be elicited. Our model tells us that besides detailed, aggregated, and historical information kept in data warehouse, we additionally need 'categorization information.

C. **Information Elicitation**: We need to elicit information *relevant* to each component of every policy. To establish this 'relevance', recall that a policy [10] is a directive governing courses of action. Courses of action, in turn, are the means to achieve ends. Thus, relevant information is about achievement of ends by policies and policy components. There are two aspects of ends. Since the success of managers [16] depends on a portfolio of Critical Success Factors, managers formulate policies that are beneficial to these factors. Thus, we need to elicit CSF-relevant information for each policy/policy component. Additionally, we need to obtain information about achievement of organizational goals/objectives by policies. For this, we use an elicitation technique that provides Ends-relevant information.

D. **Information Structuring**: The elicited information is to be organized in multi-dimensional form. For this, we propose to convert the elicited information as an ER diagram and then use available techniques [5, 9] to convert the ER schema into star schema form.

The next four sections address these four steps respectively. In Sect. 6, we present the results of a case study. Section 7 is a discussion of our work in relation to existing literature. In Sect. 8, we conclude by summarizing our work and pointing out directions for the future.

2 Representing Policies

We represent policies in the first order logic with extensions to allow variables for sets of values. The logic is defined as follows.

There are two kinds of variables, those that denote a single value, SV, and others that denote a set of values, CV. A *simple term, ST,* can either be a constant, an SV, or an *n*-adic function symbol applied to *n* SVs. A *collective term, CT,* is either a CV or an *n*-adic function symbol applied to *n* CVs.

An *atom* is an n-place predicate $P(x_1, x_2, ----, x_n)$ where any x_i is either ST or CT. There are standard predicates for the six relational operators named EQ (x, y), NEQ (x, y), GEQ (x, y), LEQ (x, y), GQ (x, y), LQ (x, y).

The formulae of the logic are defined as follows:

- Every atom is a formula
- If F1, F2 are formulae then F1 AND F2, F1 OR F2 and Not F1 are formulae
- If F1, F2 are formulae then F1 → F2 is also a formula
- If F1 is a formula then ∃sF1 and ∀sF1 are formulae. Here s is SV or CV.
- Parenthesis may be placed around formulae as needed
- Nothing else is a formula.

The precedence while evaluating the formulae is as follows:

- Universal and existential quantifiers, ∀, ∃
- Logical AND, OR, NOT

We give below two examples to illustrate the foregoing. The first example uses quantification over an SV whereas the second shows quantification over a CV.

Policy 1: Every Ayurvedic hospital must run an O.P.D.

$$\forall x[Ayu(x) \rightarrow run(x, OPD)]$$

where Ayu(x) says that x is Ayurveda hospital and Run(x, OPD) says that x must run an OPD.

Policy 2: A Semi-private ward must have area of 200 Sq. ft. and 2 beds.

$$\forall x \exists B[spw(x) \rightarrow EQ(area(x), 200) AND EQ(count(B), 2)]$$

where spw(x) says that x is a semi private ward, EQ(x, c1) says that x is equal to c1, and B is a set of beds.

We convert the well-formed formula that expresses a policy into a policy hierarchy. For this purpose, we view an expression of our logic in two parts, one on the LHS of the implication and the other on its RHS. These parts are decomposed till atoms are reached. The algorithm for arriving at the policy hierarchy is given below. We illustrate the algorithm by considering the policy "Every doctor must have a post graduate degree".

$$\forall x[doc(x) \rightarrow degree(x, MD)]$$

where doc(x) says x is a doctor and degree(x, MD) says that x has MD degree.

Algorithm: To generate policy hierarchy tree for a given policy
Input: Policy as formula
Output: Policy hierarchy
{

      addroot(formula, root) //add policy as root of the tree
      if formula contains quantifiers //(of the form $\forall x$ or $\exists x$)
          f_Q = formula minus quantifiers extracted from formula
          addchild(f_Q, root) //add f_Q to root
      if f_Q contains implication '$\rightarrow$'
          f_L = formula on left side of implication
          f_R = formula on right side of implication
          PT_L= makept(f_L) //make a postfix tree, makept, from f_L
          Attach_pt_as_child(PT_L, f_Q) //attach the postfix tree, pt, to f_Q
          PT_R = makept(f_R) //make postfix tree from f_R
          Attach_pt_as_child(PT_R, f_Q) //attach the postfix tree, pt, to f_Q
}

Step 1 of the algorithm gives us the root node, the full statement of the policy itself. In step two, we strip off the quantification from this statement and then attach the result to the root node as shown in Fig. 1. Thereafter, we make the postfix trees for doc(x) and degree(x, MD) respectively. This yields the nodes doc(x) and degree(x, MD). These are then attached as shown.

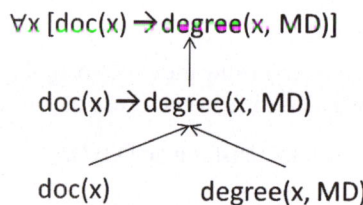

Fig. 1. Policy hierarchy for "Every doctor must have a post graduate degree"

Now, we associate **the choice set {select, modify, reject}** with each node of the policy hierarchy. If sufficient information is available in the Data warehouse, then an alternative from this choice set may be picked up to formulate the new policy using the process as follows:

Repeat until root of hierarchy is reached
      Pick node in bottom up left right manner in policy hierarchy
      Refer to Data Warehouse
      Pick alternative from choice set

Applying this to our example of Fig. 1, the choice set {select, modify, reject} applies to the two atoms doc(x) and degree(x, MD) respectively. The node doc(x) identifies that the policy under formulation is about doctors and this continues to be the case. Therefore, doc(x) is selected. Now consider the second node degree(x, MD). This is an important node since a policy decision about the minimum qualifications of doctors is being formulated. This decision requires information about the types of cases in our hospital, mortality rates, cases with post treatment complications, successfully discharged patients, admitted patients, patients refused admission due to non-availability of speci-alized treatment and so on. Let it be available in the policy data warehouse.

After consulting the relevant information, let the node (degree, MD) be modified to (degree, PDCC) The resulting leaf level of the new policy is shown in Fig. 2. The next higher node in the hierarchy is associating doc(x) with degree(x, PDCC) and we do not require any additional information to make this association. The root node provides quantification and it needs to be decided whether we should use existential or universal quantification. Again, after consulting relevant information let the latter be selected. The resulting policy is shown in Fig. 2.

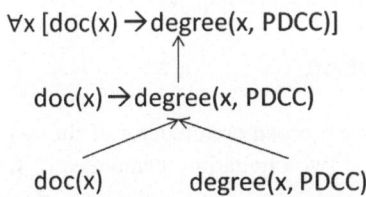

∀x [doc(x) →degree(x, PDCC)]

doc(x) →degree(x, PDCC)

doc(x)   degree(x, PDCC)

Fig. 2. The desired policy hierarchy

3   The Nature of Information

Figure 3 shows our meta-model, expressed in ER form, that elaborates the different types of information to be elicited for our warehouse. This model is an adaptation of the one of [14] and includes the 'categorized by' relationship.

As shown in the figure, Information is simple or aggregate. Simple Information corresponds to detailed information. Aggregate information is obtained as a summary by computing from simpler information. This is shown by the 'Is computed from' rela-tionship between Aggregate and Information. Further, it is possible for information to be categorized as, for example, happens when the GROUP BY is used in SQL. This means that there is a categorization relationship between information and information as shown. Aggregations may be applied to categorized or non-categorized information.

Historical information is represented by the relationship 'History of' between Infor-mation and Temporal unit (for example, hours, minutes, seconds). When a temporal unit is associated with information then we must also know the number of years of history to be maintained. This is captured, as shown in the figure, by the attribute Period.

The cardinality of 'history of' shows that it is possible for information to have no temporal unit associated with it. In such a case, only current information is to be

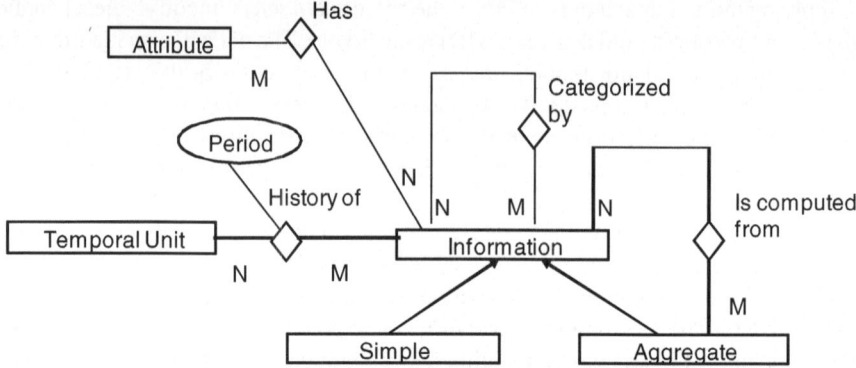

Fig. 3. Information meta-model

maintained. Further, it is possible for more than one temporal unit to be associated with Information. This allows the identification of multiple temporal units that can later be converted into temporal dimension hierarchies.

4   Eliciting Information

In this section we present the broad architecture of the requirements elicitation tool. Thereafter, we consider the two elicitation techniques of CSF Information and Ends Information elicitation.

4.1   Tool Architecture

All policies are processed by the Policy Hierarchy Maker and stored in a Policy Base of Fig. 4. The Policy Hierarchy Maker constructs policy hierarchies and stores them in textual format in the Policy Base after associating it with the name of the organization for which the policy is being formulated, the domain to which the organization belongs, and the policy type as follows.

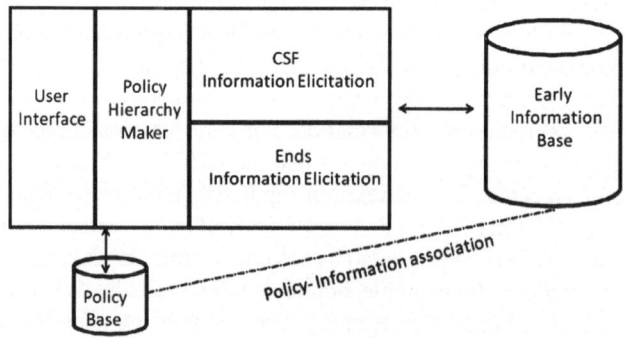

Fig. 4. The elicitation tool

The organization of the policy base is rooted in a two dimensional classification of a policy having policy type and domain as dimensions. The former dimension results from our treatment of an organization as a function. This allows us to partition policies as those governing input, output and the processing being performed, respectively. Input policies are concerned with the infrastructure, material and other inputs. Output policies deal with the amount and nature of output. Process policies provide the properties of the processing being carried out. In addition to input, output, and process there is a fourth kind that we call outcome policies. These specify the impact of the output on the organization. Along the domain dimension, policies are viewed in the context of domains, medical, life sciences, engineering etc.

Before starting a fresh policy formulation session, the requirements engineer must enter the domain and the name of the organization for which the policy is being formulated. This may be, for example, educational domain and DIT respectively. Upon getting this information, the tool can access domain specific policies available in the policy base. These can be retrieved by the requirements engineer in three ways as follows:

- Domain wise retrieval: all policies for the domain can be retrieved
- Policy Type wise: Policies of a domain but of input, output, process and outcome types are retrieved.
- Individual policies: Policies can also be retrieved based on specific terms in the policy. For example, information for all policies containing the term 'area' can be searched.

4.2   Elicitation Techniques

The model shown in Fig. 3 drives information elicitation. That is, the focus is to elicit for each node of a policy, simple information, aggregate information, category, history etc. We illustrate our elicitation techniques for the policy that for all in-patient departments, IPD, there must be at least one doctor, y, with MD degree, degree(y, MD), and the number of doctors, D, must be at least 2, GEQ(count(D), 2). This is

$$\forall x \exists y \exists D[IPD(x) \rightarrow doc(y) \text{ AND } GEQ(count(D),2) \text{ AND } degree(y, MD)]$$

The hierarchy of this policy is shown in Fig. 5.

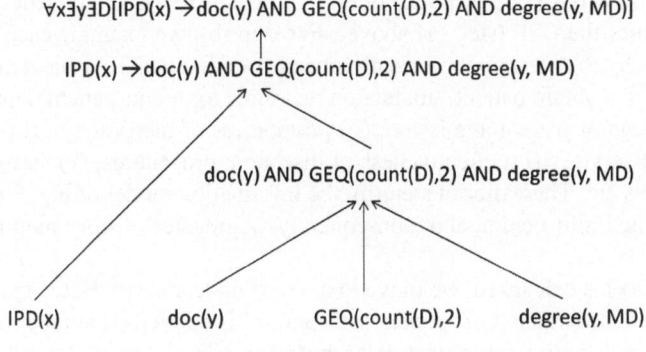

Fig. 5. Policy hierarchy

CSFI Elicitation. Critical Success Factor Information, CSFI, elicitation is a three step process consisting of (a) CSF [16] determination, (b) determination of information needed to assess CSF achievement and (c) determination of nature of the information in terms of the concepts of our meta model of Fig. 3. CSFI elicitation is terminated when all policies have been processed in this manner.

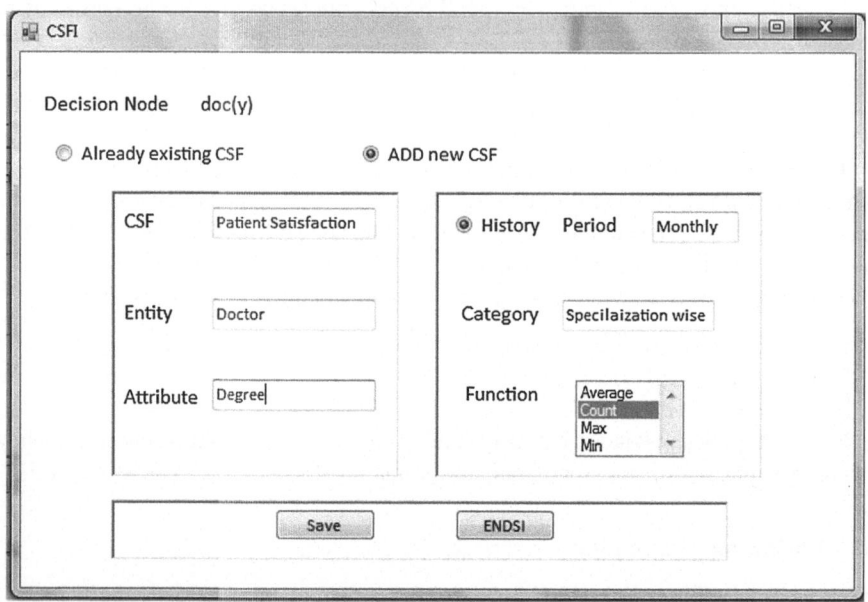

The top of the screen shows the node for which information is being elicited followed by the two options, to select an existing CSF or to add a new CSF. The panel on the left hand side of the screen shows an elicited CSF, Patient Satisfaction, and one piece of information required to assess it, Doctor, together with one attribute of this information, Degree. The panel on the right hand side allows statement of whether history is to be maintained and, if so, then the period for which it is to be maintained for one month in; the categorization of the information (specialization wise); and the function to be applied on the information,

Now, consider our example policy of Fig. 5. Let there be a CSF, 'patient satisfaction'. This determines the CSF (step (a) above). For step (b), we examine each node in the policy hierarchy to determine information needed to assess CSF achievement. For the node IPD(x), we obtain patient satisfaction measures for the in-patient department as a whole, (i) speed of patient admission, (ii) promptness of medical aid, (iii) delivery of para-medical services (iv) effectiveness of discharge procedures, (v) cases referred to other hospitals etc. Thereafter in step (c), the information model of Fig. 3 is populated with the elicited information and, consequently, aggregates, history requirements etc. are obtained.

Once IPD(x) is exhausted, we move to the next node, doc(y). Here, again, information relevant to satisfaction of 'patient satisfaction' is elicited (i) number of doctors in each specialization, (ii) experience of each doctor, (iii) roster of doctors, (iv) doctor availability for patient etc. However, unlike with IPD, a historical record of this information is required. The process of CSFI elicitation contains in this way for each node of the policy hierarchy.

The information obtained through CSFI elicitation is kept in the early information base of Fig. 4.

Ends Information Elicitation. The steps in Ends Information elicitation, EI elicitation are (i) determining Ends, (ii) determining the effectiveness measures of the Ends, and (iii) determining the information pertaining to evaluating the effectiveness. The user interface is similar to the one for CSFI elicitation and is not shown here for reasons of space.

Consider our policy of Fig. 5 again. One of the ends of the hospital is to provide comprehensive patient service (step a). The next step is to determine the effectiveness measures of this end. Again, we move in a bottom up manner. Consider IPD(x). For the in-patient department we determine effectiveness measures, (i) referrals made to other hospitals, (ii) medical services hired. For each of these, we now elicit in step (c), the information for evaluating it. For the former, we get (i) daily number of operations over a one year period, (ii) daily referrals over the last year, (iii) disease/case for which referral was done, (iii) inward referrals by other hospitals, etc. Similarly, the second effectiveness measure, medical services hired, is examined to find information like consulting doctors on panel etc.

As before, the elicited information is used to populate the model of Fig. 3 and the ENDSI elicitation process is repeated for each node of the hierarchy. The elicited information is kept in the early information base of Fig. 4.

5 Building ER Schema

Once CSF Information and Ends Information elicitation have been carried out for all candidate policies, the early information base of Fig. 4 is fully populated. We can now move build an ER diagram. We assume that name conflicts have been resolved and a given name refers to the same concept, for example, Doctor of CSF Information elicitation and Doctor of Ends Information elicitation are the same.

Construction of the ER diagram is done in two steps as follows.

Step 1: Building individualized ER diagrams for each policy: When constructing ER diagrams for individual policies, in addition to the entities elicited above, we obtain entities from the statement of the policy itself using our guideline that *All quantified simple variables refer to entities.* This follows from the notion of the first order logic that variables denote real world entities. Thus, in our example policy of Fig. 5, the bound simple variables, SV of Sect. 2, are x and y and these range over IPD and doctor respectively. Our heuristic says that IPD and doctor are two entities of the ER diagram being built. Notice that D denotes a set of variables and is not simple. Therefore, it does not identify any entity.

Step 2: Integrating individual ER diagrams: Once all individual ER diagrams are obtained, these are to be integrated into one ER diagram. As mentioned in the Introduction to this paper, we take recourse to existing schema integration techniques for this purpose. The integrated schema represents the required ER information to be kept in the DW To-Be.

For reasons of space, we do not present an example of ER construction.

6   Illustrative Case

We have applied our method to the medical domain. We considered a traditional Indian medical system which offers treatments in Ayurvedic medicine, Yoga, Unani and Naturopathy. The regulatory body is the AYUSH council. It defines policies [6] that all hospitals offering treatment using traditional medicine must comply with.

Our tool was used for the case study. The Policy Base was populated with the policies of AYUSH council. Our task was to formulate the policies of another hospital based on the AYUSH system of medicine. Since domain knowledge was required to carry out the analysis an expert in the AYUSH domain was involved in the case study. The expert used the tool and identified the information necessary to formulate policies. In eliciting information a team of doctors was consulted so that relevant information could be obtained.

The complete list of policies for AYUSH was represented in our logic. We constructed the policy hierarchy for each policy and elicited information. The statistics of the full case are as follows:

- Total number of Policies/Hierarchies = 151
- Number of nodes = 732
- Total number of decisions = 732 * 3 = 2196. This is because there are 3 alternatives, select, modify, reject for each node.

Our experience is that the structure of the policy hierarchy has a close bearing on the information elicited. The factors that influence this are as follows:

(a)   Intermediate nodes that arise due to connectives like AND and OR
(b)   Duplicate nodes on the left and right hand sides of the implication.

We consider each of these in turn.

Intermediate nodes have the potential to discover information in addition to that discovered from their component nodes. Therefore, wherever possible, a policy should be structured to yield intermediate nodes. We form the heuristic.

The intermediate node heuristic has the potential to increase the total number of nodes in a policy hierarchy. In contrast the common node heuristic considered below decreases the number of nodes to be considered.

Intermediate Node Heuristic: Merge policies using AND

We illustrate the application of this heuristic through an example. Consider the policy "A general ward must have 600 sq. ft. area, minimum 10 beds, at least 30 patients". We can represent this as three separate policies as follows. Each policy has its own policy hierarchy.

$$\forall x[G(x) \rightarrow EQ(area(x), 600)]$$

$$\forall x \exists B[G(x) \rightarrow GEQ(count(B), 10)]$$

$$\forall x \exists P[G(x) \rightarrow GEQ(count(P), 30)]$$

However, applying our heuristic we get

$\forall x \exists B \exists P[G(x) \rightarrow EQ(area(x), 600)]$ and $GEQ(count(B), 10)$ and $GEQ(count(P), 30)]$

This yields one extra node for ANDing all the individual components of the policy. The policy hierarchy is shown in Fig. 6. The intermediate node yields information additional to that discovered from the individual nodes, for example, number of patients with communicable diseases, number of cases of patient-to-patient disease transfer.

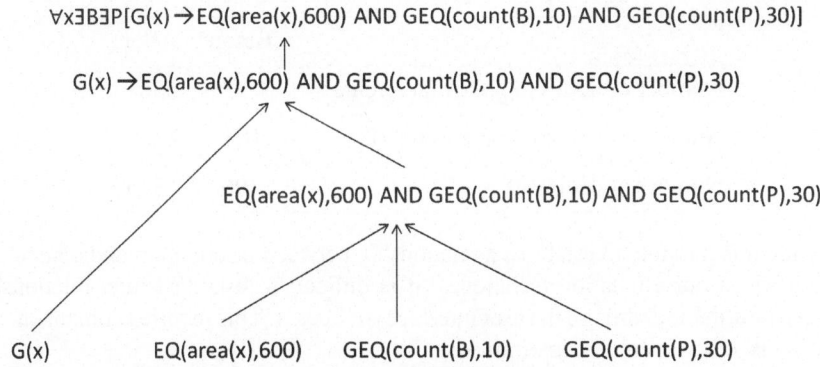

Fig. 6. The policy hierarchy

From the point of view of obtaining information, it is profitable to include intermediate nodes rather than otherwise because one needs to discover all information and not miss out on some.

Our experience is that merging policies using OR does not have an effect on information.

The intermediate node heuristic has the potential to increase the total number of nodes in a policy hierarchy. In contrast the common node heuristic considered below decreases the number of nodes to be considered.

Common Node Heuristic: For common LHS nodes between policies, elicit information only once.

Nodes can be common between policies. When nodes on the LHS of the implication are common then the information is also found to be common. For example consider two policies:

Every AYUSH hospital must have Total Patient beds ratio not higher than 1:6
$$\forall x \exists B \exists P[AYUSH(x) \rightarrow condratio(count(P), count(B), \leq, 1, 6)]$$
Bed occupancy rate for every AYUSH hospital is 50 percent
$$\forall x \exists B \exists BOCC[AYUSH(x) \rightarrow percent(count(BOCC), count(B), 50)]$$

The node AYUSH(x) occurs on the LHS of both these policies. Evidently, the same information shall be discovered for this node in both the cases. Thus, we form our heuristic that information elicitation needs to be done only once.

The implication of the Common Node Heuristic is that the number of nodes to be considered decreases. Notice however, that common nodes on the RHS do not reduce the number of decisions to be examined. This is because RHS nodes are dependent on the LHS nodes for their information elicitation context.

A comparison before and after the application of our heuristics is given below in Table 1:

Table 1. Result of heuristic application

	Before	After
Number of nodes in policy hierarchies	732	530
Number of common nodes on LHS	105	Nil
Number of decisions	2196	1590

While it is possible to establish a relationship between information and component of a policy in our elicitation techniques, it is difficult to establish inter-relationship between information through the user interfaces of Sect. 4. This requires domain knowledge and is to be separately determined.

7   Discussion

If we consider the area of Requirements Engineering holistically then we find a paucity of techniques based on reuse of requirements products. For example, in goal-oriented that carries a lot of momentum, we are unaware of any proposal for reuse of goals. This is true not only for goal-orientation in data warehousing but also in traditional, transactional systems. Perhaps, this is because policies are available in the public domain whereas goals are more personal to organizations and businesses.

Even though a policy hierarchy may seem similar to a goal reduction hierarchy three points must be noted

(a) There is a conceptual difference between goals and policies: whereas goals define what the system should do, policies are directives that govern behavior. As a result interest in goals is to determine whether they are functional or non-functional, soft or hard etc. In contrast, policies can be necessary or obligatory [11].

(b) The policy hierarchy is a different **form** of a policy expressed in our logic. No new component of a policy is discovered in building the policy hierarchy. In contrast, construction of a goal hierarchy is done to discover sub-goals. The goal hierarchy is thus not merely a different form of a goal.

(c) The policy hierarchy can be directly used for eliciting information relevant to the retention, modification, or rejection of a node. In contrast, in traditional transactional systems, the goal hierarchy forms the basis of making goals operational in real systems. When goal-orientation is applied to data warehousing, new notions like decision [12, 13], decisional goals, information goals [8] need to be introduced.

Ends analysis has been used in goal-orientation for goal reduction. We need to interpret Ends differently, what parameters are relevant to estimate Ends achievement and what is the specific information along each of these parameters. This is to arrive at the needed information to be kept in the data warehouse.

Further, we are unaware of the use of Critical Success Factors in goal-oriented data warehouse requirements engineering techniques [2–4, 8, 12, 13]. Indeed, we are not aware of these being used in goal–orientation in transactional systems as well.

Finally, we have separated the task of eliciting the needed information from that of structuring it. For the latter, we structure the elicited information, first as an ER diagram and the, in the second step, use existing techniques for conversion of ER diagrams into star schemas. This separation makes for a better focus on the elicitation task. In contrast to this, data warehouse requirements engineering has information structuring as its major concern. The proposal of Mazon et al. [8] does not propose information elicitation techniques but determines facts and measures form their intentional, decisional, and information goals. The goal-service-measure approach of [1] determines service measures from goals, organizes these in a Structured ER Model, SERM, and then arrives at the multi-dimensional structure. It is similar to our approach. However, moving from goals to services is ad-hoc, experience based and not based on guided elicitation like ours is.

8 Conclusion

Since policy assessment and re-formulation is periodically done in an organization, computer based support in the form of a data warehouse would be beneficial. The first step in development of such warehouses is that of requirements engineering. Our proposal is to reuse policies. We represent policies in first order logic that is converted into a hierarchy. The choice set, {select, modify, reject} is associated with each node in this hierarchy. Thereafter, we use Critical Success Factor Information Elicitation and Ends Information Elicitation to discover the information relevant to each alternative of the choice set. This information is converted to an ER diagram for which we have proposed some guidelines. We assume that existing techniques to are thereafter used to convert the ER into multi-dimensional form and have not addressed this issue here.

Experience with our case study leads to the formulation of the Intermediate Node and Common Node heuristics.

Our future work is motivated by our observation that policies are formulated by taking not only policy-specific but also operational, OLTP, information into account. The integration of policy-specific and operational information into one unified data warehouse is therefore an important question. What happens if this integration is not done, what are the problems that arise? Should we not develop techniques that promote integration at the requirements stage itself? These are some of the questions that we expect to address in the future.

References

1. Boehnlein, M., Ulbrich vom Ende, A.: Deriving initial data warehouse structures from the conceptual data models of the underlying operational information systems. In: Proceedings of Workshop on Data Warehousing and OLAP (DOPLAP), pp. 15–21, USA (1999)
2. Boehnlein, M., Ulbrich vom Ende, A.: Business process oriented development of data warehouse structures. In: Proceedings of Data Warehousing 2000. Physica Verlag (2000)
3. Bonifati, A., Cattaneo, F., Ceri, S., Fuggetta, A., Paraboschi, S.: Designing data marts for data warehouses. ACM Trans. Software. Eng. Methodol. **10**(4), 452–483 (2001)
4. Giorgini, P., Rizzi, S., Garzetti, M.: GRAnD: a goal-oriented approach to requirement analysis in data warehouses. Decis. Support Syst. **45**(1), 4–21 (2008)
5. Golfarelli, M., Maio, D., Rizzi, S.: Conceptual design of data warehouses from E/R schemes. In: Proceedings of HICSS-31, vol. VII, pp. 334–343 (1998)
6. GOI. Department of AYUSH, Ministry of Health and Family Welfare, Government of India, No. Z.20018/4/2000-ISM (Tech)/HD Cell, National Competitive Bidding (2000)
7. Imhoff C., White C.: DSS 2.0 -http://www.b-eye-network.com/view/8385
8. Mazón, J.-N., Pardillo, J., Trujillo, J.: A model-driven goal-oriented requirement engineering approach for data warehouses. In: Hainaut, J.-L., Rundensteiner, E.A., Kirchberg, M., Bertolotto, M., Brochhausen, M., Chen, Y.-P.P., Cherfi, S.S.-S., Doerr, M., Han, H., Hartmann, S., Parsons, J., Poels, G., Rolland, C., Trujillo, J., Yu, E., Zimányie, E. (eds.) ER Workshops 2007. LNCS, vol. 4802, pp. 255–264. Springer, Heidelberg (2007)
9. Moody, L.D., Kortink, M.A.R.: From enterprise models to dimensional models: a methodology for data warehouses and data mart design. In: Proceedings of the International Workshop on Design and Management of Data Warehouses, pp. 5.1–5.12, Stockholm, Sweden (2000)
10. OMG 14. Object Modeling Group, Business Motivation Model, release 1.3, OMG document number, dtc/14-11-07. http://www.omg.org/spec/BMM/1.3/
11. OMG-Semantics of Business Vocabulary and Business Rules (SBVR), vol. 1.0. http://www.omg.org/spec/SBVR/1.0/PDF
12. Prakash, N., Gosain, A.: Requirements driven data warehouse development. In: CAiSE Short Paper Proceedings, pp. 13–17 (2003)
13. Prakash, N., Gosain, A.: An approach to engineering the requirements of data warehouses. REJ **13**(1), 49–72 (2008)
14. Prakash, N., Prakash, D., Gupta, D.: Decisions and decision requirements for data warehouse systems. In: Soffer, P., Proper, E. (eds.) CAiSE Forum 2010. LNBIP, vol. 72, pp. 92–107. Springer, Heidelberg (2011)
15. Ross R.G.: Business Rules Manifesto, Business Rules Group, version 2.0 (2003)
16. Wetherbe, J.C.: Executive information requirements: getting it right. MIS Q. **15**(1), 51–65 (1991)

Author Index